The Embedded Internet

TCP/IP Basics, Implementation and Applications

We work with leading authors to develop the strongest educational materials in computing, bringing cutting-edge thinking and best learning practice to a global market.

Under a range of well-known imprints, including Addison-Wesley, we craft high quality print and electronic publications which help readers to understand and apply their content, whether studying or at work.

To find out more about the complete range of our publishing please visit us on the World Wide Web at: **www.pearsoned.co.uk**

The Embedded Internet

TCP/IP Basics, Implementation and Applications

Sergio Scaglia
University of Mendoza, Argentina

Harlow, England • London • New York • Boston • San Francisco • Toronto • Sydney • Singapore • Hong Kong
Tokyo • Seoul • Taipei • New Delhi • Cape Town • Madrid • Mexico City • Amsterdam • Munich • Paris • Milan

Pearson Education Limited
Edinburgh Gate
Harlow
Essex CM20 2JE
England

and Associated Companies throughout the world

Visit us on the World Wide Web at:
www.pearsoned.co.uk

First published 2007

ISBN 978 0 321 30638 8

British Library Cataloguing-in-Publication Data
A catalogue record for this book is available from the British Library

Library of Congress Cataloging-in-Publication Data
A catalog record for this book is available from the Library of Congress

10 9 8 7 6 5 4 3 2 1
10 09 08 07

Typeset by 30 in10/12pt Caslon(224) Book
Printed in Great Britain by Henry Ling Ltd, at the Dorset Press, Dorchester, Dorset

The publisher's policy is to use paper manufactured from sustainable forests.

Contents

Preface

Why embedded Internet?

Embedded systems are part of our lives. We can find them in several applications, such as home appliances, industrial plants, medical equipment, communication devices and automotive applications. Some embedded systems are generally located remotely from people that service or operate them. In such cases, tasks such as monitoring their operation, checking their performance, collecting data or upgrading the application software can be a costly and time-consuming process. Also, some applications could gain great benefits if they could remotely report their status, get remote data to process or even send remote messages to have their administrator informed about various incidents.

Many applications require huge memory and processing power to run complex algorithms that generate certain results. Owing to the limited resources in embedded systems, those kinds of applications are restricted to certain microcontroller families. If we provided Internet-connectivity to those embedded systems, they could use the Internet resources, so these complex algorithms could be resolved remotely in external servers. In this way, with few resources we could get great results using the 'external intelligence' stored in the Internet.

The demand for Internet-connected products is growing. The Internet is seen as the most cost-effective way of remotely monitoring and controlling embedded systems. As the Internet has grown, it has become the world's low-cost network, allowing data to be passed relatively cheaply across continents. So, there is no doubt at all, that while embedded system applications are still growing, Internet-connected embedded systems are the next step. With this object in mind, we need to provide programmers with 'embedded Internet' skills for the coming years.

Why this book?

As the embedded system market will grow even more over the next years, some of these systems will require their functionality to be extended through Internet connectivity. This approach will demand special skills in the embedded systems programmers.

In desktop applications development and some appliances, where reduced implementations of the desktop's operating systems have been installed (PDAs, mobile (cell) phones, set-top boxes, etc.), Internet connectivity is easy with the help of the operating system and its Transmission Control Protocol/Internet Protocol (TCP/IP) stack implementations. Nevertheless, this is not true in small embedded systems, where we would need to develop a particular solution 'from the ground'.

Although some TCP/IP stack implementations exist in embedded systems, not all of them are well suited to our specific processor architecture and/or memory restrictions. Also, some of them require a specific real time operating system use, imposing more restrictions. In addition, some commercial TCP/IP stacks implementations require an initial, and possibly a 'royalty per use', payment. However, some TCP/IP stack open (and free) implementation exists, which may be used 'as is' or as a starting point for a stack development.

In the case of 'ready' stack implementations, basic TCP/IP knowledge is required in order to troubleshoot when network problems arise. In the case of new stack development, more than this basic TCP/IP knowledge will be needed. Then, whatever the direction embedded systems designers take, they will have to acquire special skills to fill a gap in the market. This is what we are addressing with this book, facilitating from a theoretical and practical point of view all the necessary knowledge to obtain Internet connectivity for embedded systems.

The fact that these connectivity abilities will be required for many future applications makes it necessary to incorporate them in electrical engineering and computer science courses.

Who is the intended audience?

This book may be used in:

- New courses about embedded Internet developing TCP/IP theory and practice.
- Existing embedded systems courses, which incorporate Internet connectivity in the theory.
- Existing embedded systems courses, which incorporate Internet connectivity in their laboratory practices.
- Communication and networking courses using Part I of the book as the theory development guide.
- Communication and networking courses using Part II of the book as the laboratory practices.
- Final presentations or theses may take some examples of Part III of the book as a stating point for their development.
- Professionals who wish to learn TCP/IP and its applications in the embedded system field.
- Professionals who need to develop their own stacks or modify existing stacks, needing to learn both theory and practice about TCP/IP.
- Professionals who wish to get ideas about Internet applications in the embedded system field.

How is the book structured?

'*Embedded Internet: TCP/IP Basics, Implementation and Applications*' comprises three parts. Part I gives the theory behind TCP/IP. In order to know how the Internet works, it is enough to have some knowledge about the main protocols. Nevertheless, if we intend to implement real Internet applications, many details must be considered. For this reason, Part I of this book provides extensive coverage of all issues related to the protocols. All these theory chapters provide the technical background needed for the TCP/IP stack implementation.

Part II of the book shows how a TCP/IP stack may be developed for use in embedded systems. Two evaluation boards are used to program the TCP/IP in the C language. One of the boards has an Ethernet interface, whose drivers are programmed to connect the embedded system to a local area network (LAN). In the other board, a serial port is used to connect the embedded system to an Internet Service Provider (ISP), in order to get an Internet connection using a Point-to-Point Protocol (PPP) implementation. Once we get those network connections, we are ready to start developing the network and transport protocols over which the application protocols will run. Those applications show the most important Internet application protocols running on embedded systems.

Finally, Part III gives a conceptual overview about how embedded system applications may benefit from Internet connectivity. Even though some specific examples are given, they are only just a few of the enormous possibilities that Internet connectivity gives to embedded system applications, limited only by our own imagination.

The Appendices complement Part I with additional protocols information, and provide help for the use of tools required for Part II.

Description of the book

Chapter 1 provides an introduction about networking and its advantages. Assuming most students know about installing, configuring and using a computer network, this chapter simply provides general concepts needed for the subsequent chapters. In addition, the OSI Reference Model is introduced, which will be used in Chapter 2 to introduce the TCP/IP stack layered structure.

In Chapter 3, we introduce LAN technologies, where the Ethernet is presented as the most used LAN interface, and Chapter 4 describes the Serial Line Internet Protocol (SLIP) and PPP protocols provided by TCP/IP for the serial links. In Chapter 5 we introduce the Internet Protocol (IPv4), while in Chapter 6 we present the transport protocols, where User Datagram Protocol (UDP) and TCP are explained.

From Chapter 7 to Chapter 10, we see application protocols: Telnet, File Transfer Protocol (FTP), Simple Mail Transfer Protocol (SMTP), Post Office Protocol version 3 (POP3) and HyperText Transfer Protocol (HTTP). Although they are independent application protocols and they can be seen separately, some concepts from Chapter 7 are used in the others, so it is recommended that this chapter be read first. In Chapter 11, the Domain Name System is explained.

Chapters 12 to 20 constitute Part II of the book; TCP/IP stack implementations. These chapters provide a step-by-step guide to implementing, in the proposed hardware, a TCP/IP stack. Each chapter presents laboratories, which explain and show how every one of the protocols as seen in the theory, are implemented in the C language. These exercises consolidate the knowledge acquired in the first part of the book.

Chapters 21 to 24 present application examples from real life, constituting Part III of the book.

Six appendices complement the book; Appendix A provides other ways to connect to the Internet, such as Bluetooth and the IEEE 802.11 Wireless LAN Standard. Appendix B provides an overview of the next generation Internet Protocol version 6 (IPv6 and ICMPv6). Appendix C provides the Dynamic Host Configuration Protocol, while Appendix D introduces the Simple Network Management Protocol. Appendix E presents some utilities that come with Windows operating systems, which may be used to complement Part I theory with some practical exercises. Appendix F introduces a Protocol Network Analyser (sniffer) which is very useful for capturing and analysing communication packets from Internet applications. This utility will allow the reader to see the protocols 'in action'.

What knowledge does this book assume?

Part I of the book (theory) assumes the reader is familiar with computer and network concepts, as well as with the use of some Internet applications. In addition, the reader should have some knowledge of numerical representation systems, in order to recognize binary, decimal and hexadecimal numbers.

Part II of the book (implementation) assumes the reader has some knowledge about microcontroller architecture and programming in C.

Part III of the book (applications) assumes the reader is familiar with embedded systems and their applications.

What hardware and software development platform is used?

The implementation part of the book (Part II) is based on two different types of development boards with an ARM7 microcontroller, from the Philips LPC2000 family. The software platform is based on the IAR Embedded Workbench Development tool with a 32KB version of the ARM C/C++ compiler, which is included in the companion CD.

The decision to use an ARM microcontroller is given for the following reasons:

- ARM is very well-known microcontroller architecture, proved and manufactured by many companies.

- The Philips LPC2000 family are based on 32-bit microcontrollers, which are very powerful and their cost equals the lower-performance 8-bit microcontrollers.
- The performance and characteristics of memory and devices make them ideal to implement stacks that consume much memory.
- According to analysts, in five years ARM will have replaced the standard of the 8051.
- Development kits are obtained at very low prices.
- There are many software development tools available for ARM.

What's on the CD?

The CD that comes with the book includes the following components:

- IAR Embedded Workbench for ARM tools (32Kb code-size limited version).
- The 'Embedded Internet' software, with the following modules:
  - The Book Labs project files (for IAR EWARM).
  - Ethereal examples with the Labs sessions.
  - 'Embedded Internet' utilities required for the Labs.
  - A 'Getting Started' guide.
  - Datasheets and help files.
  - Additional utilities and drivers:
    - Ethereal
    - Philips LPC2000 Flash Utility
    - FTDI USB Drivers

Install each software unit following their respective instructions. See Chapter 12 for further advice.

Acknowledgements

This book would not have been possible without the contribution and support of many people; and this space allows me to express my gratitude to all of them.

First of all, I would like to thank the editors at Pearson Education: Simon Plumtree, who believed in this project from the beginning and guided me through the first steps; and Owen Knight, who had to deal with me for the rest of the book. Both of them provided me with the necessary support, and encouraged me to finish this very long project.

Secondly, I am grateful for the invaluable contribution from 'my friend' Chris Hills, at PhaedruS SystemS Ltd (**www.phaedsys.org**), who got involved with this project from the beginning and provided the necessary contacts and 'public relations' for it.

I would also like to thank:

- Georgina Clark-Mazo, from Pearson's Product Development Department, who had the difficult task of chasing after me for the proof corrections (and finally achieved it!).
- The people at IAR: Mike Skrtic, Anders Lundgren, Jason Moore, Nadim Shehayed, Francis Cheng and, especially, Robert DeOliveira, who followed the book's progress from the beginning, and Sara Skrtic, who made an excellent job of the CD's presentation.
- Niall Cooling at Feabhas (**www.feabhas.com**), who provided me with feedback and advice.
- Maria Clara Aliverti, who corrected and improved my deficient English.
- Ros Woodward (copy-editor), Jill Wallis (proofreader), and Margaret Binns (indexer).
- Axel Wolf, for providing me with a lot of technical information from NXP (founded by Philips) to include on the CD.
- The rest of the Pearson team, who I have not had the opportunity to get to know but I'm sure that they worked hard to get this book published.
- Finally, I would like to thank my family: Rosana, Venezia and Giorgo (and, why not, Tomy – my dog) for their time, because they are the actual owners of the time I dedicated to this book.

Publisher's acknowledgements

We are grateful to the following for permission to reproduce copyright material: Microsoft product screenshots reprinted with permission from Microsoft Corporation; Ethereal screenshots reprinted with permission from Ethereal Inc.

In some instances we have been unable to trace the owners of copyright material, and we would appreciate any information that would enable us to do so.

PART I

TCP/IP basics

'Welcome to the world of communications'

1

Introduction to networking

The Internet is a network of networks (or *inter-net*works), an enormous global network that allows users to share data and exchange information. For this reason, an introduction to networking helps us learn how the Internet works. In this chapter, we will review some aspects of networks in general, and we will introduce the Open System Interconnection Reference Model, which we need to know about in order to understand the TCP/IP protocol stack in the next chapter.

1.1 Networking: working with networks

Networking is the term that describes the process of working with networks and related technologies. This process may involve an entire life cycle of designing, implementing, upgrading and managing networks. Networks can be defined as a group of computers and other devices connected together to exchange information and share resources. To achieve this connection, we need certain hardware and software.

The term 'networking' can be applied, in a more general aspect, to a group of independent units connected together to share information. In the technological world, this term is used not only for computer networks, but also for telephone networks and even for electrical networks, where you plug in your electrical appliances.

Two of the most important advantages of networking are **connectivity** and **communication**. Networks connect computers and their users. The computers inside a building can be connected to Local Area Networks (LANs), and LANs in distant locations can be interconnected into larger Wide Area Networks (WANs). In this way, users can communicate with each other and exchange information using technologies such as electronic mail (e-mail) and the File Transfer Protocol (FTP).

Data sharing, one of the most important applications of networking, allows users to share data in applications such as databases, where users are able to work with the same data at the same time. It is almost impossible, in such applications, to work with different databases and then try to merge the data updated by the users, especially when one user needs to change the data already updated by other users.

Another benefit of networking is **hardware sharing**, which enables us to share different hardware (for example, an expensive colour laser printer) between several users. (See Fig. 1.1.) Of course, not all these advantages – such as the necessary hardware and software set-up costs, network administration costs, and the cost of data security concerns, among others – come free. Networking has disadvantages as well, such as the necessary hardware and software set-up costs, network administration costs and the costs of data security concerns, among others.

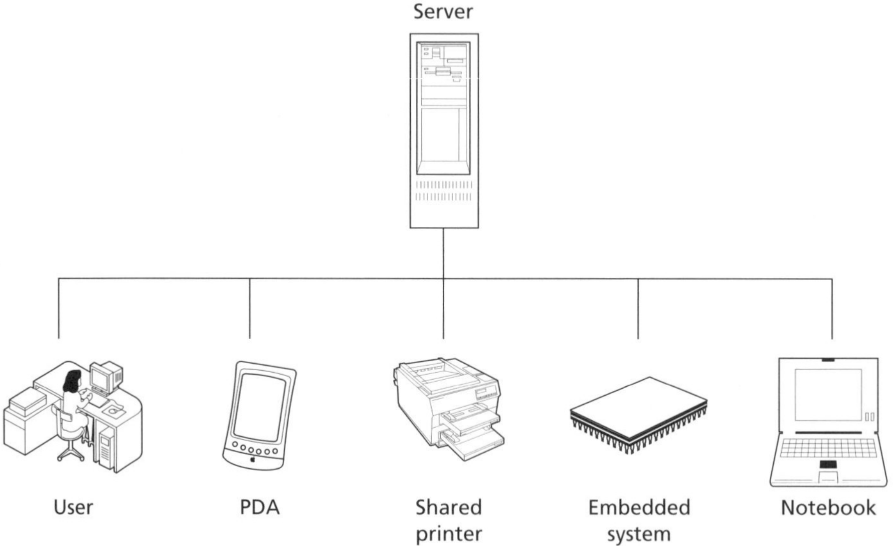

Figure 1.1 Connectivity, communication, data and hardware sharing are the most important advantages of networking.

1.2 Network fundamentals

In order to introduce the fundamentals of networks, we need to learn some network elements, such as switching networks, protocols, messages and connections.

1.2.1 Switching network types

As defined above, networks are groups of devices connected together using special hardware and software to permit them to exchange information. We can distinguish between two types of networks, according to the method the network uses to determine the right path between devices over which the information will flow:

- **Circuit switching networks**: In this type of network, before any information exchange occurs, a connection called a 'circuit' must be established. The circuit may either be fixed and always available or it may be created on demand whenever the devices need it. The information will flow exclusively over this path. The telephone system is an example of this type of network. When we call someone and they answer, we establish a circuit connection and the information will flow over this path. When we finish our communication, we hang up and this terminates the circuit. In our next call, we get a new circuit, which will probably use a different path, and the information flows over this path until the connection is terminated. (See Fig. 1.2.)

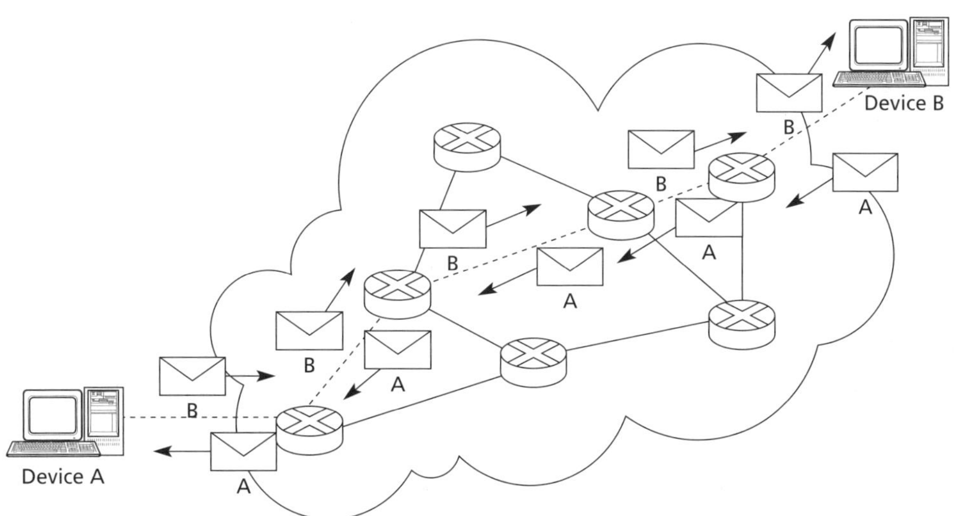

Figure 1.2 Circuit switching network.

- **Packet switching networks**: In this type of network, there is no specific path for data transfer. Instead, the data are divided into small pieces called packets, and then sent over the network. These packets flow over the network using different paths to get to their destination. As the packets could take several different paths, it is possible that a later packet will arrive before the previous ones. A packet could even be lost and never arrive. As a result, at the receiving point we need to reassemble them (collect all the packets, reclaim the lost ones, and reorder them) in order to retrieve the original data. (See Fig. 1.3.)

No network type is better than the other; they cover different needs. In circuit switching networks, once a connection has been established, the medium is dedicated to this connection and it uses certain network resources while the communication takes place. In packet switching networks, the medium is shared and network resources are available for any packet.

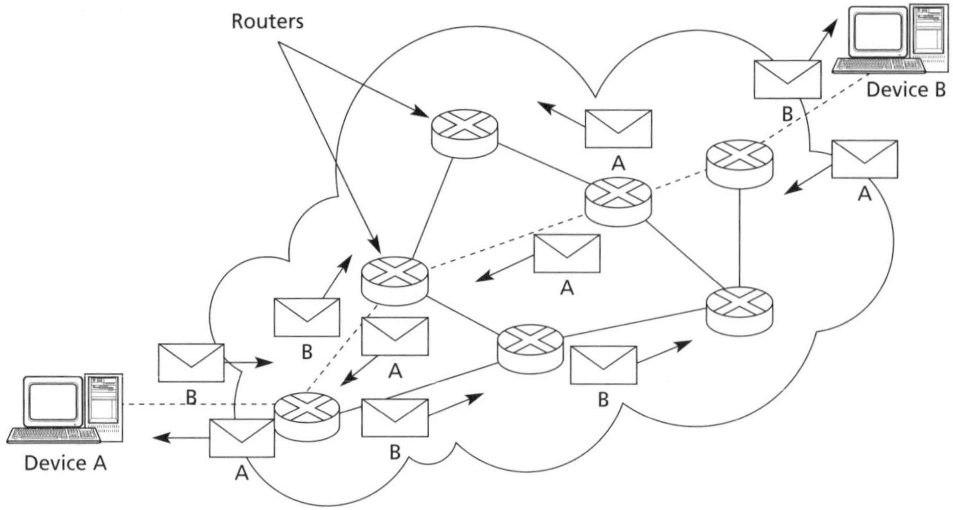

Figure 1.3 Packet switching network.

1.2.2 Network protocols

In order to connect devices, they must agree about a series of rules, messages, procedures and other types of mechanisms that allow them to communicate effectively. These sets of rules are called **protocols**. When a protocol is defined, we can follow its contents so we know what to do, and what behaviour to expect on behalf of the other communication party.

Despite being called a protocol, Transmission Control Protocol/Internet Protocol (TCP/IP) is really a **protocol suite** (or a set of protocols). TCP/IP is a protocol family, composed of several different protocols that provide different applications or services. Because of the layered structure of TCP/IP, it is sometimes called a **protocol stack**.

1.2.3 Connectionless and connection-oriented protocols

Once we have a physical path (network) over which to transfer data, we could either start sending packets to another device, or, before data transfer begins, we could establish a connection between the devices. In the second case, we would have a 'logical connection' between them. The use of either procedure must be defined in the protocol we are using. Hence, we have two protocol types:

- *Connectionless protocols*: With this type of protocol, there is no need to establish a 'logical connection', so we can start sending data as soon as we need to.
- *Connection-oriented protocols*: With this type of protocol, we need to establish a 'logical connection' between two devices before a transfer of data can take place. Once the data transfer has been completed successfully, the 'logical connection' can be broken.

We need to avoid confusing circuit switching networks and connection-oriented protocols. While in the first case, we have a dedicated 'physical connection' between devices, with connection-oriented protocols we establish a 'logical connection' between devices that is independent of the underlying physical path over which the packets flow. This 'logical connection' is implemented with a set of messages to initiate, negotiate, manage and terminate the logical link.

1.2.4 Network message structure

As we noted above, in packet switching-based networks, the data is divided into small pieces called packets and sent over the network. These packets are generically called messages. These messages may vary between different protocols or technologies, but, in general, they all have the following structure:

- **Header** is the information placed at the beginning of the message, which contains control information. A common element to include is the source and destination address, in order to let the network know how to route the message to ensure that it arrives at its destination point.
- **Data** is the portion of the message that carries the information. Sometimes it is called the 'payload' of the message.
- **Footer** is the last part of the message and may include control fields, such as the CRC (cyclic redundancy check), that allow the integrity of the message to be checked.

Owing to the layered structure of some protocols, it is common for the data portion of the message to contain the entire message (Header, Data and Footer) of the upper-layer protocol. In this way, each layer adds its own header and footer to the message it receives from the upper layer. (See Fig. 1.4.)

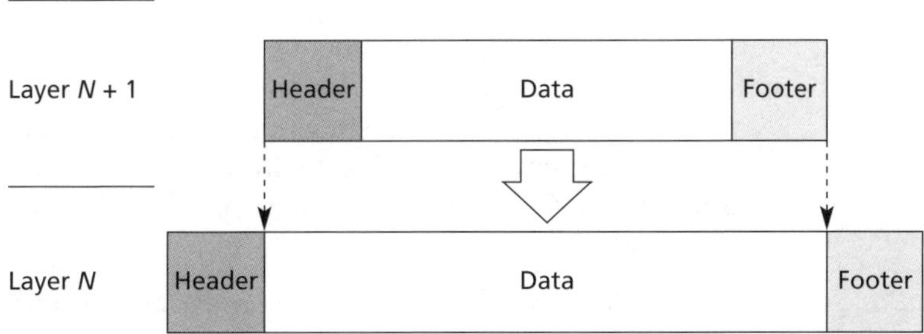

Figure 1.4 The data portion of a message contains the complete message of the upper layer.

1.2.5 Message transmission types

Until now, we have only considered the communication between two devices over a network. However, in the real world we will usually have more than two devices connected to the network. In this case, a device may want to transmit a message to only one device, to a group of devices or to all devices in the network. Therefore, we have three kinds of message transmission:

- **Unicast messages**: These messages are sent from one device to only one other.
- **Multicast messages**: These messages are sent from one device to a group of devices. This group might be composed of devices that meet certain criteria that are necessary for belonging to the group.
- **Broadcast messages**: These messages are sent from one device to all the devices on the network. Of course, this type of message is rarely used when the network is huge, because it causes a lot of traffic over the network.

1.2.6 Connection operation modes

A link between each device and the network is called a **connection**. Communication over this connection can be performed in three basic modes of operation:

- **Simplex operation**: In this mode, the communication over the connection can take place only in one direction. In order to have bi-directional communication we need a couple of connections or communication channels between the device and the network. One example of this is fibre-optic communication, where data is sent in each direction over a pair of fibres combined into one cable. Simplex operation is also used by some Internet providers who use a satellite connection to download data, and a dial-up modem to upload it.
- **Half-duplex operation**: In this mode, the communication can take place in both directions over the connection, but not at the same time. In the case of using cable or radio frequency as a medium, the connection must use half-duplex operation. In the Ethernet, for example, devices can transmit one at a time (not simultaneously), so from this point of view, this medium operates in half-duplex mode.
- **Full-duplex operation**: In this mode, communication can take place in both directions over the connection, even at the same time. For example, some frequency-multiplexed techniques are adequate for this operation mode; in these cases, data is sent in both directions over different frequency carriers.

As the connection operation mode is a 'concept' that can be applied to connections, links, channels or media, we could say that a full-duplex channel may be composed of a pair of simplex links. For example, in the case of the fibre-optic cable described above, we can consider it as two simplex connections, or just a full-duplex channel composed of two fibre strands.

1.3 Network models

As mentioned above, one of the most important uses of a network is the sharing of resources. In this way, we could design a network where some computers have the role of providing services to other computers. In these networks, the computers that offer their resources are called servers, while the others (the ones that use these resources) are the clients.

We could also design a network with no specific roles assigned to any computer. In this schema every computer in the network, called a peer, may offer its resources throughout the network, and it may use the resources of the others computers.

In this way, we have the following network models (see Fig. 1.5):

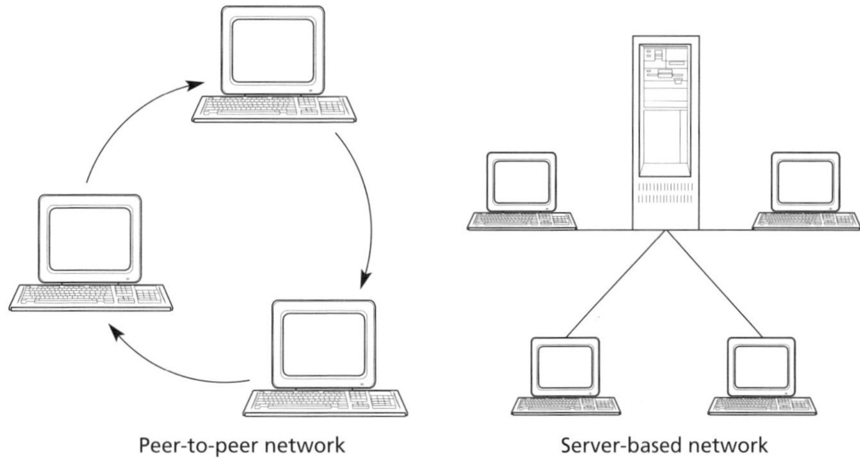

Figure 1.5 Different network models.

- **Peer-to-peer networking**: In this model, there are no assigned roles for any computer, so every computer in the network is an equal.
- **Client–server networking**: Some computers perform the server role and provide services to other computers, while client computers may use the resources that the servers offer.

1.4 Network types

Networks are distinguished by the relative distance between the devices they connect, and the general communication method they use (wire or wireless).

1.4.1 Local Area Networks (LANs)

These networks connect devices that are relatively close to each other, perhaps within the same building. The technology used in these networks has some distance limitations, defining the area that contains the devices. (See Fig. 1.6.)

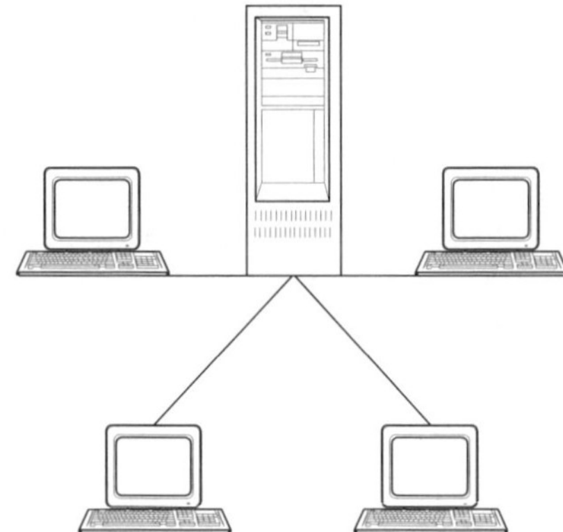

Figure 1.6 Local Area Network.

1.4.1.1 LAN topologies

In a LAN, the different ways the devices could be connected to each other determine the network topology. This topology will depend on the network architecture selected (Ethernet, token ring, FDDI (Fibre-Distributed Data Interface), etc.). Figure 1.7 shows different network topologies.

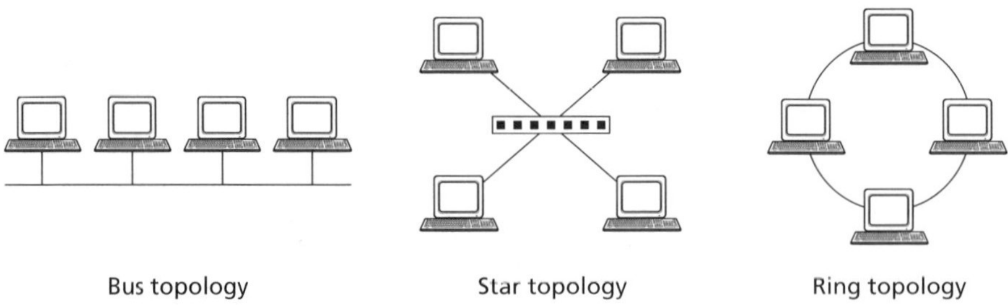

Figure 1.7 Network topologies.

1.4.2 Wireless Local Area Networks (WLANs)

These networks connect devices without wires, using radio frequencies or infrared. Owing to the distance limits of the technology used, the devices must be reasonably close to each other. (See Fig. 1.8.)

1.4.3 Wide Area Networks (WANs)

These networks use technology that allows the connection of devices over greater distances, and, in most cases, these networks connect distant LANs by means of **routers**. (See Fig. 1.9.)

The technology used to link both routers may be either a **dedicated leased line** (a communication channel between two points leased by an organization for its exclusive use) or a **packet switching network**, which uses WAN protocols such as Frame Relay or ATM. There are also other types of networks,

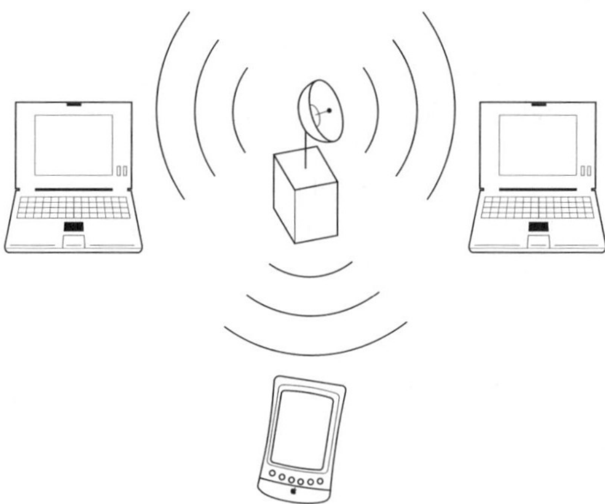

Figure 1.8 Wireless Local Area Network.

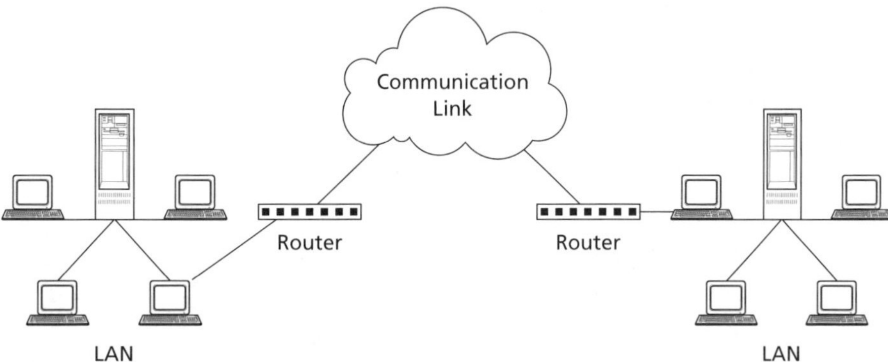

Figure 1.9 Wide Area Network.

such as Campus Area Networks (CANs), and Metropolitan Area Networks (MANs), which are intermediate options between LANs and WANs in terms of scale and complexity.

1.5 The Open System Interconnection (OSI) Reference Model

1.5.1 Introduction

Whenever we have complex systems, we use models to simplify the problem and make it easy to understand. In this case, the OSI Reference Model is used to provide a framework for both designing networking systems and for explaining how networking systems work.

This model consists of seven conceptual layers, numbered from one to seven. The layer number represents the position of the layer in the model, with the lowest layer (number one) corresponding closest to the hardware used to implement the network, while the highest layer (number seven) is the Application layer, which deals with the network users' high-level applications.

Each layer has specific functions and provides services for the layer immediately above it. In this way, each time a packet is received by the hardware, each layer processes the packet received and gives it to the layer above. When an application wants to send a packet over the network, it starts with the layer number seven, which uses the services of the layer immediately below it, and so on, until the packet is sent over the network.

1.5.2 The seven-layer model

The following is a detailed description of each layer's functions.

1.5.2.1 Layer 1: Physical layer

The Physical layer provides the most basic level of connectivity. Here the data is physically moved across the network interface. For example, if a computer is connected to a LAN, the network interface card allows it to send electrical pulses over a wire to communicate with other computers. However, the Physical layer does not necessarily have to be a wire. It can use microwave radio signals or light pulses across a fibre-optic 'cable'. In other words, the Physical layer is the way that devices signal each other. (See Fig. 1.10.)

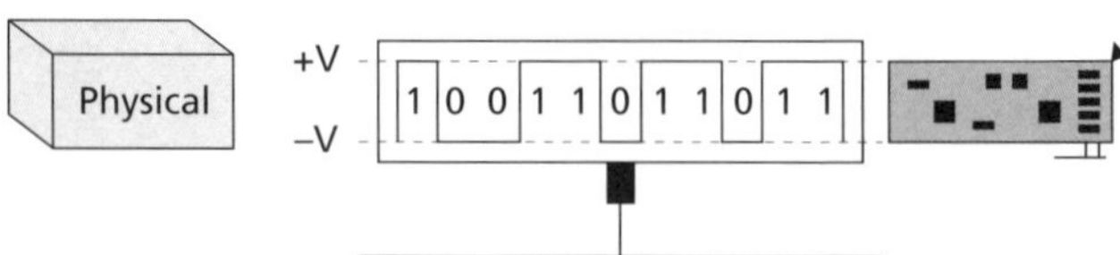

Figure 1.10 The Physical layer transforms logical bits into electrical pulses (and vice versa) and transmits (and receives) them over the network.

Some devices such as repeaters and hubs operate at this layer. They do not operate at a logical level (zeros and ones); they only understand electrical pulses. While repeaters are used to extend the connection of devices (like signal amplifiers, allowing driving a longer cable), hubs are used in Ethernet to interconnect devices using twisted pair cable (10BASET), creating a star topology.

1.5.2.2 Layer 2: Data Link layer (DLl)

This layer defines the rules about how the Physical layer will be used. Here the electrical pulses are converted into zeros and ones. This layer is responsible for logical link control, media access control, hardware addressing, error detection and handling; and defining Physical layer standards. Some protocols associated with layer 2 are Ethernet, Token Ring, FDDI, IEEE 802.11, SLIP and PPP. (See Fig. 1.11.) This layer is often divided into two sub-layers: the Logical Link Control (LLC) and the Media Access Control (MAC).

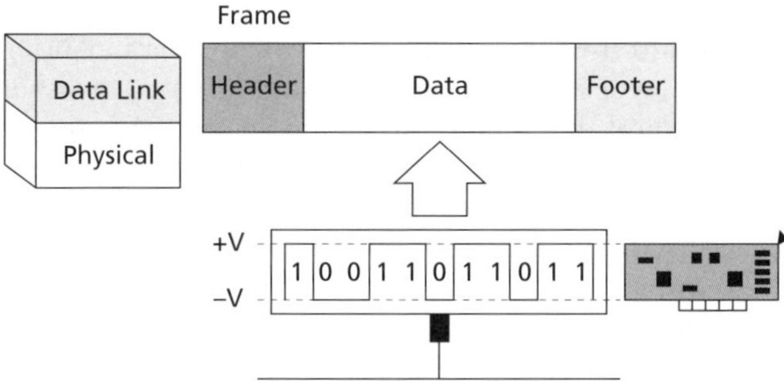

Figure 1.11 The Data Link layer encapsulates messages from the upper layer, and provides addressing, error detection and handling to deal with the local network.

The Physical layer and the Data Link layer are so closely related that many types of hardware are associated with the Data Link layer.

1.5.2.3 Layer 3: Network layer

This layer defines the link between networks and provides the necessary tasks to transform individual networks into inter-networks. It is responsible for inter-network addressing, datagram encapsulation, routing, fragmentation, error handling and diagnostics. (See Fig. 1.12.)

Routers are devices that operate at this layer. Their main function is to receive a datagram (packet), analyse the destination address, and route it in the best way according to the traffic information it contains. These routers communicate with each other using special routing protocols that inform them about networks traffic status.

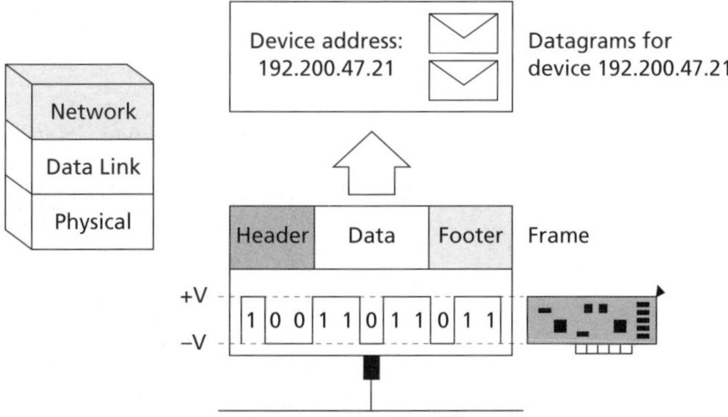

Figure 1.12 The Network layer provides the addressing for inter-networking routing, fragmentation and error handling.

1.5.2.4 Layer 4: Transport layer

While the Physical layer handles the bits, the Data Link layer deals with local networks, and the Network layer does the same with routing between networks, the Transport layer is like a 'mediator layer' between the three lower layers, and the three higher 'software application' oriented layers.

This layer introduces addressing at the process level. Hence, we could have several different applications on the same device moving data through the same lower-layer protocol implementation. As a result, the transport layer acts as a multiplexer, serving different applications from which the data is received and moving it through the lower layers to the network; and as a de-multiplexer, receiving the data from the lower layers and sending it to the appropriate application, according to the application address.

While the network layer fragments the data into small pieces according to what the Data Link layer requires, the Transport layer fragments the data according to the Network layer's requirements.

As explained above, some protocols are 'connection-oriented', meaning that before devices can exchange data they need to establish a 'logical connection', and after a successful data transfer, they may terminate this link. In such cases, this layer's responsibility involves the creation of a connection (a 'virtual circuit') and the destruction of the connection upon completion.

In cases where an implemented protocol offers a reliable delivery of data, the Transport layer has the responsibility of reordering any packets that have arrived out of sequence, requesting that any lost packets are retransmitted and providing flow control features. (See Fig. 1.13.)

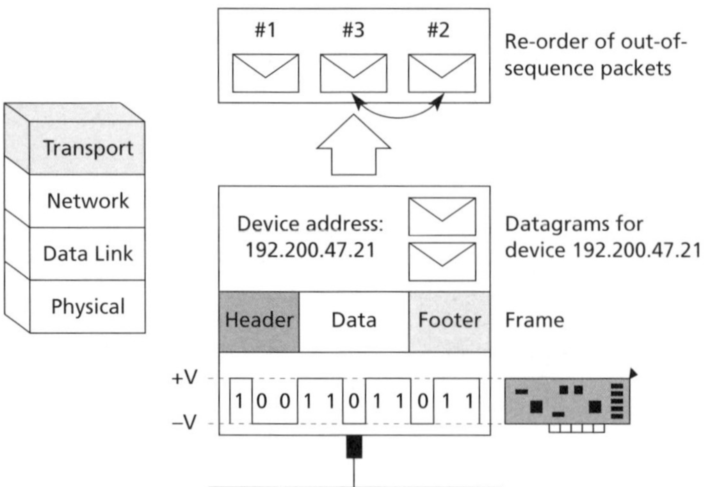

Figure 1.13 The Transport layer is responsible for providing process addressing, and in some cases reliable communications, so it can re-order out-of-sequence packets, and even request to re-transmission of lost ones.

1.5.2.5 Layer 5: Session layer

This layer provides the implemented functions necessary to establish and manage software process sessions. In this way, two software processes can 'dialogue' or interact over a persistent logical link during a specific period. As a result, a device can simultaneously communicate with many other devices by assigning each connection its own session. (See Fig. 1.14.) This layer opens, controls and then closes the session between two network devices.

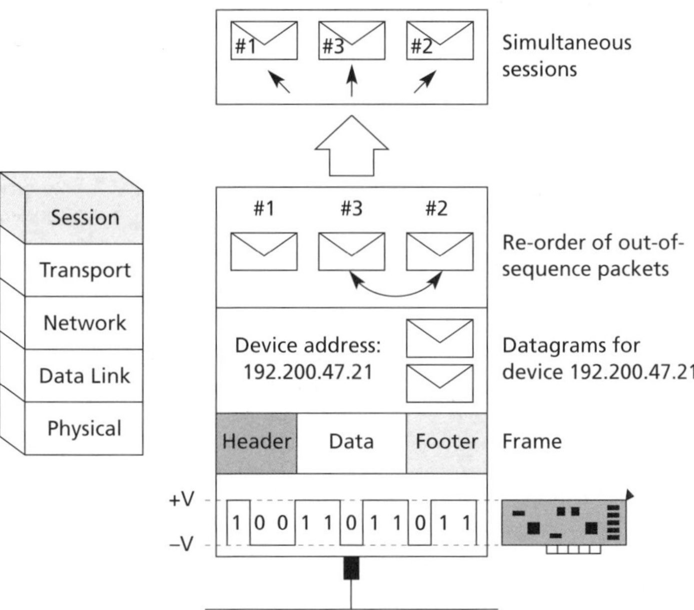

Figure 1.14 The Session layer allows the computer to communicate with many other computers by assigning each connection its own session.

This functionality is implemented as an application program interface (API), and it provides connection services to the layers above. As a result, network programmers are free from worrying about a lot of low-level details.

1.5.2.6 Layer 6: Presentation layer

As networks can consist of many different types of devices with highly varied hardware (platform) and software (operating systems), in some circumstances it is necessary to represent data in different ways. This translation job is handled by the Presentation layer.

If compression (and decompression) is required to improve data throughput, or encryption (and decryption) is needed for security reasons, this layer provides such functionalities. (See Fig. 1.15.)

1.5.2.7 Layer 7: Application layer

This layer provides the user with interface and it implements the services required from applications. This does not mean that the applications or programs reside in this layer, but that programs use the protocol services residing in this layer. Application layer protocols include HTTP, FTP, SMTP and POP3. For example, a web browser program does not reside in the

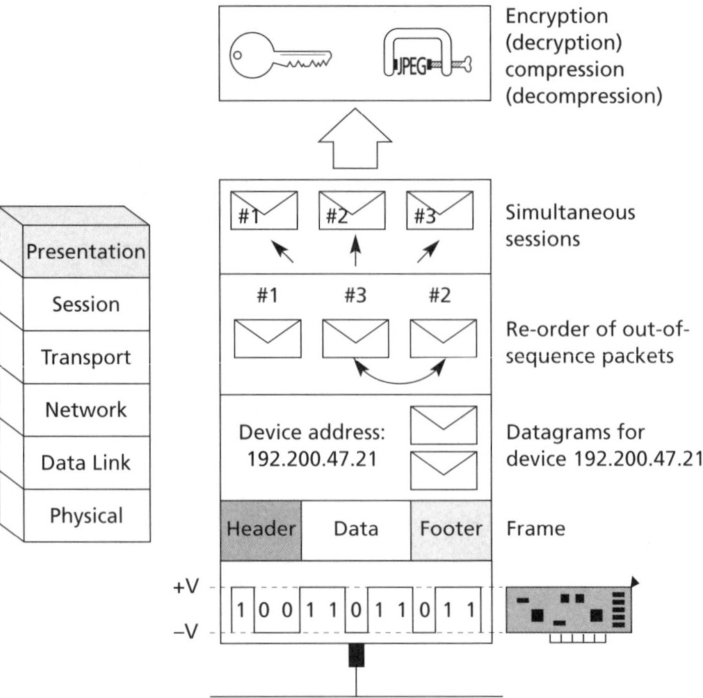

Figure 1.15 The Presentation layer performs translation jobs, as well as encryption/decryption and compression/decompression services.

Application layer, but it uses the HTTP protocol services that have functions on this layer. (See Fig. 1.16.)

It is important to notice that not all programs have to use the services offered by the Application layer; there are programs (including the operating system) that use services directly from other layers down in the stack, such as the transport services offered by User Datagram Protocol (UDP) and TCP.

1.5.3 Inter-layer communications

In the OSI model, two different kinds of communication take place between layers. Since devices are physically connected only at layer 1, all other layers must 'pass down' their data in order to transmit it over the network. In the same way, all data arriving at a layer must first pass through the physically connected layer 1. This means that there is a **vertical** communication between layers within the same device. The word 'interface' is used to describe the mechanism for communication between 'adjacent' layers in the model.

However, this is not the only communication process that occurs between layers. Although layer 1 is the only one physically connected to provide actual communications, the other layers are logically connected with the same-level layer in other devices. For example, when a layer needs to send data to other devices, this data is received by the same-level layer in the

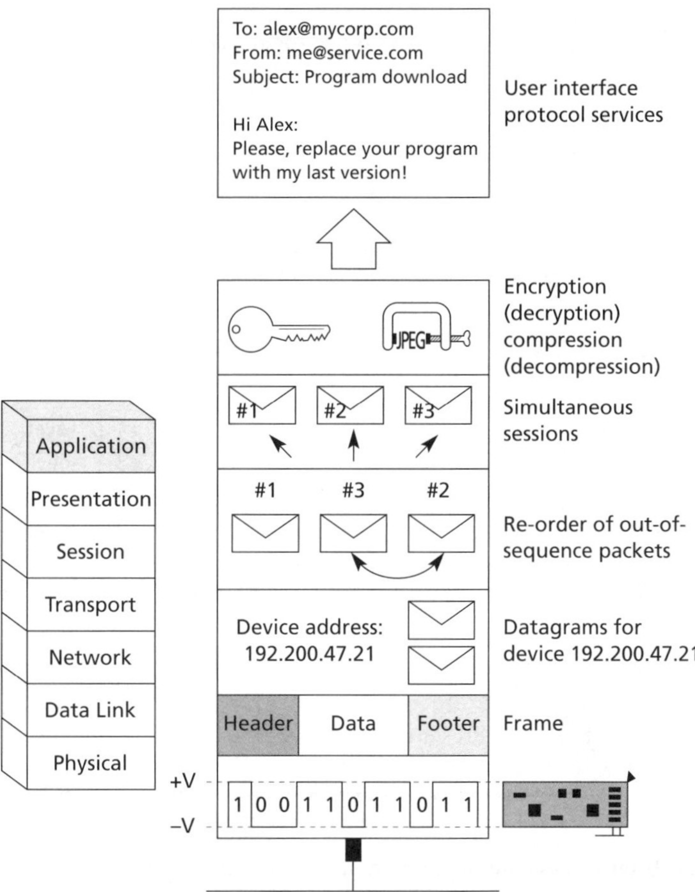

Figure 1.16 The Application layer presents specific user applications and functions.

receiver device. This means that there must be a logical connection between these layers, like an inter-layer dialogue, and this is called **horizontal** communication. (See Fig. 1.17.)

1.5.4 Message routing

In section 1.4, we saw WANs as distant LANs, interconnected with the appropriate technology. (See Fig. 1.9.) We also saw that a router device connects a LAN with other networks (represented by a cloud). Indeed, when we described a packet switching network (Fig. 1.3), we stated that the packets flow through router devices. However, we did not explain how these routers do their job. Now, with the OSI model in mind, we will describe how messages are routed through the network.

Suppose we have two LANs connected by a router, with two devices (A and B) from each LAN. If device A wants to send a message to device B (in a different LAN), the Application layer in device A will pass it down through the stack to send it over the local network. However, as device A knows that

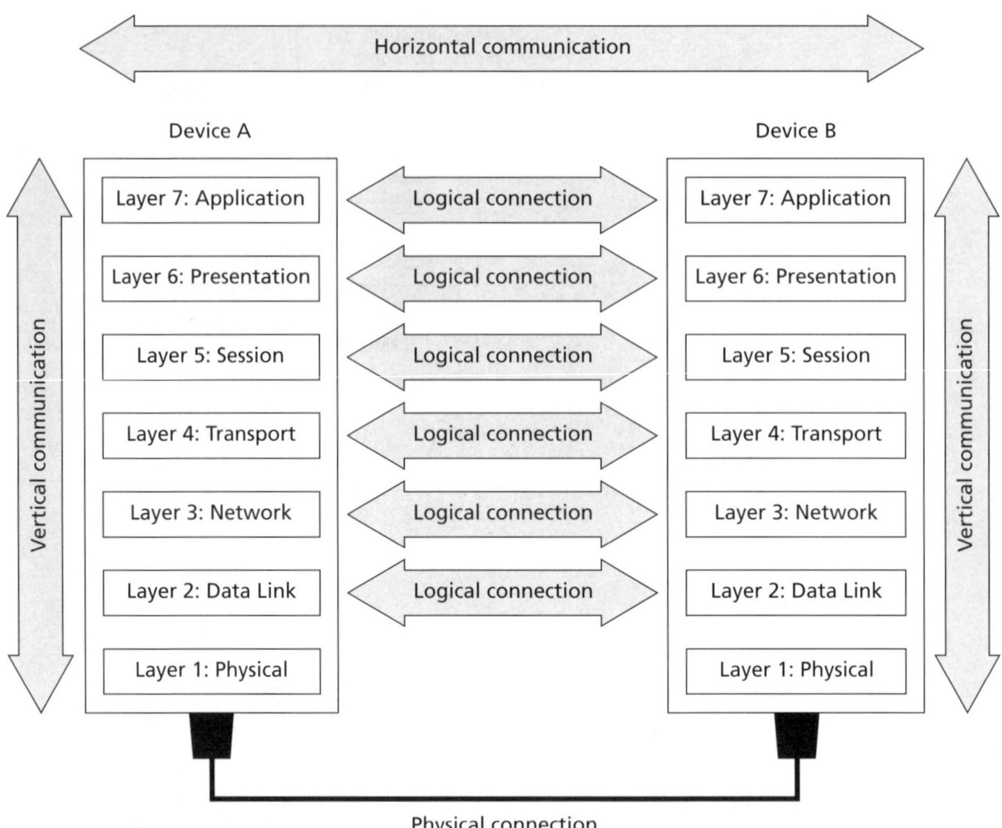

Figure 1.17 Inter-layers communication process in the OSI model.

device B is on a different network, this packet is first directed to the router. (Device A knows that device B is in another LAN by comparing the logical address of device B with the sub-net mask of the LAN where device A belongs. This will be clarified when, in a subsequent chapter, we see the IP addressing scheme of TCP/IP.) Notice that device A, sub-net A, and the router interface to sub-net A, all are on the same LAN (logical address 130.10.24.X), while device B is on a different LAN (device B logical address 130.10.45.2)

After layer 1 of the router receives the packet from device A, it processes it and passes it to the upper layers, where (after layer 2 performs its job), the packet arrives at layer 3. Now the router must know if device B is in the same LAN or in another LAN not connected to it. In the second case, the packet must be redirected to another router in order to follow its appropriate journey.

In this case, the router sends the package to device B because they are on the same LAN (sub-net B). Finally, the Physical layer of device B will receive the packet, and it will send it to the upper layers, arriving at the Application layer. Therefore, in this process, we can see how the Application layer in device A creates a 'dialogue' with the Application layer in device B, sending a message by horizontal communication. (See Fig. 1.18.)

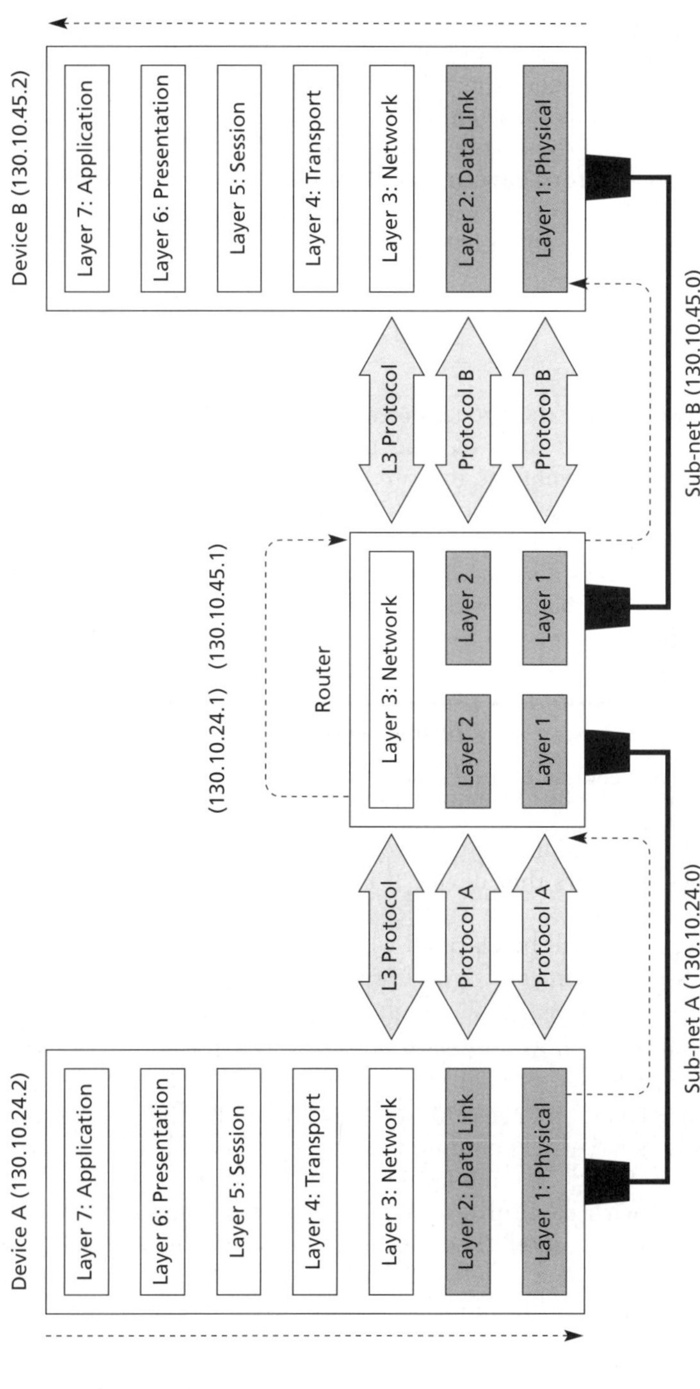

Figure 1.18 Message Routing in the OSI Model.

Note that the router has two interfaces, and each one is connected to different LANs (sub-net A and sub-net B). For this reason, each interface has a different logical address assigned to it. However, some routers can have more than two interfaces.

Observe that, as a router can connect two different LANs (for example Ethernet and Token Ring) the router can have different layer 1 and layer 2 implementations for each interface to each network. However, layer 3 (the inter-network protocol) remains the same for both interfaces.

Finally, routers have internal tables with the necessary information to decide the best way to conduct the packets. This information is exchanged between routers, and it is handled by specific protocols.

1.6 Summary

- Networking is the process of working with networks and associated technologies. Networks can be defined as a group of devices connected together to exchange information and share resources. The most important advantages of networking are connectivity, communication, data sharing and hardware sharing.
- A protocol is a series of rules, messages, procedures and other types of mechanism that allow devices to communicate effectively with each other. There are two types of protocols: *connection-oriented protocols*, which need to establish a 'logical connection' before data transfer can take place; and *connectionless protocols*, which do not need this 'logical link', so devices can start sending data as soon as they need to.
- Messages can have a similar structure consisting of a header, the data and a footer. The header may include the source and destination addresses and the footer may include a message integrity check control field. Different types of message transmission include unicast, multicast and broadcast.
- Different types of network can be distinguished based on their model (peer-to-peer and client–server networks); on the relative distance between devices and the type of media used (LANs, Wireless-LANs and WANs); or on their topology (bus, star and ring).
- The OSI Reference Model divides the overall communication process into seven layers, forming a 'protocol stack'. Each layer is responsible for different functions required in the process. Each layer provides services to its upper layer, and uses the services offered by the lower layer. As a result, there is a 'vertical communication' between adjacent layers on the same device. However, same-level layers from different devices can also communicate with each other('horizontal communication'), by establishing a 'logical connection'. The routing process (messages passing between different devices over a network until they reach their final destination) is an integral part of this model.

2

The TCP/IP stack

At the end of the previous chapter, we considered the OSI Reference Model, and its layered structure (protocol stack). In this chapter, we will introduce the TCP/IP stack, and we will use the OSI model as a reference. We will present the TCP/IP stack architecture, the protocols that constitute it, and the dependencies between them. But first, we will see the history behind this protocol development, and different perspectives about the services offered. At the end of this chapter, we describe the Internet Protocol standardization process, the request for comments documents and the organization behind this work.

2.1 The need for a new protocol: the birth of the Internet

In the first introductory chapter, we explained the advantages of networking: **connectivity** and **communication**. These advantages were the main motivation for connecting universities and research centres worldwide with an inter-network. In this way, the challenge was to interconnect networks (LANs) from each point. But, in most cases, these networks were very different, since they had different computer hardware, operating systems, network technology and software. In order to have these networks interconnected, it was necessary to have a new set of rules, messages and procedures that supported those different platforms; in other words, a new protocol was required.

The United States Defense Advanced Research Projects Agency (ARPA) developed the ARPAnet, as a part of packet switching networks research, using a number of protocols adapted from the existing technologies. However, the developers realized that a new protocol would be necessary in order to have the ARPAnet scaled to a larger size.

In 1973, the ARPA developed the Transmission Control Program (TCP), the first version of the intended protocol. This version was revised, and formally documented in RFC (Request For Comments – see section 2.6) 675 'Specification of Internet Transmission Control Program', in December 1974. Version 2 of TCP was documented in March 1977.

Until this version arrived, the protocol presented only one core (without a structured layer). In August 1977, the Internet pioneer Jon Postel published a document where he suggested a layered structure in order to separate the host level end-to-end protocol, and the Internet packaging and routing protocol. In this way, the TCP core split into TCP at the Transport layer, and the IP at the Network layer. Now, the protocol's name became 'TCP/IP'. Even though this process began in version 3 of TCP, written in 1978, the first formal standards were created in 1980, with version 4. So, the first version of IP is version 4. After this, TCP/IP became the standard protocol running the ARPAnet, having more and more networks connected to the ever-growing ARPAnet using TCP/IP protocols, and the Internet was born.

2.2 Two perspectives of the TCP/IP services

As already mentioned, the TCP/IP stack is structured into functional layers, where each layer provides services to the upper layer, and uses services from the lower layer. In this way, each layer is responsible for different functions required for the overall communication process. This perspective shows the internal process of taking services between layers from an internal point of view.

However, from an external point of view, considering the TCP/IP stack as a whole, we could distinguish two different perspectives, depending on the service consumer.

2.2.1 End-user perspective: Application level services

The end-user makes use of applications such as an Internet browser, e-mail or FTP clients, in order to communicate or share information over the Internet. But these client programs use TCP/IP Application layer protocols, which, in turn, use services provided by the lower-level protocols. Of course, all these details are hidden from the end-user. From the end-user's perspective, the TCP/IP services enable them to make use of the power of the Internet.

2.2.2 Developer perspective: Network level services

The developer, who probably needs to send and receive data from different machines over the Internet, will take services from the lower-level layers, which provide transport functions such as TCP or UDP (User Datagram Protocol). From the developer's perspective, the TCP/IP services provide a way to transport data over the internet.

2.3 The TCP/IP stack architecture

The OSI Reference Model is very useful to describe the task required to implement a network. In order to describe the TCP/IP model, we will establish a correspondence between these two models (even though the OSI Reference Model was created after the TCP/IP stack, we could use it as a reference model for our comparative purpose).

The TCP/IP model uses four layers to implement the network. These four layers cover the OSI layers from 2 to 7. (See Fig. 2.1.) The Physical layer (layer 1 in the OSI model) is not implemented in the TCP/IP model. In fact, the TCP/IP implements a network between existing networks, so these existing networks already have their own network technology; for example, Ethernet, FDDI or Token Ring. So, the OSI layer 1 is already implemented in each existing network.

The TCP/IP layers are as follows:

- *Network Interface layer*: Also called the link layer, it is where the higher protocol layers interface with the local network. For this reason, on many TCP/IP networks, there is no TCP/IP running at this layer. For example; if we have TCP/IP over an Ethernet local network, the Ethernet drivers handle layer 1 (Physical) and layer 2 (Data Link) functions. And the same occurs with AppleTalk, FDDI or Token Ring, among others. However, for some technologies that do not have their own layer 2 implementation, such as direct serial line connections or dial-up telephone networking, this layer provides implementations like the Serial Line Interface Protocol (SLIP) and the Point-to-Point Protocol (PPP). In these cases, this layer provides the necessary interface between the Internet layer and the Physical layer. It corresponds to layer 2 in the OSI model.
- *Internet layer*: This layer is responsible for inter-network addressing (IP address), data encapsulation, routing, fragmentation, error handling and diagnostics. It corresponds to layer 3 in the OSI model. In this layer, we have running the IP protocol, the ICMP protocol and several routing protocols.
- *Transport layer*: This layer is responsible for transporting data between devices over an inter-network, in order to send data reliably or unreliably. This constitutes an end-to-end communication. In this layer, specific source and destination address are assigned to different process (port numbers), so several applications may be running in the same machine. The TCP and UDP belong to this layer.

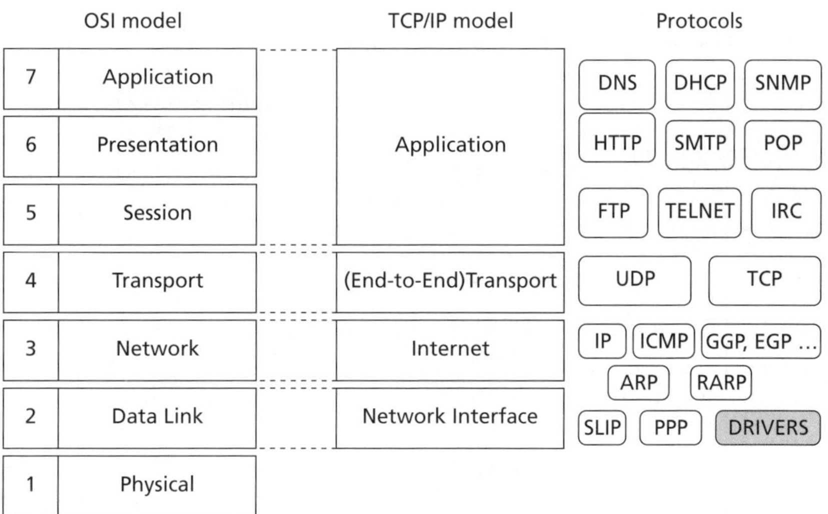

Figure 2.1 The OSI Reference Model and the TCP/IP model.

- *Application layer*: This layer spans layers 5 to 7 in the OSI model. The user's applications use protocols running in this layer, such as; Domain Name System (DNS), Dynamic Host Configuration Protocol (DHCP), File Transfer Protocol (FTP) and the Hypertext Transfer Protocol (HTTP), among others.

2.4 The TCP/IP suite

As we said before, the TCP/IP is a family of protocols, sometimes called a protocol suite. Each protocol is in charge of certain responsibilities, and it runs in a specific layer, according to its functionality. The core of the protocol suite, which provides the basic operation, comprises the IP, TCP and UDP.

Table 2.1 describes the most important (perhaps, the most known) protocols of the suite.

Table 2.1

TCP/IP layer	Functionality	Protocol	Description
2 Network interface	Network drivers	**SLIP** – Serial Line Interface Protocol	Provides a hardware driver for connections between two devices over a serial cable.
		PPP – Point-to-Point Protocol	As SLIP, but provides a better support for WAN links, adding authentication, encryption and other features.
2/3	Address translators	**ARP** – Address Resolution Protocol	Maps layer-3 IP address to layer-2 physical network address.
		RARP – Reverse Address Resolution Protocol	Provides layer-3 address of a device, from its layer-2 address.
3 Internet layer	Internet Protocol	**IP** – Internet Protocol	Is responsible for addressing and routing functions, providing encapsulation and delivery of Transport layer datagrams over a network.
		IP NAT – IP Network Address Translation	Translates addresses on a private network to different addresses on a public network, for security and sharing benefits.
		IP Sec – IP Security	Improves the IP transmission security.
		Mobile IP – IP Mobility Support	Provides an IP framework for mobile devices.
	IP Support Protocols	**ICMP** – Internet Control Message Protocol	Provides support for error handling and diagnosis.
	IP Routing Protocols	**RIP, GGP, HELLO, IGRP, BGP, EGP**, etc.	Supports the IP datagrams routing and the exchange of information between routers.

Table 2.1 Continued

TCP/IP layer	Functionality	Protocol	Description
4 Transport layer	End-to-end transport	**TCP** – Transmission Control Protocol	Transports data reliably, establishing and managing connection between devices.
		UDP – User Datagram Protocol	Connectionless protocol that transports data unreliably (it does not guarantee the delivery of data, but it has a better performance).
5-6-7 Application layer	World Wide Web	**HTTP** – Hypertext Transfer Protocol	Transfers hypertext documents between browsers and web servers, allowing the World Wide Web.
	File transfer	**FTP** – FileTransfer Protocol	Allows the transport of files between two devices.
	Interactivity	**Telnet** – Telnet Protocol	Allows a remote terminal session working on one device from another one.
		IRC – Internet Relay Chat	Allows chat between users.
	Electronic mail system	**RFC 822** – Electronic Mail Message Format	It describes the form, structure and content of an electronic mail message.
		MIME – Multipurpose Internet Mail Extensions	Extends the RFC 822 mail message format to support multimedia, binary files and character sets other than ASCII.
		SMTP – Simple Mail Transfer Protocol	Used for the delivery of mails between SMTP servers.
		POP3 – Post Office Protocol v.3	Allows the users to access and retrieve mail from their SMTP server.
		IMAP – Internet Message Access Protocol	Provides more flexibility for users in the way they access and retrieve mail messages.
	Newsgroups	**NNTP** – Network News Transfer Protocol	Implements the Usenet online community transferring news messages between news servers.
	Name system	**DNS** – Domain Name System	Resolves domain names into their corresponding IP address.
	File sharing	**NFS** – Network File System	Enables sharing files over TCP/IP networks.
	Host configuration	**DHCP** – Dynamic Host Configuration Protocol	Provides IP address and configuration to TCP/IP devices.
	Network management	**SNMP** – Simple Network Management Protocol	Allows remote management of networks and devices.
		RMON – Remote Monitoring	Used for remote monitoring of network devices.

2.5 TCP/IP stack protocol dependencies

We already know the layered structure of the TCP/IP stack, and we mentioned that protocols, running in these functional layers, provide services to other protocols. In this way, we might find some dependency between protocols running at one layer and protocols running at the lower layer. We could even find protocol dependency between protocols running at the same layer. In Figure 2.2, we see the protocol dependencies.

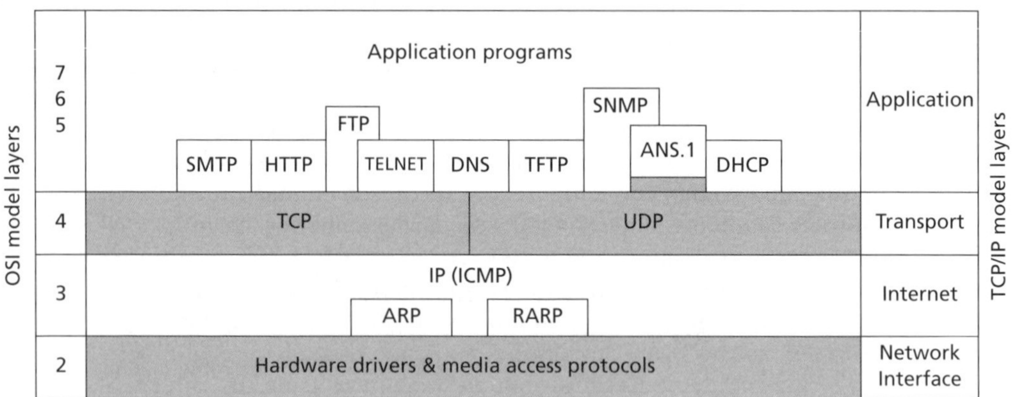

Figure 2.2 TCP/IP Protocol dependency.

The figure shows that some application protocols, such as SMTP, HTTP, FTP, TELNET and DNS, depend on TCP for their purpose. But other protocols, such as TFTP, SNMP, DHCP and DNS, depend on UDP. All those application protocols depend on the transport protocols running at the lower layer. The DNS protocol can use both TCP and UDP.

Moreover, some application protocols such as FTP (and SNMP), depend on other application protocols like TELNET (and ANS.1) running at the same layer. The ANS.1 (Abstract Syntax Notation) does not use the UDP protocol, and that is the reason for the greyed box between ANS.1 and UDP.

The TCP and UDP protocols running at the Transport layer depend on the IP running at the Internet layer. The IP depends on the protocols and drivers running at the Network Interface layer to effectively transmit and receive the data. In some cases, the IP depends on ARP to map the IP address into the physical (network interface) address.

Finally, the application programs, which provide the user with an interface and interact with him or her, depend on the application protocols to make use of the TCP/IP functionality. But, as Figure 2.2 suggests, some application programs could make use of the Transport layer functionality, using TCP or UDP.

2.6 The Internet Protocol standardization process

The Internet, like all the networking technologies, has standards associated with it. In the case of the Internet, these standards are *open*, meaning that nobody owns them, and anybody may contribute to them. Internet standards are described in documents called **Request For Comments** (RFC). As the name suggests, the document describes a proposal and request for comments and feedback about its contents.

The RFC development process starts with a new idea or proposal described in a document called an **Internet draft**. After many reviews and feedbacks, if this proposal is considered to be valuable, it is placed on the **Internet Standards Track**, starting as a **Proposed Standard**. Once the new idea or technology proposed in this document, which has undergone several tests and experiments, reaches sufficient maturity and is widely accepted, its status is changed into **Draft Standard**. Only when this specification is very mature and widely implemented, is its status changed to the final stage as **Internet Standard**, and an 'STD' standard number assigned to it. The whole process is fully documented in RFC 2026.

This RFC development process can take a long time (months and even years), and many RFC documents never get the Internet Standard status. However, as the Draft Standard is considered stable enough, many of them have been implemented in products without getting the Internet Standard status. Not all RFC documents describe standards; many of them just give additional information or comments about technologies or other standards.

All the RFC development process is in the charge of the Internet Engineering Task Force (IETF), through its working groups, and overseen by the Internet Engineering Steering Group (IESG) and the Internet Architecture Board (IAB). The RFC Editor office publishes the RFC documents, so we can find them at **http://www.rfc-editor.org/rfc-index.html**.

Whenever we need the complete specification for a TCP/IP process, we could get it from its corresponding RFC document, as the official source for the protocol implementation.

2.7 Summary

- The TCP/IP suite of protocols was developed as a challenge to interconnect very different networks, with different hardware, operating system, network technology and software, introducing a new set of rules, messages and procedures.
- TCP/IP offers services from two different perspectives: the end-user's perspective, which uses *Application level services* in order to communicate or share information over the Internet; and the developer's perspective, which uses *Network level services*, as a way to transport data over the Internet.

- In order to describe the TCP/IP stack architecture, we use the OSI Reference Model. The TCP/IP model uses four layers to implement the network: Network Interface layer, Internet layer, Transport layer and Application layer, and it covers the OSI layers from 2 to 7.
- The TCP/IP is a protocol suite (several protocols), rather than a single protocol. Each protocol has certain responsibilities, and it runs in a specific layer, according to its functionality. The core of the protocol suite is the Internet Protocol (IP), Transmission Control Protocol (TCP) and the User Datagram Protocol (UDP).
- Owing to the layered structure of the TCP/IP stack, where each protocol running in these functional layers provides services to other protocols, we might find some *dependency* between them. For example, SMTP, HTTP and FTP depend on TCP, while TFTP and DHCP depend on UDP. TCP and UDP depend on IP.
- The Internet, like all the network technologies, has standards associated with it. Internet standards are open (nobody owns them), and are described in documents called *Request For Comments*. The RFC development process can take a long time, and starts with a new idea or proposal described as an *Internet Draft*. After many reviews and feedbacks, the document status is changed to *Proposed Standard*. The next steps would be the *Draft Standard* and, finally, the *Internet Standard*, but the specification must be very mature and widely implemented to get to the final stages.

3

LAN technologies: Ethernet

In the last chapter, we described the TCP/IP layered structure. As we have seen there, the network interface layer is where the higher protocol layers interface with the local network, such as Ethernet, Token Ring and FDDI. This means that, in those cases, there are no TCP/IP protocols running at this layer. Instead, the LAN drivers handle the Physical and Data Link layers of the OSI model. After all, TCP/IP was designed to interconnect the existing LAN technologies (using its own drivers) rather than replace them. Even when Ethernet is not formerly part of the TCP/IP stack, it is important to see what it is and how it works, in order to fully understand how the TCP/IP Internet layer operates over it. We will also review the IEEE 802 model, which standardized the already existing LAN networks; and we will describe the IEEE Ethernet, which differs from the original specification. Since the Ethernet is the most common LAN implementation, it is worth the time we will spend looking at it.

3.1 Why Ethernet II and IEEE Ethernet?

Ethernet was developed by the DIX development group (initially Xerox, but later joined by Intel and Digital), which introduced the first version in 1980. At that time, the American Institute of Electrical and Electronic Engineers (IEEE) started the standardization of the newly developed network technologies. As a result, the current version of Ethernet was submitted and the 802.3 CSMA/CD (or IEEE Ethernet) standard was created, based on the Ethernet version at the time.

However, in 1982, the DIX group released version 2 of their own specifications, which differed from the already specified IEEE 802.3 standards. Since then, both specifications have been modified. As a result, two different versions of Ethernet are found: the IEEE 802.3 Ethernet and the non-IEEE commonly named Ethernet II. Although both standards are very similar, they differ in some aspects, especially in the frame formats, as we will see later.

The 802.3 Ethernet was not the only LAN technology standardized by the IEEE. Others include the 802.5 Token Ring and the 802.11 Wireless.

3.2 Ethernet II

3.2.1 Principles of operation

In this type of LAN, the devices communicate with each other, transmitting messages through a shared medium; like the coaxial cable in a bus topology network, or unshielded twisted-pair (UTP) cable where all the devices are connected via a central hub, forming a star topology network.

The messages are transmitted in packets called frames. Electrical signals are used to encode the data with specific encoding techniques. When one station transmits a frame, it drives the shared medium with an electrical signal encoded with the message data. Each device connected to the same shared medium, receives the applied electrical signal which is amplified and decoded retrieving the transmitted frame. As the frame is received, a cyclic redundancy check is calculated, in order to validate the frame data integrity. Then, the frame destination address field is compared with the device hardware address, in order to decide whether this message was transmitted to this station. If so, the data is available to read. In case the message destination address does not match the device address, the message is discarded. There are special addresses like the broadcast address (all 1s) that is accepted by all stations; and the multicast address where a message is intended for a group.

The Ethernet hardware can be programmed with an individual address, a group (or multicast) address, and the possibility to accept or reject broadcast and multicast messages. (See Fig. 3.1.) As a shared medium, if two or more devices transmit messages at the same time, the other stations will receive a garbled frame. This situation is called a collision. When this happens, the overlapped electrical signals at the medium raise the electrical levels, and the receiving circuits are able to detect the collision. In order to handle the collisions, a mechanism is needed to manage the medium. The solution is the CSMA/CD method.

3.2.2 CSMA/CD access control method

The Carrier Sense Multiple Access (CSMA) is a 'listen to the medium before talking' approach. That is, when a node (device or station) needs to transmit, it senses the medium to see if another node is transmitting. If the medium is busy, the node waits a few microseconds and tries again. When the node senses no activity in the medium, it starts transmitting.

Special cases might occur, for example, when two nodes sensed the medium was quiet and they start transmitting simultaneously, or maybe one node started transmitting but the electrical signal did not arrive at the second node when the last one was sensing the medium (it takes some time for the electrical signal to propagate from one node to the other through the medium). In both cases, a collision will occur after they started transmitting, even though they had sensed a quiet medium. For this reason, it is necessary for the node to sense the medium as it transmits, in order to detect the collision produced in such cases.

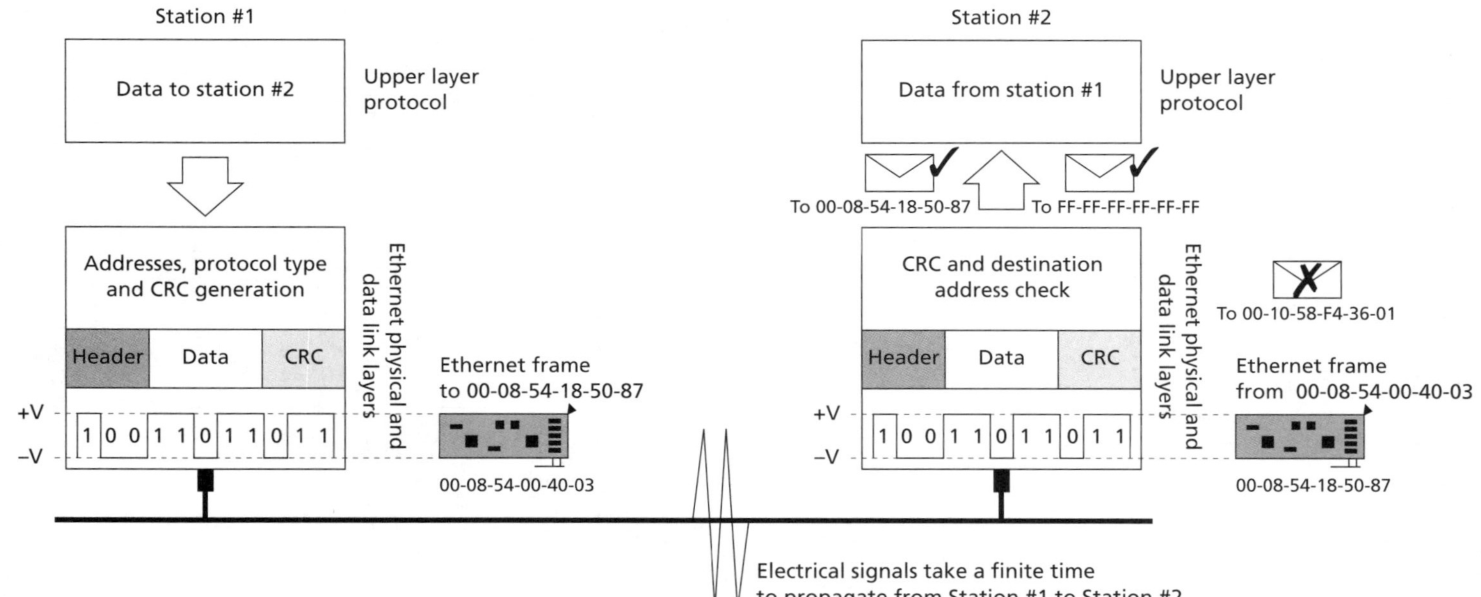

Figure 3.1 Data from upper layers are encapsulated in an Ethernet frame and delivered to the intended destination over the LAN.

Once the collision has been detected, the nodes transmit a jamming signal to notify the other nodes that a collision has occurred and the current message must be disregarded. Then, the nodes wait for a random amount of time before attempting to retransmit. As each node delays a different amount of time, the probability of a new collision is low. However, in case both nodes produce a collision again, they wait for a longer time (on an exponential basis) to retransmit, making the probability of a new collision even lower. This process is repeated a number of times before a transmission error is accused. This is known as an exponential random back-off algorithm. This collision detecting (CD) technique completes the CSMA/CD access control method.

The CSMA/CD method requires maximum and minimum length of network cable; as well as maximum and minimum frame size in order for the wait times the nodes needs to detect the collisions.

3.2.3 Ethernet II frame format

The Ethernet II frame format is shown in Figure 3.2. The **preamble** notifies the receiving nodes that a frame is beginning, and consists of seven bytes with pattern 10101010, followed by a last byte with pattern 10101011. The preamble is not formally part of the frame.

Each frame has a **destination address** field and a **source address** field. In this way, the receiving nodes compare the destination address with their own Ethernet address, and if they match, the frame is accepted. If they do not match, the frame is discarded. The destination node knows which node has sent the frame through the source address field.

The **Type** field, also called **EtherType**, designates the protocol type of the data field. With this information, the network drivers are able to pass the data to the appropriate protocol stack or layer. RFC1700 assigns common EtherType values.

The **Data** field contains the data received from upper layer protocols. The length of this field must be between 46 and 1500 bytes. If the data are less than 46 bytes, the upper layer protocols must pad the data to reach this minimum.

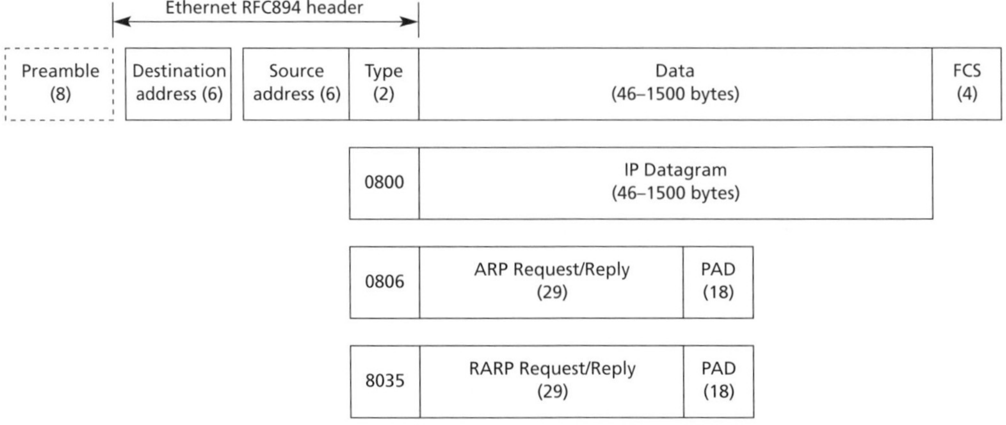

Figure 3.2 ETHERNET II frame format.

The **FCS** is a 32-bit code used to detect transmission errors, and consists of a cyclic redundancy checksum (CRC) calculation of all fields except the preamble and the FCS. When the frame is received in the destination node, the CRC is recalculated and compared with this field. If this comparison matches, it is assumed that no transmission error has occurred.

3.3 The IEEE 802 model (ISO 8802)

In order to standardize the local area networks, in February 1980, the IEEE created the 802 Networks Standards Committee. As a result, the IEEE 802 model was developed. It was also adopted by the ISO as an international LAN standard, and it was called ISO 8802. This model relates to the two lowest layers of the OSI model; the Physical and Data Link layers. In fact, the 802 model divides the related Data Link layer into three sub-layers; the Logical Link Control (LLC 802.2), the Bridging (802.1) and the Medium Access Control (MAC) layers. As the MAC layer depends on the Physical layer technology used, different standards apply; for example, 802.3 MAC is defined for CSMA/CD LANs, while 802.11 is defined for wireless LANs. (See Fig. 3.3.)

3.3.1 Logical Link Control layer (LLC – 802.2)

The LLC sub-layer provides the delivery service and multiplexing/de-multiplexing functions

The *delivery services* layer provides link services between nodes in the LAN. This means that upper layer protocols use these services in order to transmit data from one station to another. At the LLC level, the data packet is called a Protocol Data Unit (PDU). As different applications may have different requirements, the LLC defines different types of delivery service, to address those needs.

OSI model	802 model				
Data Link	802.2 Logical Link Control				
	802.1 Bridging				
	802.3 MAC	802.5 MAC	802.11 MAC	802.12 MAC	802.15 MAC
Physical	802.3 PHY CSMA/CD	802.5 PHY Token Ring	802.11 PHY Wireless LAN	802.12 PHY Demand Priority Access	802.15 PHY Wireless Personal Area Networks

Figure 3.3 The IEEE 802 model relates to the two lowest layers of the OSI model.

Three distinctive delivery services are offered:

- *Type 1 service: Unacknowledged connection-less service*. There is no need to establish a data link connection in order to transmit data (connection-less mode). This mode does not perform flow control or error recovery procedures.
- *Type 2 service: Acknowledged connection-oriented service*. In this type of service, a data link must be established prior to the transmission of data. This service offers frame sequencing, flow control and error recovery.
- *Type 3 service: Acknowledged connection-less service*. Like type 1, this service is connection-less, but the transmitted PDU must be acknowledged. In this way, there are some kinds of frames ordering and error recovery.

The upper layers would select the most appropriate type of service used, according to the application and the physical medium. For example, wireless LANs are less reliable than wired LANs, so it could be desirable to use acknowledged service for wireless LANs, and unacknowledged service for the wired LANs.

Multiplexing/de-multiplexing is needed because different applications or upper layers could also need to use the delivery services. In order to distinguish the data transmitted (received) from (for) those different applications, it is assigned an identification number called LSAP (Link Service Access Point). In this way, each upper layer, or application, that intends to use the LLC services accesses those services through this access point.

No matter what kind of network technology is used, the LLC is the same. In this way, the LLC constitutes a common entry point for upper layers to use any type of network (CSMA/CD, Token Ring, Wireless LAN, etc.) independently of the underlying technology. As a result, it is very easy to deal with different LAN technologies, while the same LLC services are used.

3.3.1.1 LLC PDU format

All LLC PDU must have the structure shown in Figure 3.4. As the LLC layer is common for any network technology, this is the PDU format for any kind of network.

The Destination Service Access Point (DSAP) address identifies the one or more service access points to which the PDU's information is intended. The Source Service Access Point (SSAP) address identifies the service access point that originated the PDU's information. (See Fig. 3.5.)

Figure 3.4 LLC PDU format.

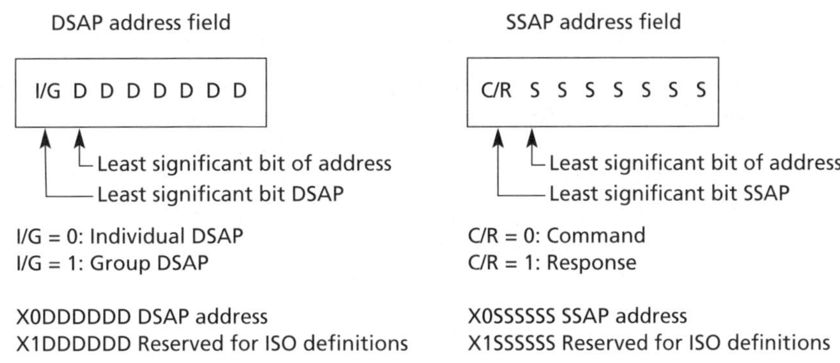

Figure 3.5 DSAP and SSAP address field formats.

The Control field consists of 8 or 16 bits, and it is used for command and response functions. It may contain sequence numbers. (See Fig. 3.6.)

The Information field is the data received from the upper layers to transmit to other station (outgoing packets), or the data received from other station to pass to the upper layers (incoming packets).

3.3.2 Bridging layer (802.1)

This layer covers the Media Access Control (MAC) bridges, which enable all types of IEEE 802 LANs to be interconnected. In this way, each station could connect itself to others at different LANs, as if they were attached to a single LAN.

The implementation of this layer is optional, and it is generally not implemented in small networks. This layer is described in IEEE 802.1 standard.

LLC PDU Control field bits

	1	2	3	4	5	6	7	8	9	10 – 16
Information transfer command/response (I-format PDU)	0	N (S)							P/F	N (R)
Supervisory commands/responses (S-format PDUs)	1	0	S	S	0	0	0	0	P/F	N (R)
Unnumbered commands/responses (U-format PDUs)	1	1	M	M	P/F	M	M	M		

N (S) = sender sends sequence number (bit 2 = least-significant bit)
N (R) = sender receives sequence number (bit 10 = least-significant bit)
S = supervisory function bit
M = modifier function bit
P/F = poll bit – command LLC PDUs
final bit – response LLC PDUs

Figure 3.6 The LLC PDU Control field formats.

3.3.3 The Media Access Control layer (802.X MAC)

This sub-layer provides the method to access the shared network medium. As this depends on the underlying technology, there are different MAC implementations for each type of network (CSMA/CD, Token Ring, Wireless, etc.). In this way, as the MAC layer relates too much to the Physical layer, they are both described in the same standard. See for example, the 802.3 standard entitled: 'CSMA/CD Access Method (MAC) and Physical (PHY) Layer Specifications'.

The MAC layer is responsible for addressing, frames generation and reception, and error detection.

3.3.4 The Physical layer (802.X PHY)

This standard describes the specific hardware implementation and its operation. As mentioned above, the Physical layer is described with the corresponding MAC layer for each network type, i.e. for each network technology there is a standard that describes both the MAC layer and the Physical layer.

3.3.4.1 802 physical addresses

One design goal was uniformity among the various LAN protocols. In addition, the same physical address scheme contributes to that. As the physical addresses are defined at the MAC layer, they are called MAC addresses. The most common format is a 48-bit address. (See Fig. 3.7.)

Bit 47 is the I/G (individual/group) bit. If this bit is 0, the address refers to an individual address. If this bit is 1, the address refers to a group (multicast). An address with all 1s refers to all the station (broadcast).

Bit 46 is the U/L (universally/locally administered) bit. If this bit is 0, the address follows the universal address format. In this case, the following 22 bits are an identifier assigned to the organization that manufactures the network interface board, while the last 24 bits confirm the unique address assigned by the organization. If this bit is 1, the 46 bits are part of a locally administered address, generally assigned by the network software.

Remember that each device in the network has a network interface controller (NIC), and the address of each device must be unique, in order to distinguish one station from the others. Therefore, the NIC manufacturer

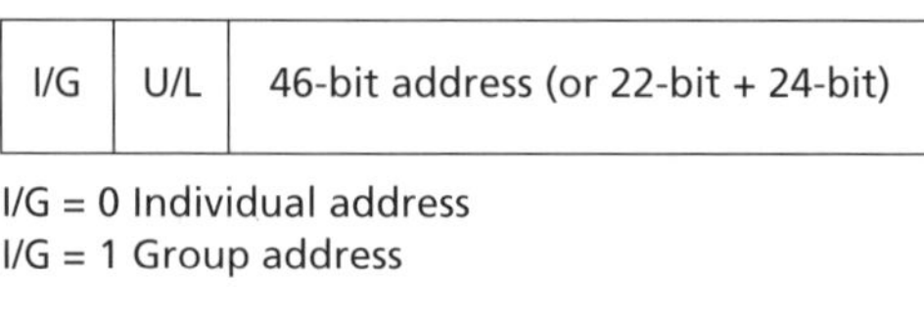

I/G = 0 Individual address
I/G = 1 Group address

U/L = 0 Universally administered address
U/L = 1 Locally administered address

Figure 3.7 Address field format.

must provide a unique address for each controller it produces. To achieve this, the manufacturer has a unique identifier assigned that constitutes the 22-bit field, and assigns a unique 24-bit address for each NIC manufactured. If you would like to know your PC NIC manufacturer identifier, you would get the MAC address with the ipconfig /all command (in Windows). For example, you get 00-08-54-18-5D-87. Then, it is necessary to query the IEEE website **http://standards.ieee.org/regauth/oui/index.shtml** where you can search the organizationally unique identifiers (OUI) with the first three bytes. If you enter 00-08-54 you will get the following message:

Here are the results of your search through the public section of the IEEE Standards OUI database report for 00-08-54:

```
00-08-54   (hex)              Netronix, Inc.
000854     (base 16)          Netronix, Inc.
                              3F-1, No. 31, Hsin-Tai Road,
                              Chupei City, Hsinchu Hsien
                              TAIWAN, REPUBLIC OF CHINA
```

[Note that bit 47 is 0 (individual address) and bit 46 is also 0 (universally administered).]

3.3.5 Sub-Network Access Protocol (SNAP)

We have already seen how the LLC layer provides LSAP as a way to share the LLC services among multiple protocols. In order to use this functionality, the protocols use the DSAP and SSAP address scheme. One half of the LLC address space was assigned to standard network layer protocols. The other half of the LLC address space is available for other protocols. Therefore, each protocol must use different LLC addresses.

However, there is another way in which several protocols can share the same LLC address. In this case, there is a particular reserved LLC address to use in conjunction with the Sub-Network Access Protocol (SNAP), which permits multiplexing and de-multiplexing of public and private protocols among multiple users of a data link, making use of the same LLC address (or link-service access point). (See Fig. 3.8.)

The SNAP PDU follows the LLC PDU header, and is composed of five bytes of header and *N* bytes of data. The header is called the protocol identifier, and the three first bytes are the OUI (the same used for the LAN MAC addresses) of the protocol owner organization, while the last two bytes are a number assigned by the organization itself. In this way, each public or private protocol can share the same LSAP address using different SNAP with different protocol identifiers.

The particular reserved LLC address, the so-called SNAP address, is AA or AB (hexadecimal values) depending on the context in which it appears. The LLC PDU control field is 03, corresponding to unnumbered information. (See Fig. 3.9.)

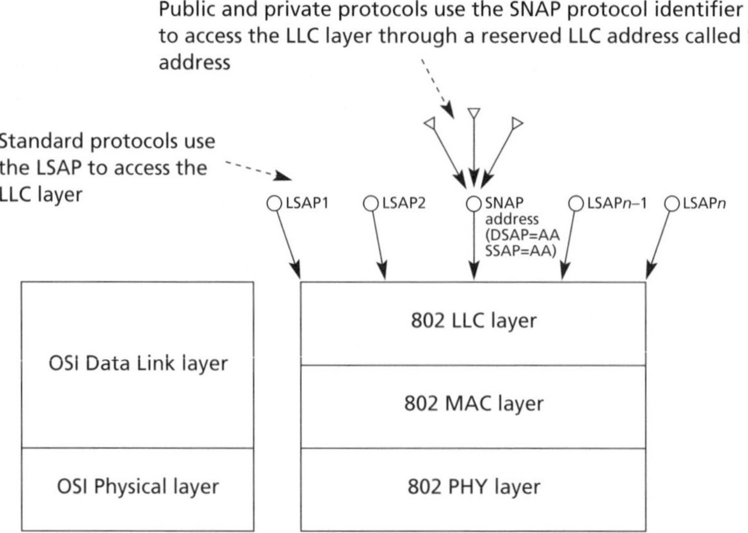

Figure 3.8 The LLC layer is shared by multiple standard protocols which use the LSAP to access the LLC services. SNAP uses one of these LSAPs (the SNAP address) to later share this access among multiple public and private protocols.

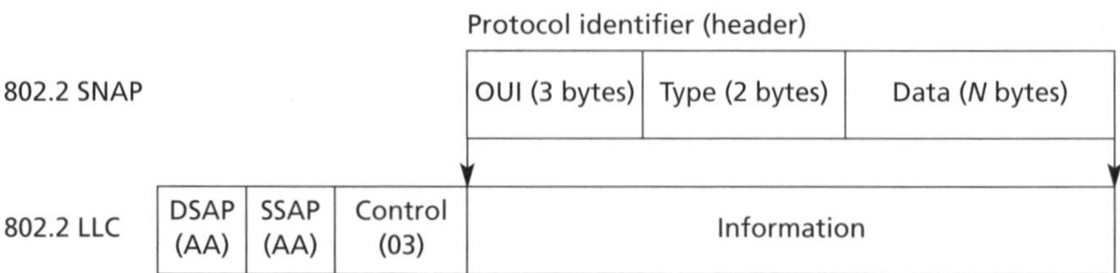

Figure 3.9 The SNAP PDU header acts as an extension of the LLC PDU header.

The original implementation of TCP/IP on Ethernet networks was based on the EtherType field found in Ethernet II frames. However, this field is not supported by the IEEE 802 standards. So, in order to have the IP datagrams transmitting over IEEE 802 Networks, the EtherType field is encoded using SNAP, as described in RFC1042. In this case, the SNAP fields take specific values, as shown in Figure 3.10.

3.4 802.3 CSMA/CD (IEEE Ethernet)

The original Ethernet technology was submitted to the IEEE for standardization. As a result, the 802.3 standard for CSMA/CD LANs was created. In fact, 802.3 LANs use the same CSMA/CD access control mechanism and the same media, and the hardware is interchangeable. The main difference is in the frame format. However, both frames can be used in the same LAN as long as the software is able to recognize each frame type.

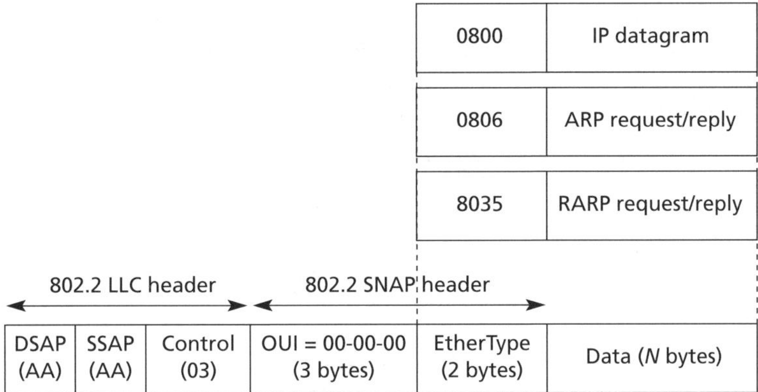

Fig. 3.10 The transmission of IP datagrams over IEEE 802 Networks, requires SNAP.

3.4.1 802.3 Media

Several cable standards can be adopted as a media. They are designated as a three-part name, for example, 10BASE5, where there is a 10 Megabits per second as a rate, BASE as a Baseband operation (or BROAD from Broadband operation) and 5, indicating segments length up to 500 metres.

Typical cable configurations are the following:

- 10BASE5: Operates at a 10 Mbps rate and it uses a low-loss thick (50 Ω) coaxial cable, with segments length up to 500 metres. It is expensive and very difficult to work with.
- 10BASE2: Operates at a 10 Mbps rate, using a low cost thin coaxial cable, with segments length up to 185 metres.
- 10BASET: Operates at a 10 Mbps rate, and it uses an unshielded twisted-pair (UTP) cable, where each segment is connected via a hub.
- 100BASETX: Operates at a 100 Mbps rate, and it uses a high-grade UTP (category 5), and a hub to connect each segment.
- 100BASEFX: Operates at a 100 Mbps rate, using optical fibre.

3.4.2 802.3 Frame format

We now have enough elements to understand the IEEE 802.3 frame structure used to transmit IP protocol datagrams. (See Fig. 3.11.)

The **preamble** consists of 56 bits alternating 1s and 0s (7 bytes with the 10101010 pattern), forming a square wave. This is necessary to adjust the receiver's automatic gain circuit and synchronize the receiver's clock. Following the preamble there is a **start delimiter frame**, with pattern 10101011, announcing the start of the frame. Both the preamble and SDF are handled by the physical layer, so we will not see them in the frame information.

The **destination** and **source MAC addresses** respond to the format already described in the 802 physical addresses section. The source MAC address is

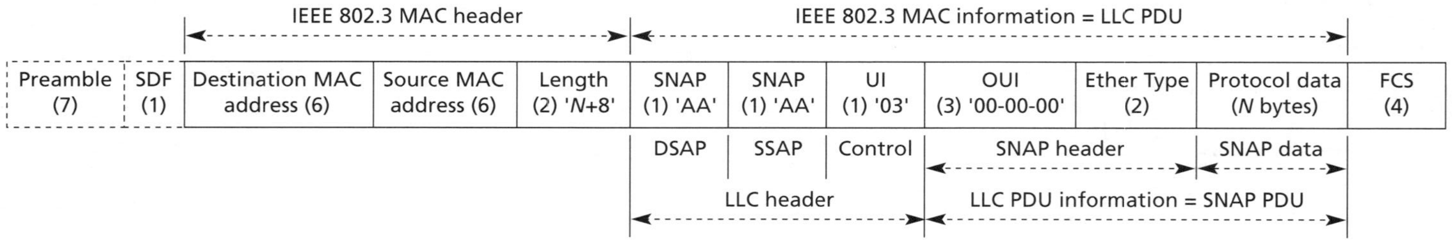

IEEE 802.3 MAC header | IEEE 802.3 MAC information = LLC PDU

Preamble (7)	SDF (1)	Destination MAC address (6)	Source MAC address (6)	Length (2) 'N+8'	SNAP (1) 'AA'	SNAP (1) 'AA'	UI (1) '03'	OUI (3) '00-00-00'	Ether Type (2)	Protocol data (*N* bytes)	FCS (4)
					DSAP	SSAP	Control	SNAP header		SNAP data	
					LLC header			LLC PDU information = SNAP PDU			

Figure 3.11 IEEE 802.3 Frame format.

the physical address of the station that sends the message, while the destination MAC address is the address of the station that receives it.

The **length** field consists of two bytes and informs the number of bytes in the LLC PDU (LLC header plus LLC information). This value must be in the range of 46 to 1500, because the total frame length (including both MAC addresses (6 + 6), length (2) and FCS (4)) must be in the range of 64 to 1518.

The Destination MAC address, the Source MAC address and the Length constitute the **802.3 MAC Header**.

Following the MAC header it is the **802.3 MAC information** field, where the LLC PDU received from the LLC layer is allocated. If the size of the data is less than 46 bytes, bytes with pattern 0x00 (hexadecimal value) must be appended to pad the field to the minimum length. This LLC PDU consists of a LLC PDU header, a SNAP header, and the protocol data field, as described in the corresponding sections. Remember that the SNAP header has the **EtherType** field, which indicates the type of protocol the data protocol field carries.

The last field in the 802.3 frame is the **Frame Check Sequence** (FCS), consisting of a 32-bit checksum value used to detect transmission errors.

3.5 IEEE 802.3 and Ethernet II networks comparison

IEEE 802.3 uses the same CSMA/CD access control mechanism developed for Ethernet II. Both networks use the same media signalling techniques, and the hardware is interchangeable.

The main difference between IEEE 802.3 and Ethernet II is in the frame formats, specifically with the Type/Length field. In the IEEE 802.3 frame, this field represents the length of the LLC PDU (maximum 1500 bytes or 05DC hexadecimal); and the protocol type in the Ethernet II frame. However, this protocol type code is always greater than 05DC hexadecimal, so it is easy to differentiate both frames by checking this field value.

The Ethernet II frame is used in most PCs and it is embedded TCP/IP network implementations due to its simplicity, avoiding the overhead superimposed by the LLC/SNAP fields. Ethernet frames with LLC/SNAP fields are IEEE 802.2 compliant.

3.6 Summary

- Ethernet, the most widely used LAN technology was developed by the DIX group, which introduced the first version in 1980. By 1982, the second version, known as Ethernet II, had been released.
- In this type of LAN, devices communicate with each other by transmitting messages through a shared medium, like coaxial cable or unshielded twisted-pair (UTP) cable. The messages are transmitted in packets called frames, using electrical signals to encode the data. As the medium is shared by all devices, simultaneous transmissions cause collisions, deforming the transmitted signals. In order to handle the collisions, the CSMA/CD method is used.

- The Carrier Sense Multiple Access (CSMA) part of the method consists of a 'listen to the medium before talking' approach. The collision detect (CD) part detects possible collisions after the frames started transmitting.
- The Ethernet II frame format consists of a preamble to synchronize the receiving clocks, destination and source addresses necessary to correctly deliver the frame, the EtherType field which designates the protocol type carried by the frame, the data as received from the upper layers, and the FCS used for error detection.
- In February 1980, the IEEE created the 802 Networks Standards Committee as a way to standardize the already existing LAN networks. As a result, the IEEE 802 model was developed.
- The IEEE 802 model relates to the two lowest layers of the OSI model. In fact, the Data Link layer is subdivided into three sub-layers; the Logical Link Control (LLC 802.2) the Bridging (802.1) and the Medium Access Control (MAC) layers. As the MAC layer depends on the Physical layer technology used, different standards apply: 802.3 MAC for CSMA/CD LANs, 802.5 MAC for Token Ring and 802.11 MAC for Wireless LANs, among others. Each standard describes both the MAC and the Physical layers for the specific network technology.
- The Logical Link Control layer provides link services through three distinctive types of delivery. It also provides the Link Service Access Point (LSAP) that allows several applications to access the link services through this access point. The LLC layer constitutes a common entry point for upper layers to use any type of network, independently of the underlying technology. The Sub-Network Access Protocol (SNAP) allows public and private protocols to share the same Link Service Access point.
- The main difference between IEEE 802.3 and Ethernet II is in the frame formats, specifically with the Type/Length field. This value must be checked to distinguish both types of frames. Ethernet frames with LLC/SNAP fields are IEEE 802.2 compliant.

4

Network interface: SLIP and PPP

In the previous chapter, we saw Ethernet as the most used LAN technology. These LANs provide their own Physical and Data Link layers, allowing TCP/IP to run over them. In this chapter, we will see a special communication solution that does not provide the necessary Data Link layer: the **serial links**. In order to provide a solution, TCP/IP has two protocols that do run at the network interface layer: the Serial Line Interface Protocol (SLIP) and the Point-to-Point Protocol (PPP), which were designed for those technologies such as serial connections that did not have their own Data Link layer implementation. Before that, an introduction to the RS-232 serial is necessary to fully understand why SLIP and PPP were designed to have TCP/IP running on serial lines.

4.1 Point-to-point network solutions

As we saw above, the TCP/IP was designed to interconnect the already existing networks, such as Ethernet and Token Ring. Each LAN network provides the Physical and Data Link layers, encapsulating the Internet layer data (IP datagram), and transmitting it over the network. Therefore, the Data Link provided by the LAN layer is necessary for the TCP/IP to run.

However, LANs are not the only structure that enables devices to communicate with each other. Other solutions, such as the serial lines, allow two devices to send and receive data. This is a point-to-point solution, and it is mostly used in dial-up connections. (See Fig. 4.1.)

In these cases, computer serial ports such as RS232 or the most recent USB are connected to analogue public telephone lines through a modem. As analogue telephone lines have a narrow bandwidth (they were designed for voice use), computer digital signals must be converted. This is the function of the modem (**MO**dulator/**DEM**odulator) which transmits a carrier (analogue signal) modulated by the digital data.

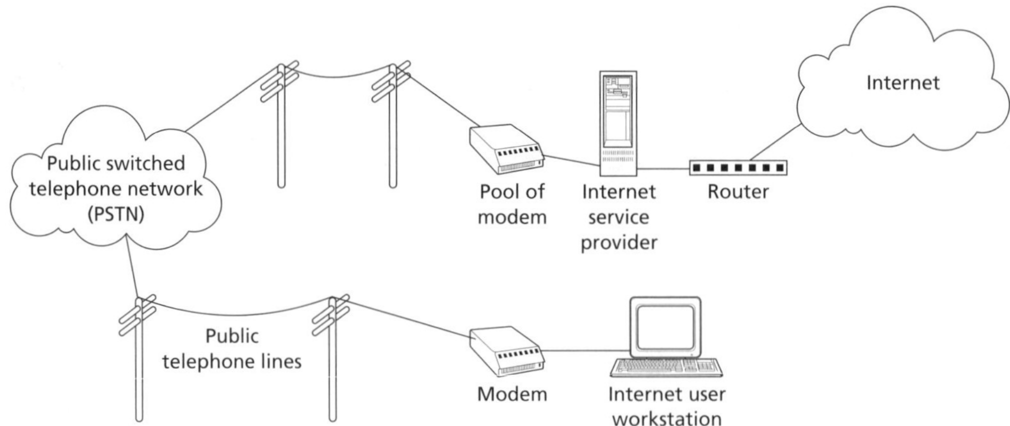

Figure 4.1 Internet dial-up connections use serial lines as point-to-point solutions.

4.2 Serial line interfaces

4.2.1 RS-232 serial port

RS-232 is a recommended standard used in serial lines for asynchronous communications with data transfer rates up to about 115 Kbaud (and even more in some cases). Distances between devices can be about 15 metres.

The standard defines two types of device: the data terminal equipment (DTE) and the data communication equipment (DCE). In order to link both devices, they must follow the RS-232 recommendations. The recommendations include details of:

- Electrical specifications: the voltages to be used on the signal lines.
- Mechanical specifications: the connectors to be used and the pin distribution
- Protocol specifications: the data format to be used for data transmission.

4.2.1.1 RS-232 electrical specifications

The voltages levels used range from –3 V to –15 V for the Logic 1 (also called 'Mark'), and from +3 V to +15 V for the Logic 0 (also called 'Space'). (See Fig. 4.2.)

Since most microcontrollers are powered with +5 V DC (some require +3.3 V DC), an RS-232 converter IC is required in order to translate –V/+V RS-232 voltage levels into the +V/0 V levels that the microcontroller can understand. Examples of such ICs are MAX232 and MAX233 chips from Maxim Corp.

4.2.1.2 RS-232 mechanical specifications

Two types of connectors are used: DB25 (25 pins) and DB9 (9 pins) (male for the DTE and female for the DCE). The distribution on the pins depends on the type of device, and is shown in Table 4.1.

The terms DTR, DSR, RTS and CTS are used for hardware flow control. When the terminal (DTE) is ready, it asserts the DTR signal (it sets it to 'true'). The DSR is asserted (true) when the modem (DCE) is ready. When

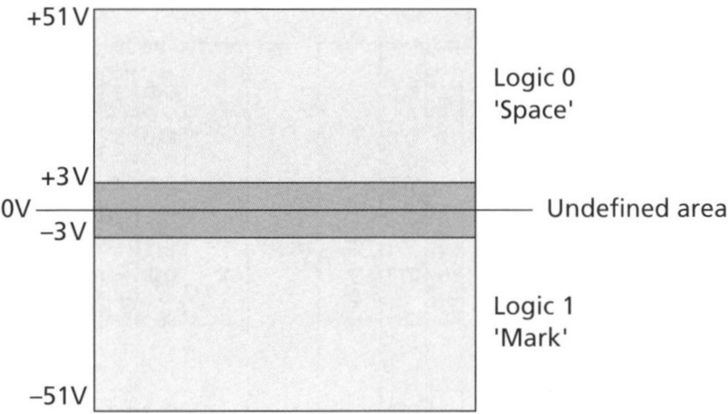

Figure 4.2 RS-232 Voltage levels.

Table 4.1

		DTE (Terminal)			DCE (Modem)	
Term	Description	DB-9m	DB-25m	Direction	DB-25f	DB-9f
TxD	Transmit Data	2	3	→	2	3
RxD	Receive Data	3	2	←	3	2
RTS	Request to Send	4	7	→	8	5
CTS	Clear to Send	5	8	←	7	4
DSR	Data Set Ready	6	6	←	4	20
DCD	Data Carrier Detect	8	1	←	1	8
DTR	Data Terminal Ready	20	4	→	6	6
RI	Ring Indicator	22	9	←	9	22
SG	Signal Ground	7	5	---	5	7

the terminal needs to transmit, it asserts the RTS pin, and it should wait for the modem to assert the CTS pin. Under this condition, both devices can start transmitting and receiving using the TxD and RxD pins.

The DCD is asserted when the modem detects the carrier signal. The RI indicates when the modem is receiving a call from the other party.

4.2.1.3 Cable configurations

The cable that links both devices must be quite straightforward, connecting all the pins as shown in Table 4.1. But some types of connections, such as PC to PC, where both devices are DTE, require a different cable. In this case, a null-modem cable is used. (See Fig. 4.3.)

There is a special case that connects two PCs with a three-wire cable. In this case, the TxD of each device is connected to the RxD of the other, and the third cable joins the grounds (SG pins). In this easy configuration, the hardware flow control is not possible, so software flow control must be used in order to avoid loss of data.

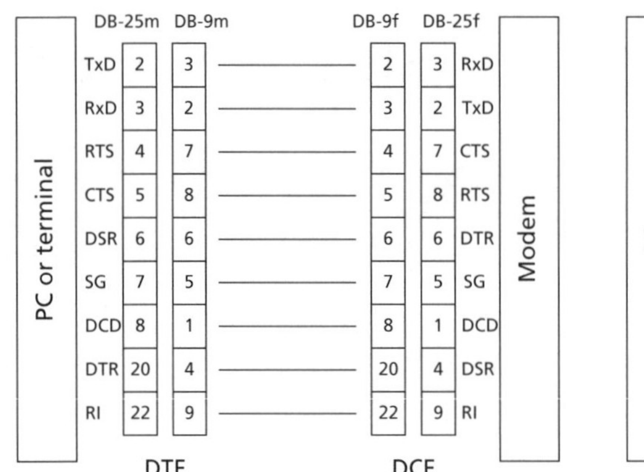

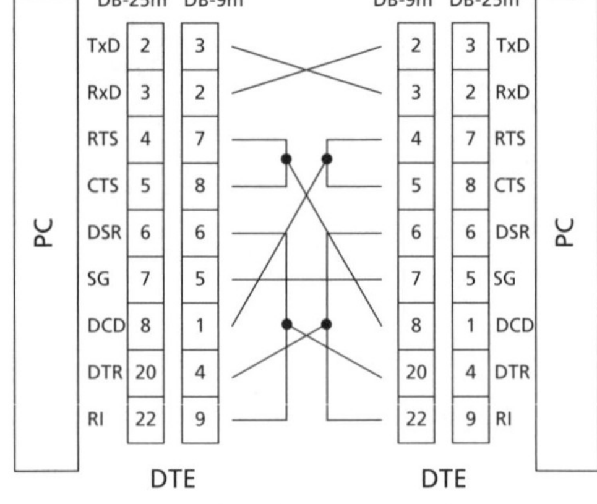

Figure 4.3 Typical cable configurations.

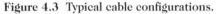

4.2.1.4 RS-232 Protocol specifications

As RS-232 is a character-oriented protocol; data is transmitted as single bytes (8-bit). Preceding the data byte, there is a Start bit, indicating the start of transmission. Then, the data transmits bit by bit (least significant bits first). To indicate the end of transmission, a Stop bit is transmitted. This Stop bit could be 1, $1\frac{1}{2}$ or 2 pulses wide.

Data can be 8 bits or 7 bits with a parity bit (odd or even parity), and generally encoded in ASCII. (See Fig. 4.4.)

As an asynchronous protocol, no clock signal is transmitted with the data. Both ends must have the same receiver clock rate. The start bit helps in

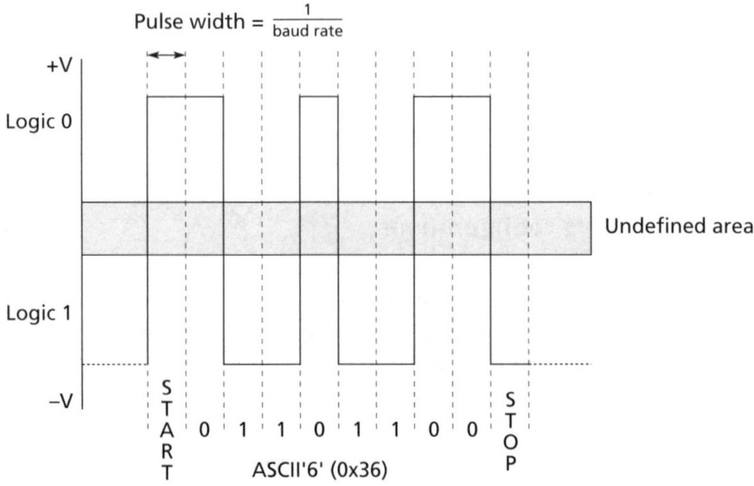

Figure 4.4 RS-232 timing specification.

clock synchronization. Typical baud rate range includes 1200, 4800, 9600, 14 400, 19 200, 28 800, 33 600, 56 000, 115 000 and, in some cases, 330 000, with 9600 being the most usual in embedded systems. In the last case, the pulse width between bits is 104 ms.

4.2.1.5 Flow control

When one device transmits data over a serial line, the other end must receive the data and process it. If the receiver device does not have enough time to receive and process the transmitted bytes, some data could be lost. In order to avoid this, the receiving devices must notify the transmitter device when data can be transmitted. This mechanism is called flow control.

There are two types of flow control: by hardware or by software. In the hardware flow control, some special terms such as DTR and RTS are used to indicate to the other device when it is ready to receive data. In addition, DSR and CTS are sensed for the same purpose. The specific procedure depends on the particular implementation. Of course, if both devices are linked with a three-wire cable, the hardware handshaking is not possible, so the receiver must process the incoming data as soon as it is possible, to avoid received data being lost; or otherwise it must use a software flow control.

In the software flow control, two special characters are used for this purpose. When the receiver cannot accept more data, it sends an XOFF control character (0x13) to the transmitter, which suspends the transmission. When the receiver device is ready for more data it sends an XON control character (0x11) to the transmitter, who resumes the data transmission.

4.2.2 Universal Serial Bus port (USB)

The RS-232 port is being replaced with the new Universal Serial Bus (USB) port. New PCs now rarely have RS-232 ports. Unfortunately, USB is more complex than the legacy serial, and it is beyond the scope of this book.

However, lots of specific ICs and converters are used to adapt RS-232 to USB, and vice versa. In this way, if we had, for example, a USB modem, we could use one of these adapters and still apply the RS-232 port programming to handle the USB peripheral. In addition, some microcontrollers come with the USB port included.

4.3 Serial line protocols

The serial lines used in point-to-point network solutions allow us to transmit data over long distances, using a modem to connect the serial port to the telephone public lines. However, in order to have TCP/IP running over these connections, we will need a Data Link layer which encapsulates the Internet layer IP datagrams for its transmission (as all LANs have). As the serial line interface does not provide this Data Link layer, the TCP/IP suite provides its own: the simplest SLIP, and the more complex and robust PPP.

4.4 Serial Line Internet Protocol (SLIP)

As the RFC1055 entitles it, SLIP is a 'Non-Standard for Transmission of IP Datagrams over Serial Lines'. This protocol provides a very simple framing structure to encapsulate the IP datagrams, allowing the TCP/IP upper layers to run over serial lines.

SLIP defines a delimiter character called the SLIP END character, with value 192 (0xC0), and it is appended at the end of the IP datagram. This character serves to notify the receiver device when the datagram ends.

Some better implementations send this END character at the beginning of the datagram too, in order to eliminate some spurious bytes that could be produced by electrical noise. In this way, when the first END character has been received, only the following characters up to the second END character will be considered as part of the datagram. The bytes (if any are produced by noise) between this second END character and the next END at the beginning of a new datagram are considered garbage, and so discarded. As a result, the noise that could affect the line when no datagrams are transmitted will not have an effect on the transmitted data (it will of course have a direct effect if the noise affects the line at the precise moment in which a datagram is being transmitted over the line).

Now, suppose that the IP datagram has a 0xC0 character (END) inserted in some part of the data. When this data character is received by the receiver's device, it will think that the datagram has ended. Wrong! In order to avoid this situation, 0xC0 characters appearing as data in the datagram must be marked with some kind of flag. The character used is called SLIP ESC character, and its value is 219 (0xDB) (it has no relation to the ASCII ESC escape character). In this case, when the character 0xC0 must be transmitted as data, it is replaced by the sequence of 0xDB 0xDC (two characters), avoiding the use of the END character. At the receiving point, when this sequence is received, it must translate it into 0xC0 (as data and not as a control).

The same happens if we need to transmit the x0DB character (ESC control) as data. In this case, it is replaced by 0xDB 0xDD, and translated back to 0xDB at the receiver. (See Fig. 4.5.)

Since SLIP is very simple, it lacks lots of features necessary for serial lines, such as error detection, layer protocol type identification, authentication support, encryption and compression. Perhaps for this reason, it has never reached the standard status.

4.5 Point-to-Point Protocol (PPP)

PPP was designed to make up for the lack of features in SLIP, providing the Data Link layer for synchronous and asynchronous serial lines, ISDN B channels, and similar lines; allowing multiple layer-three protocols to run over the same link. In addition, PPP provides features such as error detection, authentication, compression and encryption, among others.

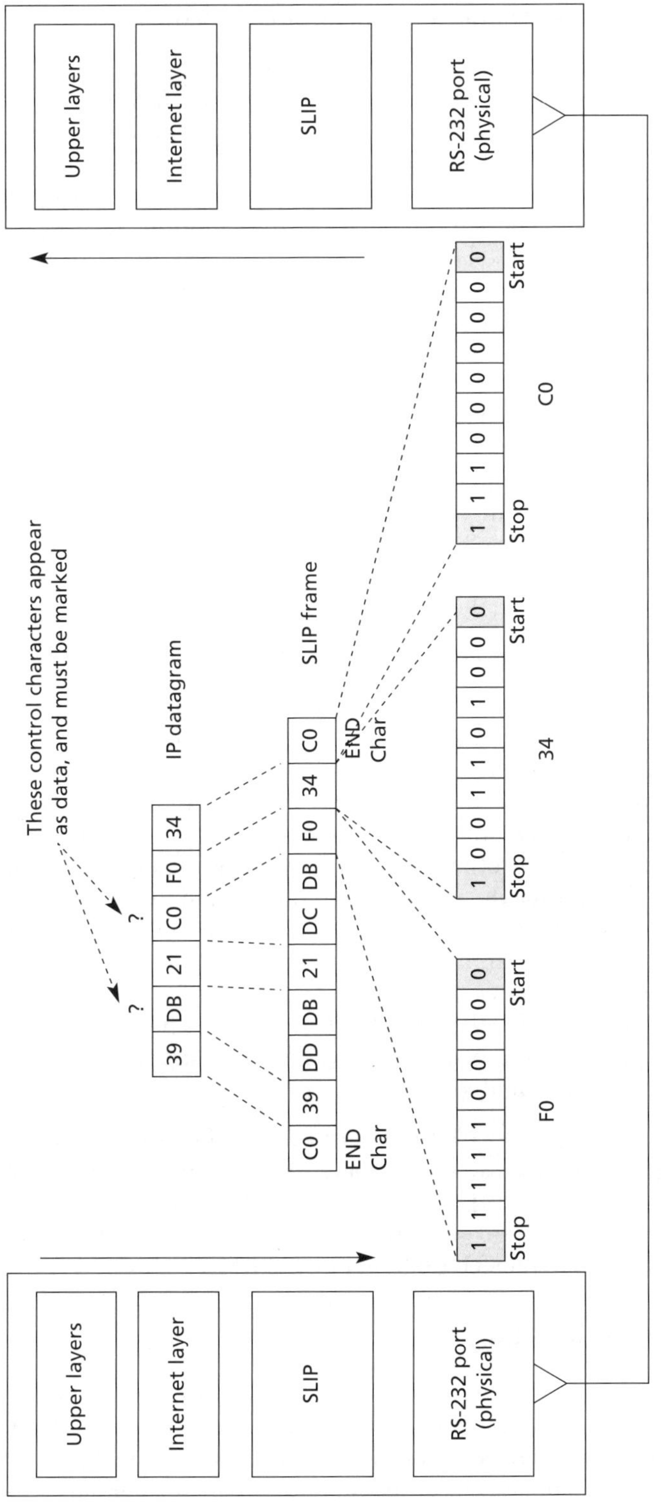

Figure 4.5 The IP datagram is encapsulated in the SLIP frame and transmitted byte by byte over the serial line.

PPP is a protocol suite rather than a protocol, as it is composed of several components. The *main* components are as follows:

- PPP encapsulation method: As a layer-two protocol, the main function is to encapsulate layer-three messages (from IP, IPX or other protocols), and send them over the Physical layer for transmission. In order to accomplish this, PPP must use an appropriate frame format. For compatibility reasons, an HDLC-like protocol frame format was adopted (High-level Data Link Control Protocol defines an HDLC frame format used in protocols such as X.25 and Frame Relay).
- Link Control Protocol (LCP): Before two devices can use the link, they must agree on how the link will be used. For this purpose, a series of link parameters must be negotiated during the link set-up. LCP provides the mechanism to set up, maintain and terminate the link between devices.
- Network Control Protocols (NCPs): PPP was designed to support several layer-three protocols, and some of them could require additional set-up before using the link. Each specific NCP will be called for each layer-three protocol that will be used, in order to set up its requirements before making use of the link. In this way, each layer-three protocol has its own NCP specification. For example, for IP datagrams, the Internet Protocol Control Protocol (IPCP) is negotiated between devices.

Additional (and *optional*) protocols are:

- Authentication Protocols (Password Authentication Protocol and Challenge Handshake Authentication Protocol): used to restrict access for unauthorized users.
- Compression Control Protocol (CCP): used to improve performance, transmitting the same information in less bytes (compressed data).
- Encryption Control Protocol (ECP): provides security encrypting the data, so intruders getting the frames do not understand the transmitted information.
- Link Quality Monitoring (LQM): provides devices a way to generate reports to its peer, about the quality of the link. The Link Quality Report (LQR) Protocol may be used for this purpose.
- PPP Multilink Protocol (PPP MP): improves performance by allowing one logical link using two or more physical links. In this case, the link bandwidth is incremented.

Several new protocols were *derived* from PPP to work with other technologies, even when these technologies already provide the Data Link layer. In those cases, the exceptional features and advantages of PPP are used. Some examples are PPP over Ethernet (PPPoE) RFC2516, and PPP over ATM – Asynchronous Transfer Mode – (PPPoA) RFC2364.

4.5.1 PPP link overview

In order for two devices to exchange data using a PPP connection, once a Physical layer connection has been established, a link must be set up between those devices. This set-up process is in charge of the LCP component, and it consists of an exchange of control messages to negotiate and agree the parameters under which the link will work. Each device sends a Configure-Request message with a list of the desired parameters. The other device must reply with different messages depending on whether it accepts the proposed parameters. When both sides have received accepted configuration request messages, the LCP configuration negotiation is successful, and the LCP link is open. If one of the negotiated parameters determines the requirements of authentication, the negotiated Password Authentication Protocol (PAP) or Challenge Handshake Authentication Handshake (CHAP) will be invoked by LCP, in order to validate the access.

After the successful authentication, the general set-up of the LCP link is completed. Then, in order to have different layer-three protocols using the PPP link, the specific configuration for each one is performed invoking the appropriate NCP. For example, if IP datagrams will use the PPP link, the IPCP will need to set up specific protocol requirements, such as an IP address, and header compression (specific parameters for the TCP/IP protocol).

In other words, once the physical link connection has been established, one LCP link with negotiated general parameters must be established; and several NCP links with layer-three protocol-specific parameters must be established (one for each of the upper layer protocols), in order to have each of the layer-three protocols running over PPP. (See Fig. 4.6.)

Do not get confused with the term 'virtual link'. There is no actual 'pipe' where LCP packets are transmitted or NCP 'pipes' for each different layer-three protocol. The term 'virtual' means that before transmitting packets a link must be established. This link does not physically exist, but is 'virtual'. In fact, the only true 'pipe' is the physical link where all the packages (LCP, NCP and protocol frames) are transmitted.

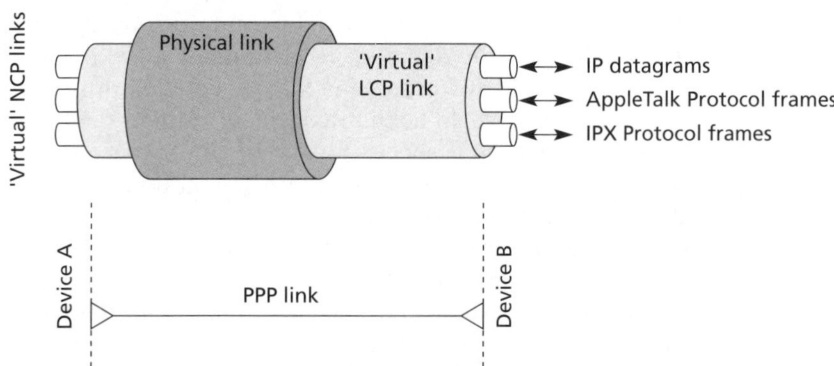

Figure 4.6 The PPP link is analogous to having one Physical link, containing a 'virtual LCP link, which in turn contains several 'virtual' NCP links, each one for each layer-three protocol using the PPP link.

4.5.1.1 PPP link phases

The PPP link's life cycle consists of configuring, maintaining and terminating the point-to-point link. In order to accomplish this, transition through different phases occurs, as shown in Figure 4.7.

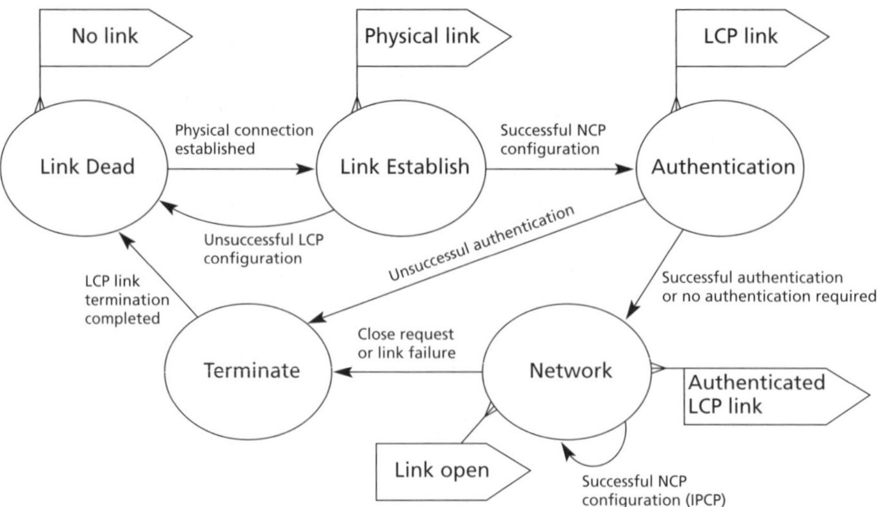

Figure 4.7 The life of a PPP link has several states, called PPP phases.

- **Link Dead**: The PPP link always begins and ends in this phase. At this point, no physical connection exists between both devices. When modems from both devices establish the physical connection, the PPP link goes to the Link Establish phase. In the case of a direct cable connecting both devices, the Link Dead phase is short as both devices detect the link.
- **Link Establish**: In this phase, the physical link is established. However, in order to use the PPP link, a 'virtual' LCP link must be set up. For this reason, both devices must send configure request message to each other with a list of parameters to negotiate. This message can be replied with an acknowledgement, if the proposed parameters are agreed; or a negative acknowledgement or rejection, when one or more proposed parameters are not accepted (this process is further detailed in section 4.5.2). Once both devices receive an acknowledgement to their configure request message, the negotiation is successful and the link proceeds to the next phase. If the negotiation process fails, the physical link is terminated, and the link goes to the Link Dead phase.
- **Authentication**: Although this phase is not mandatory, most ISPs will use this feature in order to restrict access from non-customers. The selected authentication protocol (PAP or CHAP) is one of the parameters negotiated in the Link Establish phase. If authentication is successful (or authentication was not required), the link goes to the Network phase; if it fails, it proceeds with the Termination phase.
- **Network**: At this stage, the general set-up of the LCP link is completed, and the access authenticated. Now, each network layer protocol needs to configure its specific requirements. For this reason, the corresponding NCPs are invoked, such as IPCP, IPXCP, etc. As each NCP protocol successfully configure the link, the link is considered open and the corresponding network layer protocol is able to transmit its frames over the PPP link. Several NCP links can be open when they are needed, and

closed when they are no longer needed. At this point, the PPP link is fully operational. Protocols such as CCP and ECP will negotiate their options at this phase. This phase continues until a Close Request is received, or a physical link failure is produced. When this occurs, the link goes to the Link Terminate phase.

- **Link Terminate**: In this phase, the device that wants to terminate the link sends a Termination Request message, and the receiver acknowledges it. The link then goes back to the initial Link Dead phase. In case the termination was required by a Close Request and not by a Physical link failure, the software must enforce the physical layer to terminate the connection.

4.5.1.2 PPP general frame format

As we explained above, for compatibility reasons, the PPP frame format was derived from the HDLC-like protocol frame format. (See Fig. 4.8.)

- **Flag** (1 byte): the Flag field is a frame delimiter indicating both the start and the end of the PPP frame, having a value 0x7E (01111110 in binary).
- **Address** (1 byte): is the destination address field in HDLC frames. However, in PPP, where only two devices are exchanging messages, this address is not needed, thus the fixed value 0xFF (11111111 in binary) (broadcast address) is used.
- **Control** (1 byte): this is a control field used in HDLC, but in PPP its value is fixed to 0x03 (00000011 in binary).
- **Protocol** (2 bytes): identifies the protocol of the data (or control messages) encapsulated in the information field of the PPP frame. Some values are given in Table 4.2.
- **Information** (variable): the data to be encapsulated are placed in this field. It consists of zero or more bytes of upper layer protocol data, or control messages from the PPP control frames.
- **PAD** (variable): it may be necessary, in some circumstances, to add dummy bytes (0x00 value) to reach the minimum PPP frame size.
- **FCS** (2 or 4 bytes): this is the Frame Check Sequence field that holds a CRC computation over the Address, Control, Protocol, Information and Pad fields. It can be either 16 or 32 bits, and its usage enables detection of errors in transmissions.

4.5.1.3 PPP frame encapsulation

As the Data Link layer provides encapsulation services to the Network layer, the PPP Information field will be filled with the data received from that layer. Nevertheless, before any frame can be transmitted over the PPP link, an LCP link and one or more NCP links must be established. In order to establish

Flag	Address	Control	Protocol	Information	Pad	FCS	Flag

Figure 4.8 The PPP frame format derived from the HDLC format.

Table 4.2

Protocol field value	Protocol encapsulated
0021	Internet Protocol version 4
0023	OSI Network Layer
0029	AppleTalk
002B	IPX (Novell)
003F	NetBios
8021	PPP Internet Protocol Control Protocol
8023	PPP OSI Network Layer Control Protocol
8029	PPP Appletalk Control Protocol
802B	PPP IPX Control Protocol
803F	PPP NetBios Frames Control Protocol
C021	PPP Link Control Protocol (LPC)
C023	PPP Password Authentication Protocol (PAP)
C025	PPP Link Quality Report (LQR)
C02B	PPP Bandwidth Allocation Control Protocol (BACP)
C02D	PPP Bandwidth Allocation Protocol (BAP)
C223	PPP Challenge Handshake Authentication Protocol (CHAP)

those links, a series of control messages must be exchanged between devices at both ends of the line. This control message also travels on the Information field of the PPP frame.

In other words, the PPP frame format will be used to carry datagrams provided by the Network layer protocols (IP, IPX, etc.); or control information used by LCP, PAP, CHAP and IPCP among others, to set up and manage the PPP link. In both cases, data or control is encapsulated by the PPP frame. (See Fig. 4.9.)

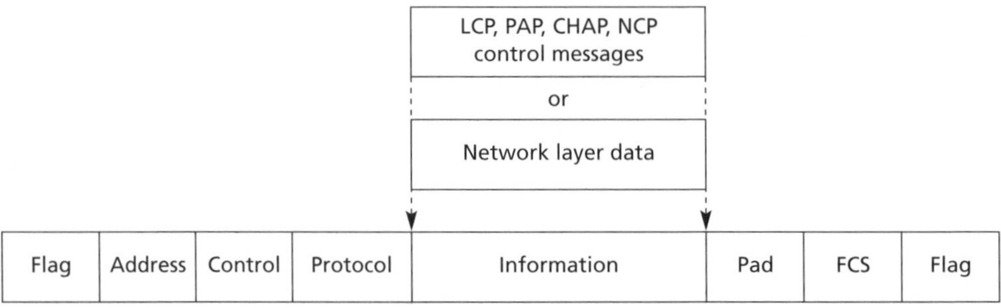

Figure 4.9 The PPP frame information field is filled with Network layer data or LCP, Authentication and NCP control messages.

4.5.1.4 PPP control message format

When the PPP frame is used to encapsulate control messages (as used by LCP, PAP, CHAP and IPCP), the Information field of the PPP frame is filled with a control message structure, as Table 4.3 shows.

Table 4.3

Field name	Size (bytes)	Description
Code/type	1	Indicates the type of control message.
Identifier	1	Used to match the reply with the request message (the reply must have the request Identifier value).
Length	2	As the Data field is variable, length is needed to indicate the total length, including Code, Identifier, Length and Data.
Data	Variable	Information specific to the control message.

The Data field could be filled with an **Option format**, as well, which consists of one or more groups with the structure in Table 4.4.

Table 4.4

Field name	Size (bytes)	Description
Type	1	Identifies the option
Length	1	The length of the option
Data	Variable	Specific data for the configuration option

Figure 4.10 shows the relationship between the PPP frame format, the control message structure and the option groups.

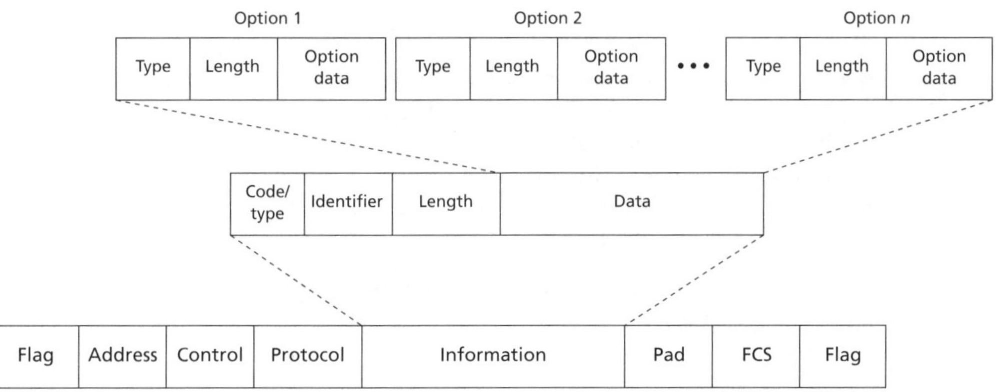

Figure 4.10 The PPP frame encapsulates a control message structure, whose data field could have one or more options used to negotiate link parameters.

4.5.1.5 PPP field compression

As the PPP frame format uses the HDLC-like framing structure, it has the Address and Control fields which are not really used in a PPP link where only two devices communicate which each other. For this reason, they always have a fixed value (Address = 0xFF and Control = 0x03). In order to improve performance, especially on slow serial links, it would be desirable to suppress those fields, reducing the header size and incrementing the efficiency. This option is called Address and Control Field Compression (ACFC), and must be negotiated during the LCP phase.

Even when both devices agree to use the ACFC option, they must still be capable of receiving both compressed and uncompressed frames. In order to distinguish both frames, if the two bytes that follow the initial flag have a value 0xFF03, the frame is uncompressed; for any other value, the frame is considered compressed. As this value is not a valid Protocol field value (the next field following the Address and Control fields), there is no way for confusion. With this option activated, we save two bytes at the PPP frame header.

It is also possible to compress the two-byte Protocol field. This option, called Protocol Field Compression (PFC), must also be negotiated during the LCP phase, and it consists of the suppression of the first byte of the two-byte Protocol field if its value is zero. For example, if the Protocol field value is 0x0021, it can be compressed to 0x21. As the first byte of the Protocol field is always even, and the second is odd, examining the next byte after the Control field (or the initial Flag field in case the ACFC is used) will tell us if the Protocol field is compressed or not. If this byte is not even (as the first byte must be), the frame has the Protocol field compressed. With this option activated, we save one byte at the PPP frame header (only when the PPP frame encapsulates protocols whose value has 0x00 in its first byte, as the case of the network layer protocols).

4.5.2 PPP Link Control Protocol

This is the most important protocol in the PPP suite. The LCP has different tasks according to the stage of the PPP link life:

- *Configuration*: before a PPP link can be used, both devices must negotiate and agree the parameters under which the link will work. The LCP provides a mechanism to allow this.
- *Maintenance*: when the link is open, the LCP must manage it.
- *Termination*: when the link is no longer needed (or the physical link fails), the LCP must close the link.

In order to accomplish those tasks, LCP uses a mechanism that consists of an exchange of messages between both devices. There are three types of LCP packets: for configuration, maintenance and termination.

4.5.2.1 Configuration phase

In order to establish a link, both devices must negotiate the parameters upon which the link will work. For this purpose, each device must send a Configure-Request message with the proposed parameter values (only those

Table 4.5

'Link life' stage	Code	Definition	Comment
Configuration	0x01	Configure-Request	Used to send a proposed link parameters.
	0x02	Configure-Ack	Used to acknowledge a request when all parameters are recognized and acceptable.
	0x03	Configure-Nak	Used to not acknowledge a request when one or more parameters are recognized but not acceptable (but willing to negotiate).
	0x04	Configure-Reject	Used to reject a request when one or more parameters are not recognized or not acceptable for negotiation.
Termination	0x05	Terminate-Request	Used to request the link termination.
	0x06	Terminate-Ack	Used to acknowledge the link termination request.
Maintenance	0x07	Code-Reject	Used to accuse the receipt of an LCP packet with an unknown code (Code/Type not recognized).
	0x08	Protocol-Reject	Used to accuse the receipt of a PPP frame with an unknown protocol (protocol not recognized).
	0x09	Echo-Request	Used to send a message for testing purposes.
	0x0A	Echo-Reply	Used to reply to an echo message.
	0x0B	Discard-Request	Used for debug and test purposes.
	0x0C	Identification	Used to identify the device to its peer.
	0x0D	Time-Remaining	Used to notify the peer of the time remaining in the session.

different from the default values). To match the reply to this request, an identifier is used. If the reply is received with a different identifier, it must be discarded. The device that receives this requesting message, must reply with one of the following options:

- Configure-Ack: when all parameters are recognized and their values are acceptable, this message must be sent with the same identifier as the request, and the received list of options (neither re-ordered nor modified).
- Configure-Nak: when all parameters are recognized, but one or more values are not acceptable this message must be sent with the same identifier as the request, and the list of unacceptable values, replaced with the values that the device would accept. The acceptable options must be filtered out, and the rest of the list must not be re-ordered. Default values can be used, in case they are different from those proposed in the request.
- Configure-Reject: when one or more parameters are not recognized, or its values are not acceptable (and not negotiable), this message must be sent with the same identifier as the request, and with the list of parameters rejected.

This negotiation process is finished when both devices receive a Configure-Ack to their Configure-Request. As the option parameters have default values that all implementations must fulfil, it is expected that the negotiation converge in some point. Table 4.6 shows some available configuration options.

In order to appreciate the configuration options format, Figure 4.11 shows an LCP Configure-Request packet example, in a PPP frame.

Table 4.6

Type	Name	Default value	Option data length	Comments
0x00	Reserved	–		
0x01	MRU (Maximum Receive Unit)	1500	2 bytes	Maximum byte size of the Information field of the PPP frame.
0x02	ACCM (Async. Control Character Map)	0xffffffff	4 bytes	Dictates which control characters (ASCII codes below 0x20) must be 'escaped' (preceded by the escape byte 0x7D and then XORed with 0x20). (XOR = Exclusive OR)
0x03	Authentication Protocol	Not used	2 or more (optional) bytes	Used, if any, in order to validate the access. PAP=0xC023, CHAP=0xC223
0x04	Quality Protocol	Not used	2 or more (optional) bytes	The Quality Protocol used, if any. For example: Link Quality Report (0xC025)
0x05	Magic Number	Not used	4 bytes	Used to detect looped back links and some anomalies in the connection.
0x07	Protocol Field Compression	Not used	–	Used in PPP frames format.
0x08	Address and Control Compression	Not used	–	Used in PPP frames format.

4.5.2.2 Maintenance phase

When a packet is received with an unknown code/type, a Code-Reject must be sent indicating this anomaly. In addition, if a PPP frame has an unknown Protocol field, a Protocol-Reject must be sent. In order to provide a loop-back mechanism for debugging and testing purposes, Echo-Request and Echo-Reply are used. Once the LCP link is open, both Echo messages can be used. Upon receipt of an Echo-Request, an Echo-Reply must be sent. In addition, for debugging purposes, a Discard-Request message can be used.

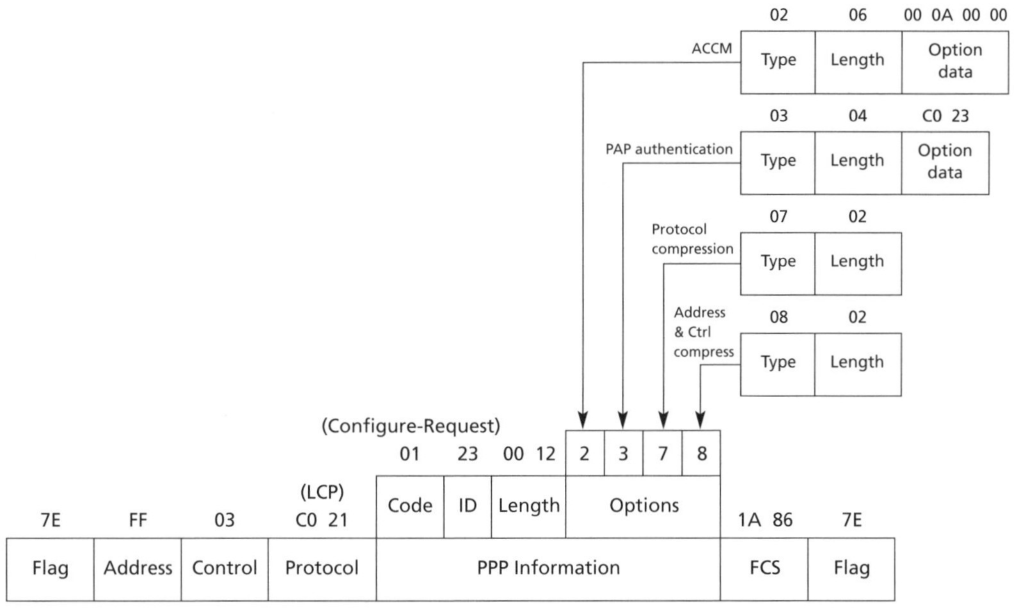

Figure 4.11 An example of PPP frame with an LCP Configure-Request packet.

4.5.2.3 Termination phase

In order to close the connection, a Terminate-Request must be sent. This packet must be continuously sent until a Terminate-Ack is received, a Physical layer is disconnected, or sufficient packets were sent concluding that the other device is down. Once a Terminate-Request is received, a Terminate-Ack must be sent.

Figure 4.12 shows how a sequence of LCP messages is exchanged in order to establish, maintain and terminate a PPP link (only LCP messages are considered). Full details about implementation are given in RFC1661.

4.5.3 PPP authentication protocols

In some cases, it is necessary to have an access control in order to restrict access to unwanted users. This is the case of the ISPs, who want to allow only their customers to connect using PPP for remote dial-up.

The PPP suite has a couple of authentication protocols, in order to provide this access control. During the LCP configuration phase, the requirement of authentication and the authentication protocol to be used is negotiated. If so, once the LCP configuration phase has been completed, the selected authentication protocol is called. If authentication is successful, the link can proceed to the following phase (NCP configuration).

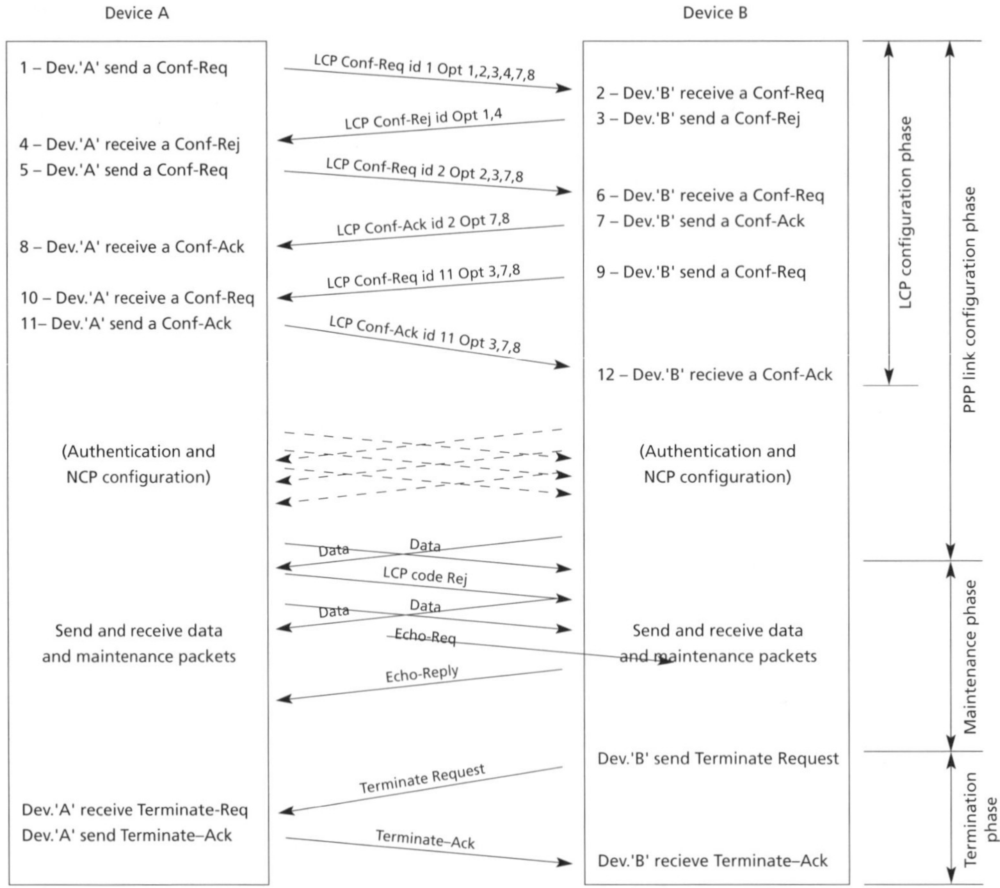

Figure 4.12 LPC sequence of packets exchanged in each 'link life' stage.

4.5.3.1 Password Authentication Protocol (PAP)

This is a very simple authentication protocol, consisting of two steps:

1 Authentication-Request: the initiator sends this message which contains the username and password.
2 Authentication-Reply: the responder receives the authentication message and, based on the username and password, decides to accept the user and notify sending an Authentication-Ack; or denies the access and sends an Authentication-Nak.

Table 4.7 shows the three PAP messages formats and Figure 4.13 shows the three PAP messages encapsulated by a PPP frame.

The most important problem with PAP is that the username and password are included in the message in ASCII code (not encrypted) so they are very easy to find.

Table 4.7

<table>
<tr><th>PAP message</th><th>Code/type</th><th>Identifier</th><th>Length</th><th>Data</th></tr>
<tr><td>Authentication-Request</td><td>1</td><td>Different for each message</td><td>6 + user length + password length</td><td><table><tr><th>Subfield</th><th>Size (bytes)</th><th>Description</th></tr><tr><td>User length</td><td>1</td><td>Length of user field</td></tr><tr><td>User</td><td>Variable</td><td>User name</td></tr><tr><td>Password length</td><td>1</td><td>Length of password field</td></tr><tr><td>Password</td><td>Variable</td><td>Password</td></tr></table></td></tr>
<tr><td>Authentication-Ack</td><td>2</td><td>The same as the request, to match the reply with the request</td><td>5 + length of message</td><td>Contains a Message-Length field (1 byte with the length of the message) and the Message-Data (variable length). The specific message depends on the implementation.</td></tr>
<tr><td>Authentication-Nak</td><td>3</td><td>The same as the request, to match the reply with the request</td><td>5 + length of message</td><td>Contains a Message-Length field (1 byte with the length of the message) and the Message-Data (variable length). The specific message depends on the implementation.</td></tr>
</table>

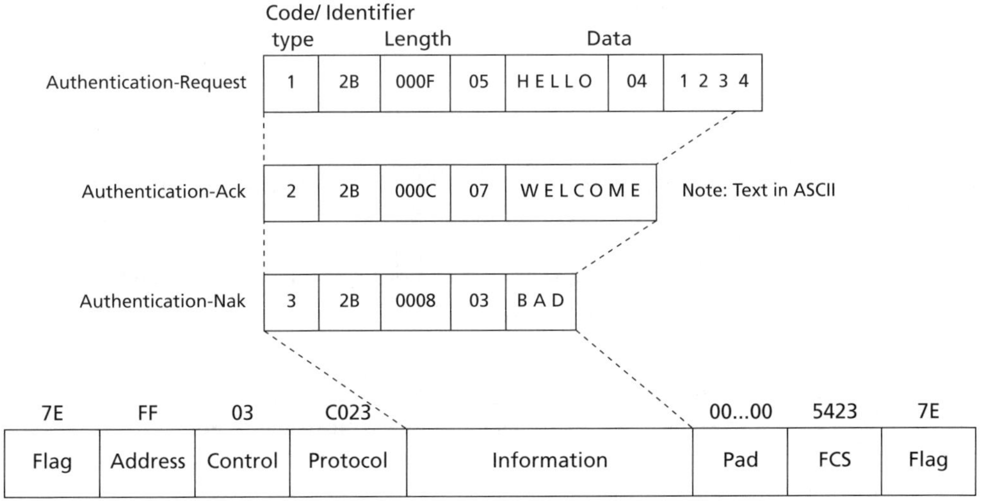

Figure 4.13 The PAP messages format encapsulated in a PPP frame.

4.5.3.2 Challenge Handshake Authentication Protocol (CHAP)

The problem with PAP is that it sends the password in the message (and, even worse, not encrypted). CHAP solves the problem in the following way: the authenticator device (generally the server) instructs the client device to use the password to perform an operation and sends the result to check if both get the same result. If so, the password is correct.

The process consists of a three-way handshake:

1. *Challenge*: the authenticator sends a Challenge message to the client with the Challenge text (a simple text message).
2. *Response*: the client uses its password to encrypt the challenge text, and the result is sent back to the authenticator. This encryption is made using a cryptographic hash function, such as MD5 (Message-Digest algorithm 5).
3. *Success or failure*: the authenticator performs the same operation and compares the result with the client's result. If both are the same, the client has the correct password.

In this authentication protocol, the password is never sent in the message. In addition, the authenticator changes the Challenge text for each authentication process, so CHAP is more secure than PAP. The format of the messages used in CHAP is shown in Table 4.8.

Table 4.8

<table>
<tr><th>Message</th><th>Code/type</th><th>Identifier</th><th>Length</th><th>Data</th></tr>
<tr><td>Challenge</td><td>1</td><td>Different for each message</td><td rowspan="2">5 + length of value + length of name</td><td rowspan="2"><table>
<tr><th>Subfield</th><th>Size (bytes)</th><th>Description</th></tr>
<tr><td>Value-length</td><td>1</td><td>Length of the value sub-field</td></tr>
<tr><td>Value</td><td>Variable</td><td>Challenge text (in challenge), or result (in response)</td></tr>
<tr><td>Name</td><td>Variable</td><td>Used to identify the device that sends the message</td></tr>
</table></td></tr>
<tr><td>Response</td><td>2</td><td>The same as the challenge, for which this is a reply</td></tr>
<tr><td>Success</td><td>3</td><td rowspan="2">The same as the response, for which this is a reply</td><td rowspan="2">4 + length of message</td><td>Message to send if authentication was successful (optional)</td></tr>
<tr><td>Failure</td><td>4</td><td>Message to send if authentication failed (optional)</td></tr>
</table>

4.5.4 PPP Network Control Protocols

Even though PPP was designed to carry IP datagrams (layer-three of TCP/IP), its design is so flexible that it allows other layer-three protocols (such as IPX, AppleTalk and NetBIOS) to run simultaneously over a PPP link. As each layer-three protocol could have its own requirements, it is convenient to have a separate protocol to negotiate these particular parameters, instead of having the LCP protocol doing this task. This modular approach avoids changing the LCP module each time the different layer-three protocols modify their requirements (only the specific module must be changed).

These protocols that negotiate the specific parameters for each layer-three protocols are called PPP Network Control Protocols (NCP) and take different implementations (and names) according to the specific layer-three protocol. For example, PPP Internet Protocol Control Protocol (IPCP) is the NCP for TCP/IP; while PPP AppleTalk Control Protocol (ATCP) is the NCP for AppleTalk, and PPP Internetworking Packet Exchange Control Protocol (IPXCP) is the NCP for IPX.

Once LCP establishes the LCP link, and after authentication is successful (if required), each of the appropriate NCP modules for the layer-three protocols that will use the PPP link must be called in order to establish the respective NCP link. Once the NCP link is open, the corresponding protocol can start transmitting frames over the PPP link.

The process of the NCP negotiation is similar to that of the LCP, consisting of different messages exchanged during three phases (Table 4.9). Remember that in order to have a layer-three protocol using a PPP link, the NCP link must be open. In addition, more than one layer-three protocol can be opened at the same time. When the link is no longer needed, the NCP link can be closed. This will not close the LCP link, and there is no need to close the NCP link when the LCP link is terminated.

Table 4.9

NCP link phase	Code	Definition	Comment
Configuration	0x01	Configure-Request	Used to send the particular layer-three protocol parameters.
	0x02	Configure-Ack	Used to acknowledge a request.
	0x03	Configure-Nak	Used to not acknowledge a request.
	0x04	Configure-Reject	Used to reject a request.
Termination	0x05	Terminate-Request	Used to request the NCP link termination (does not terminate the LCP link).
	0x06	Terminate-Ack	Used to acknowledge the NCP link termination request.
Maintenance	0x07	Code-Reject	Used to accuse the receipt of an invalid NCP frame.

As our concern is TCP/IP, we will only look at the PPP IPCP used to configure the IP protocol to use the PPP Link. Information about other NCP protocols can be found in the appropriate RFC document.

4.5.4.1 PPP Internet Protocol Control Protocol (IPCP)

When IPCP is invoked to establish the NCP link for IP datagrams, a Configure-Request message is sent, and Table 4.10 shows how to negotiate the required parameters.

Table 4.10

Type	Name	RFC	Comments
0x02	IP Compression Protocol	1332	Negotiates the use of a compression protocol
0x03	IP-Address		Used to specify an IP address or request an IP address assigned.
0x81	Primary DNS Server Address	1877	Request a DNS server address.
0x83	Secondary DNS Server Address		

The IP Compression Protocol option allows the compression protocol to be selected, such as 'Van Jacobson TCP/IP header compression' (RFC1144), compressing the size of TCP and IP headers to save bandwidth. The following is an example of this option format (in hexadecimal values):

IP compression option format

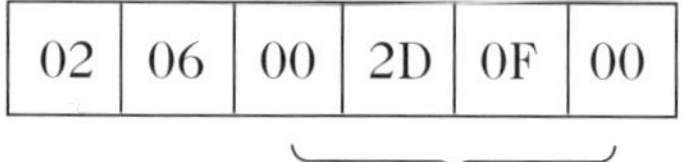

Type Length Option data

Here 0x02 is the option **Type** field (IP Compression Protocol), 0x06 is the option **Length** field, and the option **Data** field will have 0x00 0x2D as the Compression Protocol Code assigned to the 'Van Jacobson TCP/IP header compression' protocol, and 0x0F 0x00 as specific parameters of this compression protocol.

The IP-Address option (0x03) specifies the IP address of the device. As this is mainly used for dial-up connections, the client device sends a Configure-Request message to the server with the IP-Address option with 0.0.0.0 (an invalid IP address). Then, the server device will reply to this request with a Configure-Nak, supplying a valid IP-Address. The client sends a new Configure-Request with the supplied IP-Address and the server will send a Configure-Ack as a reply. In this way, the client device configures its IP-Address validated by the server device.

In the case of the DNS Server Addresses (Primary and Secondary) the procedure is the same as for the IP-Address. Figure 4.14 shows an IPCP Configure-Request packet example.

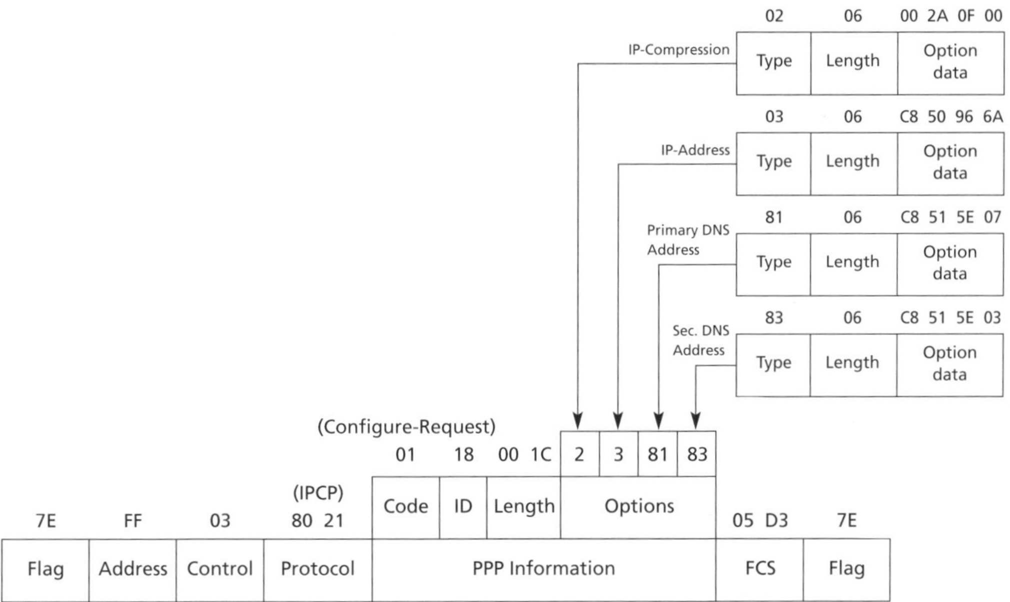

Figure 4.14 An example of PPP frame with an IPCP Configure-Request packet.

4.5.5 PPP additional protocols

There are several optional protocols that contribute to the PPP suite, improving its performance and security. We will describe them briefly; it is sufficient to know that they exist and what they do. More information is given in the appropriate RFC document.

4.5.5.1 PPP Compression Control Protocol (CCP)

As serial links are relatively slow compared with other network technologies, one way to improve performance is by compressing the data sent in the frame (not in some fields of the header such as Address and Control Compression, or Protocol Compression). As a result, the same information (in compressed format) will need fewer bytes to be sent, so it takes less time to be transmitted. An example of this is provided by the modems using compression, although at the Physical layer.

In order to use compression, two components are required:

- **PPP Compression Control Protocol (CCP)**: is responsible for negotiating and managing the use of compression on a PPP link.
- **PPP compression algorithms**: the compression algorithms that perform the data compression and decompression.

CCP acts like any other NCP protocol, using the Configuration, Maintenance and Termination phases messages in order to negotiate if compression will be used and, if so, the compression algorithm to be used. Before compressed frames can be transmitted over the PPP link, a CCP link must be established (as with NCP links).

Two new messages are used in the maintenance phase, called Reset-Request and Reset-Ack. They are used to reset the CCP link when a failure is detected in decompression.

Table 4.11 gives some of the possible compression algorithms that can be used. In order to indicate that a frame is compressed (it is necessery to know whether we need to decompress the frame at the receiving device) the Protocol field of the PPP frame is filled with 0x00FD. And what about the original Protocol field (since it is necessary to know the layer-three protocol using the frame)? This value is appended at the beginning of the data before compression.

At the receiving point, when the received frame has a value 0x00FD in the Protocol field, the data must be decompressed (using the already negotiated algorithm) and the first two bytes of the data are used to restore the original Protocol field.

When Multilink (explained below) is used, and the links are compressed independently, the value 0x00FB is used in the Protocol field instead.

Table 4.11

CCP option type	Compression algorithm	RFC
0	Proprietary (Not Standard)	--
1, 2	Predictor Compression	1978
17	Stac LZS Compression	1974
18	Microsoft PPP Compression	2118

4.5.5.2 PPP Encryption Control Protocol (ECP)

Sometimes we need to transmit data in a secure way. In normal PPP frames, data is very easy for someone to read. Encryption may be used to provide security.

In order to use encryption, two components are required:

- **PPP Encryption Control Protocol (ECP)**: is responsible for negotiating and managing the use of encryption on a PPP link.
- **PPP encryption algorithms**: the encryption algorithms that perform the encryption and decryption of data.

Like CCP, ECP acts like any other NCP protocol, using the Configuration, Maintenance and Termination phase messages in order to negotiate whether encryption will be used, and, if so, the encryption algorithm to be used. Before encrypted frames can be transmitted over the PPP link, an ECP link must be established (as with NCP links).

Two new messages are used in the maintenance phase, called Reset-Request and Reset-Ack, and they are used to reset the ECP link when a failure is detected in decryption.

Table 4.12 gives the encryption algorithms that can be used. The way to indicate whether a frame is encrypted is the same as that for compression (see section 4.5.5.1), except for the value of Protocol field which must be 0x0053. If compression is used with encryption, data is compressed before it is encrypted.

Table 4.12

ECP option type	Compression algorithm	RFC
0	Proprietary (Not Standard)	–
2	Triple-DES Encryption	2420
3	DES Encryption version 2	2419

4.5.5.3 PPP Link Quality Monitoring/Link Quality Report (LQM/LQR)

PPP can be used on several kinds of links, which can be very different in terms of quality. Although devices have a way to detect errors (CRC in the frames, for example), there is no way to obtain information about the status of the link, in order to take an appropriate action (for example, down the line if so many errors have accumulated).

For this reason, PPP provides a feature that allows devices to know the quality of the link between them. This feature is called PPP Link Quality Monitoring. At present, the only monitoring function is provided by the Link Quality Report Protocol, which allows devices to request reports about the link statistics from the other device on a time period basis. The LQR feature is negotiated in the Configure phase of the LCP negotiation (with option type 0x04). The reporting time period is specified in the configuration options.

In order to keep track of link statistics, a number of counters are used: frames sent/received, bytes sent/received, errors occurred, frames discarded and quality reports generated. To keep track of the time between reports, a timer is used. Each time the timer expires, the quality report is generated, and the information is sent to the other device using a PPP frame, with the Protocol field value 0xC025.

4.5.5.4 PPP Multilink Protocol (MP)

As we have already seen, serial links are relatively slow compared with other network technologies. In other words, they have a low bandwidth. If we wanted to double this bandwidth, we would use two serial links (in parallel), making this 'double link' faster. Or we could even triplicate the initial bandwidth, having three serial links in parallel. And so on…

If this solution were more economical than a state-of-the-art broadband technology (for example, ADSL or cable modem) it could be a better option. This multiple serial configuration could be used on demand (only when needed), whereas the technological change would be permanent.

In order to have these 'multiple links' working as a single high-capacity link, we would need a sub-layer (a) to spread the network layer data to send into those physical connections, (b) to take all the fragmented frames received through the multiple physical connections and (c) to reassemble the original frame to pass the data to the upper layer, simulating a single high-capacity bandwidth link. This sub-layer work is accomplished by the PPP Multilink Protocol.

Figure 4.15 shows how the PPP multilink sub-layer acts as an intermediate protocol between the layer-three protocols and the multiple PPP links over each physical connection. A datagram sent by the layer-three protocols is received by the PPP multilink sub-layer. This datagram is fragmented, and each fragment is sent in a frame over each physical link. In order to recognize these frames as fragmented frames, the Protocol field is set to 0x003D, and the original Protocol field value (only one byte) is appended at the beginning of the information field of the first fragmented frame. In addition, all the fragmented frames have two bytes appended at the beginning of the Information field. These two bytes have two bits indicating if the frame is a beginning fragment, or an ending fragment; and a sequence number necessary to reorder the fragmented frames.

When frames are received by the PPP multilink sub-layer, the 0x003D value in the Protocol field indicates that the frame has a fragmented datagram. Then, the reassembly process produces the original datagram. The first fragment contains the original Protocol field value, necessary to pass the datagram to the right layer-three protocol. In order to use PPP multilink, both devices must negotiate it in the Configure phase of the LCP, using specific parameters defined for this purpose.

Two other protocols, the Bandwidth Allocation Protocol (BAP) and the Bandwidth Allocation Control Protocol (BACP), are used to dynamically add or drop links according to the bandwidth needs.

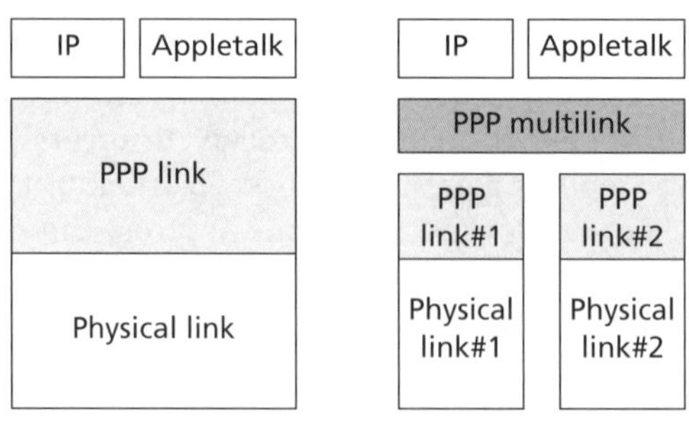

Figure 4.15 The PPP multilink architecture allows mulitple protocols to use more than one physical connection.

4.5.6 PPP Request for Comments summary

Table 4.13 enumerates the RFC documents for the PPP suite.

Table 4.13

Standard name	RFC
LCP and framing	
The Point-to-Point Protocol (PPP)	1661
PPP in HDLC-like Framing	1662
PPP LCP Extensions	1570
Authentication	
PPP Authentication Protocols	1334
PPP Challenge Handshake Authentication Protocol (CHAP)	1994
NCP	
The PPP Internet Protocol Control Protocol	1332
The PPP OSI Network Layer Control Protocol	1377
The PPP AppleTalk Control Protocol (ATCP)	1378
The PPP Internetworking Packet Exchange Control Protocol (IPXCP)	1552
The PPP NetBios Frames Control Protocol (NBFCP)	2097
IP Version 6 over PPP	2472
Additional protocols	
The PPP Compression Control Protocol (CCP)	1962
The PPP Encryption Control Protocol (ECP)	1968
PPP Link Quality Monitoring	1989
The PPP Multilink Protocol	1990
The PPP Bandwidth Allocation Protocol/Control Protocol	2125
Derived protocols	
PPP over ISDN	1618
PPP in Frame Relay	1973
Mobile IPv4 Configuration Option for PPP IPCP	2290
PPP over AAL5 (ATM)	2364
PPP over Ethernet (PPPoE)	2516

4.6 Summary

- Serial lines are used as a point-to-point network solution. They are most used as dial-up connections. There is a recommended standard (RS-232) which defines electrical, mechanical and protocol specifications.

- As serial lines do not provide a Data Link layer necessary to run TCP/IP, this last developed two serial line protocols: SLIP and PPP.
- The Serial Line Internet Protocol (SLIP) is very simple as it only provides a delimiter feature to encapsulate IP datagrams, and transparency for two special characters (escaped characters). However, SLIP lacks several desirable features.
- The Point-to-Point Protocol is a full featured serial line protocol that provides the Data Link layer for synchronous and asynchronous serial lines. It features encapsulation, error detection, authentication, compression, encryption, link quality monitoring and a multi-link support option.
- In order for two devices to exchange data using a PPP connection, a physical connection must exist, where the Link Control Protocol (LCP) establishes its own 'virtual circuit'. Once this LCP link has been established, and after the Authentication phase has been invoked, each layer-three protocol that intends to use the PPP link must establish its own 'virtual circuits'.
- The PPP frame format was derived from the HDLC-like protocol frame format. The information field of the frame can carry both layer-three protocols data, and LCP, Authentication and NCP protocols control messages. To improve performance, Address and Control fields can be compressed. In addition, the Protocol field can be compressed when the frame carries layer-three protocol data.
- The LCP is in charge of the configuration, maintenance and termination of the LCP link. Upon the configuration phase, Configure-Request messages are used to negotiate and agree the parameters under which the link will work. The messages carry several LCP options for different purposes. Configure-Ack, Configure-Nak and Configure-Reject messages are used to accept, negotiate or deny the requests. Once both devices have received the Configure-Ack for their requests, the configuration phase is finished. At the maintenance phase, each packet received with an unknown code or protocol is rejected sending a Code-Reject or Protocol-Reject message. Also, for debug or test purposes, Echo-Request and Echo-Reply can be used. During the termination phase, Terminate-Request and Terminate-Ack are exchanged.
- The authentication protocols are used to restrict access to unwanted users. The use of an authentication protocol must be negotiated during the LCP configuration phase. Two protocols are defined: PAP, a simple authentication protocol, which consists of a request sending the user and password information, and a response, which can accept or deny the access; and CHAP, a more sophisticated authentication protocol, which consists of a three-way handshake process, where the password is not sent in any message. The CHAP protocol is more secure than the PAP protocol.
- Once the LCP link has been established, and the authentication (if required) is successful, each layer-three protocol that intends to use the PPP link must open its own Network Control Protocol (NCP) link. The NCP negotiates the specific layer-three configuration parameters. Each layer-three protocol has its own NCP implementation: Internet Protocol Control Protocol (IPCP) is the NCP for TCP/IP, AppleTalkControl Protocol (ATCP)

is the NCP for AppleTalk, and PPP Internetworking Exchange Control Protocol (IPXCP) is the NCP for IPX. Several messages are used for configuration, maintenance and termination NCP phases.

- The Internet Protocol Control Protocol (IPCP) is used to negotiate the specific parameters required by the Internet Protocol (IP) in order to send IP datagrams over a PPP link. In the configuration phase, the IP Compression Protocol, the IP Address, and Primary and Secondary DNS Server Addresses are negotiated and configured.
- PPP additional protocols improve performance and security. The Compression Control Protocol (CCP) allows compression/decompression of data, so improving performance. The Encrypted Control Protocol (ECP) encrypts/decrypts the data, providing security to the transmitted information. The Link Quality Monitoring (LQM) feature, together with the Link Quality Report (LQR) protocol, allows the device to have a status about the link. The Multilink Protocol (MP) allows the use of multiple physical connections working as a single high-capacity link.

5

The Internet layer: IP and ICMP

We have arrived at one of the most important chapters about TCP/IP. So far, we have seen the TCP/IP layered structure, the Ethernet Data Link layer, and the Serial Line Protocols designed for serial links. Even when the TCP/IP stack provides SLIP and PPP, they are at the Data Link layer (OSI model) or the Network Access layer (TCP/IP model). For this reason, strictly speaking, they should not be considered as part of the TCP/IP stack, as the Data Link layer has to do with networks, and not with inter-networks, which was the main reason behind the TCP/IP design. The IP layer is the layer mainly responsible for having made the Inter-Network real, and it has several functions. But IP is not alone at the Internet layer. It has an assistant: the ICMP protocol, which helps the IP in error reporting and testing. Finally, two protocols will be viewed: ARP and RARP. Those protocols provide a mapping between IP addresses and the Data Link addresses.

5.1 Internet Protocol (IPv4)

5.1.1 Introduction

The Internet Protocol (IP – RFC791), perhaps the most important piece of the TCP/IP, is the foundation of the whole suite. It is at the Internet layer, providing services for the Transport layer (UDP and TCP), and requesting services from the Network Access layer (LAN drivers, SLIP and PPP).

TCP/IP was developed with one main objective: *to interconnect the already existent LAN technologies*. As these LAN technologies were so different in terms of hardware and software, the new design would need to provide a high degree of flexibility in order to use them. In other words, the aim was that all devices in the same network could communicate with each other using the existing LAN hardware and software. Moreover, IP must allow devices to communicate with each other even when devices are not on the same local network (LAN). In this way, IP creates a 'virtual network' that interconnects different technology networks, allowing all devices to communicate with each other as if all were on the same network. (See Fig. 5.1.)

In order to accomplish this objective, IP relies on the Data Link layer of the underlying LAN technology. For those technologies that do not provide

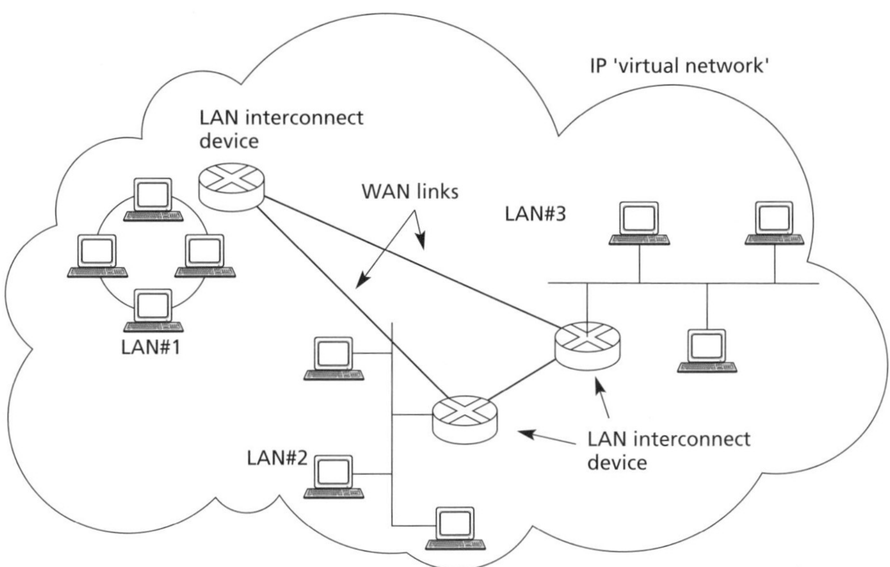

Figure 5.1 The main objective of IP is to interconnect LANs creating a 'virtual network', where all devices can communicate with each other, even when they are on distant LANs.

this Data Link layer, such as serial links, TCP/IP provides its own protocols (SLIP and PPP, as shown in Chapter 4). The IP layer, then, must provide a way to transmit those frames coming from one device at some LAN to another device at a distant LAN.

Suppose an application program running on host #1 wants to send a message to an application program running on host #2. If both hosts were on the same LAN, the Data Link layer would be able to accomplish this job for itself. However, if host #2 is on a distant LAN #2, IP must be used to deliver this message through both LANs.

Some special devices, called **routers**, are used to interconnect the distant LANs with a WAN link. Then, the message from host #1 will use the LAN #1 to get the interconnect device #1. As these devices have two (or more) network interfaces (LAN and WAN), they have separate Physical and Data Link layers for each interface. In this way, the message will use the WAN link to arrive at the distant point, where it will use the LAN #2 to arrive at host #2.

The IP layer will then pass the message to the application running at host #2, which was the original intended destination. As the routers are specially designed to deal with IP datagrams, they have only one IP layer, but a Physical and Data Link layer for each of their network interfaces. (See Fig. 5.2.)

As seen in Figure 5.2, the LAN by itself, through its Data Link layer, can only handle the transmission of frames over the local networks. In the routers, the IP layer is needed to act as a 'bridge' between the two different Data Link layers (#1 and #2) provided by each network interface (LAN and WAN router interfaces). In this way, the IP layer allows frames (called data-

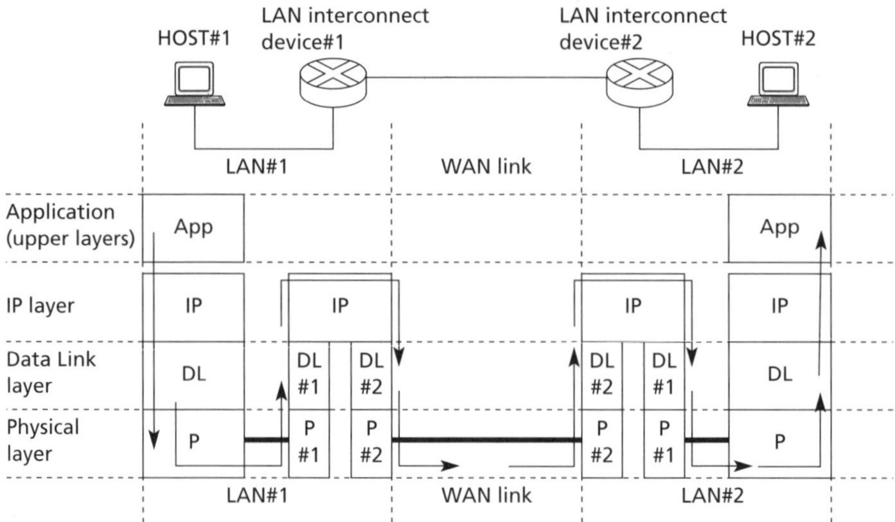

Figure 5.2 The IP layer allows the transmission of packets (datagrams) between hosts at distant LANs.

grams at this layer) to be transmitted through distant points, presenting the whole network as one 'virtual network' to the upper layers.

In order for IP to accomplish this job, several functions are needed:

- *Encapsulation*: the IP layer receives the data from the upper layer protocols, which must be passed down the stack in order to be transmitted over the LAN or WAN links. Before that, certain information, such as source and destination address fields, and control fields are included in order for the IP layer to work correctly. This operation is called encapsulation.
- *Fragmentation/reassembly*: as the IP layer relies on different LAN and WAN technologies to transmit messages over its links, and those technologies could have their own frame size limitation, the IP must have a mechanism that allows it to adapt to those different sizes. This is called fragmentation. Of course, at the destination, these fragments must be reassembled into the original message.
- *Addressing*: the devices have a unique address (MAC address) within the LAN where devices belong; the hosts must also have a unique address (IP address) in the IP 'virtual network'. Besides, in order to facilitate the delivery of IP datagrams between distant hosts, a convenient addressing scheme must be provided, where the networks and their hosts can be easily identified.
- *Delivery and routing*: the IP layer is responsible for the delivery of messages over the 'virtual network' (or inter-network). The IP layer running at the routers must decide when and where to deliver an IP datagram to other networks, allowing the delivery of messages through the inter-network.

Each of these functions will be viewed in detail, in the following sections.

5.1.2 IP encapsulation

Encapsulation is the process by which data received from the upper layers is packaged with some control information necessary to manage the layer's tasks. The new packet (encapsulated data) is then passed down to the lower layers for its processing.

In the IP layer case, data is received from the Transport layer, where protocols such as UDP or TCP use IP for its data delivery across the inter-network. Other protocols such as ICMP and the like can also use the IP layer for delivery purposes.

The data received is then encapsulated in a so-called IP datagram. Other fields are included to help IP do its job. This additional fields form the IP header. This IP datagram is conceptually similar to a frame used in Ethernet (or the equivalent in other LAN technologies). However, the IP datagram was designed to facilitate the transmission along a 'virtual network', while the Data Link frames were designed for transmission over a physical network.

Then, after data encapsulation, the IP datagram is passed down to the Data Link layer to be transmitted along the internetwork. (See Fig. 5.3.) That is, the IP datagram will be encapsulated in a LAN frame, and transmitted over the physical network to the router, where the IP datagram is removed from the Data Link frame. The router analyses the IP header information and determines the best route for the IP datagram. The IP datagram is again encapsulated, now in a WAN frame, and transmitted to other routers, until the IP datagram reaches the physical network where the destination host resides. As we see, in the delivery process, the IP datagram is encapsulated and removed many times, until it arrives at its final destination.

Sometimes, the router attached to the physical network is called a 'gateway', because it is the means by which the network communicates with the 'outer world'. This must not be confused with the gateway equipment used to act as a bridge between networks of different technologies that use different frame formats.

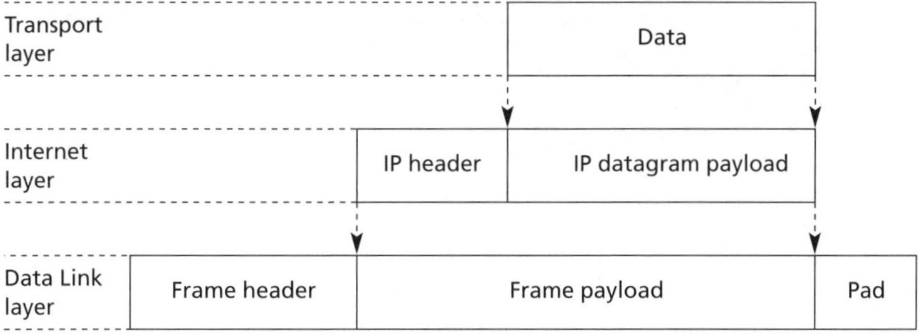

Figure 5.3 The Transport data is encapsulated in an IP datagram for 'virtual network' delivery. In turn, the IP datagram is encapsulated by a Data Link layer frame, for 'physical network' delivery.

5.1.2.1 IPv4 datagram format

The datagram format used in version 4 is shown in Figure 5.4. The field description is as follows:

- **Version** (4 bits): identifies the version of IP. Its value is 0x04 for IPv4.
- **Internet header length** – IHL (4 bits): the length of the total header (including options and padding), in 32-bit words. If no header options are present, this field has a value 0x05 (20 bytes; where 1 word = 4 bytes)
- **Type of service** – TOS (1 byte): indicates the quality of service desired.
  - **Precedence** (bits 0–2): the higher this value, the more precedence it will have over other datagrams.
  - **Delay** (bit 3): set to 1 if low delay is required.
  - **Throughput** (bit 4): set to 1 if higher throughput is required.

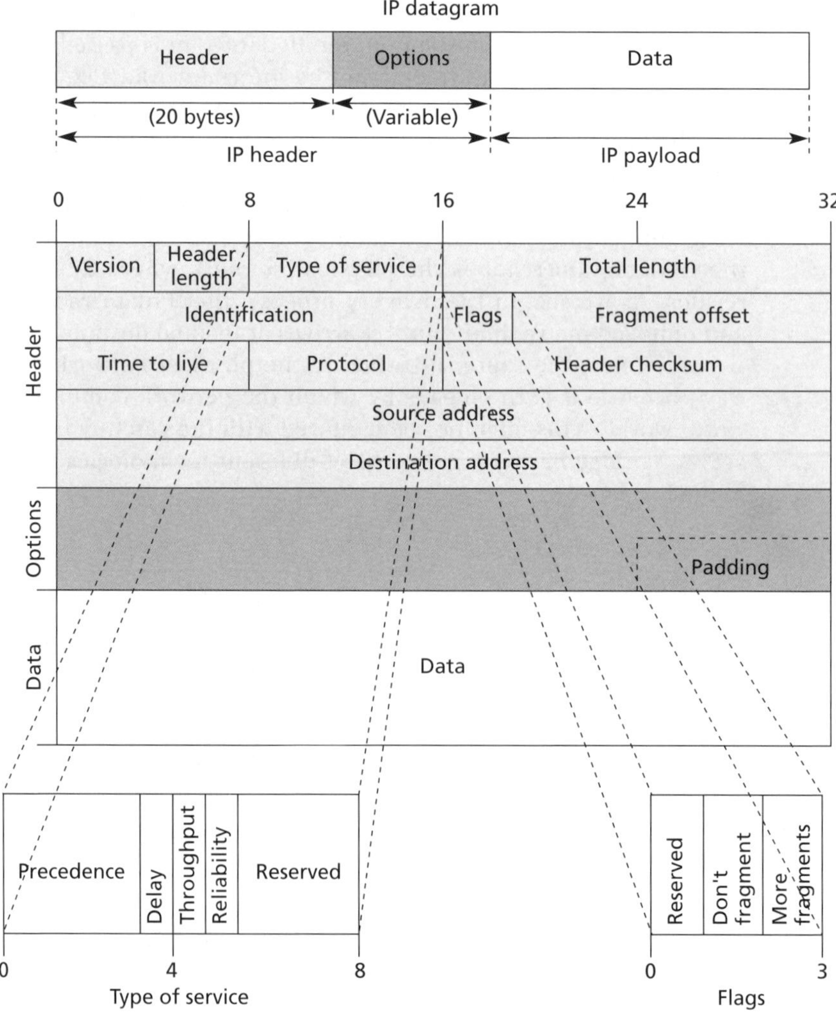

Figure 5.4 The IPv4 datagram format.

  - **Reliability** (bit 5): set to 1 if higher reliability is required.
  - **Reserved** (bits 6–7): not used.
- **Total length** (2 bytes): specifies the total length (in bytes) of the IP datagram (maximum 65 535 bytes).
- **Identification** (2 bytes): used in fragmentation, having all the fragments from the same message the same identification number. As mixed fragments from different messages could be received, this number helps in grouping the fragments from the same original message.
- **Flags** (3 bits): used for fragmentation.
  - **Reserved** (bit 0): not used.
  - **Don't fragment** (bit 1): used to specify that this datagram information field should not be fragmented.
  - **More fragments** (bit 2): set to 1 to indicate that more fragments are coming. If set to 0, this datagram is the last fragment, or it is not fragmented.
- **Fragment offset** (13 bits): when fragmentation is used, indicates the position of this fragment in the original message. It is specified in 8-byte units, so we need to multiply by 8 to get the correct position.
- **Time to live – TTL** (1 byte): used to prevent a datagram from being circulated indefinitely through the routers (in case it is incorrectly routed). As a datagram passes by each router, this value is decremented. If zero, the datagram is discarded.
- **Protocol** (1 byte): identifies the higher-layer protocol loaded in the payload. Some values are given in Table 5.1. (check www.iana.org/numbers.htm for a complete list):
- **Header checksum** (2 bytes): a 16-bit checksum computed over the IP header. It is used to verify the datagram header integrity. When it is received, a checksum is re-calculated and compared with this field value; if values do not match, the datagram is discarded.
- **Source address** (4 bytes): the 32-bit IP address of the device that created the datagram.

Table 5.1

Decimal	Hexadecimal	Protocol
0	0x00	Reserved
1	0x01	Internet Control Message Protocol
2	0x02	Internet Group Management Protocol
3	0x03	Gateway to Gateway Protocol
4	0x04	IP in IP Encapsulation
5	0x05	Stream
6	0x06	Transmission Control Protocol
8	0x08	Exterior Gateway Protocol
17	0x11	User Datagram Protocol

- **Destination address** (4 bytes): the 32-bit IP address of the intended recipient of the datagram.
- **Options** (variable): zero or more options. See Options field description below.
- **Padding** (variable): if options are included, the Option field size must be a multiple of 32 bits. If not, padding bytes must be used.
- **Data** (variable): the data to be transmitted (or a fragment where the original datagram was fragmented).

5.1.2.1.1 *IPv4 datagram header options*

The IP header may contain zero, one or more options. Each option can be either a single byte or multiple bytes. If more than one option is used, they must be in sequential order. The total size of the Options field must be a multiple of 32 bits. If necessary, a Padding field can be used to fulfil this last requirement. According to RFC791, the maximum IP header length is 60 bytes, so 40 bytes are available for this Options field.

There are two possible formats for the Options field. (See Fig. 5.5.) The Options field description is as follows:

- **Option Type** (1 byte): this field is divided into three sub-fields:
  - **Copied** (1 bit): this flag is set to 1, if the option must be copied into all fragments when the datagram is fragmented.
  - **Option Class** (2 bits): used as an Option classification. The value 0 indicates 'Control', while the value 2 indicates 'Debugging and Measurement'.
  - **Option Number** (5 bits): identifies each option, according to Table 5.2.
- **Option Length** (1 byte): is used in option format 2, and it specifies the total option size (2 bytes + the Option Data size)
- **Option Data** (Variable): is used in option format 2, and it contains the data for the option.

The Record Route option is very useful as it could supply the complete route the datagram took from the source to the destination. In the case of the Internet Timestamp option, we could have the time it took for the datagram to travel between routers.

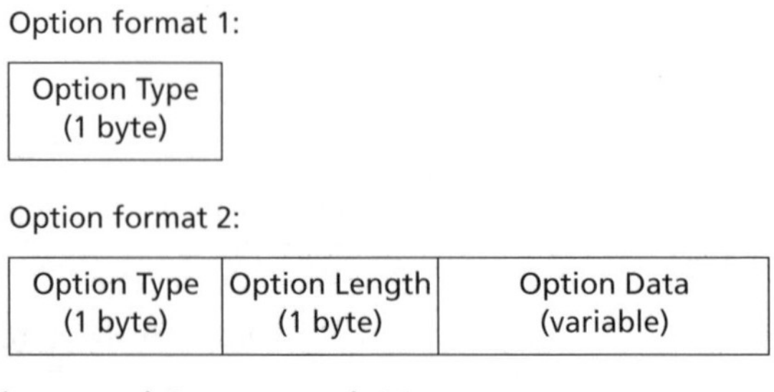

Option format 1:

Option Type (1 byte)

Option format 2:

Option Type (1 byte)	Option Length (1 byte)	Option Data (variable)

Figure 5.5 Two formats of the Options field.

Table 5.2

Class	Option number	Option length	Option format	Option name	Description
0	0	–	1	End of Option List	Used to mark the end of the list of options.
0	1	–	1	No Operation	May be used to align to a 32-bit boundary.
0	2	11	2	Security	Used to send parameters related to the military.
0	3	Variable	2	Loose Source Routing	The option includes a list of IP addresses of the routers that must be followed in sequence (others also allowed).
0	9	Variable	2	Strict Source Routing	The option includes a list of IP addresses of the 'only' routers that must be followed in sequence (others not allowed)
0	7	Variable	2	Record Route	Each router that handles the datagram, records its IP address in the Option Data.
0	8	4	2	Stream ID	Used to carry the Stream identifier.
2	4	Variable	2	Internet Timestamp	Each router that handles the datagram, records a Timestamp in the Option Data.
2	18	12	2	Traceroute	Used to implement Traceroute utility (see ICMP messages, Type 30).

Even when routers decide the path the datagrams must take through the network, we could specify the path using the Source Routing. With this option, the Option Data has a list of the IP addresses of the routers specifying the path the datagram must follow. If the Source Routing is strict, the path must be followed exactly, not allowing other routers to handle the datagram. If it is loose, the path must be followed, but other routers can be allowed in the path.

5.1.3 IP fragmentation/reassembly

As we have seen, IP delivers data over the 'virtual network' using the underlying 'physical networks'. In the previous section, we saw how the IP datagram is encapsulated by the frame used at the Data Link layer, in order to be transmitted over the physical network.

As the inter-network consists of many different network technologies interconnected, the IP datagram will be encapsulated by very different frames as it travels along the interconnected networks. In addition, each technology has its own frame format and characteristics. One of them is the maximum data size it could carry. This is called the Maximum Transmission Unit (MTU). Some example values are 4470 bytes for FDDI (fibre-optic) technology, 1500 bytes for Ethernet and 1500 bytes defaults for PPP.

This means that the IP datagram size must be equal to or less than the MTU value of the specific physical network, under which the IP datagram must be transmitted. As this would not always be the case, and considering that new network technologies with low MTU could appear, the IP protocol must be flexible enough to adapt itself to different MTU values. This adaptation is the message fragmentation (and later the reassembly) process.

The fragmentation process involves the division of the original IP message (datagram's Information field) into several smaller datagrams that the physical network can handle. If those fragmented datagrams arrive at a network with a smaller MTU, further fragmentation of the already fragmented IP datagrams can occur. Each router can further fragment the datagram as needed. However, the reassembly process is only done at the recipient device. Figure 5.6 shows this process (arbitrary MTU values were chosen).

Although the length of the IP datagram can be 65 535 bytes (as a maximum), the RFC791 admits that such long datagrams are impractical for most hosts and networks, and specifies that all hosts must be prepared to accept datagrams of up to 576 bytes. It also recommends hosts not to use larger datagrams unless they are sure the destination is prepared to accept them. As this value was specified as the minimum in the IP standard, it has become a common default MTU value for IP datagrams. Using 576 bytes as a datagram size will ensure that no fragmentation will be required by intermediate routers.

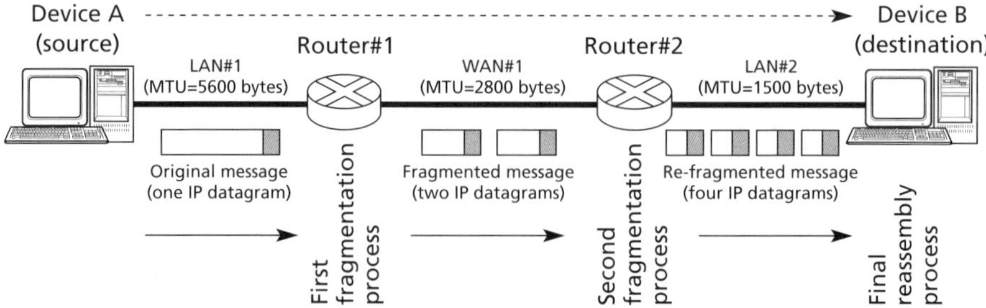

Figure 5.6 The original IP message must be fragmented because network technologies have different MTUs.

5.1.3.1 Fragmentation process

If the original message must be fragmented, several datagrams will be sent (one for each fragment). At the recipient, those fragments must be reassembled into the original message. But, as we know, IP is an unreliable protocol, so that several datagrams may not arrive in sequential order, and some of them may not even arrive at all. Besides, if more than one message is fragmented and all fragmented datagrams are sent at the same time, the recipient may receive those datagrams in any order, making it essential to recognize what datagrams belong to each original message. In order to overcome these problems, some fields of the IP header are used: Identification (2 bytes), More Fragments (1 bit) and Fragment Offset (13 bits).

All datagrams from the same original message have the same Identification value. This is useful to classify datagrams that belong to different messages. The More Fragments bit is set to indicate that more fragments will come. The last datagram must have this bit cleared to zero, indicating the last fragmented datagram.

In addition, the Fragment Offset will give us the position of this fragment in the original message (as it is specified in 8-byte units, this offset value must be multiplied by 8 to have the correct position). If a fragmented datagram must be further fragmented, the More Fragments bit of the re-fragmented datagrams are all set to one, except for the last one (only one fragmented datagram with the same identification number can have this bit in zero). (See Fig. 5.7.)

In the first fragmentation example, if the network MTU value is 2800, the total length of the IP datagram (header plus data) cannot exceed this value. As the maximum IP header length could be 60 bytes, the maximum fragment of the original message should not exceed 2740 bytes. The next lower value multiple of 8 is 2736, so this fragment will be sent in the first fragmented datagram. Then, 5400 – 2736 = 2664 bytes must be sent in a second and last

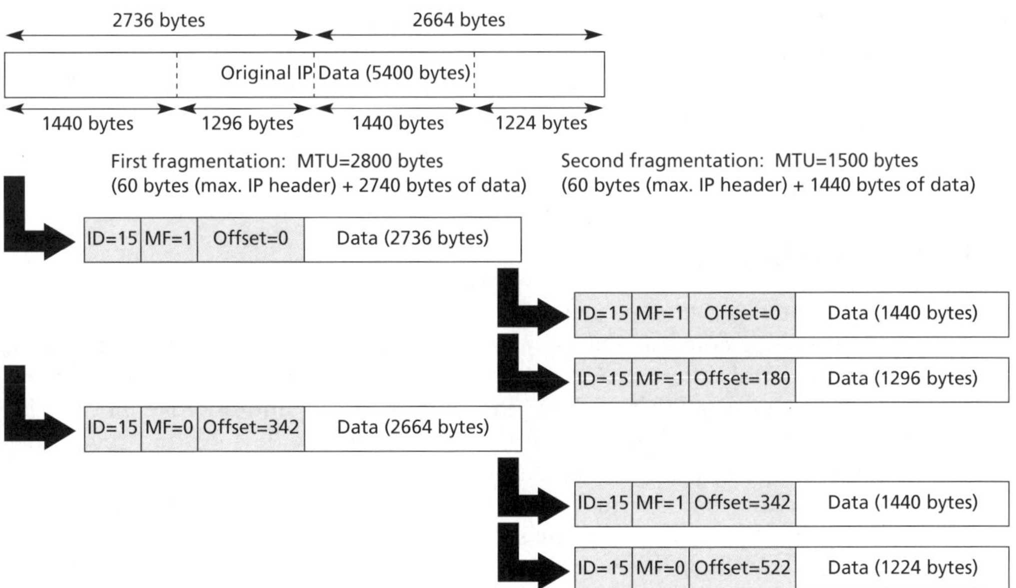

Figure 5.7 The fragmentation process divides original Data into manageable datagrams. Further fragmentation may be used as needed. (Only fragmentation relevant header fields are shown.)

fragmented datagram. For the last fragment, the More Fragments bit must be cleared to zero.

The same principles apply to the second fragmentation example. The MTU values adopted in the examples, were arbitrary chosen.

5.1.3.2 Reassembly process

When a datagram is fragmented, the recipient device must collect all fragmented datagrams and reassemble them into the original message. The fragmented datagram header has the necessary information to accomplish this job.

The reassembly process begins when the first received fragmented datagram is recognized. If the More Fragments bit is one (all fragmented datagrams except the last), or the Fragment Offset is a value other than zero (all fragmented datagrams except the first), that will tell us that it is a fragmented datagram.

A buffer must be initialized to store the fragments until the completion of the entire message. A table could be used to keep track of the filled fragments and those needed to complete the message. After receiving the last fragmented datagram (with More Fragments bit as zero), we know the original message length [(Fragment Offset * 8) + (total length – header length)].

The message identifier must be based not only on the Identification field, but also on the source address, destination address and protocol. The reason for this is that two devices could accidentally use the same Identification value and send a fragmented message to the same destination device, at the same time. In this way, the receiving fragmented datagrams would have the same Identification, and the process would not recognize them as different. Using other fields as the source address will help us to distinguish both datagrams.

A timer is needed in order to time out if some fragmented datagram never arrives. The process finishes when the message in the buffer is filled with all the fragmented datagrams received, and the original message is passed to the upper layers as would happen with normal datagrams. If the timer expires before that, the fragments are discarded and an ICMP Time Exceeded message is generated. (The ICMP protocol will be viewed later.)

5.1.4 IP addressing

In Chapter 3, when we saw LAN technologies, we realized that in order to have devices communicating over the same network, each device must have a unique and different address. Otherwise, how will we know which device sent the message if both have the same address, and one of them sends a frame? Moreover, how we will know which of the devices that receive the frame was the intended destination?

As the Internet is a network of networks, and the Internet layer deals with inter-networking, this layer must have a way to uniquely identify each device in the whole inter-network. This is accomplished by the IP address. Then, in order for one device to be able to communicate over the Internet, it must have an IP address, and this address must be unique.

As devices are grouped in networks, it would be convenient for IP addresses to uniquely identify both each device and networks that group these devices. An IP addresses scheme is necessary to order this addressing space, facilitating the exchange of datagrams across the whole inter-network.

In the following sections, we will see some IP address basics, and the different addressing schemes that were introduced to accomplish the above issues. As is common, when we talk about devices, we will refer to them as hosts.

5.1.4.1 IP address notation

In IP version 4, the IP address is a 32-bit binary number. As this number is very difficult for us to handle, it is depicted as 4 bytes separated by dots, and each byte is in decimal format. (See Fig. 5.8.)

Bit position	1 8	16	24	32
Binary	1100 1000	1000 1000	0111 0000	0100 1011
Hexadecimal	C 8	8 8	7 0	4 B
Decimal	2 0 0	1 3 6	1 1 2	7 5
Dotted decimal	200.136.112.75			

Figure 5.8 IP address notation (binary to dotted decimal conversion).

5.1.4.2 IP addresses per device

We said that each device (or host) must have a unique IP address in order to be identified. However, it does not mean that they must have only one IP address. In fact, devices such as routers, which are used to inter-connect two or more networks, have more than one IP address; one for each network interface. In this way, they can route datagrams from one network to others, allowing the inter-network to work like a whole network. (See Fig. 5.9.)

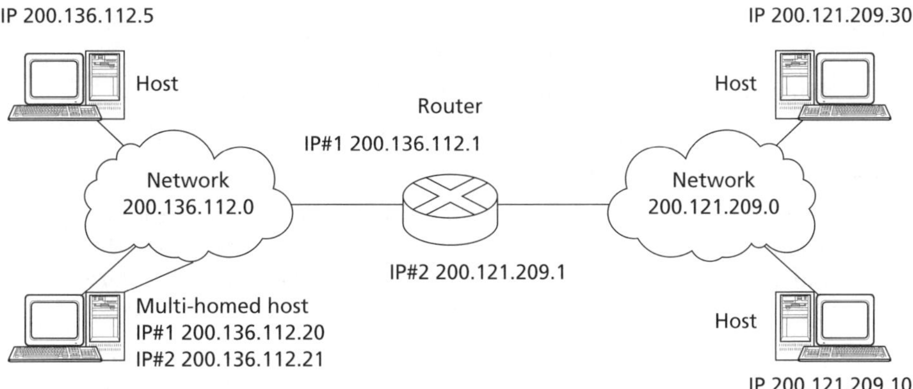

Figure 5.9 Some devices can have more than one IP, such as routers, and multi-homed hosts.

Some hosts can also have more than one IP address, so-called multi-homed. In these cases, the hosts could have two or more network interfaces to the same network (perhaps for performance reasons), or to different networks. In this last case, the host could act like a router if it has the appropriate software running.

A practical example of this would be if we had a PC with an Ethernet card connected to internet with ADSL or cable modem technology, and a modem configured to dial-up with an ISP. In this case, our PC would have two network interfaces (Ethernet and PPP over the serial port) with two IP addresses belonging to different networks (except that both ADSL and dial-up are provided the ISP from the same network). Even when we normally talk about host IP address, we need to have in mind that we are referring to its network interface IP address.

5.1.4.3 IP address structure

As the inter-network consists of interconnected networks, and each network has several hosts (or devices) attached to it, the natural way of dividing the IP address would be into two components: network ID and host ID. (See Fig. 5.10.) This structure facilitates the routers' task, as they need to know if the destination host is in the same network or in a different network from the host sending the datagram. In this way, comparing the Network ID portion of the IP address, a decision is taken. If both Network IDs are the same, both hosts are in the same network. If they differ, the router must route the datagram into a different network.

How many bits from the 32-bits IP address are dedicated to the Network IP and how many for the Host ID depends on the IP Addressing scheme used.

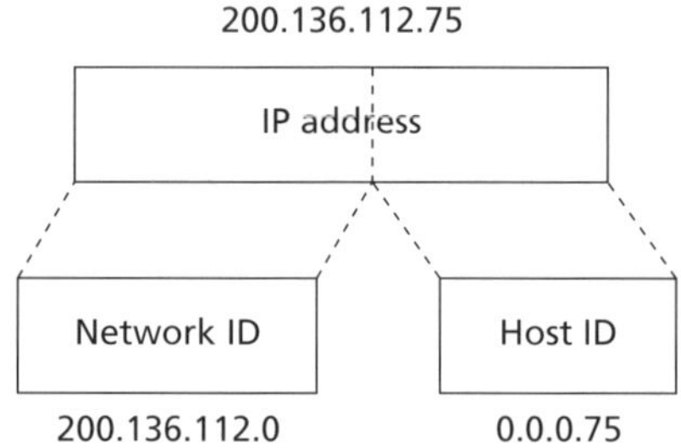

Figure 5.10 IP Address main components: Network ID and Host ID.

5.1.4.4 IP addressing scheme

Different addressing schemes were created in order to provide solutions to the fast and enormous Internet growth. The first in the list, the IP Classed Addressing, is no longer used; while the last, the Classless Addressing, is the one being used at present. Between them, some improvements were developed.

5.1.4.4.1 *IP Classed Addressing*

Initially, the whole IP address space was divided according to a Classed Addressing scheme. Although this scheme is no longer used, it is important to understand it, since it presents important concepts.

In this addressing scheme, three main classes are assigned according the network size (the number of hosts it can have). (See Fig. 5.11.)

- Class A address: uses 7 bits for the Network ID and 24 bits for the Host ID.
- Class B address: uses 14 bits for the Network ID and 16 bits for the Host ID.
- Class C address: uses 21 bits for the Network ID and 8 bits for the Host ID.

Two additional classes (Classes D and E) were assigned for multicast and experimental purposes.

If a Class 'A' network has 24 bits for the Host ID, this means it could have up to 16 777 216 hosts. In fact, all zeros as a Host ID is invalid as it is used as a network address (for example, an address with the Network ID 200.136.112.0 is considered the address of the network to which this address belongs); while all ones as Host ID is used for broadcasting (all the hosts on the network). Thus, the total possible number of hosts would be $2^{24} - 2 = 16\,777\,214$

Also in Class 'A', two Network ID values are reserved (all zeros and all ones), so the first byte range is from 1 to 126 (instead of 0 to 127).

Table 5.3 shows the possible network, host and address ranges for each class (only the three main classes are shown). In the IP address, the first byte defines the class to which it belongs. For example, the address 200.136.112.75 belongs to a Class C address (first byte range from 192 to 223).

In order for the routers to know the address class, the first bits were reserved as an Address Class identification; being the discriminator algorithm, this was very simple: if the first bit of the address is zero (0), then the address is Class 'A'. If not, the following bit is analysed. If it is zero, the address is Class 'B', and so on. When the first four bits are all ones, the address is Class 'E' and it is used for experimental purposes.

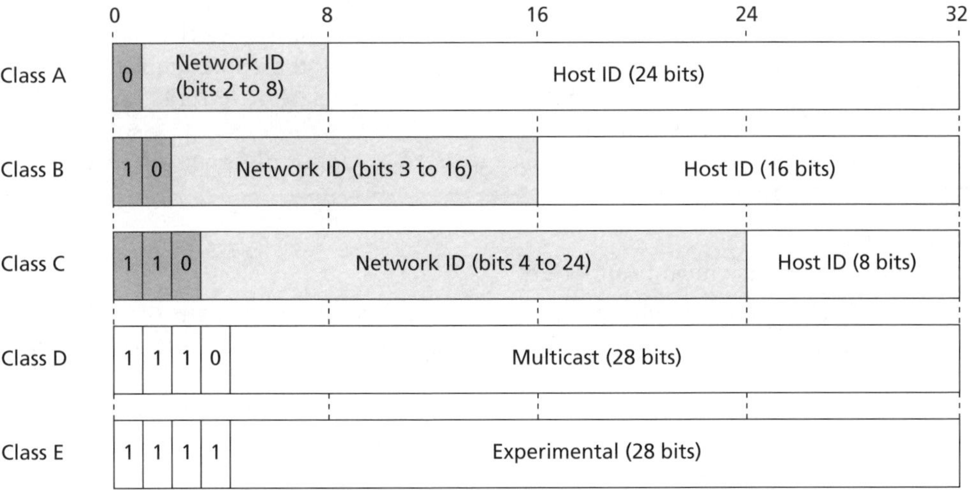

Figure 5.11 IP address class assignments.

Table 5.3

IP Address Class	First byte range	No. of networks	No. of hosts per network	IP address range
Class A	1 to 126	126	16 777 214	1.0.0.1 to 126.255.255.254
Class B	128 to 191	16 384	65 534	128.0.0.1 to 191.255.255.254
Class C	192 to 223	2 097 152	254	192.0.0.1 to 223.255.255.254

5.1.4.4.1.1 Reserved IP addresses

Among the IP addresses defined in the main three classes, there are some IP addresses ranges that cannot be used. They are reserved for the following:

- *Private networks*: suppose a company wants to configure its private TCP/IP network (not connected to the Internet), so a range of addresses must be selected. If the used range is already reserved in the Internet for another company, a potential problem may arise if the private network is accidentally connected to the Internet. If so, those addresses would not be unique. In order to prevent this situation, the RFC1918 defines special blocks of addresses just for private use. Those reserved addresses do not exist in the public Internet, and the routers ignore them, so are non-routable addresses. This avoids the potential address conflict between private and public networks. This is the address blocks reserved:

Class 'A':	from	10.0.0.0	to	10.255.255.255
Class 'B':	from	169.254.0.0	to	169.254.255.255
	from	172.16.0.0	to	172.31.255.255
Class 'C'	from	192.168.0.0	to	192.168.255.255

- *Loopback*: the address range from 127.0.0.0 to 127.255.255.255 is reserved for loopback test purposes. In fact, when an IP datagram is sent to a 127.X.X.X address, the datagram is not passed to the Data Link layer to be sent out by the Physical layer. Instead, the datagram is 'looped back' to the source at the Internet layer. It is like a 'short-circuit' on the IP layer for this address range.
- *Other purposes*: some ranges were reserved for different purposes, such as experimentation.

5.1.4.4.1.2 Address Assignment Authorities

This address scheme required a centralized management organization, in order to preserve IP address uniqueness. Thus, the Internet Assigned Number Authority (IANA) was responsible for allocating IP addresses. Later, the Internet Corporation for Assigned Names and Numbers (ICANN) was created, taking responsibility for this function as well the Domain Name System (DNS) name registration.

5.1.4.4.1.3 Problems with the Classed Addressing schemes

The biggest problem with this addressing scheme was the inefficient use of the address space. Suppose an organization has 8000 hosts: a Class 'B' network address should be assigned in this case. As this class has a maximum of 65 534 hosts per network, with only 8000 IP addresses used, we are wasting 87% of the possible IP addresses. We could assign about 32 Class 'C' network addresses (32 × 254 = 8128), but in this case, the routers would need to have 32 entries in their routing tables just for this organization. Imagine this kind of solution applied to lots of organizations.

Another problem is that this scheme does not match very well in large networks, because these kinds of networks are structured like several sub-networks under the whole network. Moreover, this hierarchical model is not allowed in this model.

5.1.4.4.2 ***IP Subnet Addressing*** **(Subnetting)**

In order to better match the Classed Addressing scheme with the large networks, the subnetting technique (RFC950) introduces a new hierarchical level in the Host ID part of the IP address. In this way, the Network ID remains the same. However, within the network, the Host ID can be further divided into several Subnets with hosts inside. (See Fig. 5.12.)

As the Network ID remains the same, the changes are only visible inside the organizations; for the rest of the Internet, the several subnets are seen as a whole network. No changes are required on routers outside the organization, because they work on the Network ID part of the address. Only routers inside the organization must deal with Subnetting, in order to decide if both source and destination addresses are on the same subnet, on a different subnet on the same network, or on different networks.

The Host ID part of the IP address is further divided in two components: the Subnet ID and the Host ID. How many bits are available for the Subnet ID, and how many for the Host ID? Well, it depends on how the network is

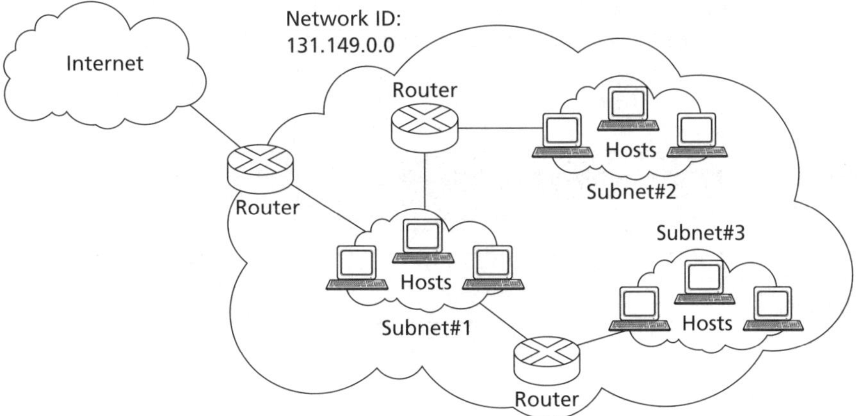

Figure 5.12 The Subnetting technique introduces a new hierarchical level inside the networks, allowing the creation of subnets under the whole network.

structured. Suppose we have a Class B network, where the original Host ID is 16 bits; then, in Subnetting, we need to take some of these bits to make the Subnet ID. Let's say we have 21 subnets, so we will need 5 bits ($2^5 = 32$) for the Subnet ID, and 11 bits that rest for the Host ID. If the maximum number of hosts per subnet does not exceed 2046 (2^{11}–2), this configuration will work well. (See Fig. 5.13.)

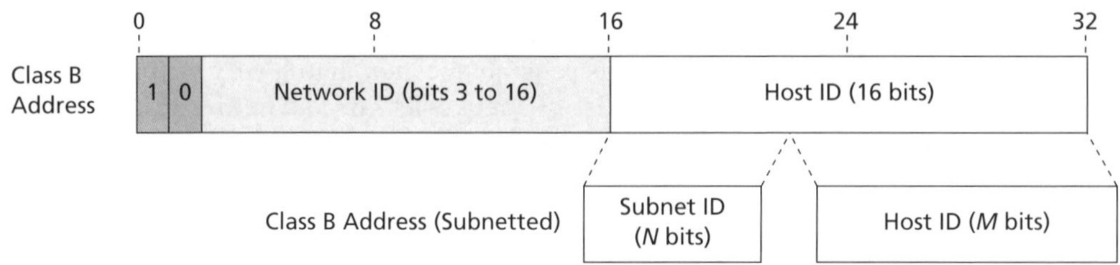

Figure 5.13 Subnetting a Class B address.

A good question is: If we can take different numbers of bits for the Subnet ID and Host ID, given any address, how will we know how many bits are used for Subnet ID and how many for the Host ID? Remember that, in the Classed Addressing, the first bits of the address indicate the class of the address; in other words, where the dividing line between the Network ID and the Host ID is.

However, in Subnetting, this dividing line between Subnet ID and Host ID is neither fixed, nor indicated by anything. In order to know this, each IP address must be accompanied by the subnet mask. In this subnet mask, the corresponding bits of both the Network ID and Subnet ID are ones, while the bits used for the Host ID, are zeros. Then, given an IP address, if we make a logical AND between this IP address and the subnet mask, the result will have only the Network ID and the Subnet ID parts. The routers, then, as they know which bits are used for the Network ID (according to the class of the address), can know which the Subnet ID would be. See Figure 5.14 for details. In this case, for example, a Class B IP address would be 131.149.75.27 and the subnet mask would be 255.255.248.0.

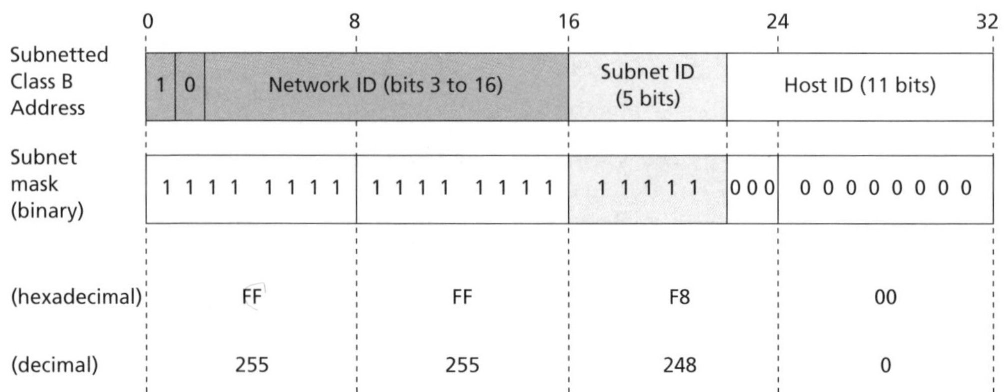

Figure 5.14 Configuring the subnet mask.

Another way to denote the IP/mask pair is 131.149.75.27 /21, where the /21 means that 21 bits are used for Network ID and Subnet ID (the first 21 bits in the subnet mask that are ones).

5.1.4.4.3 *The Variable Length Subnet Masking (VLSM) technique*

Even when Subnetting improves the Classed Addressing, it still has one weakness: it allows division of the network into subnetworks, but all subnetworks must have the same size (maximum number of hosts).

Suppose we have an organization with the following structure:

Subnet #1:	106 hosts
Subnet #2:	52 hosts
Subnet #3:	28 hosts
Subnet #4:	26 hosts

Total: 4 Subnetworks with 212 hosts

As the total number of hosts is 212, a Class 'C' network assignment fits well (up to 254 hosts). Also, as we have four Subnetworks, we need two bits for the Subnet ID. Then, six bits can be used for the Host ID. However, with these six bits, we can only address up to 62 hosts, so Subnet #1 could not be configured with its 106 hosts. Even when the total number of hosts' requirement has been fulfilled, the different sizes of the subnetworks make it difficult to apply Subnetting in these cases.

In order to solve this problem, a technique called Variable Length Subnet Masking (VLSM) was developed. This method introduces further hierarchical levels allowing splitting the network address space into several subnetworks with different sizes.

With this technique, the network address space is divided into two. Then, one half (or both) can be further divided until the needed quantity and sizes of subnetworks are obtained. It is like cutting a pie and getting some slices bigger than others. (See Fig. 5.15.) Figure 5.16 shows another way to apply VLSM in a Class 'C' /24 network to solve the problem presented in the example above.

5.1.4.4.4 *Classless Inter-Domain Routing (CIDR)* – Supernetting

Even when Subnetting and VLSM improve the classed addressing scheme, the inefficient use of the IP address space is still a problem. For example, in the case of an organization with 8000 hosts, a Class 'B' address assignment would waste about 87% of the available IP address space. One solution to this problem would be the assignment of several Class 'C' addresses instead of just one Class 'B' address, but the increasing number of entries in the router's tables just for that organization will start a new associated problem.

The main problem with classed addresses is that three classes on their own cannot accommodate the diversity of different sized networks that exist. In other words, between a Class 'C' network (up to 254 hosts) and a Class 'B' network (up to 65 534), there are so many companies with different sized networks that cannot easily be accommodated in these classes. The gap between these classes' sizes is very large. And the same happens between Class 'B' and Class 'A'.

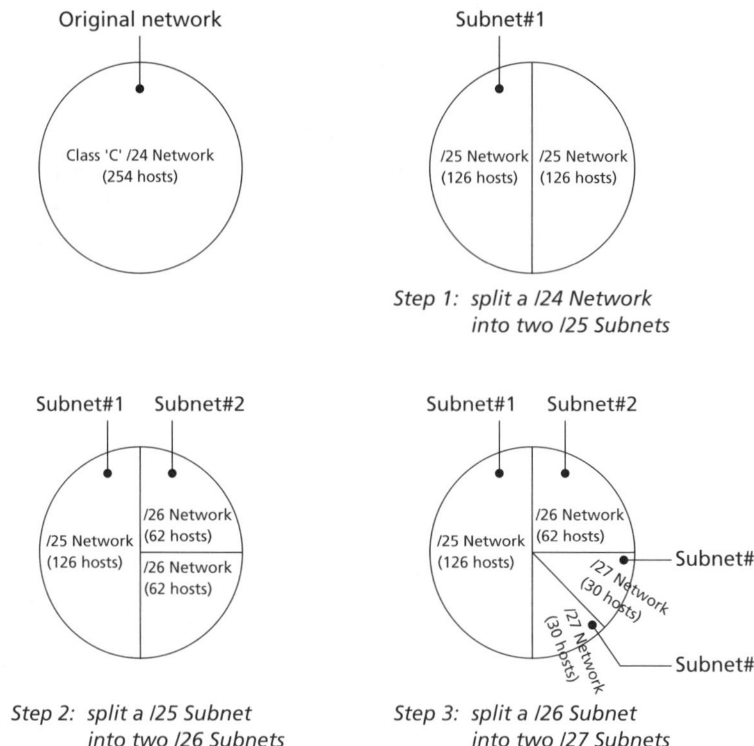

Figure 5.15 Applying the VLSM technique to a Class 'C' /24 network.

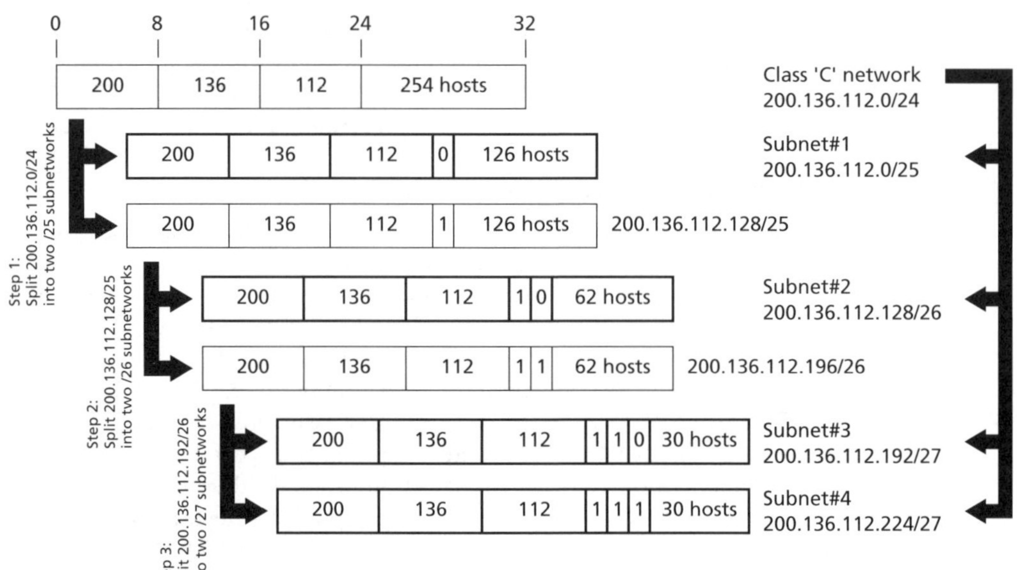

Figure 5.16 The Variable Lenght Subnet Masking (VLSM) introduces several hierarchical levels allowing the configuration of different size Subnetworks within a Network.

The consequences of this problem would be a lack of available IP address space. The new version of IP (IPv6) will solve this lack of space as it provides a greater IP address space (the IP address size is increased from 32 bits to 128 bits). However, it will take a long time before the transition to this new version is complete.

For these reasons, a new Classless address scheme was developed, called Classless Inter-Domain Routing, and documented in RFC1517, 1518, 1519 and 1520. The concept of CIDR is to apply Subnetting to the entire Internet (that is the reason why it is called 'Supernetting'). This idea is valid, because the Internet is composed of networks. In this way, each network would be a subnet of the whole Internet. Besides, as networks are very different in sizes, the VLSM technique will solve this problem. So multiple hierarchical levels can be used to split the entire Internet into several Subnets, and then split these into new Sub-subnets, and so on; as many times as needed.

As the Subnetting concept is already included in CIDR, the IP address structure only has a Network ID and a Host ID components. But the dividing line between both components can be in any place (though the Host ID must have at least two bits) allowing the assignment to be adjusted to the network size. So how could we know where this dividing line is? Again, with the Subnet mask. However, instead of using the 32-bit mask notation, the slash notation is used for simplicity purposes. This notation is called CIDR notation. An example is: 200.136.112.0 /24.

In the classless addressing scheme, as classes do not exist, the first bits of the address now form part of the Network ID. This adds complexity in the routers' job, as those bits facilitated the extraction of the Network ID component from the IP address.

Supposing that we have the IP address 200.136.112.115 /26. This means that the first 26 bits of this IP address are the Network ID, while the 6 remaining bits are the Host ID. Figure 5.17 shows how this IP address is interpreted, and how the /26 notation converted to a dotted decimal subnet mask. It is important to note that, under CIDR, those addresses reserved for private networks and loopback may still be present. In addition, this new addressing scheme needs hardware and software to be updated in order that it can be properly interpreted.

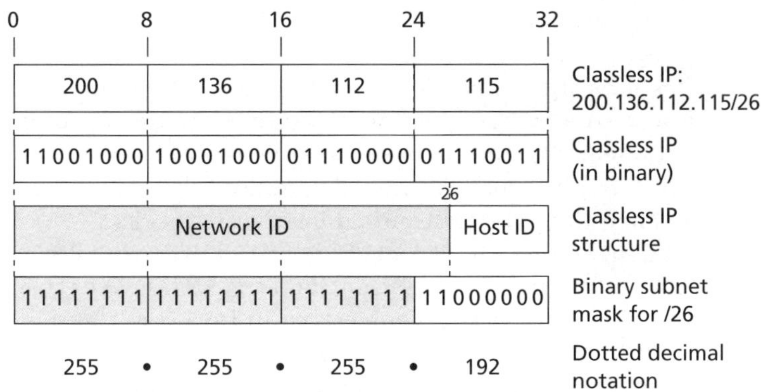

Figure 5.17 Classless IP address and subnet mask interpretation.

One of the major advantages of this addressing scheme is the efficiency in respect to the address space allocation, because several sized address blocks can be assigned to better accommodate the network needs (the only restriction is that the size must be a power of 2 less 2 (e.g. $x^2 - 2$). Also, its multiple hierarchical level structure allows a fewer number of router's table entries to handle a large number of networks. Of course, these advantages are not free; and the cost is the increasing complexity of these addressing schemes.

The same hierarchical multilevel structure of CIDR was used for the IP Assignment Authority Organizations. So IANA delegates the assignment process to regional Internet registries (such as APNIC, LACNIC, ARIN and RIPE), which in turn delegate blocks of address to national and local Internet registries (NIRs and LIRs).

Finally, we should note that the CIDR addressing scheme is the one currently used on the Internet at the time of writing.

5.1.5 IP delivery and routing

When Host A sends a message to Host B, the IP layer must encapsulate this message into a datagram (possibly several if fragmentation is needed), and must deliver this datagram from Host A to Host B, wherever this host might be. The delivery of the datagram is one of the main responsibilities of the IP layer when a message needs to be sent over the 'virtual network' or inter-network. If both hosts are on the same LAN, the message is locally delivered by the Data Link layer (as devices communicate over the existing LAN networks). This is called direct delivery.

However, in the case of the Internet, those hosts would generally be in different and distant networks. In these cases, called indirect delivery, the message delivery is performed by special LAN interconnected devices, called **routers**, which transmit the message from network to network, until the destination network where the message is locally delivered by the Data Link layer to the destination host.

The routers are the devices that interface the network with the external world (other networks). Each host must be configured with an IP address; a subnet mask (to know if source and destination are on the same network); and the default gateway (the IP address of the router which sends messages to other networks).

The host sending a message must decide if the destination host is on the same network or not. The subnet mask will help the device in this task, so if both source and destination message addresses have the same Network ID (or Subnet ID), the message must be delivered locally to the host over the LAN. If not, the message must be locally delivered to the router (default gateway) in order to be transmitted to other networks.

When we talk about locally delivered, we are talking about the physical LAN communication between the attached devices. Consider an Ethernet network: if Host A sends a message to Host B at the same physical network, the IP datagram is transmitted in an Ethernet frame from Host A to Host B. However, the Ethernet frame needs the MAC address of the destination in order to accomplish this task. And the IP messages only have the destination

IP address. The question is, how could we know the MAC address of the destination host from the IP address? The answer is the Address Resolution Protocol (ARP), which provides a mapping between both address types. This protocol will be examined in section 5.3.

When messages are sent between hosts belonging to different and possibly distant networks, the datagram must follow a path from the source, across network to network, until the final destination. This path or route is decided by the routers, which interconnect the networks. When a datagram arrives at a router, it examines the IP destination address, and decides the next step (called a hop) the datagram needs to take to follow the convenient path. The router bases this decision on information organized as tables (called routing tables). Each table entry (routing entry) has information about network addresses and the route to take to get there (the router to pass the datagram). In Figure 5.18, we see an example of an internetwork with four routers.

The routing table entries have the network address, the next router needed to reach this network, and the hops between the router and the network. The hops could be used to measure 'how distant' the network is from

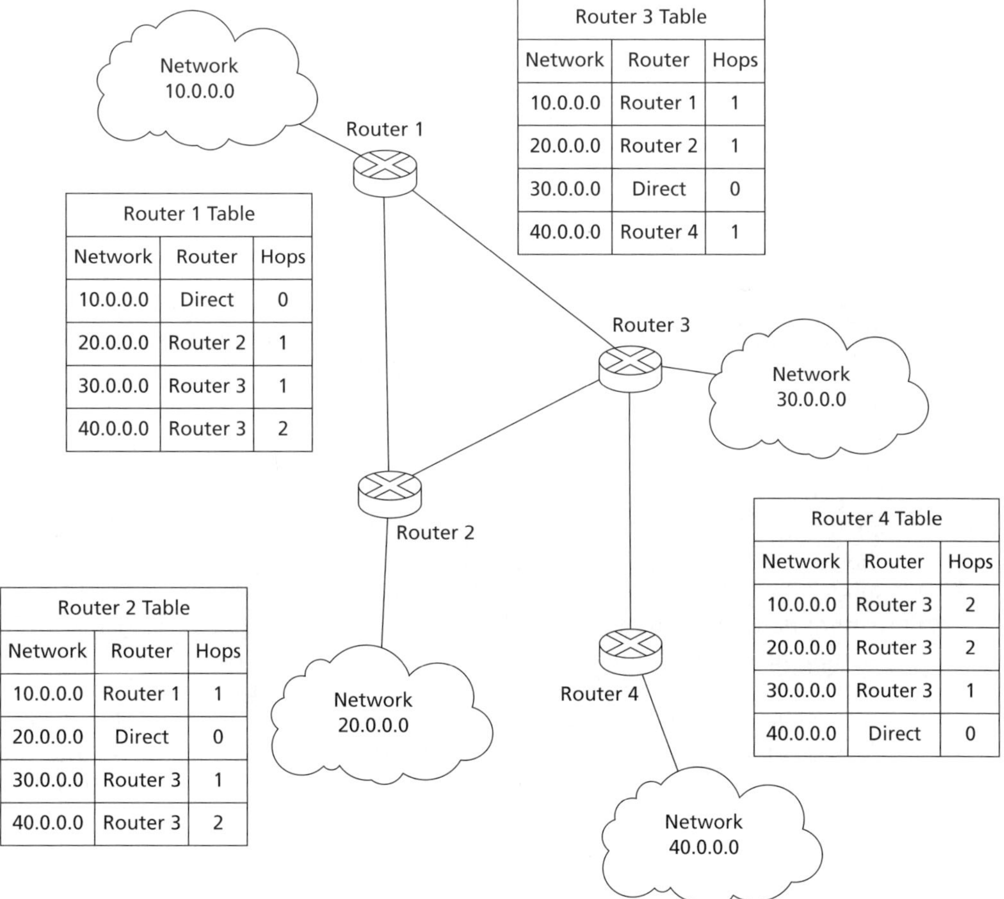

Network
10.0.0.0
Router 1
Router 3 Table
Network | Router | Hops
10.0.0.0 | Router 1 | 1
20.0.0.0 | Router 2 | 1
30.0.0.0 | Direct | 0
40.0.0.0 | Router 4 | 1
Router 1 Table
Network | Router | Hops
10.0.0.0 | Direct | 0
20.0.0.0 | Router 2 | 1
30.0.0.0 | Router 3 | 1
40.0.0.0 | Router 3 | 2
Router 3
Network
30.0.0.0
Router 2
Router 4 Table
Network | Router | Hops
10.0.0.0 | Router 3 | 2
20.0.0.0 | Router 3 | 2
30.0.0.0 | Router 3 | 1
40.0.0.0 | Direct | 0
Router 2 Table
Network | Router | Hops
10.0.0.0 | Router 1 | 1
20.0.0.0 | Direct | 0
30.0.0.0 | Router 3 | 1
40.0.0.0 | Router 3 | 2
Network
20.0.0.0
Router 4
Network
40.0.0.0

Figure 5.18 An example of IP routing and the routing tables.

this router. That is, each router in the path is one hop. The routers do not know the whole path to get on different networks. They only know the next hop to take the best way (it could be multiple ways) in order to get the right path. Otherwise, the routers would have a routing entry for each network in the inter-network, making the system impractical. As a result, a datagram is sent from router to router, getting closer to the final destination.

The CIDR addressing scheme, with its multi-level hierarchy, allows routers to have relatively few entries, as each network hides the implementation of multiple sub-networks. That is, many smaller networks can be represented using a single, higher-level network using only one table entry at the routers.

The routers communicate with each other exchanging information about routing, using routing protocols such as Routing Information Protocol (RIP) and Border Gateway Protocol (BGP). With this information, the routing tables are permanently actualized. These protocols are outside the scope of this book.

5.2 Internet Control Message Protocol (ICMPv4)

As we have seen, the IP running at the Internet layer is responsible for the data delivering between devices generally located at distant networks, across the 'virtual network'. The IP provides this service for the upper layers, receiving its data, and transmitting it within a datagram across the inter-network to the recipient, where the receiving IP layer removes the data from the datagram and passes it to the upper layers.

However, in order for an IP to provide this data transfer service, some management and maintenance work is needed. That is, the IP layer needs to detect some error conditions, as well as have information from others nodes of the virtual network. This is provided by a protocol called Internet Control Message Protocol (ICMP), which presents a framework for 'internal IP layer communication' for maintenance, diagnostic and test purposes. For this reason, it is said that ICMP is like a 'worker assistant' for IP, doing the IP layer internal task. The ICMP protocol is fully documented in RFC 792.

As the IP is not reliable, a feedback mechanism is needed. This way, when an IP datagram cannot be delivered, an ICMP message will be sent back to the source. A typical example of this is shown in Figure 5.19, where Device A sends an IP datagram to Device B. But some router R2 detects a problem and cannot deliver the IP datagram. Then, it sends an ICMP message back to the source device, informing it about the problem. 'Destination Unreachable' could be the message type and Device A could change the route it uses.

Certain rules must be applied in order to avoid 'potential loops' in case one device detects an error and sends an ICMP message to the source, and this message is received with a problem so a new message is sent to the first device, getting a 'forever' condition. These rules are described in RFC 792 and RFC 1122 ('Requirements for Internet Hosts – Communication layers').

ICMP messages are usually used either for reporting errors or for exchanging information about the conditions of the 'virtual network' nodes. Each

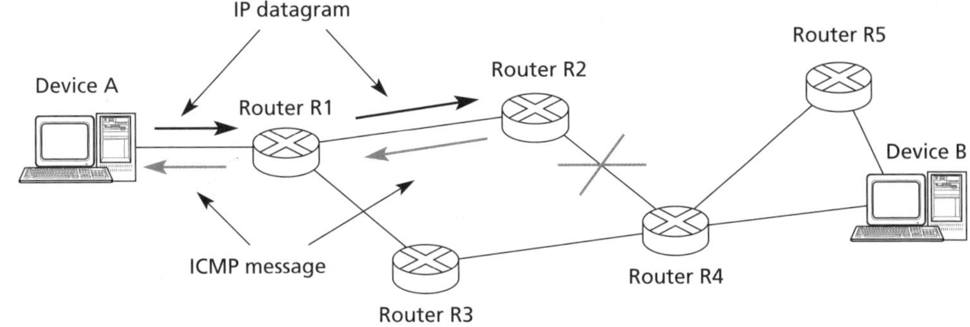

Figure 5.19 A typical example where a router detects a problem, and sends an ICMP message to the datagram source device.

type of information has a specific ICMP format, although all of them share some common fields. ICMP is not used for delivering the information; instead, IP datagrams are used.

In this way, IP datagrams may transmit a 'customer data' from the upper layers or 'internal data' such as ICMP messages. It's like a courier company providing delivery services for other companies, and using this service for delivering its own 'internal documentation'. (See Fig. 5.20.)

Although the IP layer uses the ICMP messages, it is also possible for other protocols to use these messages. As ICMP only provides the message mechanism, the protocols using ICMP must define how to use it.

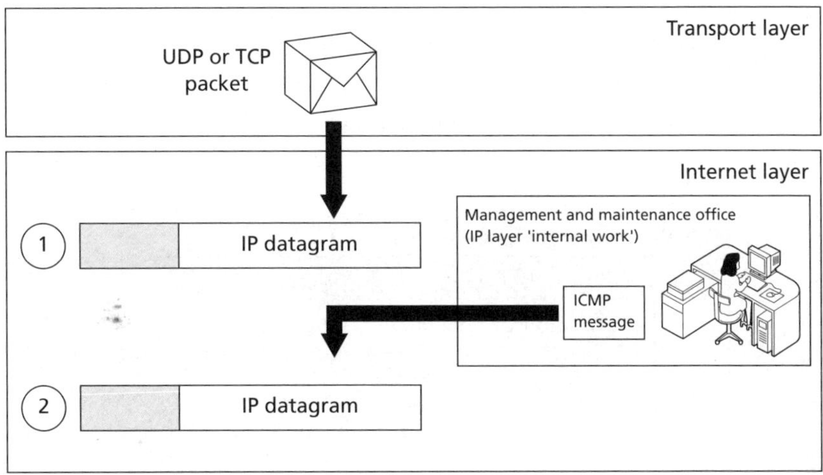

Figure 5.20 IP datagrams are used to encapsulate and transmit either Transport layer data (to service upper layers) or ICMP messages (Internal service).

5.2.1 ICMP general message format

The ICMP protocol provides a mechanism by which any IP device can send control messages to another device. These devices can be hosts or routers, depending on the type of message. Figure 5.21 shows the ICMP general message format. The first three fields are common to all ICMP messages:

- **Type**: identifies the type of message.
- **Code**: indicates different 'subtypes'.
- **Checksum**: provides error detection over the ICMP message, and is calculated over the whole ICMP structure. It consists of the 16-bit one's complement of the one's complement sum of the ICMP message starting with the ICMP Type. For computing the checksum, the checksum field should be zero.
- **Data**: depends on the specific type of message. Generally, in messages reporting errors, a portion of the original IP datagram that could not be delivered, is included in this field.

Table 5.4 shows different types of ICMP messages, as defined at RFC 792, used for error reporting. The rest of the messages are shown in Table 5.5. Be aware that as IP is unreliable, the generated ICMP message may not arrive at its desti-

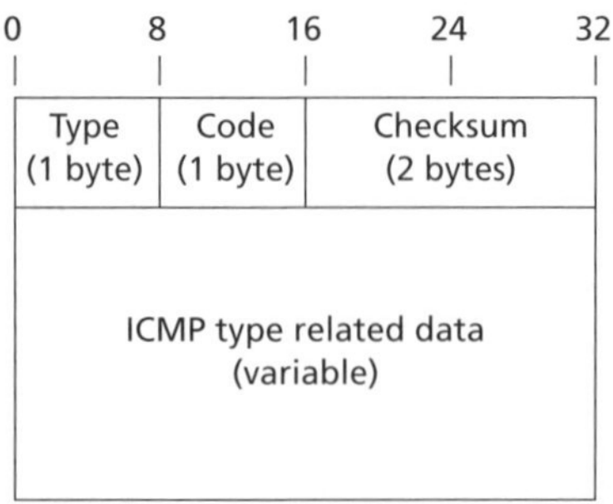

Figure 5.21 ICMP general message format.

Table 5.4

ICMP error reporting messages		
Type	**Name**	**Usage**
3	Destination Unreachable	When a datagram could not be delivered, giving more information in the Code field.
4	Source Quench	If device cannot process datagrams as received, it could request the source to slow down the rate at which it sends traffic.
5	Redirect	A router could inform a host about a better route to send datagrams.
11	Time Exceeded	The Time To Live field has expired, so a datagram is discarded.
12	Parameter Problem	Problem delivering the datagram, specifying the problem in the Code field.

Table 5.5

Information exchange messages			
Type	**Name**	**RFC**	**Usage**
0	Echo Reply	792	A response to an Echo Request.
8	Echo	792	Request used to test connectivity.
9	Router Advertisement	1256	Used by routers to advise hosts about them (the hosts must configure a router address).
10	Router Solicitation	1256	Request a Router Advertisement from routers.
13	Timestamp Request	792	Used to propagation time calculation.
14	Timestamp Reply	792	A response to a Timestamp request.
17	Address Mask Request	950	Used to request a subnet mask from a device.
18	Address Mask Reply	950	Reply to a request, containing a subnet mask.
30	Traceroute	1393	Utility for testing and debugging.

nation. The ICMP protocol is not intended to provide reliability to the IP protocol. Instead, it provides a feedback about the network environment.

In the following two sections, we will see some ICMP specific message formats.

5.2.2 ICMP error reporting messages

5.2.2.1 Destination Unreachable message

This ICMP error reporting message is used when delivery problems occur. Such errors could be, for example: the router not being able to reach a particular network, the intended host being down, the destination port being invalid, the datagram needing fragmentation but the DF bit is set, etc. The **Type** value is 3, and the possible **Code** values are shown in Table 5.6.

Figure 5.22 shows the Destination Unreachable message format. The **unused** field is reserved for later extensions, and must be zero when sent. It must not be used at the receiver except to calculate the checksum.

The **portion of the original IP datagram** is included in the ICMP message in order for the device that sent it to be able to recognize the undelivered datagram. The full IP header is included, and the first eight bytes of the data, which represents the first eight bytes of the transport layer (UDP or TCP) message header.

As datagrams are unacknowledged, the source could send several datagrams without noticing whether they had arrived or not. When it receives an ICMP message, the originator device needs to know which of the sent datagrams have not been delivered. This information is included in the portion of the original IP datagram.

Table 5.6

Code	Problem	Description
0	Network Unreachable	Routing problems or a Network ID is bad.
1	Host Unreachable	The network is accessible, but the host is not.
2	Protocol Unreachable	The protocol is invalid.
3	Port Unreachable	The port is invalid.
4	Fragmentation needed and DF bit set	The router needs to fragment the datagram, but the DF bit is set, so the datagram must be discarded.
5	Source Route failed	The route specified in the datagram can not be fulfilled.
7	Destination Host unknown	The host is unknown. Bad address.
9	Communication with Destination Network is Administratively Prohibited	The source is not allowed to send to the network where the device belongs.
10	Communication with Destination Host is Administratively Prohibited	The source is not allowed to send to this device.
11	Destination Network Unreachable for Type of Service	The network cannot be reached because the type of service specified cannot be fulfilled.
12	Destination Host Unreachable for Type of Service	The host cannot be reached because the type of service specified cannot be fulfilled.

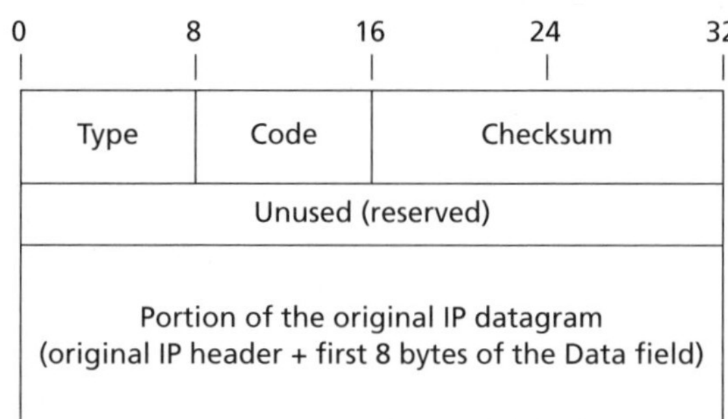

Figure 5.22 ICMP Destination Unreachable message format.

5.2.2.2 Source Quench message

As datagrams are received, they are buffered in memory, to be processed later. This memory buffer allows compensating the different rates at which datagrams are received and processed. But the buffer is limited, and it may happen that, if the sender's transmit rate is high, the device might not have the necessary buffer space to allocate the incoming datagrams, and so must discard them. When this happens, the receiving device generates an ICMP Source Quench message to ask the source device to slow down the rate at which it is sending the datagrams. The receiver device sending this ICMP message could be a router or a host.

In this type of message, the **Type** value is set to 4, and **Code** is 0. Except for these values, the message formats are like those for the previous message, as shown in Figure 5.22.

5.2.2.3 Time Exceeded message

This message is sent whenever 'timer-related' problems occur. As we saw in the IP header fields description, the Time To Live field is intended to avoid the possible router loops. Each time the datagram is handled by a router, this field value is decremented. If this value reaches zero before it arrives at its intended destination, it must be discarded. In this way, the datagram will not be 'looping forever'. Under these circumstances, when the datagram is discarded, an ICMP Time Exceeded message (**Type** value set to 11) is sent to the original source address to inform it about this error. In this case, the **Code** value is set to 0.

However, this ICMP Time Exceeded message is used in another circumstance as well: it has to do with the reassembly process with fragmented datagrams. Let's recall that in that process, we needed to wait for all fragmented datagrams in order to complete the original message. As a timer is used to avoid a 'waiting for ever' condition, the timer expiration prior to receiving all the needed fragments will cause the device to discard all received fragments. In this instance, an ICMP message is sent, and **Code** value is set to 1.

The ICMP Time Exceeded message format is the same as shown in Figure 5.22.

5.2.3 ICMP Information Exchange messages

5.2.3.1 Echo and Echo Reply messages

These are the most popular ICMP messages as they are used in the famous 'ping' utility (Ping.exe program). This utility implements an Echo test for diagnostic purposes. Each device on the Internet must implement this function, so in order to test if a device is operational, a ping message can be sent to it. The device must reply to the echo message with the same data received, reversing the source and destination address of the IP datagram. The echo request sender must match the sent message with the reply, and the time taken between both messages can be used for diagnostic and statistical purposes.

This is the same principle as the sonar submarine, which sends a signal and waits until the bounce signal is received, calculating the distance to the bouncer according to the time it took.

Figure 5.23 shows the Echo and Echo Reply message formats. The **Type** field must be 8 for Echo Request and 0 for Echo Reply. The **Code** field is not used, and must be 0.

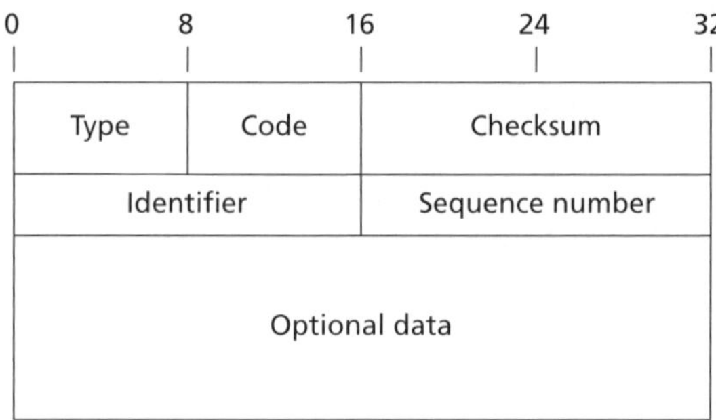

Figure 5.23 ICMP Echo (Type=8) and Echo Reply (Type=0) message format.

Since more than one echo message could be sent to the same or different devices, the receiving echo reply could come from different echo requests. In order to match the reply with the request, an **Identifier** field is provided. Also, the **Sequence** field could be incremented in each message. However, the use of this field is up to the particular implementation.

Optional data may be used in the appropriate field.

5.2.3.2 Router Advertisement and Router Solicitation messages

As hosts rely on local routers (routers at the same networks as the hosts') for delivering datagrams outside the local network, they must be configured with the router address (default gateway). Although this router address could be manually configured, an automatic method is used in order for hosts to discover local routers.

For this purpose, the Router Advertisement message is sent by routers on a regular basis. These messages are received by hosts, which are informed about the routers' existence as well as such important information as their address and the time the hosts should retain this information. (This information expires every given time period; so if a router fails, the host discards this information after the information expires and it looks for other routers.) Figure 5.24 shows the Router Advertisement message format.

The **Type** field must be 9, and the **Code** field is normally set to 0. The **Number of Addresses** indicates the number of addresses the router has, and the **Address Entry Size** is set to 2, indicating the number of 32-bit words of each entry size (32-bit address and 32-bit preference level). The **Lifetime** field indicates the number of seconds the host should consider this information as valid.

Each router address entry (one for each router interface) has a **Router Address** and the **Preference Level**. The higher this last value is, the more the host has a preference for this interface.

When a host powers on, if it has not manually configured any router, it should wait until a local router sends an Advertisement message. Instead of doing this, the host may send an ICMP Router Solicitation, in order for the router to send an Advertisement message immediately. Figure 5.25 shows the ICMP Router Solicitation message format. The **Type** value is set to 10, and the **Code** is not used, so it must be set to 0. The **Reserved** 4 bytes must be set to 0.

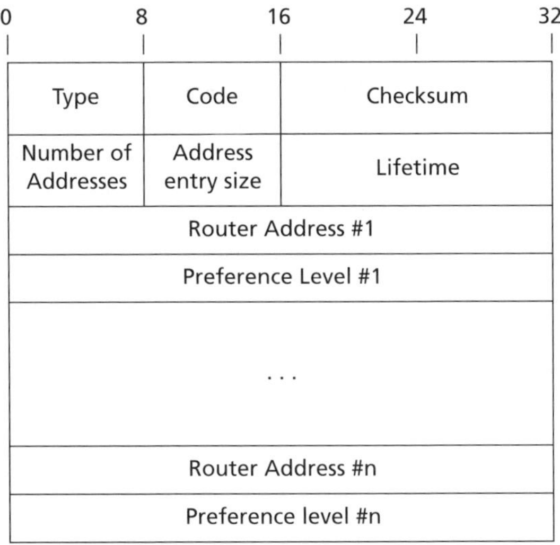

Figure 5.24 ICMP Router Advertisement (type 9) message format.

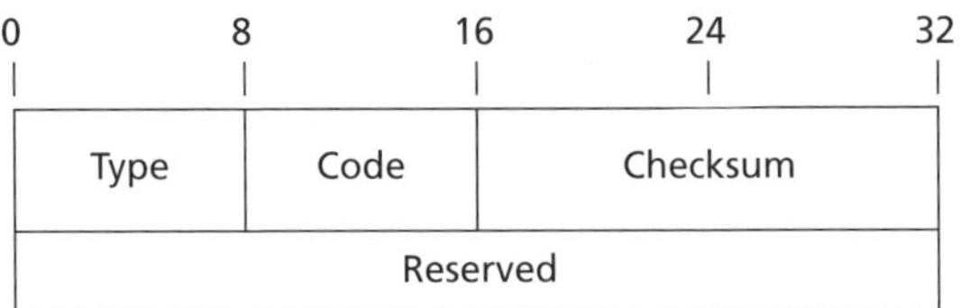

Figure 5.25 ICMP Router Solicitation message format.

Although this default gateway configuration is valid, there is another option like Dynamic Host Configuration Protocol (DHCP) to automatically configure the hosts. The RFC 1256 describes the ICMP Router Discovery Messages, and it provides full description about both messages.

5.2.3.3 Address Mask Request and Reply messages

In a Subnetting environment, in order for a device to properly interpret the IP address, a subnet mask must be known. This could be configured manually. Another way to know this value is using a couple of ICMP messages: Address Mask Request and Reply. In this way, when a host needs to know the subnet mask to use, an ICMP Address Mask Request is sent to the local router, which must reply with the subnet mask using the ICMP Address Mask Reply message.

Figure 5.26 shows the Address Mask Request and Reply Messages formats. The **Type** field must be 17 for Address Mask Request, and 18 for Address Mask Reply. The **Code** field is not used, and must be 0.

An **Identifier** and a **Sequence Number** are also present, but not used, as there is no need to a match multiple request with its replies. That is, only one Address Mask Request message is sent, in order to ask for the subnet mask.

The **Address Mask** field is the subnet mask filled by the router in the Reply message.

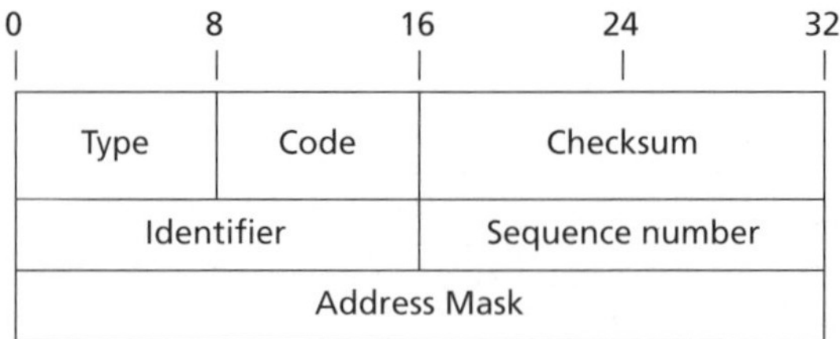

Figure 5.26 ICMP Address Mask Request and Reply message format.

Although this alternative is valid, another way to find this value is using a host configuration protocol such as Dynamic Host Configuration Protocol (DHCP).

5.2.3.4 Traceroute message

The idea behind this kind of message is not only to test the communication between two devices (as Echo messages do), but also to know the exact sequence of routers used to pass the datagram from one device to the other. The Tracert.exe utility implements this task.

One way to accomplish this task would be to send a series of datagrams incrementing the Time To Live parameter in each successive message. As a result, the first datagram, with TTL set to 1, will generate a Time Exceeded error (TTL = 0) at the first router, sending an ICMP message to the source; the second datagram, with TTL = 2, will generate the same error at the second router; and so on. Then, the source will receive several ICMP messages from each router the datagrams use to go from one device to the other.

First implementations of the Traceroute were based on the above method. But it presents a couple of problems. First, we need to generate several messages in order to know the complete route. Second, datagrams could take different paths (routers) for each message sent.

A better implementation is defined in RFC 1393, and it uses an IP option (Option Number 18) to implement Traceroute. When a router receives an IP datagram with the Traceroute option, it generates an ICMP Traceroute message and sends this message back to the datagram source. The ICMP Traceroute message format is shown in Figure 5.27.

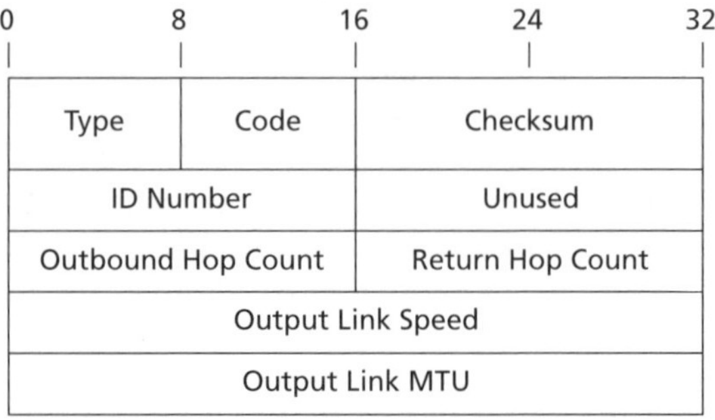

Figure 5.27 ICMP Traceroute message format.

The **Type** field must be 30. The **Code** field is set to 0 if the router passed the datagram to the next router, or set to 1 if the datagram was discarded due to a failure.

The **ID Number** is the same that the datagram has in the Traceroute option, and it is used to match the ICMP Traceroute message with the datagram used for this test. The **Unused** field is set to 0.

The **Outbound Hop Count** is set with the number of routers the IP datagram has already passed through. The **Return Hop Count** is set with the number of routers the ICMP returned message has passed through. The **Output Link Speed** is set with the speed of the link over which the Traceroute message is being transmitted (bytes per second). The **Output Link MTU** is the Maximum Transmission Unit of the link over which the Traceroute message is being transmitted (bytes).

5.3 Address Resolution Protocol (ARP)

As we have said before, the IP protocol allows devices from different physical networks to communicate with each other as if they were on the same network. In this way, several different types of network can be interconnected by routers creating a 'virtual network', where messages are transmitted in packets called datagrams. But the actual transmission occurs at layer two, where devices communicate using frames across the physical network, and routers pass the datagram from network to network, until the destination network where the recipient device resides.

In addition, as the new 'virtual network' is composed of several networks of very different technologies, each physical network has its own 'physical address' type (for example, while Ethernet has a 48-bit address, ArcNet has an 8-bit address). In this way, IP provides a common addressing scheme for the overall virtual network, making it possible for each device to be addressed the same way.

Then, each device has two different network addresses: the physical address used in the local physical network and the IP address used in the virtual network. This physical network is used to transmit frames over the local physical network, while the IP address is used to route the datagrams from network to network, across the 'virtual' inter-network.

Now, suppose that at layer three, Host A needs to send a message to Host B. To do this, the source device needs to know the IP address of the destination. Then, the message is encapsulated in a datagram, where both IP addresses are copied (source and destination), and passed down to the Data Link layer which will encapsulate the datagram into a frame to transmit it across the physical network. But how does this layer know the physical address of the destination device? We need a way to find, given an IP address, the corresponding physical address of the device. One way to do this is using the Address Resolution Protocol (ARP), which translates IP addresses into physical addresses.

When a device has the IP address of the destination device, but needs its hardware (or physical) address, a broadcast frame containing an ARP message is sent. The ARP message contains the IP address (called the protocol address) of the destination device (target device). As a broadcast frame is received by all stations, the ARP message is analysed and the device that has this protocol address must reply to the message's sender, sending its hardware address in the message. In this way, after these ARP Request/Reply messages, both devices will know their protocol and hardware addresses (the sender also sends its protocol and hardware addresses in the ARP request message). Figure 5.28 shows the ARP mechanism.

Note that the device could be a host or a router. That is, when the host needs to send the datagram to another host in a different network, indirect delivering is accomplished by sending the datagram to a local router. In this way, the MAC address of the local router must be known, so ARP is used for this purpose. When an ARP message with the router IP address as a Target Protocol address is broadcast, the router will reply to the ARP message with its own hardware address (the MAC address of the interface attached to the physical network).

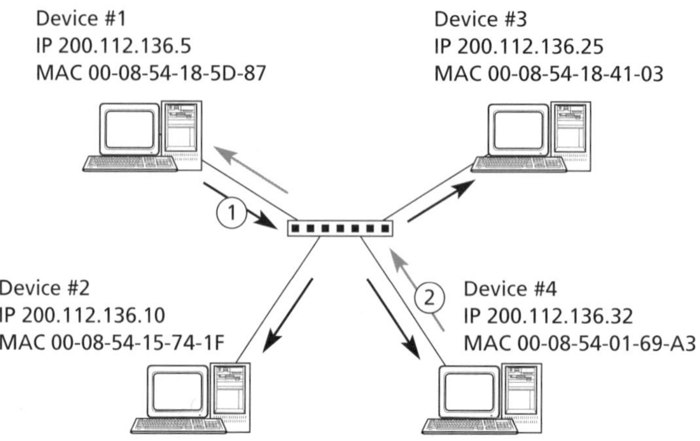

Figure 5.28 The ARP mechanism allows Device #1 to find Device #4 MAC address providing its IP address.

5.3.1 ARP message format

Although RFC 826 has the title 'An Ethernet Address Resolution Protocol', this protocol can be used to translate any layer-three protocol addresses into any layer-two hardware addresses. As such, special fields such as the hardware address length and the protocol address length are provided to be used with any sized addresses. In addition, hardware type and protocol type fields are used to specify the physical network type and protocol type used.

Figure 5.29 shows the ARP message format when it is used to translate IP addresses into Ethernet addresses. Table 5.7 describes the ARP message fields. Figure 5.30 shows an ARP Request and ARP Reply Messages examples.

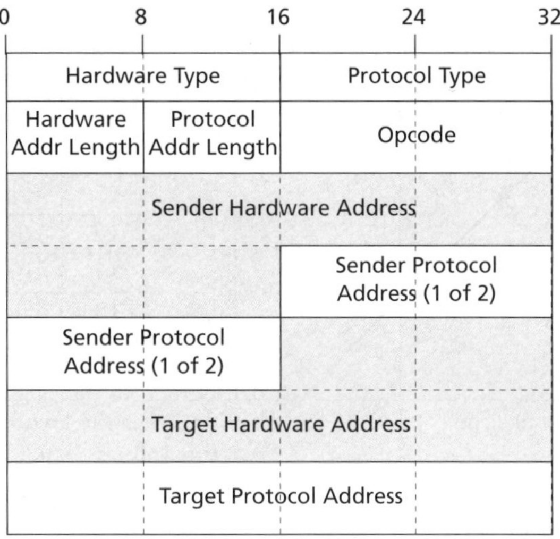

Figure 5.29 The ARP message format when used to translate IP addresses into Ethernet addresses.

5.3.2 ARP resolution caching

If every time we needed to send a frame we used the ARP mechanism, the overall performance would be very poor. Instead, a caching technique is used: that is, the software running at each device maintains a table with equivalences between IP addresses and hardware addresses. So, the first time, the ARP mechanism is used to resolve the IP address; but then the equivalence is caching (added to the table). After that, each time we need the device hardware address, we can look at it in the table.

In addition, as the ARP Request message is broadcast (sent to all devices at the physical network), all the stations should capture the IP and hardware addresses from the sender device, and add them to their resolution table. So, for future reference, this equivalence is already resolved, and there will be no need to use the ARP mechanism for that address.

Of course, the table entries should expire after a certain period. If not, if some device changes its Ethernet card, the MAC address will also change. So the equivalence stored at the resolution table will not be valid. The same will happen if for any reason the device must change its IP address, the host is down or the device is removed from the physical network.

Table 5.7

<table>
<tr><th>Field</th><th>Size (bytes)</th><th>Description</th></tr>
<tr><td>Hardware Type</td><td>2</td><td>Specifies the layer-two hardware type. Some values are:
<table>
<tr><th>Value</th><th>Physical network</th></tr>
<tr><td>1</td><td>Ethernet 10Mbps</td></tr>
<tr><td>6</td><td>IEEE 802 Networks</td></tr>
<tr><td>7</td><td>ArcNet</td></tr>
<tr><td>15</td><td>Frame Relay</td></tr>
<tr><td>16</td><td>ATM</td></tr>
<tr><td>17</td><td>HDLC</td></tr>
<tr><td>18</td><td>Fibre Channel</td></tr>
<tr><td>20</td><td>Serial Line</td></tr>
</table></td></tr>
<tr><td>Protocol Type</td><td>2</td><td>Specifies the layer-three protocol type. For IPv4, this value is 0x0800.</td></tr>
<tr><td>Hardware Address Length</td><td>1</td><td>Specifies the hardware address length. For Ethernet, this value is 6.</td></tr>
<tr><td>Protocol Address Length</td><td>1</td><td>Specifies the protocol address length. For IPv4, this value is 4.</td></tr>
<tr><td>Opcode</td><td>2</td><td>As this message format may be used for other message types, the Opcode specifies the type:
<table>
<tr><th>Opcode</th><th>Message type</th></tr>
<tr><td>1</td><td>ARP Request</td></tr>
<tr><td>2</td><td>ARP Reply</td></tr>
<tr><td>3</td><td>RARP Request</td></tr>
<tr><td>4</td><td>RARP Reply</td></tr>
<tr><td>5</td><td>DRARP Request</td></tr>
<tr><td>6</td><td>DRARP Reply</td></tr>
<tr><td>7</td><td>DRARP Error</td></tr>
<tr><td>8</td><td>InARP Request</td></tr>
<tr><td>9</td><td>InARP Reply</td></tr>
<tr><td>10</td><td>ARP-NAK</td></tr>
</table></td></tr>
<tr><td>Sender Hardware Address</td><td>Variable</td><td>The layer-two (hardware) address of the device sending the message.</td></tr>
<tr><td>Sender Protocol Address</td><td>Variable</td><td>The layer-three (protocol) address of the device sending the message.</td></tr>
<tr><td>Target Hardware Address</td><td>Variable</td><td>The layer-two (hardware) address of the device receiving the message.</td></tr>
<tr><td>Target Protocol Address</td><td>Variable</td><td>The layer-three (protocol) address of the device receiving the message.</td></tr>
</table>

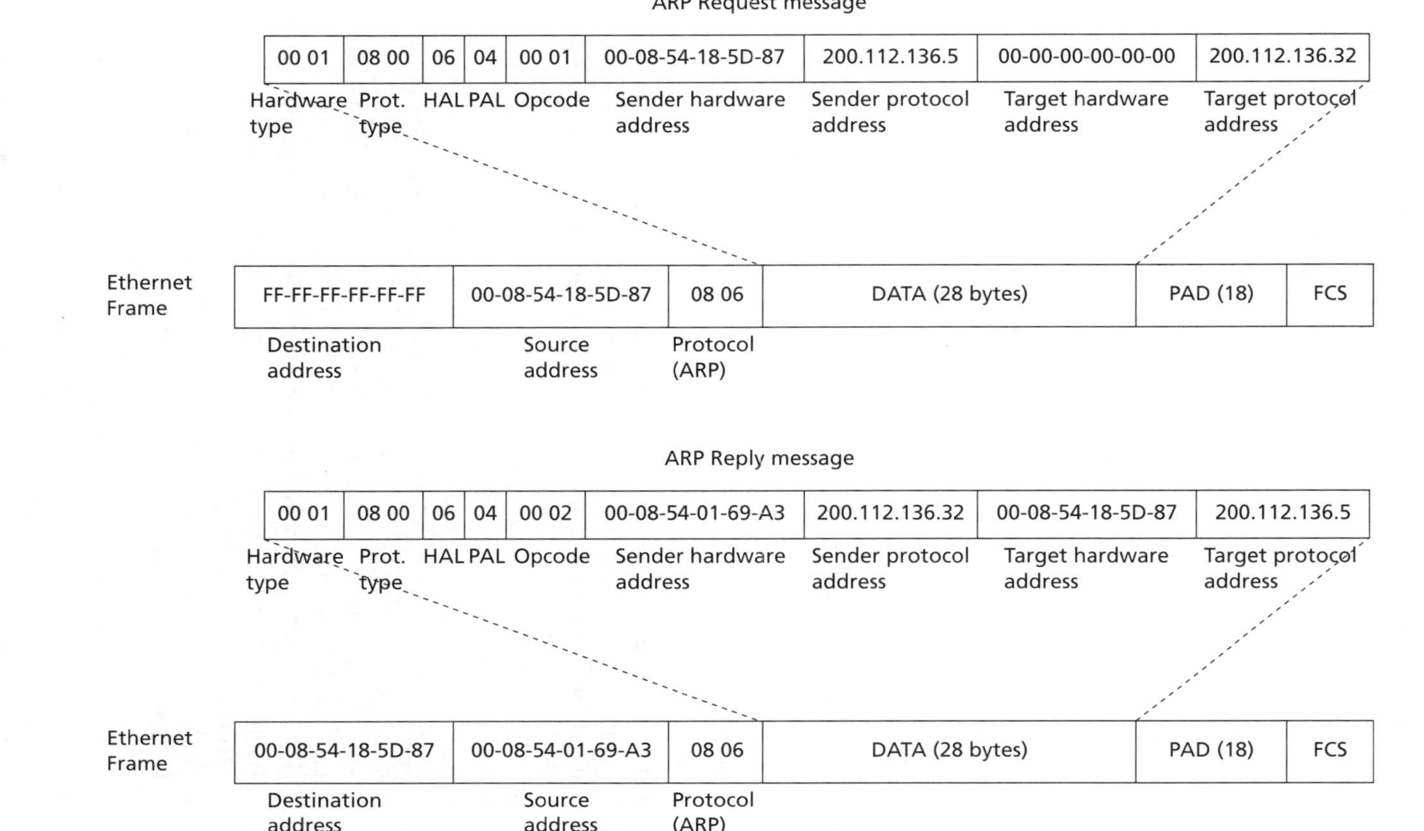

Figure 5.30 An example of ARP Request and ARP Reply messages.

5.4 Reverse Address Resolution Protocol (RARP)

As we have seen, the ARP protocol allows us to know the hardware address of a device, having its IP address. Now, could it be possible to know the IP address having the hardware address? The answer is yes, and RFC 903 defines 'A Reverse Address Resolution Protocol' which uses the same ARP message format, but with different Operation Code (Opcode) (see Table 5.7).

But, why would a device need to use RARP? Well, some hosts are diskless, as well as most embedded systems, meaning that they do not have a way to have their IP address configured. When these hosts boot up, they need to know their IP address in order to communicate with other devices using TCP/IP. As the hardware address is hardwired in the Ethernet controller, using RARP the device could provide its hardware address and ask for its IP address.

For this purpose, an ARP message with Opcode 3 (RARP Request) is broadcast. Then, an RARP server will reply to that request by sending an ARP message with Opcode 4 (RARP Reply), including the solicited IP address. Of course, there must exist at least one RARP server containing a hardware and IP address equivalence table.

Although this protocol can be used in such cases, other methods are preferred, such as the BOOTP and DHCP protocols. See Appendix C for a description of the DHCP protocol.

5.5 Summary

- The Internet Protocol is at the Internet layer and is responsible for interconnecting different LAN technologies, creating a 'virtual network' which allows all devices to communicate with each other as if they all were on the same network.
- The main functions of the IP layer are encapsulation, fragmentation/reassembly, addressing, and delivery and routing.
- Encapsulation is the process by which upper layer data is held in a datagram with other control fields, in order to pass this packet down the lower layers of the stack for its transmission.
- The IP fragmentation process consists of the IP datagram division into several smaller size datagrams, in order to overcome the frame size limitation that some networks would present to handle such large datagrams. At the recipient, the reassembly process must reconstruct the fragmented datagrams into the original datagram.
- Each device connected to the IP 'virtual network' or inter-network must have a unique IP address. Each IP address has a Network ID component, and a Host ID component. A convenient addressing scheme is provided in order to facilitate the network and host identification. The first scheme introduced was Classed Addressing, which classified the whole address space into several classes for different sized networks. This scheme was very inefficient in the use of address space and did not suit large networks

very well. The Subnetting technique was introduced to allow the internal division of networks into sub-networks. The weakness of this scheme was that all sub-networks had to be the same size. This limitation was overcome by the Variable Length Subnet Masking (VLSM) technique, although it still made inefficient use of the address space. Finally, the Classless Inter-Domain Routing (CIDR) scheme (also called Supernetting) was introduced, which applies the subnetting technique to the whole Internet. Under this classless scheme, each network would be a subnet of the whole Internet. Besides applying the VLSM technique, multiple levels can be used to split the entire Internet into several Subnets, and then split these Subnets into new Sub-subnets, and so on; as many times as needed. This addressing scheme is very efficient in regard to the use of the address space, and is the one currently used on the Internet.

- The IP layer is responsible for the delivery of messages over the 'virtual network' or inter-network. Direct delivery is performed in the local network by the Data Link layer. Indirect delivery is performed by routers, which transmit the messages from network to network, until they reach the destination network where the message is delivered to the recipient host using direct delivery. Routers decide the most convenient path to forward the messages based on information contained in the routing tables. Routers communicate with each other, exchanging information about the routes, using routing protocols.
- The Internet Control Message Protocol (ICMP) is like 'worker assistance' for IP, providing some feedback about the conditions of the inter-network. It is used mainly for maintenance, diagnostic and test purposes. ICMP messages are usually either used for reporting errors, or for exchanging information about the conditions of the 'virtual network' nodes.
- The Address Resolution Protocol (ARP) is used to map IP addresses into physical (hardware) addresses. The ARP Request message is broadcast to the network, and the device matching the target protocol address of the request replies to the message, sending its hardware address. The mapping is cached in a table for performance reasons.
- The Reverse Address Resolution Protocol (RARP) is used to map hardware addresses into IP addresses, and it is used in situations such as diskless hosts, which do not have a way of knowing their IP address at boot up.

6

The Transport layer: UDP and TCP

In the last chapter, we saw how the IP protocol transmits datagrams between devices over the inter-network. But sometimes this service is very far from what applications really need. First, several applications could be running at the same device, so the IP address should be shared among those programs. Then, some further addressing scheme will be required for assigning identification to each application. Secondly, while some applications require a full feature connection-oriented reliable transport service, others simply need a fast method for transmitting information, even admitting that some data could be lost. Then, appropriate services should be offered, covering different needs. In order to address those issues, a new Transport layer is introduced, where two protocols, TCP and UDP, are responsible for the host-to-host transport function. Each protocol provides a solution to address different application requirements.

6.1 Transport layer introduction

The Physical layer moves bits over the shared mediums, the Data Link layer moves frames on a physical network and the Internet layer moves datagrams on a virtual network. The Transport layer, then, provides 'host-to-host' communication services for the Application layer in the TCP/IP stack. This Transport layer also provides the network level services, from the developer perspective, providing a way to transport data over the Internet.

The Transport layer is like an intermediary between the hardware-oriented lower layers and the software-oriented upper layers. That is, while the three lower layers work as a team to move datagrams over an inter-network, the Transport layer uses these services in order for the Application layers to communicate over the Internet.

The Transport layer services are presented in two versions: the User Datagram Protocol (UDP) and the Transmission Control Protocol (TCP), where each protocol covers different transport service requirements. If the Internet layer provides message delivery between two distant devices, why is the Transport layer needed? Do the applications need more services than those provided by the Internet layer? Well, sometimes some extra characteristics are needed.

As we saw in Chapter 5, the Internet layer offers the IP datagram delivery over the inter-network. However, some limitations are revealed when we examine how IP works. For example, we saw that the datagrams could take different routes from one host to another, meaning that datagrams could arrive disordered or that some do not arrive at all. While in a physical network, the frame is transmitted directly from one device to the destination; in the virtual network lots of routers take part in the delivery process, so there is a higher probability that a fault or an error will occur at some point, making the datagram fail to arrive at its destination. As a result, the Internet layer delivery is unreliable. As we also saw in the last chapter, the ICMP messages were provided in order to have some feedback about the communication environment, but they were not intended to make IP more reliable.

One way to improve the delivery mechanism is to acknowledge the received datagrams. In this way, if a device sends a datagram, the receiver must send back an acknowledge message. Then, if the source does not receive this acknowledgement, it could retransmit the datagram. However, the Internet layer does not provide this characteristic.

Also, as the Internet layer is connectionless, meaning that no connection is required before transferring the data, the source device could send a datagram, but if this datagram does not arrive, the destination device has no way of knowing the intentions of the source regarding data transfer. That is, if a prior connection were required before starting data transfer, when the destination device receives the connection request, it would expect the source device to transmit data to it. Once connected, if data transfer never happens, the destination could suspect that some error occurs. In this way, a connection-oriented communication is like saying: 'Here is my connection request – wait for the data I will transfer to you.'

Making an analogy with the postal service, the first-class postal option is simple and cheap, but is unreliable, in the sense that the source has no way of knowing if the destination received the letter, since no one has confirmed reception. That is, even when the service works well most of the time, there is no guarantee that letters always arrive at their destination. However, using 'a proof of delivery' type of service, the source is notified when the destination has received the letter. Of course, this last service is more expensive than the first. Concluding the analogy, the Internet layer is similar to the simpler and cheaper postal service. In other words, while the Internet layer transmits datagrams over the inter-network using its 'best possible effort', there is no guarantee that these datagrams will arrive at the intended point.

In order to transmit data in a reliable way, some mechanisms are needed to establish connections, acknowledge received datagrams and retransmit lost data. However, these mechanisms generate more network traffic, and take more time. As a result, a higher cost is paid in terms of both time and bandwidth.

The next question one might ask is why IP does not include such characteristics. The answer is that not all the applications need them. While some applications need to count on a reliable data transmission, others do not. Below, we will see some kind of applications that require data delivery to be efficient and fast, even if a few datagrams never arrive at their destination.

As a result, it is better to have a new layer, called the Transport layer, offering services that cover different requirements: a higher-cost connection-oriented, reliable transport service; or just a simpler and faster transmission unreliable transport service. Each application will use one of these services according to its transmission requirements.

It is worth noting that 'unreliable' does not mean the datagrams will never arrive at their destination. It means that there is no guarantee about it. All the data may arrive with no problem, but, the application must consider the possibility that some datagrams may be lost.

Then, we have two different protocols running at the Transport layer:

- **Transmission Control Protocol (TCP)**: is a full featured transport protocol, connection-oriented, with flow control, acknowledged transmissions, and retransmission mechanism.
- **User Datagram Protocol (UDP)**: is a simple, efficient and fast transport protocol, although unreliable.

Perhaps the fact that some applications need a reliable transport system is easy to understand, but the opposite is not. That is, why would an application be interested in an unreliable transport system? In fact, some applications are not directly looking for unreliability, but prefer a simple and fast transport method, even when some part of data could be lost. Therefore, they accept unreliability.

For example, audio signals must be digitalized in order to be processed by digital systems. For this, the signal is sampled at a specific rate. The better the rate, the more samples there will be; and the digitalized signal will be of a better quality. If the data is transmitted over an inter-network, and a few samples never arrive, the quality could be poor but the message would still be understood at the receiving device. Even more important, if the lost sample were retransmitted later, it would not be useful since samples must follow an ordered sequence in order to interpret the overall message. The applications with stream multimedia data prefer a simpler, faster, although unreliable, transport protocol.

Other applications, perhaps, have their own internal procedure that allows them to provide the required reliability by themselves. Consider an application where one end must transmit some information and requires a receipt number from the other end before sending the next piece of information. If the receipt number is not received, a retransmission could be sent. By nature, an implicit acknowledgement system is implemented, so using TCP as a transport protocol could mean duplicating efforts. Another example would be found in the case where two applications exchange time information to synchronize their clocks, at certain time periods. As this functionality is not critical, if one of the messages is lost the system may wait for the next message without a problem.

The last question would be: if some applications require reliable transport while others prefer a simpler and faster method, what if we left each application to implement its required functionality and use the Internet layer as a delivery protocol? In these case, each application would be duplicating efforts trying to provide the same mechanisms necessary to make the transport a reliable method. It is preferable to make this effort only once, implemented in the TCP protocol, and to make it available for all those applications that require it.

6.1.1 Transport layer addressing: ports

As we saw in Chapter 5, the Internet layer provides the IP addressing by which each device in the inter-network may be uniquely identified. The device has one IP address for each of its network interfaces. The IP addresses are used as source and destination for the datagrams sent over the inter-network.

However, it is common for each device to have more than one application running, so the IP address of the device should be shared among those applications. This means that each application sending datagrams has the same IP source address. At worst, each datagram received by the device has the same IP destination address. Therefore, how does the transport layer know what application is the intended recipient, if all datagrams have the same IP destination address? The answer is the port address.

Since many applications could be running simultaneously at the same device (for example, an e-mail client, a Web browser and an FTP client), different software processes may be using the TCP/IP stack. To accomplish this, the data transmitted from these processes must be multiplexed and passed down the stack to be transmitted over the inter-network. In addition, when data are received, the data must be demultiplexed in order to pass it correctly to the right process. Figure 6.1 shows how many processes are multiplexed and demultiplexed by the Transport layer.

In order to distinguish these processes, the Transport layer assigns a different port address for each process. Then, the data received from the application is encapsulated by the Transport layer, where source and destination ports are inserted. As a result, at the receiving device, the Internet layer receives the datagram and passes the data to the Transport layer, which uses the destination port to pass the message to the correct application.

Then, if ports are used at the Transport layer to address different processes, each time an application needs to transfer data to an application

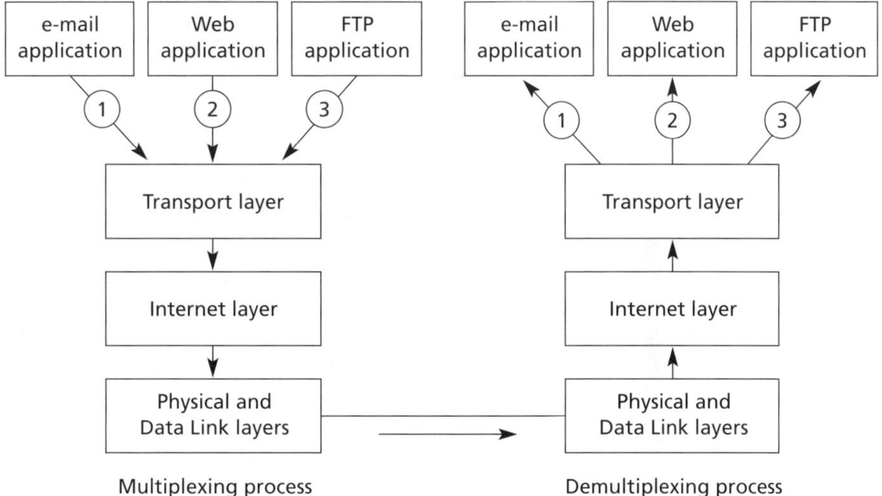

Figure 6.1 In order for many processes to use the TCP/IP stack, the application data is multiplexed and then demultiplexed by the Transport layer.

running at a different host, the host IP address and the application port address of the recipient must be known. How will applications know these port addresses? The best way is to assign a default value for every application.

As the Transport layer has two different protocols serving the applications, UDP and TCP, and the port address fields are 16 bits in length, each protocol has 65 536 ports available. These port numbers are divided into ranges and assigned to different purposes.

The application protocols use the client/server model, where the client device always initiates the communication by sending a message to the server, who receives the request, processes it and then replies to the client. The server is listening for client requests and thus never initiates the communication. The client program that initiates the communication needs to know the destination port where the server application is receiving the data. The server then uses the source port of the received message to know the client port. Thus, the server application processes have assigned port numbers in the range from 0 to 1023, called well-known port numbers.

Figure 6.2 shows some ports assigned to different server applications. Datagrams received by the IP layer of the server device are passed to the appropriate transport protocol, depending on the IP Header Protocol field

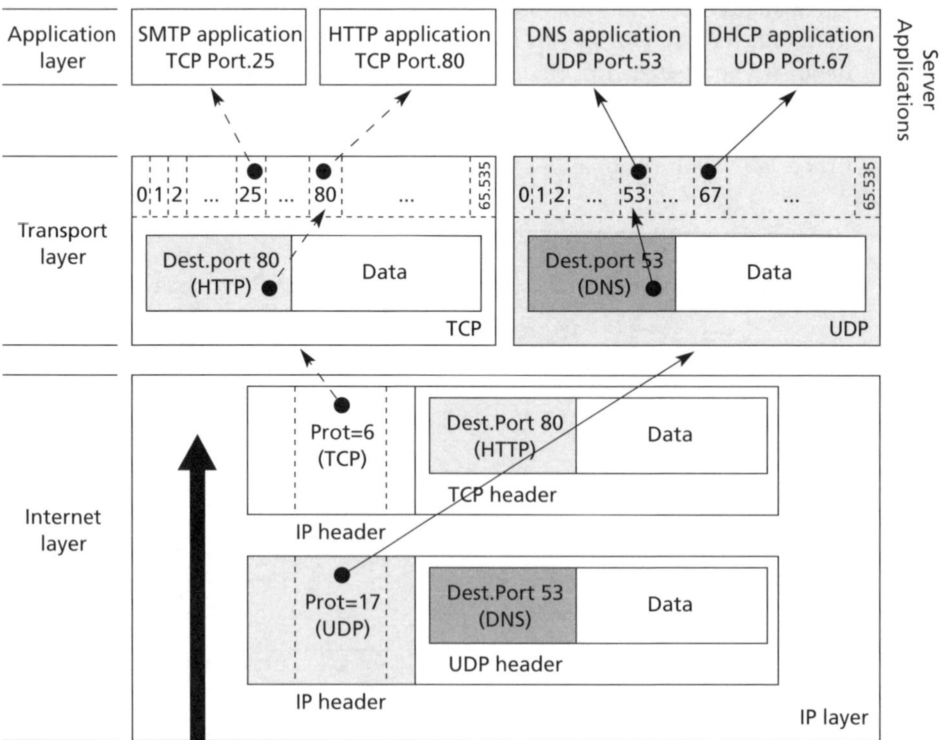

Figure 6.2 Application server assigned port values.

value. Then, according to the destination port value, the data is passed to the corresponding application process. The server application processes use well-known assigned ports, in order to facilitate the client application requests. As the service provided by the application can be accessed through these ports, they are sometimes called 'service contact ports'.

6.1.2 Server process ports assignment

The TCP and UDP port number assignment for server processes is divided into three ranges:

- **Well-known port numbers (0–1023)**: these port numbers are managed by IANA, and reserved for the universal TCP/IP applications. This range defines the 'service contact ports' for the most common internet applications. Table 6.1 shows some common well-known port numbers and the application that uses them.

Table 6.1

Port	Transport protocol	Name
7	TCP–UDP	**ECHO**
13	TCP–UDP	**Day Time** Protocol
20	TCP	**FTP-DATA:** File Transfer Protocol (data)
21	TCP	**FTP:** File Transfer Protocol (control)
23	TCP	**Telnet** Protocol
25	TCP	**SMTP**: Simple Mail Transfer Protocol
53	TCP–UDP	**DNS:** Domain Name Server
67	UDP	**BOOT/DHCP:** Bootstrap Protocol/Dynamic Host Configuration Protocol (server)
68	UDP	**BOOT/DHCP:** Bootstrap Protocol/Dynamic Host Configuration Protocol (client)
69	UDP	**TFTP:** Trivial File Transfer Protocol
80	TCP	**HTTP:** Hyper Text Transfer Protocol (World Wide Web)
110	TCP	**POP3:** Post Office Protocol (version 3)
119	TCP	**NNTP:** Network News Transfer Protocol
123	UDP	**NTP:** Network Time Protocol
143	TCP	**IMAP:** Internet Message Access Protocol
161	UDP	**SNMP:** Simple Network Management Protocol
162	UDP	**SNMP TRAP:** Simple Network Management Protocol – Trap
194	TCP	**IRC:** Internet Relay Chat

- **Registered port numbers (1024–49 151)**: other applications not universally known like the one above can be registered in order to avoid conflicts with each other. Companies such as Microsoft, Oracle, HP and Symantec have their own protocols running on port numbers from this range.
- **Dynamic and/or private port numbers (49 152–65 535):** these ports are not maintained by IANA, and can be used for any purpose and by any organization.

The complete list of port number assignments is maintained by IANA, and it can be checked out at www.iana.org/assignments/port-numbers. (The RFC 1700 had this information, but it is now obsolete.)

6.1.3 Client process ports assignment

Even when the client application process could make use of the same port values assigned to the server, it is not convenient since this would not allow the client and the server to run the same application on the same host. That is, as both client and server application must use the same protocol (UDP or TCP) the same port could not be used. To avoid this, the TCP/IP stack assigns to the client process a temporal port value from a different range depending on the particular stack implementation. A typical range could be from 1024 to 4999. Each time the client application is launched, a different port value is assigned.

6.1.4 A client/server message exchange example

Suppose a web browser (client application) is launched on a host with IP address 200.136.112.75, and the temporary port 2520 is assigned to this process. If this client needs to retrieve some data from an HTTP server running on a host with IP address 205.122.63.20, it will need to send a request with the following addresses:

- Destination IP address: 205.122.63.20 (IP address of the server)
- Destination Port address: 80 (well-known port for HTTP)
- Source IP address: 200.136.112.75 (IP address of the client)
- Source Port address: 2520 (temporary port for the client process)

In this way, the client needs to know only the server IP address, as the port is well known for the service it will access (HTTP service). When the request arrives at the server, it will use the source port address to send the reply to the correct application. For this reason, it does not matter if the client port number changes each time the application is launched. Figure 6.3 shows this example.

6.1.5 Client and server association: TCP/IP sockets

A socket is a communication-end identifier, and it is specified by the IP address and the port number: for example, <200.136.112.75:2520>. Sockets are related to the TCP/IP Application Program Interface (API), where each function needs a socket as an identifier.

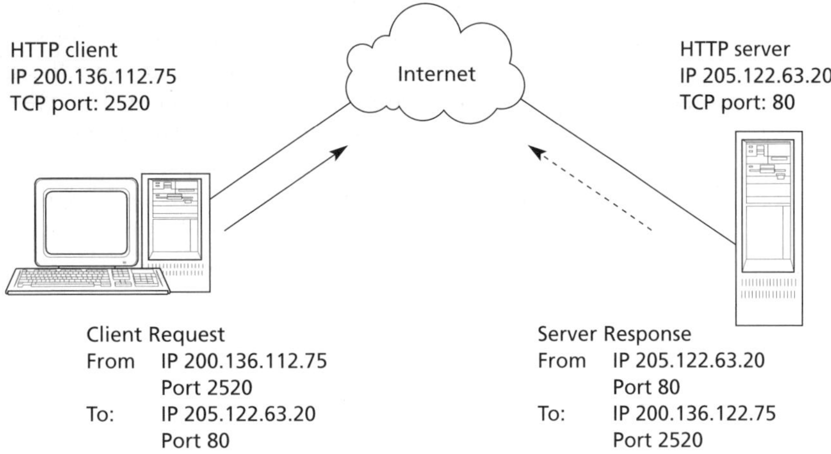

Figure 6.3 A client/server message exchange example.

The Windows version of this API is the Windows Sockets or WinSock. Figure 6.4 shows the relation between the WinSock Model and the OSI and TCP/IP models. Two types of socket exist: the stream (TCP) and the datagram (UDP). For two sockets to communicate as client and server, they must be the same socket type.

The exchange of data between two devices may be described as messages sent from a socket on one device to a socket on the other. Both sockets create an association, annotated as <200.136.112.75:2520, 205.122.63.20:80>. The elements of the association are the protocol (socket type of both client and

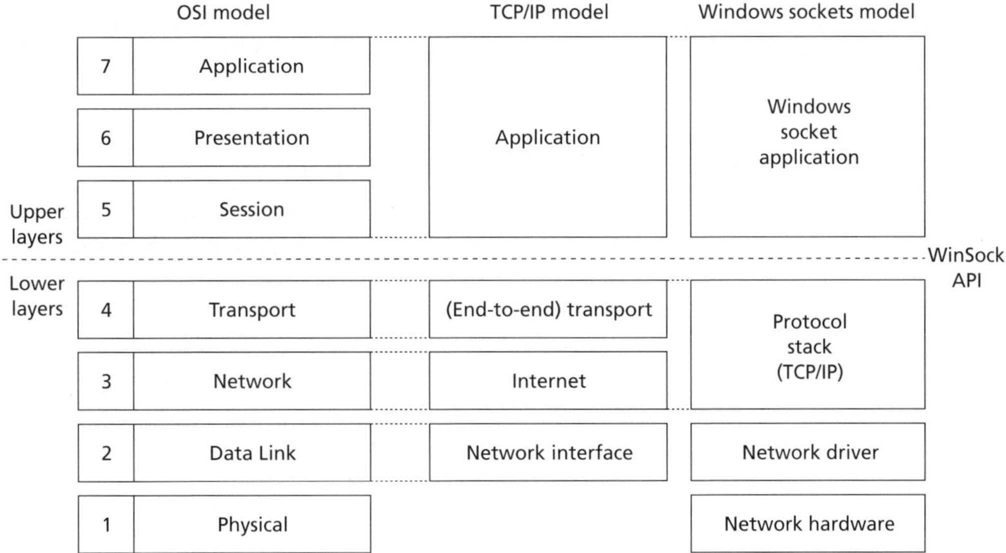

Figure 6.4 The Windows socket model and its relation with the OSI Reference Model and the TCP/IP model.

server sockets), the client IP address, the client port number, the server IP address and the server port number.

In a stream (TCP) socket, as a connection-oriented protocol, the life of an association relates to the creation and destruction of the TCP virtual circuit. In a datagram (UDP) socket, a connectionless protocol, the association would be created and destroyed with each packet transmitted.

Multiple sockets could be created, allowing several applications to share the same device IP address. In addition, several associations may exist on a device, meaning that it has multiple simultaneous connections with other devices.

6.2 User Datagram Protocol (UDP)

The User Datagram Protocol (UDP) was designed for those applications that need a simple and fast transport protocol, even when the delivery and duplication of messages are not guaranteed, or the retransmission (at a later time) would not make sense.

The UDP is so simple that it just implements the port addressing, and provides an optional checksum for error detection. The rest of the job is done by the underlying Internet protocol. The complete standard is described under RFC 768.

6.2.1 UDP encapsulation

The UDP protocol takes the higher-layer message (application data) and encapsulates it into the Data field of the UDP datagram. The header is filled with the source port of the application sending the message, and the destination port of the intended recipient application. A checksum may also be calculated. Then, the UDP message is passed down to IP for transmission. See Figure 6.5 for details.

6.2.2 UDP message format

The UDP message consists of an 8-byte fixed length header, and the data field used to encapsulate the upper layer messages. Figure 6.6 shows the UDP message format.

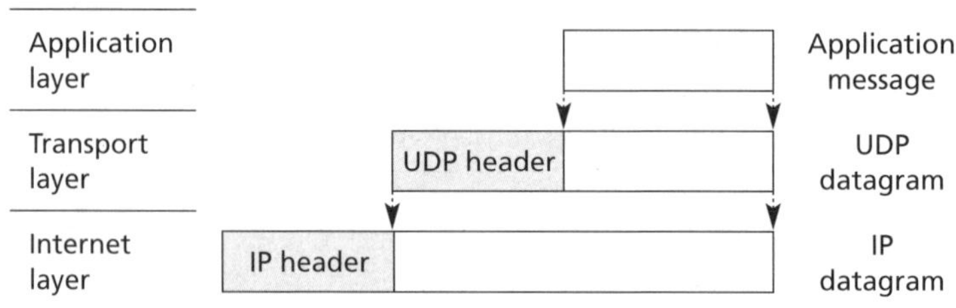

Figure 6.5 The application message is encapsulated into a UDP datagram.

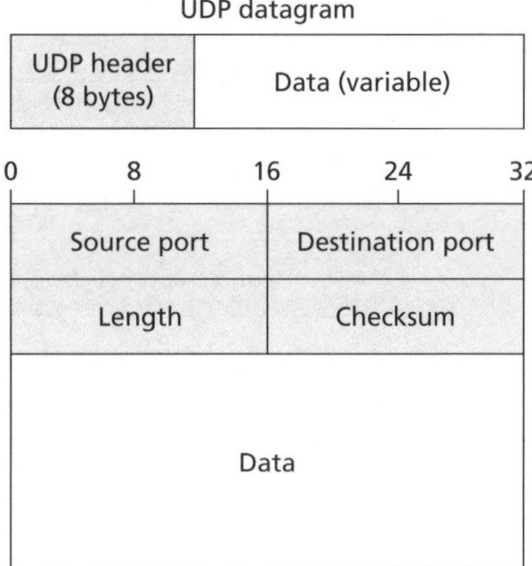

Figure 6.6 UDP message format.

The field description is as follows:

- **Source port** (2 bytes): a 16-bit port number of the process that sent the message. Normally, it could be a client process in a Request, or a server process in a Reply. Although RFC 768 describes it as an optional field, it must be used in order for the server to know the port number to which to reply the message.
- **Destination port** (2 bytes): a 16-bit port number of the recipient process on the destination device. Normally, it could be a server process in a Request, or a client process in a Reply.
- **Length** (2 bytes): the length of the whole UDP datagram, including the header and the data field.
- **Checksum** (2 bytes): an optional 16-bit checksum that provides an error-detecting feature. See the next section about how to calculate this field value.
- **Data** (variable): the encapsulated application message to be sent.

6.2.3 UDP checksum calculation

The checksum is the 16-bit ones complement of the ones complement sum of the computed fields. Instead of calculating the checksum over just the regular UDP datagram, a pseudo header is constructed with some fields from the IP datagram, and attached to the UDP message. In this way, the checksum is calculated over this pseudo-header, the UDP header, and the UDP payload or data, padded with zero bytes at the end, if necessary to make a multiple of two bytes. These IP datagram fields are the IP source and destination addresses, a zero byte for padding, the protocol type (value 17 for UDP), and the UDP length field which is then computed twice in the checksum (it is found in the pseudo-header and in the UDP header). Figure 6.7 shows the structure of this pseudo-header.

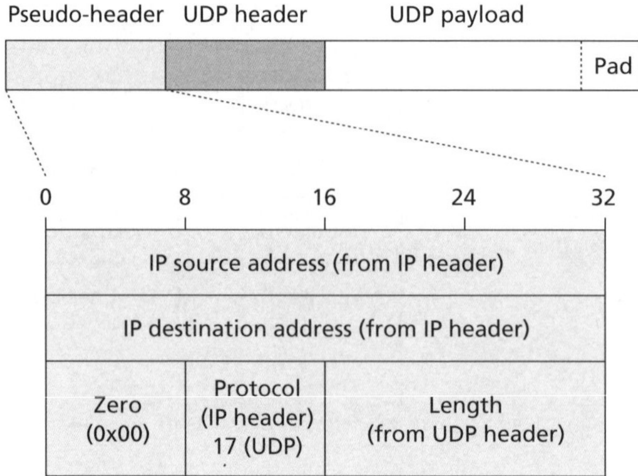

Figure 6.7 UDP Pseudo-header format used for checksum.

The reason for computing this pseudo-header with the IP addresses is to provide an extra error check to ensure that data has arrived at the right destination from the right source, avoiding the delivery of messages between incorrect addresses. In addition, it provides protection for datagrams delivered to wrong protocol layers (IP protocol field error detection), and UDP datagrams in which one part has been accidentally omitted or lost (incorrect UDP datagram length error detection).

The pseudo-header is used only for the checksum calculation and it is then discarded, so it is not included in any message. The resulting checksum value is held in the checksum field of the UDP header. The UDP checksum field is optional, and set to zero if not used. But if used, and the checksum results in a zero value, to avoid confusion at the destination, which may think the checksum is not enabled, this zero value is replaced with all ones (65 535 decimal).

6.2.4 UDP-based applications

As we have seen, UDP is simple and fast, but also it is unreliable, unacknowledged and connectionless. Except for the port addressing and the optional checksum, using UDP is like using IP. Some applications can benefit from the efficiency of UDP, but they must also contemplate its limitations.

Two kinds of applications could benefit from UDP:

- **Request-reply applications**: those applications that use this mechanism, using small messages, are very suitable for UDP. As the client sends a request message and must wait for a reply from the server, if a datagram has been lost, the client will never receive the reply so it could retransmit the request message. In this way, lost messages are detected and can be retransmitted.
- **Streaming data applications**: in applications that handle stream data such as a multimedia program streaming a video clip or an audio file over the

Internet, the performance is the most important requirement in order to keep the stream flowing continuously. Moreover, if a datagram is lost and few bytes are missing from the stream, it is not so important, and in some cases, it is even imperceptible by the users. Moreover, as a multimedia stream consists of an ordered sequence of data, if those lost datagrams were detected and retransmitted, they would arrive late (and out of their corresponding sequence), so the retransmission feature is not useful in this kind of application.

Table 6.2 shows some UDP applications.

Table 6.2

Protocol	Description	Server port
DNS	Exchange request/reply messages for domain name resolution.	53
BOOTP/DHCP	Request/reply message for host configuration.	67/68
TFTP	Transfer of small files, implementing its own acknowledged system to avoid file corruption.	69
SNMP	Uses short messages for network management.	161/162
RIP/RIPng	Exchange route information updated every a certain period, or under a request/reply message.	520/521

Even when an application could use UDP as a transport layer, and could implement all the features that UDP lacks but TCP has, it is obvious that TCP would be more suitable. However, when an application needs only some of the full set of features that TCP provides, it would be reasonable to consider the use of UDP implementing only the required features at the application level.

6.3 Transmission Control Protocol (TCP)

The Transmission Control Protocol (TCP) is a full-featured transport protocol, connection-oriented, with flow control, acknowledged transmissions, and retransmission mechanism; designed to provide applications a reliable way to send data as a stream of bytes, using the unreliable Internet Protocol, over the inter-network.

The RFC 793 is the defining standard for TCP, but there are several other documents with additional information describing how TCP works, and some enhancements developed over the years. Table 6.3 shows some of these documents. Even though TCP was designed to work with IP as an underlying network protocol, it may be adapted to work with any other network protocol.

Table 6.3

Document	Content	RFC
Transmission Control Protocol	The defining standard for TCP.	793
Window and Acknowledgment Strategy in TCP	Describes problems with the sliding window acknowledgment system, and presents solutions to correct them.	813
Increasing TCP's Initial Window	Discusses the advantages and disadvantages of the higher initial window.	3390
The TCP Maximum Segment Size and Related Topics	The importance of the Maximum Segment Size (MSS), and its relation with the IP datagram size.	879
Computing TCP's Retransmission Timer	Describes issues related to the TCP Retransmission Timer.	2988
Requirements for Internet Hosts–Communications Layers	Details about TCP implementation on hosts.	1122
TCP Alternate Checksum Options	Defines a mechanism for an alternative checksum method.	1146
TCP Extension for High Performance	Defines extensions to TCP for high-speed links.	1323
TCP Selective Acknowledgment Options	A method for selectively specifying segments for retransmission.	2018
Congestion Control in IP/TCP Internetworks	Congestion problems and their solutions.	896
TCP Congestion Control	Describes algorithms used for congestion control: slow start, congestion avoidance, fast retransmit and fast recovery.	2581

6.3.1 TCP characteristics

The most important characteristics of TCP are as follows:

- *Connection-oriented*: before data transfer can take place between the devices, a connection must be established. This creates a 'virtual circuit' which must be managed and terminated after all the data has been transferred.
- *Multiple connections*: TCP provides a method for identifying connections, which allows a device to have multiple connections opened without conflicts, either to the same IP device or different IP devices.
- *Full-duplex:* once a connection is established, data can be transferred in both directions.

- *Stream-oriented*: even when IP works with blocks of data, TCP allows the application to send data as a continuous stream of bytes. TCP must then packet this data as blocks to pass it to IP.
- *Data-unstructured*: as data are passed as streams of bytes, there is no way to separate data elements inside the stream. Therefore, the application must provide a way of knowing how to deal with this. Suppose the application passes three database records as a stream, TCP will treat this information as only one piece. Then, the destination application must know how to separate this data into the original three database records. In UDP, which is block-oriented, the application could pass one record at a time, so the record separation is natural.
- *Reliable*: as TCP ensures that all transmitted data items arrive at their destination, the communication is reliable.
- *Acknowledged*: each message transmitted by TCP is acknowledged by the recipient. In this way, TCP knows if a message has not arrived, and can retransmit the lost data.
- *Flow control*: when one device transmits data at a rate that the receiver cannot process, TCP provides a mechanism by which the receiver notifies the transmitter to slow down the transmission rate, or even to stop sending data at all, until the receiver could start receiving again.
- *Process-addressing*: as different processes or applications may be running at the same device sharing the same IP address, TCP provides a way for identifying each process and multiplexing the data passed to the IP layer. At the receiving point, TCP must demultiplex the data and pass it to the intended process. This transport layer-addressing scheme is accomplished with the port numbers.

All these characteristics allow us to understand the TCP functions; what it does, and how it works. For this reason, each of them will be described in the next sections.

6.3.2 TCP message unit: segments

Until now, the communication process has been described as a batch of messages (block of data) between layers at the TCP/IP stack. That is, if an application must transmit a message, it passes the data to the Transport layer where, for example, the UDP encapsulates this data, adds its header, and passes this datagram to the IP layer. The IP layer encapsulates the UDP message in its own datagram as well, and passes it to the Data Link layer where it is further encapsulated in a frame, and finally passed to the Physical layer to be transmitted over the network.

As we have seen above, data is passed between layers as a block. So the application is forced to divide its data into blocks in order for the UDP to process it. However, there are many applications that need to send information as a stream of bytes; and they want to pass the data as it is, without worrying about dividing it into chunks of data. Or perhaps, the messages could be so long that it would be impossible to pass them to the UDP without dividing them into smaller parts. For such cases, the TCP provides a way to transmit data as a stream of bytes, and the application does not need to worry about how to 'package' data in order to pass it to the Transport layer.

Even when TCP is stream-oriented, its underlying IP layer is not, so TCP must divide the received stream into appropriate blocks of data, in order to pass it to the IP layer. Those blocks of data are then encapsulated into so-called 'segments', which constitute the message unit in the TCP transport protocol. In addition, the 'appropriate blocks of data' mean that the segment length will be a convenient one, as we will see later on.

The fact that the TCP accepts data as a stream from the applications has a direct implication: the data received by an application using TCP is unstructured. For example, if the application needs to send three database records to another application, selecting UDP as the transport protocol, it could send three messages, one for each record. In this way, the receiver application would get those records separately in different messages.

However, using TCP, the application will pass all the data as a stream of bytes; that is, the three records as only one chunk of bytes, with no 'dividing lines' between each record. After that, the TCP will divide this stream into segments where most of the time, each segment will not be coincident with each record. Once the application receives the data, there is no way to know exactly where each record ends and where the next one starts. As a result, the application protocols using TCP need to determine a way for applications to recognize how the unstructured data of the stream is organized. For example, in the database records example, a special character could indicate the end of each record.

TCP uses messages for several purposes. One of them, of course, is data transfer. As data is passed like segments of the overall data stream passed between devices, the TCP messages are called 'TCP segments'.

6.3.3 TCP segment format

As TCP segments were designed both to carry data and to control information, they are used for data transfer as well as for other purposes, such as establishing a connection, managing the open connection, sending acknowledge messages, notifying flow control and terminating the connection.

A single format is used for all segments, including header information that allows one segment to perform more than one function, reducing the number of segments sent. For example, one segment could transfer data, acknowledge a prior received segment and send flow control information all in the same message, resulting in a reduced network traffic. However, this flexibility is not free; the TCP header is 20 bytes (or more with TCP options) in length, against the 8 bytes of the UDP header. Figure 6.8 shows the TCP segment format. The field description is as follows:

- **Source port** (2 bytes): a 16-bit port number of the process that sent the segment on the source device. Normally, it could be a client process in a Request, or a server process in a Reply.
- **Destination Port** (2 bytes): a 16-bit port number of the recipient process on the destination device. Normally, it could be a server process in a Request, or a client process in a Reply.
- **Sequence number** (4 bytes): it is used by the sliding window acknowledgment system as the sequence number of the first byte of data in the segment. In case the SYN bit is set (Connection Request message), it indicates the Initial Sequence Number (ISN).

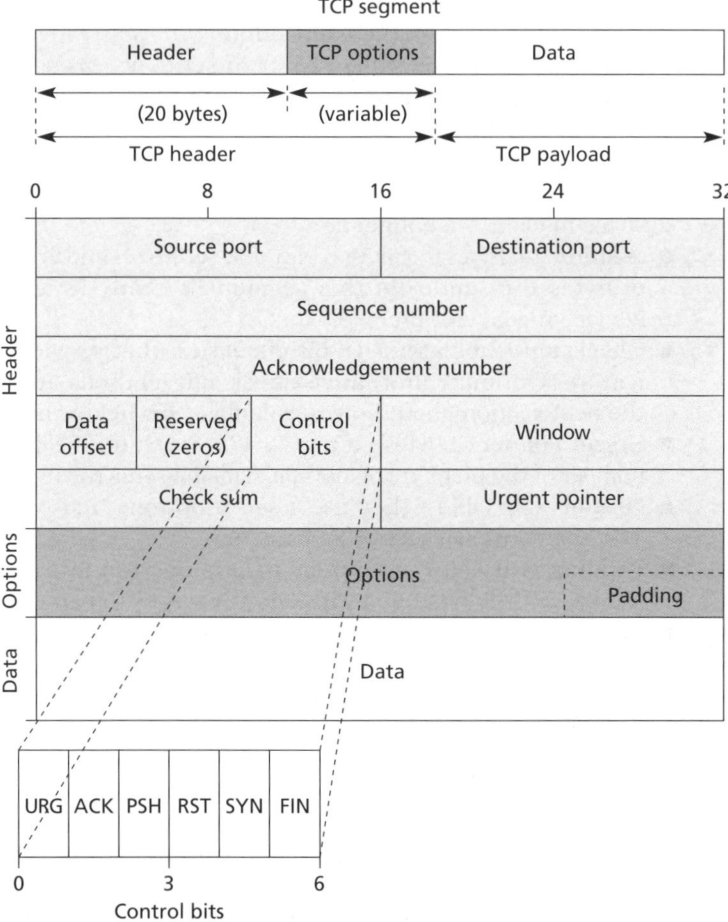

Figure 6.8 The TCP segment format.

- **Acknowledgement number** (4 bytes): if the ACK bit is set, this field is valid and contains the acknowledgment number used by a device to acknowledge the received data.
- **Data offset** (4 bits): indicates how many 32-bit words the start of the data is offset from the beginning of the TCP segment. In other words, it specifies the length of the header in 32-bit words. This value must be multiplied by four, to have it in bytes (1 word = 4 bytes).
- **Reserved** (6 bits): reserved for future use. It must be zero.
- **Control bits** (6 bits): used for control information.
  - **URG (Urgent bit)** (1 bit): if set to 1, it indicates that the segment contains Urgent Data, which is pointed by the Urgent Pointer field.
  - **ACK (Acknowledgment bit)** (1 bit): if set to 1, it indicates that this segment is an acknowledgment, and the Acknowledgment Number field is valid.
  - **PSH (Push bit)** (1 bit): if set to 1, the data in this segment must be immediately sent and pushed to the application on the receiving device. Otherwise, this data would be sent when more data was passed to TCP to complete the segment size (see 'PUSH' function).

- **RST (Reset bit)** (1 bit): if set to 1, the sender has detected a problem and wants to reset the connection.
- **SYN (Synchronize bit)** (1 bit): if set to 1, this segment is a request to synchronize sequence numbers and establish a connection. The Sequence Number field contains the Initial Sequence Number (ISN) of the sender, used for this connection.
- **FIN (Finish bit)** (1 bit): if set to 1, the sender of the segment is requesting to close the connection.

- **Window** (2 bytes): it is used for flow control, and it indicates the number of bytes the sender of this segment is ready to accept from the other device, at a given time.
- **Checksum** (2 bytes): a 16-bit checksum that provides an error-detecting feature. Optional alternative checksum methods are also supported. See the next section about how to calculate this field value.
- **Urgent Pointer** (2 bytes): if the URG bit is set, this field contains the sequence number of the first byte of 'normal' data following the urgent data.
- **Options** (variable): they are a set of options that can be included in the TCP segment. See section 6.3.4 below.
- **Padding** (variable): if Options field is not a multiple of 32 bits in length, the Padding field is filled with enough zeroes to pad the header.
- **Data** (variable): the bytes of data sent in the segment.

6.3.4 TCP segment header options

The TCP segment header may contain zero, one or more options. Moreover, each option can be either a single byte or multiple bytes. They are a multiple of 8 bits in length, and the total size of the options field must be a multiple of 32 bits. If necessary, a Padding field can be used to fulfil this last requirement.

There are two possible formats for the Options field. (See Fig. 6.9.) The field description is as follows:

- **Option-Kind** (1 byte): specifies the option type.
- **Option-Length** (1 byte): the length of the entire option in bytes, including the three sub-fields.
- **Option-Data** (Variable): the data used in the option.

Option format 1:

Option-kind (1 byte)

Option format 2:

Option-kind (1 byte)	Option-length (1 byte)	Option-data (variable)

Figure 6.9 Two formats of the TCP options.

Table 6.4 shows some of the most common TCP options. Note that some of the options appear only on the connection request (SYN) segments, while others appear in regular data segments, if needed.

Table 6.4

Option name	Option-Kind	Option Length	Option-Data	Option format	Description
End of Option List	0	–	–	1	Used to mark the end of all options included in the segment, if the end of the options does not coincide with the end of the TCP header.
No-Operation	1	–	–	1	Used to align a subsequent option on a 32-bit boundary.
Maximum Segment Size	2	4	Maximum Segment Size Value	2	Used in Connection Request to inform the largest segment the device wishes to receive.
Window Scale Factor	3	3	Window Size Shift Bits	2	Used to allow the use of much larger windows than the Window field permits. The Option-Data value specifies the power of 2 that the Window field must be multiplied to get the window size of the sliding window system.
Selective Acknowledgment Permitted	4	2	–	2	Used to specify that the device supports the selective acknowledgment (SACK) feature.
Selective Acknowledgment	5	Variable	Blocks of Data Selectively Acknowledged	2	Used to acknowledge non-contiguous blocks of data received. In this way, the recipient informs the non-contiguous blocks of data received, to avoid unnecessary retransmissions.
Alternate Checksum Algorithm	14	3	Alternate Checksum Algorithm	2	Used to request the use of an alternative checksum algorithm, instead of the default standard.
Alternate Checksum	15	Variable	Alternate Checksum	2	Used to place the alternative algorithm checksum value, in case it does not fit in the regular 16-bit checksum field.

It is worth noting that there is a special case (Option-Kind = 4) that belongs to option format 2, but has zero bytes of data, and the Option Length is 2. Such a case should belong to option format 1 instead, as the Option-Length field does not contribute with valuable information. I am still wondering why…

6.3.5 TCP checksum calculation

The checksum is the 16-bit ones complement of the ones complement sum of the computed fields. Instead of calculating the checksum over just the regular TCP segment, a pseudo-header is constructed with some fields from the IP datagram, and attached to the TCP message. In this way, the checksum is calculated over this pseudo-header, the TCP header and the TCP payload or data, and padded with zero bytes at the end, if necessary, to make a multiple of two bytes. These IP datagram fields are the IP source and destination addresses, a zero byte for padding, the protocol type (value 6 for TCP), and the TCP length field which is then computed twice in the checksum (it is found in the pseudo-header and in the TCP header). Figure 6.10 shows the structure of this pseudo-header.

The reason for computing this pseudo-header with the IP addresses is to provide an extra error check, ensuring that data has arrived at the right destination from the right source, avoiding the delivery of messages between incorrect addresses. It also provides protection for datagrams delivered to incorrect protocol layers (IP protocol field error detection), and TCP segments in which one part has been accidentally omitted or lost (incorrect TCP segment length error detection).

The pseudo-header is only used for checksum calculation and is then discarded, so it is not included in any message. The resulting checksum value is held in the checksum field of the TCP header. In addition, an alternative checksum algorithm can be used if both devices agree on this during connection establishment.

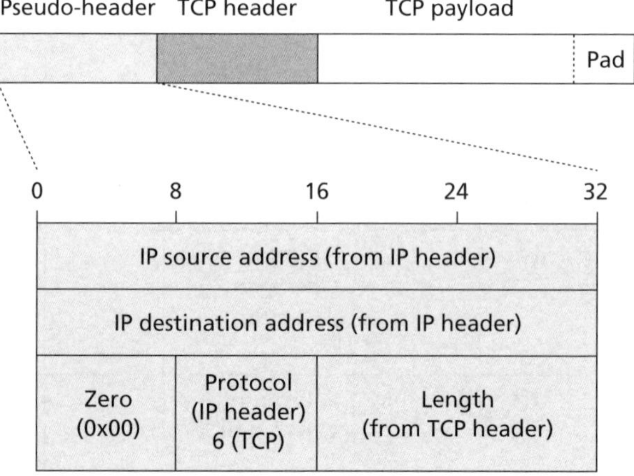

Figure 6.10 TCP pseudo-header format used for checksum.

6.3.6 TCP Maximum Segment Size (MSS)

As the application passes the data stream to the TCP layer, this data is buffered in memory. Then, the TCP forms segments to transmit the data through the IP layer. The maximum size of the segment will depend on how long it could be, in order to avoid the fragmentation at the IP layer, for performance reasons. Of course, this parameter will depend on the Maximum Transmission Unit (MTU) of the different underlying networks by which the segment will be transmitted.

On the other hand, if the segment size is too short, it will result in an inefficient use of bandwidth. For example, suppose we decide to make very short segments, carrying just 30 bytes of data in each segment. Then, the TCP header is a minimum of 20 bytes (or more if options are used). In addition, the IP header of the datagram, which will carry the TCP segment, is 20 bytes in length (or more if options are used). In this way, we are using a 70-byte datagram just to carry 30 bytes of usable data. In this case, the overhead is very high, resulting in an inefficient use of the available bandwidth.

Then, the Maximum Segment Size (MSS) must be selected, avoiding the IP fragmentation and, at the same time, providing an efficient use of the bandwidth. For this, a good starting point could be considering the minimum MTU for IP networks of 576 (see section 5.1.3). As we know, all networks are required to handle this IP datagram size, without fragmentation. Subtracting 20 bytes of the TCP header and 20 bytes of the IP header, we get the 536 bytes of the standard MSS for TCP.

However, even using this MSS standard value, some datagrams could still get fragmented, because some TCP options or IP options result in a datagram size greater than 576. But if we try to use a lower value to eliminate fragmentation, we lower the efficiency, so it is better to have only a few datagrams fragmented and the rest with better efficiency, than no fragmentation but all datagrams with poor efficiency.

Sometimes, the default MSS value is not convenient, so a device can inform another of the MSS value it wants to use. This is accomplished in the connection establishment phase (SYN message), using a TCP Option called Maximum Segment Size (Option-Kind = 2). In this way, each device may determine its own desired MSS parameter, which defines the MSS it wishes to receive.

While the segment size should not exceed the MSS parameter, it could be smaller because the flow control mechanism allows each device to notify each other about how much data they are ready to accept at any given time. In this way, even when the segment could be large, the device may accept only short segments until it can process all the data waiting in the buffer. As a result, the segment size has an MSS parameter as a maximum, but it could be smaller.

6.3.7 The 'PUSH' function for immediate data transfer

As we have already seen, the data stream is passed from the application to the TCP layer where it is buffered in memory. Then, TCP forms segments of appropriate size to transmit to the IP layer. These segment sizes must be large enough to avoid inefficiencies, so if the application passes few data to the TCP layer, it is possible that this data remains in the buffer until more data arrives in order to complete a segment with the appropriate size.

However, in some applications, this could have a negative impact. Suppose we are using Telnet, a highly interactive protocol where the user presses a command and waits for a response from the server. In these cases, probably the command will consist of a few characters, so when the user types the command, the Telnet applications will pass these few bytes of data to the TCP layer, which waits for more data in order to form a larger segment to send to the IP layer. As a result, the user who typed the command is now waiting for a response from the server, which will not respond since it has not received the data because TCP is still waiting for more data to complete the segment. So, TCP is waiting for more data from the user, but the user is waiting for a response from the server, and the server is waiting a command from the user (which is retained by TCP in its buffer): big problem, isn't it?

In order to resolve this problem, TCP has a special 'PUSH' function. When applications pass data to the TCP layer, but this data must be sent immediately, the application invokes the 'PUSH' function. Then, TCP forms a segment, and sends it with the PSH control bit set to 1.

When the recipient receives this segment and sees the PSH control bit activated, it must pass the data directly to the application without delay. In this way, the 'PUSH' function provides immediate data transfer when required.

Finally, we must note that this problem does not arise when large amounts of data are passed (as in file transfer applications), because TCP has enough data to form appropriate sized segments which are transmitted immediately.

6.3.8 The 'URGENT' function for priority data transfer

As applications pass the data to the TCP layer in a particular sequence, TCP uses this same order to transmit it. That is, all data is treated as equal in importance. However, in some circumstances, while lots of data is being transmitted, some important 'urgent' information must be transmitted to the receiver, without waiting for its corresponding turn.

For example, if we are transferring a file and at some point we realize this is the incorrect file we wanted to transfer, we would need to abort the operation. If at this moment we send the abort command (encoded in a few bytes of data), this data will wait to be transmitted until all the data previously stored in the buffer is transmitted. In these cases, it would be desirable to have an 'URGENT' function that allows sending priority data. This is sometimes called 'out of band' data.

When an application invokes the 'URGENT' function, TCP takes this 'urgent' data and forms a segment for its immediately delivery. This special segment will have the URG control bit set to 1. However, this segment could also have been completed with 'normal' data from the buffer, for a special TCP Header Urgent Pointer field indicates the end of the 'urgent' data and the beginning of the 'normal' data. (Strictly speaking, the Urgent Pointer field indicates the sequence number of the first byte of 'normal' data.)

When the recipient receives this segment with the URG bit set to 1, TCP extracts the 'urgent' data (from the first byte of data up to the Urgent Pointer field, excluding this last), and passes it urgently to the application. The rest of the data ('normal' data) is appended to the previous data stored in the buffer, which is later passed to the application, as a normal procedure.

While the 'PUSH' function deals with the problem of too few data to send the segment immediately, the 'URGENT' function deals with the problem that too much data is buffered and it cannot wait until its turn, as the data is 'urgent'. For this, when the 'urgent' data is passed, it is immediately delivered because there is enough data to form the appropriate sized segments.

6.3.9 TCP connection: establishment, management and termination

As TCP is a 'connection-oriented' protocol, before any data transfer can take place, a TCP connection must be established. Once the connection has been established, it must be managed in order to resolve problems that could arise. After all the data has been transferred, the connection may be terminated, although there is no restriction about the time the connection can remain open.

The connection progresses through a series of states during its lifetime. Upon the reception of certain events, the connection may progress from one state to another. These events may come from user calls (like OPEN, SEND, RECEIVE, CLOSE, ABORT and STATUS), incoming segments (with control bits activated like SYN, FIN, ACK and RST) and timeouts.

In order for two devices to establish a connection, one of them (generally the client) must send a request, while the other (the server) must 'listen' for incoming requests (must be prepared to accept this request). For these tasks, the OPEN user call is used. An 'Active OPEN' is used for the client to send a request message, while a 'Passive OPEN' is used for the server to prepare it to listen to incoming requests.

Because of the multiple-connection characteristics of TCP, many connections may exist simultaneously, where each connection is identified by a pair of sockets (IP address and port number) from both devices at each end. The process of setting up, managing and terminating a connection must be performed independently for each connection.

As a result, a special data structure is created at the connection set-up, in order to maintain the specific data for each connection. This structure is called the Transmission Control Block (TCB), and it contains important information such as the pair of sockets identifying the connection, the pointers of the incoming and outgoing data buffers, and the variables used by the sliding window system (explained in section 6.3.11) to keep track of transmitted and received data. Each device has its own TCB for the connection.

Unlike the connection request when is normally initiated by the client, the termination request may be initiated by any device at any time, when it considers the connection should be terminated. When a connection is terminated, the corresponding TCBs are deleted.

As the TCP segment format is the same for all messages, including data and control messages, the control bits are used for connection messages; the connection request message consists of a segment with a SYN bit set, the termination request message has a FIN bit set, and the acknowledgment message has the ACK bit set. This last message is used to confirm the reception of the message from the other device. Each SYN and FIN message received by a device must be acknowledged by sending an ACK message back to the sender, allowing this to know about the reception of its sent message.

The following is a list of the connection states:

- CLOSED: the initial state that represents no connection at all.
- LISTEN: it represents the server waiting for a connection request from any client device.
- SYN-SENT: it represents the client, after having sent a connection request (SYN message), waiting for the acknowledgement (ACK message) and SYN messages from the server.
- SYN-RECEIVED: it represents the server, after having received the client request and having sent its message with the acknowledgement and its own request to the client, waiting for the acknowledgement from the client.
- ESTABLISHED: it represents an open connection. Data transfer can take place at this state.
- FIN-WAIT-1: it represents the waiting time for an acknowledgement for its termination request sent. Although this is a normal procedure, in some cases it could be possible that both devices want to terminate the connection at the same time (called Simultaneous Close), and each one sends the termination request to each other. Then, it is possible that before the device receives the acknowledgement for its request sent, it receives a termination request from the other device.
- FIN-WAIT-2: the device, which already sent a termination request and received its acknowledgement, is waiting for the termination request from the other device.
- CLOSING: it represents the simultaneous close situation where the device sent a termination request and, before it receives its acknowledgement, it receives the termination request from the other device.
- TIME-WAIT: it represents waiting for a timeout to assurance that the remote device receives the acknowledgement for its termination request.
- CLOSE-WAIT: it represents waiting for the termination request from the application.
- LAST-ACK: it represents the waiting time for the acknowledgement for its termination request sent.

Figure 6.11 shows a simplified states diagram that implements the TCP connection lifetime cycle, explained in the following sections. The area denoted as 'Open: Server path', for example, means the states form a path that follows the server when it performs the Open user call.

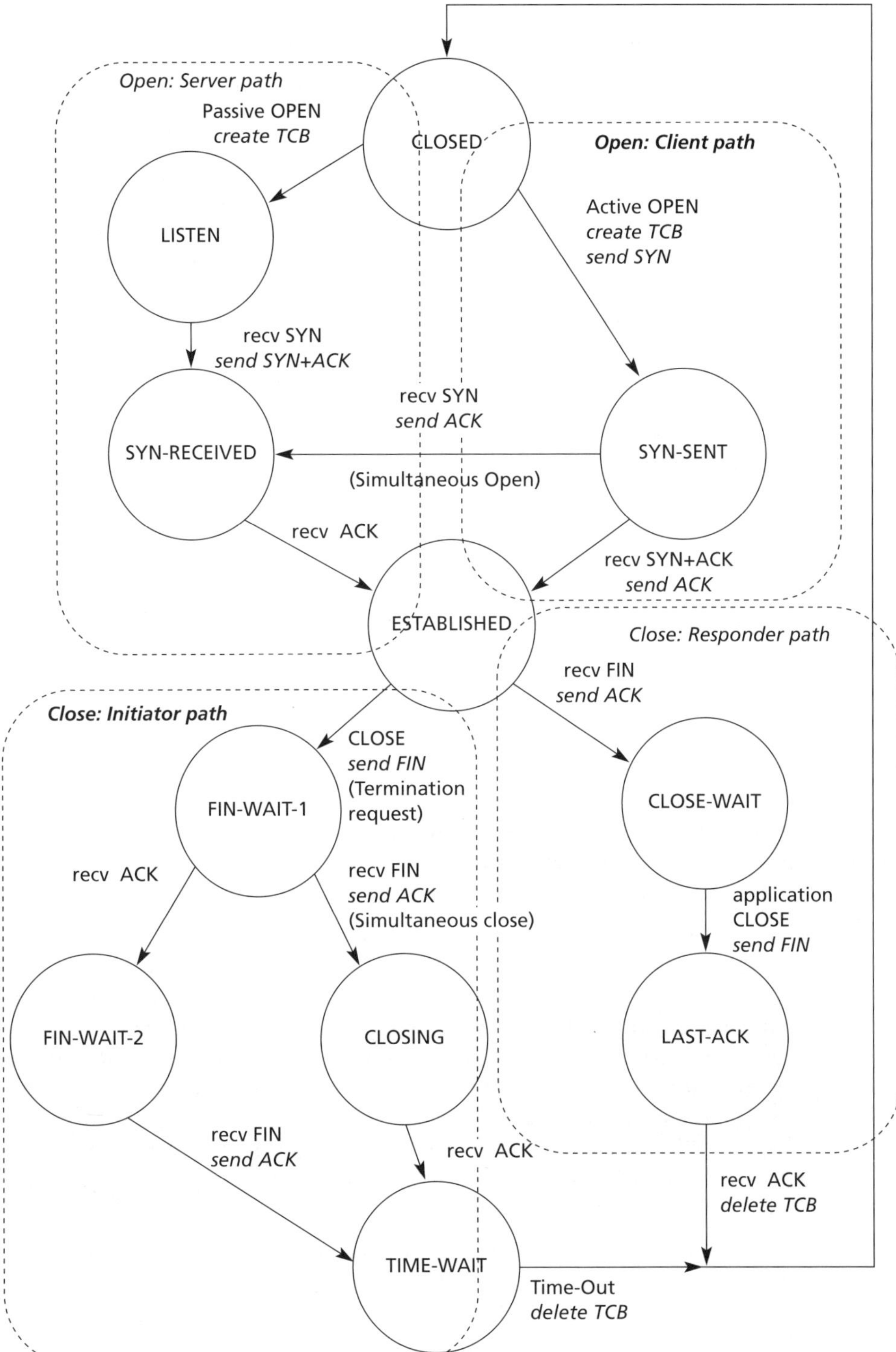

Figure 6.11 The TCP states diagram for the connection lifetime cycle, showing the states (circles), the events (in bold), and the action taken (in italic).

6.3.9.1 Connection establishment

The request message (SYN message) consists of a TCP segment with the SYN bit set, meaning that the Sequence Number field is carrying the Initial Sequence Number (needed for the sliding window system to know what bytes are sending in the message when transferring data; we will see this later on). Some TCP options may also be sent in this segment, as we saw in section 6.3.4. Once the server has received this client request, it must acknowledge it by sending a segment with an ACK bit set back to the client. But as the server must also inform the client about its own Initial Sequence Number, instead of sending two separate messages, the server only sends one segment with the ACK and SYN bits set (noted as SYN+ACK message). After the client receives this message, it must acknowledge the SYN part of the server message sending an ACK (a segment with the ACK bit set) message back to the server. This procedure is called a TCP 'three-way handshake', and is illustrated in Figure 6.12.

A special case is presented when two clients send a connection request to each other at the same time. For example, client A sends a SYN message to client B, and instead of receiving a SYN+ACK (as it would from a server), it receives a SYN message from the client B, which is trying to request a connection establishment at this moment. Thus, both clients receive the SYN message, and then they send the corresponding ACK message. The original 'three-way handshaking' is now converted into a 'four-way handshaking'. This situation is represented in the TCP states diagram with the transition from the SYN-SENT state to the SYN-RECEIVED state, marked as 'Simultaneous Open'. However, this rarely happens as the client uses temporary port numbers, which change each time the client application starts, so it is difficult for a client to know another client's port numbers at a certain moment (this is different from the situation of the servers, which use the well-known port numbers that every client knows).

The connection establishment process involves three objectives:

- *Initial communication*: the client initiates the connection request sending a SYN message (TCP segment with the SYN flag set), which is acknowledged by the server. This last also sends a SYN message (in the same message in which it acknowledges the client's request), which is acknowledged by the client. In this message exchange between client and server, some information is carried to accomplish the two following objectives.
- *Sequence number synchronization*: each device informs the other about the Initial Sequence Number it wants to use for its first transmission.
- *TCP options parameters exchange*: some TCP options that will be used in the TCP connection are exchanged by the devices.

As we will see later on, the sliding window system uses two fields of the TCP segment header to provide reliability. This involves keeping track of lost messages, and re-transmitting them. In order to know which messages arrive and which do not, TCP assigns a sequence number for each byte transmitted in the segment. The byte immediately following the header is the lowest numbered, while the following bytes are numbered consecutively. Then, the Sequence Number field is used to state the sequence number assigned to the

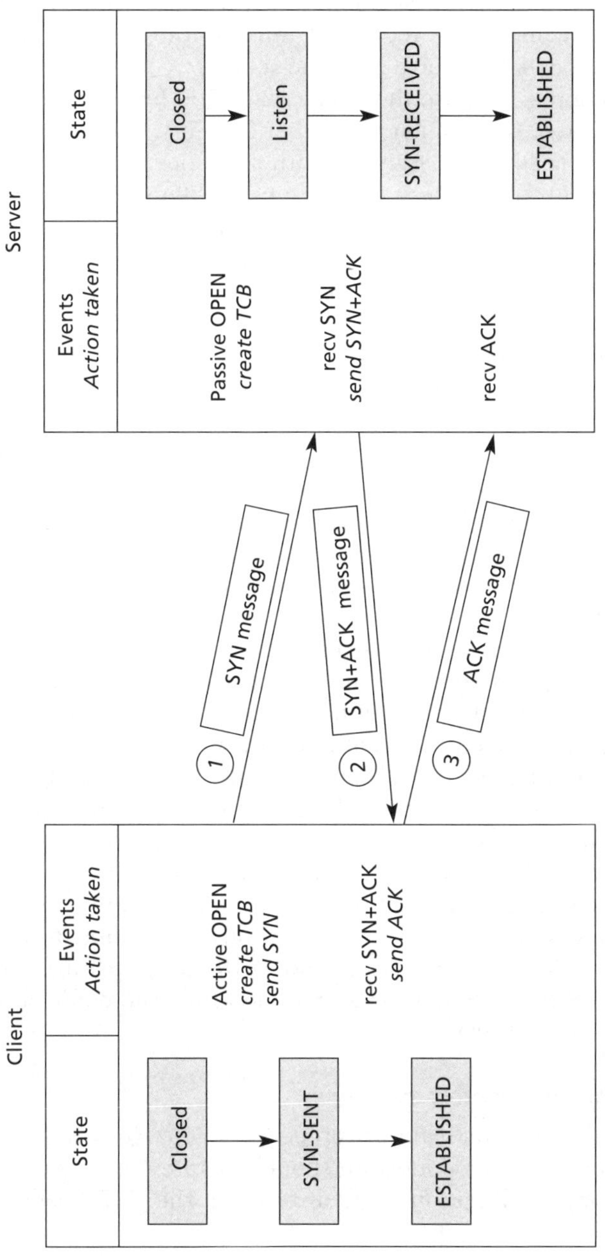

Figure 6.12 The TCP 'Three-way handshake' connection establishment process.

first byte of the data segment, transmitted in each message. Once this segment has been received by the recipient, it must acknowledge all the receiving bytes of data. For this reason, it sends an acknowledgement message with the Acknowledgement Number field equal to the sequence number of the last byte in the segment received, plus one. In other words, this Acknowledgement Number field informs the next sequence number the receiver expects to receive from the source.

For example, suppose the client sends 500 bytes of data to the server in a message where the Sequence Number field is 1. This means that the last byte sent in the segment is assigned with sequence number 500. When this segment is received by the server, it must acknowledge this reception with an ACK message where the Acknowledgement Number field must be 501, meaning that the next data segment that it expects to receive from the client, must be started with a byte numbered as 501.

6.3.9.1.1 *Initial Sequence Number (ISN)*

In the previous example, we saw how the client device used the number one to start assigning a sequence number to each byte of the data segment. However, this is avoided for the following reason. As a connection can be used repeatedly, some problems could arise regarding how to identify duplicate segments from previous incarnations of the connection. These problems are possible if the connection is being opened and closed in quick succession, or with a re-established connection after the connection breaks and memory is lost.

In those cases, we must prevent segments from different incarnations having the same sequence numbers. To accomplish this, each new connection must use a different ISN provided by an ISN generator. This generator acts as a 32-bit clock incremented every 4 microseconds. Thus, the ISN cycles approximately every $4\frac{1}{2}$ hours. Since we assume the segments will stay in the network no more than the Maximum Segment Lifetime (MSL), which is less than $4\frac{1}{2}$ hours, we can assume that each ISN will be unique. The MSL is defined in RFC 793 as the time a TCP segment can exist in the internetwork system, and is arbitrarily defined to be 2 minutes.

This ISN is informed in the connection establishment process, sending the ISN as the Sequence Number field in the SYN message. This is called the Sequence Number Synchronization, and thus the connection establishment message is called 'SYN' message.

6.3.9.1.2 *TCP options parameters exchange*

The connection establishment process is in charge of the exchange of parameters about how the connection should operate. These parameters come from the available TCP options, and are sent in the TCP header options field, as we saw in section 6.3.3.

One of these options, the MSS option, is used when value other than the default is required. Other options such as the Window Scale Factor, the Selective Acknowledgment Permitted and the Alternate Checksum Request can also be used in these connection establishment segments.

Figure 6.13 gives a more completed example of the TCP 'three-way handshake' connection establishment process, showing the sequence number synchronization and some TCP options parameter exchange.

6.3.9.2 Connection management

Once the connection has been established, both devices can start transferring data to each other. If some problem arises when the connection is established, the TCP connection management must take charge.

Both devices of the connection will remain on their Established state until one of the following conditions occurs:

- *Connection termination*: one of the devices (or both in the simultaneous termination case) sends a termination request message.
- *Connection disruption*: some problems may arise and interrupt the connection.

Regarding the termination request, there is a specific procedure to follow, as we will see in the next section.

Connection disruption could happen when, for example, one device has a software crash or the hardware hangs in the middle of the connection. In these cases, this device would go to the Close state, while the other device remains in the Established state because it does not know that the first has

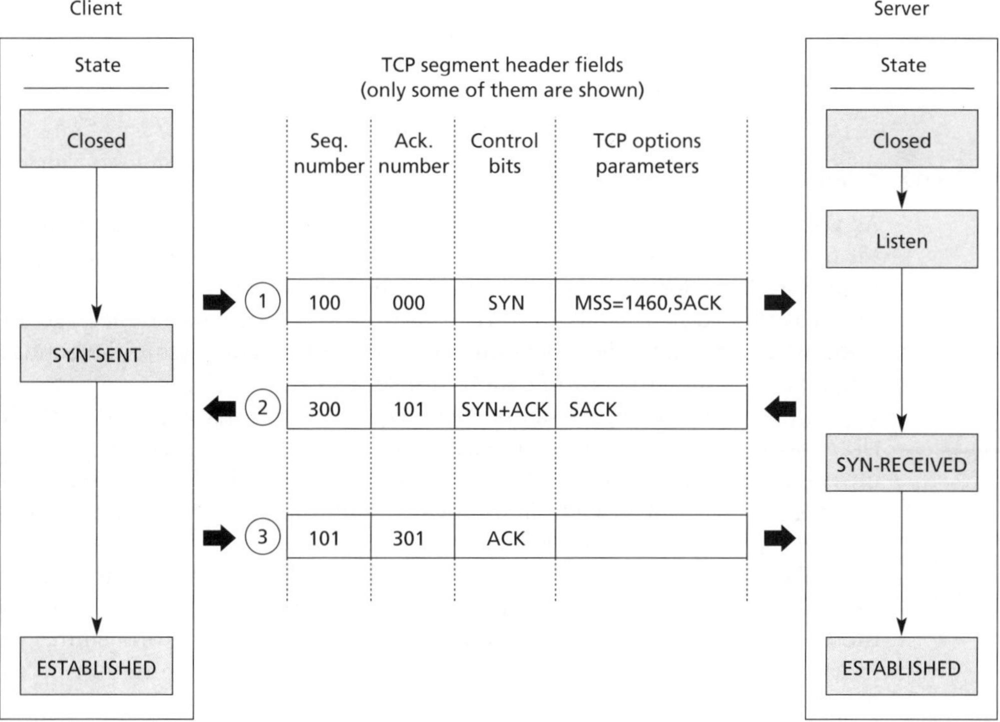

Figure 6.13 TCP Sequence Number Synchronization and options parameter exchange.

problems. This is called a 'half-open' connection. Then, the device having problems once it gets to the normal operation state can use a special Reset (RST) function to reset the connection so it can then be re-established.

The connection Reset function consists of a segment with the RST bit set in the header's control bits field. This function is generally used in unexpected situations, such as a device receiving an acknowledgement for a segment that was not sent, or receiving a segment with data from a device with which it has no connection at this time. In addition, if a message is received with an incorrect sequence number or acknowledgement number indicating it is a spurious message, a Reset function may be used.

When a device receives a segment with the RST bit set, this Reset segment is validated checking that the Sequence Number field value is inside the sliding window range. If this is not the case, it is considered spurious. If a Reset segment is received as a response to a SYN message, it is acceptable if its Acknowledgement Number field value acknowledges the SYN message.

Assuming the reset is valid, the following actions are taken according to the state of the device that received it:

- If the receiver was in the LISTEN state, the reset is ignored.
- If the receiver was in the SYN-RECEIVED state, and had previously been in the LISTEN state, then the receiver returns to the LISTEN state.
- If the receiver was in any other state, it aborts the connection and goes to the CLOSED state. The user is notified about this situation.

Finally, some implementations can send messages with no data, in order to test the connection, especially when a long time passes without messages being exchanged. These messages, called 'Keepalives', are used to see if the connection is still active for both devices. However, this feature is not strictly necessary and as it is 'unofficial', there is no wide acceptance on its use.

6.3.9.3 Connection termination

As we saw in the last section, when one device (or both in the simultaneous termination) decides to close the connection, the connection termination procedure is performed. As Figure 6.11 shows, this termination procedure is rather complex, because both devices must send a termination message and acknowledge them to allow pending data to be transferred before the connection ends, avoiding the lost of data in transit.

The termination request message consists of a regular segment with the FIN (finish) bit set, and it could carry data like any other message. This FIN message must be acknowledged by the receiver device. The connection is considered terminated when both devices send the FIN segment and receive the corresponding ACK message.

Unlike the connection request, where it is usually the client who initiates the connection and the server who responds to it, in the termination request, the client as well as the server may initiate the termination procedure. For that reason, we sometimes will refer to them as the close initiator and the close responder.

When the initiator sends the termination request, it is possible that the responder has pending data to send. Then, the responder after receiving the initial FIN message must send an acknowledgement and inform the application about the close request, waiting until the application is ready to shut down. During this time, the responder may still send data and the initiator must receive it. However, the initiator cannot send data.

Once the application at the responder side is ready to close the connection, the responder sends its own FIN message. The initiator receives this message and sends the corresponding acknowledgement, but it cannot go immediately to the CLOSE state, since it must wait some time to allow the ACK message it sent to arrive at the responder. Therefore, it goes to the TIME-WAIT state where, after a time-out period, it goes to the CLOSED state. Although the standard defines this time-out period as twice the MSL, this 4 minutes time-out is an exaggeration, so each implementation chooses lower values.

Figure 6.14 shows the connection termination procedure. As the TCP states diagram shows, a special case is possible where both devices decide to close the connection at almost the same time. In this case, called 'simultaneous close', each device sends a FIN message, and before they receive the acknowledgement, a FIN message from the other device shows up. The state diagram shows the different states each device takes as messages are exchanged. In all cases, when the device goes to the CLOSED state, the TCB created for the connection is destroyed.

6.3.10 Providing reliability and flow control

TCP is a transport protocol that provides reliable transfer of data even when it uses the underlying Internet protocol, which is unreliable by nature. For this reason, TCP must provide the mechanism by which unreliable transmission is converted into a reliable transport of data. In this way, applications requiring a reliable communication can rely on TCP without the need to implement their own mechanism, and they could concentrate their efforts on the application specifics.

As we have already said, when we talk about reliable transmissions, we are guaranteeing that the sent messages will be received by the recipient. As a result, if the transmission fails, the message should be retransmitted. Of course, this type of reception guarantee excludes those cases in which transmissions are impossible owing to hardware or software failures at some point of the inter-network. Then, unsuccessful retransmissions occur a predetermined number of times before an error is passed to the application.

In principle, the mechanism needed to provide reliability would be based on the acknowledgement for each sent message. In this way, each message device A sent to device B should be acknowledged by the last one, in order for the first one to know about its message reception. That is, device A sends a message to device B. When device B receives the message, it sends an acknowledgement to device A. Upon the reception of this acknowledgement by device A, the feedback loop is completed and a new message may be sent from device A to device B. If for any reason, either the message does not arrive at device B (thus it will not send the acknowledgement to device A) or the acknowledgement does not get back to device A, the original message

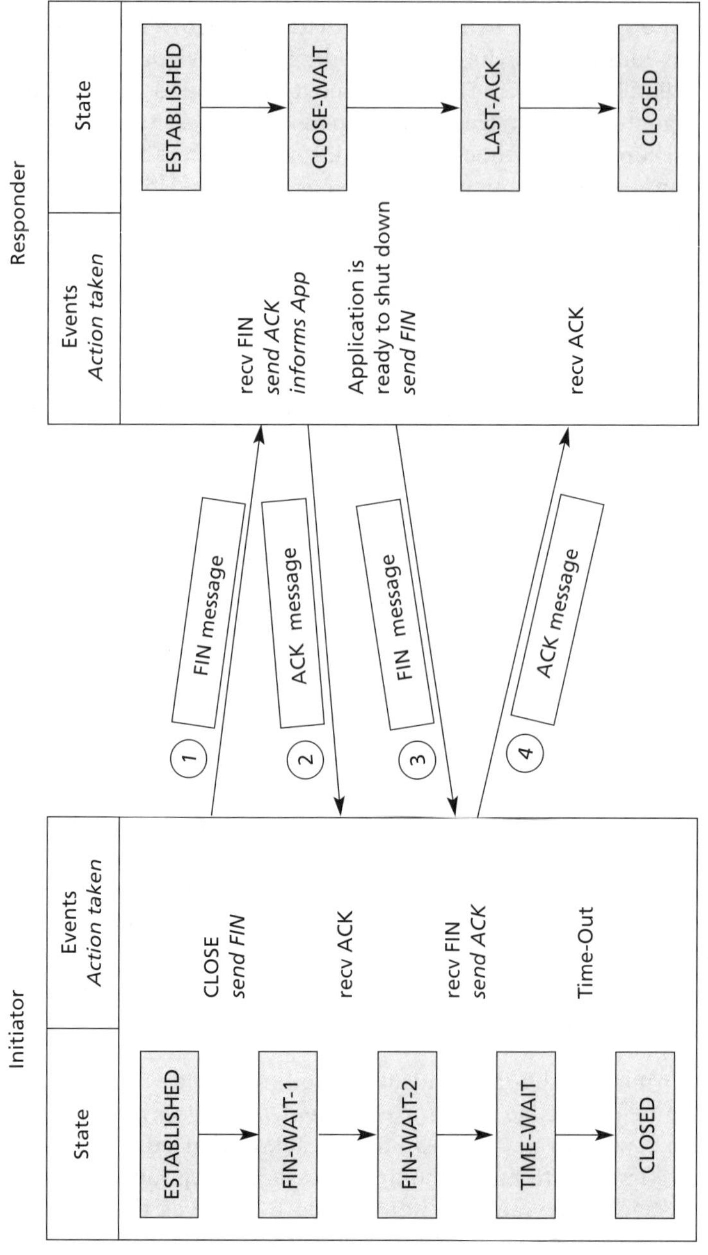

Figure 6.14 The TCP connection termination procedure.

must be retransmitted. Working in this way, we guarantee that all data transmitted from device A will be received by device B.

When device A sends a message to device B, it must wait for the acknowledgement from B. However, this acknowledgement could arrive very soon, or could be delayed and arrive late, or it could even not arrive at all. For this reason, in order for device A not to be waiting for ever for the acknowledgement message from device B, a timer must be started when the message is sent. Once the timer expires and the acknowledgment for the message has not appeared, a problem is assumed and the message is retransmitted.

The above mechanism is known as Positive Acknowledgment with Retransmission (PAR), and it is shown in Figure 6.15. Observe that only one message is in transit at a time.

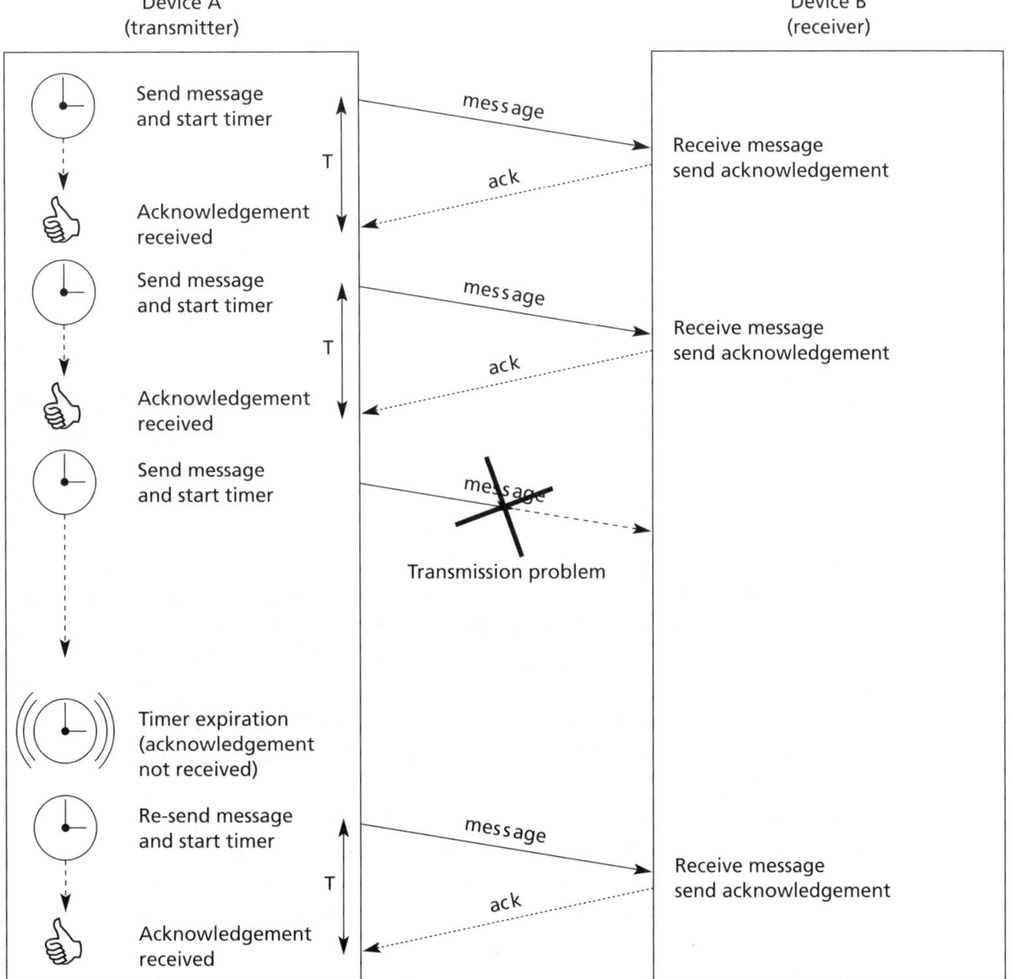

Figure 6.15 Positive Acknowledgement with Retransmission (PAR) mechanism.

The PAR mechanism works fine for some transmission protocols, but is extremely slow when used in TCP. That means that device A sends a message and waits for the acknowledgement from device B. Now that device A is sure that device B received its message, it may send the next message. However, since device A sent the message and received the acknowledgement a period of time T has elapsed. Supposing for simplicity that the average time for this time is T = 300 milliseconds, we must wait 3 seconds to have only 10 messages sent and acknowledged.

In order to overcome this inconvenience, an enhancement to the PAR mechanism is used. Instead of sending a message and waiting for its acknowledgement before sending the next, several messages are sent together. Of course, device B will be receiving each message and acknowledging it, and thus device A will receive lots of acknowledgements from device B. Nevertheless, how does device A know which acknowledgement belongs to each sent message? Remember that using IP as an underlying protocol, the messages could arrive out of order (some messages could take different paths over the inter-network). Then, a solution for this is to identify each message and its acknowledgement, allowing device A to know which sent message was received by device B and which was not. Device B may also order the receiving messages in the correct sequence.

When a sent message is not acknowledged and its timer expires, the sending device must retransmit the original message until it is sure about the reception of the message. Once the message is retransmitted and successfully acknowledged, normal operation is restored. Under these conditions, the mechanism allows fast transmission, and delays only occur when messages are lost. Figure 6.16 shows this enhanced mechanism. In this case, unlike the basic PAR mechanism, multiple messages are in transit at any time, with a better performance.

We can look at a different graphic showing the outgoing data buffer memory of device A, that is, the data to be transmitted to device B. At a certain moment, some data of the buffer has already been sent and acknowledged by the receiver, while another portion of the data has already been sent but is waiting for its corresponding acknowledgement. Of course, the rest of the data is waiting to be transmitted. Some pointers are used to delimit these portions of data at the buffer. See Figure 6.17, which shows how the data at the outgoing data buffer can be classified according to the sent and acknowledged messages. For example, the *unacknowledged data pointer* marks the start of the data sent but not yet acknowledged, meaning that the data to its left is already sent and acknowledged. The second pointer marks the end of the sent but not acknowledged data and the start of the data not yet sent.

As acknowledgement messages are received, the *unacknowledged data pointer* moves toward the right. Also, as new data is sent (and not yet acknowledged) the *non-sent data pointer* moves toward the right. Therefore, it appears that the sending device may send all the buffer at once (all the data that it has to transmit), and wait for the corresponding acknowledgement. Well, this is not exactly the case. Sometimes it happens that the receiver device cannot process all the arriving messages at once, because it is

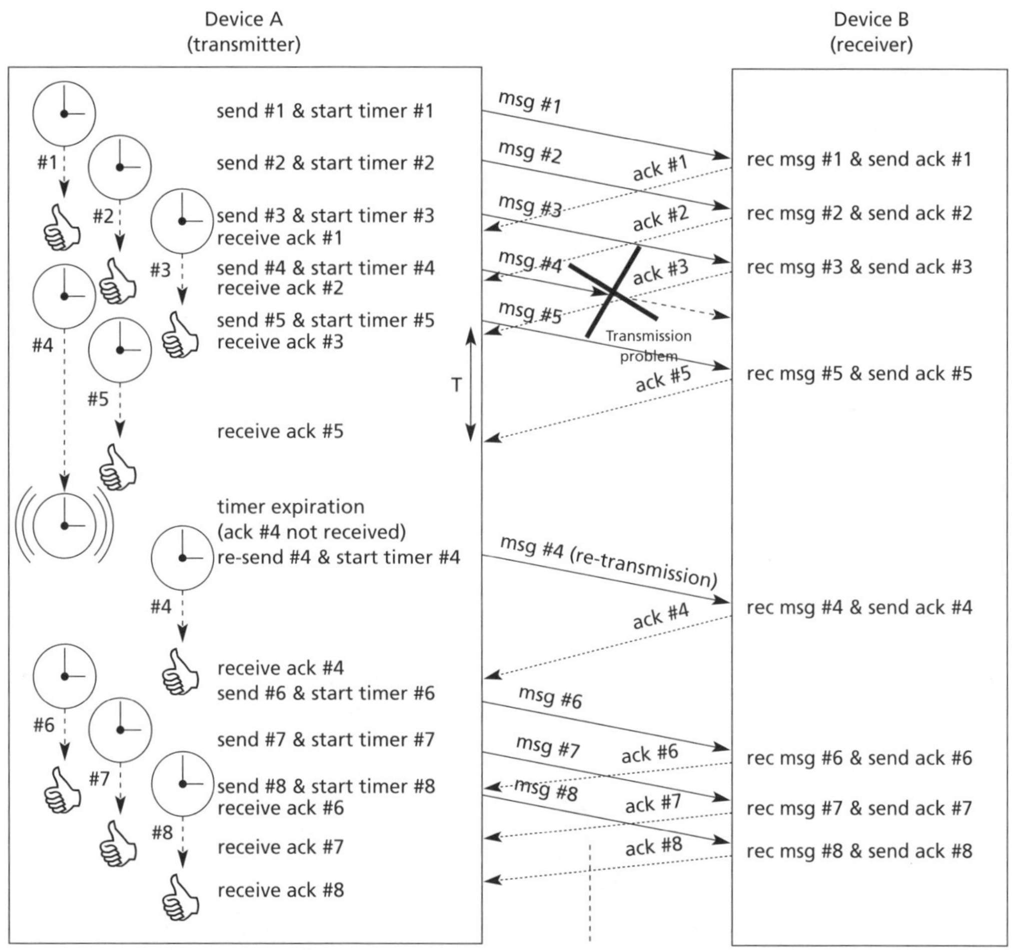

Figure 6.16 Enhanced Positive Acknowledgement with Retransmission (PAR) mechanism.

busy with other tasks. When data is received, it is held at the incoming data buffer for the subsequent process. However, this buffer has a limited size, so if it gets full and more data arrives at the device, this data will be lost. As a result, the transmitter device should not send more data than the receiver device can process, at a given time. There needs to be a mechanism by which the receiver can inform the transmitter about how much data it can receive. This mechanism is called flow control.

Flow control allows the receiver device to inform the transmitter how much data it can receive at a given moment. Then, if the receiver is busy, it could make the transmitter slow down the rate at which it is sending data, or even stop the transmission if the receiver needs some time to process other tasks. Thus only a portion of the data waiting to be sent (not yet sent portion of the buffer in Figure 6.17) can be transmitted, according to how much data the receiver is willing to accept. Then, a new division is obtained distinguishing between data not yet sent for which the recipient is ready, and data not

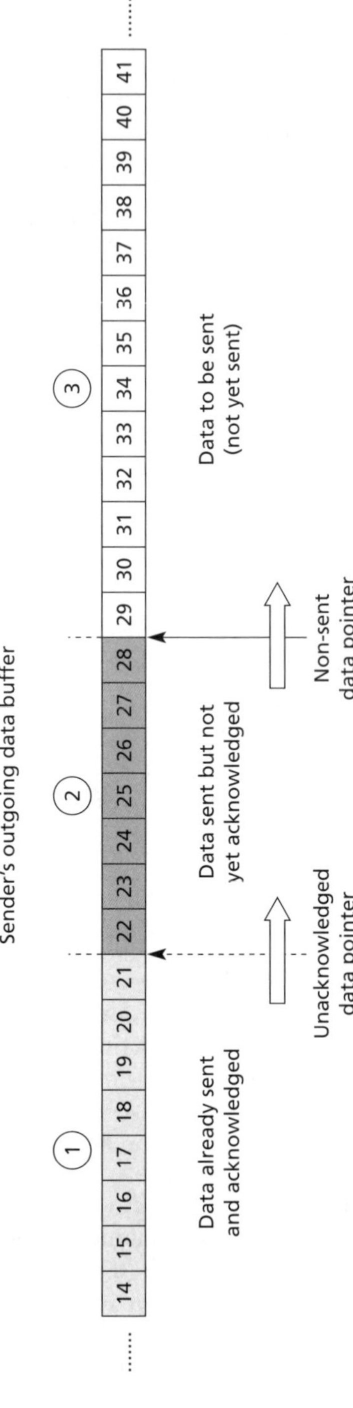

Figure 6.17 Data classification at the sender's outgoing data buffer.

yet sent for which the recipient is not ready. A new pointer, which we will call the *flow control pointer*, marks the division line between these areas. As the receiver informs that it is ready to accept more or less data, this pointer will move toward the right or left respectively.

Figure 6.18 shows the sender's outgoing data buffer with this new pointer, implementing the flow control feature. Our new transmission mechanism allows data to be sent reliably through an acknowledgement system and it provides flow control. We could further define a fictitious rectangle enclosing portions 2 and 3 of the data inside it, where the unacknowledged data pointer defines the left edge and the control flow pointer defines the right edge. This rectangle will move as the pointers do so, simulating a sliding window. This model approximates the mechanism used by TCP to provide reliability and flow control through an acknowledgement system, which we will see in the next section.

6.3.11 The TCP Sliding Window Acknowledgement System

The Sliding Window Acknowledgement System is the mechanism used by TCP to provide reliable transmissions and flow control. As it is a very complex subject, the best way to approach it is to start with an elemental mechanism like the PAR described in the last section. Then, continuing with the PAR enhancements, and arriving at the sender's outgoing data buffer that is very similar to the sliding window concept.

Now, we will see some differences between the sliding window and the enhanced PAR. The first difference is that as TCP is a stream-oriented protocol, in the sliding window each 'identified message' (as shown in Fig. 6.18) is replaced by a sequence of bytes. Of course, TCP does not send only one byte at a time in each segment, but a range of bytes. Then, in order to identify the transmitted message, all bytes have a sequence number, and each TCP segment transmits a range of bytes, where the Sequence Number field of the TCP header has the sequence number of the first byte in the range. Remember that in the connection establishment section, we saw the Initial Sequence Number (ISN) as a way of informing the other device what would be the sequence number of the first byte of the data being transmitted. The following data segments must follow this sequence numeration in order for the receiver to order the received data.

The second difference relates to the way the receiver acknowledges the received messages. While in the enhanced PAR the receiver acknowledged the received message with the same message identifier, in the sliding window the receiver acknowledges each segment with the sequence number of the last byte of the data plus one, meaning that this must be the sequence number of the next segment the transmitter can send. In other words, the acknowledgement system is accumulative, so the acknowledgement segment a transmitter receives has an Acknowledgement Number field indicating that all bytes with sequence number below this value have been received.

For example, if the transmitter sends a segment with byte numbers ranging from 501 to 650, the Sequence Number field will have the value 501. When this message is received by the recipient, it will send an acknowledge-

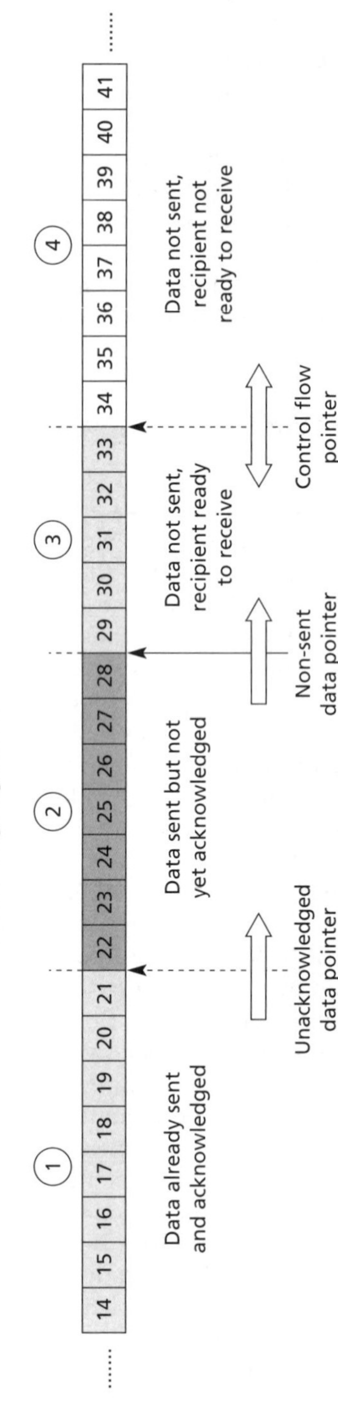

Figure 6.18 Flow control implementation.

ment segment with the Acknowledgement Number field value as 651, meaning that all the transmitted bytes with sequence number below to 651 have been received. Where the recipient receives two (or more) data segments, with ranges such as 651–790 and 791–940, it can send only one acknowledgement for all received segments, with the Acknowledgement Number field value of 941. Where the recipient receives two (or more) non-contiguous data segments, with ranges such as 651–790 and 941–1060, it can only acknowledge with Acknowledgement Number field value of 791, because if it uses 1061 it would be indicating the reception of the data segment with ranges from 791 to 940, which, of course, has not arrived yet.

Both devices at each side of the connection must implement the sliding window to keep track of the transmitted bytes as well as the received bytes. Then, two types of sliding window exist: the **Send Window** and the **Receive Window**.

The Send Window works with three pointers, which divide the stream of bytes into four areas (as those shown in Fig. 6.18):

1 Bytes sent and acknowledged.
2 Bytes sent but not yet acknowledged.
3 Bytes not yet sent, recipient ready to receive.
4 Bytes not yet sent, recipient not ready to receive.

The terminology used for the three pointers is as follows:

- SND.UNA: The **Send Unacknowledged** pointer has the sequence number of the first byte of data that has been sent but not acknowledged yet. This pointer divides area one from area two.
- SND.NXT: The **Send Next** pointer has the sequence number of the first byte of data to be sent to the other device. This pointer divides area two from area three.
- SND.WND: The **Send Window** pointer has the size of the send window. Then, the sum of SND.UNA and SND.WND marks the first byte of area four, dividing this area from area three.

The SND.WND pointer is stated in each segment header, as a Window field, and it informs the other device about how much more data it is ready to receive, implementing the flow control feature. The left edge of the Send Window is given by SND.UNA while the right edge is given by SND.UNA + SND.WND.

Area three is the number of bytes that the transmitter can send at any point in time, and since this is the data that it could use to transmit, this area is called Usable Window, and it is given by the equation SND.UNA + SND.WND – SND.NXT. Figure 6.19 shows the TCP Send Window.

The term 'pointer' is used with a different meaning from the memory pointer used in the C language, which holds memory address. Here, it is called a pointer because it marks the beginning of different areas, but it holds values such as sequence numbers and window sizes that have nothing to do with memory address values.

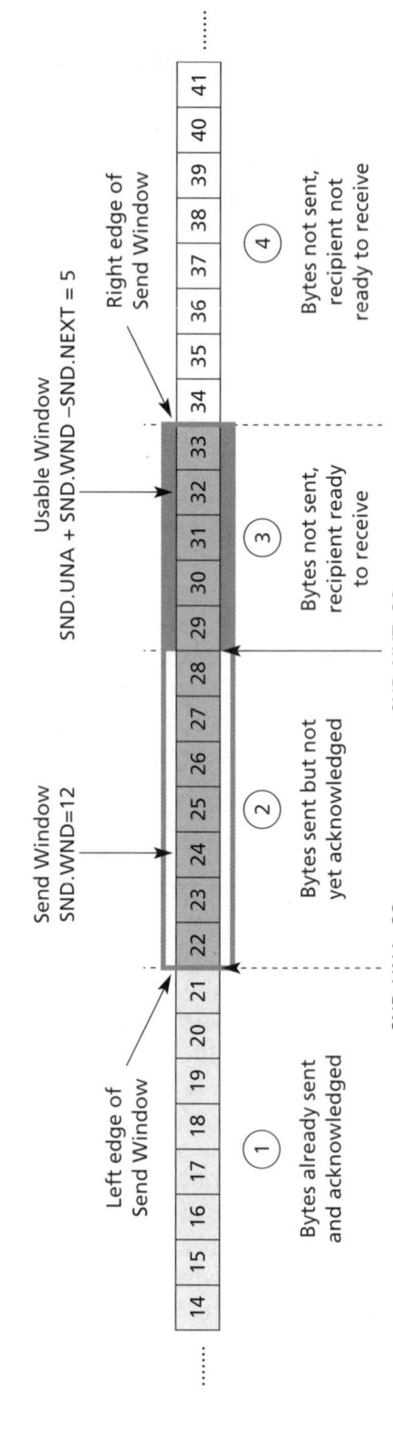

Figure 6.19 TCP Send Window.

The *Receive Window* uses only two pointers, which divide the stream of bytes into three areas:

1 Bytes received.
2 Bytes not yet received, ready to receive.
3 Bytes not yet received, not ready to receive.

At the receiving side, as the device acknowledges each segment as soon as it receives it, it has no need to keep track of unacknowledged bytes (unlike the transmitter, which has to wait a time *T* between sending the segment and receiving the acknowledgement. See Fig. 6.15).

The terminology used for the two pointers is as follows:

- RCV.NXT: The **Receive Next** pointer has the sequence number of the first byte of data that it expects from the other device. It marks the beginning of area two and it divides this area from area one. It also defines the left edge of the Receive Window.
- RCV.WND: The **Receive Window** pointer has the size of the Receive Window and it refers to the number of bytes the device is ready to accept from the transmitter at any point in time. This is the value of the TCP Segment Header Window field, used to inform the transmitter about how much more data the receiver is ready to receive, implementing the flow control mechanism. This value depends on the size of the buffer allocated for receiving data for this connection. As it is a relative pointer, the sum of RCV.NXT and RCV.WND gives the beginning of area three and it divides this area from area two. This sum also defines the right edge of the Receive Window.

Figure 6.20 shows the TCP Receive Window.

As the communication takes place, and segments are sent and received, the pointers are updated using the Sequence Number, Acknowledge Number and Window fields from the TCP Segment header. All these pointers as well as the local and remote socket numbers, and memory pointers for the send and receive buffers, current segment and the retransmit queue, are stored in the Transmission Control Block (TCB), created at the connection establishment process, as we saw in section 6.3.9.

Assuming a client/server communication, data is transferred to both sides. Then, when the *client* transmits data it uses the *Send Window* to keep track of the *transmitted bytes*, while the *server* uses the *Receive Window* to keep track of the *received bytes*. In this sense, the *Send Window* of the transmitter and the *Receive Window* of the receiver are complementary. Of course, the same happens when the server transmits data to the client.

Since the Send Window of one device is the Receive Window of the other device, the SND and RCV pointers have the same values. However, as at any given time some bytes could be in transit, those values will not always line up exactly between the two devices. This can be seen comparing Figure 6.19 with Figure 6.20 where bytes from 22 to 28 have been transmitted but not yet received by the recipient. Then, each device must maintain for each connection, a set of sliding windows (Send and Receive Windows), incoming and outgoing data buffers, and the corresponding TCB. Let us remember that each connection is identified by a pair of sockets, also stored at the TCB.

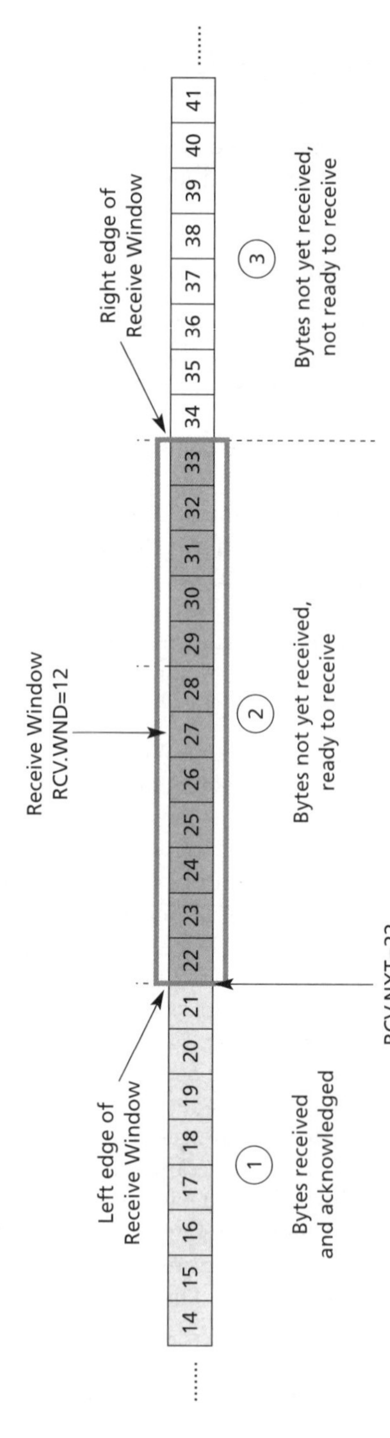

Figure 6.20 TCP Receive Window

Figure 6.21 gives a data transfer example showing how at each moment (represented by different events), the Send and Receive Window pointers are updated as messages are exchanged. The significant fields from the exchanged messages are also shown, to demonstrate how devices synchronize their variables with the information carried by the TCP segment header fields.

Figure 6.21 starts from the connection-established state, where the Initial Sequence Number from each device was exchanged. Then, each device maintains a couple of variables (not shown in the figure) called the Initial Send Sequence (ISS), the one used by the device to start sequencing the data, and the Initial Receive Sequence (IRS), which consists of the other device Initial Sequence Number selected to sequence its data. These variables will fill the initial values for the SND.UNA pointer and the RCV.NXT pointer respectively.

We can see in Figure 6.21 that, after the connection establishment phase, the initial conditions establish that the client has 200 as the ISN and a window size of 400, while the server has selected 150 as the ISN and a window size of 300. We can also see how the client's send pointers complement the server's receive pointers and vice versa (although some delays exist owing to the time the message takes to arrive at its destination, after which the pointers are updated). The pointers shown in a filled box mean that they have not changed since the last event, providing a better way to follow the pointer value changes.

This data transfer example can be represented by showing the same events but from the view of the send and receive sliding windows. Figures 6.22 (events 1 to 4), 6.23 (events 5 to 8) and 6.24 (events 9 to 11) show, step by step, how the pointers are being updated, and the windows are 'sliding' while the data transfer takes place.

Note that in these figures, the client side has the Send Window above and the Receive Window below; but at the server sides, these positions are changed to help see the complementary nature of both types of windows.

Let us describe how data transfer takes place. In event number 2 (Fig. 6.22), where the client sends 120 bytes of data to the server, we see how the SND.NXT pointer shifts towards the right, having 320 as a new value. This marks the sequence number of the first byte ready to be sent, while the SND.UNA remains with the same value as the data just sent is not acknowledged yet. As the SND.WND is 300 bytes in size, only 180 bytes can be transmitted (300 – 120 = 180), defining the USABLE window as 180 bytes, and lowering the amount of data the client can send to the server at once.

Then the transmitted message sent by the client will carry 120 bytes of data (ranging from sequence number 200 to 319), a Sequence Number field with 200, and a Window field with 400, informing the other device how much data it can receive at once.

When the message arrives at the server (in event number 3), the server receives the data, and stores it in the incoming data buffer. The RCV.NXT pointer now points to the first byte of the free area of the receive buffer, with sequence number equal to 320. The Receive Window, then, 'slides' to the right. The data stored at the left of the Receive Window, is ready to be passed to the application layer.

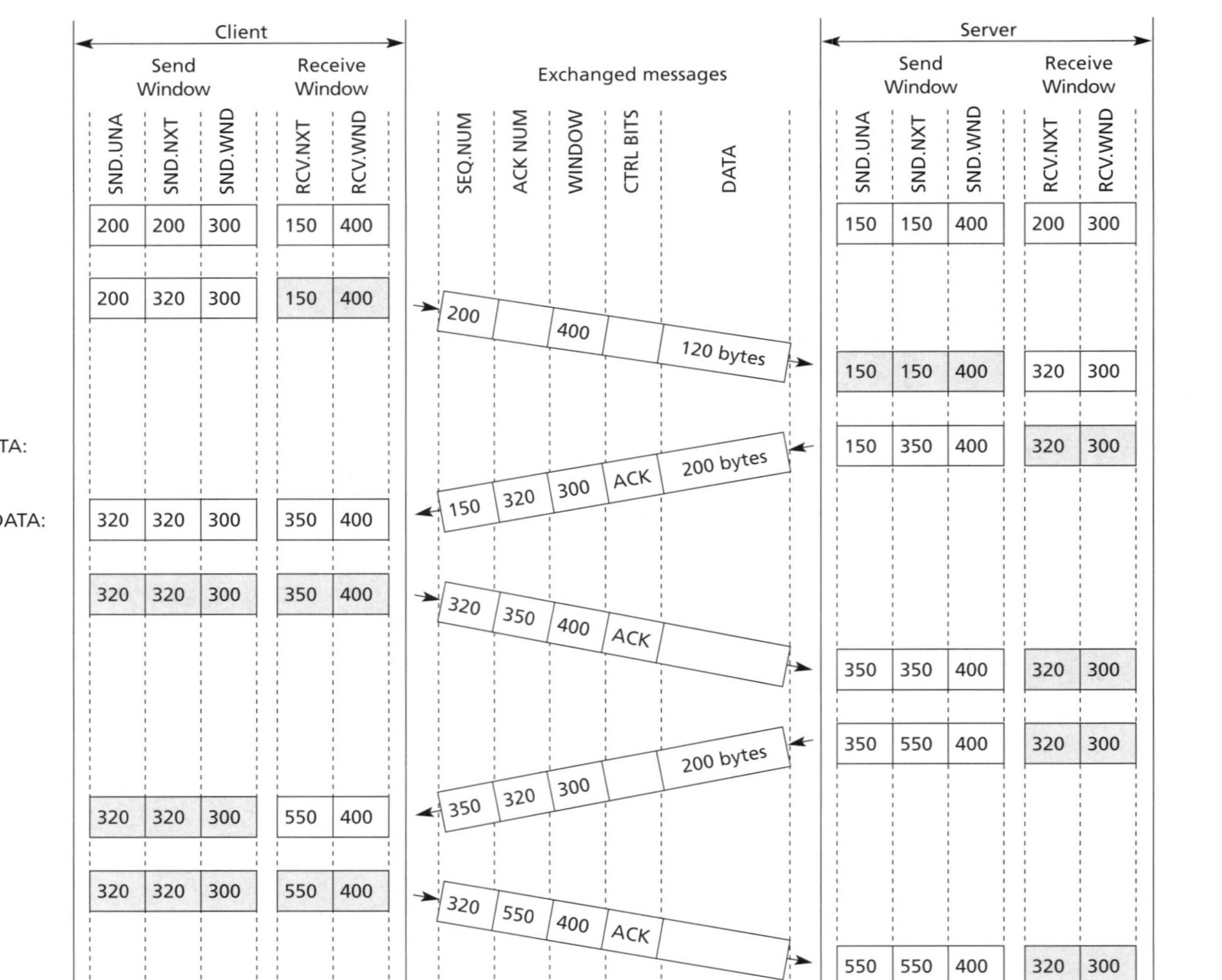

Figure 6.21 TCP data transfer example showing the send and receive pointers.

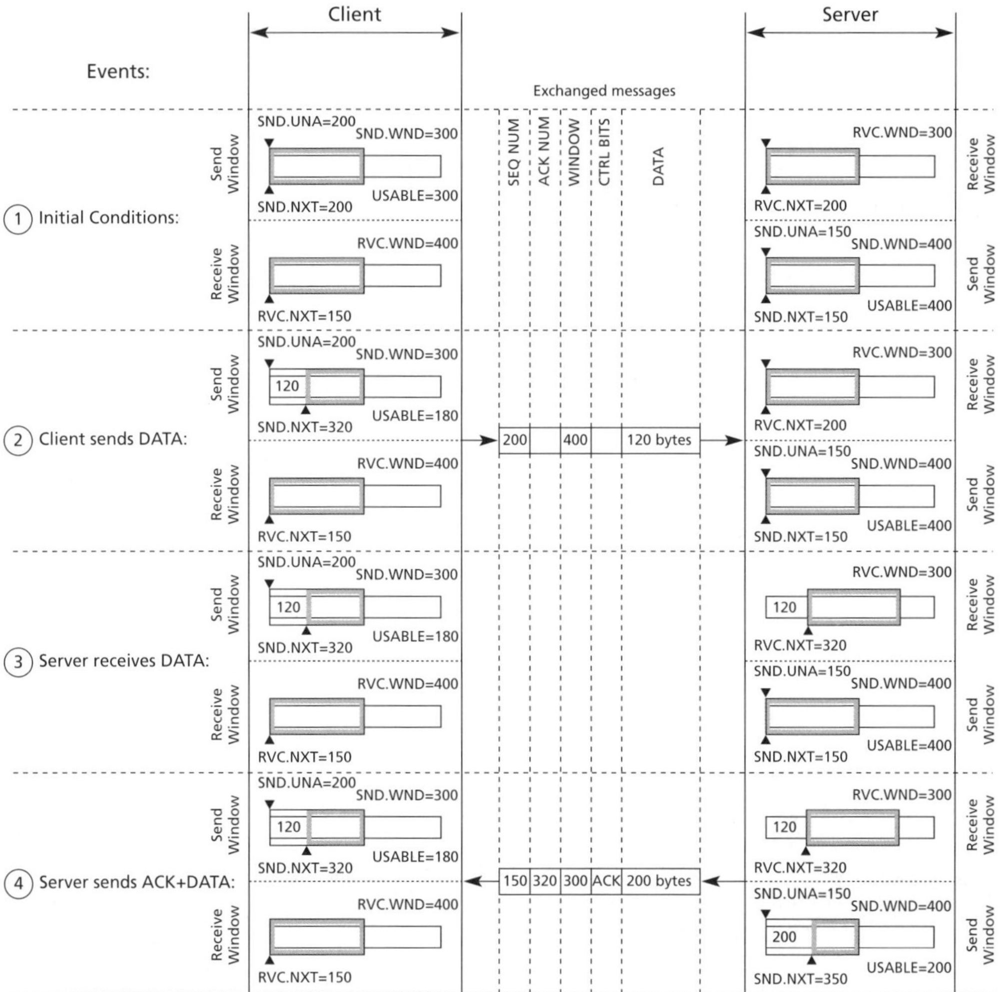

Figure 6.22 TCP data transfer example showing the send and receive sliding windows (Part 1 of 3).

Once the server acknowledges the received data and transmits the ACK segment (as well as its own data for the client), in event number 4, which arrives at the client in event number 5 (Fig. 6.23), the client send pointers are updated. The SND.UNA takes the value 320, so the client send window 'slides' toward the right. The USABLE window is also 300 again, increasing the amount of information the client can send to the server at once.

One interesting characteristic to note is how, when the transmitter device sends data, the usable window is stretching, meaning that the flow control feature is limiting the amount of bytes the sender may transmit to the device.

The above example, though it seems somewhat complex, is still being simplified. One simplification is based on the assumption that each message transmitted was received by the recipient, ignoring the associated complexity

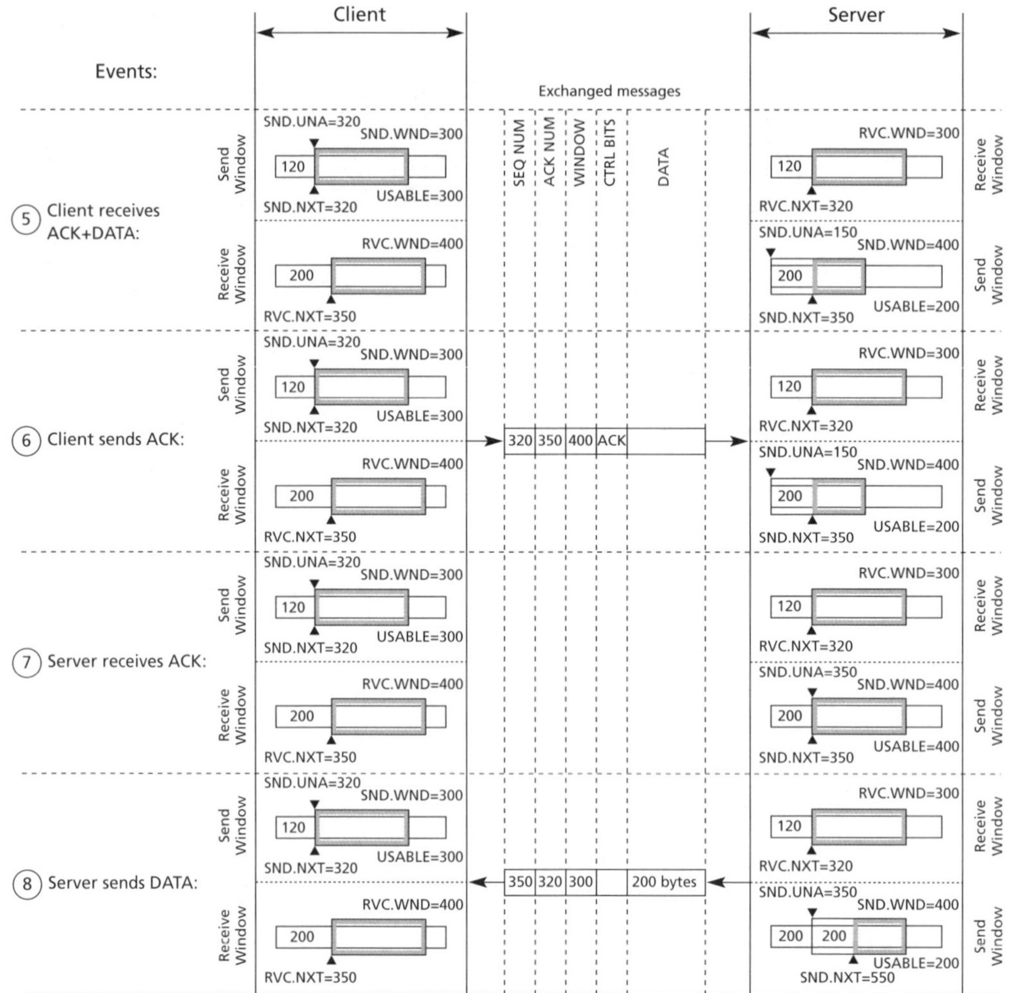

Figure 6.23 TCP data transfer example showing the send and receive sliding windows (Part 2 of 3).

that re-transmission aggregates. The other simplification comes from the fact that, in all cases, the window sizes have remained the same. However, in practice, as those windows implement the flow control mechanism, these sizes will vary. These subjects will be approached in the next sections.

6.3.12 TCP segment retransmission scheme

We have already seen how TCP uses the acknowledgement messages scheme to inform the sender about the recipient's received data. We have also seen that a timer is needed, to start when the message is sent, in order to avoid waiting for the acknowledgement for ever. If the timer expires and the acknowledgement of the sent message does not show up, the segment is considered lost and it must be retransmitted.

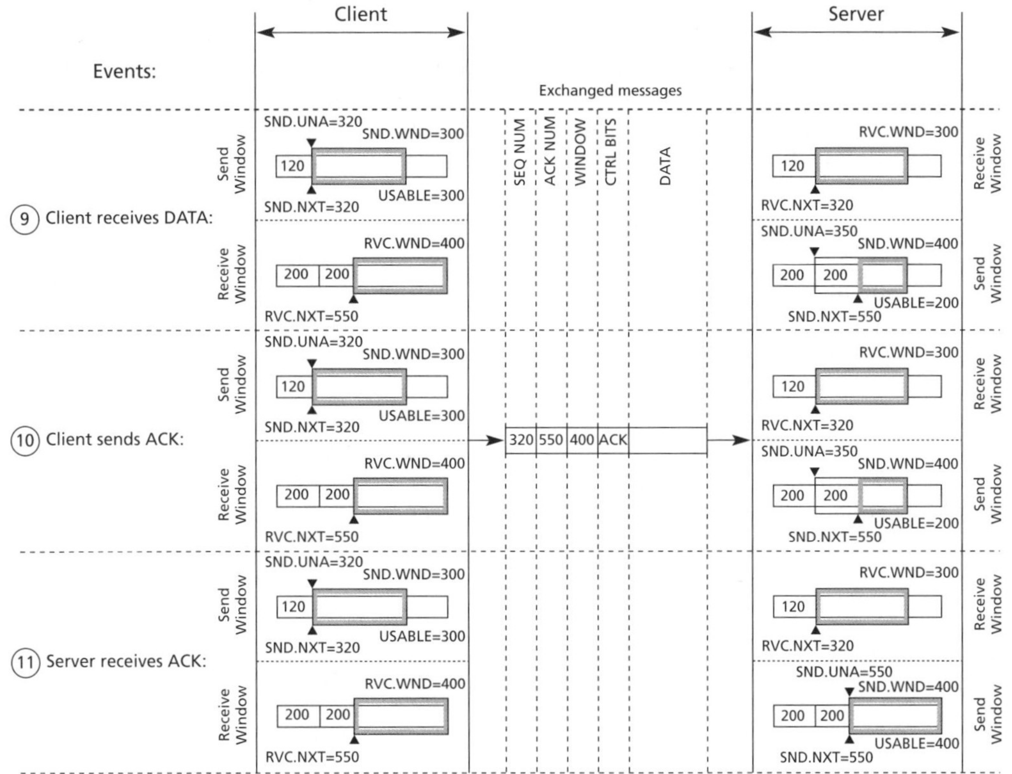

Figure 6.24 TCP data transfer example showing the send and receive sliding windows (Part 3 of 3).

The retransmission scheme consists of the following procedure:

- For each segment sent, an assigned timer is started and a copy of the segment is placed in the *retransmission queue*.
- If an acknowledgement is received for this segment before its timer expires, the segment is removed from the *retransmission queue*.
- If the timer expires, and the acknowledgement does not show up, the segment is automatically retransmitted. The timer is started, and the segment remains in the *retransmission queue*, until a successful acknowledgement is received.
- If successive retransmissions are performed, and no acknowledgements are received, the software may consider that some permanent problem exists at some part of the network, terminating the connection and informing the application about this.

6.3.12.1 TCP retransmission timer value: round trip time (RTT)

In the last section, we explained that each time a segment is transmitted (or retransmitted) a timer is started. This timer is used to know how long to wait for a segment acknowledgement until the segment is considered lost.

Nevertheless, what we did not explain was the value this timer should have. The timer value is critical as if we select too low a value, the timers may expire too soon, while the acknowledgements are coming, and we make unnecessary retransmissions. However, if the timer value selected is too long, we could waste time waiting for an acknowledgement that will never arrive. Then, the first case will increment the bandwidth use, while the last will reduce the overall performance.

The ideal value for this timer would be a value slightly larger than the time it takes to send a segment from one device to other and the acknowledgement to return to the first device. This time is called round trip-time (RTT). The problem with this solution is that this time varies notably because of several factors, such as the distance that separates both devices, the internetwork congestion and the router loads.

Instead of using a single fixed value, an adaptive method may be used where TCP adjusts this value according to the RTT variations. RFC 2988 'Computing TCP's Retransmission Timer' gives a complete approach to this subject. The adaptive method consists of the RTT measurements getting the New_RTT_Sample values, which are used to calculate the new RTT value, which will replace the Old_RTT value. The New_RTT_Sample value is measured taking the time between the segments being sent, and their acknowledgements being received.

The RTT value is calculated from the following formula:

$$RTT = (\alpha * Old\_RTT) + ((1 - \alpha) * New\_RTT\_Sample)$$

where α is a smoothing factor between 0 and 1. This factor determines how the RTT will react to the abrupt changes of the New_RTT_Sample measures. If α is close to 0, the calculated RTT value will follow the New_RTT_Sample value measured; while if α is close to 1, the RTT calculated value will almost not be affected by the New_RTT_Sample values.

6.3.12.2 Karn's algorithm

Although the above method works fine with normal segments, it has a problem when retransmission occurs. Suppose a client sends a segment to a server, and after some time, the timer expires. This indicates that the segment must be retransmitted, waiting for a new acknowledgement. However, sometimes, the segment or its acknowledgement does not get lost, but has simply been delayed. However, the timer has expired and the segment has been retransmitted. This means that, in these cases, the original acknowledgement as well as the retransmitted acknowledgement will be received by the client. As both the segment and the retransmitted segment are equal (and so are the acknowledgements), how will we know which of the acknowledgements is the correct one for the RTT measurement?

Remember that by the nature of the underlying IP protocol, it is possible that the acknowledgement of the retransmitted segment can arrive before the acknowledgement of the original segment. This is called acknowledgement ambiguity. Karn's algorithm solves this problem through two premises:

- Do not use measured RTT values for retransmitted segments, to avoid the acknowledgement ambiguity.
- Incorporation of a timer backoff scheme for retransmitted segments, starting the timer with the current RTT value for normal transmissions. When a segment is retransmitted, the timer is 'backed off' (multiplied by 2) to increment the timer value. This timer continues to be increased (up to a certain value) until the retransmission is successful. Then, the timer is kept at this value until a new RTT value can be measured on a segment sent without retransmission.

The backoff scheme is needed because, if we do not use the measured RTT values for retransmitted segments, we will not have any feedback in such cases where some problems arise, causing the retransmissions. For example, suppose a congestion problem appears, so the RTT value must be increased in order to reflect the present delay of the network. As when a segment is sent, the new RTT has not yet been updated, and this longer delay will cause the segment to be retransmitted. However, as retransmissions are not taken into account when calculating the new RTT, the timer would still be with the old RTT value, and the retransmitted segments will never succeed. With the backoff scheme, we will have some feedback for the retransmitted segments, avoiding the problem described above.

6.3.12.3 Retransmission handling

We already know that each unacknowledged segment must be retransmitted. And, we know that the acknowledgement system is cumulative. These concepts may create some doubts about how to handle certain situations when retransmission is needed.

Suppose a device sent five segments, named Segment #1 to Segment #5. Also, let us suppose that Segments #1 and #2 have been already acknowledged using Acknowledgement Number 341. After some time, the timer for segment #3 expires, indicating that this segment must be retransmitted. The question is, what happened to Segments #4 and #5? As the acknowledgement system is cumulative, perhaps the recipient received these segments but it couldn't acknowledge them as it needed the segment #3 which had not arrived (possibility 1). Or perhaps, Segments #4 and #5 did not arrive at the recipient and neither did the Segment #3 (possibility 2).

As the sender does not know what happened to Segments #4 and #5, and the recipient does not have a way to tell the sender, the retransmission of the unacknowledged segments can be made in two different ways:

- Retransmit only Segment #3 (for which the timer expires), and wait for the acknowledgement for the rest of the segments. This decision assumes that possibility 1 has occurred.
- Retransmit all segments (not only Segment #3, but also Segments #4 and #5). This decision assumes that possibility 2 has occurred.

The strategy of retransmitting only the unacknowledged segment is conservative as it sends only Segment #3 which it is sure has not arrived, but if Segments #4 and #5 were never acknowledged, they must be retransmitted later, wasting a considerable amount of time. The strategy of retransmitting all the subsequent segments is correct where Segments #4 and #5 never get acknowledged, but we could be wasting the available bandwidth retransmitting unnecessary segments.

This is a weakness of the cumulative acknowledgement system when there are non-contiguous segments to acknowledge. This weakness is based on the lack of information the sender receives about the non-contiguous data segment received by the recipient.

6.3.13 Selective Acknowledgement (SACK)

This feature is used to inform the transmitter when non-contiguous data segments have been received, which cannot be acknowledged by the cumulative acknowledgement system. In this way, the transmitter has the necessary information to take the decision about the kind of strategy to follow with the subsequent transmitted segments, when a segment must be retransmitted.

In order for both devices to use this feature, it must be enabled through the Selective Acknowledgement Permitted (SACK-Permitted) option (Option-Kind = 4) in the SYN message used for connection establishment.

Once the SACK option is enabled, the receiver can inform the sender about the non-contiguous blocks of data received using the TCP header options (Option-Kind = 5) of a segment.

Going back to the above example: where a device sent five segments and Segments #1 and #2 were acknowledged, Segment #3 got lost, and Segments #4 and #5 arrived but were not acknowledged by the cumulative acknowledgement system. Then the receiver could use the SACK option of a segment to include information about these received blocks of data from segments #4 and #5. This is like an 'unofficial' way to acknowledge the received segments.

When a segment containing SACK data arrives at the transmitter, the device marks those segments at the retransmission queue with a SACK flag set to 1. When the devices need to retransmit some unacknowledged segments, the segments with SACK = 1 are not retransmitted.

Once the retransmission of lost segments is successfully acknowledged (Segment #3 in the example), the rest of the arrived segments can be acknowledged by the cumulative acknowledgement systems (Segments #4 and #5 in the example), and the segments are deleted from the retransmission queue.

The Option-Data format for the SACK option consists of a list of blocks of contiguous sequence space occupied by the data that has been received but could not be acknowledged. Each block is described by two 16-bit fields: the *Relative Origin*, the sequence number of this block, relative to the Acknowledgement Number field in the TCP header (or the left edge of the receive window); and the *Block Size*, the size in bytes of the block.

In the above example, as Segments #4 and #5 form a contiguous block, the Option-Data would consist of four bytes; two bytes for the relative origin (equal to the size of Segment #3), and two bytes for the block size (the sum of the sizes of Segments #4 and #5) of this unique block. Of course, the whole SACK option should be completed with the Option-Kind = 5, and the Option-Length which in this case would be 6.

6.3.14 Sliding window size adjustment

Until now in the given examples the size of the Receive Window of a device remained fixed. In that way, the device limits the amount of data the other device can transmit to it. However, this cannot reduce, or even stop, the amount of data sent in a way, as may be necessary in some cases. For that purpose, it is necessary to adjust the size of the window in accordance with the conditions.

When we saw the sliding window acknowledgement system, all the examples had one simplification based on the assumption that the receiver would store the received segments in the receiver buffer, and then pass this data immediately to the application. Even when this should happen in this way, it is not always possible, for various reasons.

In fact, at the receiving point, several processes exist for different purposes. One process must receive the segments and store them in the receiver buffer. The acknowledgement for the segment must also be sent immediately (otherwise, the sender timer would expire). Meanwhile, other processes must take the data from the buffer and pass it to the application. All these tasks run concurrently, and the operating system must assign a limited processor time to each process in order to ensure completion; perhaps, this assignment should be based on a priorities basis. However, when a segment arrives it should be stored immediately in the receiver buffer, to avoid the following segments overwriting the first. Once this is accomplished, the data is extracted from the buffer and passed to the application. In this way, the buffer balances the different rates at which the segments are arriving and the data is being extracted from the buffer. However, remember, this buffer size could be very large, but it is limited and in certain circumstances the buffer could be exhausted.

The device receiving the segments, at a certain moment, could, however, be very busy dealing with lots of other connections, and possibly with other processes that have nothing to do with segments and buffers. These last processes also consume processor time. As a result, it could happen that as a first process is receiving lots of segments and storing them in the buffer, a second process is not extracting data and passing it to the application, or at least not at the same rate as the first process is doing its task. This difference in process rates will quickly exhaust the buffer. As a result, the first process would overwrite the old segment not yet transferred to the application by the second process.

Note that even when the sender is sending the same amount of data, the slow performance of the second process causes this problem. The sender will also transmit this data as long as the receiver acknowledges it, although if the receiver does not acknowledge the data, when the retransmission timers expire, the sender would retransmit the data anyway.

In such conditions, it is not sufficient to limit the amount of data the sender transmits, but it is sometimes necessary to slow down or even stop the rate at which the data is transmitted. In this cases, the sliding window must be resized according to the circumstances.

Figure 6.25 shows an example of a data transfer where the buffer is filled more quickly than drained, meaning that at some point the buffer will be exhausted. The window must then be closed, until the buffer has some free space. In this example, we are assuming the client has lots of data to send to the server so it will try to send as much data as it can. However, the server is attending lots of simultaneous connections and has lots of processes running, meaning that some processes are running very slowly.

The server buffer consists of 400 bytes (shown as four blocks of 100 bytes each). The four blocks of the buffer are initially free. Then, the server Receive Window and client Send Window is 400 bytes. The Initial Sequence Number the client selected is 200. All this is shown as the initial condition, in step 1.

In step 2, as the client is so anxious to send data, it sends 400 bytes (the limit imposed by the size of the Send Window). Then, the server receives the segment and stores it in the buffer, using blocks 1 to 4. However, as the

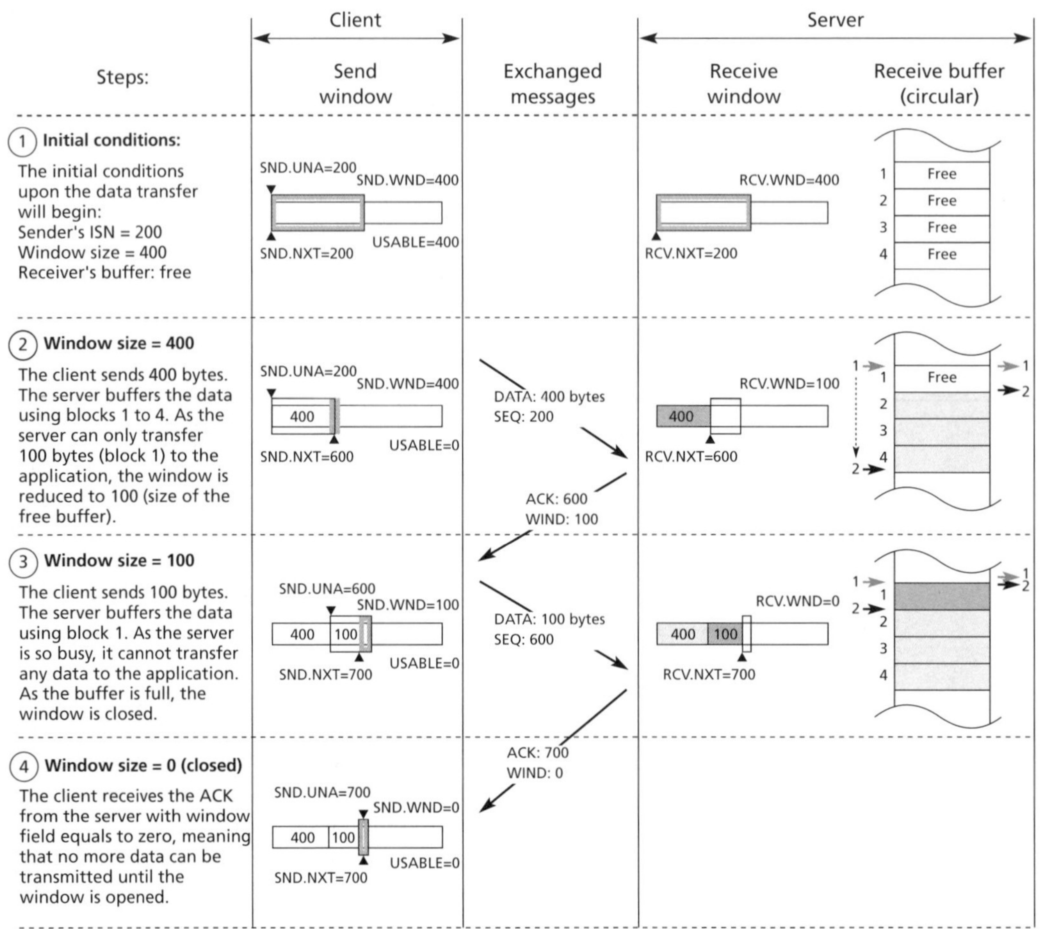

Figure 6.25 TCP sliding window size adjustment.

server is so busy with several tasks, it can only transfer block 1 (100 bytes) of the buffer to the application. In these conditions, the buffer will only have 100 bytes free, so the server acknowledges the received data, but adjusts the window size to 100.

In step 3, the client receives the acknowledgement and actualizes its pointers. As a result, the Send Window size is now 100 bytes. The left edge of the window moves toward the left, as does the right edge, but at a slower rate. As the client needs to send as much data as it can, it will send the whole window length again, consisting of a segment with 100 bytes of data. When this segment arrives at the server, it stores the data at the only one available buffer block (block 1). However, as the server is so busy, it cannot transfer anything to the application, meaning that the buffer remains totally full. Then, the server acknowledges the received data, but in this case, as it cannot receive more data, it sends the window size equals to zero.

In step 4, when the client receives the acknowledgement, the window size goes to zero, and the window closes. The right edge of the window remains fixed. In this condition, the client cannot send more data until the server releases space from the buffer (transferring data to the application). When this happens, the server must inform the client about it, sending an acknowledgement with the window field different from zero. This message re-opens the window, allowing the client to continue sending data to the server. However, as the underlying Internet protocol does not guarantee the delivery of this acknowledgement and because the reception of acknowledgements is not confirmed, it could be possible that the server acknowledgement never arrives at the client, meaning that the window will be closed for ever. In order to avoid this condition, the client can regularly send special 'probe' segments to ask the server to send back a segment containing the current window size.

In this way, the window size is adjusted in order to regulate the rate at which the sender sends data, implementing the flow control mechanism.

6.3.15 Receive buffer resize problem (shrinking the window)

Sometimes, and for any reason, the operating system can run out of memory. In such case, the receive buffer for each connection could be reduced to gain memory allowing the server to continue processing other tasks. Let us assume that the server has a buffer of 400 bytes, and the client sends 200 bytes to the server. Then, the client will have a Send Window of 400, and a Usable Window of 200. When the server receives this segment, it stores the data in the buffer. As the server is so overloaded, it cannot transfer the data to the application, so the server acknowledges the data informing a window with 200 bytes.

If the operating system asks the application to reduce its receive buffer, the new buffer size could be 350 bytes. As the data still stored occupies 200 bytes, the new available free space is 150 bytes. Then, the server should acknowledge the received data with a window of 150 bytes instead of the 200 bytes as before. When the client receives this 'new' acknowledgement, it must resize the Send Window to 150 bytes, which is less than the Usable Window that it has. This means that the right edge of the Send Window moves back to the left, causing the window to shrink.

A potential problem with this is that before the acknowledgement is received by the client, as it has an 'old' value of 200 as Usable Window, it could send 200 bytes to the server. And if this happens, when this 200 bytes arrive at the server, as its buffer was resized, only 150 bytes could be buffered, and the remaining 50 bytes will be discarded. This will force retransmission of the data, which is inefficient.

A solution to this is that the acknowledgement cannot provide a window size less than the Usable Window of the device receiving the acknowledgement. In other words, it is not permitted to shrink the window. Instead of this, devices must reduce their window size in a more gradual way.

6.3.16 The 'silly window' syndrome

In Figure 6.25, we saw how the window closes in those situations where the device (the server in that case) is so busy that it is impossible to transfer data to the application, causing the buffer to become full. Under this condition, the client must stop sending data until the server gets free space in its receive buffer, and notifies this, sending a message to the client with the window field greater than zero (re-opening the window). When the client receives this notification, it can start sending data to the server again.

However, some undesirable conditions would happen if the server started transferring data to the application (and then freeing the buffer) very slowly. For example: suppose the server is still very busy, but it can transfer one byte to the application. As soon as this happens, the closed window is re-opened and the server sends a message to the client with the Window field equals to 1. The client will re-open its Send Window with the size of one byte, and since it has lots of data to transmit, it will send a segment with only one byte of data. If this situation remains the same for a while, the client would be sending lots of segments with only one byte of data – a drastically inefficient way to transmit data over the inter-network. This condition would waste the available bandwidth and the processor time necessary to process lots of transmitter and receiver segment headers, just for a few bytes being transmitted. This anomaly is called the 'silly window' syndrome (SWS), and it arises because the sliding window system sets no minimum size on transmitted segments.

In order to prevent this, some changes called SWS avoidance algorithms are introduced at both the sender and receiver. At the receiver, once the window closes, it must not advertise the sender about the window size until this size gets one-half the buffer size or the Maximum Segment Size (MSS), whichever is less. When this happens, the sender will be notified with a window size enough to send efficient segments.

At the sender, it must avoid sending data as soon as possible (ignoring the segment size); instead, it should wait until it can send a segment of a reasonable size. In this case, Nagle's algorithm is used:

- If there is no unacknowledged data outstanding on the connection, the data passed from the application using the 'PUSH' function is sent immediately.
- If there is unacknowledged data, the passed data from the application will not be sent until either all the unacknowledged data is acknowledged, or the data is enough to send a segment with a MSS size; even if the application requested the 'PUSH' function.

This algorithm is well suited for both low data rate applications such as Telnet, and high transfer demands such as file transfer applications. In the case of Telnet, the first keystroke will be sent immediately as there is no unacknowledged data. Nevertheless, the subsequent keystrokes will not be sent until the acknowledgements are received.

However, these acknowledgements will be received before the next keystroke from the user, as the RTT is probably less than the time the user takes to press two consecutive keys from the keyboard. In the case of file transfer applications, where a large amount of data is passed from the application, there will be enough data to send segments with a MSS size, enabling the data to be transmitted immediately.

6.3.17 TCP congestion handling

Sometimes, the inter-network becomes very busy, since it has to transmit lots of IP datagrams. The routers that pass these datagrams from network to network may be receiving lots of datagrams to process, and may become overloaded. The incoming datagrams are held at a queue to be further processed and retransmitted. However, as the queue (or buffer) gets full, the next datagrams received will be discarded. In this situation, the speed at which segments are carried between both devices of a connection will be reduced. And worse still, some datagrams will get lost. This is called congestion.

The TCP flow control mechanism only considers what is happening on each device on the connection, not what is going on with the inter-network, which joins both devices. As devices do not have information about the internetwork status, when the inter-network is congested, devices only perceive that datagrams are delayed, or perhaps lost. In these circumstances, devices retransmit segments, incrementing the amount of traffic on the network and the inter-network congestion. This eventually results in a congestion collapse.

The TCP should realize when congestion occurs, assuming that the reason why the segments do not arrive at their destination is because the router got overloaded, discarding datagrams. In addition, detecting the rate at which segments were sent but not acknowledged, TCP could know about the level of congestion on the inter-network between both devices.

The RFC 2001 'TCP Slow Start, Congestion Avoidance, Fast Retransmit, and Fast Recovery Algorithms' describes changes for implementations in order to handle the inter-network congestion. Basically, the Slow Start means that as soon as the connection is established, the sender does not send as much data as it would need; instead, it would start sending a MSS-sized segment, and it would wait for its acknowledgement. Then, it could send another, and increment the amount of data sent until the window size is reached or a congestion is detected. *Congestion Avoidance* proposes slowing down the rate at which the sender transmits segments, when congestion is detected. Then, it uses the *slow start* again to increase the transmission rate until it gets back the original throughput. Both algorithms work as a whole.

Fast Retransmit dictates that when three or more acknowledgements are received with the same Acknowledgement Number, giving account of a segment sent but not yet received, this segment must be retransmitted without waiting for its timer expiration. *Fast Recovery* dictates that when *Fast Retransmit* is used, *Congestion Avoidance* can be used, but *Slow Start* should not be used. This is based on the fact that if the sender receives several acknowledgements (three or more as *Fast Retransmit* dictates), the inter-network would be not so congested as it seems, so using the *Slow Start* would decrease performance unnecessarily.

6.3.18 TCP common applications

Table 6.5 shows some TCP applications.

Table 6.5

Protocol	Description	Server Port
FTP	Used to transfer files.	20/21
TELNET	Allows users to use a remote device.	23
SMTP	Used to send electronic mail messages.	25
DNS	Exchange Request/Reply messages for domain name resolution.	53
HTTP	Used to retrieve documents in the World Wide Web.	80
POP3	Used to retrieve electronic mail messages.	110
NNTP	Used for transferring newsgroup messages.	119
IMAP	Another email retrieval protocol.	143
IRC	An interactive protocol that allows user's Chat.	194

6.4 Summary

- The Transport layer provides a 'host-to-host' communication service for the Application layer in the TCP/IP stack. This layer is like an intermediary between the more hardware-oriented lower layers, and the more software-oriented upper layers. The Transport services are presented in two versions: the User Datagram Protocol (UDP) and the Transmission Control Protocol (TCP), where each protocol covers different service requirements.
- The Transport layer provides process addressing allowing more than one application to share the same IP address. In this way, each process is assigned with a different port number. The server application processes have assigned port numbers in the range from 0 to 1023, called well-known port numbers, allowing the clients to know the server port number according to the application they will contact. Client processes have assigned a temporal port number, each time the application is launched.

- A socket is a communication-end identifier, and it is specified by the IP address and the port number. The socket type depends on the protocol used. A connection may be represented by an association of two sockets: the client socket and the server socket. The association allows a device to identify each connection from multiple simultaneous connections.
- The User Datagram Protocol (UDP) is a simple, efficient and fast transport protocol, although unreliable. It provides port addressing and an optional checksum for error checking. It is more appropriate for those applications such as multimedia programs streaming video clips or audio files over the Internet; or those applications that use a request-reply mechanism, using small messages.
- The Transmission Control Protocol (TCP) is a full-featured transport protocol, connection oriented, with flow control, acknowledged transmissions and retransmission mechanism; designed to provide applications a reliable way to send data as a stream of bytes, over the inter-network.
- As TCP is a stream-oriented protocol, the overall data passed between devices is performed in segments of data. For this, the TCP message is called 'Segment'. A single format is used for all segments, including a header information that allows one segment to perform more than one function. The segment size must be small enough to avoid fragmentation, but sufficiently large to get an acceptable performance. The Maximum Segment Size (MSS) limits the maximum size of a segment. If a device wants to use an MSS value other than the default (536 bytes), it must announce this at the establishment phase of the connection, using a TCP option. However, the segment size could be smaller than the MSS owing to the flow control mechanism.
- As TCP is connection-oriented, it must establish, manage and terminate connections. During its lifetime, the connection progresses through a series of states, upon the reception of events. A SYN message is used to request the connection establishment. At this phase, a TCB is created to hold the pointers and variables used for each connection. In addition, an Initial Sequence Number and some TCP options parameters exchange occurs at this initial phase. The connection establishment phase is performed through the 'three-way handshake'. Once the connection is established, if a 'half-open' connection occurs, a Reset message is generated. This procedure forms part of the management phase. When one device or both decide to close the connection, the termination phase is performed, and each device must send a FIN message and must receive its acknowledgement. After that, the connection is considered closed.
- The sliding window acknowledgement system provides reliability and flow control for the TCP transmissions. Each message sent must be acknowledged by the receiver. In order to identify each sent message, the Sequence Number field has the number of the first byte of the data sent. The acknowledgement informs the reception of data, sending an Acknowledgement field equal to the next Sequence Number it expects to receive from the sender. Each device of the connection must implement the sliding window for its transmission (Send Window) and its reception (Receive Window). The Send Window of one device is the Receive Window

of the other, and vice versa. As data transfer takes place, i.e., data is sent and acknowledged, the windows slide toward the right. The Window field from each message provides the size of the Receive Window (or receive buffer size) of the device sending the message. The device receiving this message updates its Send Window size from the Window field. The Usable Window is the portion of the Send Window indicating the amount of bytes that the receiver is willing to accept from the sender. When a receiver needs to slow down the rate at which the sender is transmitting messages, the Window size is reduced, limiting the amount of bytes the sender can transmit to it. In this way, the flow control feature is implemented.

- The retransmission scheme keeps track of sent segments and retransmits them when needed. For each segment sent, a timer is started and a copy of the segment is placed in a retransmission queue. If an acknowledgement is received before the timer expires, the segment is removed from the queue. However, if the timer expires and the acknowledgement does not arrive, the timer is started again, and the segment is retransmitted. The segment remains in the queue until a successful acknowledgement is received, or the software considers that a permanent error occurs, after consecutive unsuccessful retransmissions. The value used for the timers is based on the round trip-time (RTT). Karn's algorithm is used to avoid acknowledgement ambiguity.
- As the cumulative acknowledgement system cannot acknowledge non-contiguous received segments, the sender lacks information about those transmissions, and an incorrect retransmission decision could be taken, causing a waste of bandwidth or performance inefficiency. The selective acknowledgement (SACK) option allows a receiver to inform the sender about the reception of those non-contiguous received segments, so the sender can take the right decision deciding which segment should be retransmitted.
- The sliding window does not only limit the amount of data the sender can transmit to the receiver, but can also slow down the rate at which it transmits data, and may even stop sending data. This is implemented adjusting the sliding window size. However, this adjustment must be gradual in order to avoid 'shrinking the window'. The acknowledgement cannot inform a window size less than the usable window of the device receiving the acknowledgement, to avoid inefficiency problems. Also, in order to avoid the 'silly window' syndrome, the receiver cannot re-open the window until its size gets one-half the buffer size or the Maximum Segment Size, whichever is less; while the sender must use Nagle's algorithm to avoid sending small segments, causing inefficient transmissions. The TCP congestion handling provides changes for implementations, in order to deal with the problem without further incrementing the inter-network congestion. The algorithms are Slow Start, Congestion avoidance, Fast Retransmit and Fast Recovery.

7

Remote access: Telnet

In this chapter, we will start describing the application protocols. These protocols use the Transport layer for data transmission, and provide the user with specific tools to take advantage of the inter-network resources. These are the applications that the users really value, as they provide solutions to their needs. Generally, users do not know and do not worry about the internal structure of the TCP/IP stack. They only value the advantages the inter-networking gives them: the end-user perspective of the TCP/IP services, as we have seen in Chapter 2. The first application protocol we will see is Telnet. It is, perhaps, the earliest of the application protocols developed for the Internet. It is probably unknown to most users, although lots of people use it.

7.1 Introduction

Some years ago, perhaps in the 1960s and 1970s, computers were big machines, very different from the personal computers we are used to today. These computers were shared between several users who accessed them through terminals consisting of a keyboard for user input and a monitor (a Cathode Ray Tube or CRT) to display the computer's output.

Generally, the user accessed a multi-user system from the terminal, where they had to login by sending their username and password. After a successful authentication, a session could start where the user could execute a program and use some computer resources. Those computers were proprietary, having very different hardware and operating systems. Of course, the terminals also differed among computers of different brands, since they were specifically designed for each type of computer.

When the inter-network allowed these computers to interconnect, the idea of accessing remote computers began to be considered. In this way, users could connect to a remote computer (perhaps located many kilometres from them), start a session, and use programs and resources on that computer as if they were local. For this purpose, a new application protocol was developed, called Telnet.

The RFC 97 'First Cut at a Proposed Telnet Protocol', published in February 1971, was the first document defining Telnet. After that, several revisions and discussions were documented in different RFCs. The final version of the protocol is documented in RFC 854 'Telnet Protocol Specification'. Several updates are found in RFC 856–860, 885, 1091, 1096 and 1184.

Telnet allows users to access a remote host and use it as if they were connected locally. As Telnet needs to start a session on the remote computer, the natural Transport layer it must use is TCP. In principle, the Telnet job seems very easy; it must get the keyboard input from the user and send it to the remote computer, while the output from the remote computer must be sent to the user terminal and display to the user. (See Fig. 7.1.)

As we have already said, computers were so different in hardware and software that data representation could be very different in those systems. As old computers had developed with no standards, they differed in many aspects, such as the keyboard and keystrokes used, the character set used to encode data and control functions, and even the screen resolution. For this, each computer needed its own terminal to access its system.

Therefore, it was probable that when a user sent some characters, the remote system could not correctly interpret them. And the same could happen with the computer output sent to the user. The idea of accessing 'remote systems' (and different computers) from the same 'local terminal' was only made possible by providing a 'common language', which all systems could understand. This commonality is provided by the Network Virtual Terminal (NVT), which must be used and interpreted for all Telnet implementation on every system.

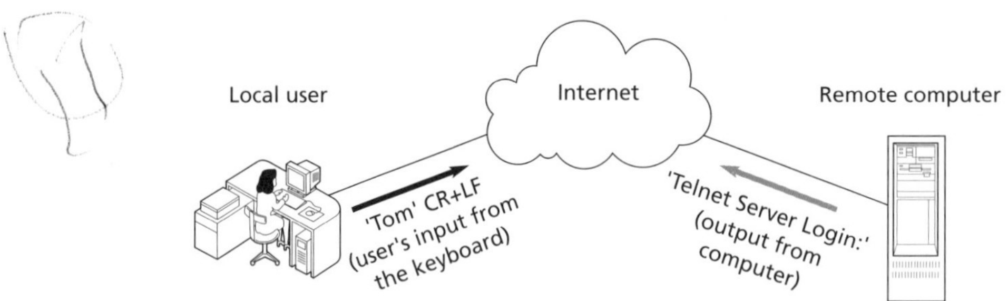

Figure 7.1 A Telnet session: the user accesses a remote computer.

7.2 The Network Virtual Terminal

The Network Virtual Terminal (NVT) defines a standard configuration that all Telnet implementations must understand. The character set used is called NVT-ASCII, which refers to the 7-bit US ASCII character set. The eighth bit is zero. The end of line is terminated using CR+LF characters (Carriage

Return 0x0D and Line Feed 0x0A). The default transmission mode is half-duplex, allowing for the fact that old computers would not transmit at full-duplex mode. This minimum configuration should allow all computers to understand each other.

In this way, the user's input from the keyboard will be translated to the NVT-ASCII character set by the Telnet client implementation running on the local terminal, and sent to the remote computer over the inter-network, using TCP. The Telnet server, running at the remote computer, will receive this data and will convert it to the character set used by the remote system. The computer's output will also be converted to the NVT-ASCII by the Telnet server, and sent to the terminal, where it will be converted to the character set used in the local terminal, by the Telnet client. (See Fig. 7.2.)

Although this minimum configuration allows basic communication, extra facilities can be provided upon negotiation. Some of these options are using an extended ASCII or a full 8-bit binary data, and a full-duplex communication mode, among others. As those facilities are optional, they must be agreed by both ends. Both ends could even agree to simulate a different terminal type, with better features than the basic NVT. Later on, we will see these and other Telnet options.

7.2.1 NVT-ASCII control codes

The Telnet standard specifies that all implementations must handle the 'printable' characters (codes 32 to 126), and it dictates how the NVT-ASCII control codes (codes 0 to 31 and 127) should be interpreted. Only control codes 0 (NUL), 10 (LF), and 13 (CR) are mandatory, the rest are optional. Table 7.1 shows the control codes that should take effect on the NVT terminal output. Note that the word 'print' instead of 'display' from the standard reflects the past where printers were used for output instead of monitor screens.

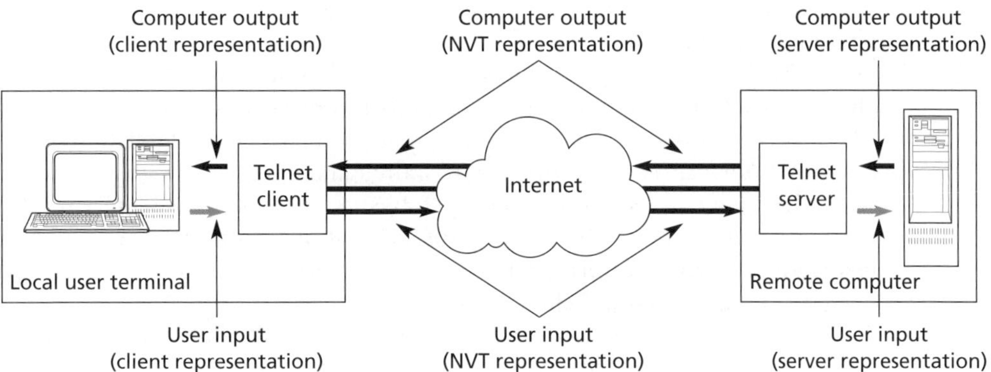

Figure 7.2 The Network Virtual Terminal provides a 'common' data representation.

Table 7.1

Name	Code (decimal)	Description	Implementation
Null (NUL)	0	No operation.	Mandatory
Line Feed (LF)	10	Moves the printer to the next print line, keeping the same horizontal position.	
Carriage Return (CR)	13	Moves the printer to the left margin of the current line.	
Bell (BEL)	7	Produces an audible or visible signal (does not move the print head).	Optional
Back Space (BS)	8	Moves the print head one-character position towards the left margin.	
Horizontal Tab (HT)	9	Moves the printer to the next horizontal tab stop (does not specify where such tab stops are located).	
Vertical Tab (VT)	11	Moves the printer to the next vertical tab stop (does not specify where such tab stops are located).	
Form Feed (FF)	12	Moves the printer to the top of the next page, keeping the same horizontal position.	

7.3 The Telnet client/server model

As Telnet functionality is based on a local user accessing a remote computer, the client/server model is well adapted. In this way, the client is running at the local terminal where the user accesses services from a server running on a remote computer.

The Telnet session is developed over a TCP connection. In this way, the client must initiate a connection establishment with a server on Port 23, which is the well-known port for the Telnet protocol. This establishment procedure is performed as a 'three-way handshake', as we saw in Chapter 6. Once the TCP connection has been established, both ends can start sending data and commands. The commands allow the terminal to send special instructions such as 'Interrupt a Process' or 'Abort', and they allow both ends to agree about the use of Telnet options.

A classical Telnet session would start with the TCP connection open, and the server sending to the client a welcome message and a login prompt (interspersed with commands asking for options). The user provides its username and its password in order to be authenticated. After that, if authentication is successful, the remote computer system shell could be presented to the user (similar to the classical c:\> prompt in DOS). Then, the user could use the system as if he or she were connected locally.

However, it is not necessary for the operating system shell to be presented to the user; instead, an application could automatically start presenting its menu to the user. This could be the case of a Telnet server running embedded systems, where they do not have a shell (system user interface), but they could have an application that allows users to inspect some internal data or read some input ports, as well as set specific parameters or control some output ports.

The TCP connection would be maintained as long as the Telnet session was active. It could be alive for a long time without restrictions. The full-featured TCP guarantees the received data to be complete and in the correct order, while the flow control assures both ends adapt its transmission rates.

As TCP allows multiple connections identified by a pair of sockets from both ends, Telnet can handle multiple sessions from different users. In addition, TCP allows full-duplex communication mode, so each end could ask to agree on the use of this mode, overriding the default half-duplex mode of the NVT specifications. When the Telnet session is ended, the TCP connection is terminated according to the normal TCP termination procedure.

7.4 Telnet commands

Besides the 'normal' data transmitted over the Telnet session, some commands are used by both ends for several purposes. For example, in order for both ends to agree an option, some commands are used, while other commands allow a 'break' key to be sent, or a process to be interrupted. Those commands allow the user to control the remote computer operation. As those command may already exists on different systems, but use different codes, they must be represented with 'common command codes' (for example, the 'backspace' could have different code on different systems). Table 7.2 shows the Telnet protocol commands.

7.4.1 Telnet command structure

As data and commands are sent interspersed using the same TCP connection, there must be a way to distinguish them. Thus, all commands are preceded by a special character named Interpret As Command (IAC) with the value 255 decimal (0xFF hex). For performance reasons, it is preferable to precede commands instead of data, as commands are less used than data.

For example, the **Interrupt Process** command should be sent as:

IAC	**IP**	**(Mnemonics)**
<255>	<244>	(Decimal)
<0xFF>	<0xF4>	(Hexadecimal)

Table 7.2

Command name	Command code	Value (decimal)	Description
Subnegotiation End	SE	240	End of subnegotiation parameters.
No Operation	NOP	241	No operation.
Data Mark	DM	242	The data stream portion of a Synch. See Telnet Interrupt handling.
Break	BRK	243	The 'break' key pressed on the terminal.
Interrupt Process	IP	244	Used for suspend, interrupt, abort or terminate a user process.
Abort Output	AO	245	Used to continue the process, but without sending the output to the terminal.
Are You There	AYT	246	Used to check if the remote computer is still 'alive'. The system must return a 'life signal'.
Erase Character	EC	247	Used to delete the last undeleted character.
Erase Line	EL	248	Used to delete all the data in the current line of input.
Go Ahead	GA	249	Used in half-duplex mode, to indicate to the other party that it may transmit.
Subnegotiation	SB	250	Indicates the start of subnegotiation of the indicated option.
Will Perform an Option	WILL	251	Indicates the device sending this code is willing to perform or continue performing the indicated option.
Won't Perform an Option	WONT	252	Indicates the device sending this code refuses to perform or continue performing the indicated option.
Do Perform an Option	DO	253	Indicates the request that the other party perform, or confirmation that you are the other party to perform, the indicated option.
Don't Perform an Option	DONT	254	Indicates the demand that the other party stop performing, or confirmation that you are no longer expecting the other party to perform, the indicated option.
Interpret As Command	IAC	255	Indicates a command follows (precedes a command).

In the case where the commands use some option, the option is sent following the command, as we will see in the next section. If we need to send a data byte with value 255 (0xFF), we must send this character twice, to avoid the receiver confusing this data with an escaped command. When the recipient receives an IAC character, it knows that the following byte is a command (except if the following byte has the value 255 (0xFF), which indicates it is a data byte), and if this command has an option, this last follows the command byte.

7.4.2 Telnet options

The NVT specification provides a way for computers with different hardware, software and data representation (for example, ASCII, EBCDIC) to understand each other. However, this minimal configuration provides only a very basic communication between devices. For those computers that could support more advanced functions or special capabilities, Telnet provides a set of options and a mechanism by which both devices can negotiate the options to use. In this way, a more advanced communication between devices is provided on demand.

One example of this is the half-duplex communication mode that the NVT has as a default. In this mode, as both devices cannot send data simultaneously, each device must send a Go Ahead command after each transmission, to signal the other party that it can transmit (similar to communications through 'walkie-talkies'). This command increments the network traffic. While this mode would be well suited for old computers, it does not take advantage of the new hardware with full-duplex capabilities. In this case, an option called Suppress Go Ahead could be negotiated, using a full-duplex communication mode, and eliminating the need to send the Go Ahead command. Table 7.3 shows some Telnet options.

7.4.3 Telnet option negotiation

A particular Telnet option can be enabled if both the client and server agree on its use. For this reason, any device may initiate the negotiation, and the other must respond, agreeing or refusing the request. Figure 7.3 shows the negotiation process and the commands used.

A particular option may be enabled, using one of the following ways:

- The WILL command is sent by the initiator (1) to indicate that it wants to use a particular option. The responder sends a DO command (2a) if it agrees on the option use, or sends a DONT command (2b) if it refuses the option use.
- The DO command is sent by the initiator (3) to request the other device use a particular option. The responder sends a WILL command (4a) if agreeing on the option use, or sends a WONT command (4b) if refusing the option use.

A DO response to a WILL command, or a WILL response to a DO command, enables the particular negotiated option.

Table 7.3

Option	Option code	Description	RFC
0	**TRANSMIT -BINARY**	Allows the use of data in 8-bit binary form.	856
1	**ECHO**	Implements several echo modes, so when the user presses a key, this character appears on the user's screen.	857
3	**SUPRESS-GO-AHEAD**	Eliminates the use of the Go Ahead command, when devices use full-duplex communication mode.	858
5	**STATUS**	Used to request the status of a Telnet option.	859
6	**TIMING-MARK**	Used to negotiate the insertion of a timing mark into the data stream, for synchronization.	860
10	**NAOCRD**	Output CR Disposition: used to negotiate how *carriage return* will be interpreted.	652
11	**NAOHTS**	Output Horizontal-Tab Stops: used to agree on *horizontal tab stop* positions for output display.	653
12	**NAOHTD**	Output Horizontal-Tab Stop Disposition: used to agree on how *horizontal tabs* will be handled and by which device.	654
13	**NAOFFD**	Output Form-Feed Disposition: used to agree on how *form feed* will be handled.	655
14	**NAOVTS**	Output Vertical-Tab Stops: used to agree on *vertical tab stop* positions for output display.	656
15	**NAOVTD**	Output Vertical-Tab Stop Disposition: used to agree on the disposition of *vertical tab stops*.	657
16	**NAOLFD**	Output Line-Feed Disposition: used to agree on how *line feed* will be handled.	658
17	**EXTEND-ASCII**	Used to negotiate the use of extended ASCII, and how it will be used.	698
24	**TERMINAL -TYPE**	Used to negotiate the use of a specific terminal type.	1091
31	**NAWS**	Used to agree on the size of the terminal window.	1073
32	**TERMINAL -SPEED**	Used to inform the terminal speed.	1079
33	**TOGGLE-FLOW -CONTROL**	Enables and disables flow control between both devices.	1372
34	**LINEMODE**	Allows the client to send data one line at a time, instead of one character at a time, improving performance.	1184
37	**AUTHENTICATION**	Used to negotiate the use of authentication.	1416
255	**EXOPL**	Extended-Options-List: used for future extension of this list.	861

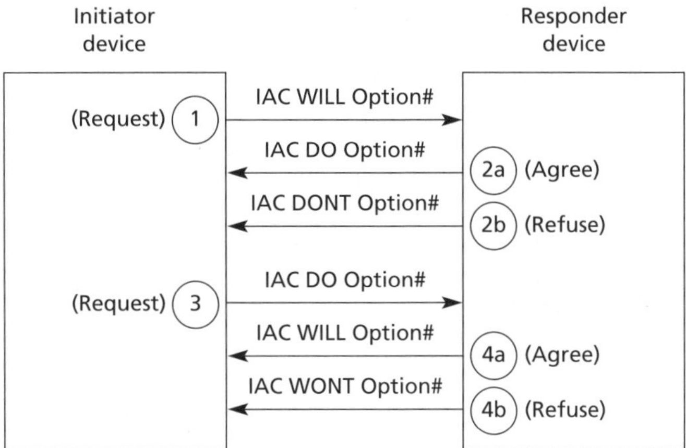

Figure 7.3 The Telnet option negotiation process.

In order to avoid potential loops in negotiation, the initiator should not send WILL or DO just to confirm an option already in use; similarly the responder should not acknowledge a request using DO or WILL if the option is already in use.

Once a particular option is activated (both devices agree on its use), it may be disabled by any device at any time, using one of the following ways:

- A device sends a WONT command indicating that it is going to stop using an option. The other device must confirm with a DONT command.
- A device sends a DONT command indicating that it wants the other device to stop using an option. The other device must confirm with a WONT command.

Even when some options enable special capabilities, they are not mandatory. For this minimal implementation, as those for embedded systems with limited resources, they could deny all requests, providing the basic communication that Telnet standard offers. For this, all WILL requests should be responded to with DONT commands, while all DO requests should be responded to with WONT commands.

Figure 7.4 shows a Telnet session negotiating the use of the 'Suppress-Go-Ahead' option. In this example, the initiator sends a DO command requesting to use the Suppress-Go-Ahead option (value 03 decimal), and the responder sends a WILL command agreeing to the request. After this option negotiation, the connection uses a full-modem communication mode.

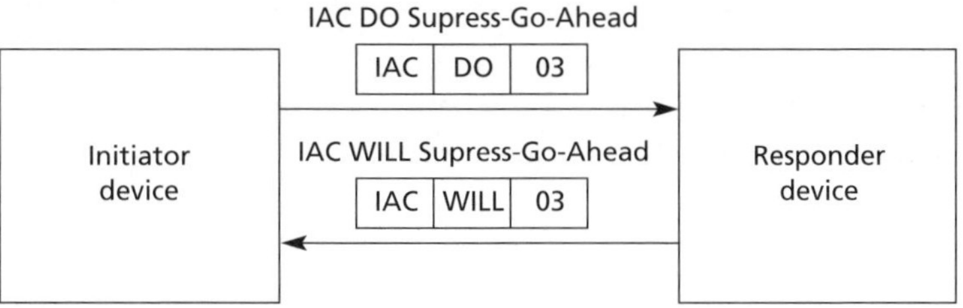

Figure 7.4 A Telnet option enable example.

7.4.4 Telnet option sub-negotiation

While some options have only two states (enabled/disabled), others need additional parameters to control how the option works. In these cases, the Sub-negotiation command is used, allowing devices to send data related to the option. This data is sent in a specific sequence, starting with an SB command, followed by the option number and the parameters required by the option, ending the sequence with an SE command. Figure 7.5 shows an example.

In this example, the initiator requests the use of the Terminal-Type option (value 24 decimal) sending a DO command, and the responder agrees on the request sending a WILL command with the Terminal-Type option. As the option was enabled and since it requires additional data to specify the type of terminal to use, the initiator sends a Sub-negotiation command with a Terminal-Type option called SEND (value 01), requesting the other device to send the type of terminal (see RFC 1091 'Telnet Terminal-Type Option'). Then, the responder sends a Sub-negotiation command with a Terminal-Type option called IS (value 00) followed by a string of the terminal type, in this case 'ANSI'. Both Sub-negotiation commands are delimited by the IAC SB and IAC SE commands.

This example shows how, even when the NVT provides a 'common terminal' that each implementation understands, an option exists to override it and to use instead a specific terminal type that the user may have, taking advantage of all the capabilities that some terminals can provide. As the server must be capable of simulating different types of terminals, it initiates the use of this option if it is prepared to do so.

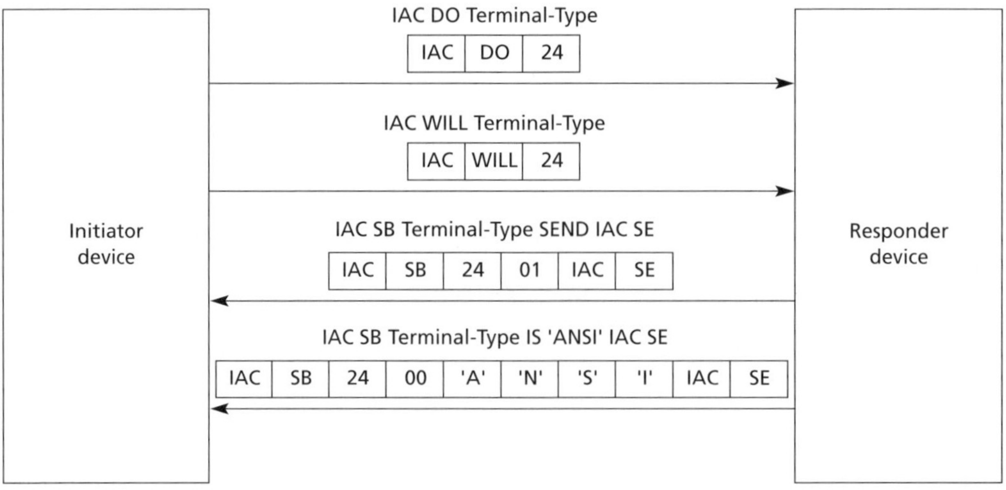

Figure 7.5 A Telnet option sub-negotiation example.

7.5 Telnet Synch function

As Telnet uses the same connection to transmit data and commands, the bytes sent by one device are received in the same order by the other device. This could generate some problems with such commands as Interrupt Process or Abort Output. For example, if the user needs to abort a process running at the remote computer, he or she could make use of the Interrupt Process command. When this command is issued, two bytes (IAC IP) are sent to the remote computer.

However, if the user has previously sent lots of data, these two bytes would be stored at the outgoing buffer, following the data waiting to be transmitted, until its turn. As a result, the process would not be interrupted immediately as the user wishes. Even if the process entered in a forever loop (and for this reason the user wanted to interrupt it), without reading the incoming data, the command would remain in the buffer and the process would never be interrupted.

In order to solve this problem, Telnet makes use of the 'Urgent' function provided by TCP to immediately transfer this command to the receiver. Telnet calls this the Synch function, which provides a way of Out-Of-Band signalling. When the Synch function is invoked, the device sends the Data Mark (DM) command which indicates the end of the 'interesting' commands (Interrupt Process, Abort Output, Are You There), and instructs the TCP layer to use its 'Urgent' function.

When this segment with the URG bit set arrives at the recipient, TCP passes the data directly to the Telnet application. Telnet process its data searching for 'interesting' commands, discarding intervening data. When the Data Mark command is encountered, it indicates that any special signal has already occurred and the recipient can return to normal processing of the data stream. In this way, the Synch function allows special commands to be immediately processed.

7.6 Summary

- Telnet was developed to allow users to access remote computers and use them as if were locally connected. In this way, the user input from the keyboard is sent to the remote computer, and the output from the computer is sent to the local terminal to be presented to the user. However, as computers and terminals were so different in hardware, software and data representation, a 'common' language was needed in order to have any terminal connected to any computer.
- The Network Virtual Terminal (NVT) defines a minimal configuration that all Telnet implementations must understand. It uses the NVT-ASCII, based on the 7-bits US ASCII character set, a half-duplex communication mode, and the CR+LF characters as the end-of-line mark. This standard provides very basic communication. However, additional capabilities are provided upon its negotiation, through the Telnet options and its negotiation

mechanism. In this way, communication can be improved according to the capabilities of each device.

- Telnet is based on a client/server model, where the client runs at the local terminal, and the server runs at the remote computer. As Telnet uses TCP as a transport protocol, the client must initiate a TCP connection establishment with the server on Port 23. Once the connection has been opened, data and commands can be transmitted over the TCP connection. A classical Telnet session starts with the server sending the user a welcome message and requesting its username and password for login purposes. After the successful authentication, the user can use the remote computer as if they were connected locally. Multiple Telnet sessions can be handled, and each TCP connection will be terminated when the Telnet session ends.
- Some Telnet commands are used to negotiate options while others are intended for the user to control the remote computer operation. 'Common command codes' are provided that all the implementations can understand. As data and commands are transmitted over the same connection, a special character 'Interpreted As Command' (IAC) precedes each command, for distinction purposes.
- For those devices supporting more advanced features, Telnet provides a set of options and a mechanism by which both ends can negotiate the option to use. In order for the option to be activated, any device can initiate its request, but both devices must agree on its use. For this negotiation process, four commands are used: WILL, DO, WONT, DONT. Once the option is activated, it may be disabled by any device at any time. Minimal implementations could deny all options requested, as options are not mandatory. While some options have two states (enabled/disabled), others require additional parameters related to the option. In such cases, the Sub-negotiation command structure is used, where the command and parameters are delimited with special SB and SE commands.
- Telnet provides a Synch function for those commands such as Interrupt Process and Abort Output, which should be used like Out-Of-Band signalling. The 'Urgent' function provided by TCP is used coupled with the Data Mark command, which indicates the end of 'interesting' commands (Interrupt Process, Abort Output, Are You There). Once this 'Urgent' segment is received by the recipient, the 'interesting' commands are immediately passed to the application. After the Data Mark has been encountered, the recipient can return to the normal processing of the data stream.

8

The File Transfer Protocol: FTP

In this chapter, we will examine the File Transfer Protocol (FTP), which is one of the oldest application protocols developed for the Internet. It is used to transfer files between two devices, even when each device has a different hardware and/or operating system. Even though users now use the HTTP and e-mail protocols to receive and send files, the FTP is still widely used as a way to transfer files over the Internet. Although it could be seen as rather complex at first, it is actually very simple in its operation and implementation. As one of the most important application protocols from the historical point of view, it is worth finding out about it.

8.1 Introduction

The FTP allows a user to transfer files between two devices over an internetwork. The word 'transfer' does not mean that the original file is removed from the sending device (moved from one device to other); instead, the file remains in the sending device, so a copy of the file is transferred to the destination device.

FTP is still one of the most used application protocols. The first FTP standard was RFC 114, published in April 1971. However, this version of FTP used the Network Control Protocol as network transport (before the existence of TCP and IP as separated layers). After that, several RFCs were published, but the first standard for modern FTP designed for the present TCP/IP, was RFC 765 'File Transfer Protocol', in June 1980. In October 1985, RFC 959 'File Transfer Protocol (FTP)' was published, including new commands and it is the present FTP base specification. Several updates exist on RFC 2228, 2640 and 2773, with security extensions, internationalization and encryption features, respectively.

8.2 FTP overview

FTP uses TCP as a Transport layer, allowing two devices to establish a connection using a reliable transmission of data. One of these devices is the client initiating the connection while the other device acts as a server listening for incoming connections on a well-known port.

Once the TCP connection has been established, the client must be authenticated for security reasons. After that, an FTP session is started using the established connection, called **FTP Control connection**. This connection is used to pass commands using the same Telnet's NVT specification to ensure communication compatibility between both devices. The client sends FTP commands and the server replies with succeed or failure messages. Some commands provide a way to manage the transfer, while others are specific to send and receive files. Once the commands have successfully configured the data transfer and a send or receive command has been issued, the data transfer begins. For this, a new TCP connection is established called **FTP Data connection**, which is used for the transmission of the file's data.

Once the data transfer is completed, the FTP Data connection is closed, while the FTP Control connection is still open to continue the FTP session, which can be closed once the user instructs it with the appropriate command. Figure 8.1 shows a typical configuration for an FTP session.

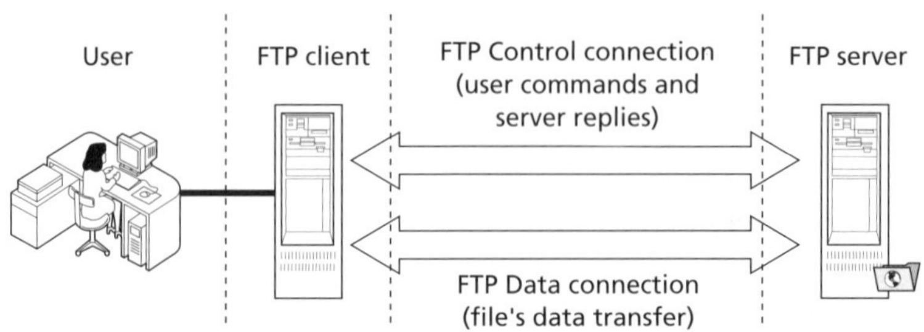

Figure 8.1 A File Transfer Protocol typical configuration.

The FTP is very flexible about how the FTP Data connection is established, in the sense that the initiator of the FTP Data connection could be the client or the server. This configuration is determined by the client using FTP commands. The client, then, can instruct the server that initiates the FTP Data connection to a specific IP address and port number. In this way, even, the IP address could be a third device (rather than the client itself) which accepts the FTP Data connection, and receives or sends the files. This configuration is called third-party file transfer or Proxy FTP.

Figure 8.2 shows this configuration. The user instructs two servers in order to transfer files between them. This could be very useful in backup operations. Note that all these connections (control and data) are flowing through the Internet, so the user could transfer files between two remote and distant servers, even when in a different location.

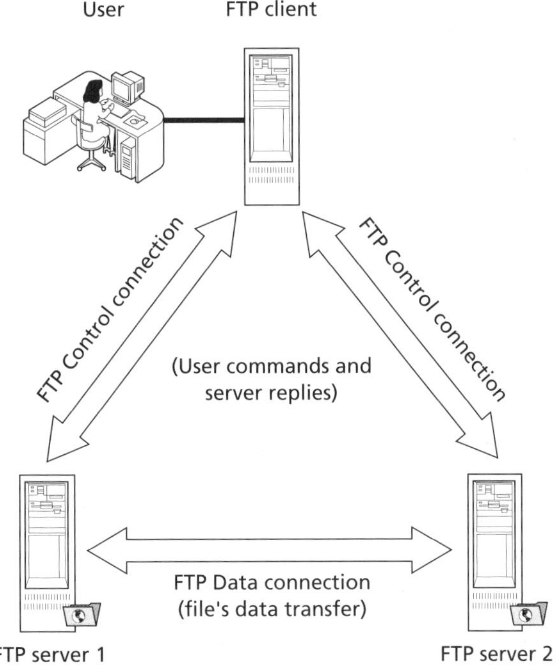

Figure 8.2 A File Transfer Protocol third-party configuration.

8.3 The FTP model

As FTP is a client/server protocol, the standard defines two software processes: the User-FTP Process and the Server-FTP Process, each running at the client and the server devices, respectively.

As we have already said, FTP uses two TCP connections as communication channels between the User-FTP Process and the Server-FTP Process:

- *FTP Control connection*: is created when the FTP session is established, and it is used by the client to send commands to the server, and by the server to send replies to the client. It is not used for file transfers, and this connection remains over the entire FTP session.
- *FTP Data connection*: is created on demand when the file transfer begins, and it is closed when the file transfer ends.

Different software processes handle each of the connections: the Protocol Interpreter (PI) manages the FTP Control connection, where commands and replies are sent and received, while the Data Transfer Process (DTP) is responsible for the actual file transfer between client and server devices. Both processes reside on the client as well as on the server. A third component, called User Interface (UI) resides only on the client, and it is this process that interacts with the user. (See Fig. 8.3.)

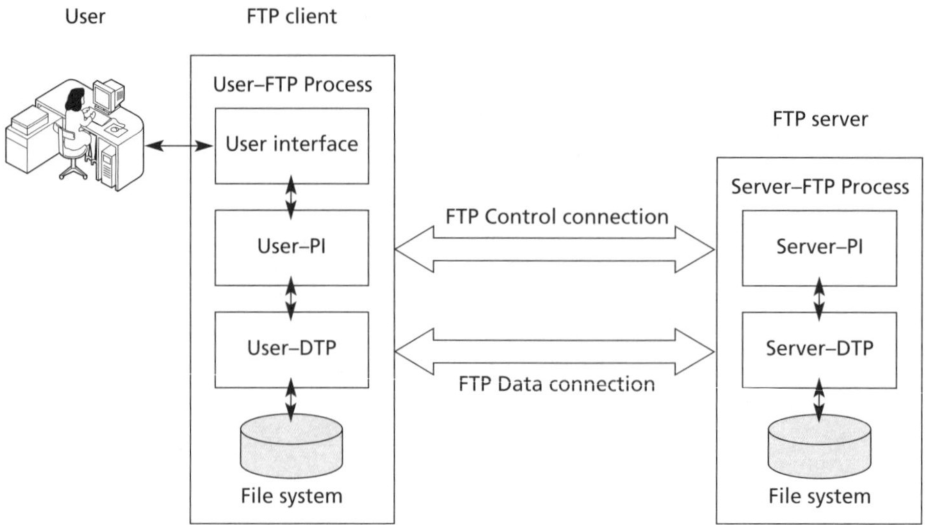

Figure 8.3 FTP client and server process components.

8.3.1 Server–FTP Process components

The Server–FTP Process has two modules running on the server device:

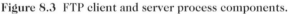

- **Server-PI (Server Protocol Interpreter)**: it is responsible for managing the FTP Control channel on the server. It listens on the well-known port 21 for incoming connection requests from clients. Once the connection is established, it receives commands from the User-PI, sending back the command replies. This module also manages the server data transfer process.
- **Server-DTP (Server Data Transfer Process)**: it is responsible for sending or receiving data to or from the User-DTP. It either establishes the TCP connection for the FTP Data channel or listens on a certain port for a connection request from the client. It interfaces with the server's local file system to read and write files.

8.3.2 User–FTP Process components

The User-FTP Process runs on the client's device, and has three software modules:

- **User-PI (User Protocol Interpreter)**: it is responsible for managing the FTP Control channel on the client. It sends the connection request to the server on port 21. Once the connection has been established, it processes the user's commands received from the User Interface, sends internal commands to the Server-PI, and receives command replies from the Server-PI. This module also manages the client data transfer process.
- **User-DTP (User Data Transfer Process)**: it is responsible for sending or receiving data to or from the Server-DTP. It either establishes the TCP connection for the FTP Data channel or listens on a certain port for a con-

nection request from the server. It interfaces with the client's local file system to read and write files.

- **User Interface**: it provides a 'friendly' FTP interface to the user with simpler 'user commands' that avoid the use of the somewhat complicated 'internal commands' used by both the User-PI and the Server-PI modules. It also presents the user with information about the command replies and the FTP session status.

8.4 FTP Control Connection

As the FTP model shows, the FTP Control Connection is established between the User-PI module on the client, and the Server-PI module on the server. Over this communication channel, the user sends commands to set up and manage the data transfer, and the server responds to these commands with replies in order for the user to know whether the commands have succeeded or failed.

The FTP Control Connection is initiated as a TCP connection request (SYN message) from the client to the server, which is listening on the well-known port 21 reserved for the control connection for the FTP protocol. Then, the 'three-way handshake' procedure is performed, and the TCP connection is established between the client and the server. Over this TCP connection, the FTP server begins the User Login procedure.

8.4.1 User Login

The User Login is the procedure performed by the server in order to authenticate FTP users. In this way, the server restricts access, allowing only authorized users to use system resources. For this, the user must send its username and password, which are validated by the server against its user database. If the username/password is valid, the server sends a positive reply and the session may start. If it is not valid, the user is requested to attempt authentication again, until a certain number of authentication failures after which the server may terminate the connection.

The User Login procedure also allows the server to customize the access rights and the available resources, depending on the authenticated user. For example, some users could have read/write access right for some files, while others could only have read access right for those resources. A particular initial 'home directory' could also be assigned to each authenticated user.

8.4.2 Anonymous FTP

Many companies and organizations allow users to freely access information, documents and even software. One example of this are the PC components manufacturers who make information and device drivers available in order for the users to update them in their systems. In these cases, the system administrator would have to set up a user's account for each person intending to use the resources available from the organization. Instead of this, a better solution consists of creating an 'anonymous' account, which everybody could use. RFC 1635 describes this technique. The username used for this is 'anonymous' and the server will request the user sends its 'email address' as a password, in order for the server to log who is accessing it.

Of course, this 'guest' user will have limited access rights to the server files, as well as some operating restrictions. Generally, guest users may only list the directory contents and retrieve files. The directories and files would also be a limited set of the authenticated users' available resources.

8.5 FTP Data Connection

Once the FTP session has been established, after a successful user authentication, commands and replies are exchanged between user and server, using the FTP Control Connection. When a file transfer or a directory list is requested by the user, the data is transferred using a separate communication channel called FTP Data Connection. This communication is based on a new TCP connection established between the User-DTP and the Server-DTP modules on the client and server respectively.

There are two ways to create this data connection: an Active Data Connection, where the server initiates a TCP connection with the client; and a Passive Data Connection, where the server executes a 'passive' action listening on a port and the client initiates a TCP connection to the server on that port. This second method exists for security concerns, as we will see later on.

8.5.1 Active Data Connections

This is the default method, and the Server-DTP module initiates the data channel by opening a TCP connection to the User-DTP module. The server uses port 20 (the well-known port for FTP-Data), while the user, by default, uses the same temporary port used for the Control Connection.

For example, suppose the User-PI uses the temporary port assigned 2309 and establishes a Control Connection to the Server-PI at port 21. Then, when data transfer is required, the Server-PI instructs the Server-DTP to initiate the Data Connection using its port 20 to the User-DTP at the same port 2309 used by the User-PI. Once the User-DTP acknowledges this connection, the data transfer could begin in either direction, depending on the user's command.

However, as having the control and data connection on the same port complicates the operation, it is strongly recommended that the user chooses a different port for its data connection. For this, the user sends the PORT command (before using the specific transfer command) specifying the port it wishes to use, for example port 2317, so the Server-DTP will initiate the data connection to the client's 2317 port instead of the 2309 as before.

Figure 8.4 shows an FTP Active Data Connection. We can see the PORT command specifying the IP address (200.112.143.3) and the port number (9, 13). This last must be interpreted as (0x09, 0x0D) in hexadecimal, thus 0x090D is the port number, which in decimal is represented as 2317. In addi-

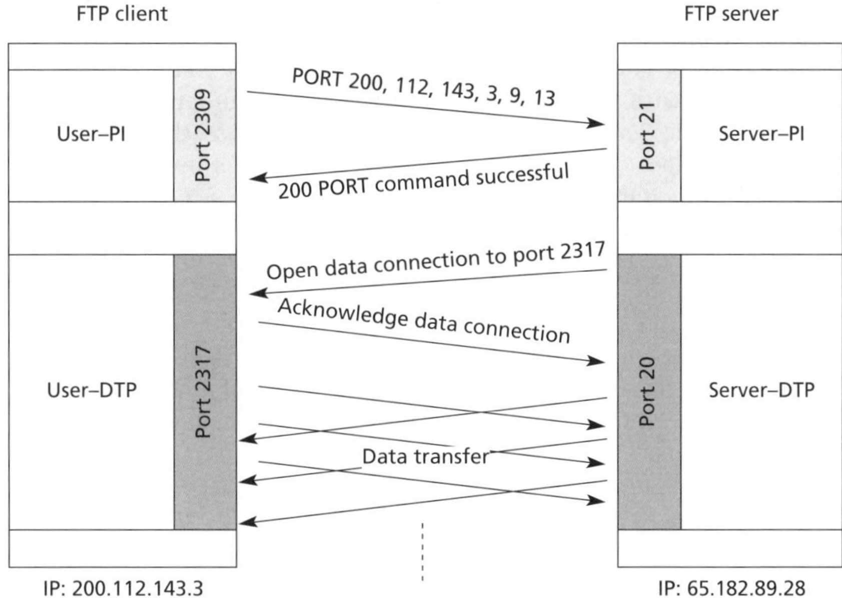

Figure 8.4 FTP Active Data Conntection.

tion, we need to take into account that the messages shown represent control and data at the application layer, so the TCP SYN and ACK messages are not really shown, but they do exist.

Actually, the PORT command allows not only the port the client will use for Data Connection to be specified, but also the IP address. In this way, the IP address and port number could be belonging to another device, allowing the user to configure a third-party configuration very easily. Therefore, the Server-DTP will open a Data Connection to a third device that is different from the client's device.

8.5.2 Passive Data Connections

In this method, the client instructs the server to be 'passive' in the data connection, meaning that the server will be listening on a certain port, while the client will initiate the TCP connection to the server on that port. For this, the client sends a PASV command to the server, which must reply with the IP address and port number that will be listening for incoming connections from the client.

As the data communication channel is created and destroyed each time transfer is needed, the server will choose a different port number each time a transfer is performed (to have enough time between the end of one connection and the beginning of the next, avoiding possible mixed segments). For this, the well-known port number 20 assigned for FTP Data is not used in the Passive Data Connections. The client, by default, uses the same temporary port number used for Control connections, but it is strongly recommended that the client chooses a different port for this Data connection.

For example, suppose the User-PI uses the temporary port assigned 1771 and establishes a Control connection to the server at port 21. Then, when data transfer is required, the User-PI sends a PASV command and the Server-PI replies with its IP address and the port number 2851. The Server-PI instructs the Server-DTP to listen on port 2851, and the User-DTP chooses a temporary port 1773 and initiates a TCP connection to the Server-DTP at port 2851, establishing the Data channel. Figure 8.5 shows an FTP Passive Data Connection.

Generally, the client's devices initiate connections rather than accept them. After all, the client/server model dictates a client-sending request to the server, and the server replying to the client. As a result, clients are suspicious of accepting incoming connections from other devices, and they usually use firewalls to protect against any class of attacks from the Internet. In these cases, the firewall would need to be configured to unblock the client port to be used for data connection, but as this port changes for each data transfer, it is necessary to unblock a range of ports, attempting to the client security. As servers are generally used to accepting incoming calls from clients, the passive connection is preferred for client's security concerns.

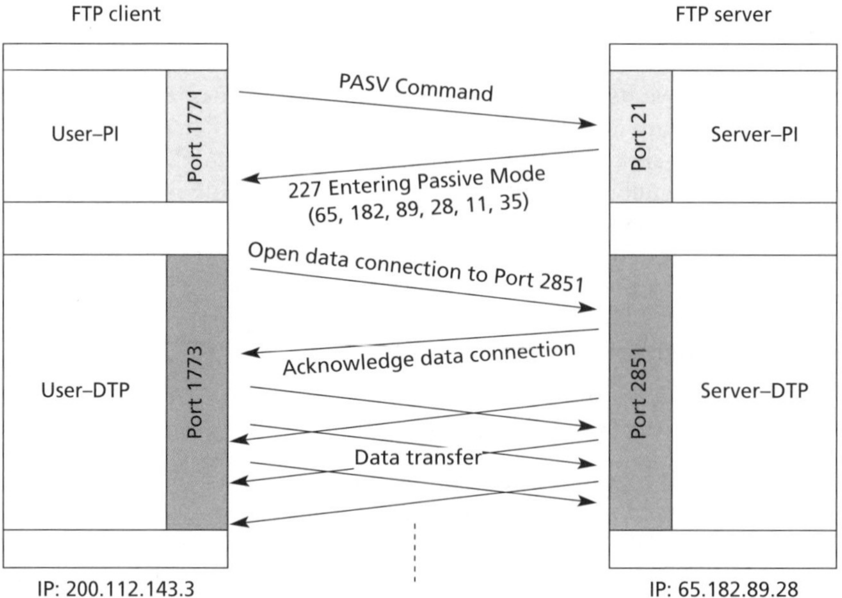

Figure 8.5 FTP Passive Data Connection.

8.6 FTP transmission modes

Once the Data Connection has been established between the user-DTP and Server-DTP, data can be transferred in either direction, depending on the User command issued (receive or send file).

There are different ways to send data over the opened data connection, defining three transmission modes: stream, block and compressed.

8.6.1 Stream mode

This is the default mode and it consists of sending data as a continuous stream of bytes, without a defined data structure. As there are no header messages that could indicate the end of the data transfer, the data connection must be closed in order for the receiving device to know when data transfer is complete. This is the simplest and most efficient transmission mode, as it does not use headers, causing overhead. As it is the default mode, all implementations must support it.

8.6.2 Block mode

In this mode, data is sent in blocks, where each block has a three-bytes header. The first byte of this header is the Descriptor. This Descriptor would indicate: a Data Block Restart (DBR, code 0x10) specifying if the sender wants to cancel the current file transfer and begin sending the file again; a Data Block Error (DBE, code 0x20), specifying the sender is suspecting the data block has errors; a data block End Of File (EOF, code 0x40), specifying the block is the last block of the file; or a data block End Of Record (EOR, code 0x80), indicating the block is the end of the record. The remaining two bytes of the header represent the length of the bytes in the block. A special algorithm is used to detect and restart interrupted transfers.

8.6.3 Compressed mode

In this mode, data is sent in blocks too, but a compression technique is used to detect repeated patterns in the data, and replace it with two bytes where the first indicates the number of times the byte is repeated, while the second represents the data to be repeated. In this way, the compressed block takes fewer bytes than the original.

8.7 FTP data representation

As different systems could have different internal data representation, FTP uses the NVT-ASCII representation used by Telnet, in order to provide a 'common language' between all system types. A problem arises with text files where the character codes are represented in different ways through different systems. For example, the NVT-ASCII is represented as 8-bit EBCDIC code in IBM mainframes, while it is represented as 7-bit (eighth bit is zero) ASCII codes in Windows. Another difference exists with the End-Of-Line character, where it is used: a LF (line feed) on Unix, a CR (carriage return) on Apple, and CR+LF (both carriage return and line feed) on Windows systems.

Then, when a text file is transferred from one system to a different one, it becomes necessary to make some conversions in order for the file to be correctly interpreted by the second system. For example, if we transfer a text file from a Unix system to an Apple system, each LF will be changed to CR+LF (NVT-ASCII acting as a 'common language') for transfer, and then changed to CR in order for the Apple system to recognize it as an End-Of-Line character. For this reason, the size of the transferred data could change from one system to other. However, as image or binary files are composed by data (not character codes) they must not be converted in any way, so they should be transferred 'as is'. As a result, in order for FTP to be able to interpret each type of file being transferred, making conversions only when needed, the correct data type must be specified.

8.7.1 FTP data types

The user can issue the TYPE command to specify the data type of the file to transfer. The standard specifies four types:

- *ASCII*: the file is a text file, using ASCII as a character set, and CR+LF as the line termination code. This is the default type, and it must be accepted by all FTP implementations.
- *EBCDIC*: the file is a text file, using EBCDIC as a character set. It is preferred in such cases where both hosts use EBCDIC for their internal character representation.
- *Image*: the data is sent as contiguous bits, packeted as 8-bit for transfer. The file has unstructured data and it is sent without any conversion. This data type is recommended to be accepted by all FTP implementations.
- *Local*: the data is transferred in logical bytes of the size specified by a second parameter: the byte size. In this way, data may be stored in logical bytes with a number of bits other than 8, allowing the destination system to store the data according to its local representation (strictly speaking, 8 bits form an 'octet', and a byte could have a different size in bits in other systems).

The ASCII and image are the most common data types. The ASCII data type is used to transfer text files, and the conversions allow the destination system to interpret this type of file correctly. The image data type is used to transfer graphics, ZIP and executable files, and it is also called binary data type.

8.7.2 FTP format control

As a text file (ASCII or EBCDIC) may be transferred to a host for different purposes, like printing, processing or simply storing the file, the receiver should know how to interpret the vertical format. In this way, the FTP standard defines an optional parameter called format control, which is used for both the ASCII and EBCDIC types, and it is used to indicate what kind of vertical control, if any, is associated with the file.

There are three options:

- *Non-print*: is the default format to be used if the parameter is omitted. Non-Print format must be accepted by all FTP implementations. The file must not contain vertical format information, and it is generally used for files transferred for processing or storage.

- *Telnet format controls*: the file contains ASCII/EBCDIC vertical format controls, like CR, LF, NL, VT, FF, which the printer will interpret appropriately.
- *Carriage controls*: the file contains ASA (FORTRAN specification) vertical format control characters. The first character of each line is not to be printed, and it should be used to determine the vertical movement of the paper, which should take place before the rest of the line is printed.

8.7.3 FTP data structures

The standard also allows specifying the file's data structure, according to the following possibilities:

- *File structure*: the file is considered as a continuous sequence of data bytes, with no internal structure. This is the default mode and it must be accepted by all FTP implementations.
- *Record structure*: the file consists of a set of sequential records, delimited by the End-Of-Record code. It must be accepted for text files (type ASCII or EBCDIC) by all FTP implementations.
- *Page structure*: the file consists of independent indexed pages.

8.8 FTP Internal commands and replies

As we have seen, the FTP Control Connection is established in order for the client and server to exchange commands and replies. These commands allow the user to manage the data transfer. 'Internal Commands' are used between the User-PI and Server-PI, while 'User Commands' are available through the User-Interface module, allowing the user to issue more 'friendly' commands. Table 8.1 shows the FTP 'internal commands'

The standard categorizes the internal commands according to the function type, distinguishing three command groups, as Table 8.1 shows in the last column:

- **Access control commands**: group of commands used for the user to login and resource access.
- **Transfer parameter commands**: group of commands used for specifying the type of Data connection; and how the data transfer will occur (data type, file structure and transmission mode).
- **FTP service commands**: group of commands used to perform file transfer operations (send and receive files), as well as support function such as rename files, create, delete and list directories, among others.

Remember that the commands are 'internal commands' used between User-PI and Server-PI modules. The user uses 'user commands' provided by the Client-Interface module, which are slightly different.

Table 8.1

CODE	Command	Description	Command group
USER	User Name	Used to identify the user of the FTP session.	**Access control**
PASS	Password	Used to send the password for authentication.	
ACCT	Account	Specifies an account for the user (in some systems)	
CWD	Change Working Directory	Allows the user to change the directory in the server directory structure.	
CDUP	Change To Parent Directory (Change Directory Up)	Used to go to the directory one level up in the server directory structure.	
SMNT	Structure Mount	Used to mount a file system.	
REIN	Reinitialize	The FTP session returns to the initial state as if the control connection is just established. The user must login again.	
QUIT	Logout	Used to terminate the FTP session and close the control connection.	
PORT	Data Port	Used to specify the port for active data connection.	**Transfer parameter**
PASV	Passive	Used to request a passive data connection.	
TYPE	Representation Type	Specifies the file data type (ASCII, EBCDIC, Image, or Local), and optionally, the format control (Non-Print, Telnet, or Carriage Control).	
STRU	File Structure	Specifies the file data structure (File, Record, or Page).	
MODE	Transfer Mode	Specifies the transmission mode (Stream, Block, or Compressed).	
RETR	Retrieve	Used to receive a file from the server.	**Service**
STOR	Store	Used to send a file to the server.	
STOU	Store Unique	Same as STOR, but instructs the server to make sure the file name is unique, avoiding file overwriting.	
APPE	Append (With Create)	Same as STOR, but if the file already exists, the data transferred is appended to this file.	
ALLO	Allocate	Used to reserve storage space to accommodate the new file to be transferred.	
REST	Restart	Used for block or compressed transfer modes, to restart file transfer at a specific server marker.	
RNFR	Rename From	Specifies the old name of a file to be renamed. Must be followed by an RNTO command.	

Table 8.1 *Continued*

CODE	Command	Description	Command group
RNTO	Rename To	Specifies the new name of a file to be renamed. Must be preceded by an RNFR command.	**Service**
ABOR	Abort	Used to abort the previous FTP service command and any associated transfer of data.	
DELE	Delete	Deletes a file on the server.	
RMD	Remove Directory	Deletes a directory on the server.	
MKD	Make Directory	Creates a directory on the server.	
PWD	Print Working Directory	Used to display the current directory where the user is, in the server's file system.	
LIST	List	Request a directory list (file names, sizes, dates, etc.) from the server (like a 'Dir' DOS command, or 'ls' UNIX command).	
NLIS	Name List	Same as LIST, but only returns the file names.	
SITE	Site Parameters	Used for site-specific functions.	
SYST	System	Request information about the server's operating system.	
STAT	Status	Request from the server a status of the current data transfer.	
HELP	Help	Request help information from the server.	
NOOP	No Operation	Used to request the server, which sends a message to verify if the control channel is still active.	

Each internal command sent by the User-PI through the control connection, is replied by the Server-PI. These replies represent an acknowledgement for the client about its command reception by the server. The reply consists of a three-digit Reply Code and a variable length Reply Text. The Reply Code allows the User-PI to process the command reply and know if the command succeeded or failed. The Reply Text is displayed for the user so that he or she has some status about the operation, in a better 'friendly' way. This text may change among different implementations.

Table 8.2 shows the FTP Server Replies, as presented in the RFC 959 in a numeric order list. The Reply Code is a three-digit code where each digit has a specific meaning. The first digit is used to indicate the success or failure of the command: in case of success, it also indicates if the command accepted is complete or is still processing; while if the command fails, it indicates if the failure is transient or permanent. Table 8.3 gives more details about the Reply Code first digit interpretation.

Table 8.2

1st digit	2nd digit	Reply Code	Reply text
Positive Preliminary Reply	Information	110	Restart marker reply.
	Connections	120	Service ready in 'nnn' minutes.
		125	Data connection already open; transfer starting.
	File System	150	File status OK; about to open data connection.
Positive Completion Reply	Syntax	200	Command OK.
		202	Command not implemented or superfluous at this site.
	Information	211	System status or system help reply.
		212	Directory status.
		213	File status.
		214	Help message.
		215	'NAME' system type.
	Connections	220	Service ready for new user.
		221	Service closing control connection.
		225	Data connection open; no transfer in progress.
		226	Closing data connection.
		227	Entering Passive Mode (h1, h2, h3, h4, p1, p2).
	Authentication and Accounting	230	User logged in, proceed.
	File System	250	Requested file action OK, completed.
		257	'PATHNAME' created.
Positive Intermediate Reply	Authentication and Accounting	331	User name OK; need password.
		332	Need account for login.
	File System	350	Requested file action pending further information.
Transient Negative Completion Reply	Connections	421	Service not available, closing control connection.
		425	Cannot open data connection.
		426	Connection closed; transfer aborted.
	File System	450	Requested file action not taken. File unavailable.
		451	Requested action aborted: local error in processing.
		452	Requested action not taken. Insufficient storage space in system.

Table 8.2 *Continued*

1st digit	2nd digit	Reply Code	Reply text
Permanent Negative Completion Reply	Syntax	500	Syntax error, command unrecognized.
		501	Syntax error in parameters or arguments.
		502	Command not implemented.
		503	Bad sequence of commands.
		504	Command not implemented for that parameter.
	Authentication and Accounting	530	Not logged in.
		532	Need account for storing files.
	File System	550	Requested action not taken. File unavailable.
		551	Requested action aborted: page type unknown.
		552	Requested file action aborted. Exceeded storage allocation.
		553	Requested action not taken. File name not allowed.

Table 8.3

Reply Code format	1st digit meaning	Description
1yz	Positive Preliminary Reply	The command has been accepted but still in progress. The user should wait for a new message before sending a new command.
2yz	Positive Completion Reply	The command has been successfully processed and completed.
3yz	Positive Intermediate Reply	The command has been accepted, but not processed yet, as the user must provide additional information.
4yz	Transient Negative Completion Reply	The command was not accepted or processed. However, the problem is temporary, so the user could try the command again.
5yz	Permanent Negative Completion Reply	The command was not accepted or processed. As the error is permanent, a new command will generate the same reply.

The second digit of the Reply Code groups the messages according its functionality. Table 8.4 shows the Reply Code second digit interpretation. The third digit of the Reply Code indicates a specific type of message within each group as defined by the second digit.

Table 8.4

Reply Code format	2nd digit meaning	Description
x0z	Syntax	Replies with syntax error, unimplemented or superfluous commands.
x1z	Information	Replies to request for information, such as status or help.
x2z	Connections	Replies referring to control or data connections.
x3z	Authentication and Accounting	Replies for the login process and accounting procedures.
x4z	Unspecified	Not defined.
x5z	File System	Replies related to the Server's file system.

8.8.1 Multiple-line text replies

The Reply Text could have more than one line of text. In this case, each line has a Reply Code and a Reply Text separated by a hyphen character (–), indicating that more lines follow, all pertaining to the same reply. The last line will have a space character between the Reply Code and the Reply Text, as single-line replies do, indicating that it is the last line of the reply.

8.9 FTP user commands

As we have already said, the User-Interface module provides a more 'friendly' set of commands for the user, facilitating the FTP User operations. The commands take the form of 'natural' commands, rather than the four-letter internal commands used by the User-PI module. In addition, one user command may represent more than one internal command, releasing the user about certain operation details.

The FTP User commands may vary between different implementations. Figure 8.6 shows the User commands provided by the Windows FTP implementation (run the ftp.exe program from the system prompt, and use '?' or 'help' to display the set of user commands). Also, 'help dir' will provide additional information about the 'dir' user command). Note that some commands have different names but serve for the same purpose, as the case of ? and help, send and put, recv and get, and bye and quit.

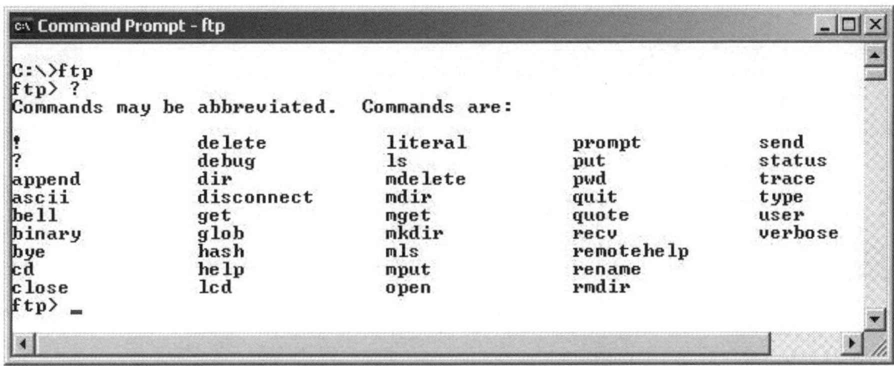

Figure 8.6 Windows FTP user commands.

8.9.1 FTP session example

Table 8.5 shows an FTP session example, using the Windows FTP client program. Typically, the user executes the FTP client program, which presents a prompt for the user to enter its commands. The user commands are interpreted by the FTP client program and the corresponding internal commands are sent to the server. The server is listening on port 21, waiting for connections.

The lines in bold are the actual messages exchanged over the FTP Control Connection (internal commands and replies). The rest are user commands, user prompts and, in italics, actions taken by the server to manage the FTP Data Connection.

8.10 FTP minimum implementation

The following minimum implementation is required for all servers:

- Type: ASCII Non-print
- Mode: Stream
- Structure: File, Record
- Commands: USER, QUIT, PORT, TYPE, MODE, STRU, RETR, STOR, NOOP.

The default values for transfer parameters are:

- Type: ASCII Non-print
- Mode: Stream
- Structure: File

All hosts must accept the above as the standard defaults.

Table 8.5

Event	Type	Actions, commands and messages
Server	action	*Waiting for control connection on port 21*
User	action	*Execute the FTP client program*
Client	display	ftp> (prompt for user commands)
User	enter	Open ftp.3com.com
Client	action	*Initiates an FTP Control Connection*
Server	reply	**220 saswh142 FTP server (version wu-2.6.2(1)) ready**
Client	prompt	User (ftp.3com.com: (none)):
User	enter	Anonymous
Client	send	**USER anonymous**
Server	reply	**331 Guest login ok, send your complete e-mail address as password**
Client	prompt	Password:
User	enter	johnsmith@mail.com
Client	send	**PASS johnsmith@mail.com**
Server	reply	**230 Guest login ok, access restrictions apply**
User	enter	Dir
Client	send	**PORT 200,136,112,58,13,16**
Server	reply	**200 PORT command successful**
Client	send	**LIST**
Server	action	*Initiates for data connection on port 3344*
Server	reply	**150 Opening ASCII mode data connection for /bin/ls**
Server	action	*Data connection transfers Directory information*
Server	action	*Close FTP Data Connection*
Server	reply	**226 Transfer complete**
Client	display	ftp: 491 bytes received in 0.00 seconds 491000.00KB/s
User	enter	get README
Client	send	**PORT 200,136,112,58,13,22**
Server	reply	**200 PORT command successful**
Client	send	**RETR README**
Server	action	*Initiates for data connection on port 3350*
Server	reply	**150 Opening ASCII mode data connection for README (546 bytes)**
Server	action	*Data connection transfers README file*
Server	action	*Close FTP Data Connection*
Server	reply	**226 Transfer complete**
Client	display	ftp: 553 bytes received in 0.01 seconds 55.30KB/s
User	enter	Close
Client	send	**QUIT**
Server	reply	**221-You have transferred 553 bytes in 1 files** **221-Total traffic for this session was 1604 bytes in 2 transfers** **221-Thank you for using the FTP service on saswh142** **221 Goodbye**
User	enter	quit (leave the FTP client program)

8.11 Summary

- The File Transfer Protocol allows us to transfer a copy of a file from one host to other, over an inter-network. FTP uses a client/server model, where two connections are used between both devices: the FTP Control Connection, used by the client to send commands and by the server to send command replies to the client; and the FTP Data Connection, used to perform the actual file transfers.
- The server's device has the Server-FTP process, which is composed of two modules: the Server-PI responsible for receiving commands from the client and sending the command replies; and the Server-DTP responsible for sending or receiving the file's data over the data connection. The client has the Client-FTP process, which is composed of three modules: the User-PI responsible for sending commands to and receiving replies from the server, the User-DTP responsible for sending or receiving the file's data over the data connection, and the client's User Interface, which interacts with the user.
- Once the FTP Control Connection has been established, the user must be authenticated in order to use the system resources. This process is known as User Login, and it is also used as a way to assign access rights according to the reported user. If the authentication fails after a certain number of times, the server can terminate the connection. Some special user accounts exist, called 'anonymous', which allow anybody to have minimal access (such as list the directory contents and retrieve some files from the system). In this case, the user must use their e-mail address as the required password. Instead, the server validates this password; it uses it to log the service access.
- There are two ways to initiate the FTP Data Connection: an Active Data Connection, where the server sends a TCP connection request and the client accepts it; and a Passive Data Connection where the client initiates the TCP connection and the server accepts it. This last is preferred by security concerns, because the clients are usually suspicious when they accept TCP connections.
- Three transmission modes define the way the data is sent over the FTP Data Connection: stream mode, where the data is sent as a stream of bytes; block mode, where data is sent as blocks with a three-byte header; and compressed mode, where data is sent in blocks but a compression technique is used.
- As data takes different internal representation among different systems, the protocol needs to make some conversion on certain types of file. For this, the standard defines four FTP data types: ASCII, EBCDIC, Image and Local. The protocol must know the file's data type in order to treat the file transfer in the correct way. In addition, as text files (ASCII and EBCDIC) may be transferred for different purposes, an optional parameter called FTP Format Control is used to define the kind of vertical control. The three options are: Non-Print, Telnet Format Controls and Carriage Controls. Finally, the file's data structure may be File Structure, Record Structure or Page Structure.

- The FTP Control Connection is used by the client to send commands, and by the server to reply the received commands. These 'internal' commands used by the client are categorized under three command groups: Access Control commands, Transfer Parameters commands and FTP Services commands. The server replies are formed by the Code Reply and the Text Reply. The Code Reply consists of a three-digit code, where each digit gives specific information about the reply. A multi-text line response is also possible, using the hyphen character to indicate that the line is not the last one of the reply.
- The User Interface interacts with the user and presents a 'friendly' set of 'user' commands. Each command the user enters is translated to the 'internal' command used by the User-PI module to send to the server. In addition, some 'user' commands may be implemented by two or more 'internal' commands, releasing the user from some operation details. The FTP user commands may differ among different implementations.

9

The e-mail protocols: SMTP and POP3

This is one of the most important chapters about application protocols because the electronic mail system not only is one of the most used application protocols of the Internet, but has also changed the way we communicate with others. E-mail has greatly contributed to the world globalization process, lowering cost and allowing people to communicate with others, previously almost impossible to talk to. (Have you ever written a letter to a book's author, asking some question? Today everyone has the chance to do it with e-mail. Have you perhaps consulted an engineer from an important computer software company?). We will start our e-mail tour by providing an electronic mail system overview, looking at its basic components that enable the overall work of this wonderful system.

9.1 An electronic mail system introduction

Since the beginning, one of the basic human needs was communication. Through first verbal and then written means, people communicated among themselves. Several systems were developed over the years in order for distant people to contact each other. The telegraph, telephone and fax systems contributed to this communication development process. However, before that, a mail postal service was created, covering ever larger areas as enabled by advances in transportation. The mail postal service is widely used today, allowing people to send and receive written messages to and from almost anyone in the world.

With the development of inter-networking, a new opportunity to improve the delivery of messages appeared, replacing the physical transportation of messages by the mail postal service with the electronic transfer of messages through the inter-network. This new idea was called electronic mail (e-mail). Even before the inter-network appeared, old mainframes with lots of users accessing from connected terminals already had some sort of electronic mail system which allowed users to communicate to each other sending written messages. However, these had limitations when it came to transmitting messages between different, distant and isolated mainframes located in different organizations.

When TCP/IP was running over an inter-network, such electronic mail systems could transfer messages to any user connected to this inter-network, using the underlying Internet technology. In order for different systems to understand a 'common message system', a new protocol was needed.

Several attempts existed to create an electronic mail system, but the first precursor of today's e-mail was RFC 772, called 'Mail Transfer Protocol', published in 1980, which used principles from Telnet and FTP. This document was revised in 1981 by RFC 780. In 1981, RFC 788, called 'Simple Mail Transfer Protocol' (SMTP), was published, and in August 1982, RFC 821 revised the SMTP, becoming the standard for the next 20 years. RFC 822 was published at the same time, defining the format of Internet messages.

9.1.1 The TCP/IP electronic mail system overview

The TCP/IP electronic mail (e-mail) system is composed of several components: the e-mail addressing scheme, the standard message format and protocols to both deliver messages and access the mailboxes where delivered messages are stored.

The process of sending a message from one user to another begins with message composition. The message must conform to the standard message format for the e-mail system. Each message consists of a header and a body. The header contains the source and recipient addresses, as well as information about the message contents (the Subject) and how the message must be delivered and processed. The body contains the actual information to be communicated. Making an analogy with the mail postal system, this step corresponds to writing a letter and putting it inside an envelope to send it to its destination.

When the message is ready, it is submitted to be delivered. The SMTP is in charge of delivering the message to the correct destination. Then, the message is sent from the user to the local SMTP system for delivery. This step corresponds to dropping the envelope into a mailbox at the local post office.

Once the message is in the sender's local SMTP system, it must be transmitted to the recipient's local SMTP system. Following the analogy, this is like the transportation of the envelope through the mail postal system using trucks and perhaps aeroplanes, to the recipient's local post office. When the message is received by the recipient's SMTP system, it is processed and placed in the user's mailbox. This corresponds to the recipient's local post office receiving the mail and, after classifying it, putting it into the destination post office box.

The user usually accesses their mailbox at their local SMTP system to retrieve any pending message for them. In this case, the most common used protocol is the Post Office Protocol version 3 (POP3), which is used for mail access and retrieval. Following the analogy, this corresponds to the final delivery from the local post office to the user's home.

9.1.2 The TCP/IP electronic mail system model

The main objective of the electronic mail system is to allow a user to send a message to one or more recipients, using a TCP/IP inter-network. This application differs from others such as Telnet and FTP in which the user interacts with a server that is always connected to the inter-network (user-to-server application). Then, the user can connect to the inter-network, establish a session, use the server's services, and then disconnect from the inter-network.

However, the electronic mail system application would require the parties (the sender and one or more recipients) to be connected at the same time; otherwise, the message could not be delivered (user-to-user application). For this, the users should always be connected to the inter-network, or at least they should be connected at the same time. As this requirement is totally impractical, the electronic mail system model had to be designed to allow a user to send and receive messages, even when the communicating parties were not connected at the same time. This is accomplished by the SMTP servers, which store the received message in a 'mailbox', allowing the user to access and retrieve the message later. In this way, the SMTP servers simulate a 'user postal mailbox'. Of course, the sender must be connected to the inter-network to send the message, but the message composition may be made when it is disconnected. Figure 9.1 shows the electronic mail system model.

As the e-mail model shows, the user sending the message uses a sender's host where the message is composed using an appropriate message editor. When the message is ready to be sent, the sender's host is connected to the Internet, and the SMTP client running at the sender's host establishes a session with the SMTP server running at the sender's local SMTP server. Then, the message is submitted to be delivered, and the user may disconnect their host from the Internet. After that, the sender's local SMTP server will connect to the recipient's local SMTP server to transfer the message. This will receive

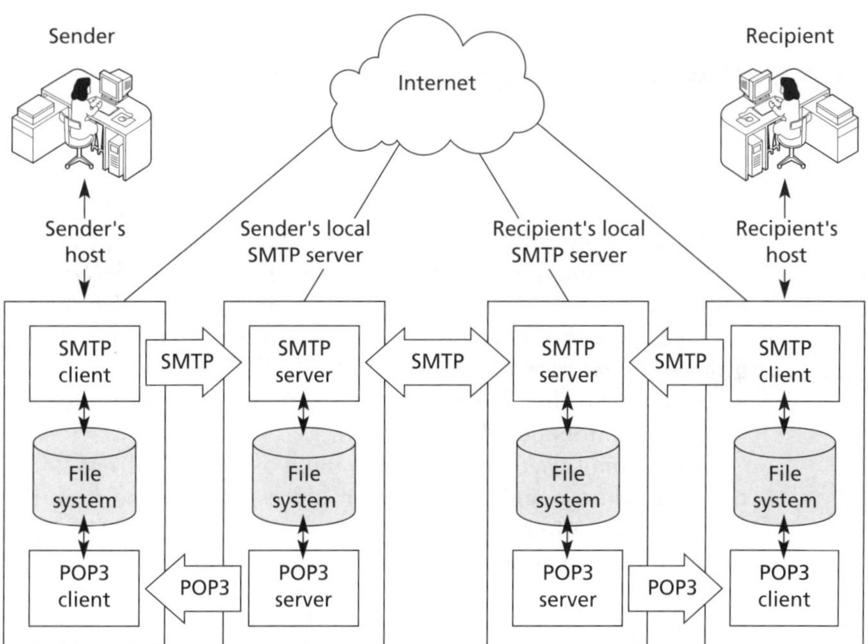

Figure 9.1 The electronic mail system model.

the message and will store it on its file system, in the corresponding user's mailbox. All this message delivery is performed using the SMTP protocol.

In this way, the recipient need not be connected to the Internet at the moment the message is delivered, because the recipient's local SMTP server will receive the message on their behalf. Later on, when the recipient users connect to the Internet, they can access the message using the POP3 protocol that allows the access to its mailbox (inbox), and retrieve the stored messages.

We may summarize the whole e-mail delivery process, from the sender to the recipient, in three steps:

- The user submits the message to the sender's local SMTP server, using the SMTP protocol.
- The sender's local SMTP server transmits the message to the recipient's local SMTP server using the SMTP protocol.
- The recipient accesses their mailbox on the recipient's local SMTP server, and retrieves the message using the POP3 protocol.

As we see, the SMTP protocol performs the major part of the tasks of the whole message delivery from the sender to the recipient.

Generally, users use e-mail client programs such as Microsoft Outlook or Eudora Mail, which already have the editor, SMTP client and POP3 client integrated, as well as other tools, to manage the sent and received messages. Another protocol also exists, called Internet Message Access Protocol (IMAP), which allows clients to access and retrieve their mail messages, like POP3 does, but with some additional benefits. However, as POP3 is widely adopted (at the time of writing), we will discuss this last.

9.2 The TCP/IP electronic mail addresses

As we have seen in the last section, in order for users to send and receive e-mail messages, two protocols are needed: the SMTP protocol, which provides the message delivery, and the POP3 (or IMAP), which provides the user's mailbox access and message retrieve. But these two protocols are not the only components needed in the TCP/IP electronic mail system. It is also necessary to provide some addressing scheme in order for the recipient to be reached. That is, when the sender composes the message, he or she needs to provide the address of the intended message recipient. This address must be in such a form that the SMTP knows where and how to deliver the message to reach the intended destination.

As an e-mail user can access its mailbox from different hosts, the conventional IP address and port number addressing scheme from these hosts can not be used. Otherwise, each time the user accesses from a different host (with a different IP address), the sender should know the recipient's new IP address. However, as the recipient's local SMTP server has a mailbox for each user, where received messages are stored, and this mailbox resides at the SMTP server which is permanently connected to the Internet through a fixed

IP address, the user's mailbox could be used as a way of addressing the user in the Internet. In this way, the user's e-mail address would consist of the IP address of the user's SMTP local server, and the username the user uses in this server to access their mailbox.

Then, the e-mail address has the following syntax:

<username>@<domain-name>

which must be interpreted as 'the user "username" at the SMTP server in the "domain-name" address'. The <domain-name> is a name specification as used by the Domain Name System (DNS) which resolves the <domain-name> into the SMTP server IP address, using a special mail exchange (MX) record. That is, when the <domain-name> needs to be resolved, the DNS server replies with the authoritative server for this domain. Once this last is queried, it finds the MX record for this domain, and replies back with the SMTP server that must be used for this domain. Also, in the additional section, the query response provides the IP address of the mail server (see Chapter 11 for information about the DNS and its protocol).

For example, if the sender sends a message to jsmith@mycompany.com, the sender's local SMTP server must resolve the domain name mycompany.com into the corresponding IP address pertaining to the recipient's local SMTP server. For this, a query is sent to the local DNS server, which replies with the authoritative server such as server.myhosting.com. The latter then replies with the name of the SMTP server, such as mail.myhosting.com, and with the IP address, such as 200.112.136.82, of this SMTP server, in the additional section of the query reply. Then, the sender's local SMTP server establishes a connection to this IP address at port 25 (the well-known port for the SMTP), and it initiates an SMTP session to send the message.

Although the TCP/IP e-mail system is the most widely used, it is not unique. But even when other electronic mail systems are not compatible with the Internet e-mail system, certain devices called gateways can be used to convert from one system to another, making it possible for users from different electronic mail systems to communicate. In these cases, the address notations used to reach users from other networks with different electronic mail systems are usually quite rare.

9.3 The Simple Mail Transfer Protocol (SMTP)

As we have already seen, the SMTP is responsible for the major part of the message delivery from the user to the recipient. Thus, its work is fundamental to the functioning of the entire system. As we saw in the introduction, the predecessor of the SMTP was the Mail Transfer Protocol (MTP), first defined in RFC 772 in September 1980, and updated in RFC 780 in May 1981. This protocol was largely based on Telnet and FTP. In fact, MTP was based on FTP but used to transfer e-mails instead of files.

As the e-mail grew in its use, the necessity of a specific protocol for e-mail delivery was fundamental. Then, RFC 788 defined the 'Simple Mail Transfer

Protocol' (SMTP), published in November 1981. This new protocol was specifically designed for the transport of e-mails. In August 1982, RFC 821 was published with a revised standard of the SMTP protocol.

Many years after RFC 821 was published, in February 1993, RFC 1425 'SMTP Service Extensions' was published, extending new capabilities to the SMTP. Sometimes, it is referred to as Extended SMTP. These extensions were revised and updated with RFC 1651 in July 1994 and RFC 1869 in November 1995. In April 2001, the RFC 2821 was published, including the extensions, and has become the current base standard for the SMTP protocol.

The SMTP protocol is used in the first two of the three steps needed for the e-mail delivery. This protocol covers the communication between the sender's host and the sender's local SMTP server (Step 1), and between the sender's local SMTP server and the recipient's local SMTP server (Step 2).

9.3.1 The SMTP client/server communication model

The SMTP communication model is based on the TCP transport protocol. As a client/server model, the communication begins with the TCP connection establishment between a client and a server. The roles of the client or the server will be covered by different hosts, depending on the step of the SMTP delivery process. That is:

- Step 1: Message submitted from the sender to the sender's local SMTP server.
  Client: *Sender's host*
  Server: *Sender's local SMTP server*
- Step 2: Message delivered from the sender's local SMTP server to the recipient's local SMTP server.
  Client: *Sender's local SMTP server*
  Server: *Recipient's local SMTP server*

The server is always listening on port 25 (the well-known port for the SMTP), while the client uses a temporary port. As we see, the Sender's local SMTP server has two different roles in the communication process: as a server in Step 1, and as a client in Step 2. See Figure 9.2 for details. We will refer to the client as the SMTP Sender, and the server as the SMTP Receiver, to clarify who is sending and who is receiving the message.

9.3.1.1 Communication relaying and direct delivery

If we read RFC 821, we see some SMTP commands such as:

RCPT TO: <forward-path> <CRLF> (used as the message destination)

and

MAIL FROM: <reverse-path> <CRLF> (used as the message source)

As the document mentions, the forward-path is more than just a mailbox. It provides a source routing list of hosts and destination mailbox. The first host in the forward-path is the host receiving the command. Also, the reverse-path is a reverse-source routing list of hosts and the source mailbox, and the first host in the reverse-path is the host sending the command. In other

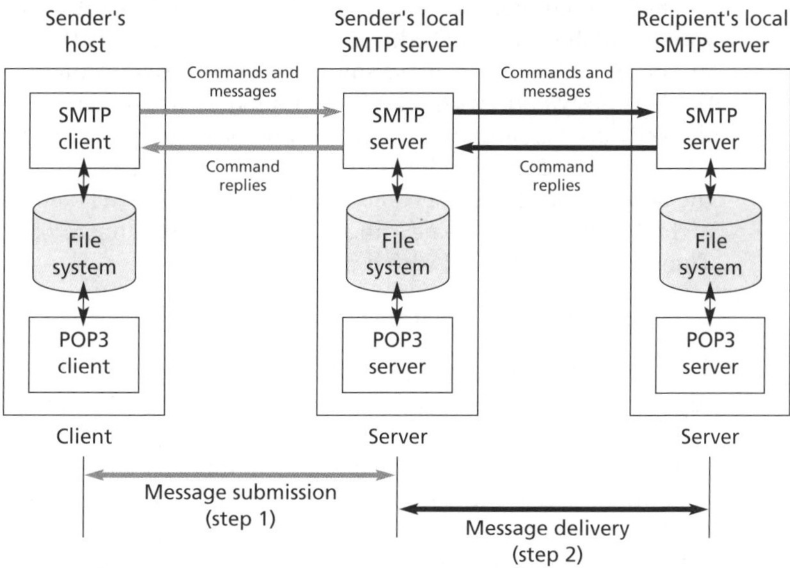

Figure 9.2 The SMTP client/server communication model.

words, the forward-path is used to provide the sequence of SMTP servers that the message must follow to reach the destination.

The reverse-path is the route to follow to reach the source, to report errors in case the delivery fails. This process is called **relaying**, and it was used at the time when the Domain Name System did not exist. In this way, the message was transmitted through intermediate SMTP servers, in a similar way to how IP routing works using routers.

With the increasing use of the DNS, the relaying communication was replaced by **direct delivery**. Using the process described in section 9.2, the SMTP Sender gets the IP address of the SMTP Receiver, and establishes communication directly with the server where the recipient's mailbox resides. As a result, this communication method is faster and more efficient and reliable.

Even when SMTP still supports relaying, it is little used as it delays message delivery and it is inefficient. Also, for security reasons and to avoid the use of the server for spam (unsolicited sending of e-mails), some SMTP servers do not allow the use of relay.

9.3.2 The SMTP session establishment and termination

The delivery of electronic mail uses the SMTP protocol to exchange e-mail messages between SMTP servers. The SMTP servers are responsible for the delivery of the submitted messages, as well as the reception of messages for local recipients. In some cases, they also receive messages for relaying to other servers. The overall process is performed over an SMTP session.

Once the TCP connection is open, the SMTP session begins. The SMTP Sender sends commands to the SMTP Receiver, which replies with SMTP Reply Codes. The messages are sent using a mail transaction process.

The TCP connection is initiated by the SMTP Sender as a normal 'three-way handshaking' procedure. Then, once the SMTP Server accepts the incoming connection, it sends the 'service ready' message consisting of the 220 reply code with a reply text such as the domain name of the server, the software version, date and time, and perhaps other information.

When the SMTP Sender, acting as a client, receives this message, it starts the session using the SMTP commands. The first SMTP command to be used is the HELO <domain-name>, including the domain name of the SMTP Sender. The server will respond with a message like this

250 smtp.myhosting.com at your service!

This initial command and its reply are for the sender and the receiver to identify each other. It also serves to confirm that both sender and receiver are in the initial state, and there is no transaction in progress. After this, the mail transaction may begin, using specific commands. Once all the messages have been transmitted, the session may be terminated. The SMTP Sender sends the QUIT command, and the SMTP Receiver responds with the 221 Reply Code. After that, the TCP connection is terminated. See Figure 9.3 for details.

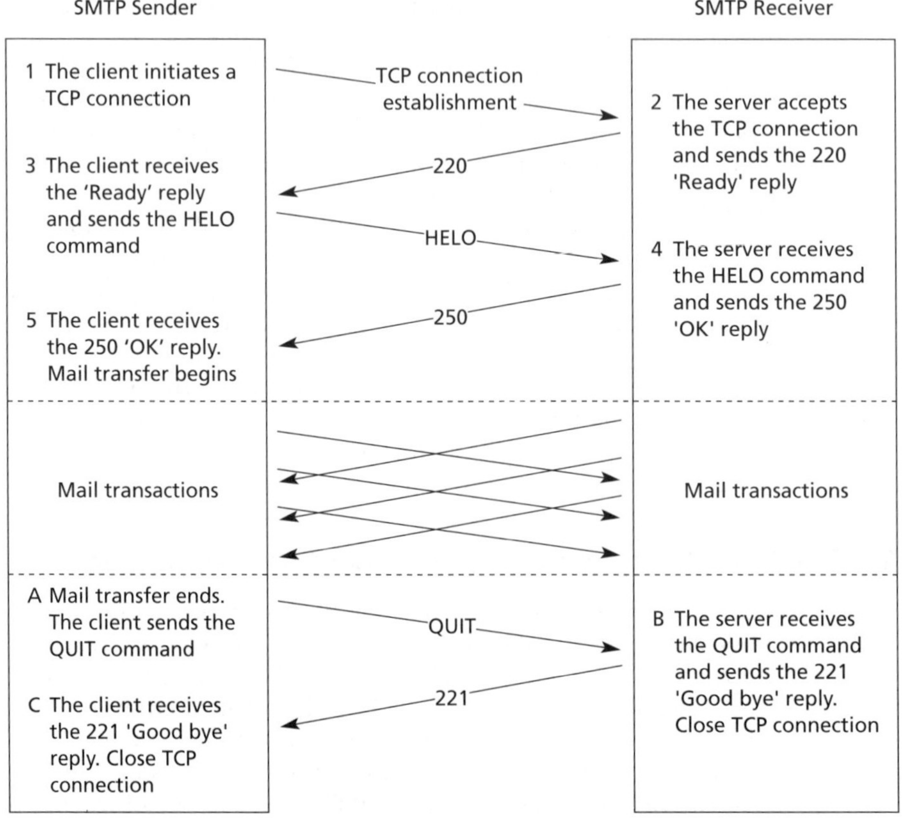

Figure 9.3 SMTP session establishment and termination.

9.3.3 The SMTP mail transaction process

The mail transaction process consists of three steps:

1 The SMTP Sender *initiates* the mail transaction using the MAIL command, providing the e-mail address of the sender, in order to *identify the sender*.
2 The SMTP Sender uses the RCPT command, providing the e-mail address of the recipient, in order to *identify the recipient*.
3 The SMTP Sender uses the DATA command to begin the *mail transfer*. The receiver treats the data that follows the command as mail data. The transfer ends with the special sequence of <CRLF>.<CRLF> (a period between two end of line terminations). In order to provide transparency, if a line must begin with a period, the SMTP Sender adds another period at the beginning of the line. When the SMTP Receiver checks the line, if it starts with a single period it is the end of the line; if the line starts with two periods, the first one is deleted.

Even though the sender and recipient e-mail addresses are given in Steps 1 and 2, they are also present in the message itself transferred in Step 3. That is, going back to the analogy with the mail postal service, the first two steps provide the information on the envelope, while step 3 provides the letter contents. Then, with the 'origin' and 'destination' addresses on the envelope, the SMTP servers can handle the message in the correct way.

The following is an SMTP mail transaction example:

Sender:	**MAIL FROM: <jsmith@mysite.com>**
Receiver:	*250 <jsmith@mysite.com>... Sender Ok*
Sender:	**RCPT TO: <lparker@yoursite.com>**
Receiver:	*250 <lparker@yoursite.com>... Recipient Ok*
Sender:	**DATA**
Receiver:	*354 Enter mail, end with "." on a line by itself*
Sender:	**From: John Smith <jsmith@mysite.com>** **To: Luis Parker <lparker@yoursite.com>** **Subject: Call me** **Date: Tue, 1 Feb 2005 18:30:26 –0300** **Hi Luis:** **I need to talk to you... Please, call me.** **John.** **.**
Receiver:	*250 199 bytes received in 00:00:01; Message accepted for delivery*

9.3.4 The SMTP extensions

There are many SMTP extensions that add functionality to the basic SMTP standard. These extensions were defined in successive RFC documents, and are listed in Table 9.1.

Table 9.1

Keyword	Extension	Description	RFC
8BITMIME	Use 8-bit data	Support for 8-bit in MIME.	1652
CHECKPOINT	Checkpoint/Restart	Allows an interrupted SMTP transaction to be able to be restarted at a later time, without having to repeat all the commands and message content prior to the interruption.	1845
SIZE	Message Size declaration	Provides information about the message's size before transmitting it, so the SMTP server can decide whether to receive it or not.	1870
DSN	Delivery Status Notification	The SMTP Receiver may notify the sender if a problem occurs in delivering the message.	1891
ENHANCED STATUSCODES	Enhanced Status Codes	Extends extra codes to the reply code, providing more information.	2034
AUTH	Authentication	Implements an enhanced security.	2554
PIPELINING	Command Pipelining	Multiple commands may be transmitted at once, rather than sending a command and waiting for its response before sending the next.	2920
STARTTLS	Start TLS	Allows the use of Transport Layer Security to protect communications.	3207
NO-SOLICITING	No Soliciting	Provides to electronic mail the equivalent to the 'No-Soliciting' sign in the real world (anti-spam).	3865
MTRK	Message Tracking	The mail's client may mark a message for future tracking.	3885

9.3.4.1 Connection establishment using SMTP extensions

As not all SMTP servers may support all the extensions, in order to use the available extensions for the particular SMTP server, the client (SMTP Sender) must request the list of supported SMTP extensions. For this, the client initiates the session with the command EHLO instead the conventional HELO. Then, the server will respond with a list of the supported SMTP Extensions.

The following is an example of a connection establishment using SMTP extensions:

Sender:	**<establish a TCP connection...>**
Receiver:	*220 smtp.myhosting.com ready.*
Sender:	**EHLO mail.mysite.com**
Receiver:	*250-smtp.myhosting.com at your service!* *250-SIZE* *250-ENHANCEDSTATUSCODES* *250-DSN* *250-PIPELINING* *250-CHECKPOINT* *250 STARTTLS*

The SMTP Sender, then, can start using any of these SMTP extensions supported by the SMTP Receiver.

9.3.5 SMTP commands

The SMTP commands sent from the SMTP Sender to the SMTP Receiver are used in plain text using the Telnet NVT-ASCII specification, with the CR+LF as the end of line. Some commands require a parameter, which is sent after the command with a space character between them.

Table 9.2 shows the SMTP Commands, as described in RFC 2821. Some extensions add new commands, like the AUTH command from the Authentication extension; while others define new parameters for the existing commands, like the SIZE parameter which can be used with the MAIL command to inform the receiver the size of the message to be sent.

Table 9.2

Command	CODE	Parameter	Description
Hello	HELO	Sender's domain name	Initiates an SMTP session.
Extended Hello	EHLO	Sender's domain name	Initiates an extended SMTP session.
Mail Transaction	MAIL	'FROM:' and the message's originator (and possibly other parameters)	Initiates a mail transaction.
Recipient	RCPT	'TO:' and the message's recipient (and possibly other parameters)	Specifies the recipient mailbox.
Mail Data	DATA	None	Used to inform that the sender is ready to transmit the mail message.
Reset	RSET	None	Aborts a mail transaction.
Verify	VRFY	E-mail address of the mailbox to be verified	Used to validate an e-mail address on the receiver.
Expand	EXPN	E-mail address of a mailing list	Used to validate and get a list of a mailing list.
Help	HELP	Command name (optional)	Used to get help information.
No Operation	NOOP	None	Used to test if the communication remains alive.
Quit	QUIT	None	Terminates the SMTP session.

9.3.6 SMTP replies

Each command the SMTP Sender sends is replied by the SMTP Receiver. In this way, the sender has an acknowledgement about the reception of its command, as well as knowing if the command was successful or failed. Some replies also provide details about the status of the transaction.

The SMTP Receiver replies consist of a Reply Code and a Reply Text. The Reply Code is formed by a three-digit code, where each digit provides specific information. The Reply Text is information for human intervention, and it is not processed by the server programs. These Reply Texts may also change between different implementations.

Table 9.3 shows some of the most common SMTP Reply Codes. The first digit is used to indicate the success or failure of the command; in the case of success, it also indicates if the accepted command is completed or is still processing; while if the command has failed, it indicates if the failure is transient or permanent. The second digit of the Reply Code groups the messages according to their functionality. The third digit of the Reply Code indicates a specific type of message within each group as defined by the second digit. This scheme of Reply Codes follows an equivalent structure to those defined for FTP.

9.3.6.1 Multiple-line text replies

The Reply Text could have more than one line of text. In this case, each line has a Reply Code and a Reply Text separated by a hyphen character (–), indicating that more lines follow, all pertaining to the same reply. The last line will have a space character between the Reply Code and the Reply Text, as single-line replies do, indicating that it is the last line of the reply.

9.3.7 An example of a typical SMTP session

The following is a typical example of a complete session using SMTP for an e-mail delivery:

```
Sender:     <establish a TCP connection...>
Receiver:   220 smtp.myhosting.com ready.
Sender:     HELO mail.mysite.com
Receiver:   250 smtp.myhosting.com at your service!
Sender:     MAIL FROM: <jsmith@mysite.com>
Receiver:   250 <jsmith@mysite.com>... Sender Ok
Sender:     RCPT TO: <lparker@yoursite.com>
Receiver:   250 <lparker@yoursite.com>... Recipient Ok
Sender:     DATA
Receiver:   354 Enter mail, end with "." on a line by itself
Sender:     From: John Smith <jsmith@mysite.com>
            To: Luis Parker <lparker@yoursite.com>
            Subject: Call me
            Date: Tue, 1 Feb 2005 18:30:26 –0300

            Hi Luis:

            I need to talk to you... Please, call me.
            John.

            .
Receiver:   250 199 bytes received in 00:00:01; Message accepted for delivery
Sender:     QUIT
Receiver:   221 smtp.myhosting.com closing connection
            <close the TCP connection>
```

Table 9.3

1st digit	2nd digit	Reply Code	Reply Text
Positive Completion Reply	Information	211	System status or system help reply
		214	<help explanation...>
	Connections	220	<domain> Service ready
		221	<domain> Service closing transmission channel
	Mail System	250	Requested mail action Ok, completed
		251	User not local; will forward to <forward-path>
		252	Cannot VRFY user, but will accept message and attempt delivery
Positive Intermediate Reply	Mail System	354	Start mail input; end with <CRLF>.<CRLF>
Transient Negative Completion Reply	Connections	421	<domain> Service not available, closing transmission channel
	Mail System	450	Requested mail action not taken: mailbox unavailable (busy)
		451	Requested action aborted: local error in processing
		452	Requested action not taken: insufficient system storage
Permanent Negative Completion Reply	Syntax	500	Syntax error, command unrecognized
		501	Syntax error in parameters or arguments
		502	Command not implemented
		503	Bad sequence of commands
		504	Command parameter not implemented
	Mail System	550	Requested action not taken: mailbox unavailable (not found, no access, rejected for policy reasons)
		551	User not local; please try <forward-path>
		552	Requested mail action aborted: exceeded storage allocation
		553	Requested action not taken: mailbox name not allowed
		554	Transaction failed

It is worth noting that some SMTP servers, concerned with security and precluding use by spammers and hackers, require different techniques in order to validate the user's mailbox authenticity, before accepting an outgoing mail from the user.

9.4 The Post Office Protocol version 3 (POP3)

As we have seen in section 9.1.2, while the submission and delivery of the message are performed using the SMTP protocol, the Post Office Protocol version 3 (POP3) is used for mailbox access and message retrieval from the SMTP Receiver server to the recipient's host.

The first version of the POP protocol was published in 1984 as RFC 918. It consisted of a simple sequence of commands for authentication, which opened the mailbox and copied its contents, deleted the messages and closed the mailbox. It was very simple, although limited.

In February 1985, RFC 937: 'Post Office Protocol version 2' was published, introducing the ability to select the messages to read, rather than download the entire mailbox. The present version of the POP protocol (version 3) was published in 1988 and documented as RFC 1081. But this document was made obsolete by RFCs 1225, 1460, 1725 and 1939. Since May 1996, RFC 1939 has defined the standard for POP3, and later documents such as RFCs 1957 and 2449 only updated and provided an extension mechanism for the standard.

9.4.1 The POP3 client/server communication model

As any other client/server model, the clients request services from the server, which replies with codes, indicating the success or failure of the operation of the commands, as well as providing the requested services. The POP3 server must be running in a server machine with file access to the SMTP server's mailboxes (it could be running in the same machine as the SMTP server, or at least, in the same LAN, in order to have access to the user's mailbox). The POP3 server will be listening for incoming connections on port 110 (the well-known port for POP3 servers).

As POP3 uses TCP as a Transport layer, the POP3 clients (implemented by software such as Microsoft Outlook, Eudora Mail and Incredible Mail) must initiate a connection establishment to the POP3 server in order to establish a POP3 session. Once the TCP connection has been established, the POP3 session begins when the client sends commands to the server, and the server replies with codes and the e-mail message contents.

The POP3 client's commands are sent using the Telnet NVT-ASCII convention, that is, in plain ASCII text and terminated with CR+LF. The POP3 server's command replies consist of the following responses:

- +OK: (Positive Response) indicates the command or action was successful.
- -ERR: (Negative Response) indicates an error has occurred.

An additional text message may accompany those responses, depending on the particular server implementation.

9.4.2 The POP3 session states

Once the TCP connection has been established, the POP3 session begins. During its lifetime, the session progresses through three states:

1 **Authorization State**: initiated by the server sending a greeting message to indicate it is ready for commands. The client must be authenticated in order to access its mailbox.
2 **Transaction State**: once successfully authenticated, the client may use several commands to list and retrieve messages and mark those for deletion.
3 **Update State**: when the client ends, it sends the QUIT command and the session goes to this state in order to update the transactions (the messages marked for deletion are actually deleted). As the session finishes, the TCP connection is terminated.

The following sections describe each session state in detail.

9.4.2.1 POP3 Authorization State

As soon as the TCP connection is established (initiated by the client, and performed as a normal three-way handshake procedure), the POP3 session begins. The server sends a positive reply with a greeting message such as '+OK POP3 server ready'. The client then proceeds with the authentication in order to have access to its mailbox. With this authentication procedure, the server validates the client's mailbox access rights as well as identifying the corresponding client's mailbox.

The client uses the USER command followed by the username (sometimes the e-mail address is used as the username) to start the authentication process. The server always replies with a positive response, even when the username does not match any existent mailbox. Otherwise, someone could try the USER command several times with different 'guessed' usernames, until it gets a valid response for one of them. But as the server will wait for the client to send the password to give the error message 'Unknown user or incorrect password', we have no way to know if the 'guessed' user is correct or incorrect.

After the USER command, the client sends the PASS command followed by the user's password. If login is valid, the server responds with a positive message indicating the successful authentication, and possibly, the number of messages and their size in bytes pending in the user's mailbox. If login failed, the server responds with a negative message and the client should try the authentication process again. After several client authentication attempts, the server could terminate the TCP connection. Sometimes, the authentication may also fail due to other technical problems not directly related to the user/password, such as the server being momentarily unable to lock the mailbox.

The following example is a typical POP3 user authentication process:

Client:	**<establish a TCP connection...>**
Server:	*+OK server ready*
Client:	**USER jsmith@mysite.com**
Server:	*+OK jsmith@mysite.com*
Client:	**PASS mydog**
Server:	*ERR Unknown user or incorrect password*
Client:	**USER jsmith@mysite.com**
Server:	*+OK jsmith@mysite.com*
Client:	**PASS mycat**
Server:	*+OK 1 message 1085 bytes*
Client:	**<start transaction state>**

An alternative authentication method exists, called *APOP*, which uses the MD5 digest string encryption algorithm. This technique is more sophisticated, and it is described in the POP3 standard. In addition, RFC 1734 describes the AUTH command which allows the use of other authentication mechanisms.

Once the user's authentication is valid, the POP3 session moves to the next state.

9.4.2.2 POP3 Transaction State

After the user's successful authentication, the Transaction State begins. In this state, the user issues commands to access its mailbox and retrieve the messages. Table 9.4 shows the commands valid in the transition state.

Table 9.4

Implementation	Command	CODE	Parameters	Description
Mandatory	Status	STAT	None	Requests status information, such as the number of messages in the mailbox and their size in bytes.
	List Messages	LIST	Message number (optional)	Provides one line containing information for each message. The list is terminated with a line with a single dot. If a message number is provided, only one line with this message information is provided.
	Retrieve	RETR	Message number	Retrieves a message from the mailbox.
	Delete	DELE	Message number	Marks a message to be deleted.
	No Operation	NOOP	None	Used to test if the session remains alive.
	Reset	RSET	None	It restarts the session at the start of the transaction state.
Optional	Retrieve top of message	TOP	Message number and number of lines	Retrieves only the specified number of lines (from the body) of the specified message.
	Unique-ID listing	UIDL	Message number (optional)	Returns a unique identification code for the specified message (all if none specified).

Although there is no a strict sequence of commands to follow, a typical POP3 mail exchange sequence would look like the following transaction process:

	<Authentication successful>
Client:	**STAT**
Server:	*+OK 2 12449*
Client:	**LIST**
Server:	*OK 2 messages 12449 bytes*
	1 4109
	2 8340
Client:	**RETR 1**
Server:	*+OK 4109 bytes*
	(Message 1 data)
	.
Client:	**RETR 2**
Server:	*+OK 8340 bytes*
	(Message 2 data)
	.
Client:	**DELE 1**
Server:	*+OK Message deleted*
Client:	**DELE 2**
Server:	*+OK Message deleted*
Client:	**QUIT**

Remember that the text message sent by the server depends on the particular implementation. Some client implementations may also be configured not to delete the retrieved messages, so, after reading the new messages, they would still be in the server and may be viewed from a web-based e-mail, or later downloaded on a different machine.

9.4.2.3 POP3 Update State

When the client issues the QUIT command, the session enters its final state, called the Update State. Any messages previously marked for deletion in the Transaction State, are now actually deleted. This two-step message deletion procedure is a precaution to avoid the accidental loss of messages.

If any problem arises in the TCP connection, or a RSET command is issued before the QUIT command, the previously marked messages will not be deleted, and the client would then be able to retrieve them again. After the server deletes the retrieved messages, a confirmation message is sent to the client; a +OK positive message if everything was fine, or a -ERR negative message if some error was produced in the data update. After the server update process, and its corresponding confirmation message, the POP3 session ends, and the underlying TCP connection is terminated.

As there are no restrictions about the time a POP3 session may take, it is convenient that the server implements a timer to detect long periods of inactivity, perhaps due to a client problem, and terminate the connection to avoid 'waiting for ever'. Of course, in these cases, the messages marked for deletion are not actually deleted.

9.5 TCP/IP electronic mail message format

In previous sections, we described two protocols used for electronic mail delivery from the sender to the recipient: the SMTP for delivery and the POP3 for mailbox access and message retrieval. Although both protocols are different and each one performs different tasks, they both share something: the e-mail message format.

The first standard for message format was published in 1977, with RFC 733 'Standard for the Format of ARPA Network Text Messages'. Later, in August 1982, RFC 822 was published, defining the e-mail message format for the next 20 years. In 2001, RFC 2822 updated the standard, and it is the current standard for the e-mail message format. However, the message format is still known as RFC 822.

It is worth noting that, unlike the case of IP, UDP or TCP where each protocol has its own message format, the e-mail message format is independent of the protocols that use it, such as SMTP or POP3. That is, the message format was designed specifically for the application and not for the protocols.

9.5.1 The RFC 822 e-mail message format

The RFC 822 messages use plain ASCII, rather than a binary format such as IP, UDP, or TCP. In this way, RFC 822 uses the Telnet NVT-ASCII specification, where each line consists of printable characters, and the end of the line is represented with the CR+LF pair. The maximum line length is 998 (excluding CR+LF), although the recommended line length is 78 or less (excluding CR+LF).

The entire message is made up of a set of text lines, ended with CR+LF. As any text file, it can be created or edited by a simple text editor, and it can be viewed and easily interpreted by humans (unlike IP, UDP or TCP messages, which seem like 'encrypted data' to the human eye). The message is composed of a header and a body. The header consists of several lines with information fields such as the sender, the recipient, the date and the subject. The body of the message carries the message itself. The header and the body are separated by an empty line (a line with CR+LF only).

The header fields must follow the following format:

```
<field-name>: <field-body>
```

For example:

```
Subject: Please, call me.
```

Some field bodies are defined as unstructured, with no restrictions other than to be ASCII characters; while others are defined as structured, which are sequences of specific lexical tokens.

The field body portion of the header field can be split into a multiple line representation, called 'folding'. In this way, a lengthy line may continue in a new line, beginning with 'at least' one space or tab. For example:

```
TO: tom@mail.com, john@mail.com,
    ronie@mail.com, jane@mail.com
```

9.5.1.1 Header field definitions

The standard defines several header field types, organized into header field groups. It is worth noting that in the message header, there is no need to follow a certain sequence in the header lines, so the relative position of each field is not important.

9.5.1.1.1 *Origination date field*

This specifies the date and time at which the message was completed and ready for delivery. It is a *mandatory* field; e.g.

Date: Wed, 23 Mar 2005 01:04:17 -0500 (EST)

9.5.1.1.2 *Originator field*

This specifies information about the sender of the message. It may consist of the following fields:

- The 'From:' field is the e-mail address (or a comma-separated list of addresses) of the author(s) of the message. This field is *mandatory*; e.g.

  From: john@myhosting.com

- The 'Sender:' field is the e-mail address of the person who is sending the message (who may be different from the person who actually creates the message). This field is *optional* and it should be used only if the sender is different from the author of the message. If the 'From:' field has more than one e-mail addresses, the 'Sender:' field *must* be used with only one e-mail address; e.g.

  Sender: info@mycompany.com

- The 'Reply-To:' field is an *optional* field indicating the e-mail address (or a comma-separated list of addresses) to which to reply the message. If this field is not present, the 'From:' address is used to reply the message; e.g.

  Reply-To: thisaddress@mail.com

9.5.1.1.3 *Destination address field*

This specifies the recipient(s) of the message. It may consist of the following fields:

- The 'To:' field contains the address(es) of the primary recipient(s) of the message. This field should *always* be present; e.g.

  To: mycoworker@mycompany.com

- The 'Cc:' (Carbon Copy) field contains the address(es) of others who receive a copy of the message. This field is *optional*; e.g.

  Cc: mychief@mycompany.com, mymanager@mycompany.com

- The 'Bcc:' (Blind Carbon Copy) field contains the address(es) of others who receive a copy of the message, but those address(es) are not revealed to the other recipients of the message. When the message is received by the recipients, the 'Bcc:' field does not appear in the message. This field is *optional*; e.g.

  Bcc: myauditor@mycompany.com

9.5.1.1.4 *Identification field*

This specifies information to identify the message. It may consist of the following fields:

- The 'Message-ID:' field which contains a single unique message identifier. It is created by the host, and several algorithms may be used for this purpose. It is convenient to include a domain (or its IP address) in order to provide a globally unique identification. Although it is an *optional* field, it should be present on every message; e.g.

  Message-ID: <002b01c52fae$e2952f90$558870c8@server>

- The 'In-Reply-To:' field is used when the message is a reply to other, and it has the 'Message-ID:' field of the original message. It is *optional*, but normally present in replies; e.g.

  In-Reply-To: <002901c52f9c$aaadd5d0$558870c8@server>

- The 'References:' field identifies other messages related to this message, and it may be used to identify a 'thread' of identification. It is an *optional* field; e.g.

  References: <000001c3ef3f$9bf66460$b328fea9@sistemas1>

9.5.1.1.5 *Informational fields*

These contain information about the message contents.

- The 'Subject:' describes the 'topic' of the message. In the replies, this field may start with the string 'Re:' (from the Latin *res*, in the matter of), followed by the subject of the original message. Although it is *optional*, it *is normally present*; e.g.

  Subject: Embedded Internet Book
  Subject: Re: Embedded Internet Book (in replies)

- The 'Comments:' field contains any additional comments on the text of the body of the message. It is an *optional* field; e.g.

  Comments: This is all the information I can give you...

- The 'Keywords:' field contains a comma-separated list of important words and phrases that might be useful for the recipient, in order to later search messages about a particular matter (using those words as the 'keywords search'). It is an *optional* field; e.g.

  Keywords: business, car, salesman, lower prices

9.5.1.1.6 *Resent fields*

These are used when a message is resent, to preserve some original fields. When a message is resent, these fields are *required*.

'Resent-Date:', 'Resent-From:', 'Resent-Sender:', 'Resent-To:', 'Resent-Cc:', 'Resent-Bcc:' and 'Resent-Message-ID:' are used to specify the date, originator, recipient, and other information of the resent message; e.g.

Resent-Date: Wed, 23 Mar 2005 01:04:17 -0500 (EST)
Resent-From: mymail@mycompany.com
Resent-To: mycoworker@mycompany.com
Resent-Message-ID: <002b01cfae$e2952f90$558870c8@server>

9.5.1.1.7 *Trace fields*

These are used to describe the path the message has taken, as it was delivered over the inter-network. These fields are inserted by the SMTP server, and they consist of an optional 'Return-Path:' field, and one or more 'Received:' fields.

- The 'Return-Path:' field contains a pair of angle brackets that enclose an optional address specification; e.g.

  Return-Path: <jsmith@muhost.com>

- The 'Received:' field contains a (possibly empty) list of name/value pairs followed by a semicolon, and a date-time specification; e.g.

Received: from portone0.portnow.com ([63.72.123.221])
    by smtp.brinks.com (Brink Mail 1) with ESMTP id IYG74540
    for <jsmith@mycompany.com>; Wed, 23 Mar 2005 01:03:19 -0500

9.5.1.2 User-defined header fields

Additional client's specific header fields can be defined, as long as they respect the above header's syntax, e.g.

X-Priority: 3
X-MSMail-Priority: Normal
X-Mailer: Microsoft Outlook Express 6.00.2800.1106
X-MimeOLE: Produced By Microsoft MimeOLE V6.00.2800.1106

9.5.1.3 An RFC 822 e-mail message format example

The following example shows a typical e-mail message format used in the Internet:

```
Received: from server ([200.112.182.185])
    by smtp.brinks.com (Brink Mail 1) with ASMTP id YG74540
    for <info@theproducts.com>; Wed, 23 Mar 2005 12:09:02 -0500
Message-ID: <000201c52fca$f0920d90$558870c8@smtpserver>
From: "John Smith" <jsmith@myhost.com>
To: <info@theproducts.com>
Subject: Question
Date: Wed, 23 Mar 2005 13:17:56 -0300
X-Priority: 3
X-MSMail-Priority: Normal
X-Mailer: Microsoft Outlook Express 6.00.2800.1106
X-MimeOLE: Produced By Microsoft MimeOLE V6.00.2800.1106

Hi:
I would like to ask you about the products your company offers.
Please, send me information about availability and prices.
Best regards;
John
```

9.5.2 The Multipurpose Internet Mail Extensions (MIME)

As the e-mail application goes back to the times where computers were text-based (rather than with the graphical interface that most computers now have), it is natural that the electronic mail message system developers designed a text-based message format like the RFC 822 to use with that system. In addition, as the e-mail pioneers used the English language, no other language was initially supported.

In this way, even though the plain text format for the e-mail messages provided by the RFC 822 format was easy to create and understand, it lacks the ability to carry types of information other than plain text, such as graphic files, binary program files and multimedia information. At the same time, it does not support other languages, which use special characters that the NVT-ASCII cannot represent.

Thus, those user needs dictated that it was necessary to develop a new format in order to allow users to send any kind of data files in addition to the plain text, and use languages in addition to English. However, as the e-mail system working with the RFC 822 message format was widely adopted and largely used at the Internet, a change to a new message format required protocols to change the way they worked. That would be a great problem for users, developers and ISPs.

The Multipurpose Internet Mail Extensions (MIME) development was an 'effective' and 'elegant' solution to these requirements, allowing messages still to use the RFC 822 plain text message format, and providing the ability to send any kind of files as well as the use of other languages. The technique used by MIME consists of encoding non-text information (such as graphics or binary data) into ASCII text characters. In this way, the message still uses ASCII characters, but after decoding the message, this is converted into binary data. Special headers are used in the message header to indicate how the information is encoded.

Since SMTP servers that deliver the mail messages, like POP3 servers that retrieve the messages, do not look at the message body contents, they do not notice that the message they are transporting is using MIME. The only change required by MIME is in the e-mail client software at both ends of the communications (sender and recipient) in order to encode and later decode the messages. At the present, almost all e-mail client software supports MIME.

The first MIME standards appeared in RFC 1341 and 1342, published in June 1992. Later documents updated the standard, published in RFC 1521, 1522 and 1590. The last standard documents about MIME comprised five parts, and are documented as RFC 2045, 2046, 2047, 2048 and 2049, published in November 1996. Some updates are found in RFC 2184, 2231, 2646, 3023 and 3798.

9.5.2.1 MIME structures

There are two basic structures in which a MIME message may be presented:

- *Discrete media*: MIME messages with this structure carry a single media type, such as a text message or a graphic (only one media type).
- *Composite media*: MIME messages with this structure may carry multiple different media contained in the same message, such as a text message *and* a graphic (more than one media type). The body of these messages contains several MIME body parts.

9.5.2.2 MIME headers

A MIME message as a whole and each of the MIME body parts (in a composite media message) are called MIME entities. In order to provide information about the MIME structure, MIME headers are used. In the case of composite media messages, MIME headers are used for each MIME body part.

The information about each MIME entity is communicated through the following MIME headers:

- MIME-Version: this header identifies the MIME version used in the message (version 1.0 at the moment). It also identifies the message as MIME-encoded. It is used only once, at the header of the whole message; e.g.

  MIME-Version: 1.0

- Content-Type: this header is used to inform about the type of data encoded in the MIME entity. It specifies a Type and Subtype (separated by a slash), and it may contain additional information. It is used in the message header indicating the type of media the message contains, as well as if the message uses a discrete or composite media. When used in the MIME body part, it indicates the type of media the part contains. As this header is *optional*, the default is plain ASCII; e.g.

  header:
  Content-Type: multipart/mixed;
  boundary="----=_NextPart_000_01C52EE3.BCF42D20"
  body part:
  Content-Type: image/jpeg; name="MyPicture.jpg"

- Content-Transfer-Encoding: specifies the method used to encode the data in the message body, or in the MIME body part. This is *optional*, and its default is plain ASCII; e.g.

  Content-Transfer-Encoding: quoted-printable

- Content-ID: it allows an identification code to be assigned. It is *optional*, and mostly used for multipart MIME messages; e.g.

  Content-ID: <id42@guppylake.bellcore.com>

- Content-Description: it allows a text description to be assigned to a MIME entity. It is *optional*; e.g.

  Content-Description: "This is the place where I live"

Additional headers were created, such as the Content-Disposition (RFC 2183), which indicates how to present the information provided in a MIME body part. For example, if its value is 'attachment', the content must be presented separate from the message (the user should take additional action to view the entity), whereas if its value is 'inline', the entity should be immediately displayed to the user.

Custom headers may be also used with the only restriction that they must start with the word 'Content-'.

9.5.2.3 MIME discrete media types

The MIME technique allows binary data to be sent encoded into an RFC 822 plain text message. In order for the recipient to know the type of data encoded into the received message, the Content-Type MIME header is used. This header allows the media type (described as top-level media types; text, image, audio, video and application) and the sub-type, which provides specific information about each media type to be indicated. Additional (and optional) parameters may be used preceded by a semi-colon, and using the *attribute* = *value* scheme.

Some discrete media types are given in Table 9.5. The application/octet-stream header is used for every file of 'unknown' file format. Some parameters are used in certain headers to provide additional information. For example, in graphic media type, a parameter is used to indicate the file name; e.g.

Content-Type: image/gif; name="MyGraphic.gif"

In other cases, as in the text/plain, the parameter is used to indicate the character set other than US-ASCII; e.g.

Content-Type: text/plain; charset="iso-8859-1"

where the –1 number represents different character sets defined for each language.

Table 9.5

Discrete media type	type/subtype	Description
text	text/plain	Plain text.
	text/html	HTML document.
image	image/jpeg	JPEG graphic format.
	image/gif	Gif graphic format.
audio	audio/basic	Audio Mono-PCM 8 kHz.
	audio/mpeg	Digital Audio.
video	video/mpeg	Digital Video.
application	application/pdf	Pdf Adobe documents.
	application/zip	Zip compressed files.
	application/octet-stream	Any 'unknown' binary file.

9.5.2.4 MIME composite media types

Two different media types are defined for the MIME composite messages:

- **Multipart**: it allows multiple entities of independent data types to be sent in a single MIME message. Each part is represented as an individual discrete media type.
- **Message**: it allows other messages to be encapsulated into this message.

9.5.2.4.1 *MIME Multipart media type*

A Multipart message consists of a single message carrying many different types of information. Each part is defined as a MIME body part. These parts may be used in different ways, depending on the specified subtype. The following are some of the defined **subtypes**:

- **multipart/mixed**: the information provided by the parts is not related. For example, we could send a single mail with many unrelated files.
- **multipart/alternative**: the parts consist of the same information, but presented in different formats, in order to provide alternatives for the recipient. For example, we could send a mail with the same file in both formats; plain text and HTML.
- **multipart/parallel**: the parts should all be presented to the recipient at the same time. For example, we could send a salutation mail with a graphic and an audio file which should be playing while the image is displayed.
- **multipart/related**: the parts are related to each other. A parameter establishes how these parts should be interpreted.

9.5.2.4.1.1 MIME Multipart message structure

The Multipart message structure consists of a MIME message with its own header and body. The body consists of many body parts, separated by a delimiter, as stated by the parameter of the Content-Type header in the MIME header. Each body part is treated like a single message with a discrete media type, and it has its own header and body. At the header of each body part, there are MIME headers that indicate the media type of the information presented at the body, as well as the method needed to decode it. Figure 9.4 shows an example of a MIME Multipart message and its corresponding structure. Here, the sender is sending a message in plain text, and attaching a graphic file in JPG format. This last is encoded using the base64 algorithm.

The boundary parameter in the 'Content-Type: multipart/mixed' header is a randomly generated delimiter used to separate each body part in the MIME body. Generally, this delimiter is prepended with many dash characters (–) in order to ensure that this random text does not exist in the information as normal data.

The preamble normally has a text that should not be displayed by the e-mail client program. If this happens, then the client would not support MIME messages. At the end of the structure, and after the last delimiter, the structure presents an area called epilogue, but it is not normally used.

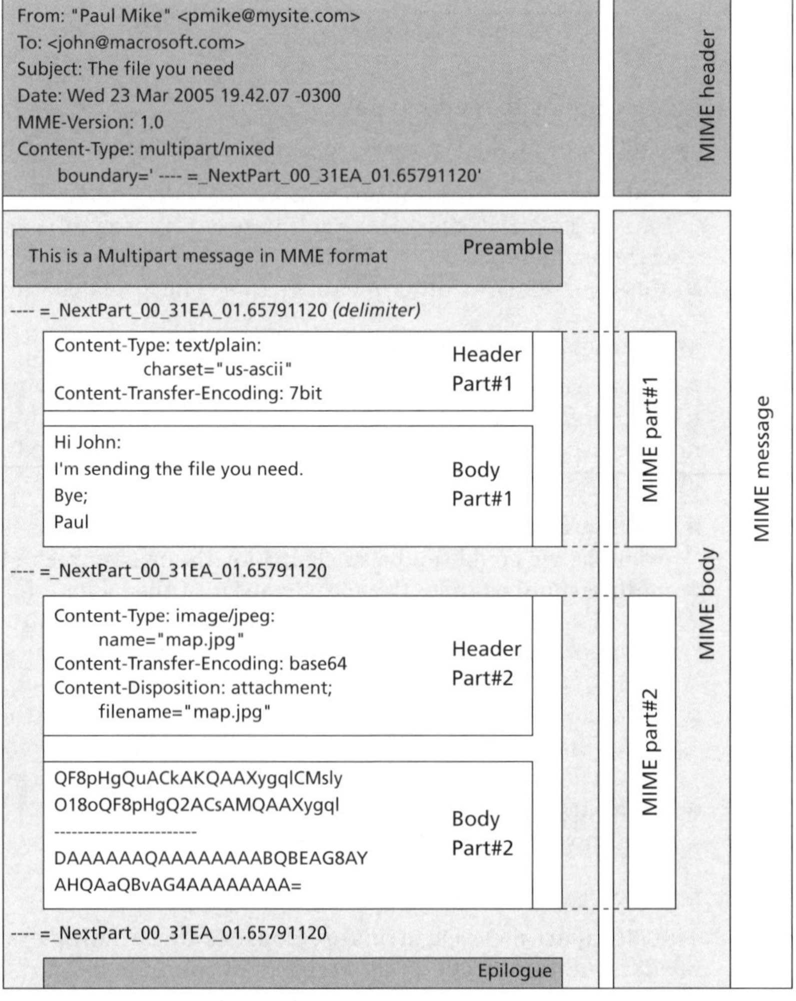

Figure 9.4 MIME Multipart message example.

9.5.2.4.2 *MIME Message media type*

This composite media type allows the encapsulation of e-mail messages within the body of another message. The following subtypes are defined in the standard:

- message/rfc822: indicates the body of the message has encapsulated an e-mail message, which follows the RFC 822 standard format.
- message/partial: allows a large message to be fragmented into smaller messages, and later reassembles them into the original one.
- message/external-body: indicates that the actual body data is not included. Instead, a reference is provided in order to access the external data. A parameter must be included, indicating where and how to access the external body.

9.5.2.5 MIME encoding methods

The MIME extensions allow the transmission of binary data using the RFC 822 plain text message format. This is possible, using encoding methods to represent non-ASCII characters with 7-bit ASCII characters. The Content-Transfer-Encoding header is used to inform the recipient which method to use in order to decode the message encoded data.

The following encoding methods are supported by MIME:

- **7-bit**: it is the default ASCII used in RFC 822 messages. Of course, it does not allow binary data to be transmitted.
- **8-bit (binary)**: it allows the transmission of messages, whose bodies may consist of a MIME message containing arbitrary octet-aligned material, in case the SMTP server supports the 8BITMIME extension. However, as SMTP servers may limit the line length up to 998 bytes, this extension does not provide a means for transferring unencoded binary via SMTP.
- **quoted-printable**: it is used when the majority part of the message is in ASCII, and only few characters must be encoded (for example, the ñ character – non US-ASCII – used in Spanish, inside a plain text message).
- **base64**: it is used to encode binary data into ASCII characters. Once the message is transmitted, the ASCII characters are decoded back into the original binary data.

9.5.2.5.1 *Quoted-printable encoding*

When most of the data is in 7-bit ASCII, and only few characters must be represented as special characters, like the accents in Spanish, the quoted-printable encoding method is preferred. In these cases, the non-ASCII characters are replaced by the equal sign (=) followed by the hexadecimal value of the character to encode. For example, the following sequence of characters (in hexadecimal);

```
0x30   0x31   0x32   0x05   0x33   0x01
```

has the following 'printable' representation;

```
0      1      2      none   3      none
```

but they would be encoded in quoted-printable as:

'012=053=01'

where the equal sign indicates that the following two characters must be interpreted as the hexadecimal value of the encoded character. In this way, the 0x05 and 0x01 non-printable characters were converted to a sequence of printable characters, like '=05' and '=01', respectively.

9.5.2.5.2 *Base64 encoding*

When binary data, such as graphics, audio and video files, or application programs, must be sent using the RFC 822 plain text message format, the base64 encoding algorithm is used to encode the binary data into 7-bit ASCII characters. The problem in sending binary data is that it is represented as 8-bit data (with values ranging from 0 to 255 decimal), while the RFC 822 message format, for historical reasons, was developed using 7-bit data (with values ranging from 0 to 127).

The base64 algorithm takes data forming blocks of 3 bytes (8-bit) each. Then, each block will have 24 bits in length. This block is then divided into 4 groups of 6 bits each. As each 6-bit group has values ranging from 0 to 63, they can be represented through the 7-bit ASCII characters, which allows up to 128 different values.

For each 64 possible values (from 0 to 63) MIME assigns a 7-bit ASCII character which will be used to carry the encoded data through the plain text message. Table 9.6 shows these assignments.

Table 9.6 MIME Base64 encoding assignments

6-bit value	7-bit ASCII Character	6-bit value	7-bit ASCII Character	6-bit value	7-bit ASCII Character	6-bit value	7-bit ASCII Character
0	A	16	Q	32	g	48	w
1	B	17	R	33	h	49	x
2	C	18	S	34	i	50	y
3	D	19	T	35	j	51	z
4	E	20	U	36	k	52	0
5	F	21	V	37	l	53	1
6	G	22	W	38	m	54	2
7	H	23	X	39	n	55	3
8	I	24	Y	40	o	56	4
9	J	25	Z	41	p	57	5
10	K	26	a	42	q	58	6
11	L	27	b	43	r	59	7
12	M	28	c	44	s	60	8
13	N	29	d	45	t	61	9
14	O	30	e	46	u	62	+
15	P	31	f	47	v	63	/

Suppose we have 8-bit binary data which must be converted into 7-bit ASCII in order to send it using the RFC 822 message format. Applying MIME base64 encoding, we must take the first three data bytes, and we encode them as Figure 9.5 shows.

The binary data is rearranged as groups of 6-bit each. Then, each group is used to look up the corresponding ASCII character in the MIME base64 encoding table. As the table is shown in decimal values, we need to convert the group's value in its decimal equivalent, but the software does not need to do this. In this way, the first three data bytes 0xF3987A are converted into '85h6' sequence of ASCII characters, which may be sent using the RFC 822 message format.

In case the length of the binary data is not a multiple of three (to complete the 24 bits necessary to form the 6-bit groups), the equals sign (=) is used as a padding character. The major disadvantage of this encoding method is its inefficiency, as it uses four ASCII characters to send only three bytes of data.

9.5.2.5.3 *MIME message header extensions for non-ASCII text*

The MIME encoding methods allow the use of an RFC 822 plain text message *body* to send binary data, using appropriate techniques. But sometimes, we need to send non-US-ASCII text in the message *headers*. This is the case where other languages are used which use a different character set than the US-ASCII.

For example:

```
--------------------------------------------------------------
From: Mónica <monica@mihost.com.ar>
To: "Raúl" <raul@miempresa.com.ar>
Subject: Reunión periódica en la empresa.
Date: Miércoles, 23 Mar 2005 13:38:14 -0300
--------------------------------------------------------------
```

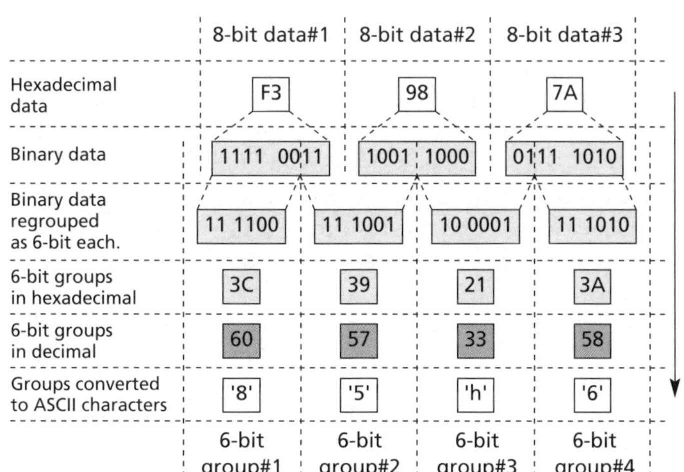

Figure 9.5 MIME base64 encoding technique.

As you see, there are lots of characters in the message header that cannot be represented with the US-ASCII character set. For these cases, the RFC 2047 provides a description to encode non US-ASCII characters text into US-ASCII RFC 822 message headers.

This technique consists of replacing the non US-ASCII text with an encoded text using US-ASCII characters. The syntax used is the following:

=?*charset*?*encoding*?*encoded-text*?=

where

=? and ?= are flags used to identify an encoded text in the headers.
? is a separator used to distinguish the different fields.
charset is the character set used, like the ISO-8859-1 (Latin 1)
encoding is the encoding technique used:
'B' is used for base64 encoding.
'Q' is used for quoted-printable encoding.
encoded-text is the non US-ASCII text encoded as US-ASCII using one of the above encoding techniques.

For example; the text 'Mónica' would be replaced with =?ISO-8859-1?Q?M=F3nica?= where the '=F3' string is interpreted as the 'ó' character (code 0xF3 hexadecimal or 243 decimal in ISO-8859-1) using quoted-printable encoding.

9.6 Summary

- The electronic mail (e-mail) system allows a user to send an electronic message to any other user through the inter-network. This system is based on four components: the e-mail message addressing scheme, the e-mail message format, and two protocols for delivering the messages (SMTP) and accessing and retrieving the messages (POP3).
- As the e-mail application is based on a user-to-user application model (rather than a user-to-server model such as Telnet and FTP), the users should be present at the time the message is delivered. To avoid this, the electronic mail system model was designed using SMTP servers, which are always connected to the Internet, and receive the user's messages until he or she later accesses the server to retrieve their messages.
- In order for a message to be delivered to the recipient, some addressing scheme must be used, so the SMTP server knows where and how to deliver the message to reach the intended destination. An e-mail address is in the form of user@domain-name, where user is the 'username' the user has in the SMTP server, and domain-name is the Domain Name System name the SMTP server has registered, which must be resolved into its corresponding IP address.
- The Simple Mail Transfer Protocol (SMTP) is used for message delivery from the sender to the recipient's mailbox, which is performed in two steps; from the sender's host to the sender's local SMTP server, and from

the sender's local SMTP server to the recipient's local SMTP server. As SMTP uses TCP for its message transport, the client establishes a connection with the server, where the mail transaction process is performed. The client sends commands to the server, which sends back replies to the client. Once the mail transaction is completed, the TCP connection is terminated. Extra functionality is added using the SMTP extensions.

- The Post Office Protocol version 3 (POP3) allows a user to access their mailbox located at the local SMTP server, and retrieve its pending messages. Using the TCP as a transport protocol, the session begins when the client establishes a TCP connection with the server. The POP3 session comprises three states. First, the Authorization State, where the user must send their username and password in order for the server to validate their mailbox access rights. Then, the Transaction State, where the client sends commands to list and retrieve, and mark messages for deletion. Finally, the Update State, where the messages previously marked for deletion are actually deleted. After that, the session finishes and the TCP connection is terminated.
- The message format used in the electronic mail system is known as the RFC 822 message format. It consists of a plain text message, where each line is terminated by a CR+LF control characters. The message consists of a header and a body, which are separated by an empty line. The header consists of several lines with specific fields detailing the source, destination, subject, date and other information; while the body contains the message itself.
- The Multipurpose Internet Mail Extensions allow the transmission of binary data (like graphics, audio, video and application files) using the RFC 822 plain text message format. This is accomplished using different encoding methods, such as the 7-bit, 8-bit (binary), quoted-printable and base64. The MIME message may be presented by two types of structures: discrete media, carrying a single media type; or composite media, allowing the transmission of multiple media types in a single message. MIME headers are used to communicate to the recipient about the MIME version and the kind of MIME message structure, as well as the type of media the message contains, and the encoding method used. Besides, the MIME composite media type may be a Multipart media type, with different subtypes, which dictate how the different types of information the message carries should be presented to the recipient; or Message media type, allowing a message to encapsulate another e-mail Message. Finally, there are MIME message header extensions that allow the use of non US-ASCII characters in the message headers.

10

The World Wide Web protocol: HTTP

We have arrived at one of the most interesting chapters of Part I, which describes the most important application of the Internet: the World Wide Web (WWW). The fact that most people refer to it as the 'Internet' demonstrates its popularity over the other applications. It has not only contributed to the explosive use and growth of the Internet, but it has also changed society itself. It has changed the way in which many companies conduct business, and the way people buy from these companies. The Internet has been incorporated into the daily life of people. Other Internet applications such as FTP, e-mail, newsgroups and discussion forums have been implemented using the web, replacing the use of traditional client programs.

10.1 Introduction

The World Wide Web is the most important and popular application of the Internet. It allows users to retrieve information from many servers (called web servers), which provide documents of any kind of media (text, graphics, audio, video, etc.) in a linked way. That is, one document may present a way to pass into another document located in any other server, as if all documents came from just one information repository. This technology is called hyperlinked documents and hypertexts. The original idea was the creation of a 'web' of electronically linked documents at the CERN (Conseil Européene pour la Recherche Nucléaire), a research centre which involved many scientists who needed to share related documents.

Other Internet applications that were used for document transfer, such as FTP and e-mail, already existed when the WWW was developed. Nevertheless, the WWW had a wide acceptance by inexperienced users because of its easy operation and intuitive user interface. The easy way a user may retrieve documents from any server through a simple click on a hyperlink constitutes one of the keys of the WWW success.

For example, the FTP protocol allows users to download information in various formats, as WWW does. However, the user must know how to operate the FTP client program. Even when the graphical version of FTP client programs facilitates this task, the user must access the FTP site and find the searched documents, which are organized as directories. In this way, users need to know the document names and the directories where they are located. Thus, FTP users cannot be inexperienced, as they need to know the FTP site structure in order to find the searched information, and the FTP commands to go through the directory structure and finally download the correct files.

The e-mail protocol allows users to transfer any kind of document from one place to another; but strictly speaking, this involves the information transfer from one user to another. That means that in order for one user to receive information, someone else must send it. This is not an appropriate use when someone is searching for information, and hopes to find it without waiting for someone to send it.

The WWW is very easy for inexperienced users, who only need to know the web address of the web site that displays the required information. Even more, some web sites provide 'search engines' to help the user to find information on the web, using 'keywords' to find web sites with related contents. From there, everything is to hand. That is, the page presents its contents and a self-description to retrieve more information through the so-called 'hyperlinks' which allow users to navigate from one server to others, as they would walk down a street and visit different stores located in that street. Of course, the servers may be located as far away as the technology allows.

10.1.1 The beginnings of the World Wide Web

The first version of the HTTP protocol was designed in 1990 by Tim Berners-Lee. Later on, web server and client programs were developed. In 1993, the MOSAIC web browser was developed by the National Center for Supercomputer Applications (NCSA). Marc Andreesen, the program developer, later formed Netscape Communications.

The WWW has had an amazing growth since its beginning, and today almost everyone knows about it. Most companies have a website, and, even more, there are companies that have a presence only in the web, selling products and services only through their web site.

Several applications went beyond its initial text documents retrieval purpose. Not only may different media types be handled, but lots of programs and interactive applications allow users to use web-based e-mail, newsgroup forums, e-commerce shopping, auctions, electronic newspapers and lots of ever-growing applications. At this time, the Internet is the most important information repository available for everybody. Its instantaneous access, availability (24 hours/365 days), free access (in most cases), worldwide availability and its presentation possibilities (any kind of media type) make this tool an excellent opportunity for any kind of application.

10.1.2 The World Wide Web technology

The WWW is based on the HyperText Transfer Protocol (HTTP), which enables the retrieval of documents from a server to a user's host. However, in order to facilitate the user's task, the retrieved documents should be 'linked' to each other, allowing movement from one document to the next in a straightforward way. The technology that allows this is called HyperText, and it is implemented with the HyperText Markup Language (HTML), constituting the main document format used in the WWW. A third component that enormously contributed to the WWW's success is the Uniform Resource Locator (URL), which allows the access of any resource from a server.

The main components of the WWW are:

- HTTP (web protocol) which enables document retrieval between the web client and the web server.
- The HTML (web document format) which allows documents to be formatted appropriately in order for the users to interact with information in a very easy and straightforward way.
- The URL (web addressing) which provides a simple way to access a resource from any server connected to the Internet.

Of course, this technology needs a basic infrastructure like the one provided by an inter-network, where lots of devices are connected, allowing host clients to use the service offered by server machines. In the case of the largest public inter-network, the Internet, the WWW service is sometimes erroneously called 'the Internet', showing the importance the protocol has.

10.2 The HyperText Markup Language (HTML)

The term hypertext suggests 'more than text', meaning than the text contains information needed to implement the hypertext functionality. This function allows a user to retrieve related documents in an interactive way. In this way, the user could start retrieving a document from one server, and then retrieve related information from any other server, in a straightforward way, using a 'hyperlink' rather than instructing the web client to do so using a different address for each different resource.

As a result, as each set of related documents is inter-connected through hyperlinks, it is very easy for the user to navigate from one document to another, by simply accessing them through these links. This facility contributed to the enormous development of the WWW. It is worth noting that the documents could also be retrieved using the FTP technology, but as the user needs to have more experience in its use, the FTP is not as successful as the WWW.

Other hypertext functionality is concerned with the way the information must be shown. That is, a series of tags are used to 'mark' the document. In this way, the document may have simple text with some tags which can instruct the web clients (browsers) to show this 'marked text' in different sizes, colours, fonts and alignments. In other words, the document continues being text based, but the tags instruct the browser to show this document with enhancements, improving the design of the simple text.

However, as the document is based on a simple text file, as opposed to a graphic file, the size is very small so its transfer from the server to the client's browser is very fast, allowing a better use of the available bandwidth, which is one of the most important concerns in the inter-network.

With this model, the browsers gain 'intelligence' needed to enhance the retrieved documents, as well as to run scripts allowing users to interact with the web site. This model distributes the 'intelligence' between the server and the client, diminishing the necessary bandwidth between browser and web server. Only when strictly needed are large graphics or multimedia files transferred between clients and servers.

10.2.1 The HTML document format

An HTML document is a plain ASCII document, where the text is interspersed with tags that define the elements of the document. Each element constitutes a part of the whole document. For example, the title, a paragraph, a hyperlink are elements within an HTML document.

The general syntax for a tag is:

```
<element-name parameter1="value1" parameter2="value2"...>
```

Some texts may be surrounded by a pair of tags, where the last tag consists of the element name preceded by a slash character, indicating the ending tag. For example:

```
<element-name>some text ...</element-name>
```

However, some elements may be entirely described by only one tag. Also, tags may be nested within each other.

The HTML document has the following structure:

```
<html>
  <head>
        head elements....
  </head>
  <body>
        body elements....
  </body>
</html>
```

where the <html> and </html> tags define the 'html' element which must enclose the whole HTML document. Also, each HTML document must have a header, with information about the document, enclosed by a pair of <head> and </head> tags; and a body, with the document content, enclosed by a pair of <body> and </body> tags.

10.2.2 HTML elements

Here are some of the most common HTML elements used to format a document:

- **Title**: it is used to display a title at the browser's caption, e.g.

```
<title>This is my web site</title>
```

- **Heading**: defines different headings in a text (from h1 for larger font sizes to h6 for smaller font sizes), e.g.

```
<h1>This is the main headline</h1>
<h3>This is a secondary headline</h3>
```

- **Paragraph**: it is used to ensure proper spacing between paragraphs of body text, e.g.

```
<p>This is a paragraph and it will be formatted accordingly to the web
browser...</p>
```

- **Line break**: it is used to introduce a new line, e.g.

```
John Smith<br>
1866 NW 67Ave.<br>
Miami, FL 33165<br>
```

- **Horizontal rule**: it is used to insert an horizontal line across the page, e.g.

```
<hr>
```

- **Text format**: it is used to format the text as bold, italics or underlined and to change the font, e.g.

```
This is <b>Bold</b>
This is <i>Italic</i>
This is <u>Underlined</u>
This is <font face='Arial' size='10'>Arial</font>
```

- **Link**: it is used to display a hyperlink to another document (the 'a' letter comes from 'anchor'), e.g.

```
<a href="http://www.mysite.com">Click here to visit us</a>
```

- **Image**: it is used to display an image. The src (source) parameter should indicate the URL for the image, while other parameters may be used to define the image alignment, size, border and the alternative text to display (for older non-graphical browsers), e.g

```
<img src="logo.gif" align="center" alt="Company Logo">
```

- **Table**: it is used to display information contained in a table. The **<tr>** and **</tr>** define a row, while the **<td>** and **</td>** define a data element.

```
<table border="1">
 <tr>
   <td>Name</td>
   <td>Phone</td>
 </tr>
 <tr>
   <td>Simon</td>
   <td>305-477-4672</td>
 </tr>
</table>
```

- **Form**: the HTML form is used to gather information from the user to submit it to the web server for its process. The form typically includes *input* or *select* elements which are used by the user to enter or choose information, e.g.

```
<form method="POST"
        action="http://www.mywebsite.com/order.html">
  <input type="text" name="Name" maxlength="15">
  <select name="CreditCard">
    <option>AMEX</option>
    <option>MasterCard</option>
    <option>VISA</option>
  </select>
</form>
```

- **Script**: it is used to include program lines in a scripting language, such as JavaScript or VisualBasicScript, e.g.

```
<script language="javascript">
... script lines
</script>
```

10.2.3 HTML attributes

In some tags, further specification may be provided using attributes (provided as a parameter='value' pair), like the ALIGN attribute, which may specify the LEFT, CENTER or RIGHT alignment; or the BORDER attribute in a table, which may specify the size of the table borders. Lots of attributes exist depending on the particular tag.

10.2.4 An HTML document example

The following is an example of a document containing HTML elements:

```
<HTML>
  <HEAD>
    <TITLE>This is my Website</TITLE>
   </HEAD>
  <BODY>
    This is <b>Bold</b><br>
    This is <i>Italic</i><br>
    This is <u>Underlined</u><br>
    This is <font face='Arial' size='10'>Arial</font>
    <hr>
    <table border="1">
      <tr>
        <td>Name</td>
        <td>Phone</td>
      </tr>
      <tr>
        <td>Simon</td>
```

continued

```
        <td>305-477-4672</td>
      </tr>
    </table>
    <hr>
    Visit us at <a href="www.mywebsite.com">www.mywebsite.com</a>
      <hr>
      <form  method="POST"    action="http://www.mywebsite.com/order.html">
      <table>
        <tr>
          <td>Name:</td>
          <td><input type="text" name="Name" maxlength="15"></td>
        </tr>
        <tr>
          <td>Password:</td>
          <td><input type="password" name="Password"   maxlength="8"></td>
        </tr>
      </table>
      <input type="checkbox" name="save" checked>Remember the password<br>
      <select name="creditcard">
        <option>AMEX</option>
        <option>MasterCard</option>
        <option selected>VISA</option>
      </select><br>
      <br><input type="submit" value="Proceed">
    </form>
  </BODY>
</HTML>
```

The above HTML code may be saved in a file with a name like Page.html, and then it may be opened with a client browser, which will display the HTML 'text document' as follows:

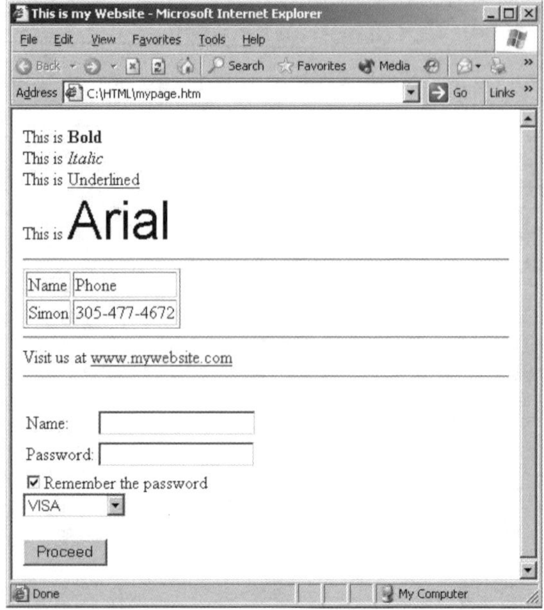

Microsoft product screenshot reprinted with permission from Microsoft Corporation.

The screenshot shows how a plain text HTML file is interpreted by the browser looking as if it were a graphic file, but the transfer takes less bandwidth since the file is small in size.

For more information about the HTML language, visit the www.htmlhelp.com site.

10.3 HTTP Uniform Resource Locators (URLs)

We have already seen that one of the keys of the World Wide Web's success is the easy way a user may retrieve documents from servers to hosts, with a simple click from a document hyperlink. In order to retrieve the document, the link should fully specify the web server and the location of the resource within that server (directory path). For this reason, the HTTP URLs were developed, allowing the full addressing of a resource in the web, using a compact notation.

According to RFC 1738 'Uniform Resource Locators', a URL is written as:

<scheme>:<scheme-specific-part>

where the <scheme> may be one of the following:

Scheme	Protocol
http	HyperText Transfer Protocol
ftp	File Transfer Protocol
mailto	Electronic Mail Address
nntp	USENET news using NNTP access
telnet	Reference to interactive sessions
File	Host-specific file names

The <scheme-specific-part> is interpreted depending on the <scheme>. Then, even when the URL was initially developed for the web, it was generalized for other protocols, allowing the location and access of resources via the Internet.

The most general HTTP URL syntax is:

http://<host>:<port>/<url-path>?<query>#<bookmark>

where

<host> is the fully qualified DNS domain name or the IP address of the web server where the resource is located. (See Chapter 11 for more information about the Domain Name System.)

<port> is the port number where the web server is listening for incoming connections. This defaults to 80, and it may be omitted.

<url-path> is the full directory path of the resource within the web server, including the resource name.
<query> is an optional information passed to the web server for query purposes.
<bookmark> identifies a specific location within an HTML document.

However, in its simplest form, an HTTP URL is presented as:

http://www.mywebsite.com

where the <port> is omitted (using the default), and the <url-path> is empty. Also, the <query> and <bookmark> are not used.

As the <url-path> consists of the directory path where the resource is located and the resource name, if the <url-path> is empty, then no resource was specified. In this case, generally, the web server has a default document (normally called index.html or default.html) which is sent to the browser. However, some web servers may be configured in order to allow web browsers to show the directory content when no specific resource was specified, although this option is really very unsafe and generally not enabled.

It is worth noting the fact that even when the <url-path> is empty, the URL notation should have the '/' (slash character) at the end of the <host>:<port> (for example, http://www.mysite.com/), but most web servers accept this omission. In a similar manner, most web browsers allow the use of 'www.mywebsite.com' rather than the complete notation specifying the 'http://' scheme for the HTTP protocol.

Other examples of HTTP URLs are:

- http://www.mywebsite.com/books/chapter1.html#introduction
- http://www.mycompany.com:8080/welcome.hml
- http://65.108.27.82/orders/music/best/basquet.html
- http://www.news.org/today.html?music

10.3.1 Relative URLs

All the URLs shown in the above examples are called **absolute URLs**, because they contain all the necessary information to access a resource. However, sometimes this full specification is not needed, because all the resources have a common '**base URL**'. In these cases, we could save lots of text by simply providing the necessary information starting from the base URL. Such cases are called **relative URLs**, and they provide information to access a resource, but relative to the base URL.

The 'base URL' may be explicitly declared, or inferred from the main document. For example, if you want to access a resource from http://www.mysite.com/index.html (absolute URL), and this main document has lots of graphic files, there is no need to use absolute URLs for each graphic. Instead we could simply provide the relative URL as 'images/graphic1.jpg' which provides information related to the base URL which would be inferred from the main document as http://www.mysite.com/.

10.4 The Hypertext Transfer Protocol (HTTP)

The HyperText Transfer Protocol (HTTP) is the application layer protocol that implements the WWW. In fact, HTTP is responsible for the actual transfer of hypertext documents (and other types of files) between the web servers and the web clients (browsers).

The first attempt of the HTTP protocol is known as HTTP version 0.9, and is a very limited protocol supporting only hypertext data transfers (electronically linked text data files). The RFC 1945 'Hypertext Transfer Protocol – HTTP/1.0', published in May 1996, was the first formal standard for HTTP. The most important change was the ability to handle many types of media.

In January 1997, the RFC 2068 described the HTTP version 1.1, which was later revised on RFC 2616 'Hypertext Transfer Protocol – HTTP/1.1'. The most important changes were the support of multiple host names (virtual hosts) and improvements related to performance achieved with caching and proxies. In addition, persistent connections were introduced, which allowed better efficiency in multiple requests from related documents. The HTTP/1.1 is the current version for the HyperText Transfer Protocol.

10.4.1 The HTTP client/server communication model

The HTTP allows a client (web browser) to request documents from the server (web server), which responds to those requests. The server responds to the client's commands with command replies and by sending the requested documents. The Request/Response pair constitutes an HTTP transaction.

Since HTTP uses TCP as the transport layer, before the client sends its request to the server, the client establishes a connection to the server's IP address on port 80 (the well-known port for HTTP). The server, which is listening on that port for incoming connections, accepts the client's connection request and the TCP connection is opened.

Once the TCP connection has been opened, the HTTP session begins and the **HTTP Transaction** occurs as follows:

1 **Client Request**: the client sends a request, called HTTP Request, to the server specifying the resource the client wants to retrieve.
2 **Server Response**: the server receives the client's request, and takes the corresponding actions. Then, the server sends back a response, called HTTP Response, which indicates the status of the processed request, and the content of the resource, if appropriate.

Both the HTTP Request and the HTTP Response must follow specific formats as we will see later on.

Figure 10.1 shows the two basic steps in the HTTP Request/Response transaction. Once the HTTP transaction ends, the TCP connection should be closed. However, this will depend on the connection scheme used, as we will see in the next section.

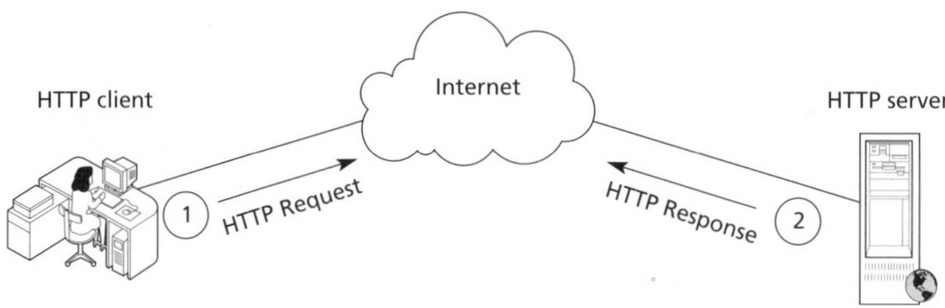

Figure 10.1 HTTP Request/Response transaction.

10.4.1.1 HTTP persistent connections

In the old HTTP versions (HTTP/0.9 and HTTP/1.0), once the server sent back its response to the client, the TCP connection was closed. This is in fact the simplest way the TCP connection would be handled. That is, for each HTTP transaction, a new TCP connection should be established and then terminated.

This simple connection scheme worked fine, when plain texts were used for the hypertext documents. That is, once the client retrieved the document, the connection was not needed so it should be closed. With the coming of the use of multimedia data in the retrieved documents, these types of connection became very inefficient. For example, suppose the client needs to retrieve a document from the server, which has a graphics and an audio file referenced within the main HTML document. Then, the client establishes a TCP connection, sends its HTTP Request, and the server sends back its HTTP Response including the requested HTML document. After that, the TCP connection is closed.

As soon as the browser processes the requested HTML document, it finds references to the graphics and the audio file, so it will also need to retrieve these documents from the server in order to display the graphics and play the audio files, completing the presentation of the whole HTML file. Then, two more HTTP transactions will be needed, but as the TCP connection has been closed, the client will need to establish a new TCP connection for each HTTP transaction. As a result, three HTTP transactions would be required to get the complete HTML document (one for the HTML itself, and two for the graphics and audio files), and three TCP connections would be established and closed for just one complete HTML document.

As a TCP connection establishment consists of 3 TCP messages, and the TCP connection termination consists of 4 TCP messages, a total of 7 TCP messages would be required for each HTTP transaction, and *twenty one* TCP messages for the whole HTML document. Obviously, this is not the best way to handle these situations.

The more file references the main HTML document has, the more inefficient the transfer will be. As newer HTML documents become more and more complicated, with lots of referenced multimedia files, a new connection scheme would be needed. The solution was: persistent connections.

With the coming of HTTP/1.1, the default connection scheme was persistent connection, where once the server replied to the client request, the connection remained opened. When the client sends the last request, and the connection should be closed, a special *Connection: Close* header is used in the HTTP Request, informing the server that after its response, the TCP connection must be closed. As a result, under this scheme, once the client establishes the TCP connection with the server, multiple HTTP transactions may occur without the use of unnecessary TCP handshaking messages. As the TCP handshaking messages take time (both open and close the TCP connection), this new scheme is also much faster than the conventional one used in older HTTP versions.

For backward compatibility, HTTP/1.1 servers still support the old connections scheme, so in case they receive an HTTP/0.9 or HTTP/1.0 request, they close the connection after they send the response. Also, HTTP/1.1 clients may override persistent connections using the *Connection: Close* header in the first HTTP Request.

10.4.1.2 HTTP pipelining

With persistent connections, the HTTP session can be prolonged as long as the browser needs in order to retrieve all the necessary files to complete the main document. The HTTP/1.1 version enables the browser to send requests one after the other in a pipelined mode, without the need to wait for a response from the server to send the next request. This also improves the efficiency of the web server since it replies to each request as soon as it can, without the need to wait for the next request.

Figure 10.2 shows how HTTP/1.1 implements persistent connections and HTTP pipelining, when the web browser requests from the server a web page with the following HTML code:

```
<HTML>
  <HEAD>
    <TITLE>This is my site</TITLE>
  </HEAD>

  <BODY>
      <img src="images\logo.jpg" alt="Company Logo" align="CENTER">
      <H1 align="CENTER">WELCOME TO MY SITE</H1>
      <img src="images\footer.jpg" alt="Page Footer" align="CENTER">
  </BODY>
</HTML>
```

As we see in Figure 10.2, when the user enters the web page URL address in the browser (step #1), the client establishes a TCP connection with the server, which is normally listening for incoming connections at port 80 (by default). Actually, before the client requests a TCP connection to the server, the server IP address is needed, so the domain name introduced by the user must be resolved using the DNS protocol (see Chapter 11).

Once the TCP connection has been established, the HTTP session is initiated and the TCP connection persists during the entire session. After that,

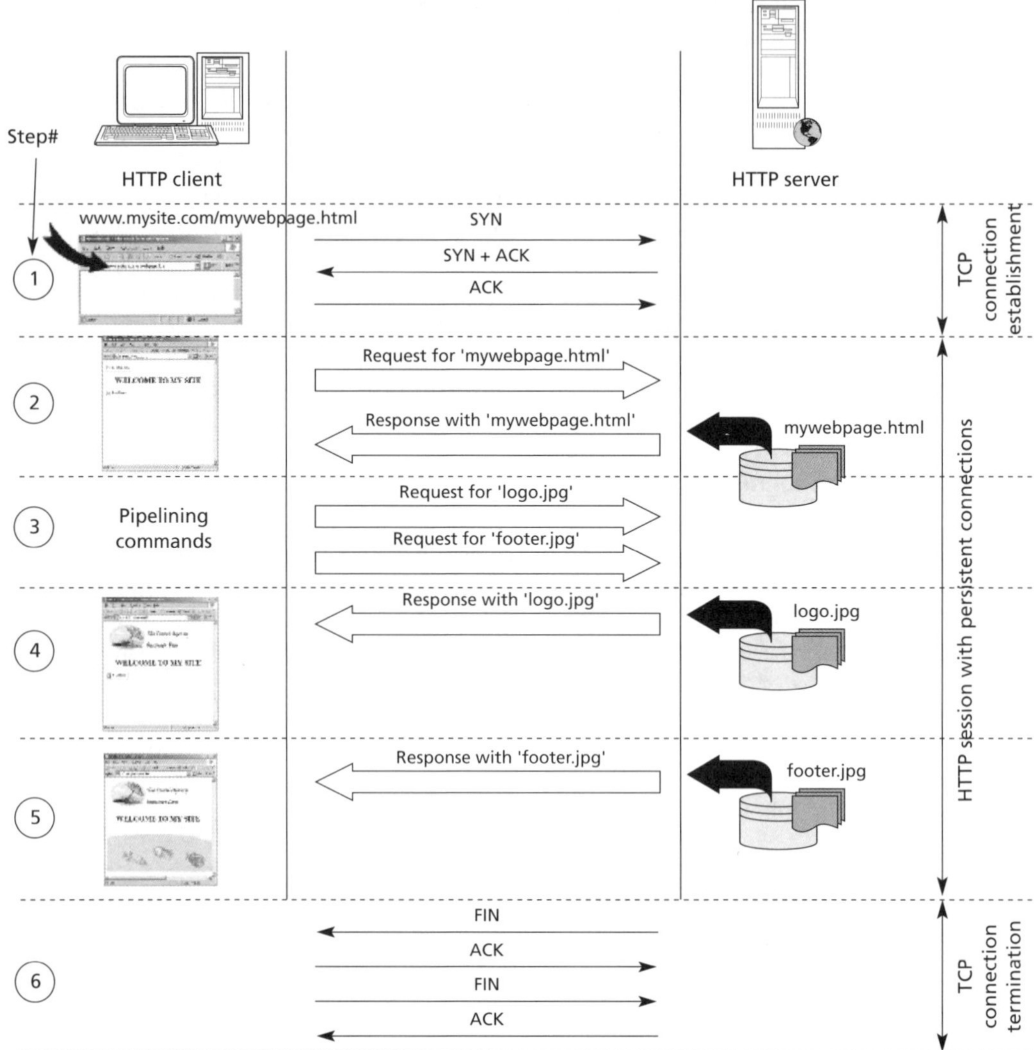

Figure 10.2 HTTP persistent connections and pipelining.

both devices terminate the TCP connection (step #6). During the HTTP session, the client requests from the server the 'mywebpage.html' file, which is provided by the server (step #2). As version HTTP/1.1 has persistent connections as default, the TCP connection is still open. As the client receives the web page, it starts displaying it in the browser (note that the graphics are not yet displayed).

As soon as the browser processes the web page, it realizes that two more files (the 'logo.jpg' and the 'footer.jpg' located in the 'images' directory) are needed to retrieve it from the server, in order to complete the page. Then the client sends two more requests for those files (step #3). Take note that both requests are sent in a pipeline mode.

In steps #4 and #5, the 'logo.jpg' and 'footer.jpg' files are received, so the browser displays these graphics, completing the web page.

10.4.2 HTTP caching

Caching is a technique used in several areas where a 'repetitive access' to some resource occurs. In the case of a 'hard disk access', where the access time is relatively high, if we need to access the same data many times, it is preferable to store this data in a memory area with a lower access time, and then retrieve the data from there each time it is needed. In this way, after the first data accesses from the hard disk, it is stored in a memory area, called 'cache', and subsequent retrieval of this data is accessed from the cache, lowering the access time and increasing the overall performance.

The same technique was used in the ARP protocol (see Chapter 5) where once the ARP message has been used to know the MAC address of some device, it is stored in a memory table (cache), which is used to retrieve the same information in subsequent queries. This avoids requesting an ARP message each time we need the device's MAC address. The same technique is also used in the Domain Name System (see Chapter 11), where once a host name is resolved, it is cached for subsequent queries.

In the case of HTTP, where a document may be accessed many times, the caching technique is very important, especially in modern HTML pages, where lots of heavy graphics and other types of media files are accessed each time the main document is retrieved. The use of caching in HTTP has two major impacts: the user will get responses faster, and the inter-network bandwidth use will be reduced. Figure 10.3 shows how caching works and why HTTP performance is improved through this technique. Two consecutive requests for the same resource are handled by the cache. In the first request, if the resource is not stored in the cache, the request is redirected to the server, which responds with the requested resource. The HTTP cache stores the server's response. The second request from the client for the same resource, as the cache already has the stored resource, is served from the cache, which responds with the cached resource.

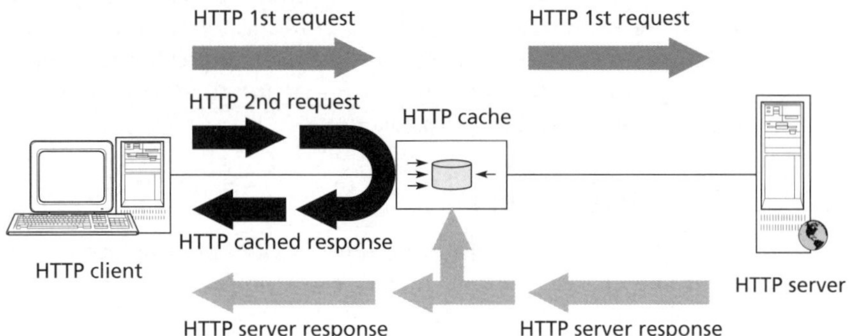

Figure 10.3 HTTP catching.

Of course, there are potential problems with caching resources. And the most important problem relates to out-of-date information. That is, once we access a resource and the cache stores it, subsequent retrieval of the resource comes from this cache. But if the original resource changes, the cache content will remain the same, and we will be getting an out-of-date version of the resource. Thus, the cache cannot keep resources indefinitely.

Even though not all the resources will change with the same frequency, we should assume that all of them will change at some point. For this reason, HTTP headers state how long a resource may be considered valid before its expiration. A process called validation exists which allows a cache to check at the server if a cached resource has been modified.

10.4.2.1 HTTP cache location

HTTP caching is a technique that may be used in different places. One place where it is used is in the user's device, as part of the HTTP client (web browser). The main advantage of this location is the faster response the user gets when a cached resource is requested, and the bandwidth saved, as the HTTP request and response messages are not actually transmitted across the inter-network. One drawback of this cache location is that it may not be shared by other devices and, for this reason, it is sometimes called a private cache.

Another place where an HTTP cache may be used is in intermediate devices, such as proxy servers, as we will see in the next section. Generally, a proxy is used in companies with many users, where it serves the group, providing many benefits. Then, the HTTP cache located in proxies is shared among many users. In this way, if any user requests a resource that is not in the cache, this resource is cached after its retrieval from the server. After this, this resource will be available for any user, until its expiration. In this way, a shared cache presents an advantage compared with a private cache. However, as the proxy cache is quite far from the web client, the response time would be higher and there may not be any bandwidth saved in the company's network.

Also, the caching technique may be used in some web servers. Obviously here there are no advantages about the response time and the bandwidth saved as in the cache used in other locations, but in some cases where the server needs to use lots of resources and there may be too much time to construct the requested web page, it could be very convenient to cache this response for a while, in case another user requests the same page again. In this way, the resources the process uses and the processing time it consumes will be greatly saved with this cache.

10.4.3 HTTP proxy servers

The proxy servers are intermediate devices that operate between the web client and the web server. In this way, the proxy intercepts HTTP requests from the client to the server, and HTTP responses from the server to the client. Thus, the proxy acts like a server for the web client, and as a client for the web server. Figure 10.4 shows a proxy intercepting the HTTP messages.

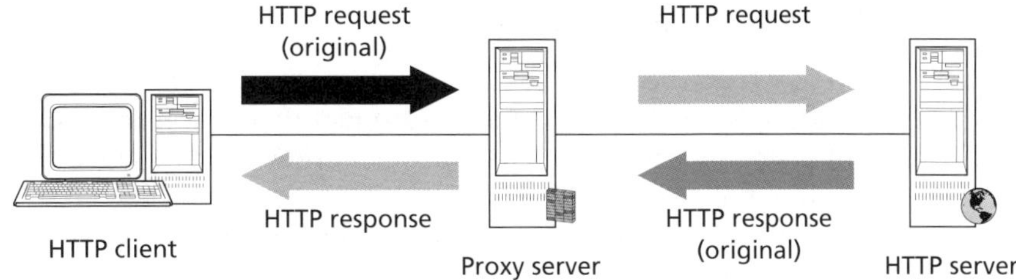

Figure 10.4 HTTP proxy servers.

Proxy servers are usually used to provide security, perhaps filtering responses with files containing viruses, or configuring them to restrict users from visiting some 'prohibited sites'. Also, proxies improve performance through the use of caching.

In order to use a proxy server, it must be explicitly configured in the web browser, where the IP address or the domain name of the proxy device must be declared. After that, all requests are sent to the proxy instead of sending them directly to each web server.

10.4.4 HTTP security and privacy

As the WWW is being used for e-commerce, surveys and other types of activity which may involve personal data, credit card details, and other private information, HTTP must prevent unauthorized access and protect private information from intruders.

RFC 2617 explains two HTTP authentication methods:

- **Basic authentication**: when a client sends a request to a server for a resource which requires authentication, the server responds to the client with a *WWW-Authenticate* header. Then, the client sends a new request with an *Authorization* header, containing a username and password, encoded using the base64 algorithm.
- **Digest authentication**: in this case, the server responds to the client with a *WWW-Authenticate* header indicating that Digest authentication is needed, and a 'nonce' (server-specified data string which is uniquely generated each time) is provided in order for the client to calculate a checksum using this nonce, the username, the password, the HTTP method and the requested URI (Uniform Resource Identifier). The default checksum algorithm is MD5, and the result is sent to the server where it is verified validating the authentication. This method is better than the Basic authentication as it does not send the username and password 'in the clear'.

HTTP does not include any mechanism in order to protect private information. For this, a protocol was specifically designed to ensure secure HTTP transactions, and it is called 'Secure Sockets Layer' (SSL). In order to access resources protected by servers using SSL, the 'HTTPS' scheme is used in their URL address.

10.4.5 HTTP state management

An HTTP transaction is based on a simple Request/Response message model. As each new request is treated independently from the previous one, the protocol is considered 'stateless'. It means that there is no 'data' that persists from one request to the next.

In order to implement web sites such as online stores, a session is needed where the customer logs in, then selects the items to purchase, and finally enters the payment methods. All these activities follow a determined sequence of steps, where each step follows the previous one. Then, some 'memory' between each HTTP request is needed in order to know which the last step was and which the next will be. In other words, we need to provide a method by which a stateless protocol like HTTP can be used as a session protocol over a period of time. RFC 2965 'HTTP State Management Mechanism' provides this method.

In order for the server to implement a state between HTTP requests, the server sends to the client a 'cookie', which consists of a small amount of data that is stored in the web client. This cookie 'remembers' such data as the username, the password, the items in the shopping card, and the web application, among others. Then, subsequent HTTP requests will use this cookie to provide information to the server, which will know which the last step was, and how to handle the new request. For each request, the cookie is updated accordingly. As a result, the cookie provides the necessary 'memory' between HTTP transactions that persist over the session.

The 'dark side' of cookies is that they store sensible and private information which could be accessed by other people. Also, some web browsers allow cookies to be stored in the user machine without the user even realizing.

10.4.6 HTTP Message Format

As we have seen already, an HTTP transaction consists of an HTTP Request message and an HTTP Response message. Both messages comply with a generic structure called HTTP Message Format. The HTTP Message Format uses plain text and consists of several lines where each line is terminated with CR+LF control codes. Figure 10.5 shows the format for each HTTP message.

The following is a description of each component of an HTTP message:

- **Start-line**: this line takes different formats depending on the nature of the message. In an HTTP Request, the request-line specifies the HTTP method, the URL, and the HTTP version. In an HTTP Response, the status-line specifies the HTTP version, the status-code and a reason-phrase.
- **Message-headers**: there are several message headers organized into groups. Only one header is mandatory; the rest are optional. Headers do not follow any order, and they must fulfil this format:

  <field-name>:<field-value>

- **Empty-line**: consists of an empty line terminated by a CR+LF control code, and it is used to separate the header from the body of the message.

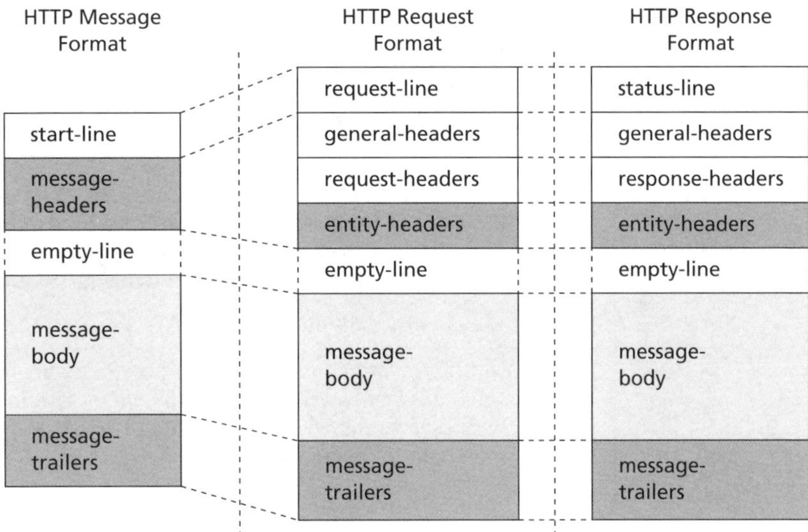

Figure 10.5 HTTP Message Format.

- **Message-body**: it is used to carry the requested resource (called an **entity** in the HTTP standard) in the response messages. In addition, it is sometimes used to provide a detailed error message in a response, and in some requests it is used to send information to the server.
- **Message-trailers**: sometimes they are used to carry entity headers acting like a message-header, but they are positioned at the end of the file.

The following sections describe each HTTP message component in detail.

10.4.6.1 Request-line

The request-line is the start-line of the HTTP Request Message. It is used to indicate the command or action the client wants the server to perform, the resource that the method refers to, and the version of HTTP the client is using. This line presents the following format:

<METHOD> <Request-URI> <HTTP-Version>

10.4.6.1.1 *Method*

The method indicates to the server the action to take. Table 10.1 describes the available methods.

10.4.6.1.2 *Request-URI*

The request-URI indicates the URI of the server's resource that the client requests. However, it does not follow the exact form as it is used in the web browser. For example, if the user specifies the following URL address in the browser:

http://www.mysite.com/orders/myorder.html

Table 10.1

Method	Description
GET	Used to retrieve the specified resource from the server. Conditional GET uses special headers to retrieve the resource if the condition is met. Partial GET is used with the Range Header, to retrieve only part of the resource.
HEAD	As GET, but only the header part of the response is sent by the server (without the body part where the resource itself is sent). It is useful to check the resource's headers without retrieving it.
POST	Used for the client to submit data to the server for its processing.
OPTIONS	Used to ask the server about available communication options. The response includes headers that provide the client with information about how the server may be accessed. If a resource is specified, information about that resource access is provided.
PUT	It is the complement of GET, and it allows the server to store the entity in the body request at the URL specified in the request-line. Generally, this method is not allowed.
DELETE	Requests the specified resource to be deleted. Generally, this method is not allowed.
TRACE	Used to receive a copy of the request that sends to the server, for diagnostic purposes.

the request-URI of the request-line will be /orders/myorder.htm, because the 'HTTP' scheme only indicates to the browser the use of HTTP protocol, and the www.mysite.com is used in the host header to identify the virtual host in a multi-host site server. Nevertheless, when a proxy server is used, the browser sends the complete URL (http://www.mysite.com/orders/myorder.html) as the request-URI in order for the proxy to process the request in the same way as the web client did.

When the OPTIONS method is used, an asterisk (*) may be used as a request-URI, indicating that the method refers to the server itself.

10.4.6.1.3 *HTTP-Version*

The HTTP-Version component indicates the version of the HTTP protocol that the client is using in its request. In this way, the server will know how to handle the request (use persistent connection or close after the response), as well as what kind of headers to include in the response. Valid values are 'HTTP/0.9', 'HTTP/1.0', and 'HTTP/1.1'.

10.4.6.1.4 *Request-line example*

Continuing with the above example, the request-line would take the following format:

```
GET /orders/myorder.htm HTTP/1.1
Host: www.mysite.com
```

10.4.6.2 Status-line

The status-line is the start-line of the HTTP Response Message. It is used to indicate the version of HTTP the server is using, and the result of the client's request (using a code and a text description). This line presents the following format:

<HTTP-Version> <Status-Code> <Reason-Phrase>

10.4.6.2.1 *HTTP-Version*

The HTTP-Version component indicates the version of the HTTP protocol that the server is using in their response. Valid values are 'HTTP/0.9', 'HTTP/1.0', and 'HTTP/1.1'. For backward compatibility issues, the server must return an HTTP version not greater than the one the client used in their request.

10.4.6.2.2 *Status-Code and Reason-Phrase*

The server response includes information about the result of the client's request. This information is provided in a three-digit number called Status-Code, which is appropriate for the web client processing; and in a text string called Reason-Phrase, which is appropriate for humans to read.

Table 10.2 shows the Status-Code and Reason-Phrase as defined in RFC 2616.

Table 10.2

1st digit Status-Code	Status-Code	Reason phrase	Description
Informational Message	100	Continue	The client should continue with its request.
	101	Switching Protocols	The server agreed to the client's request with the Upgrade Header to change the application protocol being used on this connection.
Success	200	Ok	The request has succeeded.
	201	Created	The request has been fulfilled and resulted in a new resource being created.
	202	Accepted	The request has been accepted for processing, but the processing has not been completed.
	203	Non-Authoritative Information	The request was successful, but some of the information returned came from a third party instead of from the original server associated with the resource.
	204	No Content	The server has fulfilled the request but does not need to return an entity-body to the client.
	205	Reset Content	The server has fulfilled the request and the client should reset the document view which caused the request to be sent. Used to clear the forms.
	206	Partial Content	The server has fulfilled the partial GET request for the resource.

▶

Table 10.2 *Continued*

1st digit Status-Code	Status-Code	Reason phrase	Description
Redirection	300	Multiple Choices	As the resource is represented in more than one way in the server, the client must pick the most appropriate one (agent-driven negotiation).
	301	Moved Permanently	The requested resource has been moved to a new URL permanently. The new URL should be used in future requests.
	302	Found	The requested resource resides temporarily under a different URL.
	303	See Other	The response to the request can be found under a different URL and should be retrieved using a GET method on that resource.
	304	Not Modified	The client sent a conditional GET request, but the resource has not been modified since that date/time, so the server has not sent it.
	305	Use Proxy	The client must use a proxy to access the resource. The server sends that proxy URL.
	307	Temporary Redirect	The resource is temporarily located at a different URL than that specified by the client.
Client Error	400	Bad Request	The request could not be understood by the server due to malformed syntax.
	401	Unauthorized	The client is not authorized to access the resource.
	402	Payment Required	Reserved for future use.
	403	Forbidden	The server understood the request, but it is refusing to fulfil it.
	404	Not Found	The server cannot locate the requested resource.
	405	Method Not Allowed	The requested method is not allowed.
	406	Not Acceptable	The client sent a request with Accept Headers which do not coincide with those response entities the resource is capable of generating.
	407	Proxy Authentication Required	Similar to 401, but the client must first authenticate itself with the proxy.
	408	Request Time-Out	The client did not send the request within the time that the server was prepared to wait.
	409	Conflict	The request could not be completed due to a conflict with the current state of the resource.
	410	Gone	The requested resource is no longer available at the server, and the new URL is unknown.

Table 10.2 *Continued*

1st digit Status-Code	Status-Code	Reason phrase	Description
Client Error	411	Length Required	The request requires a Content-Length header field.
	412	Precondition Failed	The precondition given in the request was not met.
	413	Request Entity Too Large	The server is refusing to process the request because the request entity is larger than what the server is willing or able to process.
	414	Request-URI Too Long	The server is refusing to process the request because the request-URI is larger than the server can process.
	415	Unsupported Media Type	The server is refusing to process the request because the entity of the request uses a media type not supported by the server.
	416	Requested Range Not Satisfiable	The Range included in the Range-Header of the request is not valid for the resource.
	417	Expectation Failed	The request included an Expect-Header that could not be satisfied by the server.
Server Error	500	Internal Server Error	The request could not be fulfilled due to a server problem.
	501	Not Implemented	The server does not support the functionality required to fulfil the request.
	502	Bad Gateway	The server, while acting as a gateway or proxy, received an invalid response from another server it accessed in attempting to fulfil the request.
	503	Service Unavailable	The server is overloading or down for maintenance, so it is temporarily unable to fulfil the request.
	504	Gateway Time-Out	The server, while acting as a gateway or proxy, timed out while waiting for a response from another server it accessed in attempting to fulfill the request.
	505	HTTP Version Not Supported	The request used a version of HTTP that the server does not support.

The first digit of the status-code defines the group under which the reply is classified. The code terminated in '00' is defined as a 'generic' status-code for the group, while other two-digit combinations are more specific responses. Where the client receives a status-code that it does not understand, it may interpret it as the 'generic' response, replacing the last two digits by '00'. For example, if the client receives a response with '430' as the Status-Code and it does not know how to interpret it, it can take '400' 'Bad Request' as an equivalent.

10.4.6.3 Message headers

The HTTP protocol is a very simple request/response message exchange model. Nevertheless, much of the functionality of the protocol is implemented by message headers, which allow clients and servers to exchange greater details about the HTTP transaction.

As Figure 10.5 shows, there are four types of message headers; *general-headers*, used for both request and response messages; *request-headers*, only used in request messages; *response-headers*, which are present in response messages; and *entity-headers*, used for both request and response messages. The next sections describe each of them.

10.4.6.3.1 *General-headers*

This type of header provides general information about the whole message and how it should be processed.

- Cache-Control: specifies how caching is performed. Some directives are for request, others for responses, and others are for both. Table 10.3 describes the available directives.
- Connection: it is used to override the default persistent connection mode in HTTP/1.1. Using the Connection: close directive, the server will close the TCP connection after the response.
- Date: it indicates the date and time when the message originated, e.g.

  Date:Wed, 13 Apr 2005 18:32:15 GMT

- Pragma: it is used to include implementation-specific directives that might apply to any recipient along the request/response chain, e.g.

  Pragma: no-cache (as Cache-Control: no-cache)

- Trailer: it lists the names of the headers included in the message-trailer section of the message. This is a warning for the message's recipient to take a look at the data after the message body.
- Transfer-Encoding: it indicates the encoding used for the body of the message. (This applies to the entire message, and not to the entity carried in the message, which is described by the Content-Encoding entity-header.)
- Upgrade: it allows the client to specify which other application protocols it supports. If the server agrees, they may 'upgrade' the connection to an alternative protocol, using a response with the status code 101 (Switching Protocols.)
- Via: included by the intermediary devices (gateways or proxies) that participate in the request/response chain. It is very useful for tracing the path of the message.
- Warning: it is used to carry additional information about the status of the message. Multiple warning headers may appear in the message, and they consist of a three-digit code and a text message, as the following list shows:

  110 Response is stale
  111 Revalidation failed
  112 Disconnected operation
  113 Heuristic expiration

Table 10.3

HTTP message	Directive	Description
Request or response	no-cache	It forces the cache to check with the server if the cached data is still valid.
	no-store	It specifies the message should not be stored in the cache.
	max-age	In requests, it specifies the maximum age the client is willing to accept. In responses, it indicates the maximum age of the response.
	no-transform	Some cache implementations transform for space saving or performance improving (for example, change the image file format). This directive forces cache not to modify the way in which cached entries are stored.
Request	min-fresh	The client requires the response remains 'fresh' for the specified number of seconds.
	max-stale	It indicates that the client is willing to accept a response that has exceeded its expiration time. If a value is provided, the exceeded expiration time should not be more than the indicated value in seconds.
	only-if-cached	It forces the response to come from the cache only (it must not come from the HTTP server).
Response	public	It indicates the response may be cached by any type of cache (including shared caches).
	private	It indicates the response should not be cached by shared caches.
	s-maxage	It indicates the maximum age for shared caches receiving the response.
	must-revalidate	It forces the cache to revalidate its cache entry for this response with the original server.
	proxy-revalidate	As must-revalidate, but only for proxies.

199 Miscellaneous warning
214 Transformation applied
299 Miscellaneous persistent warning

10.4.6.3.2 *Request-headers*

This type of directive is only used in HTTP Request messages, and informs the server about the client, the request, how to process the request, and some requirements the response should fulfil.

- Accept: it is used to indicate to the server the Internet media type the client is willing to accept in the response. Multiple media types may be specified in the header. Also, the client's preference may be indicated using the 'quality value' ('q') parameter (explained later). If it is omitted, any type of media is accepted.

- Accept-Charset: it is used to specify the character set the client is willing to accept in the response. Multiple character sets may be specified, and the 'q' parameter may be used to set the preference. If omitted, any character set is accepted.
- Accept-Encoding: it is used to specify the content encoding the client is willing to accept. It is usually used to indicate to the server if it may send content in compressed form, and what compression algorithms may be used.
- Accept-Language: it is used to specify the list of languages the client supports.
- Authorization: it is used by the client to present authentication information ('credentials') to the server, in order for the client to be authenticated when required.
- Expect: it is used to indicate that particular server behaviours are required by the client. The typical case is the 'Expect: 100-continue' header used to indicate that the client wishes the server to send the preliminary reply '100 Continue' message. If the server does not understand the parameter used with the Expect header, the 417 'Expectation Failed' reply is sent by the server.
- From: it is used to send the e-mail address of the person behind this request.
- Host: it is used to specify the Internet host DNS domain name and the port number (if other than the default) of the website the request is directed to. This is the only mandatory header in HTTP/1.1, and it allows multiple virtual hosts to share the same IP address (otherwise, we would need one IP address for each domain name).
- If-Match: it is used with the GET method to condition the response, which is only sent if the provided entity tag matches the specific entity that the client wishes to access. Otherwise, the 412 'Precondition Failed' reply is sent.
- If-Modified-Since: it is used to check if a resource has changed since it was last accessed. The server will send the requested entity only if it has been modified since the time specified in this header. Otherwise, the 304 'Not Modified' reply is sent.
- If-None-Match: it is used to condition the response, which is only sent if the provided entity tag does not match the specific entity that the client wishes to access.
- If-Unmodified-Since: it is used to specify that the resource should be sent only if has not been modified since the specified time. Otherwise, the 412 'Precondition Failed' reply is sent.
- Max-Forwards: it is used with the TRACE or OPTIONS methods, and it is intended to avoid the request loops between intermediary devices. A limit parameter is specified which is decremented each time the request is forwarded by one intermediary device in the request/response chain. If this value reaches zero, it must not be forward but rather respond back to the client (it is a mechanism similar to the Time To Live field of the IP datagrams).
- Proxy-Authorization: it is used to present authentication information ('credentials') to a proxy server. If there is more than one proxy that requires authentication, multiple headers should be used.
- Range: it is used to specify the range of bytes in the entity to be retrieved, meaning that only a portion of the entity is required. If the range provided

is valid, the server sends this part of the entity using the 206 'Partial Content' reply. If the range is not valid, the 416 'Requested Range Not Satisfiable' reply is sent.

- If-Range: it is used in combination with the Range header, and indicates that the server should only send a part of the entity (according to the Range parameter) if the entity has not been changed. Otherwise, the server should send the entire entity.
- Referrer: it allows the client to specify the URL address of the resource from which the Request-URI was obtained. For example, if the present request is generated from a link in some page, the URL of this page is sent in this header. This information is sent for trace, logs and other tasks. If the request is generated by the user entering the URL resource through the keyboard, this header is not sent (because it is not referred from another web page); e.g.

  Referrer: http://www.thatsite.com/links/mylinks.html

- TE: it is used to indicate what extension transfer-encoding it is willing to accept in the response, and whether or not it is willing to accept trailer fields in a chunked transfer-encoding (see more below on chunked transfers).
- User-Agent: it is used to provide information about the client's software, such as the name and version number. This information may be used by the server to customize the response according to the browser capabilities.

10.4.6.3.3 *Response-headers*

These types of directives are only used in HTTP Response messages. They are used by the server to pass additional information which cannot be placed in the Status-Line.

- Accept-Ranges: it is used to inform the client if the server accepts partial content requests (request with Range header). Where the server accepts the byte-range request, it may send an Accept-Ranges: byte header, while if this feature is not supported by the server, it may send an Accept-Ranges: none header, in a server response.
- Age: it is used to inform the client about the estimated age of the resource, which is calculated by the device sending the response.
- ETag: it is used to specify the entity tag (ETag) for the entity included in the response. The entity tag may be used as a reference in future requests. For example, it is used in an If-Match request header.
- Location: it is used to redirect the recipient to a location other than the Request-URI for completion of the request or identification of a new resource. When the response has a 201 'Created' status, in a response to a PUT method, the Location header indicates the location of the created resource. If the response has a 3XX reply, the Location header indicates the server's preferred URI for automatic redirection to the resource.
- Proxy-Authenticate: it is included in a 407 'Proxy Authentication Required' response to specify an authentication method and other parameters the client needs for authentication. The client will generate a new request including the Proxy-Authorization header.

- Retry-After: it may be used with the 503 'Service Unavailable' responses to indicate how long the client should wait before trying the request again. It may also be used in 3XX (Redirection) responses, indicating how long to wait before issuing the redirected request. The value of this header may be expressed in seconds or as an HTTP-date; e.g

  Retry-After: 180
  Retry-After: Wed, 13 Apr 2005 22:00:00 GMT

- Server: it is used to provide information about the server software, such as the name and version number.
- Vary: it is used to indicate the set of request-header fields that fully determine, while the response is fresh, whether a cache is allowed to use the response to reply to a subsequent request without revalidation.
- WWW-Authenticate: it is included in a 401 'Unauthorized' response to specify an authentication method and other parameters the client needs for authentication. The client will generate a new request including the Authorization header.

10.4.6.3.4 *Entity-headers*

The entity-headers provide information about the resources carried in the body of an HTTP message, called an entity in the HTTP standard. With this information, such as type and encoding method, the recipient may properly handle and present the entity to the user.

As web clients generally request resources (entities) from the servers, the entity headers usually appear in HTTP Responses. However, some HTTP Request, like those using the POST or PUT methods, may also have this type of header, as they convey information from the client to the server.

Every HTTP message containing an entity-body should have, at least, one entity header defining the media type of the body (Content-Type header).

- Allow: it is used to list all the supported methods for a particular resource. This header must be especially used in a response with the 405 'Method Not Allowed' status-line, to a request containing an unsupported method.
- Content-Encoding: it is used to specify if the entity has been compressed, and what algorithm to use in order to decompress it.
- Content-Language: it is used to specify the natural language of the intended audience for the carried entity. Multiple languages may be specified.
- Content-Length: it is used to specify the size of the entity in bytes, so the recipient knows where the message ends.
- Content-Location: it may be used to specify the location of the entity, providing their URL (absolute or relative). This may be useful when an entity is stored in multiple places, and different from the Request-URI, so the server must inform the URL from which the entities were accessed.
- Content-MD5: it provides the MD5 digest for the entity to make a message integrity check for the entity.
- Content-Range: it is used in responses where the entity is only a part of the complete resource (for example, a response to a request with a Range request-header). This header must indicate what portion of the resource

the message contains (starting from zero instead of 1), and the total size of the resource, e.g.

Content-Range: bytes 0-499/1200 (first 500 bytes of the 1200)

- Content-Type: it is used to indicate the media type and subtype of the entity. This is similar to the use of this header in MIME (see Chapter 9); e.g.

  Content-Type: text/html; charset=ISO-8859-1

- Expires: it is used to specify the date and time after which the entity should be considered stale. If a Cache-Control header with the max-age directive exists, it overrides the Expire header; e.g.

  Expires: Thu, 28 Apr 2005 12:00:00 GMT

- Last-Modified: it is used to indicate the date and time the server 'believes' the entity was last modified. The term 'believe' is used because although some entities such as files are very easy to determine since the file system of the operating system provides this information, in the case of other entities such as database records or virtual objects, it is difficult to know when the last change occurred. This header is useful where the client already has a copy of a large resource and wants to check if it was modified or not to avoid unnecessary transfers. Then, using a HEAD method, it can determine the last-modified date/time, so it may know if the resource it has is the same or if it needs updating.

10.4.6.4 Message body

The message body of an HTTP message is an optional part used mainly to transfer the resources requested by the clients from the servers. Sometimes, it may also carry error information details from the server to the client, or user information from the client to the server in such cases where the client submits data from an HTML form.

The resources carried in the message body are called entities, and HTTP supports a wide range of media for these entities. Specific entity headers, as those described above, are used to fully describe the entities carried in the message body.

10.4.6.5 Message trailers

The message trailers are the last part of an HTTP message. They are optional, and are mainly used in 'Chunked Transfers' (see later) to carry some entity header, that are only available when the dynamic-generated page content is finished, when it is too late to put those entity headers in the entity-header section of the message. That is, some entity headers need information that is not available until the page is completed (for example, the page length).

10.4.7 HTTP media type/subtype

The main goal of the HTTP protocol is to 'transfer' resources from the server to the client (although sometimes, the client may upload a resource to the server). This resource is carried in the body of the message, and it is called an **entity**. The standard defines how these entities are encoded, identified and transferred.

In the early days of the HTTP protocol, the world of computing only 'understood' text, so the first attempt (HTTP/0.9) only handled text documents. As the computing world moved to a multimedia world, later HTTP versions incorporated other kinds of media type. These required that the carried entity should be encoded and identified in such a way that the recipient would know how to decode the contents accordingly.

At the same time, the e-mail protocol developers journeyed the same way, and they resolved to develop the Multipurpose Internet Mail Extensions (MIME) to allow RFC 822 format messages to transport types of media other than text files. In order to reuse the developed technology, the HTTP developers took many concepts from the MIME technology. However, as HTTP does not strictly follow the MIME standard, it is not MIME compliant.

One of the MIME elements that HTTP adopted was the set of the standardized Internet media types. Each type is described as a type and subtype, according to the following structure:

Type/Subtype [; parameter1 ; parameter2 ; ....]

where the parameters are used to provide more information about the entity; e.g.

text/html; charset=ISO-8859-1
image/jpeg; name='MyPicture.jpg'

These media types are mostly used in the Content-Type entity header, which describes the media type of the entity that the message-body carries; e.g.

Content-Type: image/gif; name='mylogo.gif'

Also, the media types are used in the Accept request headers, where they are used to inform the server about the media types the client can handle; e.g.

Accept: image/gif ; image/jpeg ; application/ ; */**

where the 'application/*' means that the client accepts any subtypes of the 'application' type, and the '*/*' means that the client accepts any type of media (and its subtypes).

10.4.8 HTTP encoding transformations

This is an area where HTTP does not strictly follow the MIME standard. In order to provide flexibility, HTTP has two levels of encoding transformations.

10.4.8.1 Content encoding

Content Encoding is an encoding transformation applied to the entity carried in an HTTP message. It is mainly used to compress the entity before being sent, and decompress it when ultimately received. Content encoding is considered 'end-to-end' (client–server), so the possible intermediaries at the request/response chain are not involved in this transformation.

In order for the recipient to know how to decompress the transformed entity, the Content-Encoding entity header is used in the message. A client may also specify what encoding algorithm it supports, using the Accept-Encoding request header. The currently compressed algorithms in use are gzip, compress, and deflate. The client may use the Accept-Encoding : identity request header to inform the server of the use of no transformation.

10.4.8.2 Transfer encoding

Transfer encoding is an encoding transformation applied to the entire HTTP message, in order to ensure 'safe transport' between devices. As the transport occurs from device to device throughout the request/response chain (including possible intermediates), different transfer encoding may be used for each hop. For this reason, transfer encoding is said to be 'hop-by-hop'.

The transfer encoding method, if used, is indicated in the Transfer-Encoding general header of the message. The currently possible values are: chunked, identity, gzip, compress, and deflate. The client may also specify in the TE request header what extension transfer encoding it is willing to accept in the response, and whether or not it is willing to accept trailer fields in a 'chunked' transfer encoding.

Where both transfer encoding and content encoding are used simultaneously, at the receiving point, the transfer encoding is removed first. Of course, if content encoding is used to compress the entity, it makes no sense to use transfer encoding to compress the entire HTTP message, as the entity (the largest part of the HTTP message) is already compressed. The most important application of transfer encoding is related to the 'safe transport' between devices; and so the 'chunked' transformation is the most useful.

10.4.8.2.1 *Chunked transfers*

Chunked transfer is one of the available options for transfer encoding. It contributes to the purpose of ensuring 'safe transport' of messages between devices. Let's see why this would be necessary in some cases.

When HTTP/1.1 introduced persistent connections, a new issue related to the end of the message appeared. With previous HTTP versions (HTTP/0.9 and HTTP/1.0), conventional connections were used, so the server, once the HTTP response had been sent, closed the connection. Then, the client could easily identify the end of the HTTP response message. But with the HTTP/1.1 version, which works with persistent connections, several HTTP responses may be transmitted one after the other from the server, so the client does not have a way to differentiate where one response ends and where the next one begins. And this issue may negatively affect the 'safe transfer' of HTTP messages between devices, which is the main purpose of the transfer encoding.

One of the solutions for this issue is to include the Content-Length entity header, which informs the client how many bytes are included in the entity, so it may know where the message ends. Although this solution is often used, it is not appropriate in many cases.

Much of the web content is generated dynamically, and this tendency is growing. This means that in order to use the Content-Length entity header, we would need to anticipate what would be the length of the entity, which is not yet known as the message is not completed. We could generate the message and buffer it in order to calculate its length before sending it, but this would consume time and memory resources from the server. A better solution is to apply the 'chunked' transfer encoding.

When 'chunked' transfers are used, the server may send pieces of data as soon as they are generated. In this way, as the content is dynamically generated, several chunks are sent, each with its own size indicator. The following structure is used for the HTTP message-body, in a 'chunked' transfer:

```
<chunk1-size>
<chunk1-data>
<chunk2-size>
<chunk2-data>
...
<chunkN-size>
<chunkN-data>
0
<message-trailer>
<empty-line>
```

The chunk-size field is a string of **hex digits** indicating the size of the chunk. The chunked structure is ended by a 0 (zero), followed by the message-trailer which is terminated with an empty line. The message trailer may be used to include additional HTTP headers, which must be previously declared at the beginning of the message, using the Trailer general header. Using the 'chunked' transfer, the server can send the dynamically generated data as soon as they are available, while the client can know when the entire message ends.

10.4.9 HTTP content negotiation

Many resources have multiple representation options. In this way, the HTTP headers describe a list of the available or accepted options. One example of this is graphical images where they may be present in multiple formats such as JPEG, GIF, TIFF and others. In these cases, a content negotiation allows clients to choose the best selection according to their needs or preferences. Two types of negotiation exist:

- **Server-Driven Negotiation**: the client sends a request including request headers (Accept, Accept-Language, etc.) with the acceptable resource representations. The server then sends the resource in the best version matching the client's preferences.
- **Agent-Driven Negotiation**: the client sends a preliminary request for the resource. If multiple forms of the resource exist, the server responds with the 300 'multiple choices' status in the message, listing all possible representation of the resources (like offering a 'menu' with options). The client then sends a second request with the selected choice.

There is also a combination of both techniques, called **transparent negotiation**, which is used by the cache which uses agent-driven negotiation information provided by the origin server, in order to provide server-driven negotiation for subsequent requests.

The server-driven negotiation is the most used of those negotiation techniques. In this way, the 'Accept-' request headers are used to list the web client's preferences. In order to provide an order of preference within this list, a '**quality value**' parameter was introduced. The parameter syntax is '**q=d**' and follows each item in the list, where *d* is a decimal value between 1 (highest priority) and 0 (lowest priority). If no quality value is indicated, the default is 1. Here are some examples:

Accept: image/gif, image/jpeg;q=0.7, application/;q=0.3*
Accept-Language: en, es;q=0.5, fr;q=0
*Accept-Encoding: gzip;q=1.0, identity;q=0.5, *;q=0*

10.5 Summary

- The World Wide Web is the most important application of the Internet. It allows the transfer of many kinds of document between web servers and user hosts, using hyperlinks which interconnect related documents in a straightforward way. The World Wide Web uses HTTP as a web protocol, HTML as a web document format, and URL as a web addressing scheme.
- The HyperText Markup Language (HTML) consists of a plain ASCII document, where the text is interspersed with tags defining the elements of the document. The tags follow a specific syntax, and they are used to tell the browser how to format or present the specified element or enclosed text. Many elements are defined to format the text, or include links, images, forms and tables.
- The Uniform Resource Locator (URL) provides web resource addressing specifying the server, path and name of the resource to retrieve, using a compact notation. Although initially developed for the HTTP protocol, it was extended to be used in other protocols. The complete format of a URL allows the use of other ports apart from the default, as well as optional strings to use as query and bookmark purposes. Relative URLs may be used to avoid long strings, and they provide a resource path relative to a 'base URL', which may be explicitly declared or inferred from the used context.
- The HyperText Transfer Protocol (HTTP) is the application layer protocol that implements the World Wide Web. It uses TCP as the transport layer, and it is based in a client/server communication model, where the client requests resources sending HTTP Requests to the server, which replies with HTTP Responses including status information and the resource itself if appropriate.
- The current version of HTTP (HTTP/1.1) allows multiple web servers to share the same IP address (virtual servers). This version also introduces the concept of persistent connections, which use the same TCP connection for multiple resources transfer, resulting in a faster operation as well as improved efficiency and network bandwidth savings. As the persistent connection scheme is used, the client may send multiple requests in a

pipelining mode, so the server can reply to each request as soon as it can, making the overall operation much faster.

- HTTP caching is a technique used to improve HTTP performance and reduce the network's bandwidth use. It consists of storing the server's response to a requested resource in a memory area called the cache, from where next requests for that resource are served. The cached resources expire after some time, being considered out of date. A subsequent request must be served from the origin server and this fresh copy of the resource should be cached again. A mechanism of validation exists in order for the cache to validate if the cached resource has been modified in the server. The cache may be located in the user's device (integrated with the browser), in any intermediary device (as proxies), or even in the web server.
- HTTP proxy servers are intermediary devices in the HTTP Request/Response chain. They intercept HTTP Requests from the web clients, and HTTP Responses from the web servers. They are used to provide additional services such as security, virus detection, 'prohibited sites' access restriction and caching. They are generally used in companies where users share Internet access through these devices.
- In order for web servers to prevent unauthorized access from intruders, the HTTP standard provides two authentication methods. They are *Basic Authentication*, where the username and password are sent in the message, and *Digest Authentication*, which is a more sophisticated authentication method in which the server provides a nonce and the client uses it along with the username, password, method and requested URI to calculate a checksum (by default with the MD5 algorithm) and sends its result to the server, where it is validated in order to grant or deny the resource access. This last authentication method is better than the first, as it does not send the username and password in the message.
- As each HTTP Request is treated independently from the previous ones, the HTTP is considered a 'stateless' protocol. However, some web applications need some 'data' to persist over a session. Then, the server uses 'cookies' to store a small amount of data in the client, which is used in a subsequent request to inform the server about the current state of the session.
- Both the HTTP Request and the HTTP Response messages follow a generic structure called HTTP Message Format. This format uses plain text and it consists of many lines where each line is terminated with CR+LF control codes. The first line in the request includes the method, the resource's URL, and the HTTP version; while the response includes the version, status code and reason phrase of the requested command. The following lines include message headers, which are used to provide details about the HTTP transaction. An empty line separates the message header from the message body, where the resource (or entity) is carried. The last message part are the message trailers, where additional headers may be included.
- HTTP may transfer many kinds of media types between clients and servers. In order for the recipient to know how to decode the entity, the Content-Type entity header is used in the message, with the type/subtype structure specifying the media type, as used in MIME. The client may use the Accept request header, to inform the server which media types it is willing to accept.

- HTTP supports two levels of encoding transformations. The first, *content encoding*, is applied to the entity carried in the message, and it is mainly used to compress the entity before it is transferred. The second, *transfer encoding*, is applied to the entire message, and it is most commonly used for *chunked transfers* where the message body is sent as many pieces of data, called chunks, each with its own size indicator. This chunked structure is appropriate in dynamically generated pages where the entity length is not available until the whole page is generated, and, it is difficult for the client to know when the message ends. In the chunked structure, a chunk size equals zero; it indicates the end of the message.
- HTTP offers two methods for *content negotiation*, which is used in those cases where a resource presents multiple representation options. In the *agent-driven negotiation*, the client selects an option from a list provided by the server. In the *server-driven negotiation*, the client sends a request including headers specifying acceptable values, and the server decides the best option that matches the client's preference. A 'quality value' ('q') may be used by the client to specify an order of preference within the list of acceptable values.

11

The Domain Name System

In this last chapter of Part I, we discuss the Domain Name System. Even though in theory the Internet would work without this system implementation, in practical terms this would not be possible. A big part of the Internet success is due to the Domain Name System, which facilitated access to Internet resources. Without this facility, Internet users should use IP addresses instead of domain names, and would certainly not use the Internet as much as they do. The ease of use the Domain Name System provides has made it key to the sucess of the Internet, especially for the World Wide Web.

11.1 An introduction to name systems

As we saw in Chapter 5, in order for each device to transmit and receive data over an inter-network, the IP addresses must be unique. In the current version of the Internet Protocol (IPv4), these addresses are given as four bytes in decimal notation, separated by 'dots'; for example, '200.112.136.85'.

In the early days, TCP/IP users had to use an IP address in order to connect to remote systems. For small networks, it would be possible to remember or look up the IP address of the device we would like to connect to. But, as the network grows, this procedure would become cumbersome. Moreover, on a huge inter-network like the Internet we access lots of web sites every day. What if we had to access all those sites by entering their IP addresses instead of their domain names? Although this is possible, it would be inefficient and impractical.

The fact is that for most people an IP address number does not say much. It is very difficult to remember a site's IP address, or to associate this IP address with a particular website. However, it is very easy to associate a name with a particular website; for example, the name Microsoft is fully related to the Microsoft website. In this way, using a name system instead of an IP address certainly makes using the Internet much easier.

As we said before, however, devices require IP addresses and only understand IP addresses. In order to use a name system and to make this name system works, we would need to 'translate' this name into its corresponding IP address.

The name system defines a **Name Space** which describes the rules for names and their structures, and the relationship between devices in the system. As well as the IP address being unique for each device, the name for each device should be unique, too. The only way to guarantee this is to have an authorized organization registering names for devices. This process is called **Name Registration**.

The 'translation' process of converting a name into an IP address is called **Name Resolution**, and it is needed each time we connect to a device using its name instead of its IP address.

11.2 Name space

The name space constitutes the set of all possible names the devices could have. In this way, each possible name would have some limitations, such as the set of symbols or characters allowed in those names, as well as the maximum size of each name.

Another important aspect is the structure this name space would have, also called the Name Architecture. Within this, we can distinguish between a simple unstructured name space, called the flat name space; and a structured name space, called the hierarchical name space.

11.2.1 Flat name space

Initially, this would be the natural method we would use to assign a name to a device in a network. That is, instead of using the IP address to refer to each device in a network, we would use a label representing the device's name. No label would have a specific structure, and there would be no relationship between any two given names.

Of course, the name space is finite in its maximum number of available names. This limit will depend on the maximum number of characters the labels of the name may have, and the number of different symbols the labels may use. As a result, while in small networks this would not have a great impact, in an enormous inter-network such the Internet, where millions of computers are connected, this simple flat name space would prove absolutely impractical. That is, the name space would be exhausted very soon owing to the large quantity of devices connected to the inter-network, and the names of those devices would become impossible to remember as each one needs to be unique.

Another problem of the flat name space is related to the Name Registration and Name Resolution processes. With this type of name space, a single central authority is required to register the device's name, in order to avoid name duplications. The database used to resolve the name to the IP address 'translation' process would have to have all the registered names, which would be impractical in the case of the Internet, where millions of machines are connected.

11.2.2 Hierarchical name space

In this architecture, the labels use a specific structure, where the label's components are related to each other using a hierarchical 'parent/child' semantic. This hierarchical multi-level structure is similar to those used in large companies where the organizational chart describes the name and function of each executive of the company.

In the hierarchical name space, each device has been assigned a name given by a label composed of different elements, describing the hierarchical structure to which the device belongs. Figure 11.1 shows a typical example of a hierarchical name space used to assign names to computers inside a company. Here, the devices have been assigned the following names:

john.sales.acme	john.operation.acme	john.service.acme	john.administration.acme
sara.sales.acme	richard.operation.acme	matt.service.acme	bill.administration.acme
luis.sales.acme	julie.operation.acme		george.administration.acme
	robert.operation.acme		

We can see how the label John is assigned to many devices in the same company, but as they belong to different departments in the company, the complete names differ from each other.

As a result, the hierarchical name space allows the use of the same label assigned to many devices, guaranteeing the name uniqueness. Also, this architecture greatly benefits the Name Registration and Name Resolution processes, as it 'distributes' the authority and the registered database through the structure. For example, in Figure 11.1, the Acme main office (root of the whole structure) would be in charge of the processes related to the main departments, such as Sales, Operation, Service, Administration, and all the new departments which would be created in that 'level' of the hierarchy; while it could 'delegate' the authority and responsibility of the devices belonging to each department.

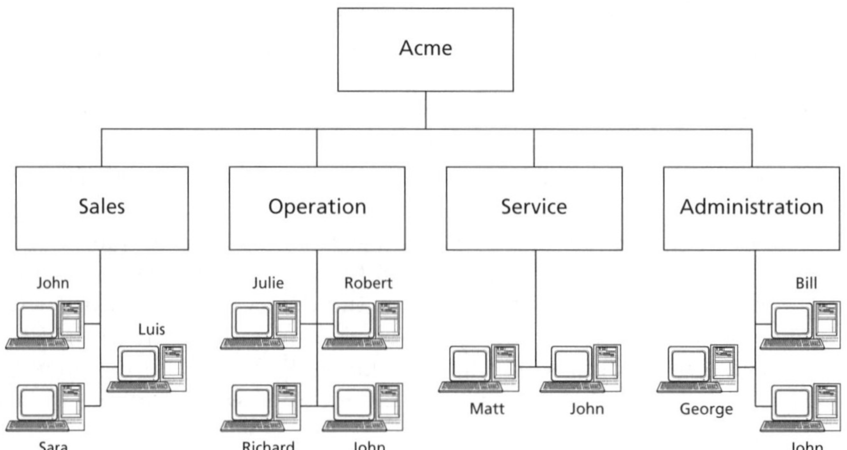

Figure 11.1 Hierarchical name space.

In this way, the registration process of new devices or changes to the existing ones, would be in the charge of each department, alleviating the work for the Acme main office (in a flat name space, this office would be in charge of the processes for the whole company). Thus, the database for the resolution process would be distributed throughout the structure.

11.3 TCP/IP host tables

The need for a name system has been recognized since the beginning of inter-networking. In the ARPAnet, the predecessor of the present Internet, where only a few machines were connected, device names were assigned. These names were listed in host tables maintained on each site. Those host tables consisted of simple text files used to map the names to addresses.

In order to avoid inconsistency with the assigned names, the mappings were published in RFC documents. Then, each host administrator made the necessary changes, which were published in a later RFC publication. Once the RFC published the information, each site administrator had to change their own host table to make the necessary corrections. The problem with this was the slow response of the system to each network modification.

A later improvement allowed the Network Information Center (NIC) to maintain a centralized copy of a 'master' host table, which could be downloaded by each host administrator. However, as the ARPAnet grew considerably, this centralized system of maintaining a text file for the whole inter-network became unmanageable.

Name Resolution is performed by each device simply reading the host table, and searching the IP address for the given name. In this way, the resolution process is completely local, without the need to contact any server in the inter-network. Of course, with a large inter-network the host table size increased enormously.

Even though the problems this system presents are well known, it is still being supported by operating systems, because it may be used in small network implementations, or as a complement to a DNS, where the host table would map the most usual sites accessed, so that the host table may provide its IP address instead of having the DNS system sending a query to resolve these site names.

11.4 TCP/IP Domain Name System

The introduction of a hierarchical name system, incorporating the domain concept, moved the host table implementation to a new Domain Name System (DNS). RFC 1034 and 1035 provide the standard for the Domain Name System, although many later RFC documents provide additional features for this system.

The following sections describe how the Domain Name System implements the three functions of a name system.

11.4.1 DNS name space

The DNS uses a hierarchical name system, based on the concept of the domain. The word domain is used as an 'area of control', meaning that some part of the structure is controlled by the same authority. For example, in the company organizational chart shown in Figure 11.1, the devices belonging to the sales department are controlled by the department's authority, so they belong to the sales domain. The rest of the devices belong to their respective department domains, while all of them are under the control of the Acme main office, which in turn delegates authority to each department.

The DNS name space may be represented through the use of a tree structure, similar to those used to store files on a computer's hard disk. In these file systems, the directory is presented as a tree structure, where the root directory is at the top of the structure, and may contain files and/or directories. Each directory itself can contain files and/or subdirectories, and those subdirectories may contain other subdirectories, and so on.

The DNS domain name structure is similar to the above described directory structure, but it deals with domains and devices, instead of subdirectories and files. The highest level is the root of the tree, which contains domains called top-level-domains (TLD). Each TLD has second-level-domains (SLD), which in turn may have sub-domains or hosts. Each sub-domain can have hosts or additional sub-domains, and so on. The hosts are represented by their assigned domain name rather than by their IP address. Figure 11.2 shows the DNS domain name structure. Text labels are used to identify the domain within the structure. Each label can be from 0 to 63 characters in length, and it may consist of any letters and numbers, including the dash ('-') symbol. Labels are not case-sensitive. The null label (zero length) is reserved and used for the root.

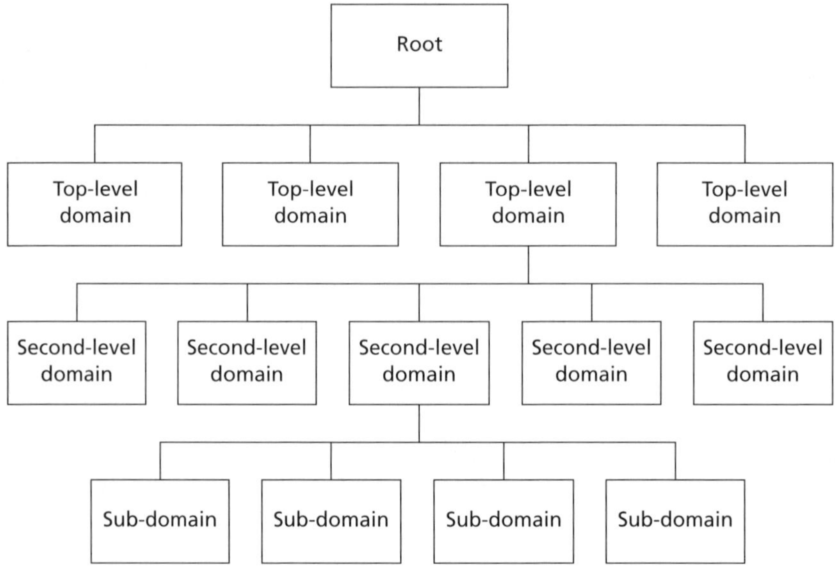

Figure 11.2 The DNS name space.

Domain names are constructed using labels separated by a dot ('.'). They must include the labels of each node describing the domain, up to the root. The complete domain name should not exceed 255 characters in length. The root is present in all domain names, but as it uses the null label (an empty label), it is symbolized with a final dot, which in practice is commonly omitted. For example: suppose a '*scientist*' top-level-domain under the root, containing a '*research*' second-level-domain, which in turn may have a '*students*' sub-domain, and lastly a '*john*' host in this sub-domain. The *fully-qualified domain name* for this host would be 'john.students.research.scientists.', where the final dot may be omitted. The fully-qualified domain name (FQDN) means the complete specification for the domain name, as opposed to *partially qualified domain name* (PQDN) where only a portion of the domain name is specified, used for convenience in some cases.

11.4.2 DNS name registration

As we said above, Name Registration is the process by which some authority controls and maintains a device's name list (or a database) in order to guarantee name uniqueness, fundamental to the appropriate working of any name system.

If a centralized organization were needed to control and maintain the list of all devices for the entire Internet, it would certainly collapse. Fortunately, the DNS Hierarchical Name Space allows the central authority to delegate part of this work to other organizations. For example, the central authorities responsible for every name in DNS are the Internet Assigned Numbers Authority (IANA) and the Internet Corporation for Assigned Names and Numbers (ICANN). They decide which TLDs are created, and they maintain them. However, IANA/ICANN may delegate control for each TLD to a different authority, which controls the creation of SLDs.

11.4.2.1 Top-level domains

There are many TLDs under which organizations and individuals may be registered. These TLDs are grouped under two main categories:

- **Organizational TLDs**: this group comprises the initially seven top domains denominated as .COM, .EDU, .GOV, .MIL, .NET, .ORG and .ARPA. These domains were created to be used for different organizations, according to their type. The .ARPA was a temporary domain used for the transition to DNS, and is now used for reverse name resolution. Later, eight additional top domains were created .AERO, .BIZ, .COOP, .INFO, .INT, .MUSEUM, .NAME, and .PRO. Different organizations were assigned to manage these top domains.
- **Country Code TLDs**: this group includes the top domain for each country, using the country code as designated in ISO 3166-1. Each country has the authority to register sub-domains as they want.

11.4.2.2 Second-level domains

These are the domains under the TLDs. In the case of the organizational TLDs, the SLDs are organizations and individuals. In the country code TLDs, the SLDs will depend on the structure the particular country has chosen; some of them register organizations directly (as 'mycompany.it' in Italy), while others use the SLDs to form an organizational domain level, under which the organizations are registered (as 'mycompany.co.uk' in the United Kingdom).

11.4.2.3 Zones of authority

The zone of authority represents an area that is administered independently. That is, throughout the hierarchy, different authority zones can be defined. Each zone includes certain segments of the DNS name tree, and it is administrated by its authority. These zones must not overlap. Every zone must have at least one DNS server (a primary DNS server) containing a set of resource records describing the zone. This server is called an authoritative server for this zone, and it is the one used to resolve queries for this zone. A secondary server is used as a backup, or for load balancing purposes.

For example, all TLDs are in the same zone under the IANA/ICANN authority. Their servers must provide information about all TLDs defined and their respective authoritative name servers. Under each TLD, the authoritative name server must provide information for the authoritative name server for each organization the TLD has registered. The organization's authoritative name server has the definitive information about this zone, including the organization's domain name, their servers' IP addresses, etc. However, when the organization is large enough, it would be convenient to define different zones of authority inside the organization itself. Then, each zone will have its own authoritative DNS name servers, providing information for the zone.

11.4.3 DNS Name Resolution

Name Resolution is the process by which a domain name is 'translated' into its IP address. This process is performed using the client/server model, where the client (normally the resolver) sends a query to a server (the name server) which replies using the information it has. However, as we will see later, name servers may also act as clients, querying other name servers.

Each zone of authority has at least one name server containing the information about the domains, sub-domains and objects in the zone. This information resides in a set of resource records, stored in the server.

11.4.3.1 DNS name servers

The name servers have information about domain names. They respond to the client's queries, sending the information they have about the requested domain. As the domain database containing all the registered domains is distributed among lots of name servers, not all servers will have the correct information to reply, but at least, they will provide details of the name server holding the requested information. In this way, name servers are linked following the authority hierarchy present in the DNS name space.

11.4.3.1.1 *DNS Master File*

As we saw above, each zone of authority has at least one name server that has stored a set of resource records describing the elements in that zone. A typical DNS Master File containing all those records for a zone may look like the following:

```
$ORIGIN mysite.com.
@  IN  SOA  ns1.myhosting.com. contact.myhosting.com. (
                 10012562     ; Serial
                 3600         ; Refresh
                 300          ; Retry
                 604800       ; Expire
                 3600 )       ; Minimum

@            IN       NS          ns1.myhosting.com.
@            IN       NS          ns2.myhosting.com.

localhost    IN       A           127.0.0.1
@            IN       A           65.185.105.32
             IN       MX  10      mail.mysite.com.
             IN       MX  20      mail2.myhosting.com.

www          IN       CNAME       @
ftp          IN       CNAME       @
mail         IN       CNAME       @
```

- The $ORIGIN directive specifies the *domain name* and it is used to complete the PQDNs. For example, if a name is given as 'support', it should be interpreted as 'support.mysite.com'. The @ sign is used as a reference to the ORIGIN.
- The SOA (Start Of Authority) record marks the beginning of the DNS zone, and it provides information such as the primary authoritative name server for the zone, an e-mail address of its administrator (without the @ between the username and the domain), and other parameters used for different purposes, which will be explained later.
- The NS (Name Server) records specify the name servers (or at least one) that are authoritative for the zone.
- The A (Address) records contains the IP address of the domain name. This is the address the resolver expects to receive as a response to its query.
- The MX (Mail Exchange) records specify the domain name of the mail servers which handle e-mail for this zone. If more than one mail server is used (for backup or other reasons), a number represents the priority (the lower the number, the higher the priority).
- The CNAME (Canonical Name) provides an alias for the domain name. In this way, the user may write www.mysite.com in the browser, and this record converts it into the real (canonical) name of the node: mysite.com.
- Even though the above example does not use them, there are other records such as PTR (Pointer): it is used for reverse resolution in the IN-ADDR.ARPA. domain and the TXT (Text String): it is used to store additional data as a string.

- Finally, the IN parameter that appears in each record is named a class, and it is used to indicate that the record is used for 'Internet'. The DNS was designed for multi-protocol support.

Also, although it does not appear in the above example, each record uses an optional TTL (Time-To-Live) parameter preceding the IN parameter, which is used to inform the cache about when this record information expires. If this parameter is omitted, a $TTL directive in the Master File is used instead.

11.4.3.1.2 *Primary and Secondary name servers*

Each zone needs at least one DNS name server which has the Master File for the zone. This Master File has a set of records describing the zone. This server is an authoritative server for the zone. This authoritative server is queried by the resolvers when they need some information about the zone.

There are many arguments that justify having more than one name server for a zone. Perhaps, the most important is to provide the redundancy needed when the name server fails, or in case it requires maintenance. Another important reason may be load balancing to improve performance.

In those cases where more than one name server exists for a zone, one of them is called the Primary, while the rest are called Secondary. For a good redundancy, the Primary and Secondary servers should be installed in distant physical sites, with different ISPs if possible. Then the administrator only modifies the Master File on the Primary name server. The Secondary name servers update their information from the Primary using a process called a zone transfer. This process is performed on a regular basis, and it is controlled by four parameters of the SOA record:

- Serial: this value indicates the 'version' of the Master File, and it is incremented each time the information is modified. In this way, when the Secondary server gets the SOA record from the Primary server (using a DNS Query for that Record Resource), and comparing this value with its own, it may know if it needs a zone transfer.
- Refresh: it indicates the period of time the Secondary server waits between checks from the Primary to see if a zone transfer is needed.
- Retry: where the last attempt to check the Primary serial failed, the Secondary server must wait the period of time indicated by this field, before trying again.
- Expire: if the Secondary cannot check the Master File serial from the Primary for a period of time given by this field, it must assume its copy of the zone is obsolete, and discard it.

If the zone transfer is needed, it is performed using a DNS Query using a question type AXFR, indicating a transfer zone is requested. The server will send the Resource Records using a series of DNS Responses. Once the Secondary has updated its information, it will continue checking for updates from the Primary, every Refresh seconds. If a problem arises when the Secondary tries to query the Primary for updates, it will try again after Retry seconds. After Expire seconds, if the Secondary is unable to check for updates from the Primary, it should discard its information.

In order to avoid the Secondary servers constantly asking the Primary about changes in the zone information, RFC 1996 'A Mechanism for Prompt Notification of Zone Changes (DNS NOTIFY)' introduced a new DNS message type called Notify. With this improvement, each time the Master File is modified in the Primary server, it sends a DNS Notify message to the Secondary server, which acts as if the Refresh timer has just expired.

Another improvement was introduced by RFC 1995 'Incremental Zone Transfer in DNS', implementing incremental updates instead of the complete zone transfer. That is, the Primary server keeps track of the recent changes made to the Master File. When the Secondary realizes about changes, it sends a query with the IXFR (incremental transfer) question type containing the serial number of its database copy. The Primary compares this serial with its own, and it may know the last changes the Secondary needs to update the zone information. In this way, as the transfer of the complete zone is avoided, it is very useful in those cases where the database is large.

11.4.3.1.3 *Root Servers*

The resolution process starts from the root of the DNS hierarchical structure. At that level, the so-called Root Servers provide information about names and addresses of the authoritative servers for each of the top-level domains. Then, the whole DNS depends on these Root Servers, where all queries start from. For this reason, there are more than a dozen of these Root Servers, strategically installed in different parts of the world. Furthermore, some of them consist of a set of 'mirrors' servers working from different places.

11.4.3.1.4 *Improving performance: caching*

Each time a name server responds to a Name Resolution request, time and resources are taken. In the case of name servers responding to lots of requests each second, this becomes a performance problem. For this reason, the caching technique is used.

Each time a Name Resolution is resolved, the response is stored in a memory area called cache. In this way, subsequent requests for the same name will be satisfied from the cache, instead of starting the resolution process again. Owing to the way most people use the browser, each time a domain name is requested to be resolved, there is a high probability that the following request will be for the same domain name. For example, if you visit a web page and request its main web page, the domain name for that site will be requested to be resolved. Further access for other web pages within the same web site, will require the same web site domain name to be resolved. Having cached the first name resolution, the next resolution requests would be satisfied from the cache.

Each time a name server responds to a request using its cache instead of querying its database, the response is marked as *non-authoritative*, so the resolver (client) may know that this information may not be up to date. Also, the name server would supply the name of the *authoritative* server that supplied this cached data. Then, the resolver may choose what to do: use this cached data or issue a new request to the appropriate name server.

Although DNS information does not change very often, it may change. For this reason, the cached responses must not be stored for ever. Thus, each resource record has associated an optional parameter called Time-To-Live (TTL), which indicates the time the corresponding resource is valid while cached. A $TTL directive in the Master File gives the default TTL value for the zone. Each resource record that explicitly indicates its own TTL, overrides the default.

In the above paragraphs, we considered the time and resource a request takes in order to be resolved. This is true even if the request results are unsuccessful. For this reason, it makes sense to also cache the unsuccessful resolution requests, in order that time and resources are not wasted on future requests. This technique is called *negative caching*. The Minimum field of the SOA record specifies how long to cache this negative information.

11.4.3.1.5 *Load balancing*

Some websites have so many HTTP requests that they need more than one server to attend to this demand. In these cases, DNS provides a technique called load balancing, consisting of having multiple IP addresses, declared in the A type resource record, for each domain (one IP address for each server). Then, for each request, the DNS server will respond with a list of IP addresses for this domain. The resolver will generally take the first IP on the list, but as the DNS changes the order for this list in each response, the HTTP request will be redirected to different IP addresses each time, and the load is then spread between multiple servers.

This same technique may be applied to spread DNS requests into multiple DNS servers, for such domains which have many requests to attend, like the case of the .COM domain which has numerous organizations registered.

11.4.3.1.6 *Dynamic updates*

RFC 2136 'Dynamic Updates in the Domain Name System (DNS UPDATE)' introduced an enhancement to the DNS operation allowing DNS zone information to be dynamically updated. In this way, it is possible to add, modify or delete resource records using a DNS Update message.

This solution was developed for those hosts which do not have a static (or fixed) IP address, but which have a dynamically assigned IP address using Dynamic Host Configuration Protocol (DHCP) or similar. In these cases, the dynamically assigned IP address may change very frequently. Then, the appropriate resources in the Master File should be modified accordingly.

11.4.3.2 DNS Resolvers

A DNS Resolver is a software module running in the user's device, and it is in charge of the process of Name Resolution. In order to accomplish this task, a set of messages are sent to DNS servers, which ultimately provide the requested information. This communication is based on a client/server model, using specific message formats.

The most important types of resolution are the standard Name Resolution (given a domain name, determine its IP address), the reverse Name

Resolution (given an IP address, determine the associated domain name), and the electronic Mail Resolution (given an e-mail address, determine the mail server's domain name which handles it).

11.4.3.2.1 *Standard Name Resolution*

The standard Name Resolution process involves the following steps:

1 Locating a name server which is authoritative for the domain name we are resolving.
2 Requesting from this authoritative name server, the A resource record containing the IP address for the domain name we are resolving.

The first step is, perhaps, the most difficult part of the whole process. This is due to the hierarchical structure of the DNS name space, the authorities that define the zones and the name servers that have the set of resource records for that zone. As we have seen, the DNS name servers are 'linked' in a way that each name server knows the name servers that are responsible for the sub-domains below it. For this reason, in order to locate the authoritative name server containing the appropriate set of resource records pertaining to a given domain name, the resolution process must begin from the root, making a request to any of the root servers, which will give us information about how to locate the top-level domain to which the given domain name belongs. Having this, the next step is to query the TLD authoritative name server, which will give us the authoritative name server for the sub-domain to which the given domain name belongs; and so forth. Having contacted the ultimate authoritative name server for the given domain name, which has the A resource record mapping the domain name with its IP address, we have performed the second step of the process. If this last is successfully responded, we will have the IP address of the domain name.

Suppose we need to resolve the following URL:

http://www.mysite.com

The resolution process needs to start from a root server which knows the authoritative name server for the .com domain. The next query to this name server will give us the authoritative name server for the mysite.com domain. After this, the next query for this name server, asking for the www.mysite.com domain name, will respond with two resource records: the CNAME resource record indicating that www is an alias and their canonical name is server1, and the A resource record with the IP address for the server1.mysite.com domain name.

As we can see, many steps are needed in order to complete the whole resolution process. However, there are two ways to accomplish these processes, using iterative resolution, or recursive resolution.

In **iterative resolution**, the client's resolver is in charge of the complete process. Then, it must send queries to each of the authoritative name servers throughout the hierarchical space, starting from a root server. Each response will contain either the authoritative name server for the requested domain name, or the name server closest to it. Finally, the query will get the authoritative name server for the requested domain name, which ultimately responds with the associated resource records from the domain zone Master File.

In **recursive resolution**, the client's resolver simply sends a query (with the *Recursion Desired* flag set) to a local name server, which will be in charge of the complete resolution process on the client's behalf. The local name server, then, will begin the resolution process as described above (iterative resolution), until the requested resource records have been received. After that, the local name server responds with this information to the client's resolver.

One important point to take into account is that not all name servers support recursive resolution; in particular root servers or other name servers like the ones managing most-used domains (such as the .com domain), which do not support recursion to avoid being exhausted with these tasks. Generally, local name servers are willing to accept recursive queries.

Every device must be configured with an IP address of a local name server. This configuration may be dynamically assigned (when the device's IP address, sub-mask and default gateway are assigned), or manually configured in the appropriate DNS configuration option. Without an assigned local name server, or if the one assigned is not properly working, the device will not be able to resolve domain names.

11.4.3.2.1.1 Name resolver caching

The Name Resolution process, in either iterative or recursive resolution, takes a relatively long time. That is, lots of DNS messages need to be exchanged in order to get the authoritative server, which ultimately provides the right information. One way to improve efficiency is with the caching technique.

Using resolver caching, once a name is resolved, it is cached. Then, the next resolutions for the same name are served from the cache, eliminating the traffic generated by the queries. The resolver cache also alleviates the DNS servers' load. Of course, the cached data is not valid for ever, so the TTL parameter specifies the time this data will expire. Although the caching technique improves efficiency, not all resolvers support it, and not even all query results are cached.

11.4.3.2.1.2 Name Resolution process example

Figure 11.3 shows a Name Resolution example using a recursive query to the local name server configured in the client's device. Suppose the user types the www.mysite.com URL in the web browser. Then, the client's resolver is invoked. The first approach is to check if this domain name is cached and still valid (Step 1). If so, the task is completed. Supposing it is not in the cache, the next step is to query the local name server (Step 2). As this local name server supports recursive resolution, the resolver uses this feature, charging the local name server with the responsibility of resolving the domain name on its behalf. The local name server checks its cache, looking for the domain name already resolved and cached (Step 3). Supposing this is

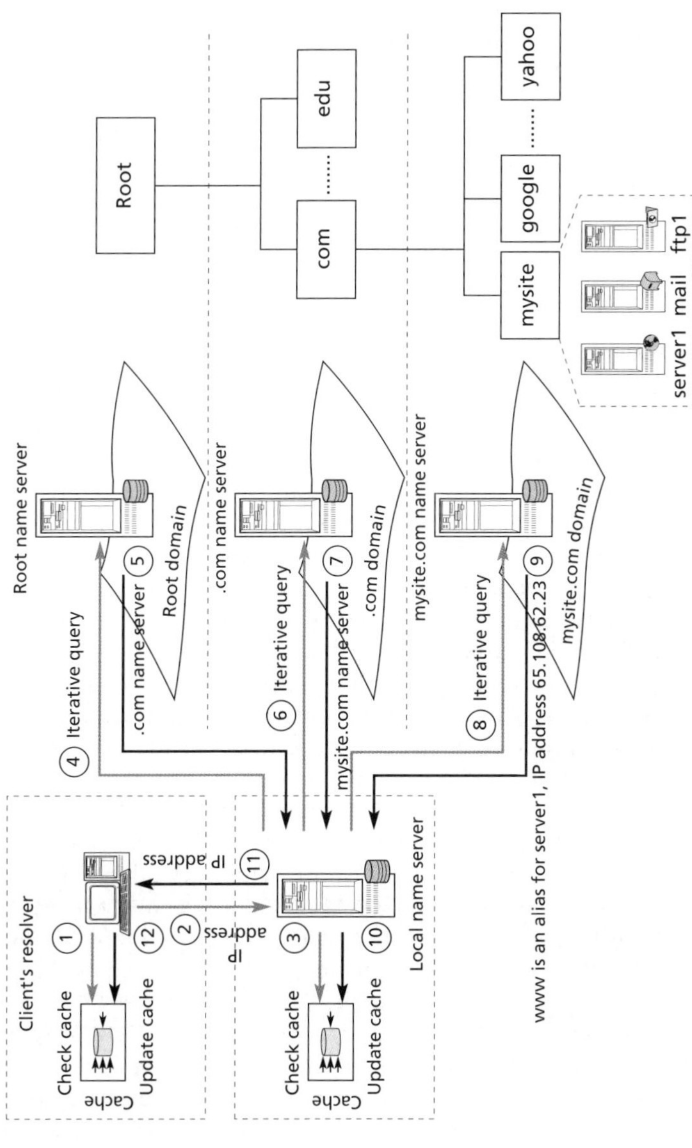

Figure 11.3 Name Resolution example for www.mysite.com

not the case, the local name server begins a series of iterative queries for each of the name servers from the DNS hierarchical name space, starting from the root, until the authoritative name server for the searched domain name is found.

The first query is for the root name server (Step 4), which responds to the .com authoritative name server (Step 5). The next query sent to the .com name server (Step 6) will provide the authoritative name server for the mysite.com domain name (Step 7).

Finally, querying the mysite.com name server about the www.mysite.com domain name (Step 8), it will respond with the CNAME resource record, indicating that www is an alias for the server1 name, and with an A resource record with the IP address for the server1.mysite.com domain name (Step 9).

The local name server updates its cache (Step 10) and sends the response to the client's resolver (Step 11), which gets the IP address to pass it to the browser, and which updates its cache (Step 12) for future references to this domain name.

11.4.3.2.2 *Reverse Name Resolution*

As we said above, reverse Name Resolution consists of determining the domain name associated with a given IP address. In order to accomplish this task, the Master File has a PTR (pointer) resource record which associates the IP address with a domain name. But the question is, given an IP address, how do we get the right domain name server to get the PTR resource record?

In standard Name Resolution, given a domain name such as www.mysite.com we start querying from the root server downwards through the hierarchy, until we get the authoritative name server for the given domain. This is possible because the name servers are 'linked' by the name. So the solution is to create an alternative hierarchical structure, but 'linked' by the IP address. This structure is created using the temporary .ARPA.

A numerical hierarchy structure is created inside the ARPA TLD, using an SLD called IN-ADDR.ARPA. In this level, there are 256 sub-domains labelled from '0' to '255' (each possible number in the first byte of the IP address). Within each of these levels, there are another 256 sub-domains, and so forth, up to four levels (representing the four bytes of IP address).

Then, given the address 200.112.136.85, we use the 85.136.112.200.IN-ADDR.ARPA to resolve this 'name' as a standard name resolution, in order to search the PTR resource which maps this address to the corresponding domain name.

The reason for using the address reversed (85.136.112.200 instead of 200.112.136.85) is because, as in the standard Name Resolution we start resolving from right to left (in www.mysite.com.root we work from the root, com, and mysite domain, in this order), so we need to present the address in this way to begin from the first byte of the address (200) instead of the last (85).

11.4.3.2.3 *Electronic mail resolution*

As we saw in Chapter 9, an e-mail address has the following format: john@mysite.com, where john is the username and mysite.com is the domain name. However, the SMTP server which handles e-mails for this domain probably has a domain name such as, for example, mail1.mysite.com.

Then, the question is how the resolver finds the mail server for the mysite.com domain name. The answer is the MX resource record from the master file in the domain's name server.

That is, the resolver queries its local name server (as we already saw in the standard resolution example), but asking for the MX resource record. Then, when the authoritative name server for this domain is found, it will answer the MX resource record containing the domain name of the mail server which handles e-mail for this domain (mail1.mysite.com in this case), and the A resource record containing the IP address associated with this mail server. Remember that, in the case where more than one mail server exists, all of them are returned with their corresponding priority number.

11.4.3.3 DNS client/server communication model

DNS Name Resolution consists of the transfer of messages between a client and a server, for the purpose of resolving domain names. The client sends queries, while the server sends back replies. The role of the client may be performed by the resolver as well as by the name server (in the recursive resolution, or in a zone transfer), while the role of the server is performed only by a name server.

DNS uses both UDP and TCP transport protocols. For simple DNS query messages, UDP is used. In such cases where large query messages (more than 512 bytes) or zone transfers are needed, TCP is used instead. The servers listen for incoming request on port 53 on both protocols (the well-known port for DNS).

11.4.3.4 DNS message format

A common message format is used by DNS for all communications (queries and responses). The message is divided into five sections; the *Header* (a fixed-length section containing 12 bytes used to control the process), the *Question* (a variable-length section used by the client to include the questions of the query), the *Answer* (a variable-length section used in the response to carry resource records answering the questions of the query), the *Authority* (a variable-length section used in the response containing resource records indicating authoritative name servers), and the *Additional* (a variable-length section used in the responses containing additional information related to the questions of the query). Figure 11.4 shows the DNS message format.

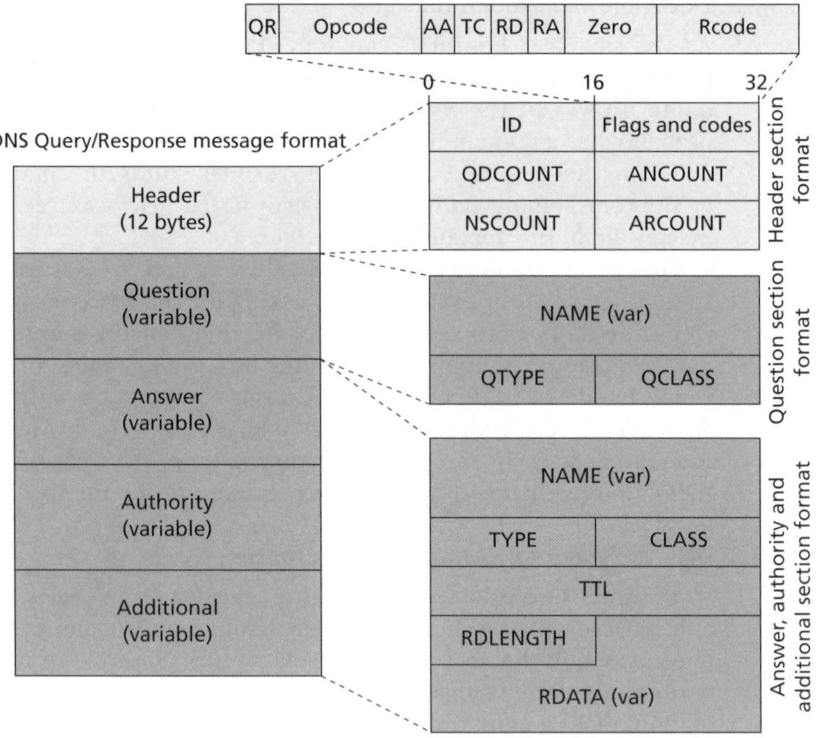

Figure 11.4 DNS general message format.

The header (12 bytes) is always present in all messages, and it consists of the following fields:

- ID (2 bytes): Identifier is a 16-bit number assigned by the requester, used to match the response with the corresponding query.
- Flags and Codes (2 bytes): It consists of many fields indicating the following:
  - QR (1 bit): Query-Response specifies if the message is a Query (0) or a Response (1).
  - **OpCode** (4 bits): Operation Code indicates the type of query in the message:

    0 (QUERY): A standard Query.
    1 (IQUERY): An inverse Query (Obsolete).
    2 (STATUS): A server status request.
    3 (RESERVED)
    4 (NOTIFY): Used by Master servers to notify Secondary servers that the zone has changed.
    5 (UPDATE): Used to implement Dynamic DNS.
    6–15 (RESERVED)

  - AA (1 bit): Authoritative Answer flag, if set to 1, indicates that the response was created by an authoritative server for the domain name specified in the question section

- TC (1 bit): Truncation flag, when set to 1, indicates that the message was truncated due to length greater than that permitted on the transmission channel (512 byte limit in UDP).
- RD (1 bit): Recursion Desired is used in the query to request (if RD set to 1) to the local name server a recursive resolution.
- RA (1 bit): Recursion Available is set to 1 in the response if the name server supports recursive resolutions.
- Z (3 bits): Zero must be all zero. Reserved for future use.
- RCode (4 bits): Response Code is used in responses, indicating the following:
  - 0 No Error – No error condition.
  - 1 Format Error – The name server cannot interpret the query.
  - 2 Server Failure – The server had a problem.
  - 3 Name Error – Used by authoritative name servers to indicate that the domain name does not exist.
  - 4 Not Implemented – The name server does not support this type of query.
  - 5 Refused – The name server refuses the operation for policy reasons.
  - 6 YX Domain – A name exists, but it should not (RFC 2136).
  - 7 YX RR Set – A resource record set exists, but it should not (RFC 2136)
  - 8 NX RR Set – A resource record set does not exist, but it should (RFC 2136).
  - 9 NOT AUTH – The server is not authoritative for the zone specified (RFC 2136).
  - 10 NOT ZONE – A name specified in the message is not within the specified zone (RFC 2136).

- QDCOUNT (2 bytes): Question Count specifies the number of questions in the Question section of the message.
- ANCOUNT (2 bytes): Answer Record Count specifies the number of resource records in the Answer section of the message.
- NSCOUNT (2 bytes): Authority Record Count specifies the number of resource records in the Authority section of the message.
- ARCOUNT (2 bytes): Additional Record Count specifies the number of resource records in the Additional section of the message.

The **Question** (variable) section is used in Queries, and copied in the Responses. All Queries should have at least one question in this section. The question section contains the following fields:

- QNAME (variable): Question Name contains the domain name for which the query is sent. The name is encoded using the DNS name notation (see the next section).

- QTYPE (2 bytes): Question Type specifies the type of question in the query. This could be a resource record or a special request as a zone transfer. The following codes are valid:

  1 A – The address resource record.
  2 NS – The name server resource record.
  5 CNAME – The canonical name resource record
  6 SOA – The Start Of Authority resource record.
  12 PTR – The pointer resource record (used for reverse resolution).
  15 MX – The mail exchange resource record (used for e-mail resolution).
  16 TXT – The text string resource record.
  251 IXFR – A request for incremental zone transfer (partial zone transfer).
  252 AXFR – A request for an entire zone transfer.
  255 * (Asterisk) – A request for all records.

- QCLASS (2 bytes): Question Class specifies the class of the query. It has the value 1 for Internet ('IN'), or 255 for 'ANY CLASS'.

The **Answer**, **Authority**, and **Additional** (variables) sections contain the resource records the name server sends in the responses. Each section may have zero or more records. These sections share the same format, consisting of the following fields:

- NAME (variable): NAME is the domain name with which the resource record is associated. The name is encoded using the DNS name notation.
- TYPE (2 bytes): TYPE specifies the type of the resource record, as described in the QTYPE field of the Question section.
- CLASS (2 bytes) CLASS specifies the class of the resource record, as described in the QCLASS field of the Question section.
- TTL (4 bytes): Time-To-Live specifies the number of seconds that the resource record can be considered valid in the cache. If this value is zero, it means that the resource record should not be cached.
- RDLENGTH (2 bytes): Resource Data Length specifies the length (in bytes) of the RDATA field.
- RDATA (variable): Resource Data contains the resource record, and its specific format depends on the particular resource type, according to Table 11.1.

11.4.3.4.1 *The DNS name notation*

As we saw in the DNS message format description, the domain names are formed using a special DNS name notation. In this scheme, the fully qualified domain name consisting of labels separated by dots is replaced by a single byte used to indicate the label length, followed by the label itself. Each label of the domain name is placed one after the other (omitting the dot). The end

Table 11.1

Resource record type	Field/ subfields	Size (in bytes)	Description
A	ADDRESS	4	A 32-bit IP address of the specified NAME.
NS	NSDNAME	variable	The name of the name server that should be authoritative for the specified NAME, using the DNS name notation.
CNAME	CNAME	variable	The canonical name of the specified NAME, using the DNS name notation.
SOA	MNAME	variable	Master Name is the domain name of the authoritative server for the zone, using the DNS name notation.
	RNAME	variable	Responsible Name is the electronic mail of the person responsible for the zone, using DNS name notation (but omitting the '@' symbol).
	SERIAL	4	Serial Number is the version of the Master File of the zone.
	REFRESH	4	Refresh indicates the period of time the Secondary server waits between checks from the Primary to see if a zone transfer is needed.
	RETRY	4	Retry is the period of time the Secondary server must wait, in case the last attempt to check the Primary serial failed, before trying again.
	EXPIRE	4	Expire is the number of seconds that the Secondary server must wait before considering the information stale, where it cannot contact the Primary server.
	MINIMUM	4	This field specifies how long a negative entry must be considered valid (Negative Caching TTL).
PTR	PTRDNAME	variable	The domain name pointed by the resource record, using the DNS name notation.
MX	PREFERENCE	2	The preference level of this mail server.
	EXCHANGE	variable	The domain name of the mail server, using the DNS name notation.
TXT	TXT-DATA	variable	A descriptive text data.

of the name is indicated using a byte with the zero value (it would indicate the root which has a zero length label). For this reason, in those fields that use this notation, it is not necessary to indicate the field length, as the name itself indicates where it ends.

For example, the domain name server1.mysite.com. is written as:

[7]server1[6]mysite[3]com[0]

where each number within brackets represents a single byte indicating the length of the label that follows.

11.4.3.4.2 *Using compression*

As the domain names are used in several fields in a DNS message, and as most of them may be in the same zone, most of these names may have many labels in common (for example, labels as mysite and com are repeated in mail1.mysite.com, mail2.mysite.com and server1.mysite.com).

In order to reduce the size of messages, the DNS uses a compression scheme which allows eliminating the repetition of domain names (or the repeated labels) in a message. In this way, the repeated part of the domain name is replaced with a pointer to a prior occurrence of this part. This consists of a 16-bit pointer where the first 2 bits are fixed at '11', and the next 14 bits form the offset from the start of the message (the ID field of the header) where the prior occurrence is found. If the offset equals zero, it points to the first byte of the ID field.

Figure 11.5 shows an example where the first instance of a domain name 'server1.mysite.com' is included in the messages using all labels. Then, when the domain name 'mail1.mysite.com' must be included in the message, only the 'mail1' label is used; and a pointer to Position 50, where the 'mysite.com' label begins. A later reference to the same domain name 'server1.mysite.com' is directly made using a pointer to Position 42, where the first instance of this name begins. Take note that all numbers (used in label length indicators and position pointers) in the example are in decimal, while the labels are represented in ASCII.

As all labels begin with the label length which does not exceed 63 (with the first 2 bits in '00'), and the pointers have values greater than 192 (with the first 2 bits in '11'), it is easy to distinguish between a label length indicator and a pointer.

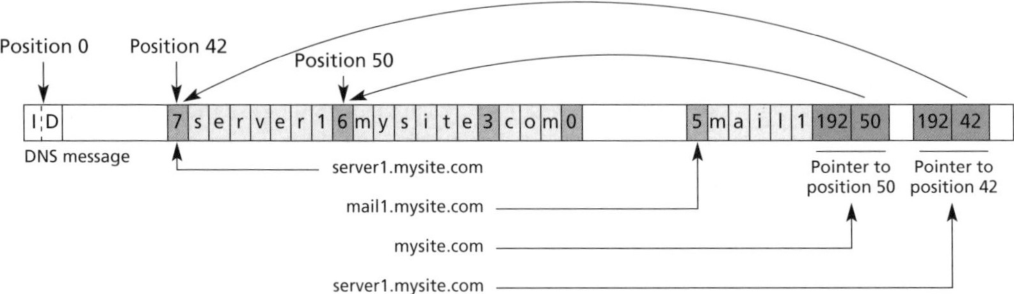

Figure 11.5 DNS message compression.

11.5 Summary

- A name system allows the use of names instead of IP addresses, which are necessary to identify devices in a TCP/IP network. All the possible assigned names define the **Name Namespace**. As well as IP addresses being unique, two or more devices may not have the same name. In order to guarantee this last condition, a central authority organization should register device names. This process is called **Name Registration**. As computers only deal with numbers, each time a name is used, a 'translation' process called **Name Resolution** is invoked, to get the corresponding device's IP address.
- The flat name space consists of an unstructured name space, where a single label is assigned to each device. The flat name is inappropriate for the Internet where millions of computers are connected. In this case, the central authority organization and its database necessary to name resolution would have to handle the entire name space, impossible in practical terms.
- The hierarchical name space consists of a structured name space, where the names are composed of multiple labels related one to the other, using a hierarchical 'parent/child' semantic. In this architecture, the Name Registration process and the database containing the mapping between names and IP addresses, may be distributed through the hierarchical structure.
- Host tables were the first attempt to use a name system in an internetwork, and consisted of simple text files located in each host, used to map the device's name with its IP addresses. In this way, the resolution process is local. Although this system may work for small networks, it is inappropriate for huge networks like the Internet.
- The TCP/IP Domain Name System was developed to implement a name system in large networks such as the Internet. It uses a hierarchical name system based on the concept of a domain. The DNS hierarchical structure starts with the root, which contains the top-level domains (TLDs). Each TLD has second-level domains (SLDs), which in turn may have subdomains or hosts. Domain names are constructed using labels separated by dots ('.').
- The IANA/ICANN is the central authority responsible for every name in the Internet. It creates and maintains the TLDs of the DNS hierarchical structure. The TLDs are grouped under two main categories; the **organizational TLDs**, which register different organizations according to their type; and the **country code TLDs**, which include the top domains for each country. The IANA/ICANN delegates the authority of each organizational TLD to different organizations. In the case of country code TLDs, each country has the authority for its own domain. The registration process is distributed through the hierarchical domain name structure, where each authority defines an independently administered area called a zone of authority. Every zone must have at least one DNS name server.
- Name Resolution is the process by which a domain name is 'translated' into its IP address. The process is performed using the client/server model, where the **resolver** (client) sends a query to a **name server** (server), which replies using the information it has about the requested domain name.

- Name servers have information about domain names. This information is stored in the DNS Master Files. The hierarchical structure is divided into zones of authority, where each name server has the resource records for this zone, and knows the authoritative name server for the sub-domains under its zone. In this way, the name servers are 'linked' following the authority hierarchy present in the DNS name space. If a name server is queried about a domain name for which it is not the authoritative server, it may respond with the authoritative name server for this domain name. Several 'root' name servers are at the top of the structure, and they provide information about each authoritative name server for each TLD. In order to provide redundancy, more than one name server is used for each zone. A mechanism called zone transfer allows the secondary name servers to update their information from the primary name server. The caching technique is used to improve performance.
- A DNS resolver is a software module running in the client's machine, and it is charged with the process of name resolution. It uses the client/server communication model to send query messages to the name servers, which reply with the requested information. The most important type of resolutions are the **standard name resolution** (given a domain name, determine its IP address), the **reverse name resolution** (given an IP address, determine its domain name), and the **electronic mail resolution** (given an e-mail address, determine the mail server's domain name which handles it).
- In standard Name Resolution, the process can be accomplished in two different ways: **iterative resolution**, where the resolver is in charge of the whole process, sending queries to each name server throughout the hierarchical space, starting from the root servers; or **recursive resolution** where the resolver sends a query to the local name server, which is in charge of the whole process, and respond to the resolver once it has the queried information.
- A common DNS message format is used for all communications between clients and servers. A message's header is used to control the whole process, while other sections allow the message to carry the queries and the responses, as well as additional information. All domain names used in the messages use a special DNS name notation. A compression scheme is provided in order to reduce the size of messages.

PART II

Embedded Internet implementation

'This is where we realize that our knowledge is never sufficient...'

12

Preparing the Labs

In this first chapter of Part II, we will start preparing all the necessary hardware and software under which the Labs will be developed. The main goal of the Labs as well as the proposed hardware and software are introduced. The required hardware and software installation and configuration steps are explained.

12.1 Labs introduction

Our goal is to develop and implement a TCP/IP stack to apply to an embedded system. For this reason, we will start with a basic application running on the proposed hardware. After our stack has been implemented, the application should be able to send and reply ping messages (ICMP Echo Request and Reply), receive and send UDP datagrams, process TCP segments, send e-mails and serve web pages to a browser.

We will provide a console interface to show the messages from our embedded systems. For debugging purposes, we will provide the stack with the ability to show the packets it receives and the actions it takes. A simple menu will be supplied, in order for the developer to interact with the embedded software. The console will be implemented using a hardware serial interface attached to a serial port on a personal computer (PC). The Window's HyperTerminal program will allow us to communicate with the software running in the embedded system.

As well as the console interface, the hardware must have a network interface in order to communicate with other devices. This network interface could be an Ethernet interface, or a serial port. Figure 12.1 presents the complete development environment under which the Labs will be developed.

The development PC will be used to load the Labs projects into the Integrated Development Environment (IDE), add or modify the program code, compile and link the project, and get the final binary code, which will be downloaded into the embedded system board using the Philips Flash Utility. Once the board is programmed, it is ready to run, so the HyperTerminal is launched in the development PC in order to be used as a system console, allowing some feedback about what is happening in the embedded system and issuing some commands to instruct the software to do

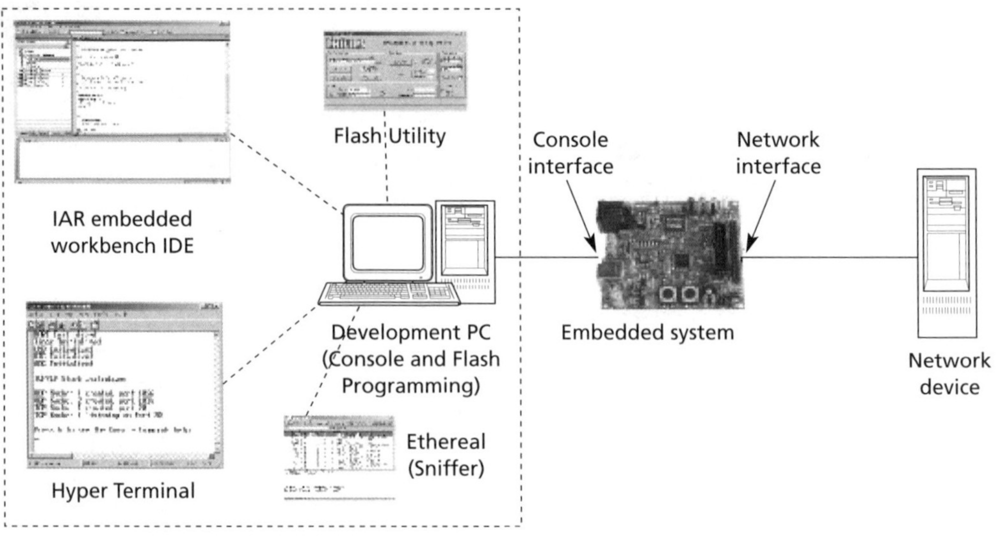

Figure 12.1 The Development Environment.

specific tasks. The embedded system will interact with the network device through the network link connected to the board's network interface.

Although in Figure 12.1 the development PC and the network device are shown as two different devices, in fact one PC can be used for both purposes. That is, the PC used for development can be used as the network device that interacts with our embedded system board. Of course, other network devices may be present in the network, as we will shortly see.

12.2 The proposed hardware

As our TCP/IP stack provides support for Ethernet and serial interfaces, two different types of hardware should be used in order to test both drivers. Once the hardware is determined and configured, and the appropriate driver or protocol is selected, the rest of the stack (upper layer protocols) works transparently.

The hardware is based on the Philips LPC2124/29 16/32 bit ARM7TDMI-S™ with 256K bytes program flash, 16K bytes RAM, RTC, 4× 10 bit ADC 2.44 uS, 2× UARTs, I2C, SPI, 2× 32bit Timers, 7× CCR, 6× PWM, WDT, 5V tolerant I/O, up to 60MHz operation. The LPC2129 version includes two CAN interfaces, which will not be used in our Labs. A standard JTAG connector with ARM 2×10 pin layout for programming/debugging with ARM-JTAG is provided, and the crystal frequency is 14.7456MHz. See the manufacturer's specifications for a more detailed description.

The above common features are presented in two different kinds of boards: the LPC-P212X with serial interfaces and the LPC-E212X with Ethernet interface.

12.2.1 Serial interface boards

The proposed hardware is based on the Olimex © LPC-P2124 or LPC-P2129 boards (IAR Kick-Start kits Part# KSDK-LPC2129 and Part# KSDK-2129-PLUS with J-Link), which present two serial ports (RS-232). The first serial port will be used as a console/Flash programming, while the other port will be used as a network link to connect to a network device (a PC) using the PPP protocol. Figure 12.2 shows this board model and the resources it presents.

The boards present Port 1 (UART 0) and Port 2 (UART 1), a power jack (7 to 9 VDC required), a power LED, a reset button and a programming jumper. Two buttons, two LEDs and a trimmer connected to a microcontroller's analogue input port (which provides a variable voltage to an analogue input port) constitute some resources used as an application input/output simulation.

12.2.2 Ethernet interface boards

The proposed hardware is based on the Olimex © LPC-E2124 or LPC-E2129 boards (IAR Kick-Start kits Part# KSDK-LPC2129E and Part# KSDK-2129E-PLUS with J-Link), which present a USB serial port and an Ethernet interface. The USB port will be used as a console/Flash programming, while the Ethernet port will be used as a network interface to connect to other devices configuring a Local Area Network. Figure 12.3 shows this board model and the resources it presents.

The boards present a USB port (the microcontroller's UART 0 port through a FTDI© USB-RS232 converter chip) and an Ethernet port with LAN activity LEDs, a power LED, a reset button, and a programming jumper. The power supply is provided by the PC through the USB interface, so no external power

Figure 12.2 The LPC-P2124/29 board.
(Copyright© Olimex Ltd)

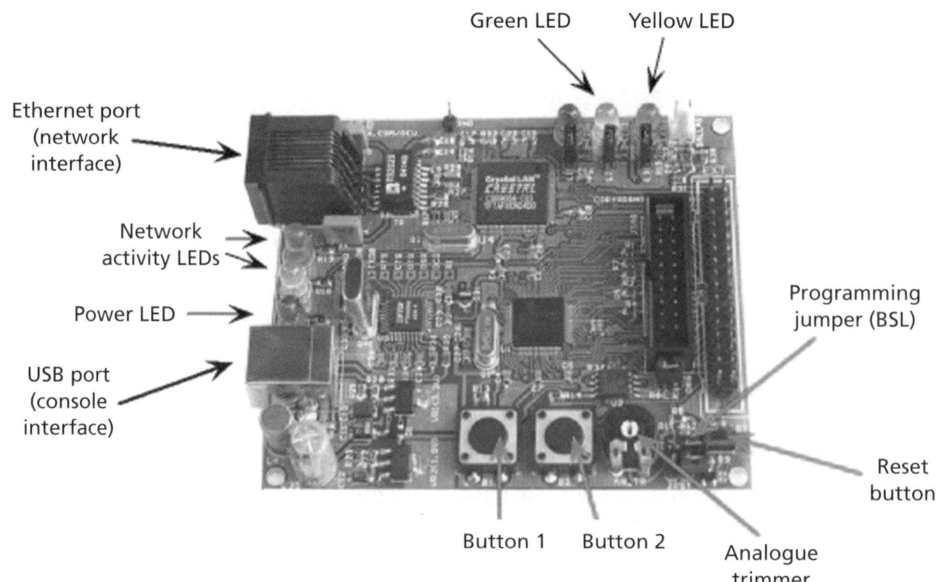

Figure 12.3 The LPC-E2124/29 board.
(Copyright© Olimex Ltd)

supply is required. Two buttons, two LEDs and a trimmer connected to a microcontroller's analogue input port (which provides a variable voltage to an analogue input port), constitute some resources used as an application input/output simulation. Although these boards also have a third LED (Red), it will not be used, so that an application will run with the same resources for any kind of board.

12.2.3 Cable configuration

The LPC-P212X board console uses a pin-to-pin serial cable to connect to the PC serial port. Figure 12.4 shows the cable pin-out specifications. In order to connect to the modem, the cable shown in Figure 12.5 may be used.

In the case of the cellular data cables, since they are ready to connect to the PC serial port, the connector is a DB-9 female so it can be directly connected to the modem serial end of the above modem cable. However, some modems would require specific cable configurations, especially cellular phone data cables. See the modem or cellular users manual for specific information.

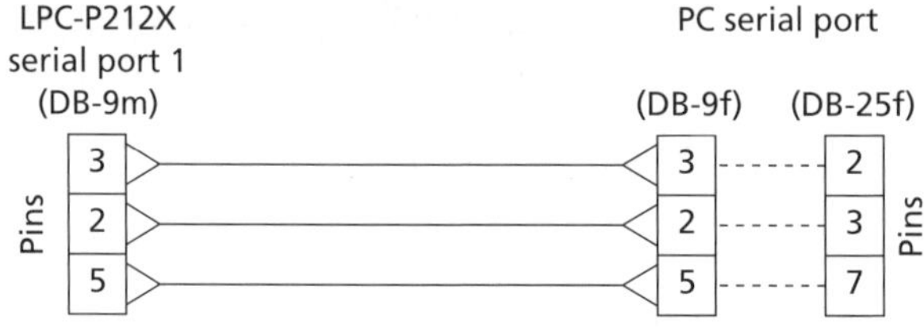

Figure 12.4 LPC-P212X console cable configuraton.

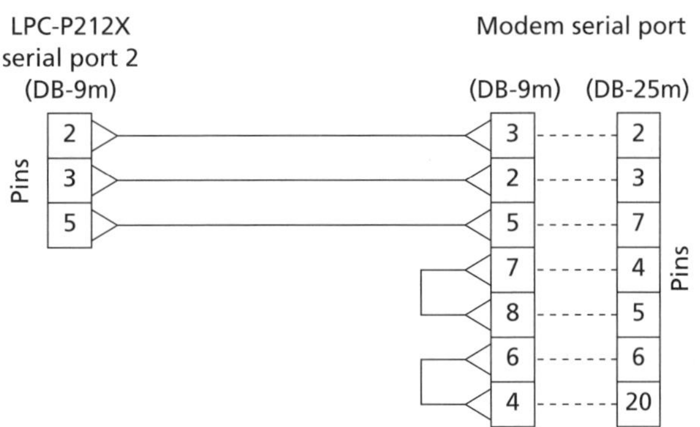

Figure 12.5 LPC-P212X modem cable configuration.

The LPC-E212X boards use a standard USB cable to connect to the PC USB port and a standard Ethernet UTP cable for the network interface.

12.2.4 Common resources

Even though each kind of board presents a specific network interface, all of them provide a common set of resources: two buttons (digital inputs), a trimmer (analogue input) and two LEDs (digital outputs). The real time clock (RTC) will be also used as a common resource from all the boards.

This set of resources will be used to simulate a 'real life' application. As a common set of resources, this application will fit in any of the presented boards, independently of the selected interface. That means the application will work the same way in any of the proposed hardware.

12.3 The proposed software

The CD provided with the book provides a free evaluation copy of the IAR Embedded Workbench IDE for ARM. IAR Systems© is a leader company that provides a range of development tools for embedded systems, including IDEs with C/C++ compilers and debuggers, starter kits, hardware debug probes and state machine design tools. The product line supports 8051, ARM, AVR, MSP430 and many other 8, 16 and 32-bit MCUs from different chip manufacturers.

Although the provided evaluation copy of the IAR Embedded Workbench IDE is a 32K code limited version, the complete Labs and examples provided in this book can be compiled without problems. For more information about IAR Systems, please visit **www.iar.com**. In addition, the CD provides the 'Embedded Internet' Getting Started guide.

12.4 Setting up the Labs hardware

The Labs hardware can be configured in many ways. It will depend on the interface the hardware presents, the kind of network we want to implement (a PPP link, a LAN, an Internet connection, etc.), and of course, the necessary equipment we can get. Let's see first some configurations for the serial interface boards.

12.4.1 Configuring the Labs for the LPC-P212X boards

The first Labs configuration we will see is shown in Figure 12.6. In this case, the LPC-P212X board will establish a PPP link with the development PC, using serial port 2. This port is connected to an external serial modem. An analogue telephone Private Branch Exchange (PBX) is used to allow the external modem to establish a circuit connection with the PC internal modem, using the PBX extensions. Serial port 1 of the board is connected to the PC serial port using an RS-232 cable. This link allows the use of the HyperTerminal program (or any other terminal emulation software) as a console to view and control the embedded software running on the board. This link is also used to Flash Programming.

In order for the embedded software to connect to the PC using a PPP Link, the PC should be configured as an RAS (Remote Access Session) server. See section 12.5. Once the PPP link is established, the LPC-P212X board will be assigned with the 192.168.0.51 IP address. Using this address, the board can be accessed from the development PC. The RAS server (the development PC) will have the 192.168.0.50 IP address. (In Windows 98, the RAS server will have the 192.168.55.1 IP address, while the LPC-P212X board will be assigned with the 192.168.55.2 IP address. These IP addresses cannot be changed.)

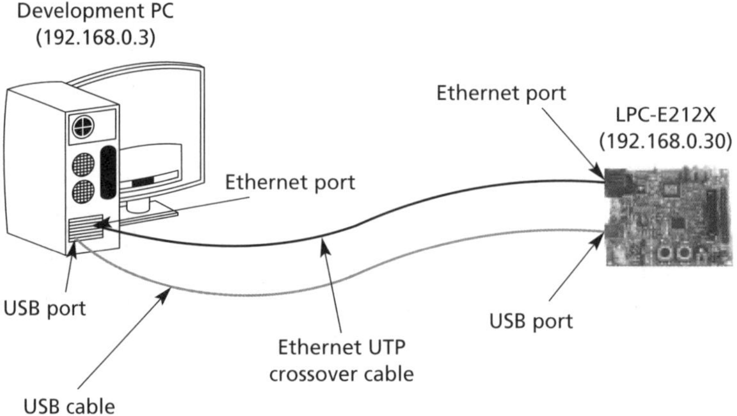

Figure 12.6 Connecting the LPC-P212X to the PC using a PPP link.

This configuration will allow us to test the TCP/IP stack from the PC. That is, a ping can be issued from and to the PC, the embedded web server may be accessed from the PC Internet Browser, and the UDP and TCP servers can be accessed from the PC. Having Internet access from the Development PC, and the RAS server properly configured (see the screenshot on page 300, where the option 'Allow callers to access my local area network' is checked), we will be able to send e-mail messages to the outside world.

In Figure 12.7, we see a similar configuration as above, but the modem is connected to a telephone line. Dialling an ISP access phone number will allow us to connect the embedded software to the Internet, over the PPP protocol. This configuration will allow us to send e-mail messages from the embedded system to any e-mail address in the world. The Web server, the ping and the UDP/TCP servers can also be tested from the outside world using any Internet connection. In Figure 12.7, once the PPP link is established, the LPC-P212X board is configured with an IP address assigned by the ISP. We can use this IP address to access the board from any device connected to the Internet.

Figure 12.8 shows the same configuration as the one shown in Figure 12.7, except for the cellular (mobile) phone which replaces the conventional analogue telephone line. In this case, the cell phone presents a modem interface connected to the board serial port, and it is handled with the 'AT commands' as any other modem. Most cell phone companies provide accesses to the Internet, using the PPP protocol. Here again, the board will be configured with an IP address assigned by the ISP (in this case, the cell phone communications service provider).

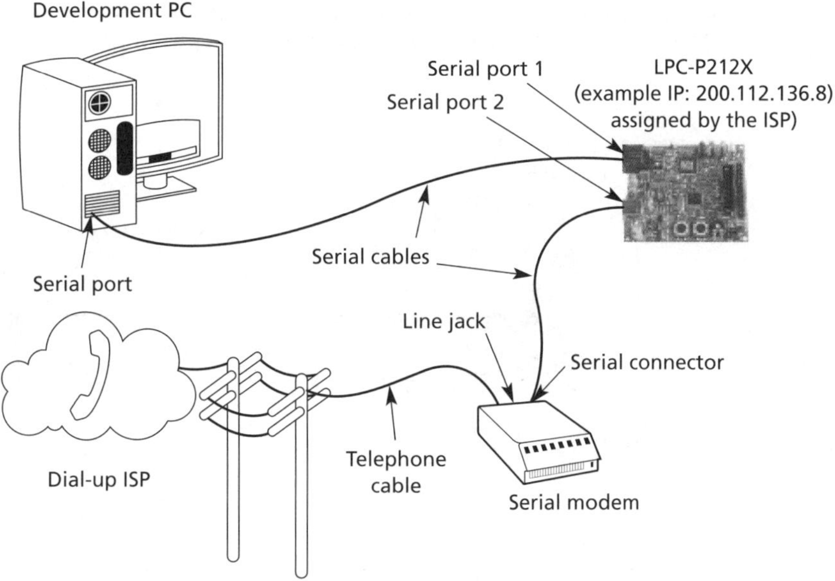

Figure 12.7 Connecting the LPC-P212X to the Internet using a telephone line.

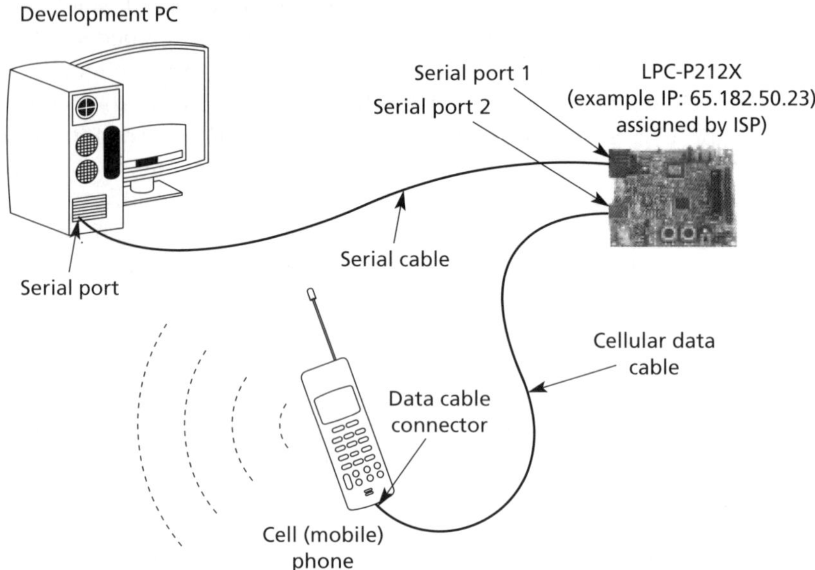

Figure 12.8 Connecting the LPC-P212X to the Internet using a cell phone.

12.4.2 Configuring the Labs for the LPC-E212X boards

In these configurations, we will have our boards connected to a LAN using the Ethernet interface. In Figure 12.9, only one cable is used to create a LAN between the PC and the LPC-E212X. This cable must be an Ethernet crossover UTP cable. The USB port of the board is connected with the PC USB port, using a USB cable. This serial link will be used as the console and flash programming. As this USB link provides the system power for the LPC-E212X from the PC, there is no need for an external power supply.

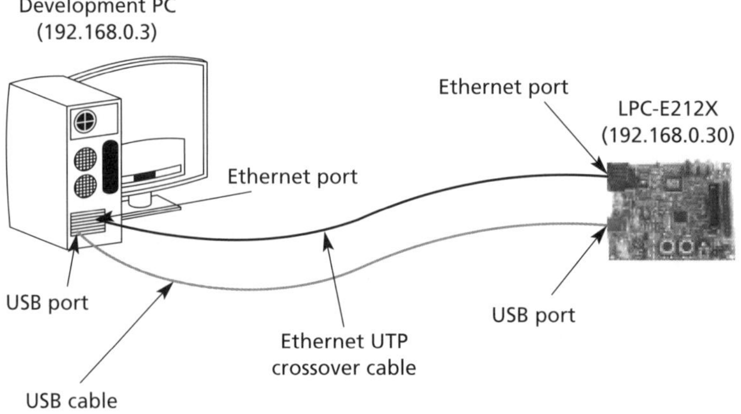

Figure 12.9 Connecting the LPC-E212X and the PC using an Ethernet Crossover UTP Cable.

As the HyperTerminal program and the Philips Flash Utility need a COM port (RS-232 serial port) in the PC, we will need to install a Virtual COM Port (VCP) provided by the USB-RS-232 converter chip manufacturer (**www.ftdichip.com**). In this way, the VCP driver emulates a standard PC serial port, allowing the programs to use the USB port as if it were a COM port.

In this case, the development PC must be configured with the 192.168.0.3 fixed IP address (see section 12.5), while the LPC-E212X board is assigned with the 192.168.0.30 IP address. Under this configuration, we may test all the TCP/IP stack features, but not send e-mail messages to the outside world, as we cannot get a connection to the Internet.

In Figure 12.10, we have a similar configuration except for the use of a hub or switch to connect more than two devices in a LAN network. In this case, we may also connect other devices to the LAN, so the TCP/IP stack features can be tested from devices in addition to the development PC. In this scheme, the configuration is the same as the above, except for other devices that may exist, which should be configured with other IP addresses such as 192.168.0.100, 192.168.0.101, and so on. Once again, as we do not have an Internet connection, we cannot send e-mails to the outside world. However, installing and configuring a local SMTP and POP3 servers, we could send e-mails from and to any of the devices at the LAN.

In Figure 12.11, we use a router, which replaces the hub/switch and provides a WAN port which connects to the Internet through a broadband connection. This configuration will allow us to test all the TCP/IP stack features, including sending e-mails to any e-mail address and sending and replying to ping messages to and from any device connected to the Internet.

In this case, the router probably has an embedded DHCP server, so the devices could be assigned with variable IP addresses. However, as our stack does not have the DHCP client implemented, we need to use a fixed IP

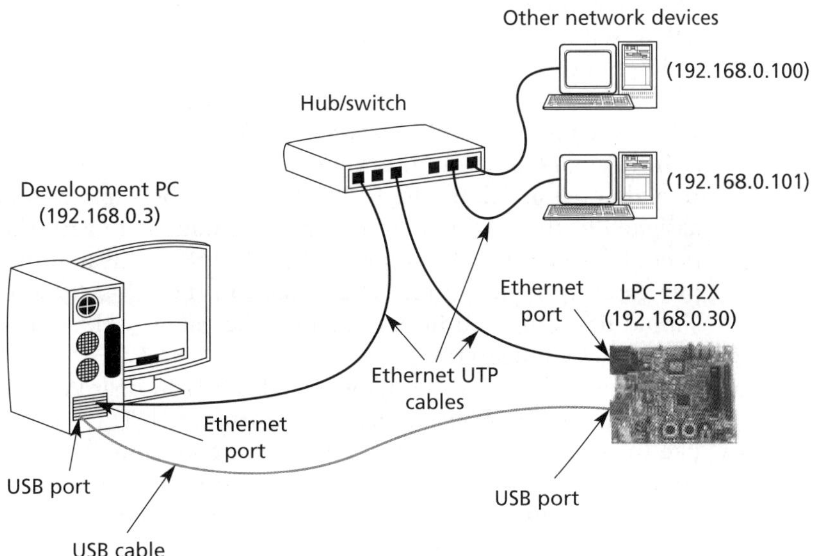

Figure 12.10 Connecting the LPC-E212X to a LAN using a Hub or Switch.

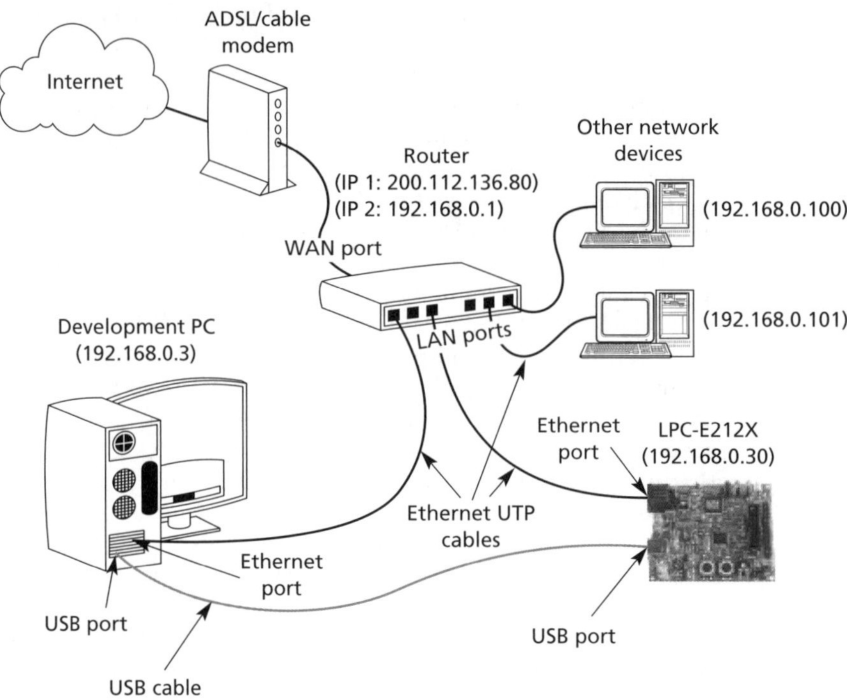

Figure 12.11 Connecting the LPC-E212X to the Internet using a router.

address such as 192.168.0.30. Most routers allow some devices to have their own fixed IP address, so this should not be a problem. The router should be configured in order have this fixed address reserved for the LPC-E212X board, and not assign it to other devices. With respect to the development PC, it may be configured with a fixed IP address or an IP assigned from the DHCP server, although it is suggested that the fixed configuration is used in order to present the same and known IP address, which makes it easy to hardcode the address in the software. If the address changes regularly, we would need to change the software configuration too.

In this configuration, the router will present two IP addresses; the 'public' IP address assigned by the ISP to the WAN port, and an 'internal' IP address assigned to the LAN port in order to communicate with the rest of the connected devices. This last may be the 192.168.0.1 IP address, and it will act as our gateway to the Internet connection. For this reason, this IP address should be configured in our stack as the gateway IP address (in fact, this is the default configuration).

Although these routers allow our LPC-E212X board to be connected to the Internet, they may have a firewall incorporated. This means that if we would like to access our board from any device connected to the Internet, we must configure the router in order to allow and redirect the incoming messages to our board. This is accomplished using the 'Virtual Servers' option, which allows an external port to be defined and protocol to be redirected to a specific internal device. For example, if we want our embedded server to be accessed from the Internet, we need to configure an external port 80 and protocol TCP to be redirected to the port 80 of the 192.168.0.30 IP address. See the specific router's documentation for configuration details. In this case, a TRENDnet TW100-BRF114 router is used (**www.trendware.com**), which works well for this purpose and it is economical (it costs about U$S50). Of course, there are lots of other brands and models, so search for the option that best fits your needs.

12.5 Installing and configuring the software

12.5.1 IAR Embedded Workbench for ARM

Follow the IAR EWARM installation instructions.

12.5.2 Philips Flash Utility

Decompress the ZIP file into any directory, and run the Set-up program. Follow the Set-up program instructions.

12.5.3 USB VCP drivers (FTDI) (only needed for LPC-E212X boards)

Decompress the appropriate driver into any directory. Connect the board to the PC using the USB cable. When Windows detects the new hardware, the 'Found New Hardware' wizard should appear. Provide the wizard with the directory where you decompressed the drivers. The wizard will install both the USB serial converter and the USB serial port drivers. Once you have finished, go to the Device Manager, which should show these drivers as below:

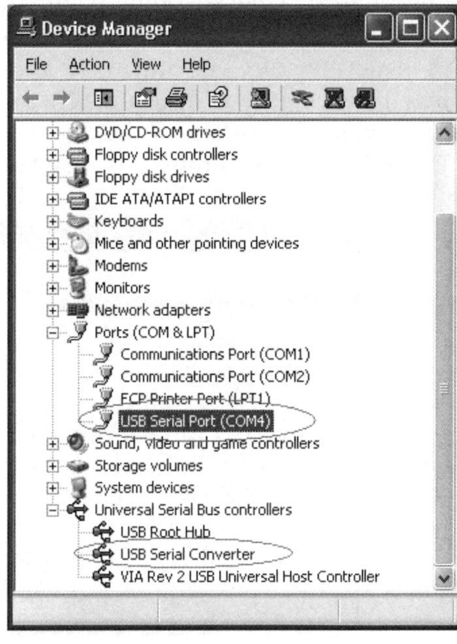

12.5.4 Ethereal and WinPcap (sniffer and the network packet capturer)

The Ethereal set-up program allows you to install both the Ethereal and WinPcap programs. Follow the installer wizard instructions.

The **Ethereal** network protocol analyser has changed its name to **Wireshark**. Nevertheless, the software is the same. Visit **www.wireshark.org** to know more about this.

12.5.5 HyperTerminal configuration (used as a console)

Go to *Start* → *All Programs* → *Accessories* → *Communications* → *HyperTerminal*. When HyperTerminal opens provide a name for the connection and press OK. Then, choose the COM Port of the PC where the console cable is connected (for the LPC-E212X boards, with USB cable, select the USB Serial Port as indicated by the Device Manager) and press OK. Finally, select 9600 (Bits per second), 8 (Data bits), None (Parity), 1 (Stop bits), and None (Flow control) as the COM properties, and press OK. The HyperTerminal is ready to use.

12.5.6 Configuring an RAS server to test the PPP protocol (needed only for the LPC-P212X boards)

12.5.6.1 Windows XP/2000

Go to Start → *All Programs*→ *Accessories* → *Communications* → *New Connection Wizard*. When the 'New Connection Wizard' window appears, press 'Next'. Select 'Set up an advanced connection' option, and press 'Next'. Select 'Accept incoming connections' and press 'Next'. Select the modem device and press 'Next'. Choose 'Do not allow virtual private connections' and press 'Next'. Check users who will be allowed to connect. Change the password using the Properties button (avoid the use of blank passwords). In addition, new users may be added using the Add button. After this, press 'Next'. The following window shows the Networking Software. Select 'Internet Protocol (TCP/IP)' and press Properties. The following window should appear:

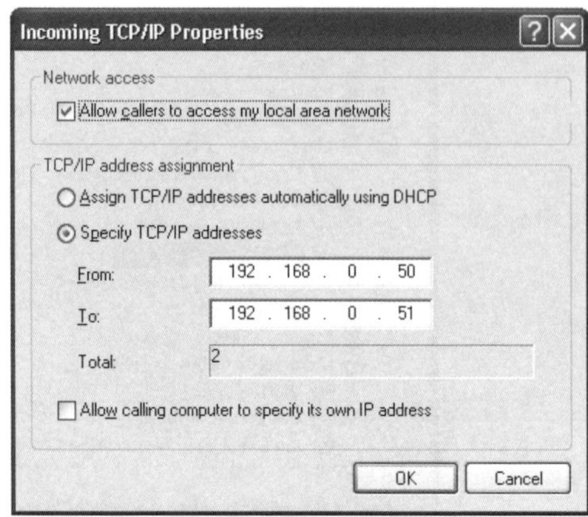

With this configuration, the LPC-P212X will always have the same address (192.168.0.51). If we specify 192.168.0.55, for example, as the second address, then the board will be assigned with a different IP address each time it connects to the PC. Press 'OK', and then press 'Finish'.

12.5.6.2 Windows 98

Go to *Start→Programs→Accessories→Communications→Dial Up Networking*. The following windows should appear:

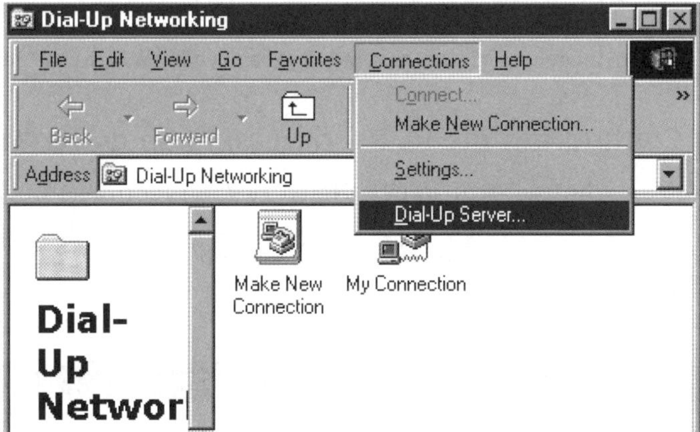

Select the 'Dial-Up Server...' option under the 'Connections' menu. Then, in the Dial-Up Server window, select the 'Allow caller access' option, and use the 'Change Password' button if you want to protect the access. Configure the 'Server Types' options as the following figure shows:

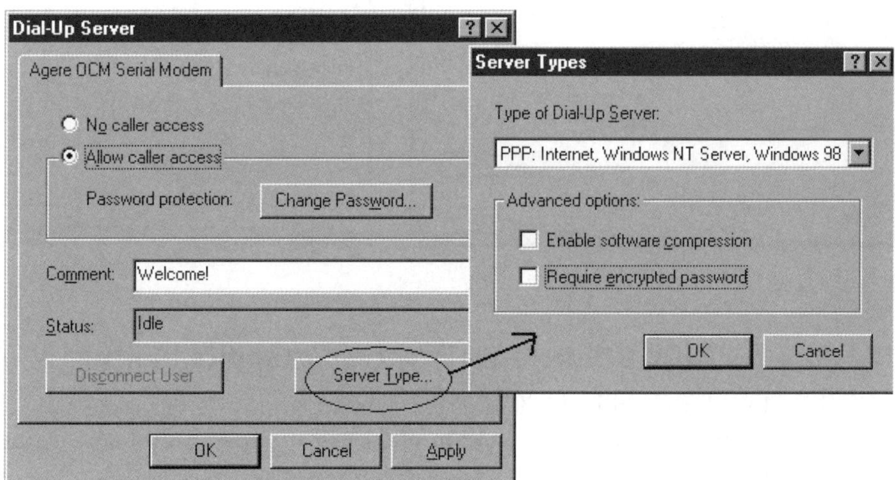

Press 'OK' on both windows, and the dial-up server will be ready for incoming connections. The Windows System Tray should show an icon indicating this.

In Windows 98, it is not possible to specify the IP addresses; the RAS server will have the 192.168.55.1 IP address, while the LPC-P212X board will be assigned with the 192.168.55.2 IP address.

If the 'Dial Up Server…' option does not appear in the 'Connections' menu of the Dial-Up Networking window, go to the *Control Panel→ Add/Remove Programs*, and select the 'Windows Setup' Tab. Select the 'Communications' component, and press Details... The Dial-Up Server component should be checked (installed). If it is not checked, then check it and press the OK button, to start the component installation.

For more information, please refer to the Windows Operating System help.

12.5.7 Configuring the PC IP address: fixed or variable

From the Control Panel, Network Connections, Local Area Connection Properties, select the 'Internet Protocol (TCP/IP)' item, and press Properties. In this window, we may configure the PC IP address as a variable IP address assigned by a DHCP server, or a fixed IP address, as we need.

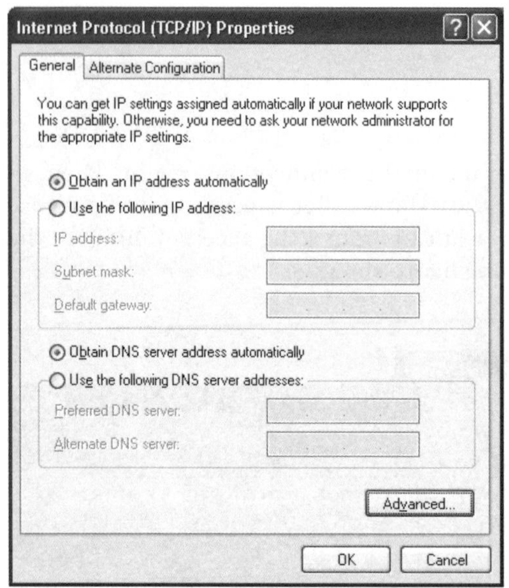

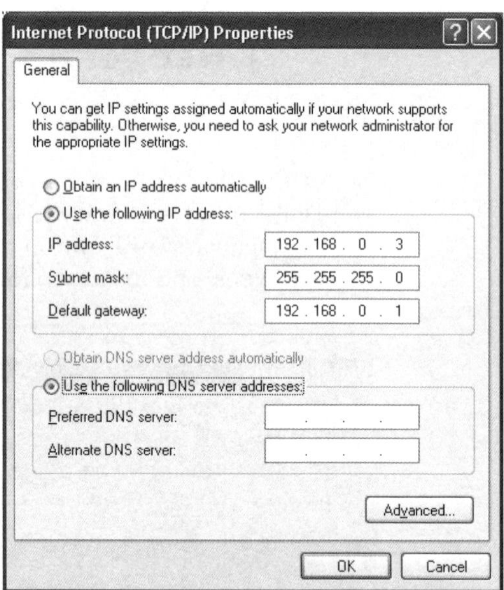

12.5.8 TCP/UDP Utilities, SMTP server, graphics utility

Install the Embedded Internet software from the CD (select the 'Embedded Internet Installations' option and click on 'Install Embedded Internet') and follow the instructions.

12.6 Steps to execute the Labs

1 Set up the hardware: connect and configure the hardware boards as stated above.
2 Compile the Laboratory project:

   Open the IAR Embedded Workbench IDE.
   Load the Lab project (or examples).
   Make (compile and link) the Lab project.

3 Download the image to the microcontroller's flash memory: launch the Philips Flash Utility and configure it with the COM port where the console cable is connected. Verify that the *Execute Code after Upload* option is checked. Select the filename of the Lab's binary code. See the following figure:

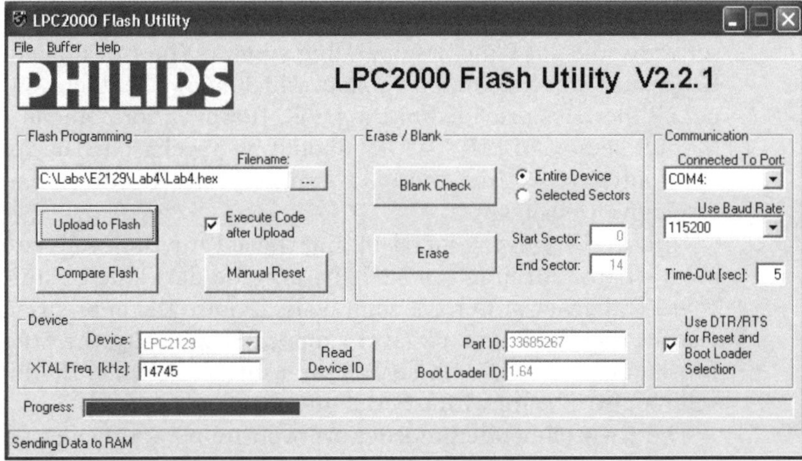

Put the *programming jumper* in the board (or press the BSL button – see notes at the end of this section) and press the Reset button. Then, take out the programming jumper (or release the BSL button). Now the microcontroller is running its internal Boot Loader program.

Press the *Upload to Flash* button (in the Flash Utility) to start programming the binary code into the microcontroller flash memory.

Note: the binary code to download is located in the following directories:

LPC_E212X board →
$INSTALL_DIR$\EmbeddedInternet\Labs\LabXX\LPC_E212X\EXE\LabXX._E212X.hex
LPC_P212X board →
$INSTALL_DIR$\EmbeddedInternet\Labs\LabXX\LPC_P212X\EXE\LabXX._P212X.hex
where XX is the Lab number.

4 Start the Laboratory program: launch the HyperTerminal program and choose the PC COM port where the console cable is connected. Select 9600,8,N,1 and None as the port configuration.

Press the Reset button on the board to start the loaded program. The HyperTerminal should show the embedded software initialization messages. Follow the Lab instructions to complete the specific test.

Note that

- It is convenient to replace the programming jumper by a switch button (BSL button) in order to make it easier each time the board is programmed.
- As the Flash Utility and the HyperTerminal use the same PC COM port, the HyperTerminal should be disconnected using the button, in order for the Flash Utility to use the COM port and download the code to the board. Once this is done, the Flash Utility releases the COM port (if *Execute Code after Upload* is checked) and HyperTerminal may be connected again pressing the button. In this way, we may have both programs opened at the same time without problems.

12.7 Where to get the hardware and software

This book has a CD with the necessary software to implement the Labs. All software runs on Windows operating system. The IAR Embedded Workbench IDE is a 32Kb code limited version, which allows loading, compiling and linking all the Labs provided in the book. However, for commercial applications the full licence of IAR EWARM should be purchased. The rest of the necessary software is free, and its updates may be downloaded from their respective websites.

Only the hardware need be purchased for the reader to complete the book's Labs. Although most Labs may be developed using either type of board (Ethernet or Serial), some Labs require the appropriate board type to test the specific Data Link layer support. Specifically, the Ethernet driver Lab will require a board with an Ethernet interface, while the PPP protocol Lab will require a board with a Serial interface.

The **www.embeddedinternet.org** website book provides detailed information about where to get the right hardware, the software, starting kits and any other resources that may help the reader to learn, such as examples, exercises and other protocols not provided with this book edition. In addition, latest updates for the Labs will be available from this website.

Please visit IAR (**www.iar.com**) for more information about the available Kick-Start kits.

13

The application and the TCP/IP stack

In this chapter, we will introduce the first Lab, which is based on a simple embedded application that simulates an industrial process. This application will be the base for the next Labs where we will start adding each of the TCP/IP stack modules, step-by-step, explaining how the module works. This Lab is important since it will allow us to check if our development environment (the boards and the software installation) is working correctly. Once this Lab has been completed, and before moving to the next Labs, we will see an overview of the complete TCP/IP stack, explaining its structure, describing its modules and showing how it is included in any project.

13.1 Embedded systems with TCP/IP stack

Typically, an embedded system consists of an embedded system hardware running an embedded system application, which controls some process. This application takes data from the digital and/or analogue inputs connected to switches and sensors, processes the data and controls the controlled process using the outputs connected to motors, valves, actuators and others.

Figure 13.1 shows an embedded system running an embedded system application and a TCP/IP stack, which allows the embedded system to communicate with other devices using TCP/IP communications. In this way, the embedded system may benefit from the use of remote monitoring and controls, e-mails sent for status/error reporting, remote software updates, etc.

Paradoxically, the TCP/IP stack and its protocols are the 'stars' of this book. In addition, the rationale of this is just because we are learning and implementing a TCP/IP stack. As a way to test our implementation, an embedded system application should be present. Moreover, 'any' application would fit this requirement. That is to say, that here, the application is not as important as our 'great' TCP/IP stack.

However, once the TCP/IP stack has been fully implemented and tested, it will only be included in those embedded systems which require some way of communication over TCP/IP. These embedded systems will run an application that will solve a 'real life problem'. This means that applications (and not TCP/IP stacks) justify the embedded system implementation.

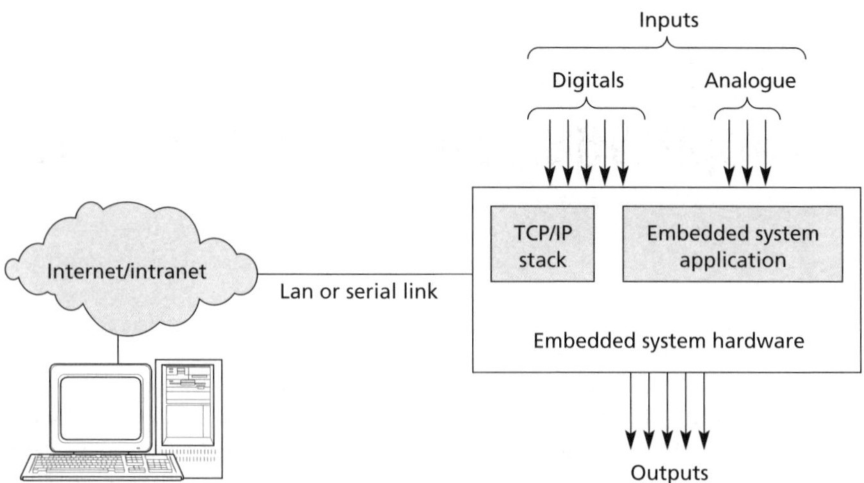

Figure 13.1 An embedded system with TCP/IP communications.

For this reason, the TCP/IP Stack should be designed and implemented as efficiently as possible. And this means that it must take as little memory and processor time as possible, in order for the application to have available as many resources as it needs to implement the solution for this 'real life' problem which justifies the implementation. Our TCP/IP stack implementation was designed with educational purposes in mind, so for commercial applications, the design should prioritize efficiency goals.

Another feature the stack should have is that it should not delay the application too much. In other words, the stack should not block the application's processes. If for any reason, the stack does not allow the application to sense its inputs, process the information and act accordingly, the 'real life' problem will not be solved by the embedded system implementation, so the stack will be more like a problem than a communication solution. For this, the stack is designed as non-blocking. For example, the PPP protocol may take about 20 seconds for the modems to establish and negotiate a link. Imagine what could happen in an industrial control process if the application is blocked during this time, and some 'critical sensors' are sensing extremely high pressure or temperature values. Once the PPP link was established, the application could send an e-mail notifying that the boiler had exploded!

13.2 Introducing the application

13.2.1 An industrial control process

Throughout this second part of the book, we will use a simple application in order to test the TCP/IP stack in a 'real life' case. The proposed application simulates an industrial process, where a tank is filled with a liquid, then a heater raises the liquid temperature, and finally the tank is emptied, concluding the process cycle.

Figure 13.2 shows the process. When the cycle starts, valve 1 is opened and pump 1 is ON, so the liquid flows filling the tank. Once the required liquid level is reached, valve 1 is closed and pump 1 is OFF, while the heater is ON. Then, the liquid temperature will rise until a given value. At this time, the heater is OFF, valve 2 is opened, and pump 2 is ON. In this way, the liquid flows emptying the tank. The complete cycle is divided into three phases: filling, heating and emptying.

In order to implement this process, we would need to sense two inputs (*1–Liquid Level, 2–Liquid Temperature*) and control three outputs (*1–Valve 1 and Pump 1, 2–Heater, 3–Valve 2 and Pump 2*). We could use switches to simulate the inputs, and LEDs to simulate the outputs. However, we would have to manually activate the switches to produce a phase change in the cycle. To avoid this manual intervention, we will use variables instead of the simulated I/O. That is, we define the *Liquid Level* as an integer, which is increased while valve 1 is opened, during the FILLING phase. After some time, the *Liquid Level* will get some value and valve 1 is closed, starting the HEATING phase. Now, the *Liquid Temperature* (an integer) will increase while the heater is ON, until it reaches a given value. At this point, the EMPTYING phase begins where valve 2 is opened, and both the *Liquid Level* and *Temperature* decrease. We use a *Cycle* variable, which allows the process to re-start automatically.

The above application may be started using *Button 1*, which starts the process cycle. We will program *Button 2* to set and clear the *Cycle* variable each time it is pressed. In order to provide a cycle phase indicator, we will program the Yellow LED to flash differently for each distinctive cycle phase.

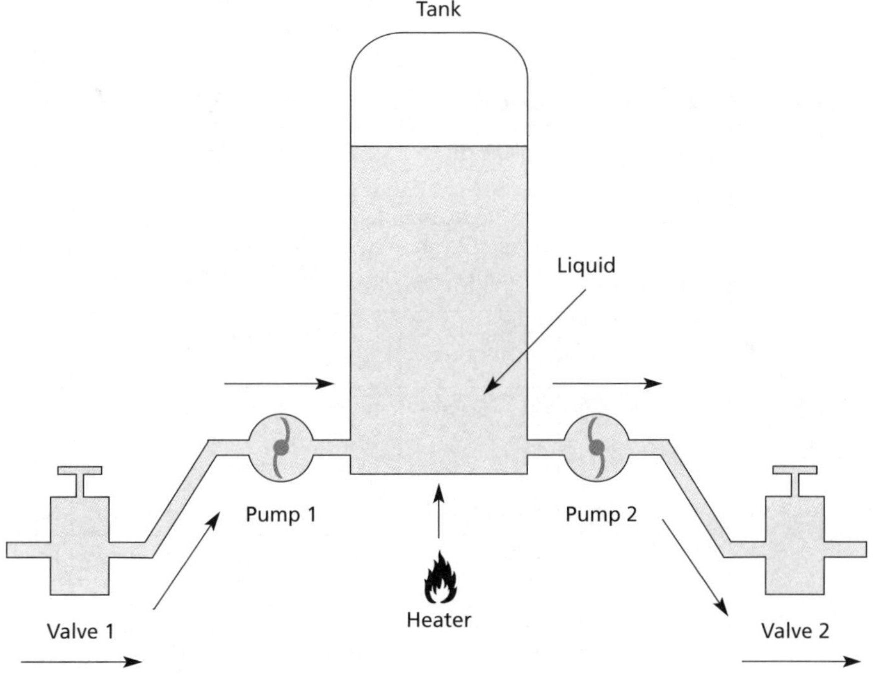

Figure 13.2 The application: a simple industrial process.

13.2.2 The board activity LED

Besides the presented application, we will include a simple process, which uses a flashing LED (green LED), indicating that the embedded program is running. We will include a LED enable variable in order to activate and deactivate the flashing LED remotely using TCP/IP.

13.2.3 Lab 1 software modules

Since the knowledge of the 'C' Language and embedded system programming is a requirement for this book, we will not describe the Lab 1 software source code. Instead, we will present a brief description in Table 13.1 for each module that constitutes the project. The reader may read this description and look at the source code in the Lab 1 project.

Table 13.1

Group	Module	Description	
		Function	Description
Source files process	app.c	This module implements the application process cycle simulation. It uses a finite state machine (FSM), going through the different cycle phases.	
		app_init( )	It initializes the FSM and all variables to an initial state.
		app_process( )	It implements the FSM and controls the process according to the cycle's phase. It also reads the buttons and controls the application's LED.
		ledappOn( )	It turns on the application's LED.
		ledappOff( )	It turns off the application's LED.
	led.c	This module implements the board activity LED. The LED changes its state (On/Off) every 500 ms. A led_enable variable allows the LED flash to be enabled/disabled from other modules.	
		led_init( )	It initializes the board activity LED to the Off state.
		led_process( )	It monitors the timer and controls the board activity LED state. It also enables/disables the LED according to the led_enable variable.
		ledOn( )	It turns on the board activity LED.
		ledOff( )	It turns off the board activity LED.
	console.c	This module implements the system console. It provides a menu for the user monitor and it controls the program from the console.	
		console_process( )	It scans characters from the console's keyboard and processes them accordingly.

Table 13.1 *Continued*

<table>
<tr><th rowspan="2">Group</th><th rowspan="2">Module</th><th colspan="2">Description</th></tr>
<tr><th>Function</th><th>Description</th></tr>
<tr><td rowspan="2">Source files</td><td rowspan="2">main.c</td><td colspan="2">This is the main routine, which provides the program entry point.</td></tr>
<tr><td>main( )</td><td>It calls the initialization function of each module, and it enters in a 'super loop', where each of the above module's processes is called in order to accomplish its task.</td></tr>
<tr><td rowspan="23">Utilities files</td><td rowspan="3">sysclock.c</td><td colspan="2">This module checks the system clock configuration and provides the peripheral's clock frequency for those modules that require it (timer, UART (Universal Asynchronous Receiver Transmitter), and RTC).</td></tr>
<tr><td>cClkFreq( )</td><td>It returns the system's clock frequency.</td></tr>
<tr><td>pClkFreq( )</td><td>It returns the peripheral's clock frequency.</td></tr>
<tr><td rowspan="6">timer.c</td><td colspan="2">This module implements the timer routines used by other modules.</td></tr>
<tr><td>timer_init( )</td><td>It initializes the Timer Counter and the Interrupt vector.</td></tr>
<tr><td>tc0( )</td><td>It handles the Timer interrupt request.</td></tr>
<tr><td>timer_start( )</td><td>It starts the timer with a given timeout value.</td></tr>
<tr><td>timer_stop( )</td><td>It stops the timer.</td></tr>
<tr><td>timer_expired( )</td><td>It checks if the timer has expired.</td></tr>
<tr><td rowspan="4">uart.c</td><td colspan="2">This module implements the routines to handle communications over the serial line (UART0), used by the system console.</td></tr>
<tr><td>uart_init( )</td><td>It initializes the UART0 with the appropriate parameters.</td></tr>
<tr><td>putchar( )</td><td>It writes a character to the UART0 transmit buffer.</td></tr>
<tr><td>getchar( )</td><td>It gets a character from the UART0 receiver buffer.</td></tr>
<tr><td rowspan="2">RTC.c</td><td colspan="2">This module implements the routine to initialize the Real Time Clock.</td></tr>
<tr><td>RTC_init( )</td><td>It configures and starts the Real Time Clock.</td></tr>
<tr><td rowspan="3">ADC.c</td><td colspan="2">This module implements the routines to handle the analog-to-digital conversion. This is used for the board's trimmer which supplies an analog voltage input.</td></tr>
<tr><td>ADC_init( )</td><td>It configures the ADC hardware.</td></tr>
<tr><td>ADC_Read( )</td><td>It waits for the ADC conversion and reads the data.</td></tr>
</table>

Once the Lab 1 project has been loaded in the IAR EWARM, the Workspace window will show the modules arranged into two groups: the Source files group, and the Utils files group. Double-clicking each module makes the editor load the source code. Each module source code contains the module functions, as described above.

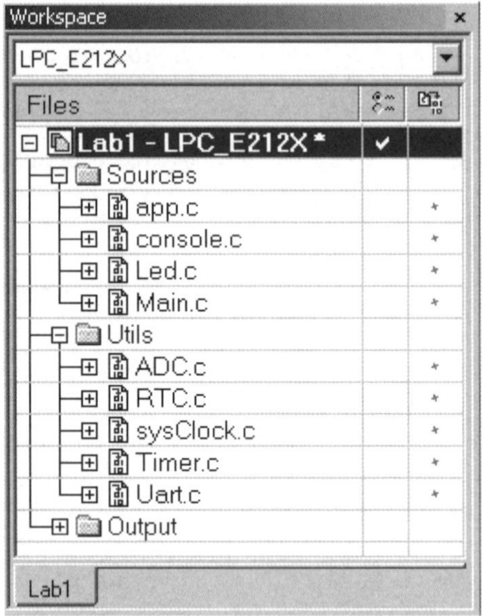

Lab 1: The application

Lab 1 introduction

In this first Lab, we will see the application, which will be used for all the Labs. This Lab will be the foundation under which we will construct our TCP/IP stack.

Lab 1 target support

This Lab supports both types of boards. Select the appropriate target board from the 'Configuration drop-down menu' in the Workspace window.

Lab 1 instructions

Complete the steps according to Chapter 12 (see section 12.6). Once the Lab is running, follow the Lab 1 exercises.

Lab 1 exercises

- Verify that the board activity LED (green LED) is flashing.
- Press the 'h' key in the console (the HyperTerminal program) to see the Help menu.
- Press the 'l' key to verify the board activity LED is disabled/enabled each time this key is pressed.

- Press the 'p' key to get the application parameters.
- Press the 's' key to start the application process cycle. Verify the yellow LED flashing with different timings while the cycle runs on each phase. Use the 'p' key to see how the application process parameters change. Use the 'c' key to have the process running continuously.
- Use Button 1 to start the application from the board. Use Button 2 to have the process running continuously.
- Use a screwdriver to rotate the trimmer, and verify using the 'p' key that the analogue input (ADC) is changing its value.

13.3 The TCP/IP stack design

In this section, we will take an overview of the TCP/IP stack that we will start implementing from the next Lab. When all the Labs have been completed, the resulting TCP/IP Stack will present the structure and modules as described in the following subsections.

13.3.1 The TCP/IP stack structure

Figure 13.3 shows the layered structure of our TCP/IP stack. The lowest layer, the Data Link layer, will depend on the network interface the hardware presents. This is the only hardware-specific layer. The rest of the layers work independently from the underlying network interface.

The IP protocol uses the Data Link layer (Ethernet or PPP), and it provides service for the Transport layer. The ICMP module uses IP to carry its messages. Both HTTP and SMTP use TCP as a transport protocol. The HTTP module provides the functionality required by web server applications, while

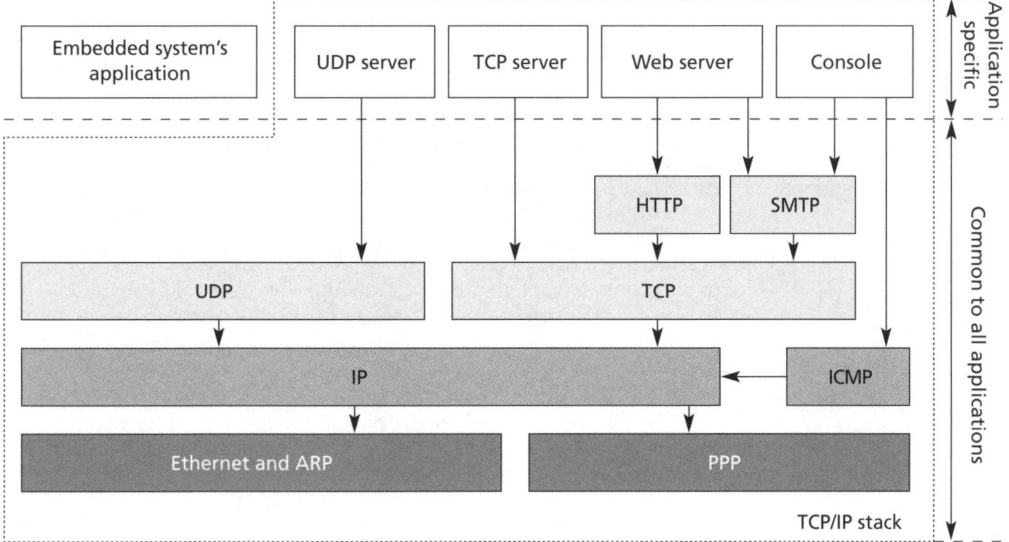

Figure 13.3 The TCP/IP stack structure.

the SMTP module implements the e-mail services. All the above comprise the TCP/IP modules that are common to all applications. That is, their functionality is independent of the application.

The highest layer contains the application's specific modules, which will be implemented according to the application needs and requirements. The console uses the ICMP module services to send ping requests, and the SMTP module to send e-mail messages to other devices or users. The web server provides the web pages that can be remotely viewed from an Internet browser. While the HTTP module provides the web server functionality, the SMTP allows the web server to send e-mail messages from any Internet browser. Both UDP and TCP servers allow remote users to interact with the application using the transport network services. All these modules must be specifically designed for each application.

13.3.2 The TCP/IP stack modules

Table 13.2 shows the modules included in the provided TCP/IP stack, and their functionality.

Table 13.2

Layer	Module	Functionality
	stack.c	This module inserts the TCP/IP stack functionality in any source code. It must be included in all sources requiring TCP/IP communications.
Network interface	ethernet.c	It implements the drivers for the Ethernet interface. It is required for the LPC-E212X boards.
	arp.c	It implements the ARP protocol, needed by the Ethernet drivers to translate IP addresses into MAC addresses.
	ppp.c	It implements the PPP protocol for the serial interface. It is required for the LPC-P212X boards.
Internet	ip.c	It implements the Internet Protocol for the Internet layer.
	icmp.c	It implements the Internet Control Message Protocol.
Transport	udp.c	It implements the User Datagram protocol for the Transport layer. It provides simple, fast, unreliable transport over the inter-network.
	tcp.c	It implements the Transmission Control protocol for the Transport layer. It provides a connection oriented, with flow control, reliable transport over the inter-network.
Application	smtp.c	It implements the Simple Message Transport Protocol, needed to send electronic mail.
	http.c	It implements the HyperText Transport Protocol, required to implement a web server.

13.3.3 How to include the TCP/IP stack in a project

Our TCP/IP stack is designed to be easily included in any project. Only one header file must be included in each source file, in order to enable the TCP/IP communications. The 'stack.h' header file accomplishes this task.

Two #defines statements specify the type of network interface, in order for the stack to include the appropriate data link drivers (Ethernet or PPP). For this, the 'hardware.h' header file defines either the Ethernet or PPP_LINK according to the type of board.

The 'stackcfg.h' header file provides a way to configure some parameters such as the MAC address, the IP address, the gateway and subnet mask, the SMTP server IP address, and the e-mail address to be used as the e-mail sender when using SMTP services.

The stack needs a timer for some internal tasks. Since most applications already provide a timer functionality, the same routines are used by the stack. Once the stack has been included in a project, the stack_init( ) and stack_process( ) routines must be called from the main.c module, in order to have the TCP/IP working. The following screenshot shows the TCP/IP stack modules, as they appear in the IAR EWARM Workspace window:

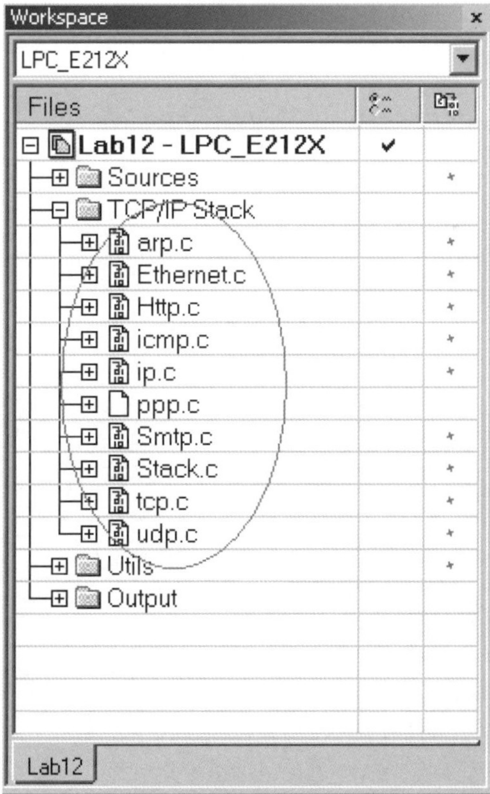

In order for an application to use the TCP/IP stack, we need to include the stack modules in the project. As these modules are common for all projects (that is, they are not specific for each application), it is convenient to include them in a separated group of source codes.

Once the TCP/IP stack modules have been included in the project, the 'stack.h' header file should be included in every source code that requires the TCP/IP stack functionality.

14

Connecting to a LAN: Ethernet and ARP

In this chapter, we will implement the Data Link layer for the Ethernet interface. We will start looking at the Ethernet engine chip architecture and how to program it. Then, we will present the Ethernet drivers and routines necessary to have the board sending and receiving frames over a network. Lab 2 will show us the Ethernet drivers in action. We will complete the Data Link layer with the ARP protocol implementation. Finally, Lab 3 adds the ARP module, providing some exercises to interact with this module.

14.1 The Ethernet interface

14.1.1 Introduction

The Ethernet interface will allow our embedded system to connect to a LAN, and use a gateway to the outside world via the Internet. This interface consists of an Ethernet engine integrated circuit (IC) which has all the necessary logic to process Ethernet frames. In our case, the kit uses the Crystal LAN CS8900A 10Base-T Embedded Ethernet Controller, from Cirrus Logic. This chip only needs isolation transformers, activity LEDs, a few resistors and capacitors, and an RJ-45 jack to transmit and receive Ethernet packets over a LAN. The information given here about the CS8900A chip is the minimum necessary to program the Ethernet drivers. For additional information, please refer to the CS8900A Product Data Sheet.

The main goal of the Ethernet interface is to transmit and receive Ethernet frames to and from the LAN. However, before this may happen, the Ethernet interface must be initialized (reset and appropriately configured). This configuration, and the proper transmit and receive operations, are made using the CS8900A internal control and configuration registers. The microcontroller must be able to write to and read these registers in order to fully control the Ethernet interface.

14.1.2 The CS8900A PacketPage architecture

The CS8900A has a 4 Kbyte internal RAM called PacketPage memory. This memory is used for temporary storage of transmit and receive frames, and for internal registers. The CS8900A allows two different operation modes: Memory Mode and I/O Space. In addition the CS8900A allows data transfer in both 16-bit and 32-bit.

In I/O Space mode (our case), PacketPage is accessed through eight 16-bit I/O Ports, as Table 14.1 shows.

Table 14.1

Address	Type	Description
0x00	Read/Write	Receive/Transmit Data (Port 0)
0x02	Read/Write	Receive/Transmit Data (Port 1)
0x04	Write-only	Transmit Command
0x06	Write-only	Transmit Length
0x08	Read-only	Interrupt Status Queue
0x0A	Read/Write	PacketPage Pointer
0x0C	Read/Write	PacketPage Data (Port 0)
0x0E	Read/Write	PacketPage Data (Port 1)

- The *Receive/Transmit Data* ports are used when transferring transmit data to the CS8900A and receive data from the CS8900A. Port 0 (address 0x00 for the LSB, and address 0x01 for the MSB) is used for 16-bit transfers. In 32-bit transfers, both port 0 and port 1 are used.
- The *Transmit Command* port is used when the microcontroller needs to transmit a frame. It writes to this port, specifying how the frame should be transmitted. Then, the *Transmit Length* port is used to specify the length of the frame to be transmitted.
- The *Interrupt Status Queue* port provides information that, in our case, will not be useful, as we will not use the interrupt resources.
- The *PacketPage Pointer* port is used by the microcontroller to address the CS8900A internal register, while the *PacketPage Data* port is used for data transfer between the CS8900A internal register and the microcontroller. Again, port 0 is used for 16-bit transfers, while port 0 and port 1 are used for 32-bit transfers.

From the above table, we will start defining the PacketPage port addresses that are important for our purposes:

```
/* CS8900 PacketPage I/O Port Definitions */
#define pp_RxTxData     0x00    // Receive/Transmit data Port 0
#define pp_TxCmd        0x04    // Transmit Command
#define pp_TxLen        0x06    // Transmit Length
#define pp_Ptr          0x0A    // PacketPage Pointer
#define pp_Data0        0x0C    // PacketPage Data Port 0
```

14.1.3 The CS8900A interface lines

The CS8900A interfaces with the microcontroller using the following lines:

- *SAB* (4 bits): the System Address Bus consists of four address lines used by the microcontroller to address the CS8900A PacketPage ports.
- *SDB* (8 bits): the System Data Bus consists of eight bi-directional data lines used to carry data to/from the microcontroller. As the CS8900A internal registers are 16 bits long, the data transfer must be done in two parts (the LSB and the MSB).
- *IOR* (1 bit): the I/O Read control line, used by the microcontroller to read data from the CS8900A.
- *IOW* (1 bit): the I/O Write control line, used by the microcontroller to write data to the CS8900A.

Refer to the board schematics for pin individualization.

Under this scheme, when the microcontroller needs to write to the CS8900A PacketPage port, it must address the desired PacketPage port using the 4-line System Address Bus, put the information into the 8-line System Data Bus, and drop the IOW line (active low), so indicating to the CS8900A that the data must be written into the addressed PacketPage port. Then, the microcontroller deactivates the IOW line, indicating that the write cycle has ended.

For a read cycle, the microcontroller should address the desired PacketPage port using the 4-line SAB, and making the IOR control line low (active low). Upon this, the CS8900A detects that the microcontroller wants to read the address's PacketPage port content, and put it into the 8-line SDB. Once the microcontroller has read the available data, it deactivates the IOR line, indicating that the read operation has finished.

The above CS8900A interface lines should be declared in the hardware.h file:

```
#define SAB      0x000000F0      // System Address Bus lines SA4-SA0
#define SDB      0x00FF0000      // System Data Bus lines  SD7-SD0
#define IOR      0x00001000      // I/O Read line
#define IOW      0x00002000      // I/O Write line
```

These lines define the microcontroller I/O pins that are assigned to interface the CS8900A in the hardware schematic.

14.1.4 Read and write PacketPage port routines

With the above CS8900A information, we are now ready to write our first routines. In order to communicate with the CS8900A, we will need a routine that accesses the content of any of the 16 PacketPage port addresses. This routine should perform the reading cycle as described above.

This routine is called with the PacketPage port address as a parameter, and it returns its content. The first two lines clear and set the address lines according to the port_address parameter. Then, the IOR control line is

```
char CS8900_read_port(char port_address) {
  char port_data;

  IO0CLR = SAB;                              // Clear Address lines
  IO0SET = (port_address<<4) & SAB;          // Set Address lines
  IO0CLR = IOR;                              // IOR=0 - Enable Read
  port_data = ((IOPIN0 & SDB)>>16);          // Read Data from CS8900
  IO0SET = IOR;                              // IOR=1 - Disable Read
  return port_data;                          // Return Data
}
```

activated, and the data is read from the CS8900A. After that, the IOR is restored, and the addressed port value is returned.

The same way, the write cycle is accomplished by the following routine:

```
void CS8900_write_port(char port_address, char port_data) {
  IO0DIR |= SDB;                             // SD7-SD0 as Outputs
  IO0CLR = SDB;                              // Clear Data lines
  IO0SET = (port_data<<16);                  // Set Data lines
  IO0CLR = SAB;                              // Clear Address lines
  IO0SET = (port_address<<4) & SAB;          // Set Address lines
  IO0CLR = IOW;                              // IOW=0 - Enable Write
  IO0SET = IOW;                              // IOW=1 - Disable Write
  IO0DIR &= (~SDB);                          // SD7-SD0 as Inputs
}
```

In this case, the routine is called with the PacketPage port address and the value to write into it. As the System Data Bus is bi-directional, the first line sets these lines as outputs, while the last line of the routine restores the lines as inputs. The rest of the lines set the data lines and the address lines, and toggle the IOW control line to direct the CS8900A to write to the addressed port. In this way, we can write any value in any of the 16 8-bit PacketPage ports (although they are logically organized as 8 16-bit ports).

14.1.5 Read and write CS8900A Internal Register routines

The CS8900A Internal Registers can be accessed through the PacketPage Pointer and Data ports. Then, with the help of the above routines, we may develop the necessary routines to access the Internal Registers.

The following routine reads the content of the specified internal register:

```
unsigned short CS8900_read_reg(unsigned short reg_address) {
  CS8900_write_port(pp_Ptr, (reg_address & 0x0FF));
  CS8900_write_port(pp_Ptr+1, ((reg_address>>8) & 0x0FF));
  return  ((CS8900_read_port(pp_Data0+1)<<8) + CS8900_read_port(pp_Data0));
}
```

The first two lines write the 16-bit internal register address (reg_address) into the 16-bit PacketPage pointer (lower byte first, higher byte after). The third line reads and returns the 16-bit internal register content. Note that even when all registers are 16 bits long, the System Data Bus is 8 bits long, so the register content must be read in two parts.

In a similar way, the following routine writes a specified internal register:

```
void CS8900_write_reg(unsigned short reg_address, unsigned short reg_data)
{
  CS8900_write_port(pp_Ptr, (reg_address & 0x0FF));
  CS8900_write_port(pp_Ptr+1, ((reg_address>>8) & 0x0FF));
  CS8900_write_port(pp_Data0, (reg_data & 0x0FF));
  CS8900_write_port(pp_Data0+1, ((reg_data>>8) & 0x0FF));
}
```

Here, the first two lines write the specified internal register address into the PacketPage Pointer port, while the second two lines write the specified value into the PacketPage Data port.

14.1.6 CS8900A Internal Register description

Although there are many internal registers, we will describe only those registers that we use in our Ethernet driver. In the same way, for each register, only the bits that we use will be described. Note that the CS8900A has many other characteristics and functionality than those described here. All registers are 16 bits long, and considered from b0 (LSBit) to b15 (MSBit).

- **Self Control Register** (SelfCTL, Read/Write, address 0x0114). SelfCTL controls the CS8900A Reset, the operation of the LED outputs and the low-power modes.

  RESET (b6): when set, the CS8900A is reset. Once reset occurs, this bit is clear.

- **Self Status Register** (SelfStatus, Read-only, address 0x0136). SelfStatus reports the status of the EEPROM interface (not used) and the initialization process.

  INITD (b7): if set, the CS8900A initialization is complete.

- **Line Control Register** (LineCTL, Read/Write, address 0x0112). LineCTL determines the configuration of the MAC engine and the physical interface.

  SerRxON (b6): When set, the receiver is enabled. When clear, non-incoming packets pass through the receiver.

  SerTxON (b7): When set, transmitter is enabled. When clear, no transmissions are allowed.

  AUIonly (b8): When set, the AUI physical interface is selected. When clear, the physical interface depends on the AutoAUI/10BT bit.

AutoAUI/10BT (b9): When set, the physical interface will be selected automatically. When clear, the 10BASE-T interface is selected.

- **Test Control Register** (TestCTL, Read/Write, address 0x0118). TestCTL controls the diagnostic test modes of the CS8900A.

  FDX (b14): When set, 10BASE-T full duplex mode is enabled. When clear, the CS8900A is configured for standard half duplex 10BASE-T operation.

- **Individual Address Register** (IndividualA, Read/Write, address 0x0158–0x015D). IndividualA is loaded with the 48-bit MAC (physical) address of the device. LSB of the MAC address in 0x0158, MSB of the MAC address in 0x015D.
- **Receiver Control Register** (RxCTL, Read/Write, address 0x0104). RxCTL defines what type of frames to accept and it configures the destination address filter.

  PromiscuousA (b7): When set, frames with any destination address are accepted.

  RxOKA (b8): When set, the CS8900A accepts frames with correct CRC and valid length (≥ 64 and ≤ 1518).

  IndividualA (b10): When set, received frames are accepted if the destination address matches the MAC address (loaded in the IndividualA register).

  BroadcastA (b11): When set, received frames are accepted if the destination address is 0xFFFF FFFF FFFF.

  CRCerrorA (b12): When set, received frames that pass the destination address filter, but have a bad CRC, are accepted. When clear, frames with bad CRC are discarded.

  RuntA (b13): When set, received frames that are smaller than 64 bytes, and that pass the destination address filter are accepted. When clear, received frames less than 64 bytes in length are discarded.

There is a Hash filter that can be programmed in order to accept frames with individual (IAHashA bit) or multicast (MulticastA bit) addresses that pass this filter, but we will not work with these options.

- **Receiver Configuration Register** (RxCFG, Read/Write, address 0x0102). RxCFG determines how frames will be transferred to the host.

  Skip_1 (b6): When set, the last committed received frame is deleted from the receive buffer.

  BufferCRC (b11): When set, the received CRC is included with the data stored in receive buffer, and its length is considered within the receive-frame length. When clear, neither the receive buffer nor the receive length include the CRC.

- **Receiver Event Register** (RxEvent, Read-only, address 0x0124). RxEvent reports the status of the current received frame.

RxOK (b8):	If set, the received frame had a good CRC and valid length.
IndividualAdr (b10):	If set (and RxOK is set), the received frame had a destination address, which matched the MAC address programmed in the IndividualA register.
Broadcast (b11):	If set (and RxOK is set), the received frame had the broadcast address (0xFFFF FFFF FFFF) as the destination address.
CRCerror (b12):	If set, the received frame had a bad CRC.
Runt (b13):	If set, the received frame was shorter than 64 bytes.

- **Bus Status Register** (BusStatus, Read-only, 0x0138). BusStatus describes the status of the current transmit operation.

  Rdy4TxNOW (b8): If set, the CS8900A is ready to accept a frame from the microcontroller for transmission.

Now, we need to define all these registers for our driver:

```
/* CS8900 PacketPage Internal Registers */
#define pp_RxCFG          0x0102     // Receiver Configuration
#define pp_RxCTL          0x0104     // Receiver Control
#define pp_LineCTL        0x0112     // Line Control
#define pp_SelfCTL        0x0114     // Self Control
#define pp_TestCTL        0x0118     // Test Control
#define pp_RxEvent        0x0124     // Receiver Event
#define pp_SelfStatus     0x0136     // Self Status
#define pp_BusStatus      0x0138     // Bus Status
#define pp_IndividualA    0x0158     // Individual Address
```

Having this, we can start writing the CS8900A drivers.

14.2 Writing the CS8900A drivers

Before the CS8900A may receive or transmit frames, some initialization must be done. This consists of a Reset procedure, and some Internal Register configurations. The CS8900A driver routines use the following references.

In the stack.h file we define:

```
#ifdef ETHERNET
 #define PACKET_BUF_SIZE          1514
 #define DATALINK_HDR_SIZE        14
#endif
```

The ethernet.c file defines the following variables:

```
char rx_buf[PACKET_BUF_SIZE];
char tx_buf[PACKET_BUF_SIZE];
char MyMAC[6] = MyMACAddress;
char MyIP[4]  = MyIPAddress;                    // device IPv4 address
char Gateway[4] = GatewayAddress;
char SubNetMask[4] = SubNetMaskAddress;
```

The first two lines define the receive and transmit buffers. The rest of the variables will hold the device's addresses configuration. These addresses can be changed from the stackcfg.h file, which has the following lines:

```
#ifdef ETHERNET
  #define MyMACAddress             {0x00, 0x08, 0x54, 0x18, 0x5D, 0x50}
  #define GatewayAddress           {192, 168, 0, 1}
  #define SubNetMaskAddress        {255, 255, 255, 0}
  #define MyIPAddress              {192, 168, 0, 30}
  #define pcIP                     {192, 168, 0, 3}
#endif
```

The pcIP constant will be used by other Labs to know the PC's IP address.

The ethernet.h file defines the Ethernet frame's header structure and some macros:

```
#define HTONS(n)  ((((unsigned short)((n) & 0xff)) << 8) | (((n) & 0xff00) >> 8))
#define FRAMEr    ((struct ethernet_hdr *)&rx_buf[0])
#define FRAMEt    ((struct ethernet_hdr *)&tx_buf[0])

#pragma pack(1)
struct ethernet_hdr {
  char destination[6];
  char source[6];
  unsigned short protocol;
};
#pragma pack()
```

The HTONS(n) macro converts between the network and processor byte order. The FRAMEr is a pointer to the Ethernet frame header structure, in order to facilitate the structure's field accesses (for example using the FRAMEr->destination syntax). While the FRAMEr pointer is defined for the receive buffer, the FRAMEt pointer is defined for the transmit buffer.

The ethernet.h header file also defines some constants and exports variables used by other modules:

```
#define ARP_PROTOCOL          0x0806
#define IP_PROTOCOL           0x0800
#define ICMP_PROTOCOL         1
#define UDP_PROTOCOL          17
#define TCP_PROTOCOL          6

extern char MyMAC[];
extern char MyIP[];
extern char Gateway[];
extern char SubNetMask[];
```

14.2.1 CS8900A initialization

The following routine initializes the CS8900A:

```
void ethernet_init(void) {
  unsigned short ret;

  /* Define pin directions */
  IO0DIR |= (SAB | IOR | IOW);   // SA3-SA0, IOR, and IOW as Outputs
  IO0DIR &= (~SDB);              // SD7-SD0 as Inputs
  IO0SET = IOW | IOR;            // Set IOR=IOW=1

  /* Reset the CS8900A */
  CS8900_write_reg(pp_SelfCTL, 0x0040);

 /* Wait for INITD=1 indicating CS8900 Reset Ok */
  while( !(CS8900_read_reg(pp_SelfStatus) & 0x0080));
...
```

The above code starts defining the directions (Input or Output) of the microcontroller I/O pins that interface with the CS8900A. Then, the CS8900A is reset via the SelfCTL register. Once the INITD bit of the SelfStatus register indicates that initialization is complete, the routine continues with the second part: the internal register configuration. The next portion of the routine shows this:

```
  /* Load parameters */
  CS8900_write_reg(pp_LineCTL, 0x0000);          // Clear all bits for 10Base-T
  CS8900_write_reg(pp_TestCTL, 0x4000);          // Set Full-Duplex bit
  CS8900_write_reg(pp_RxCTL, 0x0D00);            // Set RXOkA, IndividualA, and
                                                 // BroadcastA bits
  CS8900_write_reg(pp_RxCFG, 0x0000);            // Clear BufferCRC bit

  /* Load MAC Address */
  CS8900_write_reg(pp_IndividualA,   (MyMAC[1]<<8) + MyMAC[0]);
  CS8900_write_reg(pp_IndividualA+2, (MyMAC[3]<<8) + MyMAC[2]);
  CS8900_write_reg(pp_IndividualA+4, (MyMAC[5]<<8) + MyMAC[4]);

  /* Enable Transmitter and Receiver  */
  ret = CS8900_read_reg(pp_LineCTL) | 0x00C0;    // Set TxOn and RxOn bits
  CS8900_write_reg(pp_LineCTL, ret);             // in Line Control Register
}
```

The first four lines write the appropriate registers in order to configure the CS8900A for the 10Base-T interface, with full-duplex mode, and accept only frames with correct CRC and valid length whose destination address matches the IndividualA register address or with a broadcast address. That is, the CS8900A will only accept those frames with our MAC address as the destination address, or broadcast frames (0xFFFF FFFF FFFF as the destination address), which are sent for every device at the network. The last line clears the BufferCRC bit, so the CRC field will not be loaded at the frame buffer.

Note that if we would like to catch all the frames in the network, we should set the PromiscuousA bit at the RxCTL register. In this way, we could spy on all the network activity by seeing the frames sent for other devices.

The next three lines load the MyMAC[6] variable into the IndividualA register. In this way, we are assigning the MAC or Physical address for the device, which will run this code. With this, the CS8900A will know if the received frame is for us or not. The char MyMAC[6] is defined in the Ethernet.c file as a global variable, and the Ethernet.h file defines an extern char MyMAC[] so any other module that includes this header file may share this variable.

The last two lines enable the receiver and transmitter.

14.2.2 Receiving frames

Once the CS8900A has been initialized, we may start trying to get frames. We can tell if a frame has been received by the CS8900A by checking the RxOK bit at the RxEvent register. See the next code:

```
void ethernet_poll(void) {

  if ((CS8900_read_reg(pp_RxEvent) & 0x0100)) {       // if RxOK bit set, there is a frame
      frame_process();
  }
}
```

This routine must be regularly called from the Main Application module, in order to poll the CS8900A for received frames. If the time between polls is too long, we could lose incoming frames. Fortunately, the CS8900A has an internal 4-Kbyte memory buffer to hold the received frames.

Once a received frame is detected, the **frame_process()** routine is called. The following code shows this routine:

```
void frame_process(void) {
  if (frame_get() == 0)
    return;
  switch (HTONS(FRAMEr->protocol)) {
    case ARP_PROTOCOL:
           arp_process();
           break;
         case IP_PROTOCOL:
           ip_process();
           break;
  }
}
```

The first line calls the **frame_get()** function, which loads the frame into the receive buffer rx_buf[], and returns the frame's length. Once the frame's protocol is analysed, the appropriate function is called. Those functions belong to higher protocol layers.

The following code shows the **frame_get()** function:

```
unsigned short frame_get(void)
{
  char header[4];
  unsigned short RxLength;
  unsigned short i;

  header[0] = CS8900_read_port(pp_RxTxData + 1);
  header[1] = CS8900_read_port(pp_RxTxData);
  header[2] = CS8900_read_port(pp_RxTxData + 1);
  header[3] = CS8900_read_port(pp_RxTxData);
  RxLength = (header[2]<<8) + header[3];
  if (RxLength > PACKET_BUF_SIZE) {
    // Skip Frame  -  Set Skip bit in RxCFG register
    CS8900_write_reg(pp_RxCFG, (CS8900_read_reg(pp_RxCFG) | 0x0040));
    return 0;
  }
  for(i=0; i<RxLength; i+=2) {
    rx_buf[i]   = CS8900_read_port(pp_RxTxData);
    rx_buf[i+1] = CS8900_read_port(pp_RxTxData + 1);
  }
#if debug_ethernet
  frame_display(RxLength);
#endif  // debug_ethernet
  return RxLength;
}
```

After some variable declarations, the function initiates the frame transfer procedure. This procedure consists of repetitive reading to the Receive/Transmit Data port (pp_RxTxData). The CS8900A starts transferring a status, the frame length and then the frame's data. Remember that these ports are 16 bits long, so we need to make the reading twice (8-bit each time) to complete the transfer of a 16-bit word.

Although the status (stored in header[0] and header[1]) is not used, we need to read it in order to continue with the frame's length (stored in header[2] and header[3]). Once we know the frame's length, and after validating that it will not override the receive buffer length, we can start transferring the complete frame into the rx_buf[] area.

Once the frame is loaded into the receive buffer, if the debug_ethernet option in the Debug.h file is on, the received frame is shown at the console. After this, the function ends returning the frame length.

The following code shows the **frame_display()** function:

```
#if debug_ethernet
void frame_display(unsigned short len) {
  unsigned short i, j;

  printf("Frame Received - Length: %d bytes\r\n", len);
  printf("Destination:    %02x-%02x-%02x-%02x-%02x-%02x\r\n",
                          FRAMEr->destination[0], FRAMEr->destination[1],
                          FRAMEr->destination[2], FRAMEr->destination[3],
                          FRAMEr->destination[4], FRAMEr->destination[5]);
 printf("Source:          %02x-%02x-%02x-%02x-%02x-%02x\r\n",
                          FRAMEr->source[0], FRAMEr->source[1],
                          FRAMEr->source[2], FRAMEr->source[3],
                          FRAMEr->source[4], FRAMEr->source[5]);
  printf("Type:           %04x\r\n", HTONS(FRAMEr->protocol));
  printf("Data:\r\n     ");
  j=0;
  for(i=14; i<len; i++) {
    printf("%02x ", rx_buf[i]);
    j++;
    if (j==16) {
      j=0;
      printf("\r\n     ");
    }
  }
  printf("\n----------------------------------------------------\n");
}
#endif //debug_ethernet
```

Note that the above code will only be included if the debug_ethernet option is on. This code prints the destination and source addresses, and the Protocol types, and scans the data frame, printing each byte in hexadecimal format, forming lines up to 16 bytes each. In addition, a title and an ending line are printed before and after each printed frame.

14.2.3 Sending frames

Now, it is time to start sending frames to other devices. The following code sends the frame loaded in the Transmit Buffer (tx_buf[]):

```
void frame_send(unsigned short len) {
  unsigned short I, j=0xFFFF;

  If (len > PACKET_BUF_SIZE) {
    // if len exceeds maximum ethernet frame length, discard it
    printf("Ethernet: maximum frame length exceeded\n");
    return;
  }
```

```
CS8900_write_port(pp_TxCmd, 0xC0);
CS8900_write_port(pp_TxCmd+1, 0x00);
CS8900_write_port(pp_TxLen, (len & 0xFF));
CS8900_write_port(pp_TxLen+1, ((len>>8) & 0xFF));
do {
 j--;
} while(!((CS8900_read_reg(pp_BusStatus) & 0x0100)) && j>0);
if (j == 0) {
 printf("Ethernet: CS8900 not ready to accept a frame!\n");
 return;
}
 ....................
```

This routine is called with the frame length as a parameter. The first step is to check if the length is greater than the maximum allowable. If so, the frame is discarded. Having checked this, we need to write the word 0x00C0 into the pp_TxCmd port (bit 6 and 7 conform the TxStart option which represents the 'Start transmission after the entire frame is in the CS8900A' when both bits are set) and the frame's length into the pp_TxLen port. The following do while loop checks the pp_BusStatus register to see if the CS8900A is ready to accept the frame. The loop and a variable which is decremented allow a time-out detection in case the CS8900 is not ready (for example, if the Ethernet cable is disconnected from the board). In this way, we avoid the application hanging up to wait for the CS8900 to get ready.

After checking that the CS8900 is ready to accept the frame, we start writing the complete frame data using the pp_RxTxData port. And that's it; the CS8900A will do the rest:

```
...
for(i=0; i<len; i+=2) {
     CS8900_write_port(pp_RxTxData, tx_buf[i]);
     CS8900_write_port(pp_RxTxData+1, tx_buf[i+1]);
   }
}
```

In the **frame_send()** function, we supposed that the complete frame was loaded in the transmit buffer. However, the Data Link layer must provide a way to send data over the network for upper layers. In this way, the upper layers should call a function providing the data to send and the protocol type (IP or ARP).

The **ethernet_send()** function provides the interface for the upper layers:

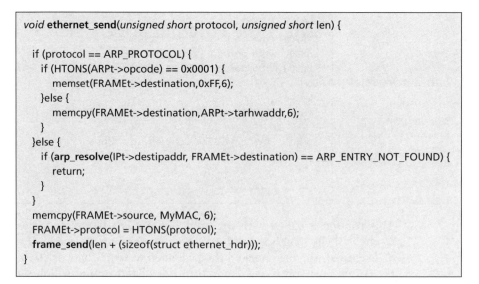

```
void ethernet_send(unsigned short protocol, unsigned short len) {

  if (protocol == ARP_PROTOCOL) {
    if (HTONS(ARPt->opcode) == 0x0001) {
      memset(FRAMEt->destination,0xFF,6);
    }else {
      memcpy(FRAMEt->destination,ARPt->tarhwaddr,6);
    }
  }else {
    if (arp_resolve(IPt->destipaddr, FRAMEt->destination) == ARP_ENTRY_NOT_FOUND) {
      return;
    }
  }
  memcpy(FRAMEt->source, MyMAC, 6);
  FRAMEt->protocol = HTONS(protocol);
  frame_send(len + (sizeof(struct ethernet_hdr)));
}
```

The above function is called from the upper layers when they already have their data loaded at the transmit buffer (tx_buf[]). Then, they call this function providing the protocol type, and the data length. The **ethernet_send()** function must construct the Ethernet header before calling the **frame_send()** function to send the packet over the network.

The Ethernet header consists of the destination address, the source address and the protocol type. The protocol type is copied from the parameter provided by the upper layer when calling this function, while the source address is taken from the MyMAC[] variable which holds the physical address assigned to the device at the Ethernet initialization phase.

The destination address is a little more complicated to solve. If the protocol that sends the packet is the ARP protocol, the destination address is the broadcast address (0xFFFF FFFF FFFF) if the message is an ARP Request (Opcode equals 0x0001). If the message is an ARP Reply, we can use the Target Hardware Address field from the ARP message to fill the destination address.

If the protocol is the IP protocol, we will need to use the ARP protocol services to find the MAC address of the destination device. The **arp_resolve()** function tries to resolve this (see the ARP code explanation).

Once we have the upper layer protocol data loaded at the transmit buffer, and the Ethernet header completed, we can use the **frame_send()** function to send the frame over the network. Note that the FCS field of the Ethernet frame is automatically appended at the end of the packet by the CS8900A.

Lab 2: The Ethernet drivers

Lab 2 introduction

In this Lab, we will see the Ethernet driver receiving and sending frames. Since the **ethernet_send( )** function needs the arp.c module which is not included in the present Lab, this function is modified to allow us to send a frame using the broadcast address. Besides this, we will use an unknown protocol type (0x0000), to avoid following the specifications for a particular protocol message.

Lab 2 target support

This Lab only supports the LPC-E212X boards with Ethernet interface.

Lab 2 options setting

This Lab requires the debug_ethernet option to be set.

Lab 2 instructions

Complete the steps according to Chapter 12 (see section 12.6). Once the Lab is running, follow the Lab 2 exercises.

Lab 2 exercises

- From the PC system command, execute a 'ping 192.168.0.30' command. See Appendix E, section E.5 for details. The board should start receiving frames. Check this in the LPC-E212X console.
- Analyse the received frames. Compare their structure with the Ethernet header structure. See the destination address field to determine if this frame was correctly received (in accordance with the *Receiver Control Register* setting). See the source address field and determine which devices sent this frame. Analyse the protocol type field to determine the higher layer protocol, which sent information in this frame.
- Modify the *Receiver Control Register* to enable the Promiscuous mode. Analyse the received frames to determine if this mode was successfully enabled.
- Press the 'f' key in the console to send a frame. Before that, open and configure the Ethereal program to have this frame captured (see Appendix F for more information). Then, analyse the captured Ethernet frame.

14.3 The ARP protocol implementation

14.3.1 Introduction

As we saw in Chapter 5 (section 5.3), the ARP protocol allows the Ethernet driver to know the MAC address associated with each device. That is, when the IP layer needs to send a message to a device, it uses the Data Link layer services, providing the destination IP address and the message itself. The Data Link layer, in this case the Ethernet driver, needs the MAC address to send the frame over the local network. Then, it calls the ARP protocol to resolve this association.

The ARP implementation requires a table to associate each IP address of a device with its MAC address. Each resolved association will be cached into this table for a given period. After this time, the association should be checked for its validity.

The entries for the ARP table may come from two sources:

- *Our device receives ARP Requests from other devices* – these requests have the MAC and IP addresses of the sender device, so this association is cached, in case our device needs it later. Remember that the ARP requests are broadcast messages, so they are received by all devices on the LAN.
- *Our device sends an ARP Request to other devices* – when the ARP protocol needs to resolve an association that it has not found in the ARP table, it needs to send an ARP Request in order for the destination device to respond with its hardware address. Once this happens, the association is cached into the ARP table for future use.

14.3.2 ARP module functions

The ARP module must implement the following functions:

- Process incoming ARP Request and update the ARP table. If this request is for us, reply with our MAC address.
- Process incoming ARP Replies and update the ARP table.
- Allocate space in the ARP table for new entries. If there are no free entries, select one entry (following some criteria) to be replaced by the new entry.
- Resolve the Resolution request searching the associations in the ARP table. If the association is not found, generate an ARP Request.
- Maintain the ARP table updating the time out value for each entry. Then check the entry validity. If the entry timed out, generate an ARP Request to update the data.

14.3.3 ARP module description

14.3.3.1 Initializing the ARP table

The first step is to design the ARP table:

```
struct arp_entry {
  char              proaddr[4];
  char              hwaddr[6];
  char              state;
  unsigned short    tout;
  char              retries;
  unsigned short    queries;
};

struct arp_entry arp_cache[ARP_CACHE_SIZE];
```

Each entry of the above table will hold an address association; the protocol address and its associated hardware (or MAC) address. The state field indicates the state of the entry; ARP_ENTRY_FREE (empty entry), ARP_ENTRY_OK (the entry is valid), and ARP_ENTRY_RESOLVING (the stack generated an ARP Request and is waiting for its response).

The tout (time-out) indicates when the entry must be validated. For this, an ARP Request is sent. If we get no reply for this request, a new request is sent until we either get a response or the entry's retries field gets zero, indicating that the device is not responding. In this case, the entry is not valid, and then it must be deleted (marked as free). The queries field indicates how many times this entry was requested. These parameters will help us decide which entry to delete, in case we need to allocate a new entry and the ARP table is full. In this way, we adopt the criteria to delete the least used entry.

The ARP_CACHE_SIZE parameter determines the size of the table. It will depend on how many devices will be in the Local Network. If the size of the table is larger than the number of devices, we were wasting memory. If there are more devices than table entries, we were using CPU time in deleting and allocating new entries.

The first task is to initialize the ARP table:

```
void arp_init(void) {
  int i;

  for(i=0;i<ARP_CACHE_SIZE;i++) {
    arp_cache[i].state = ARP_ENTRY_FREE;
  }
  timer_start(arptimer, 100);
}
```

This code initializes the ARP table and it starts the timer for the ARP module.

14.3.3.2 Processing incoming ARP messages

When the Data Link layer (Ethernet module) receives a frame containing an ARP message, the **arp_process( )** function is called. See the following code:

```
void arp_process(void) {
  int i;

#if debug_arp
  arp_display();
#endif //debug_arp

  if (differ_subnet(ARPr->senproaddr)==0)
    arp_update();
```

The first task of this function is to display the ARP message in the console, for debugging purposes (if the debug_arp option is set in the '**debug.h**' file). Then, we call the **differ_subnet( )** function to verify if the IP address of the device that sent the message is on the same network. That is, we do not need the MAC address of other network devices, as we use the Gateway's MAC address to send messages for them. If the device is on the same network, we call the **arp_update( )** function to update the entry. We will see these functions implemented later on.

```
if (! memcmp(ARPr->tarproaddr, MyIP, 4)) {           // is this ARP message for us?
  if (ARPr->opcode == HTONS(ARP_Request)) {          // is this an ARP Request?
       ARPt->hwtype = HTONS(0x0001);
       ARPt->protype = HTONS(0x0800);
       ARPt->hwaddrlen = 6;
       ARPt->proaddrlen = 4;
       ARPt->opcode= HTONS(ARP_Reply);
       memcpy(ARPt->tarhwaddr, ARPr->senhwaddr, 6);
       memcpy(ARPt->tarproaddr, ARPr->senproaddr, 4);
       memcpy(ARPt->senhwaddr, MyMAC, 6);
       memcpy(ARPt->senproaddr, MyIP, 4);
       for(i=0;i<18;i++)
         tx_buf[42+i] = 0x20;                          // padding...
       ethernet_send(ARP_PROTOCOL, sizeof(struct arp_hdr)+18);
  }
 }
}
```

The rest of the code starts comparing the target IP address with the device's IP address, to see if this message is for us. If so, after verifying if the message is an ARP Request, we compose an ARP Reply and we send it using the **ethernet_send( )** function.

Now, let's see the **arp_display( )** function:

```
#if debug_arp
void arp_display(void) {
 printf("ARP Message:\n");
 printf("HwType:    %04x\n", HTONS(ARPr->hwtype));
 printf("ProType:   %04x\n", HTONS(ARPr->protype));
 printf("HwAddrLen: %x\n", ARPr->hwaddrlen);
 printf("ProAddrLen:%x\n", ARPr->proaddrlen);
 printf("OpCode:    %04x\n", HTONS(ARPr->opcode));
 printf("Sender:    %02x-%02x-%02x-%02x-%02x-%02x (%d.%d.%d.%d)\n",
                     ARPr->senhwaddr[0], ARPr->senhwaddr[1],
                     ARPr->senhwaddr[2], ARPr->senhwaddr[3],
                     ARPr->senhwaddr[4], ARPr->senhwaddr[5],
                     ARPr->senproaddr[0], ARPr->senproaddr[1],
                     ARPr->senproaddr[2], ARPr->senproaddr[3]);

 printf("Target:    %02x-%02x-%02x-%02x-%02x-%02x (%d.%d.%d.%d)\n",
                     ARPr->tarhwaddr[0], ARPr->tarhwaddr[1],
                     ARPr->tarhwaddr[2], ARPr->tarhwaddr[3],
                     ARPr->tarhwaddr[4], ARPr->tarhwaddr[5],
                     ARPr->tarproaddr[0], ARPr->tarproaddr[1],
                     ARPr->tarproaddr[2], ARPr->tarproaddr[3]);
 printf("--------------------------------------------------\n");
}
#endif //debug_arp
```

This function shows the received ARP message, using the **printf( )** function.

The **differ_subnet( )** function compares the Network ID portion of the sender's IP address with our Network ID, in order to verify if they are on the same network. These functions return to 1 if they are on different networks, or 0 if they are both on the same network. The following code shows how it is implemented:

```
char differ_subnet(char *proaddr) {

  return    (proaddr[0] & SubNetMask[0]) ^ (MyIP[0] & SubNetMask[0]) |
            (proaddr[1] & SubNetMask[1]) ^ (MyIP[1] & SubNetMask[1]) |
            (proaddr[2] & SubNetMask[2]) ^ (MyIP[2] & SubNetMask[2]) |
            (proaddr[3] & SubNetMask[3]) ^ (MyIP[3] & SubNetMask[3]);
}
```

The **arp_update( )** function is called each time an ARP message is processed, in order to update the ARP table. The following code shows its implementation:

```
void arp_update(void) {
 int i;
 struct arp_entry * entry;

 for(i=0;i<ARP_CACHE_SIZE;i++) {
  entry = &arp_cache[i];
  if (entry->state == ARP_ENTRY_FREE)
    continue;
  if (memcmp(entry->proaddr,ARPr->senproaddr,4)==0) {
    entry->state = ARP_ENTRY_OK;
    entry->tout = ARP_ENTRY_TOUT;
    entry->retries = ARP_DEF_RETRIES;
    return;
  }
 }
```

First, the code searches in the table, to see if the device's IP address is already cached. If so, the entry is just actualized. If not, the entry must be allocated.

```
  i = arp_allocate();
  entry = &arp_cache[i];
  memcpy(entry->proaddr, ARPr->senproaddr, 4);
  memcpy(entry->hwaddr, ARPr->senhwaddr, 6);
  entry->state = ARP_ENTRY_OK;
  entry->tout =      ARP_ENTRY_TOUT;
  entry->retries = ARP_DEF_RETRIES;
  entry->queries = 0;
}
```

Then, the **arp_allocate( )** function is called. This function will return the first free entry it encounters. If the table is full, it will search for the least queried entry, in order to allocate the new entry at this position. Once we have the entry position, we must fill the table fields.

The following code shows the **arp_allocate( )** function implementation:

```
int arp_allocate(void) {
  int i, j, q;

  for(i=0;i<ARP_CACHE_SIZE;i++) {
   if (arp_cache[i].state == ARP_ENTRY_FREE) {
          return i;
   }
  }
  // there isn't a free entry...we will choose the less utilized entry
  for(i=0;i<ARP_CACHE_SIZE;i++) {
   if (arp_cache[i].queries > q) {
     q = arp_cache[i].queries;
     j = i;
   }
  }
  return j;
}
```

The first for(; ;) loop searches for the first free entry, and it returns this position if it is found. If the table is full, the function must decide to delete an entry in order to allocate the new entry. This decision uses the queries field to select the least queried entry for its deletion. We suppose that each entry, the more queries it has, the more probabilities it has to be used. The second for(; ;) loop implements this decision.

14.3.3.3 Resolving the IP address

With all the above codes, we have implemented the first three functions as stated in the ARP module functions section. The fourth function is the **arp_resolve( )**, which is implemented as the code on page 335 code shows:

The code is called by the **ethernet_send( )** function, when it needs the MAC address of a device to send a frame. The function is called with the destination IP address as a first parameter, and a second parameter where the resolved hardware address will be copied, in the case where it is found in the ARP table.

With the destination IP address (if the device is in the same network), or the gateway IP address (if the device is in a different network), the hardware address is searched for in the ARP table. If it is found, the address is copied to the second parameter and the ARP_ENTRY_FOUND value is returned. If it is not found, an **arp_request( )** is issued, and the ARP_ENTRY_NOT_FOUND is returned.

```
int arp_resolve(char * ipdest, char * hwaddr) {
  int i;
  char proaddr[4];
  struct arp_entry * entry;

  if (differ_subnet(ipdest)) {
#if debug_arp
    printf("Different SubNet: using Gateway IP address\r\n");
#endif
    memcpy(proaddr, Gateway, 4);
  }else {
    memcpy(proaddr, ipdest, 4);
  }
  for(i=0;i<ARP_CACHE_SIZE;i++) {
    entry = &arp_cache[i];
    if (entry->state == ARP_ENTRY_FREE)
      continue;
    if ( memcmp(entry->proaddr, proaddr, 4)==0) {
      memcpy(hwaddr, entry->hwaddr,6);
      entry->queries++;
      return ARP_ENTRY_FOUND;
    }
  }
  arp_request(proaddr);
  printf("ARP: Entry not found! Sending an ARP Request (Broadcast)\r\n");
  return ARP_ENTRY_NOT_FOUND;
}
```

It is worth noting that when the ARP_ENTRY_NOT_FOUND is returned, the **ethernet_send( )** function returns and the frame is not sent (see the **ethernet_send( )** code). That means the message is lost. Is this OK? Well, if we do not want this frame to get lost, we need to save the frame in some memory space. Then, once the ARP Request recently sent has had a reply, we could send the saved frame. However, how much memory space would we need to save these frames? What if while the ARP Request is sent and the device replies we have many other frames to be saved? In addition, what if the device never replies? Taking into account that each frame can be up to 1514 bytes, we realize that the cost of memory is too high to implement this strategy. Instead, we would prefer the frame was lost, because if the Transport layer sending the message is TCP, it will retry after detecting it has no response from the other device. Moreover, at this time, the device should already have responded to the ARP Request, so the device's hardware address should already be cached in the ARP table. However, if the Transport layer sending the message is UDP, the message will not be resent. After all, the UDP is supposed to be unreliable, so the Application layer using this transport protocol should foresee this situation.

For the above reason, our ARP implementation differs from others where the cached entry, once it times out, is deleted. We prefer to maintain the table by updating the entries when they expire, instead of deleting each entry and having the next frame lost.

The **arp_request( )** function is implemented as follows:

```
void arp_request(char *proaddr) {
  int i;

  ARPt->hwtype = HTONS(0x0001);
  ARPt->protype = HTONS(0x0800);
  ARPt->hwaddrlen = 6;
  ARPt->proaddrlen = 4;
  ARPt->opcode= HTONS(ARP_Request);
  memcpy(ARPt->tarproaddr, proaddr, 4);
  memset(ARPt->tarhwaddr, 0x00, 6);
  memcpy(ARPt->senproaddr, MyIP, 4);
  memcpy(ARPt->senhwaddr, MyMAC, 6);
  for(i=0;i<18;i++)
    tx_buf[42+i] = 0x20;
  ethernet_send(ARP_PROTOCOL, sizeof(struct arp_hdr)+18);
}
```

The above code assembles the ARP Request message, and then calls the Data Link layer service to send it out.

14.3.3.4 Maintaining the ARP table

The last function of the ARP module is the ARP table maintenance. The **arp_poll( )** function does this:

```
void arp_poll(void) {
  int i;

  if (timer_expired(arptimer)) {            // 100 msec has elapsed
    for(i=0; i<ARP_CACHE_SIZE; i++) {
      if (arp_cache[i].state != ARP_ENTRY_FREE)
        arp_cache[i].tout--;
    }
    timer_start(arptimer, 100);
  }else
    return;
```

Every 100 milliseconds, the ARP timer elapses. This routine is called periodically from the **stack.c** module. When the timer has expired, all non-free table entries are updated (its tout field is decremented). Then the timer is restarted.

The code looks for each non-free table entry, which tout field has expired. If the entry status is ARP_ENTRY_OK, an **arp_request( )** is called in order to check if the entry is still valid. The status now changes to ARP_ENTRY_RESOLVING.

```
for(i=0; i<ARP_CACHE_SIZE; i++) {
  if (arp_cache[i].state == ARP_ENTRY_FREE)
    continue;
  if (arp_cache[i].tout == ARP_ENTRY_TIMED_OUT) {
    switch(arp_cache[i].state) {
      case ARP_ENTRY_OK:
         arp_request(arp_cache[i].proaddr);
         arp_cache[i].tout = ARP_REQUEST_TOUT;
         arp_cache[i].state = ARP_ENTRY_RESOLVING;
         break;
      case ARP_ENTRY_RESOLVING:
         if (arp_cache[i].retries > 0) {
             arp_cache[i].retries--;
             arp_request(arp_cache[i].proaddr);
             arp_cache[i].tout = ARP_REQUEST_TOUT;
         }else
             arp_cache[i].state = ARP_ENTRY_FREE;
         break;
      default:
         printf("ARP: Invalid State!\r\n");
    }
  }
 }
}
```

If the tout field indicates that the entry has expired, and the entry status is ARP_ENTRY_RESOLVING, it means that the device has not replied the ARP Request. In this case, the request is resent until the entry retries field is zero, in which case the device is considered not to be connected, and the corresponding entry is deleted (changing its status as ARP_ENTRY_FREE).

Going back to the **arp_resolve( )** function, we may realize that the code does not check the entry status field. This means that if the function finds the requested address in an entry where the status field has the ARP_ENTRY_RESOLVING value, the function informs that entry as valid. Again, is this OK? The fact that the entry has this status means that the tout has expired, and not that the device is not responding. Then, only when the device does not respond for a while, should the entry be deleted, and the function should inform the requested entry was not found!

14.3.3.5 Showing the ARP table

Finally, the **arp.c** module has implemented an **arp_show_table( )** function, which allows the users to query the ARP table status from the console. The following code shows its implementation:

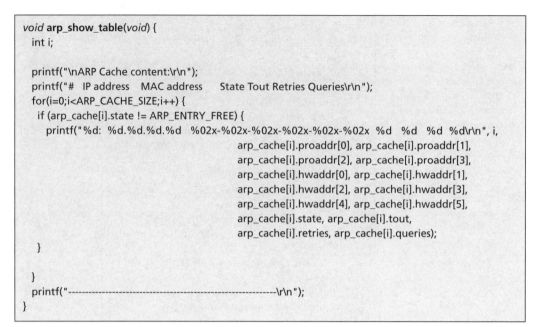

```
void arp_show_table(void) {
  int i;

  printf("\nARP Cache content:\r\n");
  printf("#  IP address   MAC address     State Tout Retries Queries\r\n");
  for(i=0;i<ARP_CACHE_SIZE;i++) {
   if (arp_cache[i].state != ARP_ENTRY_FREE) {
     printf("%d:  %d.%d.%d.%d  %02x-%02x-%02x-%02x-%02x-%02x  %d   %d   %d  %d\r\n", i,
                                       arp_cache[i].proaddr[0], arp_cache[i].proaddr[1],
                                       arp_cache[i].proaddr[2], arp_cache[i].proaddr[3],
                                       arp_cache[i].hwaddr[0], arp_cache[i].hwaddr[1],
                                       arp_cache[i].hwaddr[2], arp_cache[i].hwaddr[3],
                                       arp_cache[i].hwaddr[4], arp_cache[i].hwaddr[5],
                                       arp_cache[i].state, arp_cache[i].tout,
                                       arp_cache[i].retries, arp_cache[i].queries);
   }

  }
  printf("----------------------------------------------------------\r\n");
}
```

Lab 3: The ARP protocol

Lab 3 introduction

In the present Lab, we will examine the ARP protocol implementation. We will see how the ARP table is created and maintained.

Lab 3 target support

This Lab only supports the LPC-E212X boards with Ethernet interface.

Lab 3 options setting

This Lab requires the debug_arp option to be set.

Lab 3 instructions

Complete the steps according to Chapter 12 (see section 12.6). Once the Lab is running, follow the Lab 3 Exercises.

Lab 3 exercises

- From the PC's system command, execute a 'ping 192.168.0.30' command. See Appendix E, section E.5 for details. The board should start receiving ARP messages. Check this in the LPC-E212X console. If the board does not receive an ARP Request, you should execute an 'arp –d' command in the PC. This deletes the ARP cache table, so the next ping command will generate an ARP Request.

- Analyse the received messages. Compare its structure with the ARP message structure. See the Sender addresses to see from which device the ARP message was sent.
- Press the 'A' key in the console, to see the ARP table. It should include the PC addresses, as well as other addresses from any other device connected to the network. If other connected devices do not appear in the table, execute a 'ping 192.168.0.30' command from these devices (and execute an 'arp –d' if necessary).
- From the PC (and from each device connected to the network), execute an 'arp –a' command and check if the LPC-E212X device addresses are cached.
- Press the 'A' key in the console several times, to see how the tout parameter is decremented. Each time it gets the ARP_ENTRY_TIMED_OUT value, a request is sent and a response should be received, updating the table.
- Disconnect the Ethernet cable from the board, and check that all entries have been deleted; once the table cannot be updated (with the cable disconnected, the board will not be able to send or receive ARP messages).

15

Dial-up networking: PPP

In this chapter, we will implement the Data Link layer for the serial interface. Since serial hardware programming is very common in embedded systems, we do not describe this module here. In fact, the console is already using a serial interface module (uart.c). However, we will explain a slight modification for the **uart1.c** module used for the physical link. After this, we will see a description for each of the protocols and modules needed to get the PPP link established. Finally, Lab 4 will give us the opportunity to see the PPP implementation in action.

15.1 Serial port programming considerations

The PPP was designed to provide a Data Link layer for the serial links. This serial link may use the same driver module as the console. However, as this serial interface will handle much more information and at a higher speed than the console, we will use the driver with some modifications.

Typically, the serial ports are polled regularly in order to get the received characters. If the polling frequency is not enough, we could lose some characters. Remember that a PPP packet may have up to 1500 bytes. That means that with only one character lost, the Frame Check Sequence (FCS) will be wrong and the entire packet will be discarded. While the serial port is polled regularly by the program, the incoming characters arrive irregularly. That is, when a packet arrives, we have many characters to read from the serial port; but between packets, we may have a long time without any character arriving. A solution is to provide an input buffer to compensate the different rates at which the characters arrive and the port is read. For transmitted characters, the problem arises because of the different rates between the serial port and the processor. If the program needs to wait for the serial port to be ready to send each character, with a 1500-byte PPP packet, the program may be delayed for too long. For this reason, it is sometimes better to store the characters in a buffer, from where the characters will be sent to the serial port, at a regular time. However, an output buffer may consume too much memory, so the convenience of its implementation will depend on each particular case.

In our implementation, we will use an input buffer and an interrupt scheme for received characters. Since the UART has a 16-byte Receive FIFO, it can be programmed to generate an interrupt when the FIFO has reached the Rx Trigger Level (1, 4, 8 or 14 characters in the FIFO). Then, the interrupt handle routine (**uart1_irq( )**) will store the received characters in an *input buffer*. Each time the **getchar1( )** function is called, it will read the characters from this buffer. In our case, the application can tolerate some delays without problems, so we will not use an *output buffer*. Then, for transmitted characters, the **putchar1( )** routine will write the characters directly to the port.

15.2 Point-to-Point Protocol implementation

15.2.1 Module structures, variables and #define references

The **stack.h** header file has definitions used by **ppp.c** and other modules. For example, the packet buffer size and the data link header size are needed by the IP layer to know the buffer position where the IP datagram begins, and the maximum IP datagram size allowed by the buffer size.

```
#ifdef PPP_LINK
  #define PACKET_BUF_SIZE        1504      // we don't consider the FCS (last two bytes)
  #define DATALINK_HDR_SIZE      4
#endif
```

The ppp_status variable is exported in order for other modules to know the status of the PPP link.

```
#ifdef PPP_LINK

#define PPP_CLOSED                      0x00
#define PPP_OPENED                      0x01
#define PPP_WAIT                        0x02  // the PPP is connecting/disconnecting...
#define PPP_ERROR_MODEM                 0x04
#define PPP_ERROR_DIAL_BUSY             0x08
#define PPP_ERROR_DIAL_NO_CARRIER       0x09
#define PPP_ERROR_DIAL_NO_DIALTONE      0x0A
#define PPP_ERROR_DIAL_NO_ANSWER        0x0B
#define PPP_ERROR_NEGOTIATION           0x10
#define PPP_ERROR_AUTH                  0x20
#define PPP_ERROR_PHY_LINK              0x40
#define PPP_ERROR_SERVER_CLOSE          0x80

#define PPP_STATUS_NO_ERROR             ppp_status <= 0x02
#define PPP_STATUS_ERROR                ppp_status > 0x02
extern char  ppp_status;

#endif
```

The **ppp.c** module declares the modem_state and modem_status variables, and defines their possible values and their labels.

```
#define MODEM_DISCONNECTED        0x00
#define MODEM_RESETTING           0x01
#define MODEM_RESET_OK            0x02
#define MODEM_DIALING             0x04
#define MODEM_CONNECTED           0x08
#define MODEM_DISCONNECTING       0x10
#define MODEM_WAITING_DIAL        0x20
char modem_state = MODEM_DISCONNECTED;

#define MODEM_NO_STATUS           0x00
#define MODEM_OK                  0x01
#define MODEM_ERROR               0x02
#define MODEM_TIMEOUT             0x04
#define MODEM_BUSY                0x08
#define MODEM_NO_CARRIER          0x10
#define MODEM_NO_DIALTONE         0x20
char modem_status = MODEM_NO_STATUS;
```

In addition, the ppp_status, ppp_state and the ppp_start_stop variable are declared in this module. The labels and values for the last two variables and the MAX_RETRIES label are also defined.

```
#define PPP_INITIAL_STATE   0x00
#define LCP_ACK_SENT        0x01    // we sent an ACK
#define LCP_ACK_RCVD        0x02    // we received an ACK
#define LCP_OK              0x03
#define PAP_REQ_SENT        0x04    // we sent a PAP REQ
#define PAP_ACK_RCVD        0x0C    // we received an ACK for the user and password
#define IPCP_REQ1_SENT      0x10    // we sent an IPCP REQ (with IP: 0.0.0.0)
#define IPCP_NAK_RCVD       0x30    // we received a NAK with the assigned IP address
#define IPCP_REQ2_SENT      0x40    // we sent an IPCP REQ  (with the assigned IP)
#define PPP_OK              0x80    // we are connected!!!
char ppp_state = PPP_INITIAL_STATE;

#define MAX_RETRIES 3
char ppp_status = PPP_CLOSED;

#define PPP_NO_ACTION       0x00
#define PPP_START           0x01
#define PPP_STOP            0x02
char ppp_start_stop = PPP_NO_ACTION;
```

The following structures define the PPP packet header, the PPP Control Message header, and the variables to hold the ISP data (phone number, user and password). Also, the receive and transmit buffers are declared in this module. The id variable will hold the ID field, which must be incremented for each sent packet, while the MyIP and server variables will hold the IP addresses, once the PPP link has been established.

```
struct ppp_hdr {
  char              address;
  char              control;
  unsigned short    protocol;
};

struct ppp_ctl_hdr {
  char              type;
  char              id;
  unsigned short    length;
};

struct {
  char       number[20];
  char       user[20];
  char       pass[20];
} isp;

int c;
char      rx_buf[PACKET_BUF_SIZE+2];          // we include the FCS (2 bytes)
char      tx_buf[PACKET_BUF_SIZE+2];          // we include the FCS (2 bytes)
char      id=85;                              // we start with this id number
char      MyIP[4];                            // The IP assigned by the RAS Server
char      server[4];                          // RAS Server IP address
```

The **ppp.h** header file defines the **HTONS( )** macro which translates between network and processor byte order. The PPP is defined as a pointer to the PPP header structure in order to facilitate the header field access (for example; using the PPP → protocol syntax). In the same way, CTRL defines a pointer to the Control Message header structure. Some labels are defined for the protocols and the Control Message types.

```
#define HTONS(n) ((((unsigned short)((n) & 0xff)) << 8) | (((n) & 0xff00) >> 8))
#define PPP   ((struct ppp_hdr *)&rx_buf[0])
#define CTRL  ((struct ppp_ctl_hdr *)&rx_buf[DATALINK_HDR_SIZE])

#define LCP_PROTOCOL      0xC021
#define PAP_PROTOCOL      0xC023
#define CHAP_PROTOCOL     0xC223
#define CCP_PROTOCOL      0x80FD
#define IPCP_PROTOCOL     0x8021
#define IP_PROTOCOL       0x0021

#define ICMP_PROTOCOL     1
#define UDP_PROTOCOL      17
#define TCP_PROTOCOL      6

#define REQ               1
#define ACKW              2
#define NAK               3
#define REJ               4
#define TERM_REQ          5
#define TERM_ACK          6
```

15.2.2 PPP functions description

When the stack is included in a project, the **stack_poll( )** routine must be called regularly from the **main( )** routine. If the stack is configured for the serial interface, the **ppp_poll( )** routine will be called from the **stack.c** module. See how **ppp_poll( )** is implemented:

```
void ppp_poll(void) {

  c=getchar1();                     // Scan the modem
  if (c != -1) {
    modem_response();
    if (modem_state == MODEM_CONNECTED) {
      if (modem_status == MODEM_NO_CARRIER) {
        if (ppp_state != PPP_OK)
            ppp_status = PPP_ERROR_NEGOTIATION;
        else
            ppp_status = PPP_ERROR_PHY_LINK;
        ppp_state = PPP_INITIAL_STATE;
        ppp_start_stop = PPP_STOP;
      }
      char_process();
    }
  }
  ...
```

The routine starts calling the **getchar1( )** function to read the incoming characters from the modem. If a character is obtained (c != -1), the **modem_response( )** routine is called, which looks for a response from the modem (OK, ERROR, BUSY, NO CARRIER, NO DIALTONE, CONNECT) and sets the modem_status variable. If the modem connects, the modem_state variable is set to the MODEM_CONNECTED value.

Once the modem is connected, it looks for the modem_status variable. If it is set to MODEM_NO_CARRIER, then an error has occurred. It looks at the ppp_state variable to see if it was an error in the PPP negotiation phase, or the physical link was disconnected. In any of these cases, the PPP state is reinitialized. Finally, while the modem is connected, the **char_process( )** function is called. This routine looks for the PPP frame Flag (0x7E) character and calculates the CRC value. When a PPP packet is detected, it calls the **packet_process( )** function to process the packet according to the protocol it carries.

The last part of the **ppp_poll( )** function follows on page 345.

The ppp_start_stop variable is used to control when the PPP link begins and ends. Since the physical link is needed by the PPP protocol, the modem is connected or disconnected accordingly, using the **modem_connect( )** or **modem_disconnect( )** functions. While the modem is connected and the PPP link is not established, the **ppp_engine( )** function is called in order to send the necessary messages to get the PPP link established.

```
...
  if (ppp_start_stop == PPP_START)
    modem_connect();
  if (ppp_start_stop == PPP_STOP)
    modem_disconnect();
  if (modem_state==MODEM_CONNECTED &&
                                  ppp_state!=PPP_OK) {
    ppp_engine();
  }
}
```

The following code shows the **modem_response( )** implementation:

```
void modem_response(void) {
  static char i ;
  static char first_char;
  static char second_char;

  if (c==0x0D || c==0x0A) {
    i=0;
    first_char = 0;
    second_char = 0;
    return;
  }
  if (c==0x20)
    return;
  ...
```

The routine starts looking for a carriage return or a new line character, which would indicate that a new response could begin. The space characters (0x20) are filtered. The idea is to detect one of the following possible responses from the modem:

- **OK**
- **E**RROR
- **B**USY
- **NO C**ARRIER (**NOC**ARRIER, filtering the space)
- **NO D**IALTONE (**NOD**IALTONE, filtering the space)
- **CON**NECT

For the three responses on the left, only two characters will be needed. For the three responses on the right, we should take three characters. Once a new line is detected, the next received character will be stored in the first_char variable. The next character will be the second letter. Now, with two characters we could see if we got one of the three responses on the left (**OK**, **E**RROR, **B**USY). If not, we should store the second character in the second_char variable, and wait for the next character to see if we got one of the other responses. The following code shows this:

```
...
i++;
switch(i) {
  case 1:
    first_char = c;
    break;
  case 2:
    switch(c) {
      case 'K':
        if (first_char=='O') {
            modem_status = MODEM_OK;
            timer_stop(ppptimer);
        }
        break;
      case 'R':
        if (first_char=='E') {
            modem_status = MODEM_ERROR;
            timer_stop(ppptimer);
        }
        break;
      case 'U':
        if (first_char=='B') {
            modem_status = MODEM_BUSY;
            timer_stop(ppptimer);
        }
        break;
      case 'O':
        second_char=c;
        break;
    }
    break;
```

The *i* variable and the switch structure allow each character to be processed according to its order. The first character is stored. If the second character is K, R or U, then the first character is checked to see if OK, ERROR or BUSY was received from the modem. If the second character is O, the character is stored and we wait for the third character. This last will be processed by the code at the top of page 347.

The code looks for the NOC, NOD, or CON words to detect one of the NO CARRIER, NO DIALTONE or CONNECT responses.

Once a modem response has been detected, the modem_status or modem_state variable is set accordingly, and the ppptimer (a timer assigned for the PPP module) is stopped. This timer allows us to know if the modem does not respond in a given period of time.

```
    ...
    case 3:
      if (first_char=='N' && second_char=='O' && c=='C') {
        modem_status = MODEM_NO_CARRIER;
        if (modem_state != MODEM_WAITING_DIAL)
          timer_stop(ppptimer);
        if (modem_state == MODEM_CONNECTED)
          printf("NO CARRIER\n");
      }
      if (first_char=='N' && second_char=='O' && c=='D') {
        modem_status = MODEM_NO_DIALTONE;
        timer_stop(ppptimer);
      }
      if (first_char=='C' && second_char=='O' && c=='N') {
        modem_state = MODEM_CONNECTED;
        timer_stop(ppptimer);
      }
      break;
  }
}
```

15.2.2.1 Processing incoming characters

Each incoming character is processed by the **char_process( )** function. This routine looks for escaped data, uncompresses compressed fields and detects valid packets.

```
void char_process(void) {
  static char extended=0;
  static unsigned int chksum;
  static unsigned short index = 0;

  if (c == 0x7E) {                    // Start or End of packet
    if (index && (chksum == 0xF0B8)) {
      packet_process();
    }
    extended=0;                       // Prepare for next packet
    index = 0;
    chksum = 0xFFFF;


...
```

When the Flag character (0x7E) is detected, it means that a packet either begins or ends. If the index variable is greater than zero, and the checksum is valid, the flag would be indicating the end of a valid packet. Then, the **packet_process( )** function is called, which will pass the frame to the respective protocol handler.

```
...
}else if (c == 0x7D) {
  extended = 1;
}else {
  if (extended) {
    c ^= 0x20;
    extended = 0;
  }
  if (index==0 && c!=0xFF)            // if Address compressed, include it
    rx_buf[index++] = 0xFF;
  if (index==1 && c!=0x03)            // if Control compressed, include it
    rx_buf[index++] = 0x03;
  if (index==2 && (c&0x01))           // if Protocol compressed, include it
    rx_buf[index++] = 0x00;
  rx_buf[index++] = c;
  chksum = calc(c ^ chksum) ^ (chksum/256);
 }
}
```

If the Escape character (0x7D) is received, the next character is escaped. The **extended** variable helps in this task. The next if statements verify if the Address, Control or Protocol fields are compressed. If so, they uncompress them. The last line calculates the frame's FCS, using the **calc( )** function, which implements a CRC algorithm.

15.2.2.2 Processing incoming packets

Each time the **char_process( )** routine detects a packet, the packet is passed to the **packet_process( )** function for its process.

```
void packet_process(void) {

#if debug_ppp
  ppp_debug();
#endif //debug_ppp

  switch(HTONS(PPP->protocol)) {
    case LCP_PROTOCOL:
      lcp_process();
      break;
    case PAP_PROTOCOL:
      if (CTRL->type == ACKW) {
      ppp_state = PAP_ACK_RCVD;
      printf("PAP OK\n");
      }
      if (CTRL->type == NAK) {
        printf("PAP: Incorrect User or Password!\n");
      }
      break;
    ...
```

If the debug_ppp option is set in the **debug.h** file, the **ppp_debug( )** function is called. This function displays the frame's protocol type (LCP, PAP, IPCP, CCP and IP) in the console and the control message type (REQ, ACK, NAK, REJ, etc.). Also, the **ppp_debug( )** routine calls the **ppp_display( )** function in order to display the received frame in the console. As these two routines are very simple, we will not show them here. After this, a switch structure allows the process of each frame according to its type. The **HTONS( )** macro (defined in the **ppp.h** file) is used to convert the network byte order (big endian; big units first) to our processor byte order (little endian; little units first).

For the LCP packets, the **lcp_process( )** function is called. If the packet is a PAP response, and it has an ACKW code (the user and password are correct), the ppp_state is updated. See the continuation of the above code:

```
        ...
        case IPCP_PROTOCOL:
          ipcp_process();
          break;
        case CCP_PROTOCOL:
          memcpy(&tx_buf[4], &rx_buf[4], HTONS(CTRL->length));
          if (rx_buf[4] == TERM_REQ)
            tx_buf[4] = TERM_ACK;
          else
            tx_buf[4] = REJ;
          ppp_send(CCP_PROTOCOL, HTONS(CTRL->length));
          break;
        case IP_PROTOCOL:
           ip_process();
           break;
        default:
           printf("Unknown Protocol %04x\n", HTONS(PPP->protocol));
           break;
    }
  }
```

Under the same scheme, if the packet is an IPCP packet, then it is passed to the **ipcp_process( )** function; if it is an IP packet, it is forwarded to the **ip_process( )** function, implemented in the IP layer.

As our implementation does not support the CCP protocol, any received CCP packets will be rejected. If the peer requests to terminate the connection (TERM_REQ), we reply with an acknowledgement (TERM_ACK). The packet is sent using the **ppp_send( )** function.

15.2.2.3 Processing LCP packets

Each packet containing an LCP Control Message is processed by the **lcp_process( )** function. This routine will check each type of control message, and it will act accordingly.

```
void lcp_process(void) {

  switch(CTRL->type){
    case REQ:
      lcp_req_scan();
      break;
    case ACKW:
      if (ppp_state == LCP_OK)
        printf("LCP OK\n");
      ppp_state |= LCP_ACK_RCVD;
      break;
    case NAK:
      break;
    case REJ:
      break;
    ...
```

If the LCP message is a Request, the **lcp_req_scan( )** function scans the request for acceptable options. If the LCP message is an acknowledgement, the ppp_state variable is updated. For NAK (Not Acknowledge) or REJ (Reject) messages, no action is taken.

```
    ...
    case TERM_REQ:
      tx_buf[4]=TERM_ACK;
      tx_buf[5]=rx_buf[5];                    // id must match request
      tx_buf[6]=0;
      tx_buf[7]=4;
      ppp_send(LCP_PROTOCOL, ((tx_buf[6]<<8) + tx_buf[7]));
      printf("PPP Closed (requested by Server)\n");
      ppp_start_stop = PPP_STOP;
      modem_status = MODEM_NO_STATUS;
      if (ppp_status == PPP_WAIT) {           // if it does not reach the PPP_OK
        if (ppp_state == PAP_REQ_SENT)
          ppp_status = PPP_ERROR_AUTH;        // an error in Authentication
        else
          ppp_status = PPP_ERROR_NEGOTIATION;        //an error in negotiation
      }else {
         ppp_status = PPP_ERROR_SERVER_CLOSE;        // the server terminates
                                                     // the connection
      }
      ppp_state = PPP_INITIAL_STATE;
      break;
    case TERM_ACK:
      break;
    default:
      printf("\nLCP Unkown Type: %d\n", CTRL->type);
      break;
  }
}
```

If we receive an LCP message with a Termination Request code, we must send an acknowledgement. Then, we update the state and status variables.

15.2.2.4 Scanning LCP acceptable options

When an LCP REQ message is received, the LCP Configuration Options must be scanned. We will only accept the ACCM (Code 2), the Protocol Field compression (Code 7), the Address and Control Compression (Code 8) and PAP (0xC023) as the Authentication protocol (Code 3).

```
void lcp_req_scan(void) {
  int i;
  int rx_ptr;
  int tx_ptr;
  char result=0;                              // ACK (bit0=0 and bit1=0)
  short size;

  size = HTONS(CTRL->length)+4;               // packet size
  rx_ptr = 8;
  while(rx_ptr < size) {
    switch(rx_buf[rx_ptr]) {
      case 2:
        break;
      case 3:
        if (rx_buf[rx_ptr+2] == 0xC2)         // if CHAP
          result |= 1;                        // NAK    (bit0=1)
        break;
      case 7:
        break;
      case 8:
        break;
      default:                                // any other option
        result |= 2;                          // REJ    (bit1=1)
        break;
    }
    rx_ptr += rx_buf[rx_ptr+1];
  }
  ...
```

The above code scans the LCP Request options. Any other options than those accepted, will be rejected. If the Authentication protocol is other than PAP, the option will be NAKed. The result variable is used to hold the scan result (ACK, NAK or REJ).

If one or more of the LCP Configuration Options is not acceptable, we must send a REJ with a list of the rejected options. The if (result&2) block at the top of page 352 constructs this message.

If the result of the LCP Options scan determines that a NAK must be sent, the message with the proposed option (PAP) must be set. If the scanned LCP Options are acceptable, an ACK message with a list of those options must be sent (see bottom code, page 352).

```
...
if (result&2) {                                    // REJ
   tx_buf[4]=REJ;
   rx_ptr = 8;
   tx_ptr = 8;
   while(rx_ptr < size) {
     if (rx_buf[rx_ptr]!=2 && rx_buf[rx_ptr]!=3 &&
                 rx_buf[rx_ptr]!=7 && rx_buf[rx_ptr]!=8) {
        for(i=rx_ptr;i<(rx_ptr+rx_buf[rx_ptr+1]); i++) {
           tx_buf[tx_ptr++] = rx_buf[i];
        }
     }
      rx_ptr += rx_buf[rx_ptr+1];
   }
   tx_buf[6] = ((tx_ptr - 4)>>8)&0xFF;          // length
   tx_buf[7] = (tx_ptr - 4)&0xFF;
  }else if (result&1) {                           // NAK
    tx_buf[4]=NAK;
    tx_buf[6]=0;
    tx_buf[7]=8;
    tx_buf[8]=3;
    tx_buf[9]=4;
    tx_buf[10]=0xC0;
    tx_buf[11]=0x23;
  }else {                                         // ACK
    tx_buf[4]=ACKW;
    rx_ptr = 8;
    tx_ptr = 8;
    while(rx_ptr < size) {
              for(i=rx_ptr;i<(rx_ptr+rx_buf[rx_ptr+1]); i++) {
               tx_buf[tx_ptr++] = rx_buf[i];
              }
              rx_ptr += rx_buf[rx_ptr+1];
    }
    tx_buf[6] = ((tx_ptr - 4)>>8)&0xFF;  // length
    tx_buf[7] = (tx_ptr - 4)&0xFF;
    ppp_state |= LCP_ACK_SENT;
  }

  tx_buf[5]=rx_buf[5];                          // id must match request
  ppp_send(LCP_PROTOCOL, ((tx_buf[6]<<8) + tx_buf[7]));
  if (ppp_state == LCP_OK)
    printf("\nLCP OK\n");
}
```

The last part of the code copies the ID field from the request to the response, and uses the **ppp_send( )** function to send the message. Once an LCP ACK message has been sent and received, the LCP negotiation is done. Since we are using and accepting default values for the LCP Options, the LCP negotiation should converge in all cases.

15.2.2.5 Processing IPCP packets

The **ipcp_process( )** function processes the IPCP messages received by the stack. This protocol will assign an IP address for our device. The following code shows its implementation:

```
void ipcp_process(void) {

  switch(CTRL->type) {
    case REQ:
      if (rx_buf[8]==2) {              // IP Compression-Protocol option  (Not Allowed)
        memcpy(&tx_buf[4], &rx_buf[4], 10);
        tx_buf[4] = REJ;
        tx_buf[7] = 0x0A;
      }else {                          // only IP-Address option (Allowed)
        memcpy(&tx_buf[4], &rx_buf[4], HTONS(CTRL->length));
        tx_buf[4] = ACKW;
        memcpy(&server[0], &rx_buf[10], 4);
        printf("\Server Address: %d.%d.%d.%d \n",
                          server[0],server[1],server[2],server[3]);
      }
      ppp_send(IPCP_PROTOCOL, HTONS(CTRL->length));
      break;
    case ACKW:
      ppp_state = PPP_OK;
      memcpy(&MyIP[0], &rx_buf[10], 4);
      printf("PPP Ok - Address: %d.%d.%d.%d\n",
                          MyIP[0],MyIP[1],MyIP[2],MyIP[3]);
      ppp_status = PPP_OPENED;
      break;
    case NAK:
      ppp_state = IPCP_NAK_RCVD;
      break;
  }
}
```

If the IPCP control message is a REQ, we should reject option type 2 (IP Compression Protocol) since we do not support it. Only option 3 (IP Address) is accepted, and then we must acknowledge it upon its reception. When this option is received, we get the RAS Server IP address.

As we saw in Chapter 4 (section 4.5.4.1), for dial-up connections, the client should send an IPCP REQ with an invalid IP address (0.0.0.0). Then, the server should NAK the message with a valid IP address (the IP assigned for the client device). Finally, the client sends a REQ with the assigned IP address, and the server responds with an acknowledgement. In the last part of the above code, we see the process for the ACKW and NAK messages received from the server. The REQ message sent from our devices is shown in the **ppp_engine( )** function, as we will see later on.

15.2.2.6 The PPP engine

In the last section, we saw how each of the incoming packets is processed. However, in order for our device to get a dial-up connection, many packets must also be sent. The **ppp_engine( )** function is in charge of this:

```
void ppp_engine(void) {
  char userlen;
  char passlen;

  if (! timer_expired(ppptimer))
    return;
  switch(ppp_state) {
    case PPP_INITIAL_STATE:
    case LCP_ACK_SENT:
      memcpy(&tx_buf[4], &LCP_REQ[0], sizeof(LCP_REQ));
      tx_buf[5] = id++;                                    // id field
      ppp_send(LCP_PROTOCOL, sizeof(LCP_REQ));
      break;
    case LCP_OK:
    case PAP_REQ_SENT:                         // we still sending PAP REQ ...
      userlen = strlen(isp.user);
      passlen = strlen(isp.pass);
      memcpy(&tx_buf[4], &PAP_REQ[0], 4);
      tx_buf[8] = userlen;
      memcpy(&tx_buf[9], &isp.user[0], userlen);
      tx_buf[9+userlen] = passlen;
      memcpy(&tx_buf[10+userlen], &isp.pass[0], passlen);
      tx_buf[5] = id++;                                    // id field
      tx_buf[7] = 6 + userlen + passlen;
      ppp_send(PAP_PROTOCOL, tx_buf[7]);
      ppp_state=PAP_REQ_SENT;
      printf("PAP REQ Sent...");
      break;
      ...
```

Once the modem has been connected, the ppptimer is started to have the **ppp_engine( )** function sending a message every 1 second (ppptimer timeout value). Depending on the ppp_state variable value, different messages will be sent.

The above code starts looking for the ppptimer. Once it expires, then a switch structure allows the device to send messages according the PPP link negotiation phase. For example, at the initial state, the device will send an LCP REQ message every second, until the LCP phase is done. After this, the

PAP REQ with the user and password is sent every second until we get a PAP ACK message. The LCP_REQ and the PAP_REQ constants are defined at the start of the **ppp.c** module as follows:

```
const char LCP_REQ[]={0x01,0x00,0x00,0x0E,0x02,0x06,0x00,0x0A,0x00,0x00,
                      0x07,0x02,0x08,0x02};

const char PAP_REQ[]={0x01,0x00,0x00,0x00};
```

Once the PAP phase is done, the IPCP protocol must be negotiated. The rest of the **ppp_engine( )** code takes care of this. First, an IPCP REQ message with an invalid IP address (0.0.0.0) must be sent. For this, the IPCP_REQ array is used:

```
char IPCP_REQ[]={0x01,0x00,0x00,0x0A,0x03,0x06,0x00,0x00,0x00,0x00};
```

The structure of the above array represents an IPCP REQ message with an option type 3, and the IP value as 0.0.0.0:

```
...
    case PAP_ACK_RCVD:
    case IPCP_REQ1_SENT:
      memcpy(&tx_buf[4], &IPCP_REQ[0], sizeof(IPCP_REQ));
      tx_buf[5] = id++;                                        // id field
      ppp_send(IPCP_PROTOCOL, sizeof(IPCP_REQ));
      ppp_state=IPCP_REQ1_SENT;
      break;
    case IPCP_NAK_RCVD:
    case IPCP_REQ2_SENT:
      memcpy(&IPCP_REQ[0x06], &rx_buf[0x0A], 4);
      memcpy(&tx_buf[4], &IPCP_REQ[0], sizeof(IPCP_REQ));
      tx_buf[5] = id++;                                        // id field
      ppp_send(IPCP_PROTOCOL, sizeof(IPCP_REQ));
      ppp_state=IPCP_REQ2_SENT;
      break;
    default:
      break;
  }
  timer_start(ppptimer, 1000);
}
```

Once the IPCP NAK has been received from the server, the assigned IP address is copied into the IPCP_REQ array (for this reason, it is not defined as a constant as in the case of LCP_REQ and PAP_REQ). Now, we will send the IPCP REQ message with a valid IP, and wait for its acknowledgement from the server. When it is received, the PPP link will be established. After the switch structure, a **timer_start( )** function is called to wait a second before sending a new message.

15.2.2.7 Sending PPP packets

The **ppp_send( )** function is responsible for encapsulating the received message from other protocols and sending the packet to the modem, via the UART1 port:

```
void ppp_send(unsigned short protocol, unsigned short tx_len) {
  int i;
  unsigned short ret;

  tx_len += 4;                          // + Addr (1) + Ctrl (1) + Protocol (2)
  tx_buf[0] = 0xFF;
  tx_buf[1] = 0x03;
  tx_buf[2] = (protocol>>8)&0xFF;
  tx_buf[3] = protocol&0xFF;
  ret = tx_chksum(tx_len);
  tx_buf[tx_len++] = ret&0xFF;
  tx_buf[tx_len++] = (ret>>8)&0xFF;
#if debug_ppp
...                  (see the ppp.c source code)
#endif
  ...
```

The first lines of the above code compose the PPP packet, adding the Address, Control and Protocol fields. The **tx_chksum( )** function is called to calculate the CRC over the entire packet. The result is then added at the end of the packet, forming the FCS field. After this, there is a code fragment (not shown in the above code) for debugging purposes that displays the protocol and message type that is being sent. As it is very simple, it does not require an explanation. The rest of the code is as follows:

```
  ...
  putchar1(0x7E);
  for(i=0;i<tx_len;i++) {
    if (tx_buf[i]<0x20 || tx_buf[i]==0x7D || tx_buf[i]==0x7E) {
      putchar1(0x7D);
      tx_buf[i] ^= 0x20;
    }
    putchar1(tx_buf[i]);
  }
  putchar1(0x7E);
}
```

At this point, the PPP packet is complete, so we just need to send it out using the **putchar1( )** routine. The first line sends the starting Flag character. The for(; ;) loop sends the complete message, one byte at a time. If the character must be escaped, the escape character (0x7D) is sent, and the character is escaped before it is sent. Once the complete message is sent, the ending Flag character is sent.

15.2.2.8 Connecting and disconnecting the modem

In order for the PPP link to be established, the physical link must first be established. For this reason, the **ppp_poll( )** function calls the **modem_connect( )** or **modem_disconnect( )** routine, depending on the ppp_start_stop variable. The following is the skeleton of the **modem_connect( )** function:

```
void modem_connect(void) {
  static char retry=0;
  char dialstring[4+sizeof(isp.number)] = "ATDT";

  if (timer_expired(ppptimer) && modem_state != MODEM_WAITING_DIAL) {
    modem_status = MODEM_TIMEOUT;
    timer_stop(ppptimer);
    return;
  }
  switch(modem_state) {
    case MODEM_DISCONNECTED:
      ...
    case MODEM_RESETTING:
      ...
    case MODEM_RESET_OK:
      ...
    case MODEM_DIALING:
      ...
    case MODEM_WAITING_DIAL:
      ...
    case MODEM_CONNECTED:
      ...
  }
}
```

The code implements a finite state machine, based on the modem_state variable value. The first if statement detects when the modem has not responded after some time. The switch structure allows the execution of each step necessary to get the modem connected. The normal procedure is to reset the modem, wait for its 'OK' response, dial the RAS server phone number, and wait for the 'CONNECT' response from the modem. However, we need to be prepared for other possible responses such as 'BUSY', 'NO DIALTONE', 'NO CARRIER', etc.

As the modem_state variable is initialized with the MODEM_DISCONECTED value, the following is the first case statement that will be executed:

```
...
case MODEM_DISCONNECTED:
  printf("Modem Reset...");
  modem_command("ATM0");          // Silence command
  modem_command("ATZ");
  timer_start(ppptimer, 3000);
  modem_state = MODEM_RESETTING;
  modem_status = MODEM_NO_STATUS;
  break;
...
```

This code resets the modem and starts the timer. The **modem_command( )** function uses the **putchar1( )** function to send each of the command characters to the modem (via UART1), and complete the command with a carriage return (0x0D) character. The 'ATM0' command is optional, and it is used to have the modem working silently. The 'ATZ' command is for resetting the modem. If the modem responds with an 'OK', the **modem_response( )** function should detect it and set the modem_status variable accordingly. Since the modem_state is changed to MODEM_RESETTING, the following will be the case statement executed the next time the **modem_connect( )** routine is called:

```
...
case MODEM_RESETTING:
  if (modem_status == MODEM_NO_STATUS)
    break;
  if (modem_status == MODEM_OK) {
    printf("OK\n");
    modem_state = MODEM_RESET_OK;
  }else {
    if (modem_status == MODEM_TIMEOUT)
      printf("NO RESPONSE\n");
    else
      printf("ERROR\n");
    modem_state = MODEM_DISCONNECTED;
    modem_status = MODEM_NO_STATUS;
    ppp_start_stop = PPP_NO_ACTION;
    ppp_status = PPP_ERROR_MODEM;
  }
  break;
  ...
```

While the modem does not respond to the reset command, and the timer does not expire, the modem_status variable will not change. If the modem respond with an 'OK', the **modem_response( )** function will change the modem_status variable to MODEM_OK. In this case, the above code will assign the MODEM_RESET_OK value to the modem_state variable, and the process will continue with the next step.

If the modem responds with an 'ERROR', or the modem does not respond within three seconds (TIME-OUT value), the ppp_start_stop variable is set to the PPP_NO_ACTION value, and the modem connection process is abandoned.

Supposing the modem responded with an 'OK'. The modem_state variable would have the MODEM_RESET_OK value, so next time the **modem_connect( )** is called, the code at the top of page 359 will be executed.

Here, the phone number to dial is appended to the dialstring variable contents ('ATDT') to complete the dial command. The complete string is sent to the modem. Now, the finite state machine will go to the MODEM_DIALING state, waiting for the 'CONNECT' response from the modem. The timer is started, within 30 seconds, to give the modem time to dial, answer and negotiate the physical link.

```
...
case MODEM_RESET_OK:
  printf("Modem Dialing ");
  strcat(dialstring, isp.number);
  printf(dialstring);
  modem_command(dialstring);
  printf("...");
  if (retry > 0)
     printf("(Retry #%d) ", retry);
  modem_state = MODEM_DIALING;
  modem_status = MODEM_NO_STATUS;
  timer_start(ppptimer, 30000);
  break;
  ...
```

The following code shows the MODEM_DIALING case statement implementation:

```
...
case MODEM_DIALING:
  if (modem_status == MODEM_BUSY) {
     printf("BUSY\n");
  }
  if (modem_status == MODEM_NO_CARRIER) {
     printf("NO CARRIER\n");
  }
  if (modem_status == MODEM_NO_DIALTONE) {
     printf("NO DIALTONE\n");
  }
  if (modem_status == MODEM_TIMEOUT) {
     modem_command("ATH");        // if NO ANSWER, stop dialling...
     printf("NO ANSWER\n");
  }
  ...
```

The above code looks to see if the modem_status variable changes and, if so, it informs the modem status in the console. If the modem_status gets the MODEM_TIMEOUT value, the 'ATH' command is sent to the modem to make it stop dialling.

The code overleaf looks for the modem_status value in order to retry the connection. For this reason, the finite state machine goes to the MODEM_WAITING_DIAL state for 10 seconds, and it will restart the sequence. However, if the retry variable exceeds the MAX_RETRIES parameter, the error will be updated in the ppp_status variable, the ppp_start_stop variable is set to the PPP_NO_ACTION value, and the modem connection process is abandoned.

```
...
if (modem_status == MODEM_BUSY ||
   modem_status == MODEM_NO_CARRIER ||
   modem_status == MODEM_NO_DIALTONE ||
   modem_status == MODEM_TIMEOUT) {

   retry++;
   if (retry <= MAX_RETRIES) {
      modem_state = MODEM_WAITING_DIAL;
      timer_start(ppptimer,10000);
   }else {
      modem_state = MODEM_DISCONNECTED;
      switch(modem_status) {
        case MODEM_BUSY:
          ppp_status = PPP_ERROR_DIAL_BUSY;
          break;
        case MODEM_NO_CARRIER:
          ppp_status = PPP_ERROR_DIAL_NO_CARRIER;
          break;
        case MODEM_NO_DIALTONE:
          ppp_status = PPP_ERROR_DIAL_NO_DIALTONE;
          break;
        case MODEM_TIMEOUT:
          ppp_status = PPP_ERROR_DIAL_NO_ANSWER;
          break;
      }
      modem_status = MODEM_NO_STATUS;
      ppp_start_stop = PPP_NO_ACTION;
      retry = 0;
   }
}
break;
...
```

When the finite state machine goes to the MODEM_WAITING_DIAL state, it just waits for the 10 seconds timer to expire, in order to restart the sequence:

```
...
case MODEM_WAITING_DIAL:
  if (timer_expired(ppptimer)) {
     modem_state = MODEM_DISCONNECTED;                  // re-start the sequence
     modem_status = MODEM_NO_STATUS;
  }
  break;
  ...
```

Finally, if the **modem_response( )** function detects the 'CONNECT' response from the modem, it puts the MODEM_CONNECTED value in the modem_state variable. In such a case, the next time the **modem_connect( )** function is called, the following code will be executed:

```
    ...
    case MODEM_CONNECTED:
      retry = 0;
      if (ppp_state != PPP_OK) {
        printf("Connected!\n");
        timer_start(ppptimer, 1000);          // start timer for the ppp_status
      }
      ppp_start_stop = PPP_NO_ACTION;
      break;
  }
}
```

The retry variable is initialized for the next time it is needed; the timer is started to have the **ppp_engine( )** function sending messages every second. The ppp_start_stop variable is set to PPP_NO_ACTION, so the **modem_connect( )** routine will not be further called from the **ppp_poll ( )** function.

The **modem_disconnect( )** function is shown in the following code:

```
void modem_disconnect(void) {
  if (ppp_state == PPP_OK) {
    tx_buf[4] = TERM_REQ;
    tx_buf[5]=      id++;;
    tx_buf[6]=      0;
    tx_buf[7]=      4;
    ppp_send(LCP_PROTOCOL, ((tx_buf[6]<<8) + tx_buf[7]));
    ppp_state = PPP_INITIAL_STATE;
    printf("PPP Closed (requested by Device)\n");
    timer_start(ppptimer, 2000);
    modem_status = MODEM_NO_STATUS;
  }
  if (modem_status == MODEM_OK || modem_status == MODEM_NO_CARRIER) {
    modem_state = MODEM_DISCONNECTED;
    modem_status = MODEM_NO_STATUS;
    ppp_start_stop = PPP_NO_ACTION;
    if (PPP_STATUS_NO_ERROR)              // ppp_status <= 0x02 indicates NO ERROR
      ppp_status = PPP_CLOSED;
    printf("Modem Disconnected!\n");
    return;
  }
  if (! timer_expired(ppptimer))
    return;
  modem_command("+++ATH");
  modem_state=MODEM_DISCONNECTING;
  modem_status = MODEM_NO_STATUS;
  timer_start(ppptimer, 5000);
}
```

The first if statement checks if the PPP link has been established, to send a Terminate Request LCP message to inform the other device that the connection will shut down. Once the LCP message is sent, a two-second timer is started before shutting down the physical link. When this timer expires (last if statement), the '+++ATH' command is sent to the modem. Since the modem is connected (in data mode), the '+++' command makes the modem go to the command mode. Then, the 'ATH' command instructs the modem to hang up the line. Once the modem disconnects, the modem_state, modem_status, ppp_start_stop and ppp_status variables are updated (second if statement).

15.2.2.9 Opening and closing the PPP link

So far, we have seen many functions. However, nothing will happen until the ppp_start_stop variable is set to PPP_START. Only then will the PPP machinery start moving to get the link established. In the same way, the ppp_start_stop variable must be set to PPP_STOP to shut down the PPP link.

The above means that the ppp_start_stop variable governs the complete PPP start/stop sequence. However, this variable cannot be accessed from outside the ppp.c module. Instead, **ppp_open( )** and **ppp_close( )** must be used. The **ppp_open( )** code is as follows:

```
void ppp_open(char *number,char *user, char *pass) {

  if (ppp_status == PPP_CLOSED || PPP_STATUS_ERROR) {
    strncpy(isp.number, number, sizeof(isp.number));
    strncpy(isp.user, user, sizeof(isp.user));
    strncpy(isp.pass, pass, sizeof(isp.pass));
    ppp_start_stop = PPP_START;
    ppp_status = PPP_WAIT;
  }
}
```

The function is called with the RAS server phone number, the user, and the password as parameters. These parameters are copied into the isp (Internet Service Provider) structure, for later use. Then, the ppp_start_stop variable is set to PPP_START, and the ppp_status is set to PPP_WAIT.

The **ppp_close( )** code is shown below:

```
void ppp_close(void) {

  if (ppp_status == PPP_OPENED) {
    ppp_start_stop = PPP_STOP;
    ppp_status = PPP_WAIT;
  }
}
```

The code sets the ppp_start_stop variable to PPP_STOP, and the ppp_status to PPP_WAIT.

Lab 4: The PPP link

Lab 4 introduction

In this Lab, we will see how our embedded system gets a dial-up connection. We may use a PC as an RAS server, or an ISP (see section 12.4.1 for details).

Lab 4 target support

This Lab only supports the LPC-P212X boards with serial interface.

Lab 4 options settings

This Lab requires the debug_ppp option to be set. Also, in the **console.c** module, the **ppp_open( )** function parameters (phone number to dial, user and password) must be replaced as required.

Lab 4 instructions

Complete the steps according to Chapter 12 (see section 12.6). Once the Lab is running, follow the Lab 4 exercises.

Lab 4 exercises

- Press the 'h' key in the console to see the help menu. Verify the new items for the PPP connection to appear.
- Press the 'C' key to start the PPP dial-up connection. Verify if the modem responds with an 'OK' to the reset. Check the modem is dialling the correct number. When the modem gets connected, the Connected! message should appear in the console. After this, the received and sent packets will be shown (if the debug_ppp option is set).
- Analyse the sent and received LCP messages structure. Compare the LCP request messages sent with the LCP Response messages (ACK, NAK or REJ) received. Check that the ID field of both messages is the same. Look for the received ACK message, which acknowledges our proposed options. Check the LCP requests from the server, and the options they have. Verify the options we reject, the options we do not acknowledge, and those options that are acceptable for us. Verify that when an LCP ACK is sent and received, the LCP OK message appears, indicating that the LCP negotiation has ended.
- Verify the PAP phase, which consists of the PAP request sent and the PAP response received, indicating if the authentication was successful or if it failed. Analyse the PAP REQ message and verify the user and password sent. The PAP OK message should appear, indicating the PAP authentication has ended.
- Check if the CCP is negotiated. If so, we should reject the CCP request messages, since we do not support this protocol. If the server sends the CCP termination request message to finish the CCP negotiation phase, we should acknowledge the message. In some cases, we could find some servers that terminate the connection if the CCP protocol is rejected.
- Check the IPCP messages. If we receive an IPCP REQ message with the option 2 (IP Compression Protocol), we should reject the message. Only option 3 (IP address) will be accepted. Those IPCP REQ messages with this option will be acknowledged. This option 3 will give us the server IP address. The console should show the server IP address. Verify the IPCP REQ messages that we send. The first IPCP REQ message with an invalid IP address

(0.0.0.0) should be Not Acknowledged by the server, providing the IP address assigned for us. Our next IPCP REQ message with this assigned IP address should be acknowledged by the server. The console should show the 'PPP Ok' message and the assigned IP address. With this, the PPP link is established. Press the 'Z' key to see the PPP status. The 'PPP Link Opened' should be shown.

- Press the 'X' key to disconnect the PPP link. The 'PPP Closed (Requested by Device)' and Modem Disconnected! messages should appear. Check the LCP Termination Request and Termination Acknowledge messages. Try to close the connection from the server (using the 'Disconnect' option from the dial-up connection icon in the system tray). An LCP Termination request should be received, while our acknowledgement should be sent. The 'PPP Closed (Requested by the Server)' and 'Modem Disconnected!' messages should appear.
- Complete the Connect and Disconnect procedures as above, but now using the Ethereal sniffer program to capture the packets. We must select the WAN (PPP/SLIP) interface or the Generic NdisWan adaptor if the first does not appear. Once the packets have been captured, analyse their structure and compare them with the one shown in the console. The sniffer does not show either the PPP header (Address and Control fields) or the FCS. Instead, the packet is shown with the Ethernet header structure. The sniffer may show other unwanted captured packets, which should be filtered to facilitate the packet analysis.
- Try the connection using different users and passwords (they must be declared in the server). Try with bad passwords. Note that the isp structure has only 20 characters for each field (phone number, user and password). If you need longer fields, change them accordingly.
- Test the modem response under different conditions. For example, test the BUSY response trying to dial a phone number of a telephone line that is currently in use (perhaps, calling our own phone number). Disconnect the phone cable from the modem, to get the NO DIALTONE response. Dial a phone number of a telephone line you are sure nobody will answer, in order to test the NO ANSWER response.
- Test the dial-up connection with many ISPs. If the connection is not successful, analyse the sent and received packets to see what are the options the ISP requires, or which options we send that the ISP rejects.

16

Implementing the IP layer (IP and ICMP)

We have arrived at the foundation layer of the TCP/IP stack. This is the first hardware-independent layer, whose implementation works the same way no matter what the underlying network technology. Although simple, this layer will provide the base for the upper layers. We will start looking at the Internet Protocol implementation, and checking how it works in Lab 5. After this, the ICMP will be implemented, in order to provide the stack with a way to test network connectivity and report network-related error messages. Lab 6 will show us the ICMP in action.

16.1 The Internet Protocol implementation

16.1.1 Module structures and #define references

In order to accommodate the IP datagram header, the following structure is used:

```
struct ip_hdr {
  char            verhl;          // IP version and Header Length
  char            tos;            // type of service
  unsigned short  len;            // total length
  unsigned short  id;             // identification
  unsigned short  fragment;       // Flags and Fragment Offset
  char            ttl;            // time to live
  char            protocol;       // protocol
  unsigned short  hdrchksum;      // IP header Checksum
  char            srcipaddr[4];   // source IP address
  char            destipaddr[4];  // destination IP address
};
```

In addition, the following structure defines the pseudo-header used by the TCP and UDP checksum calculation:

```
struct pseudo_hdr {
  char            srcipaddr[4];
  char            destipaddr[4];
  char            zero;
  char            protocol;
  unsigned short  len;
};
```

As we saw in the TCP/IP stack introduction, the IP layer (and upper layers) is hardware independent. This means that whichever network interface the hardware presents, the IP layer works the same way. For this reason, the following definition is created:

```
#ifdef ETHERNET
  #define datalink_send ethernet_send
#endif
#ifdef PPP_LINK
  #define datalink_send ppp_send
#endif
```

In this way, the IP layer will always call the **datalink_send( )** function, which in turn executes the **ethernet_send( )** or the **ppp_send( )** functions, depending on the underlying hardware.

Finally, the following define statements are used:

```
#define IPr  ((struct ip_hdr *)&rx_buf[DATALINK_HDR_SIZE])
#define IPt  ((struct ip_hdr *)&tx_buf[DATALINK_HDR_SIZE])
#define IP_DATA_START      (DATALINK_HDR_SIZE + sizeof(struct ip_hdr))
#define IP_DATA_MAX      (PACKET_BUF_SIZE – DATALINK_HDR_SIZE –
                                             sizeof(struct ip_hdr))

#define SWAP(n)   ((n&0xFF)<<24) + ((n&0xFF00)<<8) +
                     ((n&0xFF0000)>>8) + ((n&0xFF000000)>>24)
```

The first line defines a pointer to the IP header structure pointing to the receive buffer where the IP datagram header begins (after the data link header). The second line defines the same but for the transmit buffer. The IP_DATA_START defines the beginning position of the IP datagram payload in the buffer, while the IP_DATA_MAX defines the maximum amount of data the IP datagram can carry. The **SWAP( )** macro converts between network and processor byte order for 32-bit data.

16.1.2 Processing IP datagrams

As we saw in the previous chapters, when a frame arrives at the network interface (Ethernet or serial link), the packet is processed and redirected to the appropriate layer. If the frame contains an IP message, then the **ip_process( )** function is called.

The following code shows the **ip_process( )** function implementation:

```
void ip_process(void) {

  unsigned short len;
  unsigned short chksum1;
  unsigned short chksum2;
  int i;

#if debug_ip
  ip_display();
#endif //debug_ip
...
```

Note that when the **ip_process( )** is called from the Data Link layer, the frame is already loaded at the receive buffer. Then, the IPr defined pointer points to the start of the IP header in this buffer.

After defining some necessary variables, there is a conditional compiler directive, which calls the **ip_display( )** function if the debug_ip option in the **debug.h** file is on. This function shows the IP datagram header at the console for debugging purposes. Later, we will see this function implementation.

The next step is to validate the IP datagram against some criteria. The first is the IP packet version. Versions other than the supported IPv4 will be discarded. In addition, in order to maintain simplicity for the IP module, neither the IP options nor the fragmented packets are supported, and so they are discarded if they are received.

```
...
if ((IPr->verhl & 0xF0) != 0x40) {
  printf("IP: packet version not supported!\r\n");
        return;
}
if ((IPr->verhl & 0x0F) != 0x05) {
  printf("IP: header options not supported!\r\n");
        return;
}
if ((HTONS(IPr->fragment) & 0x1FFF) != 0x0000) {
  printf("IP: fragmented packets not supported!\r\n");
        return;
}
...
```

The next step is to verify the IP checksum:

```
...
  chksum1 = HTONS(IPr->hdrchksum);
  IPr->hdrchksum = 0;
  chksum2 = chksum16(&IPr->verhl, (IPr->verhl & 0x0F) * 4, 0, 1);
  if (chksum2 != chksum1) {
    printf("IP: Bad Checksum %04x (it should be %04x)\n",chksum1, chksum2);
    return;                                    // returns if cheksum failed!
  }
  IPr->hdrchksum = HTONS(chksum1);             // restore checksum
  if (memcmp(IPr->destipaddr, MyIP, 4))        // is this IP datagram for us?
    return;
...
```

First, we save the checksum field of the received IP datagram (previous conversion from the big-endian – network byte order – to the little-endian – ARM7TDMI-S byte order). As the checksum must be calculated over the IP header, and with the checksum field in zero, we clear this field. After this, we call the **chksum16( )** function (which we will see later on), and the result is compared with the original value. If those values differ, the checksum failed and we return, discarding the incoming IP datagram. If the IP checksum passes, we restore the original checksum value.

The next step is to see if this IP datagram is for us. To do this, we compare the IP destination address with our device address (stored in the MyIP[] variable). Only if the datagram is for us do we continue with the packet processing:

```
...
len = HTONS(IPr->len) - ((IPr->verhl & 0x0F) * 4);          // Length of IP Data
switch (IPr->protocol) {
  case ICMP_PROTOCOL:
    icmp_process(len);
    break;
  case UDP_PROTOCOL:
    udp_process(len);
    break;
  case TCP_PROTOCOL:
    tcp_process(len);
    break;
  default:                          // send Protocol Unreachable ICMP message
    i = ICMP_DATA_START;
    // Copy original IP header + first 8 bytes of IP Data
    memcpy(&tx_buf[i+4], &rx_buf[DATALINK_HDR_SIZE], sizeof(struct ip_hdr)+8);
    ICMPt->type = ICMP_Destination_Unreachable;
    ICMPt->code = ICMP_Protocol_Unreachable;
    tx_buf[i]   = 0;                            // Unused (reserved)
    tx_buf[i+1] = 0;                            // Unused (reserved)
    tx_buf[i+2] = 0;                            // Unused (reserved)
    tx_buf[i+3] = 0;                            // Unused (reserved)
    icmp_send(IPr->srcipaddr, sizeof(struct icmp_hdr)+4+sizeof(struct ip_hdr)+8);
    break;
  }
}
```

First, we calculate the length of data, which is the difference between the IP datagram total length and the IP header length. As this data length is the length of the higher layer protocol data, we will use it as a parameter for the appropriate protocol process function call. The switch structure analyses the protocol of the IP datagram, and calls the appropriate function to process the data. If an unknown protocol is received (the default option of the switch structure), a Protocol Unreachable ICMP message is constructed and sent (using the **icmp_send( )** function that we will see later on).

16.1.3 Sending IP datagrams

In the previous chapters, we saw the Data Link layer for both the Ethernet and the serial interface. Whichever interface the hardware presents, the upper layer protocols should be the same. For this reason, the IP module always uses the **datalink_send( )** function, which is replaced by the compiler by the **ethernet_send( )** or the **ppp_send( )** function, depending on the underlying network interface (see **ip.h** file). Remember that the **hardware.h** file defines the ETHERNET or PPP_LINK option depending on the Ethernet or serial interface the hardware uses for network communications. In this way, the IP module works transparently and no matter what kind of Data Link layer is running, it will run in the same manner.

The IP module must provide a way for upper layers to send IP datagrams over the inter-network. For this, the **ip_send( )** function is created. In order for the upper layers (UDP, TCP or ICMP) to send their data, they must fill the transmit buffer with the data to send and call the **ip_send( )** function specifying the protocol, the destination IP address and the data length. The following code shows how the IP datagram is created:

```
void ip_send(char protocol, char *IPdest, unsigned short len) {

  IPt->verhl=0x45;
  IPt->tos=0x00;
  IPt->len=HTONS(len+sizeof(struct ip_hdr));
  IPt->id = HTONS(++id);
  IPt->fragment=0;
  IPt->ttl=128;
  IPt->protocol=protocol;
  IPt->hdrchksum=0;
  memcpy(IPt->destipaddr, IPdest, 4);
  memcpy(IPt->srcipaddr, MyIP, 4);                //MyIP
  IPt->hdrchksum = HTONS(chksum16(&IPt->verhl, (IPt->verhl & 0x0F) * 4, 0, 1));
  datalink_send(IP_PROTOCOL, len+sizeof(struct ip_hdr));      // Send frame
}
```

The IP header is constructed using default values. The total length is calculated by adding the IP header length to the upper layer data length. In addition, the provided protocol is used. The provided IP address is copied to the IP destination field, while the source IP address is filled with the device

IP address. In order to calculate the checksum, the checksum field must be zero. After the calculation, the checksum field receives the checksum result. Once the IP datagram is completed, the **datalink_send( )** function is called.

16.1.4 Displaying IP datagrams

The **ip_process( )** function has an option to show the IP datagram on the console screen. That is, if the debug_ip option in the **debug.h** file is on, the **ip_display( )** function is called. The following code implements this function:

```
#if debug_ip
void ip_display(void) {
  printf("IP Message:\n");
  printf("IP Version:       %d\n", (IPr->verhl>>4));
  printf("Hdr Len:          %d bytes\n", (IPr->verhl & 0x0F) * 4);
  printf("TOS:              0x%02x\n", IPr->tos);
  printf("Tot Len:          %d bytes\n", HTONS(IPr->len));
  printf("Id:               %d\n", HTONS(IPr->id));
  printf("Fragment:         0x%04x\n", HTONS(IPr->fragment));
  printf("TTL:              %d\n", IPr->ttl);
  printf("Protocol:         %d\n", IPr->protocol);
  printf("Hdr Chksum:       0x%04x\n",  HTONS(IPr->hdrchksum));
  printf("Source Address  %d.%d.%d.%d\n",IPr->srcipaddr[0], IPr->srcipaddr[1],
                                         IPr->srcipaddr[2], IPr->srcipaddr[3]);
  printf("Dest. Address:  %d.%d.%d.%d\n",IPr->destipaddr[0], IPr->destipaddr[1],
      IPr->destipaddr[2],                IPr->destipaddr[3]);
  printf("\n-------------------------------\n");
}
#endif
```

The #if compiler directive allows the complete **ip_display( )** function to be compiled only if the debug_ip option is set. Then, having defined IPr as an IP header structure pointer pointing to the receive buffer where the IP datagram starts, all the IP header fields are printed to the console, using the standard printf( ) function. Once again, the **HTONS( )** macro is used to correct the byte-order differences.

16.1.5 Calculating the IP checksum

The IP checksum is calculated using the **chksum16( )** function. Although this function is provided in the IP module, it is exposed as a public function as it is also used by the ICMP, UDP and TCP modules, when they need to perform a checksum operation. The code on page 371 shows the 16-bit checksum implementation.

The first two parameters receive a buffer pointer and the buffer length (in bytes) over which the function must calculate the 16-bit checksum. The other two parameters will be explained later. For the time being, simply consider the function called with chksum=0 and complement=1.

```
int chksum16(void *buf1, short len, int chksum, char complement) {
  unsigned short * buf = buf1;
  int chksum16;

  while(len > 0) {
    if (len == 1)
      chksum16 = ((*buf)&0x00FF);
    else
      chksum16 = (*buf);
    chksum = chksum + HTONS(chksum16);
    *buf++;
    len -=2;
  }
  if (complement)
    return (~(chksum + ((chksum & 0xFFFF0000) >> 16))&0xFFFF);
  return chksum;
}
```

The 16-bit checksum of a given data is defined as 'the 16-bit one's complement of the one's complement sum of all 16-bit words in the data'. For this reason, we need to sum every 16-bit word of the buffer's data. The while(len>0) structure does just this. That is, it takes the length of the buffer and it decrements this length by 2, to process the data in 16-bit words. These words are accumulated into the chksum variable. The **HTONS( )** macro takes care of the byte-order difference between the network and the processor. Where the buffer length is odd, the last byte should be padded with 0x00. For this reason, if (len = = 1) is true (this only happens if the buffer's length is odd), the last byte is appended to 0x00 to form a 16-bit word (consider the byte-order difference).

Having completed this sum, we need to calculate the one's complement of the sum, adding the sum of the carry bits to the result. This is accomplished by the following line:

```
chksum + ((chksum & 0xFFFF0000) >> 16)
```

Now, the routine should return the 16-bit one's complement of the previous result. The negate operator (~) provides the ones complement, while the &0xFFFF expression ensures only 16-bit were considered.

This function works fine with IP and ICMP protocols, where the checksum must be calculated over a contiguous buffer. But for UDP and TCP protocols, where the checksum is calculated using two non-contiguous buffers (the pseudo-header and the message itself), the function must be able to be called with a previously accumulated checksum value and the complement flag, which decides whether the final accumulated checksum or the 16-bit ones complement of this checksum is returned.

Then, for UDP and TCP protocols, the function must be first called with the chksum = 0 and complement = 0, when the pseudo-header checksum is calculated; and with chksum containing the previously accumulated checksum result, and with complement = 1 the second time the function is called, when the message itself is using it. In this way, the checksum process is accomplished in two parts, where the chksum and complement parameters allow the use of the function called twice with different buffers as if they were called only one time with a contiguous buffer.

Lab 5: Receiving IP datagrams

Lab 5 introduction

In this Lab, we will see the IP layer receiving datagrams from the underlying Data Link layer.

Lab 5 target support

This Lab supports both types of boards. Select the appropriate target board from the 'Configuration drop-down menu' in the Workspace window.

Lab 5 options setting

This Lab requires the debug_ip option to be set.

Lab 5 instructions

Complete the steps according to Chapter 12 (see section 12.6). Once the Lab is running, follow the Lab 5 exercises. If you use the LPC-P212X board, you must make the dial-up connection in order to send or receive messages.

Lab 5 exercises

- From the PC system command, execute a 'ping 192.168.0.30' command (or 'ping 192.168.0.51' for the LPC-P212X board). See Appendix E, section E.5, for details. Check the console to see if the board is receiving IP datagrams.
- Analyse the received datagrams. Compare their structure with the IP header structure. See the Source address field to determine the device that sent the IP datagram. Check the ID field, which should be different for each datagram. Verify the Protocol field and check it corresponds to the ICMP protocol.
- From the PC, open the browser and type http://192.168.0.30 (or http://192.168.0.51 for the LPC-P212X board). The board should start receiving IP datagrams. Check the console and verify the Protocol field corresponds to the TCP protocol.

16.2 The ICMP implementation

16.2.1 Module structures and #define references

The **icmp.h** header file declares a structure for the ICMP message header:

```
struct icmp_hdr {
  char             type;               // type of icmp message
  char             code;               // "subtype" of icmp message
  unsigned short icmpchksum;          // icmp message checksum
};
```

Then, we may define pointers to that structure as follows:

```
#define ICMPr  ((struct icmp_hdr *)&rx_buf[sizeof(struct ip_hdr) +
                                              DATALINK_HDR_SIZE])
#define ICMPt  ((struct icmp_hdr *)&tx_buf[sizeof(struct ip_hdr) +
                                              DATALINK_HDR_SIZE])
```

In addition, the following constants are defined:

```
#define ICMP_DATA_START     (DATALINK_HDR_SIZE +
                           sizeof(struct ip_hdr) + sizeof(struct icmp_hdr))

#define ICMP_DATA_MAX       (PACKET_BUF_SIZE –
                           DATALINK_HDR_SIZE – sizeof(struct ip_hdr) –
                           sizeof(struct icmp_hdr))
```

Finally, the following constants will be defined:

```
#define ICMP_Echo                          8
#define ICMP_Echo_Reply                    0
#define ICMP_Destination_Unreachable       3          // Type = 3
#define ICMP_Protocol_Unreachable          2          // Code = 2
#define ICMP_Port_Unreachable              3          // Code = 3
```

16.2.2 Processing ICMP messages

As we have already seen, each time an IP datagram is received, and after some validations, the IP module processes the datagram according to the protocol it carries. In the case of an ICMP message, the **icmp_process( )** routine is called.

The **icmp_process( )** function is called with the length of the IP data (or, what is the same, the length of the ICMP message) as an input parameter. As the ICMP header message structure was defined as a 4-byte length (considered as a common header for most of the ICMP message types), we will consider the ICMP data length as the passed length minus four bytes. The following code shows the **icmp_process( )** function implementation.

```
void icmp_process(unsigned short len) {
  unsigned short chksum1;
  unsigned short chksum2;
  short i;

#if debug_icmp
  icmp_display(len-4);
#endif //debug_icmp

  chksum1 = HTONS(ICMPr->icmpchksum);
  ICMPr->icmpchksum = 0;
  chksum2 = chksum16(&ICMPr->type, len, 0, 1);
  if (chksum2 != chksum1) {
    printf("ICMP: Bad Checksum %04x (it should be %04x)\n",chksum1, chksum2);
    return;
  }
  ICMPr->icmpchksum = HTONS(chksum1);                    // restore checksum
  ...
```

The first step is to display the ICMP message at the console, if the debug_icmp option is on, in the **debug.h** file. If so, the **icmp_display( )** function will do this (we describe this function later on).

The second step is to validate the checksum field of the ICMP message. For this reason, the field value is saved, and then cleared. After this, the checksum is calculated using the chksum16( ) function provided by the IP module. If the newly calculated and the previously saved values differ, a 'Bad Checksum' message is displayed at the console, and the ICMP message is discarded. If those values are equal, the checksum field is restored and the function continues processing the ICMP message.

The code at the top of page 375 shows how the ICMP message is processed according to its type.

First, we use a variable as an index pointing to the start of the ICMP message data. Then, a switch structure processes the ICMP message according to its type; if the message is an ICMP Echo Request (ping request), an Echo Reply is built and sent using the **icmp_send( )** function (which we will see later on). If the received ICMP message is an Echo Reply, a message is shown at the console.

If an ICMP Destination Unreachable message is received, it is further processed according to its code field (switch(ICMPr->code) statement), and showing the error at the console. Finally, if any other ICMP message is received, it is simply shown at the console as an unknown type. Of course, we could include other types of ICMP messages, but the ones included are the most representative of those encountered.

```
...
i = ICMP_DATA_START;
switch(ICMPr->type) {
 case ICMP_Echo:                                        // Echo Request (8)
  printf("ICMP: Ping Request received from %d.%d.%d.%d \r\n",
                                IPr->srcipaddr[0],IPr->srcipaddr[1],
                                IPr->srcipaddr[2],IPr->srcipaddr[3]);

  ICMPt->type = ICMP_Echo_Reply;         // Echo Reply (0)
  ICMPt->code = 0;
  tx_buf[i] = rx_buf[i];                                 // id
  tx_buf[i+1] = rx_buf[i+1];
  tx_buf[i+2] = rx_buf[i+2];                             // seq
  tx_buf[i+3] = rx_buf[i+3];
  memcpy(&tx_buf[i+4], &rx_buf[i+4], len-8);      // copy ping data
  icmp_send(IPr->srcipaddr, len);
  break;
 case ICMP_Echo_Reply:
  printf("ICMP: Ping Reply received from %d.%d.%d.%d \r\n",
                                IPr->srcipaddr[0],IPr->srcipaddr[1],
                                IPr->srcipaddr[2],IPr->srcipaddr[3]);
  break;
 ...
```

```
 ...
 case ICMP_Destination_Unreachable:
  switch(ICMPr->code) {
   case ICMP_Protocol_Unreachable:
     printf("ICMP Dest.Unreachable received: Protocol %d
                         Unreachable\n",rx_buf[i+13]);
     break;
   case ICMP_Port_Unreachable:
     printf("ICMP Dest.Unreachable received: Port %d
                         Unreachable\n",(rx_buf[i+26]<<8)+rx_buf[i+27]);
     break;
   default:
     printf("ICMP Dest.Unreachable received: Unknown Code
                         %d\n",ICMPr->code);
      break;
  }
  break;
 default:
  printf("ICMP received: unknown type %d\n",ICMPr->type);
  break;
 }
}
```

16.2.3 Sending ICMP messages

Many functions need to send ICMP messages. For example, when the IP module processes an incoming datagram which has a protocol other than ICMP, UDP or TCP, an ICMP message should be sent informing the 'Protocol Unreachable' error (see **ip_process( )** function in the ip.c module). In addition, protocols such as UDP and TCP may receive messages with an unknown port, so they must send an ICMP message informing the 'Port Unreachable' error. All these modules use the **icmp_send( )** function for this purpose.

```
void icmp_send(char *IPdest, unsigned short len) {

  ICMPt->icmpchksum = 0;
  ICMPt->icmpchksum = HTONS(chksum16(&ICMPt->type, len, 0, 1));
  ip_send(ICMP_PROTOCOL, IPdest, len);
}
```

This function only calculates the 16-bit checksum (provided by the IP module), and uses the **ip_send( )** function (from the IP module) to send the ICMP message over the inter-network. Then, the caller function must compose the ICMP message before calling the **icmp_send( )** function.

16.2.4 Sending PING (ICMP Echo Request)

In order to provide the application a way to test the network connectivity, the **icmp_ping( )** function was created. The following code shows how this function is implemented:

```
void icmp_ping(char *IPdest) {
  short i;
  static char id;

  i = IP_DATA_START;
  ICMPt->type=8;                    //Echo Request
  ICMPt->code=0;
  tx_buf[i+4] = 0x03;               // identifier (any number...)
  tx_buf[i+5] = 0x00;
  tx_buf[i+6] = 0x00;
  tx_buf[i+7] = ++id;               // sequence number
  i = ICMP_DATA_START+4;
  strcpy(&tx_buf[i],"Embedded Internet PING");
  icmp_send(IPdest, 30);
}
```

This function is called with the ping destination IP address as a parameter. As the ICMP message is encapsulated by an IP datagram, the IP_DATA_START determines the beginning of the ICMP header message. The ICMP Type and

Code fields are filled with the appropriate values, while the checksum field will be calculated by the **icmp_send( )** function. After the checksum field, the generic ICMP message data starts, as denoted by ICMP_DATA_START. In the particular case of the ping message, and both Identifier and Sequence fields must be filled. Then, some data must be sent to test the Echo Reply. Once the ICMP message is composed, the **icmp_send( )** function is called with the IP destination address and the message length as parameters.

16.2.5 Displaying the ICMP messages

As we saw in the **icmp_process( )** function, if the debug_icmp option in the **debug.h** file is enabled, the **icmp_display( )** function is called. The following code shows this implementation.

```
#if debug_icmp
void icmp_display(unsigned short data_len) {

  unsigned short i = ICMP_DATA_START;

  printf("ICMP Header:\n");
  printf("Type:       %d\n", ICMPr->type);
  printf("Code:       %d\n", ICMPr->code);
  printf("Checksum:   %04x\n", HTONS(ICMPr->icmpchksum));
  printf("Id:         %d\n", (rx_buf[i+1]<<8)+rx_buf[i]);
  printf("Sequence:   %d\n", (rx_buf[i+3]<<8)+rx_buf[i+2]);
  printf("Data:\n");
  for (i=0; i<(data_len-4); i++) {
    printf("%c", rx_buf[ICMP_DATA_START+4+i]);
  }
  printf("\n-----------------------------------\n");
}
#endif //debug_icmp
```

The above function will only be compiled if the debug_icmp option is on. This function is called with the ICMP data length as a parameter. It is worth noting that although this function can display any type of ICMP message, it is specifically designed for ping messages, as it formats the Identification and Sequence fields that belong to ping messages. Once these first four bytes of data are shown; the rest are presented as the data used to test the connectivity.

Lab 6: The ICMP in action

Lab 6 introduction

In this Lab, we will see the IP layer carrying ICMP messages. We will start receiving and sending pings (ICMP requests and replies) to test connectivity. Then, we will send ICMP messages that inform us about network errors.

Lab 6 target support

This Lab supports both types of board. Select the appropriate target board from the 'Configuration drop-down menu' in the Workspace window.

Lab 6 options setting

This Lab requires the debug_icmp option to be set.

Lab 6 instructions

Complete the steps according to Chapter 12 (see section 12.6). Once the Lab is running, follow the Lab 6 exercises. If you use the LPC-P212X board, you must make the dial-up connection in order to send or receive messages. If you use Windows XP with the Windows Firewall activated, you must check the 'Allow incoming echo request' option in the Windows Firewall window, Advanced tab, ICMP settings. Otherwise, the firewall will block these messages.

Lab 6 exercises

- From the PC system command, execute a 'ping 192.168.0.30' command (or 'ping 192.168.0.51' for the LPC-P212X board). See Appendix E, section E.5, for details. Check the console to see if the board is receiving ICMP messages.
- Analyse the received ICMP messages. Compare their structure with the ICMP message structure. Verify the Type to see if it is an Echo (Type 8) or Echo Reply (Type 0). Check if the Sequence field changes from each ICMP ping message. Verify in the PC system command if there are responses from the board.
- Press 'h' to check the help to see if new options for ping messages appear. Press the 'P' key to send a ping to the PC and verify if we get a response from the PC. Press the 'I' key to send a ping to pcIP2 address (see **stackcfg.h** file) in the outside world (the board will get responses only if it has a connection with the Internet). Use Ethereal to capture the messages and see the message structure.
- From the PC, open the browser and type http://192.168.0.30 (or http://192.168.0.51 for the LPC-P212X board). Use Ethereal to check if the board sends a 'Destination Unreachable' (Type 3) with 'Protocol Unreachable' (Code 2) ICMP message to the PC. This message is generated because the **ip_process( )** function does not encounter the **tcp_process( )** routine for the TCP_PROTOCOL, since it was disabled in this Lab.

17

Implementing the Transport layer (UDP and TCP)

From the application perspective, this is the most important layer of the stack. Most applications will use either this layer directly or at higher protocols, which ultimately use this layer for data transfers. In this chapter, we start describing the UDP implementation. Lab 7 will show us the UDP in action. After this, the TCP implementation will be examined in detail. Finally, Lab 8 will give us the opportunity to have a 'hands-on' training with the TCP.

17.1 The UDP implementation

17.1.1 Module structures, variables and #define references

In the **udp.h** header file, we have defined the following constants;

```
#define UDP_MAX_SOCKETS           3
#define UDP_INVALID_SOCKET       -1
#define UDP_PORT_ALREADY_USED    -2
#define UDP_SOCKET_ERROR         -3

#define UDP_CHKSUM_NONE           0
#define UDP_CHKSUM_SEND           1

#define UDP_EVENT_DATA            1
```

In the **udp.c** module overleaf, we start declaring a structure for the UDP datagram header.

Then, we define two pointers to that structure: one for the receive buffer, and the other for the transmit buffer.

```
#pragma pack(2)
struct udp_hdr {
  unsigned short srcport;                 // Source Port
  unsigned short destport;                // Destination Port
  unsigned short totlen;                  // total length ( header + data)
  unsigned short udpchksum;               // UDP Checksum
};
#pragma pack()
#define UDPr ((struct udp_hdr *)&rx_buf[sizeof(struct ip_hdr) +
                                                DATALINK_HDR_SIZE])

#define UDPt ((struct udp_hdr *)&tx_buf[sizeof(struct ip_hdr) +
                                                DATALINK_HDR_SIZE])
```

Since our Transport layer implementation is based on the socket concept, we need to create a table (UDP Control Block, UCB), where each entry will have the following structure:

```
#pragma pack(4)
struct ucb {
  char              state;
  unsigned short    local_port;
  char              options;
  void              (*event_handler)(int,char,char*,unsigned short,
                                     unsigned short,unsigned short);
};
#pragma pack()
```

In this way, each entry will have socket properties like the local port, options (include or do not include the checksum in sent datagrams) and the call-back routine address. This last is the address of the routine that will be called by the UDP module to notify when some events occurred (such as: data arrived). The state field is used to mark the entry as valid (UDP_SOCKET_USED) or not valid (UDP_SOCKET_FREE). This is necessary because we are using fixed length tables to avoid the complexity of the dynamic memory allocation. When the entry is not valid, it is equivalent to an empty entry.

As we will later see, when an application wants to use UDP communications, a UDP socket must be created. For this, the application uses the **udp_open_socket**( ) function, specifying the port, options and the address of the call-back function in order to be notified about some event. All these parameters are saved in a table entry.

Finally, the **udp.c** module defines the following;

```
#define UDP_SOCKET_FREE  0
#define UDP_SOCKET_USED  1

struct ucb udp_socket[UDP_MAX_SOCKETS];
static unsigned short last_port = 1024;
```

While the first two lines define the constant values for the state field of the table, the last two statements declare the **udp_socket** table and a variable necessary to keep track of assigned port values.

The **stack.h** header file defines the UDP_DATA_START and UDP_DATA_MAX values as follows:

```
#define UDP_DATA_START    (DATALINK_HDR_SIZE + 20 + 8)
#define UDP_DATA_MAX      (PACKET_BUF_SIZE - DATALINK_HDR_SIZE - 20 - 8)
```

That is, the UDP data starts after the Data Link header (14 bytes for Ethernet, 4 bytes for PPP), the IP header (20 bytes) and the UDP header (8 bytes). The maximum UDP data length will be equal to the maximum Packet Buffer size minus all these headers.

17.1.2 Initializing the UDP module

The first step is to initialize the UDP socket table to an initial state:

```
void udp_init(void) {
  int iSocket;
  struct ucb* pSocket;

  for(iSocket=0; iSocket<UDP_MAX_SOCKETS; iSocket++) {
    pSocket = &udp_socket[iSocket];
    pSocket->state = UDP_SOCKET_FREE;
    pSocket->local_port = 0;
    pSocket->options = 0;
    pSocket->event_handler = 0;
  }
  return;
}
```

The above routine starts defining an integer iSocket to be used as a table index, and pSocket as a pointer to the UCB structure. Then, all table entries are initialized as free.

17.1.3 Processing UDP datagrams

As we already saw, when the IP layer receives a UDP message, the **udp_process( )** function is called, with the length of the message (len) as a parameter.

The routine starts defining some necessary variables. After this, the **udp_display( )** function is called if the debug_udp option is set in the **debug.h** file. The len parameter is not necessary in this case, as the UDP header has a field indicating this value. For this, as it is unused, we use the dummy expression len = len, just to avoid the compiler warning.

```
void udp_process(unsigned short len) {
  struct pseudo_hdr p_hdr;
  unsigned short chksum1;
  int chksum2;
  int iSocket, j;
  struct ucb* pSocket;

#if debug_udp
  udp_display();
#endif

  len = len;                    // avoid compiler warning!
  ...
```

The next step is to verify if the UDP checksum is used (checksum field different from zero). If so, the checksum of the received datagram must be calculated and compared with the message's checksum field. If they differ, the UDP message is discarded.

```
...
if (UDPr->udpchksum != 0) {
  chksum1 = HTONS(UDPr->udpchksum);
  memcpy(&p_hdr.srcipaddr[0], &IPr->srcipaddr[0], 4);
  memcpy(&p_hdr.destipaddr[0], &IPr->destipaddr[0], 4);
  p_hdr.zero = 0;
  p_hdr.protocol = UDP_PROTOCOL;
  p_hdr.len = UDPr->totlen;
  chksum2 = chksum16(&p_hdr.srcipaddr[0], sizeof(p_hdr), 0, 0);
  UDPr->udpchksum = 0;
  chksum2 = chksum16(&UDPr->srcport,HTONS(UDPr->totlen),
                                              chksum2, 1);
  if (chksum2 == 0)
    chksum2 = 0xFFFF;
  if (chksum2 != chksum1) {
    printf("UDP: Bad Checksum %04x (it should be %04x)\n",chksum1,
                                                        chksum2);
    return;                                // returns if checksum failed!
  }
  UDPr->udpchksum = HTONS(chksum1);        // restore checksum
}
...
```

In order to calculate the message checksum, we start saving the checksum value in the chksum1 variable. This is necessary because the checksum field must be in zero when the checksum is calculated. Then, the pseudo-header structure must be filled and the **chksum16( )** function provided by the **ip.c** module must be called. The returning value (chksum2 variable) is used in the second call of the function to accumulate the result. Now, the checksum is calculated over the UDP header message, and the function returns with the one's complement of the result. If the checksum is OK, the saved value is restored, and the UDP process continues.

The next step is to search in the table for the recipient application (which port coincides with the UDP message destination port). If it is found, the application's call-back function is called, with the following parameters; the socket number, the UDP_EVENT_DATA event indicating that data has arrived, the IP and port of the source, and the start and length of the data received.

```
...
// look up the socket for the recipient port
// and call the application event_handler
for(iSocket=0; iSocket<UDP_MAX_SOCKETS; iSocket++) {
  pSocket = &udp_socket[iSocket];
  if (pSocket->local_port == HTONS(UDPr->destport) &&
                                    pSocket->state != UDP_SOCKET_FREE) {

    pSocket->event_handler(iSocket+1, UDP_EVENT_DATA, IPr->srcipaddr,
                                    HTONS(UDPr->srcport), UDP_DATA_START,
                                    HTONS(UDPr->totlen)-sizeof(struct udp_hdr));
    return;
  }
}
...
```

If the above code does not find an entry with the destination port, then the port is unreachable and an ICMP message should be sent:

```
...
// If we are here, the Port is unreachable...Send an ICMP informing that !
printf("Destination Port %d not found!\n", HTONS(UDPr->destport));
j = ICMP_DATA_START;
// Copy original IP header + first 8 bytes of IP Data
memcpy(&tx_buf[j+4], &rx_buf[DATALINK_HDR_SIZE], sizeof(struct ip_hdr)+8)
ICMPt->type = ICMP_Destination_Unreachable;
ICMPt->code = ICMP_Port_Unreachable;
tx_buf[j]   = 0;                      // Unused (reserved)
tx_buf[j+1] = 0;                      // Unused (reserved)
tx_buf[j+2] = 0;                      // Unused (reserved)
tx_buf[j+3] = 0;                      // Unused (reserved)
icmp_send(IPr->srcipaddr, sizeof(struct icmp_hdr)+4+sizeof(struct ip_hdr)+8);
}
```

17.1.4 Displaying UDP messages

The following routine displays the received UDP message. Note that it is only compiled if the debug_udp option is set in the **debug.h** file.

```
#if debug_udp
void udp_display(void) {
  int i;

  printf("UDP Message:\n");
  printf("Source Port:            %d\n", HTONS(UDPr->srcport));
  printf("Destination Port:       %d\n", HTONS(UDPr->destport));
  printf("Total Length:           %d bytes\n", HTONS(UDPr->totlen));
  printf("Checksum:               %04x\n", HTONS(UDPr->udpchksum));
  printf("Data:\n");
  for (i=0; i<(HTONS(UDPr->totlen)-8); i++) {
    printf("%c", rx_buf[UDP_DATA_START+i]);
  }
  printf("\n----------------------------------------\n");
}
#endif
```

The above routine is called for every UDP message arrived, whether the intended port exists or not.

17.1.5 Opening UDP sockets

Whenever an application needs to use the UDP transport services, it must open a UDP socket. For this, the udp_open_socket( ) function must be called. The application may choose the desired port, or it can pass a null value as a port, in which case the function will assign a port. The application has the option to use the checksum for sent messages, passing the appropriate parameter (options).

In order for the application to receive events notification from the UDP module, it must pass the address of a call-back routine. In this way, each time the UDP module receives data for this application, it will call that call-back routine to notify about the event.

```
int udp_open_socket(unsigned short port, char options,
                    void (*event_handler)(int,char,char*,
                    unsigned short,unsigned short, unsigned short)) {
  int i;
  struct ucb* pSocket;

  if (port == 0) {
    while(check_free_port(last_port++) != 1);
    if (last_port >= 49999)
      last_port = 1024;
    port = last_port++;
  }else {
    if (check_free_port(port) != 1)
      return UDP_PORT_ALREADY_USED;
  }
  ...
```

The first step of the function is to check the port parameter. If it is null, the function looks for the next available port to assign using the **check_free_port( )** function. If the application asks for a given port, the routine checks if this port is already in use; in such cases it returns with an error.

```
...
for(i=0; i<UDP_MAX_SOCKETS; i++) {
  pSocket = &udp_socket[i];
  if(pSocket->state != UDP_SOCKET_FREE)
    continue;
  pSocket->state = UDP_SOCKET_USED;
  pSocket->local_port = port;
  pSocket->options = options;
  pSocket->event_handler = (unsigned int ) event_handler;
  return (i+1);
}
return UDP_INVALID_SOCKET;
}
```

The next step is to search for a free entry at the socket's table. If no free entry is found, the UDP_INVALID_SOCKET value is returned. When a free entry is found, the entry is filled with the parameters passed to the **udp_open_socket( )** function. Then, a socket value (greater than zero) is returned. From this moment, each time the **udp_process( )** routine receives a UDP message for this port, the application event handler (the call-back routine) will be called to process the message.

17.1.6 Closing UDP sockets

Once the application no longer needs the UDP socket, it may close the sockets, calling the **udp_close_socket( )** function:

```
void udp_close_socket(int socket) {
  int iSocket = socket-1;

  if (udp_validate_socket(socket) == UDP_INVALID_SOCKET)
    return;
  udp_socket[iSocket].state = UDP_SOCKET_FREE;
  udp_socket[iSocket].local_port = 0;
  udp_socket[iSocket].options = 0;
  udp_socket[iSocket].event_handler = 0;
}
```

The application calls the function passing the socket as a parameter. Then, after validating the socket value, the socket table entry is marked as free. The rest of the entry's fields are initialized.

17.1.7 Support routines

The following routines are used for different purposes. The **udp_validate_socket( )** function checks for the validity of the passed socket. If it is invalid, it returns to the UDP_INVALID_SOCKET value; otherwise, it returns zero.

```
int udp_validate_socket(int socket) {

  if ((socket < 1) || (socket > UDP_MAX_SOCKETS)) {
    printf("UDP: Invalid Socket Error!\r\n");
    return UDP_INVALID_SOCKET;
  }
  return 0;
}
```

The **check_free_port( )** function is used to check if the passed port is free:

```
static int check_free_port(unsigned short port) {
  int iSocket;

  for(iSocket=0; iSocket<UDP_MAX_SOCKETS; iSocket++) {
    if (udp_socket[iSocket].local_port == port)
      return 0;
  }
  return 1;
}
```

The above code searches for the passed port in the table. If it is found, it means that the port is not free, and a zero is returned. If it is not found, the port is free and one value is returned.

Finally, the **udp_get_port( )** function is used to know the port number the **udp_open_socket( )** routine has assigned to the application, when this last passed a null value in the port parameter.

```
int udp_get_port(int socket) {
  int iSocket = socket-1;

  if (udp_validate_socket(socket) == UDP_INVALID_SOCKET)
    return UDP_SOCKET_ERROR;
  return udp_socket[iSocket].local_port;
}
```

Note that when an application calls the **udp_open_socket( )** function with a null value in the port parameter, the routine only gives back the socket created. So if the application needs to know the port the routine has assigned to it, it can call the **udp_get_port( )** function.

17.1.8 Sending UDP datagrams

When the application layer needs to send data using the UDP transport services, it fills the transmit buffer with its data and it calls the **udp_send( )** function, passing the socket, the destination IP address and port value, and the data length as parameters:

```
void udp_send(int socket, char *IPdest, unsigned short destport,
                                              unsigned short len) {

  struct pseudo_hdr p_hdr;
  int chksum2;
  int iSocket = socket-1;

  if (udp_validate_socket(socket) == UDP_INVALID_SOCKET)
    return;
  if (udp_socket[iSocket].state == UDP_SOCKET_FREE) {
    printf("UDP Send: the socket is free: %d\n", iSocket+1);
           return;
  }
  UDPt->srcport = HTONS(udp_socket[iSocket].local_port);
  UDPt->destport = HTONS(destport);
  UDPt->totlen = HTONS(len + 8);
  ...
```

This routine first checks for the socket validity. In addition, the socket must exist in the socket table. After these validations, the UDP header fields are filled.

If the application has opened the UDP socket with the UDP_CHKSUM_SEND option, the UDP checksum must be calculated. If not, the checksum field is put in as zero. The checksum calculation procedure is the same as that for the **udp_process( )** routine.

```
...
if (udp_socket[iSocket].options == UDP_CHKSUM_SEND) {
  memcpy(&p_hdr.srcipaddr[0], &MyIP[0], 4);
  memcpy(&p_hdr.destipaddr[0], IPdest, 4);
  p_hdr.zero = 0;
  p_hdr.protocol = UDP_PROTOCOL;
  p_hdr.len = UDPt->totlen;
  chksum2 = chksum16(&p_hdr.srcipaddr[0], sizeof(p_hdr), 0, 0);
  UDPt->udpchksum = 0;
  chksum2 = chksum16(&UDPt->srcport,HTONS(UDPt->totlen), chksum2, 1);
  if (chksum2 == 0)
    chksum2 = 0xFFFF;
  UDPt->udpchksum = HTONS(chksum2);
}else {
  UDPt->udpchksum = 0;
}
ip_send(UDP_PROTOCOL, IPdest, len+8);
}
```

After filling the UDP header, the UDP message is passed to the IP layer using the **ip_send( )** routine which sends the datagram using the underlying data link services.

Lab 7: Working with UDP messages

Lab 7 introduction

In this Lab, we will transfer information using the UDP Transport layer.

Lab 7 target support

This Lab supports both types of boards. Select the appropriate target board from the 'Configuration drop-down menu' in the Workspace window.

Lab 7 options setting

This Lab requires the debug_udp option to be set.

Lab 7 utilities used

In this Lab we will use the UDP Console Panel to send and receive UDP messages. See the 'Getting Started' guide for help on this utility.

Lab 7 instructions

Complete the steps according to Chapter 12 (see section 12.6). Once the Lab is running, follow the Lab 7 exercises. If you use the LPC-P212X board, you must make the dial-up connection before sending or receiving UDP messages. In Windows XP, check that the Windows Firewall is configured to allow outgoing destination unreachable ICMP packets, or deactivate the Firewall for this Lab.

Lab 7 exercises

- Start the UDP Console Panel utility with 192.168.0.30 remote IP address (or 192.168.0.51 for the LCP-P212X boards), remote port 1066, and 1070 as the local port. Press 'Start UDP', enter some data and send it to the remote device. Verify the message has arrived at the board. Check the IP address and the port number of the source of the message. The UDP Console Utility should get an error, because the UDP port 1066 does not exist. That is, the board should respond with a Protocol Unreachable ICMP error. Note that in the Ethernet boards, this may not happen the first time, because the ICMP message may not be sent if the destination MAC address is not found in the ARP table. Instead, the 'ARP Entry not found!' message should appear.
- Analyse the received UDP messages. Compare their structure with the UDP message structure. Check that the Source and Destination ports coincide with those specified in the UDP Console Panel. Capture the messages with Ethereal.
- Press the 'h' key to see the available help. Press 'O' to open a UDP socket at port 1066. Now, send a message from the UDP Console Panel. Check that the message arrives at the board, and no ICMP message is sent to the UDP Console Panel. This is because now the UDP socket at port 1066 is opened. A 'Data Available' message should appear at the board console.

- Press the 'S' key to send a UDP message to the PC at port 1080. Check that an ICMP Destination Unreachable (specifically port 1080 unreachable) should be received. This is just because we started the UDP Console Panel utility at port 1070. Restart this program, but now at local port 1080, and press the 'S' key to send the UDP message again. Now, the message should arrive at the PC, showing the '**Hello World!**' at the UDP Console Panel.
- Press 'O' again and check the '**Error opening a socket: Port 1066 already used**' message is displayed.

17.2 The TCP implementation

17.2.1 Module structures, variables and #define references

The **stack.h** header file defines the following;

```
#define TCP_DATA_START     (DATALINK_HDR_SIZE + 20 + 20)
#define TCP_DATA_MAX       (PACKET_BUF_SIZE – DATALINK_HDR_SIZE - 20 - 20)
```

The above defines the buffer position at which the TCP segment starts and the maximum TCP segment data length. Note that the IP header size (20 bytes) and the TCP header size (20 bytes) are taken into account in those definitions.

The **tcp.h** file defines the following constants:

```
#define TCP_MAX_SOCKETS              10
#define TCP_INVALID_SOCKET           -1
#define TCP_PORT_ALREADY_USED        -2
#define TCP_SOCKET_ERROR             -3

#define TCP_EVENT_CONN_REQ            0
#define TCP_EVENT_ESTABLISHED         1
#define TCP_EVENT_DATA                2
#define TCP_EVENT_SEND_COMPLETED      3
#define TCP_EVENT_CONN_CLOSED         4
#define TCP_EVENT_CLOSE_REQ           5
#define TCP_EVENT_RESET               6
#define TCP_EVENT_rTOUT               7
#define TCP_EVENT_cTOUT               8
```

While the first group defines the maximum TCP sockets supported and constant values that some functions return, the second group defines the events used by the TCP module to notify the applications.

The **tcp.c** module declares the following structure for the TCP segment header:

```
#pragma pack(2)
struct tcp_hdr {
  unsigned short   srcport;        // Source Port
  unsigned short   destport;       // Destination Port
  unsigned int     seq;            // Sequence Number
  unsigned int     ack;            // Acknowledgement Number
  char             data_offset;    // Data Offset
  char             flags;          // Flags (Control bits)
  unsigned short   window;         // Window Size
  unsigned short   tcpchksum;      // TCP Checksum
  unsigned short   urgent_ptr;     // Urgent Pointer
};
#pragma pack()
```

Then, the module defines pointers to that structure, pointing to the start of the TCP segment at both the receive and transmit buffers:

```
#define TCPr    ((struct tcp_hdr *)&rx_buf[sizeof(struct ip_hdr) + DATALINK_HDR_SIZE])
#define TCPt    ((struct tcp_hdr *)&tx_buf[sizeof(struct ip_hdr) + DATALINK_HDR_SIZE])
```

Since the TCP implementation is based on the socket concept, a transmission control block (tcb) is used to keep track of each TCP connection and the socket state. This tcb consists of a table where each entry corresponds to a socket. The state, local port, remote IP and port, and other parameters related to the connection are saved in the table entry.

The following is the structure used to declare the tcb table:

```
struct tcb {
  char              state;
  unsigned short    local_port;
  char              remote_ip[4];
  unsigned short    remote_port;
  unsigned short    remote_mss;
  char              flags;
  unsigned int      snduna;
  unsigned int      sndnxt;
  unsigned short    sndwnd;
  unsigned int      rcvnxt;
  unsigned short    rcvwnd;
  unsigned short    rTimer;
  unsigned short    rTimeout;
  char              retries;
  unsigned short    cTimer;
  void              (*event_handler)(int,char,char*,unsigned short,
                                      unsigned short,unsigned short);
  unsigned short    more_data;
  unsigned short    position;
  int               (*fill_buffer) (int,unsigned short *,unsigned short *);
};
```

Each of the above fields and their purposes are discussed in the description of the module implementation.

The state field of the above structure may have the following values, representing the possible states the socket may take as described in the TCP state diagrams:

```
#define TCP_SOCKET_FREE                0
#define TCP_SOCKET_CLOSED              1
#define TCP_SOCKET_LISTEN              2
#define TCP_SOCKET_SYN_SENT            3
#define TCP_SOCKET_SYN_RECEIVED        4
#define TCP_SOCKET_ESTABLISHED         5
#define TCP_SOCKET_FIN_WAIT_1          6
#define TCP_SOCKET_FIN_WAIT_2          7
#define TCP_SOCKET_CLOSING             8
#define TCP_SOCKET_TIME_WAIT           9
#define TCP_SOCKET_CLOSE_WAIT          10
#define TCP_SOCKET_LAST_ACK            11
```

The following lines define some parameters for the retransmission scheme and the connection time-out detection:

```
#define TCP_DEF_rTOUT        30     // Retransmission default Time-Out (3 sec)
#define TCP_DEF_TIME_WAIT    5      // Time-Out for the TCP_SOCKET_TIME_WAIT
                                    //state (0,5 sec)
#define TCP_DEF_RETRIES      2      // default retries = 2 (original segment and
                                    //2 retransmissions)
#define TCP_DEF_cTOUT        1200   // Connection default Time-Out (120 sec)
```

The TCP segment control bits are defined as follows:

```
#define FIN     0x01
#define SYN     0x02
#define RST     0x04
#define PSH     0x08
#define ACK     0x10
#define URG     0x20
```

Finally, the following are some declarations needed by the module:

```
#define  TCP_MSS              TCP_DATA_MAX
unsigned short                len;
unsigned short                max_len;
struct tcb                    tcp_socket[TCP_MAX_SOCKETS];
static unsigned short         last_port = 1024;
static unsigned short         opt_len = 0;
static unsigned short         data_len = 0;
static char                   tcp_options = 0;
static char                   data_to_ack = 0;
```

17.2.2 Initializing the TCP module

The first step is to initialize the sockets table (tcb). This function is called from the **stack.c** module.

```
void tcp_init(void) {
  int i;
  struct tcb* pSocket;
  char a[4] = {0,0,0,0};

  for(i=0; i<TCP_MAX_SOCKETS; i++) {
    pSocket = &tcp_socket[i];
    pSocket->state = TCP_SOCKET_FREE;
    pSocket->local_port = 0;
    memcpy(&pSocket->remote_ip[0], &a[0],4);
    pSocket->remote_port = 0;
    pSocket->remote_mss = 0;
    pSocket->flags = 0;
    pSocket->snduna = 0;
    pSocket->sndnxt = 0;
    pSocket->sndwnd = 0;
    pSocket->rcvnxt = 0;
    pSocket->rcvwnd = HTONS(TCP_MSS);
    pSocket->rTimer = 0;
    pSocket->rTimeout = 0;
    pSocket->retries = 0;
    pSocket->cTimer = 0;
    pSocket->event_handler = 0;
    pSocket->more_data = 0;
    pSocket->position = 0;
    pSocket->fill_buffer = 0;
  }
  timer_start(tcptimer, 100);
  return;
}
```

The above routine simply initializes each table entry for their default values. After this, the tcptimer is started to handle the sockets time-out.

17.2.3 Processing the TCP segments

As we have seen, when the IP layer receives a TCP message, the **tcp_process( )** routine is called for its process.

This routine is called with the message length as a parameter. Then, the options and data lengths are calculated. If the debug_tcp option is set in the **debug.h** file, the **tcp_display( )** routine is called which shows the TCP message in the console.

The next step is to verify the checksum field. For this, the checksum field is saved, the pseudo-header is filled, and the **chksum16( )** function is called to calculate the checksum over the pseudo-header. After this, the checksum

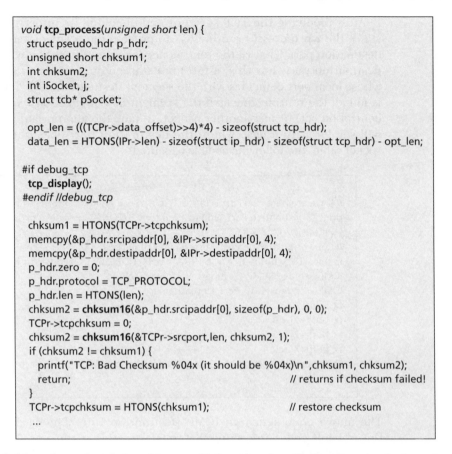

```
void tcp_process(unsigned short len) {
  struct pseudo_hdr p_hdr;
  unsigned short chksum1;
  int chksum2;
  int iSocket, j;
  struct tcb* pSocket;

  opt_len = (((TCPr->data_offset)>>4)*4) - sizeof(struct tcp_hdr);
  data_len = HTONS(IPr->len) - sizeof(struct ip_hdr) - sizeof(struct tcp_hdr) - opt_len;

#if debug_tcp
  tcp_display();
#endif //debug_tcp

  chksum1 = HTONS(TCPr->tcpchksum);
  memcpy(&p_hdr.srcipaddr[0], &IPr->srcipaddr[0], 4);
  memcpy(&p_hdr.destipaddr[0], &IPr->destipaddr[0], 4);
  p_hdr.zero = 0;
  p_hdr.protocol = TCP_PROTOCOL;
  p_hdr.len = HTONS(len);
  chksum2 = chksum16(&p_hdr.srcipaddr[0], sizeof(p_hdr), 0, 0);
  TCPr->tcpchksum = 0;
  chksum2 = chksum16(&TCPr->srcport,len, chksum2, 1);
  if (chksum2 != chksum1) {
    printf("TCP: Bad Checksum %04x (it should be %04x)\n",chksum1, chksum2);
    return;                                         // returns if checksum failed!
  }
  TCPr->tcpchksum = HTONS(chksum1);                 // restore checksum
  ...
```

field is cleared and the **chksum16( )** function is called again to calculate the checksum over the TCP segment. This time, the returned value is compared to the saved checksum. If those values differ, the TCP segment is discarded, otherwise the saved checksum is restored and the routine continues. Remember that the **chksum16( )** routine is provided by the **ip.c** module:

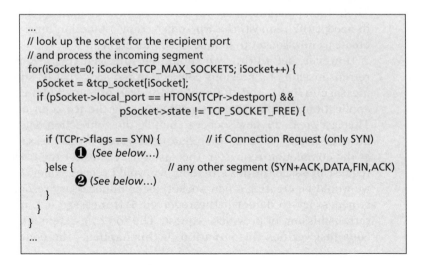

```
...
// look up the socket for the recipient port
// and process the incoming segment
for(iSocket=0; iSocket<TCP_MAX_SOCKETS; iSocket++) {
  pSocket = &tcp_socket[iSocket];
  if (pSocket->local_port == HTONS(TCPr->destport) &&
                   pSocket->state != TCP_SOCKET_FREE) {

    if (TCPr->flags == SYN) {          // if Connection Request (only SYN)
         ❶ (See below...)
    }else {                            // any other segment (SYN+ACK,DATA,FIN,ACK)
         ❷ (See below...)
    }
  }
}
...
```

After receiving the TCP segment and checking its integrity (the checksum), the **tcp_process( )** routine has to process the segment according to the destination port. That is, the routine needs to find the socket which owns the destination port. For this, a for(; ; ;) statement is used to find the socket whose local port coincides with the segment destination port. Once the entry is found, the routine checks if the segment is a connection request (the SYN control bit set) or just another packet, to take the appropriate process, as we will see later. In a case where the destination port does not exist on the socket table, the following code is executed:

```
...
// If we are here, the Port is unreachable...Send an ICMP informing that !
printf("Destination Port %d not found!\n", HTONS(TCPr->destport));
j = ICMP_DATA_START;
// Copy original IP header + first 8 bytes of IP Data
memcpy(&tx_buf[j+4], &rx_buf[DATALINK_HDR_SIZE], sizeof(struct ip_hdr)+8);
ICMPt->type = ICMP_Destination_Unreachable;
ICMPt->code = ICMP_Port_Unreachable;
tx_buf[j]  = 0;
tx_buf[j+1] = 0;
tx_buf[j+2] = 0;
tx_buf[j+3] = 0;
icmp_send(IPr->srcipaddr, sizeof(struct icmp_hdr)+4+sizeof(struct ip_hdr)+8);
}
```

The above code sends an ICMP Destination Unreachable message (Port Unreachable code), informing that the destination port cannot be reached.

Returning to the segment process, if the segment is a SYN (connection request) (see ❶, on page 393) and the socket is in the TCP_SOCKET_LISTEN state, we must inform the application that a connection request has arrived. For this, we call the application's call-back function (whose address was held at the event_handler field of the socket table), passing the socket, TCP_EVENT_CONN_REQ event, and the source's IP and port as the parameters. Then, the application may reject or accept the connection request. In order to accept the request, the **tcp_conn_accept( )** function must be called, which creates a new socket to handle the connection.

However, before this, we should be sure that this SYN message is not a retransmission of a previous connection request. That is, suppose that a SYN message arrived, and the application was informed about this. Then, the application accepted the connection calling the **tcp_conn_accept( )** function. This last created a new socket to handle the connection, and sent a SYN+ACK message acknowledging the request. However, if this message did not arrive at the connection requester, this last will retransmit the original connection request message. In this situation, we would receive a new SYN message and we would be creating a new socket, using unnecessary resources. For this, it is necessary to detect if the received SYN message is a new request or a retransmission of previous request. The for(; ;) statement in the following code just verifies this situation. If this happens, the code simply returns because our retransmission mechanism will take care of our SYN+ACK sent, retransmitting it if necessary:

```
for(j=0;j<TCP_MAX_SOCKETS;j++) { // check if this is a retransmission of a prior SYN
  pSocket = &tcp_socket[j];
  if (pSocket->state == TCP_SOCKET_SYN_RECEIVED &&
                pSocket->remote_port == HTONS(TCPr->srcport) &&
                pSocket->rcvnxt == (SWAP(TCPr->seq) + 1) &&
                pSocket->remote_ip[0] == IPr->srcipaddr[0] &&
                pSocket->remote_ip[1] == IPr->srcipaddr[1] &&
                pSocket->remote_ip[2] == IPr->srcipaddr[2] &&
                pSocket->remote_ip[3] == IPr->srcipaddr[3]) {

                    // it is a re-transmission of a previous SYN
                    // we don't have to create another socket
                    // the time-out of our SYN+ACK will re-send the segment
                return;
  }
}
pSocket = &tcp_socket[iSocket]                    // if continue, get the reference again
if (pSocket->state == TCP_SOCKET_LISTEN) {
  pSocket->event_handler(iSocket+1,TCP_EVENT_CONN_REQ,
                              IPr->srcipaddr,HTONS(TCPr->srcport),
                              TCP_DATA_START, 0);

  return;
}
```

Continuing with the segment process, for any other segment than a SYN message (see ❷, on page 393), the following code is executed:

```
if (pSocket->remote_port == HTONS(TCPr->srcport) &&
          pSocket->remote_ip[0] == IPr->srcipaddr[0] &&
          pSocket->remote_ip[1] == IPr->srcipaddr[1] &&
          pSocket->remote_ip[2] == IPr->srcipaddr[2] &&
          pSocket->remote_ip[3] == IPr->srcipaddr[3]) {

  tcp_process_segment(iSocket + 1);
  return;
}
```

After the above code verifies the arrived segment destination IP and port coincide with the socket's remote IP and port, the **tcp_process_segment( )** function is called for further processing.

17.2.4 Displaying the TCP segments

If the debug_tcp option is set in the **debug.h** file, the **tcp_display( )** routine shows the received TCP segments at the console. The following code shows how it is implemented:

```
#if debug_tcp
void tcp_display(void) {
  int i;

  printf("TCP Message:\n");
  printf("Source Port:        %d\n", HTONS(TCPr->srcport));
  printf("Destination Port:  %d\n", HTONS(TCPr->destport));
  printf("Sequence Number:    %u\n", SWAP(TCPr->seq));
  printf("Acknowledg.Number: %u\n", TCPr->ack);
  printf("Data Offset:        %d bytes (Options Length: %d bytes / Data Length: %d
                              bytes)\n", ((TCPr->data_offset)>>4)*4, opt_len, data_len);
  printf("Flags: ");
  if (TCPr->flags & FIN)
    printf("FIN ");
  if (TCPr->flags & SYN)
    printf("SYN ");
  if (TCPr->flags & RST)
    printf("RESET ");
  if (TCPr->flags & PSH)
    printf("PUSH ");
  if (TCPr->flags & ACK)
    printf("ACK ");
  if (TCPr->flags & URG)
    printf("URG ");
  printf("\nWindow:             %d\n", HTONS(TCPr->window));
  printf("Checksum:           %04x\n", HTONS(TCPr->tcpchksum));
  printf("Urgent Pointer:     %d\n", HTONS(TCPr->urgent_ptr));
  printf("Data:\n");
  for (i=0; i<data_len; i++) {
    printf("%c", rx_buf[TCP_DATA_START+i]);
  }
  printf("\n------------------------------------------\n");
}
#endif
```

The above code prints the received TCP segment header and data at the console.

17.2.5 The TCP finite state machine

As we saw in Chapter 6, the TCP is 'connection-oriented'. The connection progresses through a series of states during its lifetime. Which state the connection will move to will depend on the present state and the received events. These events may come from received messages, application commands and time-outs. In order to manage these connection states, a finite state machine (FSM) will be implemented (see Fig.6.11).

When we analysed the **tcp_process( )** routine, we saw that for any other segment than a SYN (connection request), the **tcp_process_segment( )** routine is called. This routine will process the segment depending on the socket's state, according to the TCP states diagram:

```
void tcp_process_segment(int socket) {
 struct tcb* pSocket;
 int iSocket = socket-1;

 if (tcp_validate_socket(socket) == TCP_INVALID_SOCKET)
 return;
pSocket = &tcp_socket[iSocket];          // Get the pointer to the structure
switch(pSocket->state) {
 case TCP_SOCKET_SYN_RECEIVED:
  ...
  break;
 case TCP_SOCKET_SYN_SENT:
  ...
  break;
 case TCP_SOCKET_ESTABLISHED:
  ...
  break;
 case TCP_SOCKET_CLOSE_WAIT:
  ...
  break;
 case TCP_SOCKET_LAST_ACK:
  ...
  break;
 case TCP_SOCKET_FIN_WAIT_1:
  ...
  break;
 case TCP_SOCKET_FIN_WAIT_2:
  ...
  break;
 case TCP_SOCKET_CLOSING:
  ...
  break;
 case TCP_SOCKET_TIME_WAIT:
  ...
  break;
 default:
  printf("Unknown State %d\n", pSocket->state);
  break;
 }
}
```

In the above routine we can see that different actions may be taken, depending on the socket's state. Each of these actions will be explained in the following sections, where the corresponding procedure and its graphical representation is shown.

In order to simplify the implementation, we will break down the TCP states diagram into the following procedures:

- **TCP Listen Procedure**: it is used by the application to have a socket in the listen state, in order to accept incoming connections.

- **TCP Accept Procedure**: when the application receives a connection request through the listening socket, it may call the **tcp_accept( )** function which will create a new socket to handle the new connection.
- **TCP Connect Procedure**: it is used by the application to initiate a connection to another device.
- **TCP Established Procedure**: when the socket is in the established state, data transfer can take place. This procedure must ensure the reliability of data transferred, and it must handle the connection time-out.
- **TCP Close Initiator Procedure**: it is used by the application when it needs to close the connection.
- **TCP Close Responder Procedure**: this procedure handles the close request received from the other device.

17.2.5.1 TCP Listen Procedure

When an application wants to receive incoming connections, it must have a socket in the listen state. For this, it must call the **tcp_socket_open( )** routine which creates a socket. Then, by calling the **tcp_listen( )**, the socket will be put in the listen state for the socket's local port. This socket will handle all connection request received for this port. The **tcp_listen( )** routine is implemented as follows:

```
int tcp_listen(int socket) {
  int iSocket = socket-1;

  if (tcp_validate_socket(socket) == TCP_INVALID_SOCKET)
    return TCP_SOCKET_ERROR;
  if (tcp_socket[iSocket].state != TCP_SOCKET_CLOSED &&
                    tcp_socket[iSocket].state != TCP_SOCKET_LISTEN) {
    return -1;  // Error
  }
  tcp_socket[iSocket].state = TCP_SOCKET_LISTEN;
  return 0;
}
```

This code simply puts the socket in the TCP_SOCKET_LISTEN state, if there are no errors.

The implementation for the Listen Procedure is handled by the **tcp_process( )** routine (see section 17.2.3). As we saw in that routine, the new connection requests are passed to the application, which has the following options:

- Accept the connection request, calling the **tcp_conn-accept( )** function.
- Reject the connection request, calling the **tcp_conn-reject( )** routine.
- Ignore the event, so not action is taken.

Figure 17.1 provides a graphical view of the TCP Listen Procedure. If the application decides to accept the connection request, the TCP Accept Procedure will be executed, as it is explained in the next section. But if the application wants to reject the incoming connection, the **tcp_conn-reject( )** routine is called.

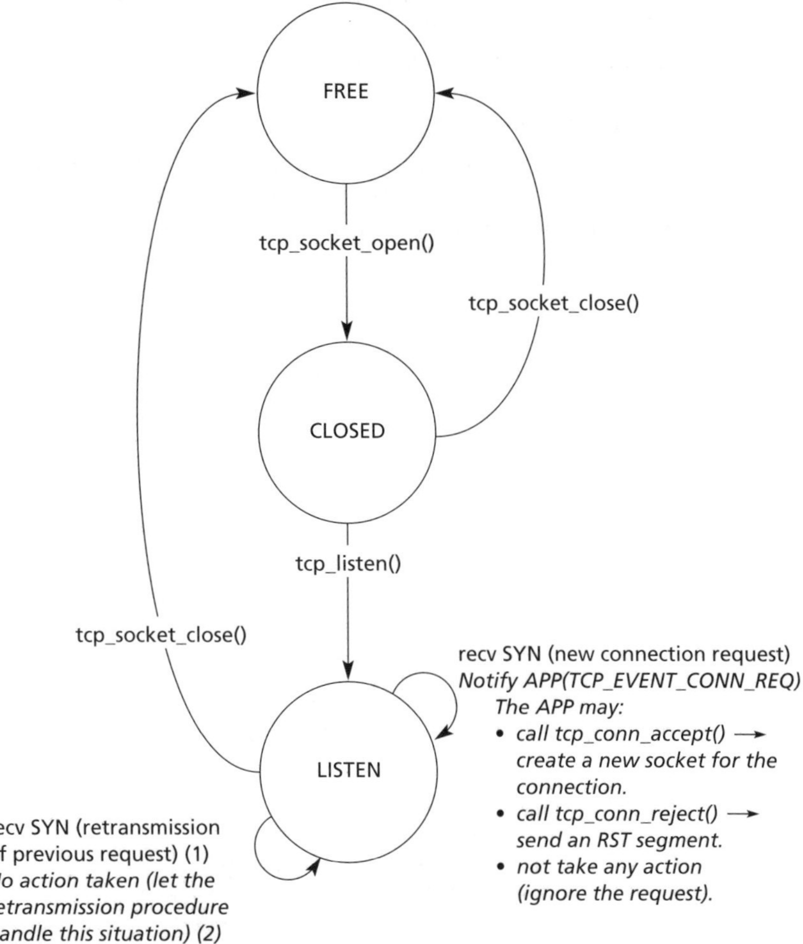

The App creates a socket and puts it in the LISTEN state, to receive incoming connection requests.

(1) It's important to detect if the SYN segment is a new Connection Request or a retransmission of a previous request, in order to avoid opening additional (and unnecessary) sockets. That is, for each SYN received (initial SYN segment and subsequent retransmissions), the program would create a new socket using more resources.

(2) If the peer retransmits a SYN segment (and supposing that we have already sent a SYN+ACK segment), it means that our SYN+ACK has not arrived at the peer. In this case, we will not receive an ACK for our segment from the peer, so that retransmission procedure will retransmit it accordingly when the rTimer expires.

Figure 17.1 The TCP Listen Procedure

```
void tcp_conn_reject(int socket) {

  if (tcp_validate_socket(socket) == TCP_INVALID_SOCKET)
   return;
  tcp_send_reset(socket,IPr->srcipaddr,HTONS(TCPr->srcport));
}
```

This routine validates the socket parameter, and sends a reset (a segment with the RST control bit set) to the requesting device, using the **tcp_send_reset( )** function, which will be explained later.

17.2.5.2 TCP Accept Procedure

The Accept Procedure creates a new socket to handle the new connection, so the original socket continues listening for incoming requests. Figure 17.2 shows the states and events involved with this procedure.

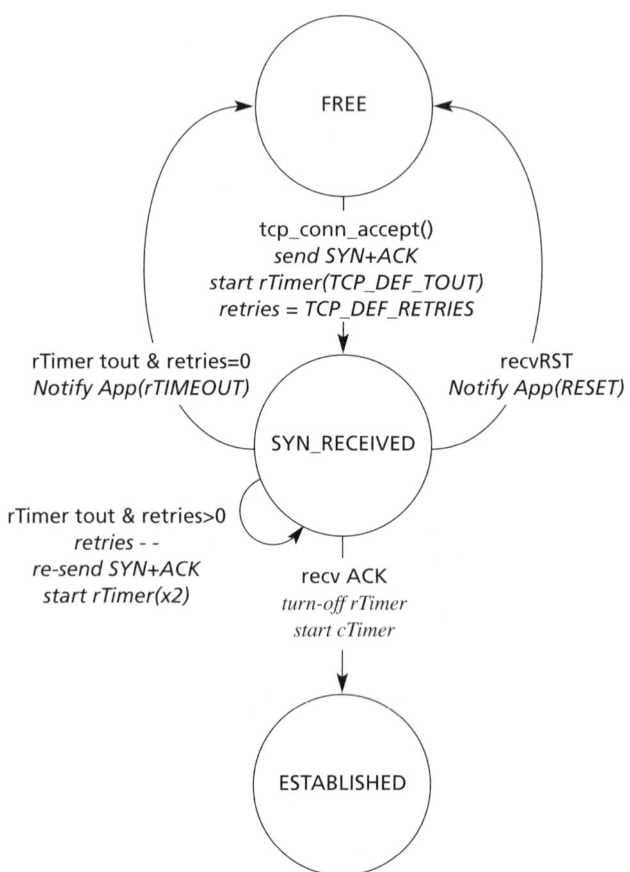

The APP calls the tcp_conn_accept() function in order to accept the incoming connection request. The TCP/IP stack creates a new socket to handle the new connection, and leaves the original socket in the listen state for new requests. The new socket will have the IP and Port addresses of the remote peer.

Notes: Each time a SYN, FIN, or a data segment is sent, the rTimer (retransmission timer) is initialized with default values. For retransmissions, the rTimer is loaded with doubled values (back-off-algorithm). In the Established state, a cTimer (connection timer) is started to avoid half-open connections.

Figure 17.2 The TCP Accept Procedure.

The **tcp_conn_accept( )** function creates a new socket (which searches for a free entry in the socket table), and fills the socket properties with the appropriate values. After this, the SYN+ACK message is sent acknowledging the connection request, and the retransmission timer is started. Once the ACK has been received from the peer, the socket moves to the ESTABLISHED state.

The following code shows the **tcp_conn_accept( )** routine implementation.

```
int tcp_conn_accept(int socket) {
  int i;
  struct tcb* pSocket;
  int iSocket = socket-1;

  if (tcp_validate_socket(socket) == TCP_INVALID_SOCKET)
    return TCP_SOCKET_ERROR;
  for(i=0;i<TCP_MAX_SOCKETS;i++) {
    pSocket = &tcp_socket[i];
    if (pSocket->state != TCP_SOCKET_FREE)
      continue;
    pSocket->local_port = tcp_socket[iSocket].local_port;
    memcpy(pSocket->remote_ip, IPr->srcipaddr, 4);
    pSocket->remote_port = HTONS(TCPr->srcport);
    pSocket->remote_mss = get_remote_mss();
    pSocket->event_handler = tcp_socket[iSocket].event_handler;
    pSocket->snduna = get_ISN();
    pSocket->sndnxt = pSocket->snduna;
    pSocket->sndwnd = HTONS(TCPr->window);
    pSocket->rcvnxt = SWAP(TCPr->seq) + 1;
    pSocket->rTimeout = TCP_DEF_rTOUT;
    pSocket->retries = TCP_DEF_RETRIES;
    pSocket->cTimer = 0;
    pSocket->state = TCP_SOCKET_SYN_RECEIVED;
    tcp_send(i+1, 0);
    return (i+1);
  }
  return TCP_SOCKET_ERROR; // there isn't a free socket to assign to this new connection
}
```

The above code shows how, after validating the socket parameter, a free table entry is searched. If it is found, the entry is filled with the connection parameters. The **get_remote_mss( )** function gets the Maximum Segment Size (MSS) from the SYN message, and the **get_ISN( )** returns a pseudo-random number used as the Initial Sequence Number (ISN) for the Connection Establishment process. Once the table entry is filled, the SYN+ACK message is sent using the **tcp_send( )** routine, and the socket moves to the TCP_SOCKET_SYN_RECEIVED state.

According to Figure 17.2, the socket will remain in the TCP_SOCKET_SYN_RECEIVED state waiting for an ACK message from the peer. Once this happens, the socket moves to the TCP_SOCKET_ESTABLISHED state, and the application is notified about the TCP_EVENT_ESTABLISHED event. If an RST message is received, the application is notified with the TCP_EVENT_RESET event, and the socket is closed. In the figure we can see that other events (such as the retransmission timer) may cause the state changes, but these events are handled by the **tcp_poll( )** routine as we will see later.

Returning to the **tcp_process_segment( )** routine, the following is the code that processes the received messages while the socket is in the TCP_SOCKET_SYN_RECEIVED state:

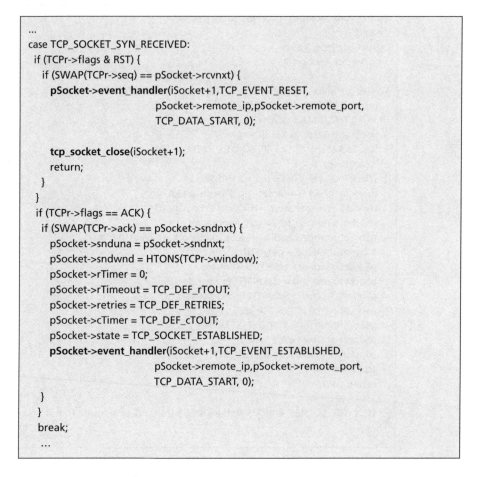

```
...
case TCP_SOCKET_SYN_RECEIVED:
  if (TCPr->flags & RST) {
    if (SWAP(TCPr->seq) == pSocket->rcvnxt) {
      pSocket->event_handler(iSocket+1,TCP_EVENT_RESET,
                             pSocket->remote_ip,pSocket->remote_port,
                             TCP_DATA_START, 0);

      tcp_socket_close(iSocket+1);
      return;
    }
  }
  if (TCPr->flags == ACK) {
    if (SWAP(TCPr->ack) == pSocket->sndnxt) {
      pSocket->snduna = pSocket->sndnxt;
      pSocket->sndwnd = HTONS(TCPr->window);
      pSocket->rTimer = 0;
      pSocket->rTimeout = TCP_DEF_rTOUT;
      pSocket->retries = TCP_DEF_RETRIES;
      pSocket->cTimer = TCP_DEF_cTOUT;
      pSocket->state = TCP_SOCKET_ESTABLISHED;
      pSocket->event_handler(iSocket+1,TCP_EVENT_ESTABLISHED,
                             pSocket->remote_ip,pSocket->remote_port,
                             TCP_DATA_START, 0);
    }
  }
  break;
  ...
```

17.2.5.3 TCP Connect Procedure

The TCP Connect Procedure is used by the application when it needs to initiate a connection to another device (generally a server). The procedure starts by calling the **tcp_socket_open()** function which creates a socket. Then, the **tcp_conn_open( )** routine will send the SYN message (Connection Request) and it will start the retransmission timer. Then, the socket moves to the TCP_SOCKET_SYN_SENT state. Figure 17.3 shows this procedure.

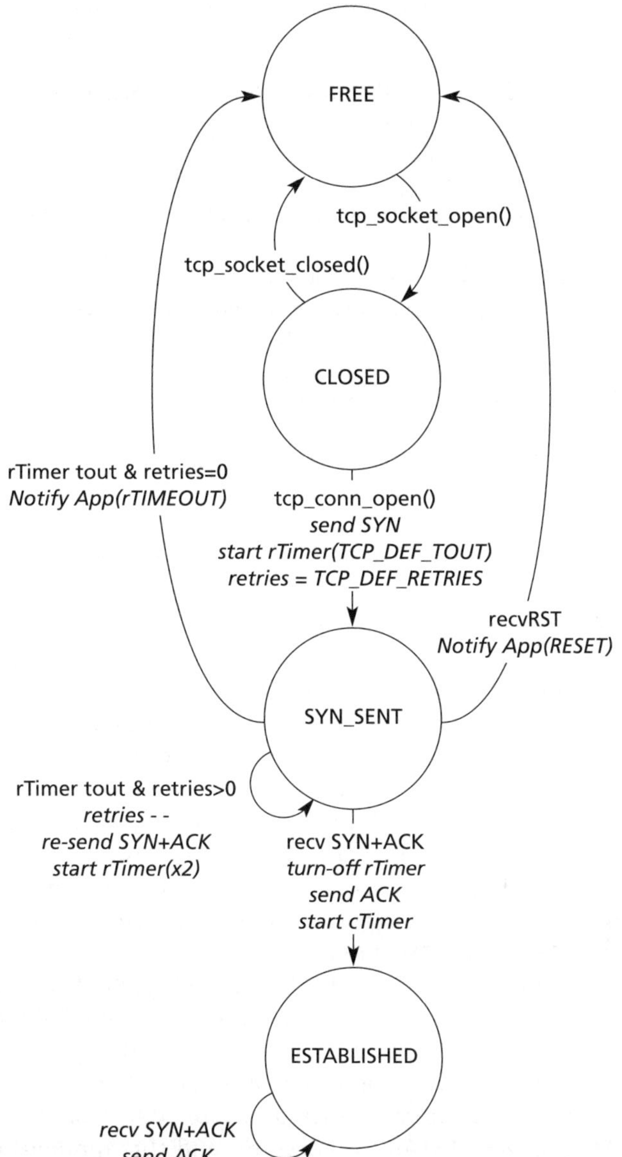

Once the App calls the tcp_socket_open() function to create a new socket, the APP must call the tcp_com_open() function in order to request a connection with a peer. The TCP/IP stack sends a SYN (connection request) segment and waits for the SYN+ACK response from the peer.

Notes: The Simultaneous Open is not considered for several reasons:

1) This implementation assumes that only sockets in the Listen state may receive SYN segments (connection requests.)

2) It makes little sense that a Client which is trying to connect to a server, receives a connection request from any other peer.

3) As the Client has a temporary port which changes from each time a new Client's socket is created, how does the peer know this port? It seems like the received segment is not a valid (intentionally sent) segment...

Figure 17.3 The TCP Connect Procedure.

The **tcp_conn_open( )** routine is implemented as follows :

```
void tcp_conn_open(int socket, char *destipaddr,unsigned short destport) {
  struct tcb* pSocket;
  int iSocket = socket-1;

  if (tcp_validate_socket(socket) == TCP_INVALID_SOCKET)
    return;
  pSocket = &tcp_socket[iSocket];
  memcpy(pSocket->remote_ip, destipaddr, 4);
  pSocket->remote_port = destport;
  pSocket->snduna = get_ISN();
  pSocket->sndnxt = pSocket->snduna;
  pSocket->rcvnxt = 0;
  pSocket->state = TCP_SOCKET_SYN_SENT;
  tcp_send(socket, 0);
}
```

After validating the socket and filling the appropriate socket table entry fields, the SYN message is sent using the **tcp_send( )** routine, and the socket moves to the TCP_SOCKET_SYN_SENT state. The **get_ISN( )** function is used to set the ISN sent in the connection request message.

The socket will remain in the TCP_SOCKET_SYN_SENT state, waiting for the SYN+ACK message from the server. When this happens, the retransmission timer is turned off and the socket moves to the ESTABLISHED state. However, since other events may arise, the routine must handle them accordingly. The code on page 405 shows the **tcp_process_segment( )** routine process for the received messages, when the socket is in the TCP_SOCKET_SYN_SENT state.

While the socket is in the TCP_SOCKET_SYN_SENT state, and the stack receives an RST message, the application is notified about this event and the socket is closed. Note that the acknowledge field of the RST message is validated in order to avoid spurious messages. However, if a SYN+ACK message is received, the timer is turned off, an ACK is sent, the socket moves to the TCP_SOCKET_ESTABLISHED state, and the application is notified about this event.

It is worth noting that in all cases, when we say that the socket is closed, it is moved to the FREE state rather than the CLOSED state. This strategy avoids the possibility of the application running out of sockets, while unused sockets remain closed, consuming resources.

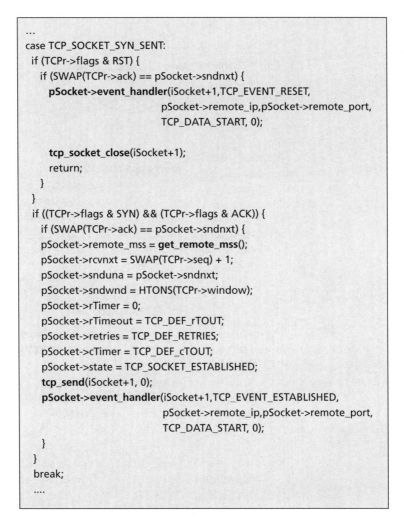

```
...
case TCP_SOCKET_SYN_SENT:
  if (TCPr->flags & RST) {
    if (SWAP(TCPr->ack) == pSocket->sndnxt) {
      pSocket->event_handler(iSocket+1,TCP_EVENT_RESET,
                             pSocket->remote_ip,pSocket->remote_port,
                             TCP_DATA_START, 0);

      tcp_socket_close(iSocket+1);
      return;
    }
  }
  if ((TCPr->flags & SYN) && (TCPr->flags & ACK)) {
    if (SWAP(TCPr->ack) == pSocket->sndnxt) {
    pSocket->remote_mss = get_remote_mss();
    pSocket->rcvnxt = SWAP(TCPr->seq) + 1;
    pSocket->snduna = pSocket->sndnxt;
    pSocket->sndwnd = HTONS(TCPr->window);
    pSocket->rTimer = 0;
    pSocket->rTimeout = TCP_DEF_rTOUT;
    pSocket->retries = TCP_DEF_RETRIES;
    pSocket->cTimer = TCP_DEF_cTOUT;
    pSocket->state = TCP_SOCKET_ESTABLISHED;
    tcp_send(iSocket+1, 0);
    pSocket->event_handler(iSocket+1,TCP_EVENT_ESTABLISHED,
                           pSocket->remote_ip,pSocket->remote_port,
                           TCP_DATA_START, 0);
    }
  }
  break;
....
```

17.2.5.4 TCP Established Procedure

When the socket is in the TCP_SOCKET_ESTABLISHED state, data transfer can take place. This means that we may receive data segments, as well as the ACK segments acknowledging the data sent by us. In addition, RST or FIN segments may be received from the peer, indicating that it wants to reset or close the connection. Even more, a SYN+ACK segment could also be received in this state, in such cases where the peer did not receive our ACK acknowledging its SYN+ACK, so the peer re-sends this last one. In all cases, we need to be prepared to receive any of the above segments. Figure 17.4 shows the TCP Established Procedure, including the connection timer (cTimer) event, as well as the retransmission timer (rTimer) event, which are handled by the **tcp_poll( )** routine.

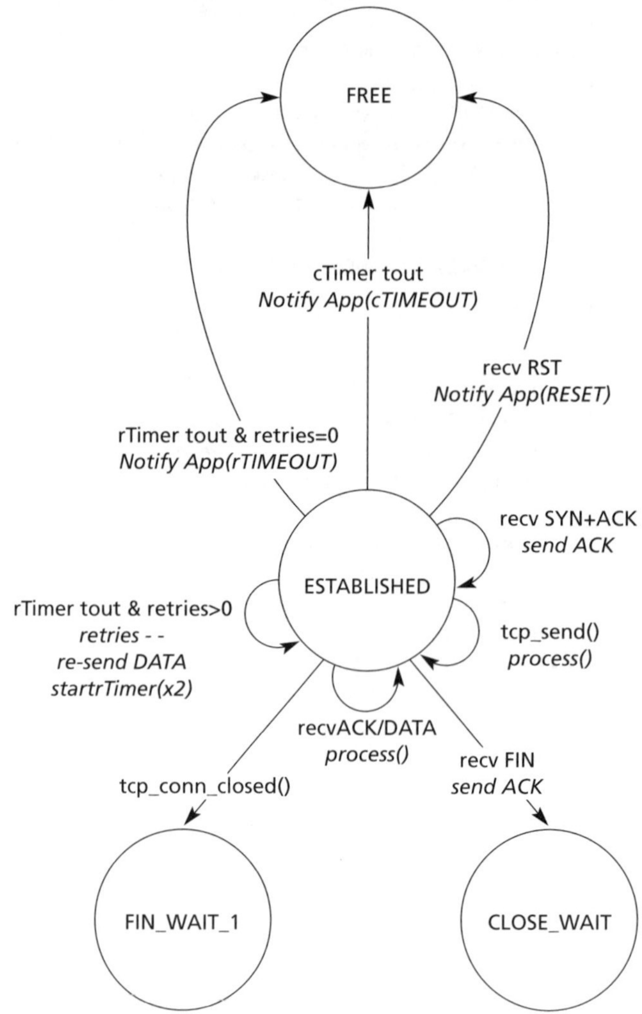

Figure 17.4 The TCP Established Procedure.

The code at the top of the page 407 shows the **tcp_process_segment( )** routine process while the socket is in the TCP_SOCKET_ESTABLISHED state.

When an RST segment is received, the application is informed with the TCP_EVENT_RESET event and the socket is closed. If a SYN+ACK is received, an ACK segment is sent.

```
...
case TCP_SOCKET_ESTABLISHED:
  if (TCPr->flags & RST) {
    if (SWAP(TCPr->seq) == pSocket->rcvnxt) {
      pSocket->event_handler(iSocket+1,TCP_EVENT_RESET,
                                    pSocket->remote_ip,pSocket->remote_port,
                                    TCP_DATA_START, 0);
      tcp_socket_close(iSocket+1);
      return;
    }
  }
  if ((TCPr->flags & SYN) && (TCPr->flags & ACK)) {
    if (SWAP(TCPr->seq) == pSocket->rcvnxt-1) {
      tcp_send(iSocket+1, 0);
      return;
    }
  }
  ...
```

```
...
if (TCPr->flags & ACK) {
  if (SWAP(TCPr->ack) == pSocket->sndnxt) {
    pSocket->sndwnd = HTONS(TCPr->window);
    if (pSocket->snduna != pSocket->sndnxt) {          // we have unacknowledged data...
      pSocket->snduna = pSocket->sndnxt;
      pSocket->rTimer=0;
      pSocket->rTimeout = TCP_DEF_rTOUT;
      pSocket->retries = TCP_DEF_RETRIES;
      if (pSocket->more_data == 0) {
        pSocket->event_handler(iSocket+1,TCP_EVENT_SEND_COMPLETED,
                                    pSocket->remote_ip,pSocket->remote_port,
                                    TCP_DATA_START, 0);
      }else {
        len = get_max_len(iSocket+1);
        pSocket->more_data = pSocket->fill_buffer(iSocket+1,
                                                  &pSocket->position, &len);
        tcp_send(iSocket+1, max_len - len);
      }
    }
  }
}
...
```

If the received segment has the ACK control bit set and is acknowledging our sent data, then, we must update our sliding window system's variables and turn off the retransmission timer. If there is more data to send (we will see the send data mechanism below), the buffer is filled by the application and the data is sent. Otherwise, the application is informed that all the data has been sent.

```
...
if (data_len > 0) {
   data_to_ack = 1;
   if (SWAP(TCPr->seq) == pSocket->rcvnxt) {
      pSocket->rcvnxt += data_len;
      pSocket->event_handler(iSocket+1,TCP_EVENT_DATA,
                              pSocket->remote_ip,pSocket->remote_port,
                              TCP_DATA_START, data_len);
   }
   if (data_to_ack) {
      tcp_send(iSocket+1, 0);
   }
}
pSocket->cTimer = TCP_DEF_cTOUT;
...
```

If we receive a segment with data, we must acknowledge it. For this, we use the data_to_ack variable, which will indicate that there is data to acknowledge. After the segment sequence validation, the socket's sliding window is updated, and the application is notified about the data received with the TCP_EVENT_DATA event. If the application has data to send, the acknowledge is included in this segment and the data_to_ack variable is cleared. Otherwise, the data_to_ack variable remains set, so an ACK segment will be sent to acknowledge the received data. The last line updates the connection timer (if we receive a segment, there is activity on the connection).

```
...
if (TCPr->flags & FIN) {
   if (SWAP(TCPr->seq) == pSocket->rcvnxt) {
      if (pSocket->snduna == pSocket->sndnxt) {
         tcp_socket[iSocket].cTimer = 0;
         pSocket->rcvnxt++;
         pSocket->state = TCP_SOCKET_CLOSE_WAIT;
         tcp_send(iSocket+1, 0);
         pSocket->event_handler(iSocket+1,TCP_EVENT_CLOSE_REQ,
                              pSocket->remote_ip,pSocket->remote_port,
                              TCP_DATA_START, 0);
      }
   }
}
break;
...
```

Finally, if a FIN segment arrives and after some validations, the connection timer is turned off and the sliding window is updated. The socket moves to the TCP_SOCKET_CLOSE_WAIT state, an ACK is sent, and the application is notified with the TCP_EVENT_CLOSE_REQ, meaning that the peer wants to close the connection. Note that the FIN segment is processed only if there is no unacknowledged data (snduna = = sndnxt).

17.2.5.5 TCP Close Initiator Procedure

This procedure is used by the application when it needs to close the connection. It starts with the application calling the **tcp_conn_close( )** routine:

```
void tcp_conn_close(int socket) {
  int iSocket = socket-1;

  if (tcp_validate_socket(socket) == TCP_INVALID_SOCKET)
     return;
  tcp_socket[iSocket].cTimer = 0;
  if (tcp_socket[iSocket].state == TCP_SOCKET_ESTABLISHED)
     tcp_socket[iSocket].state = TCP_SOCKET_FIN_WAIT_1;
  else {
     tcp_socket[iSocket].state = TCP_SOCKET_LAST_ACK;
     tcp_socket[iSocket].flags = FIN;
  }
  tcp_send(iSocket+1, 0);
}
```

After validating the socket, the connection timer is turned off. Then, the code checks if the socket is in the TCP_SOCKET_ESTABLISHED state (Close Initiator) or in the TCP_SOCKET_CLOSE_WAIT state (Close Responder), in order to decide the next state to move on. In both cases, a FIN must be sent. When the socket is in the TCP_SOCKET_FIN_WAIT_1 state, the **tcp_send( )** function sets the FIN flag automatically. Note that the **tcp_conn_close( )** routine is used in both the TCP Close Initiator and the TCP Close Responder procedures.

Figure 17.5 shows the TCP Close Initiator Procedure. When the application calls the **tcp_conn_close( )** routine, a FIN is sent and the connection timer is turned off while the retransmission timer is turned on. The socket moves to the TCP_SOCKET_FIN_WAIT_1 state, waiting for the ACK from the peer. When this happens, the socket moves to the TCP_SOCKET_FIN_WAIT_2 state and the retransmission timer is set with a doubled default value. This is to give the peer the necessary time to send out data if it needs to. However, the retries variable is cleared because we do not need to retransmit any segment.

Although the above is the most common scenario, while the socket is in the TCP_SOCKET_FIN_WAIT_1 state, we could receive a FIN segment from the peer indicating that a 'simultaneous close' situation is present. In this case, the socket moves to the TCP_SOCKET_CLOSING state. Of course, if an RST segment is received, the socket is closed.

The code on page 411 shows the **tcp_process_segment( )** routine process when the socket is in the TCP_SOCKET_FIN_WAIT_1 state.

If an RST segment is received, the application is notified and the socket is closed. If our FIN message is acknowledged (ACK segment received), the socket moves to the TCP_SOCKET_FIN_WAIT_2 state. If the 'simultaneous close' occurred, the socket would move to the TCP_SOCKET_CLOSING state and the received FIN would be acknowledged.

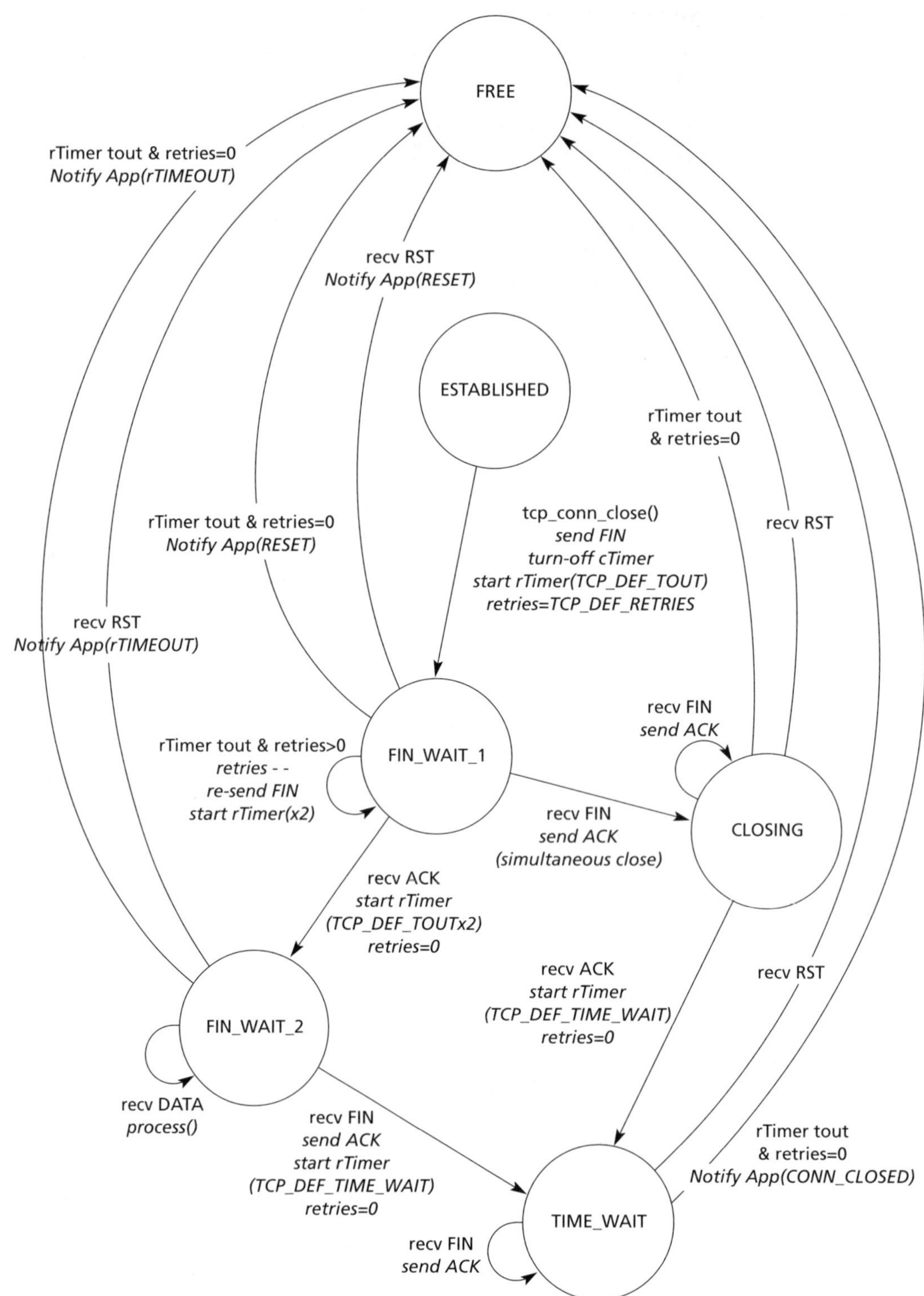

Figure 17.5 The TCP Close Initiator Procedure.

```
...
case TCP_SOCKET_FIN_WAIT_1:
  if (TCPr->flags & RST) {
    if (SWAP(TCPr->seq) == pSocket->rcvnxt) {
      pSocket->event_handler(iSocket+1,TCP_EVENT_RESET,
                             pSocket->remote_ip,pSocket->remote_port,
                             TCP_DATA_START, 0);
      tcp_socket_close(iSocket+1);
      return;
    }
  }
  if (TCPr->flags == ACK) {
    if (SWAP(TCPr->seq) == pSocket->rcvnxt) {
      pSocket->retries = 0;
      pSocket->rTimer = TCP_DEF_rTOUT * 2;
      pSocket->state = TCP_SOCKET_FIN_WAIT_2;
      return;
    }
  }
  if (TCPr->flags & FIN) {
    if (SWAP(TCPr->seq) == pSocket->rcvnxt) {
      pSocket->rcvnxt++;
      pSocket->state = TCP_SOCKET_CLOSING;
     tcp_send(iSocket+1, 0);
    }
  }
  break;
...
```

While the socket is in the TCP_SOCKET_FIN_WAIT_2 state (see code on page 412), the FIN segment from the peer should be received. In such case, an ACK is sent and the socket moves to the TCP_SOCKET_TIME_WAIT state. Of course, an RST segment or even data segments may be received from the peer, so the code must contemplate these situations.

In the 'simultaneous close' case, the socket moves to the TCP_SOCKET_CLOSING state waiting for the ACK message. If this happens, the socket will move to the TCP_SOCKET_TIME_WAIT state. However, while in the TCP_SOCKET_CLOSING state, a FIN segment could also be received. This could happen because the peer retransmitted its FIN as it did not receive our ACK for its FIN. And, of course, an RST may be received as in other cases.

```
...
case TCP_SOCKET_FIN_WAIT_2:
  if (TCPr->flags & RST) {
    if (SWAP(TCPr->seq) == pSocket->rcvnxt) {
      pSocket->event_handler(iSocket+1,TCP_EVENT_RESET,
                             pSocket->remote_ip,pSocket->remote_port,
                             TCP_DATA_START, 0);
      tcp_socket_close(iSocket+1);
      return;
    }
  }
  if (TCPr->flags & FIN) {
    if (SWAP(TCPr->seq) == pSocket->rcvnxt) {
      pSocket->rcvnxt++;
      tcp_send(iSocket+1, 0);
      pSocket->retries = 0;
      pSocket->rTimer = TCP_DEF_TIME_WAIT;
      pSocket->state = TCP_SOCKET_TIME_WAIT;
      return;
    }
  }
  if (data_len > 0) {
    data_to_ack = 1;
    if (SWAP(TCPr->seq) == pSocket->rcvnxt) {
      pSocket->rcvnxt += data_len;
      pSocket->event_handler(iSocket+1,TCP_EVENT_DATA,
                             pSocket->remote_ip,pSocket->remote_port,
                             TCP_DATA_START, data_len);
    }
    if (data_to_ack) {
       tcp_send(iSocket+1, 0);
    }
  }
  break;
...
```

The code at the top of page 412 shows the **tcp_process_segment( )** routine process for the received messages while the socket is in the TCP_SOCKET_CLOSING state.

The last state of the TCP Close Initiator Procedure is the TCP_SOCKET_TIME_WAIT state. The socket will remain in this state until the **tcp_poll( )** routine detects that the TCP_DEF_TIME_WAIT time has elapsed. Meanwhile, if an RST is received it is processed, notifying the application and closing the socket. It is also possible to receive a FIN segment from the peer (a retransmission of a previously sent FIN segment), where it has not received our ACK for that FIN.

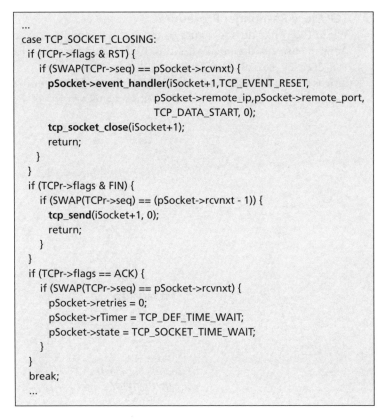

```
...
case TCP_SOCKET_CLOSING:
 if (TCPr->flags & RST) {
    if (SWAP(TCPr->seq) == pSocket->rcvnxt) {
      pSocket->event_handler(iSocket+1,TCP_EVENT_RESET,
                             pSocket->remote_ip,pSocket->remote_port,
                             TCP_DATA_START, 0);
      tcp_socket_close(iSocket+1);
      return;
    }
 }
 if (TCPr->flags & FIN) {
    if (SWAP(TCPr->seq) == (pSocket->rcvnxt - 1)) {
      tcp_send(iSocket+1, 0);
      return;
    }
 }
 if (TCPr->flags == ACK) {
    if (SWAP(TCPr->seq) == pSocket->rcvnxt) {
      pSocket->retries = 0;
      pSocket->rTimer = TCP_DEF_TIME_WAIT;
      pSocket->state = TCP_SOCKET_TIME_WAIT;
    }
 }
 break;
 ...
```

```
...
case TCP_SOCKET_TIME_WAIT:
 if (TCPr->flags & RST) {
    if (SWAP(TCPr->seq) == pSocket->rcvnxt) {
      pSocket->event_handler(iSocket+1,TCP_EVENT_RESET,
                             pSocket->remote_ip,pSocket->remote_port,
                             TCP_DATA_START, 0);
      tcp_socket_close(iSocket+1);
      return;
    }
 }
 if (TCPr->flags == FIN) {
    if (SWAP(TCPr->seq) == (pSocket->rcvnxt - 1)) {
      tcp_send(iSocket+1, 0);
    }
 }
 break;
```

17.2.5.6 TCP Close Responder Procedure

When the other device wants to close the connection, it sends a FIN segment. As we saw in the TCP Established Procedure, if the socket is in the TCP_SOCKET_ESTABLISHED state, and this FIN segment is received, the socket moves to the TCP_SOCKET_CLOSE_WAIT state. This event starts the TCP Close Responder Procedure. Figure 17.6 shows this.

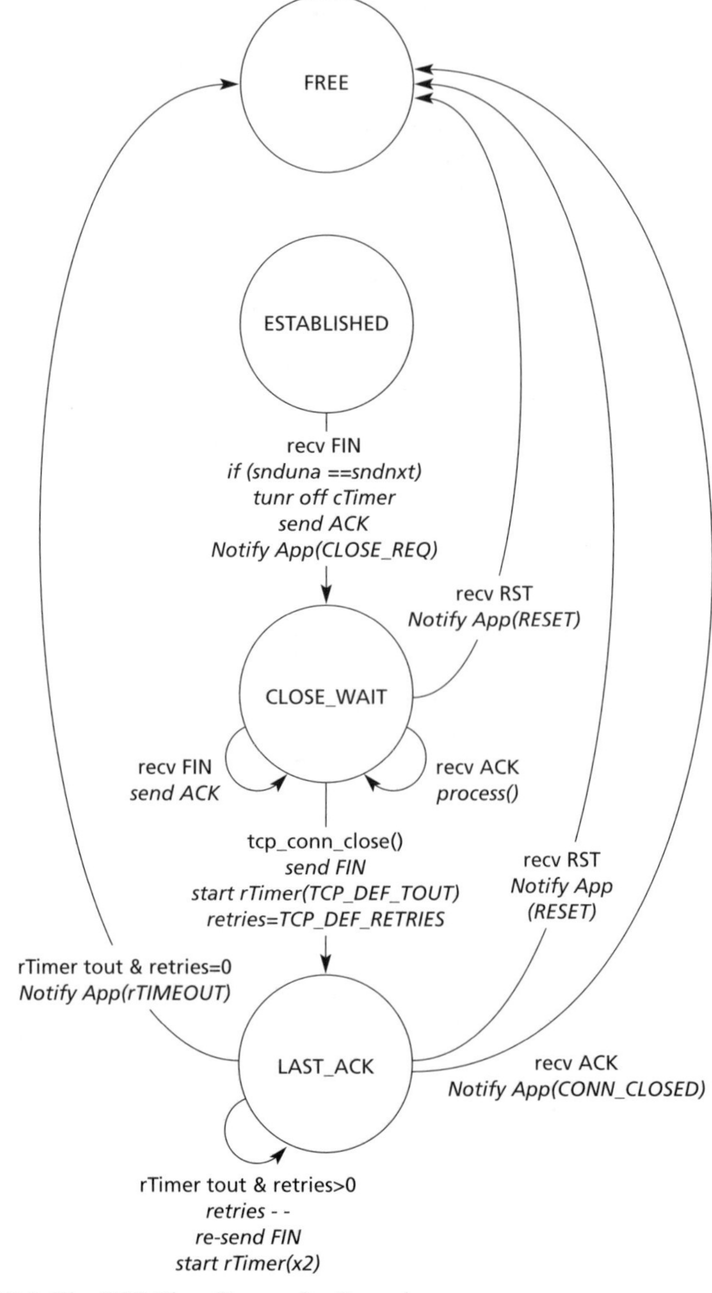

Figure 17.6 The TCP Close Responder Procedure.

The socket will remain in the TCP_SOCKET_CLOSE_WAIT state until the application calls the **tcp_conn_close( )** routine. When this happens, the socket moves to the TCP_SOCKET_LAST_ACK state. However, before the application calls this routine, it may need to send more data. In this case, incoming ACK segments must be processed. Other segments the socket may receive in this state are RST and FIN segments. This last one may be received as a consequence of a FIN retransmission from the peer if it has not received our ACK previously sent.

The following code shows the **tcp_process_segment( )** routine process for the received messages while the socket is in the TCP_SOCKET_CLOSE_WAIT state:

```
...
case TCP_SOCKET_CLOSE_WAIT:
  if (TCPr->flags & RST) {
    if (SWAP(TCPr->seq) == pSocket->rcvnxt) {
      pSocket->event_handler(iSocket+1,TCP_EVENT_RESET,
                             pSocket->remote_ip,pSocket->remote_port,
                             TCP_DATA_START, 0);
      tcp_socket_close(iSocket+1);
      return;
    }
  }
  if (TCPr->flags & FIN) {
    if (SWAP(TCPr->seq) == (pSocket->rcvnxt - 1)) {
      tcp_send(iSocket+1, 0);
      return;
    }
  }
  if (TCPr->flags & ACK) {
    if (SWAP(TCPr->ack) == pSocket->sndnxt) {
      pSocket->sndwnd = HTONS(TCPr->window);
      if (pSocket->snduna != pSocket->sndnxt) {  // we have unacknowledged data...
        pSocket->snduna = pSocket->sndnxt;
        pSocket->rTimer=0;
        pSocket->rTimeout = TCP_DEF_rTOUT;
        pSocket->retries = TCP_DEF_RETRIES;
        if (pSocket->more_data == 0) {
          pSocket->event_handler(iSocket+1,TCP_EVENT_SEND_COMPLETED,
                                 pSocket->remote_ip,pSocket->remote_port,
                                 TCP_DATA_START, 0);
        }else {
          len = get_max_len(iSocket+1);
          pSocket->more_data = pSocket->fill_buffer(iSocket+1,
                                     &pSocket->position, &len);
          tcp_send(iSocket+1, max_len - len);
        }
      }
    }
  }
  break;
...
```

In the above code, if an RST is received, the application is notified with the TCP_EVENT_RESET event, and the socket is closed. If a FIN message is received, the ACK is sent.

If the received segment has the ACK control bit set, it is acknowledging our sent data. Then, we must update our sliding window system's variables and turn off the retransmission timer. If there is more data to send, the buffer is filled by the application and the data is sent. Otherwise, the application is notified that all the data has been sent.

Finally, in the TCP_SOCKET_LAST_ACK state, the socket is waiting for the ACK from the peer. When this arrives, the application is notified with the TCP_EVENT_CONN_CLOSED event. The application should call the **tcp_socket_close( )** routine to close the socket. If an RST segment arrives, it is processed as usual. See the code implementation:

```
...
case TCP_SOCKET_LAST_ACK:
 if (TCPr->flags & RST) {
   if (SWAP(TCPr->seq) == pSocket->rcvnxt) {
     pSocket->event_handler(iSocket+1,TCP_EVENT_RESET,
                             pSocket->remote_ip,pSocket->remote_port,
                             TCP_DATA_START, 0);

     tcp_socket_close(iSocket+1);
     return;
   }
 }
 if (TCPr->flags == ACK) {
   if (SWAP(TCPr->seq) == pSocket->rcvnxt) {
     pSocket->event_handler(iSocket+1,TCP_EVENT_CONN_CLOSED,
                             pSocket->remote_ip,pSocket->remote_port,
                             TCP_DATA_START, 0);
   }
 }
 break;
 ...
```

17.2.6 Opening and closing TCP sockets

In order for an application to use the TCP transport services, it has to get a TCP socket. For this purpose, the **tcp_socket_open( )** function is provided.

This function is called by the application, which specifies a port number (optional), and the address of the call-back function, which the stack notifies about events related to this socket.

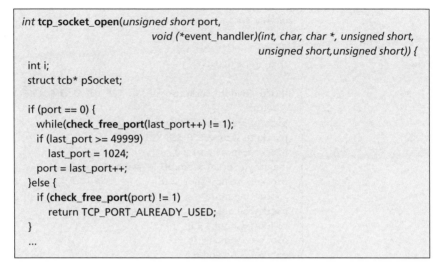

```
int tcp_socket_open(unsigned short port,
                    void (*event_handler)(int, char, char *, unsigned short,
                                          unsigned short,unsigned short)) {
 int i;
 struct tcb* pSocket;

 if (port == 0) {
   while(check_free_port(last_port++) != 1);
   if (last_port >= 49999)
     last_port = 1024;
   port = last_port++;
 }else {
   if (check_free_port(port) != 1)
     return TCP_PORT_ALREADY_USED;
 }
 ...
```

If the application passes zero as a port value, the stack will assign a free port, using the **check_free_port( )** function.

```
 ...
 for(i=0; i<TCP_MAX_SOCKETS; i++) {
   pSocket = &tcp_socket[i];
   if(pSocket->state != TCP_SOCKET_FREE)
     continue;
   pSocket->state = TCP_SOCKET_CLOSED;
   pSocket->local_port = port;
   pSocket->rTimeout = TCP_DEF_rTOUT;
   pSocket->retries = TCP_DEF_RETRIES;
   pSocket->event_handler = (unsigned int ) event_handler;
  return (i+1);
 }
 return TCP_INVALID_SOCKET;
}
```

The for(; ;) statement checks for the first free entry in the socket's table, and initializes the entry with the passed parameters and some defaults. The resulting socket is returned (as sockets are numbered from one instead of zero, the socket number is the index of table plus one). If there is not a free entry to assign, the TCP_INVALID_SOCKET is returned as error.

Once the application no longer needs the socket, it must close it. For this, the **tcp_socket_close( )** function is used. This function simply puts the socket in the TCP_SOCKET_FREE state, and clears the table entry fields:

```
void tcp_socket_close(int socket) {
  struct tcb* pSocket;
  int iSocket = socket-1;
  char a[4] = {0,0,0,0};

  if (tcp_validate_socket(socket) == TCP_INVALID_SOCKET)
     return;
  pSocket = &tcp_socket[iSocket];
  pSocket->state = TCP_SOCKET_FREE;
  pSocket->local_port = 0;
  memcpy(pSocket->remote_ip, &a[0], 4);
  pSocket->remote_port = 0;
  pSocket->remote_mss = 0;
  pSocket->flags = 0;
  pSocket->snduna = 0;
  pSocket->sndnxt = 0;
  pSocket->sndwnd = 0;
  pSocket->rcvnxt = 0;
  pSocket->rTimer = 0;
  pSocket->rTimeout = 0;
  pSocket->retries = 0;
  pSocket->cTimer = 0;
  pSocket->event_handler = 0;
  pSocket->more_data = 0;
  pSocket->position = 0;
  pSocket->fill_buffer = 0;
}
```

17.2.7 Sending control and data segments

The **tcp_send( )** routine sends messages using the TCP segment format. It is called passing the socket and data length (len) as parameters:

```
void tcp_send(int socket, unsigned short len) {
  struct pseudo_hdr p_hdr;
  int chksum2;
  int iSocket = socket-1;

  if (tcp_validate_socket(socket) == TCP_INVALID_SOCKET)
    return;
  if (tcp_socket[iSocket].state == TCP_SOCKET_FREE) {
    printf("TCP Send: the socket is free: %d\n", socket);
    return;
  }
  switch (tcp_socket[iSocket].state) {
    case TCP_SOCKET_SYN_RECEIVED:
    case TCP_SOCKET_SYN_SENT:
     tcp_socket[iSocket].flags = SYN;
     //send a MSS=1460 TCP Option
     tx_buf[TCP_DATA_START] = 0x02;
```

```
      tx_buf[TCP_DATA_START+1]= 0x04;
      tx_buf[TCP_DATA_START+2]= TCP_MSS>>8;
      tx_buf[TCP_DATA_START+3]= TCP_MSS;
      tcp_options = 4;
      break;
    case TCP_SOCKET_FIN_WAIT_1:
      tcp_socket[iSocket].flags = FIN;
      break;
}
if (len>0)
  tcp_socket[iSocket].flags |= PSH;
if (tcp_socket[iSocket].state != TCP_SOCKET_SYN_SENT)
  tcp_socket[iSocket].flags |= ACK;
...
```

The first lines of the code validate the socket and its state. After this, the Control Bit is set according to the socket state. If a SYN is sent, the MSS option is added. If data is sent, the PSH flag is set. The ACK flag is set in all segments except the first SYN segment in the connection request (there is nothing to acknowledge).

```
...
TCPt->srcport = HTONS(tcp_socket[iSocket].local_port);
TCPt->destport = HTONS(tcp_socket[iSocket].remote_port);
TCPt->seq = SWAP(tcp_socket[iSocket].sndnxt);
TCPt->ack = SWAP(tcp_socket[iSocket].rcvnxt);
TCPt->data_offset = ((sizeof(struct tcp_hdr) + tcp_options)/4)<<4;
TCPt->flags = tcp_socket[iSocket].flags;

TCPt->window = tcp_socket[iSocket].rcvwnd;
TCPt->tcpchksum = 0;
TCPt->urgent_ptr = 0;
...
```

The next step is to complete the TCP segment header as above. After this, the checksum must be calculated:

```
...
// Calculate checksum
memcpy(&p_hdr.srcipaddr[0], &MyIP[0], 4);
memcpy(&p_hdr.destipaddr[0], tcp_socket[iSocket].remote_ip, 4);
p_hdr.zero = 0;
p_hdr.protocol = TCP_PROTOCOL;
p_hdr.len = HTONS(len+tcp_options+20);
chksum2 = chksum16(&p_hdr.srcipaddr[0], sizeof(p_hdr), 0, 0);
chksum2 = chksum16(&TCPt->srcport,len+tcp_options+20, chksum2, 1);
TCPt->tcpchksum = HTONS(chksum2);
 ...
```

Now, the TCP segment can be sent using the IP layer:

```
...
ip_send(TCP_PROTOCOL, tcp_socket[iSocket].remote_ip,
                        len+tcp_options+sizeof(struct tcp_hdr));
if (tcp_socket[iSocket].flags != ACK)
  tcp_socket[iSocket].rTimer = tcp_socket[iSocket].rTimeout;        // Init timer
if (len>0) {
  tcp_socket[iSocket].sndnxt += len;
}else {
  if ((TCPt->flags & SYN) || (TCPt->flags & FIN))
    tcp_socket[iSocket].sndnxt++;
}
data_to_ack = 0;
tcp_socket[iSocket].flags = 0;
tcp_options = 0;
}
```

The above code sends the segment and starts the timer for any segment other than an ACK (if the ACK bit is the only flag set). The sliding window variables are set accordingly. Lastly, some variables are cleared.

There is a special case when we need to send an RST segment using a socket, which does not have a remote IP and port associated. This is the case for the socket in the listen state, where a connection request is rejected using the **tcp_conn_reject( )** routine. This routine needs to send an RST segment to the connection requester. However, as the listener socket does not have a remote socket associated, a special **tcp_send_reset( )** routine is provided, which accepts the remote IP and port as parameters.

17.2.8 Sending stream-oriented data

As we saw in Chapter 6, TCP is a 'stream-oriented' protocol. This means that TCP allows applications to send data as a continuous stream of bytes. However, the above **tcp_send( )** routine sends data sized up to MSS = 1460.

As the application should not be concerned about splitting its data into the appropriate slices, we need to implement a mechanism that allows us to let the application believe it is sending data in a continuous manner. Figure 17.7 shows how this mechanism works.

Suppose an application needs to send 3500 bytes, and that the MSS of the peer is 1460 bytes. This means that the application data must be divided into three blocks to be sent using the **tcp_send( )** routine. The mechanism starts with the application calling the **tcp_send_data( )** function (1). This routine, after some initialization, calls the **fill_buffer( )** application call-back function (2) in order for the application to fill the first block (A) of data to be sent. The **fill_buffer( )** function is called with the socket, the initial position, and the maximum length to fill as parameters. After filling the transmit buffer, this function returns 1 if there is still more data to send, or 0 if there is not.

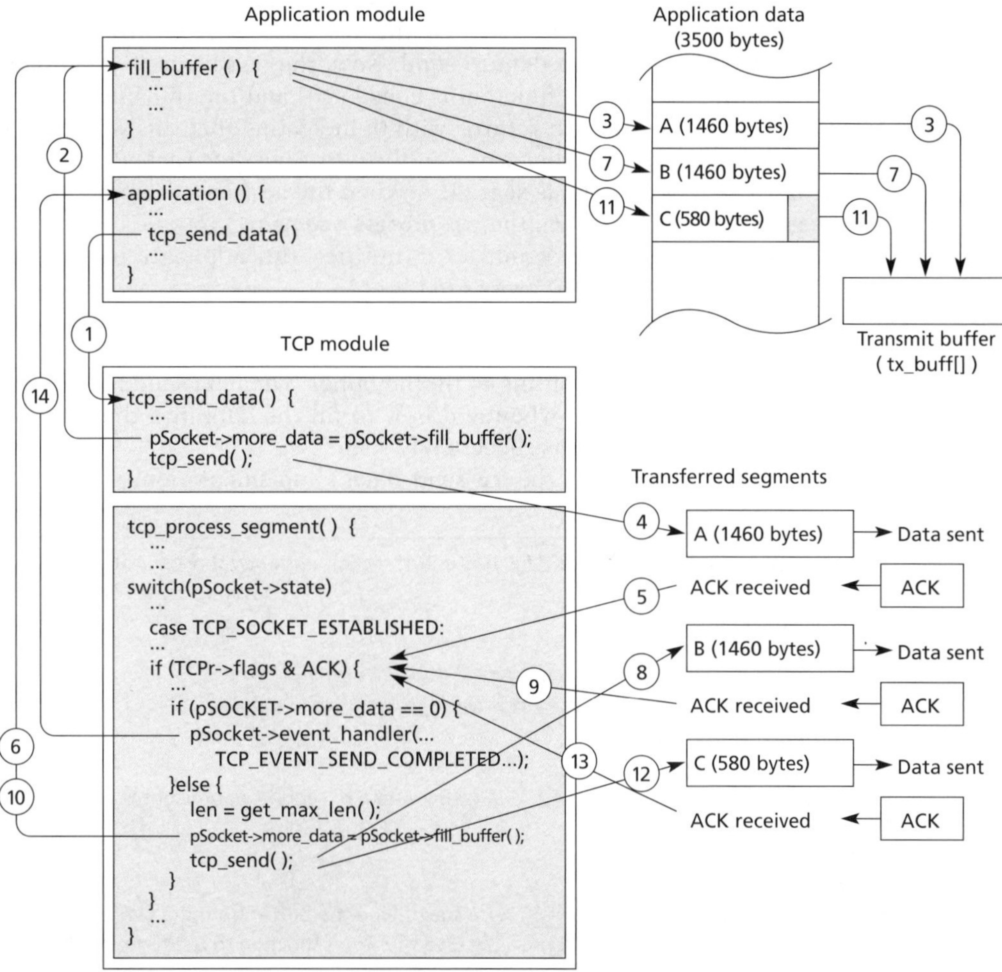

Figure 17.7 The TCP 'stream-oriented' data send mechanism.

This returning value is saved in the **more_data** field of the socket table. As well, the final position is saved in order for the function to know where to get the following data, the next time it is called. In this case, the **fill_buffer( )** function fills the transmit buffer with the (A) block (3), and returns 1 indicating there is more data to send.

Now, the **tcp_send( )** routine sends the first data segment (4). Once the acknowledgement for this segment has been received (5), the **tcp_process_segment( )** routine (checking the ACK flag under the case TCP_SOCKET_ESTABLISHED statement) checks if there is more data to send. If so, the **fill_buffer( )** function is called again (6) with the previously saved position, to have the routine correctly fill the second block of data (B) into the transmit buffer (7). This routine returns with 1, which means that there is more data to send. Both the final position and the returning value are saved in the respective socket table field.

The second block of data (B) is sent using the **tcp_send( )** routine (8). When this data is acknowledged (9), the **tcp_process_segment( )** routine checks if there is still more data to send. Now, the last block is pending to send. Then, the fill_buffer( ) function is called (10) and the transmit buffer is filled (11). Now, the function returns with 0, indicating that this was the last block of data. This value is then saved in the corresponding socket table field.

The last block of data (C) is sent (12). When the acknowledgement for this data segment is received (13), the **tcp_process_segment( )** routine checks that there is no more data to send, so it notifies the application with the TCP_EVENT_SEND_COMPLETED event (14).

In this way, the application does not worry about how much data it can send in each segment. The application just needs to call the tcp_send_data( ) function and to provide a routine to fill the buffer. The data send mechanism will inform the application when and how to fill the data into the transmit buffer, and when the data was successfully sent.

The following code shows the **tcp_send_data( )** implementation:

```
int tcp_send_data(int socket, int (*fill_buffer)(int socket, unsigned short *position,
                                                  unsigned short *len)) {
  struct tcb* pSocket;
  int iSocket = socket-1;

  if (tcp_validate_socket(socket) == TCP_INVALID_SOCKET)
    return TCP_INVALID_SOCKET;
  pSocket = &tcp_socket[iSocket];
  if (pSocket->more_data > 0)          // Is there data to send from previous request?
    return TCP_SOCKET_ERROR;
  // Setup the socket
  pSocket->more_data = 0;
  pSocket->position = 0;               // start filling the buffer from the beginning
  pSocket->fill_buffer = fill_buffer;  // save the App's function to call to fill the buffer
  // Now call the function
  len = get_max_len(socket);
  pSocket->more_data = pSocket->fill_buffer(socket, &pSocket->position, &len);
  tcp_send(socket, max_len - len);
  return 0;
}
```

After validating the socket, the function checks if there is more data to send from a previous request. If so, an error is returned. Assuming it continues, the more_data and position fields are initialized, and the application **fill_buffer( )** function address is saved for future reference. The **get_max_len( )** function is called to determine the maximum length the application may use to fill the transmit buffer. Although in principle this length is determined by the MSS of the remote peer, other parameters such as the remote window size (sndwnd) and the TCP_DATA_MAX (which depends on the transmit buffer size) may affect this maximum length. The **get_max_len( )** function saves its returning value in the max_len variable.

With these parameters, the **fill_buffer( )** function (or whichever name the application calls it) is called through the pSocket->fill_buffer pointer. Please note that the len parameter passed as a reference (the variable's address) to this function is the maximum length the application's routine may use. However, this function may need to fill fewer bytes than the maximum. For each byte filled, the len variable is decremented. After the function returns, the (max_len – len) will give us the actual number of bytes filled into the buffer. This value is used to send the segment using the **tcp_send( )** routine.

Finally, we need to explain that in some cases, where the data to send will never exceed the maximum allowable, the application **fill_buffer( )** function implementation is very simple. For an example of a complex implementation of this function, see the **create_content( )** function in the http.c module in Chapter 20, where the data to send (HTML pages) exceeds the segment maximum lengths.

17.2.9 The Sliding Window Acknowledgement System implementation

Now that we have seen the process for received and sent segments, we may look at the sliding window implementation in detail. The Send Window keeps track of the transmitted bytes. The socket table entry has three fields that serve for this purpose; the snduna, the sndnxt and the sndwnd.

The sndnxt field holds the sequence number of the first byte of data to be sent. The **get_ISN( )** function provides the initial sequence number for this field (see **tcp_conn_open( )** or **tcp_conn_accept( )**). When a segment is assembled, the seq header field is filled with the sndnxt value. Once the segment is sent, the sndnxt field is incremented by the data length (if a data segment was sent) or by one (if a SYN or FIN segment was sent). See the **tcp_send( )** routine. When a segment is received, its ack header field must be validated against the sndnxt field.

The snduna field is used to hold the sequence number of the first byte that was sent but not yet acknowledged. This value is initialized with the same value as the sndnxt, but only updated when a received segment acknowledges our sent data (in the **tcp_process_segment( )** routine). The difference between the sndnxt and the snduna are the bytes sent and waiting to be acknowledged from the remote device.

The sndwnd field saves the receive window size of the remote device, which consists of the maximum size of bytes the other device is willing to accept; that is, how much data we are able to send to this device. This value is taken into account by the **get_max_len( )** function. The sndwnd field is filled with the window header field of the received segments.

The receive window keeps track of the received bytes. The socket table entry has two fields for this purpose; the rcvnxt and the rcvwnd fields. The rcvnxt field has the sequence number of the first byte of data that the device expects to receive from the remote device. This field is filled with the ISN sent from the other device in the connection establishment process. After this, the rcvnxt field is updated each time a segment is received; incrementing its value by the data length (if a data segment was received) or by one (if a

SYN or FIN segment was received). See the **tcp_process_segment( )** routine. The rcvnxt field is used to fill the ACK header field in outgoing segments. When a segment is received, its seq header field must be validated against the rcvnxt field.

The rcvwnd field holds the size of the device's receiving window. This size is the maximum size in bytes our device is willing to accept. In our case, this value is fixed with the TCP_MSS constant. The rcvwnd field is used to fill the window header field for all outgoing segments.

17.2.10 The segment retransmission scheme

As TCP is a reliable transport protocol, we need a way to ensure that all the transmitted segments arrive at their destination. One way to ensure this is to detect those segments that fail to arrive at their destination, and retransmit them.

In order to detect failed transmissions, we make use of the acknowledgement system. Each time a segment other than an ACK is sent, a retransmission timer (rTimer) is started (ACK segments are not acknowledged). If the reception of the sent segment is acknowledged before the rTimer expires, the transmission is considered a successful one. If the rTimer expires and the acknowledgement was not received, the segment is considered lost and it must be retransmitted. This retransmission is tried a few times (TCP_DEF_RETRIES) before a network problem is assumed.

The timers are managed by the **tcp_poll( )** routine which is called periodically from the **stack_process( )** routine in the **stack.c** module. The following is the **tcp_poll( )** routine implementation:

```
void tcp_poll(void) {
  int i;

  if (timer_expired(tcptimer)) {                    // 100 msec has elapsed
    for(i=0; i<TCP_MAX_SOCKETS; i++) {
      if (tcp_socket[i].rTimer > 1)
        tcp_socket[i].rTimer--;
      if (tcp_socket[i].cTimer > 1 && tcp_socket[i].state ==
                                        TCP_SOCKET_ESTABLISHED)
        tcp_socket[i].cTimer--;
    }
    timer_start(tcptimer, 100);
  }else
    return;
    ...
```

When the TCP is initialized with the **tcp_init( )** routine, a 100 milliseconds timer (tcptimer) is started. Each time the **tcp_poll( )** routine detects this time has elapsed, both the retransmission (rTimer) and the connection (cTimer) timers from each socket table entry are decremented. Then, the tcptimer is started again.

```
...
for(i=0; i<TCP_MAX_SOCKETS; i++) {
  if (tcp_socket[i].rTimer == 1) {        //retransmission socket timer has expired
    if (tcp_socket[i].retries == 0) {
      if (tcp_socket[i].state == TCP_SOCKET_TIME_WAIT) {
        tcp_socket[i].event_handler(i+1,TCP_EVENT_CONN_CLOSED,
                              tcp_socket[i].remote_ip,tcp_socket[i].remote_port,
                              TCP_DATA_START, 0);
      }else {
        tcp_socket[i].event_handler(i+1,TCP_EVENT_rTOUT,
                              tcp_socket[i].remote_ip,tcp_socket[i].remote_port,
                              TCP_DATA_START, 0);
      }
      tcp_socket_close(i+1);
    }else {
      tcp_socket[i].rTimeout = tcp_socket[i].rTimeout * 2; // BackOff Algorithm
      tcp_socket[i].retries--;
      tcp_resend(i+1);
    }
  }
  if (tcp_socket[i].cTimer == 1 && tcp_socket[i].state ==
                                    TCP_SOCKET_ESTABLISHED) {

    tcp_socket[i].event_handler(i+1,TCP_EVENT_cTOUT,
                              tcp_socket[i].remote_ip,tcp_socket[i].remote_port,
                              TCP_DATA_START, 0);

    tcp_send_reset(i+1,tcp_socket[i].remote_ip,tcp_socket[i].remote_port);
    tcp_socket_close(i+1);
  }
 }
}
```

The above code loops for the entire socket table. For each entry, if the retransmission timer has expired and the retries variable is greater than zero, this variable is decremented and the segment is retransmitted using the BackOff algorithm (the time is duplicated). If the retransmission timer expires, and no retries are left, the application is notified with the TCP_EVENT_rTOUT event and the socket is closed. Note that the rTimer is also used when the socket is in the TCP_SOCKET_TIME_WAIT state to wait a time before closing the socket, so if the socket is in this state, the application is notified with the TCP_EVENT_CONN_CLOSED event instead of the TCP_EVENT_rTOUT event.

The second part of the code detects a connection time out (the cTimer expired while the socket was in the TCP_SOCKET_ESTABLISHED state). In this case, the application is notified with the TCP_EVENT_cTOUT event, an RST segment is sent to the remote device, and the socket is closed.

The above procedures follow the time-out procedures described in the TCP states diagrams (Figures 17.2–17.6).

Once the loss of a segment is assumed, it must be retransmitted using the **tcp_resend( )** routine:

```
void tcp_resend(int socket) {
  unsigned short len=0;
  int iSocket = socket-1;

  if (tcp_validate_socket(socket) == TCP_INVALID_SOCKET)
    return;
  if (tcp_socket[iSocket].state == TCP_SOCKET_ESTABLISHED) {
    len = tcp_socket[iSocket].sndnxt - tcp_socket[iSocket].snduna;
    tcp_socket[iSocket].position – = len;
    tcp_socket[iSocket].more_data = tcp_socket[iSocket].fill_buffer(socket,
                                        &tcp_socket[iSocket].position, &len);
    len = tcp_socket[iSocket].sndnxt - tcp_socket[iSocket].snduna;
    tcp_socket[iSocket].sndnxt = tcp_socket[iSocket].snduna;
    printf("Resending...\r\n");
    tcp_send(socket, len);
    return;
  }
  if (tcp_socket[iSocket].state == TCP_SOCKET_CLOSING ||
                        tcp_socket[iSocket].state == TCP_SOCKET_LAST_ACK)
    tcp_socket[iSocket].flags = FIN;
  tcp_socket[iSocket].sndnxt = tcp_socket[iSocket].snduna;
  tcp_send(socket, 0);
}
```

This routine starts validating the socket. After this, the last segment sent by this socket must be retransmitted. This means that we need to reconstruct the segment as it was sent. Note that our implementation does not use a retransmission queue as mentioned in Chapter 6. In such case, it would be very easy to recover the segment from the queue. However, the stack implementation for embedded systems is restricted in the memory usage, so no retransmission queue is used. In fact, the application does not have a buffer to store the data before it is being sent. Instead, the application creates the data to be sent 'on the fly' at the time the TCP module requests it for its transmission.

Now, if the socket is in the TCP_SOCKET_ESTABLISHED state, the last segment was a data segment. The unacknowledged data (sndnxt – snduna) will give us the length of data (len). We need to adjust the position, and then call the **fill_buffer( )** function to fill the segment with the same data which contained the last segment sent. As this function changes the len variable, we need to re-calculate the length of data. Lastly, the sndnxt pointer is put as before the segment was sent, and the complete segment is retransmitted using the **tcp_send( )** routine.

However, if the socket is in the TCP_SOCKET_CLOSING or TCP_SOCKET_LAST_ACK states, the last segment sent was a FIN, so this flag is set. Then, the sndnxt pointer is put as before the segment was sent, and the segment is retransmitted using the **tcp_send( )** routine. Note that this last routine will set the appropriate flags for any other socket state.

17.2.11 Support routines

In this section, we will see the rest of the functions of the **tcp.c** module. The following is the **tcp_validate_socket( )**;

```
int tcp_validate_socket(int socket) {

  if ((socket < 1) || (socket > TCP_MAX_SOCKETS)) {
    printf("TCP: Invalid Socket Error!\r\n");
    return TCP_INVALID_SOCKET;
  }
  return 0;
}
```

This function simply checks if the passed socket has an invalid value. If so, it returns the TCP_INVALID SOCKET value.

The **tcp_get_port( )** function is implemented as follows:

```
short tcp_get_port(int socket) {
  int iSocket = socket-1;

  if (tcp_validate_socket(socket) == TCP_INVALID_SOCKET)
    return TCP_SOCKET_ERROR;
  return tcp_socket[iSocket].local_port;
}
```

The above function returns, after validating the passed socket, the local port assigned to this socket.

The **check_free_port( )** function searches in the socket's table to see if the passed port exists:

```
int check_free_port(unsigned short port) {
  int i;

  for(i=0; i<TCP_MAX_SOCKETS; i++) {
    if (tcp_socket[i].local_port == port)
      return 0;
  }
  return 1;
}
```

The **get_ISN( )** function returns a pseudo-random number to be used as the ISN in the TCP Connection Establishment session:

```
unsigned int get_ISN(void) {
  return ((rand()<<16)+rand());
}
```

The **get_remote_mss( )** function searches for the remote device's MSS value:

```
unsigned short get_remote_mss(void) {
  int i;

  for (i=0;i<opt_len;) {
    if (rx_buf[TCP_DATA_START+i]<2) {
      i++;
    }else {
      if (rx_buf[TCP_DATA_START+i]==2) {
        return ((rx_buf[TCP_DATA_START+i+2]<<8) +
                                        rx_buf[TCP_DATA_START+i+3]);
      }
      i += (rx_buf[TCP_DATA_START+i+1]);
    }
  }
  // if mss option is not found , return default 536
  return 536;
}
```

This function searches for the option-kind 2 (the MSS) in the TCP header options of the SYN or SYN+ACK message received from the remote device, during the TCP Connection Establishment process. If this option is found, the option-data value is returned. Otherwise, the default value (536) is returned instead.

The **get_max_len( )** function returns the maximum allowable segment data size:

```
short get_max_len(int socket) {
  int iSocket = socket-1;

  if (tcp_validate_socket(socket) == TCP_INVALID_SOCKET)
    return TCP_SOCKET_ERROR;
  max_len = tcp_socket[iSocket].remote_mss;
  if (max_len > tcp_socket[iSocket].sndwnd)
    max_len = tcp_socket[iSocket].sndwnd;
  if (max_len > TCP_DATA_MAX)
    max_len = TCP_DATA_MAX;
  return max_len;
}
```

The function first validates the passed socket. After this, the remote's MSS is considered. If this value is greater than the send window size (the maximum data size the receiver is willing to accept), the sndwnd is adopted. Finally, the function checks the size does not exceed the TCP_DATA_MAX value. The resulting value is saved in the max_len variable and returned to the caller.

Finally, the **tcp_sockets_show( )** routine display the socket's table in the console:

```
void tcp_sockets_show(void) {
  int i;
  char state[10];
  struct tcb* pSocket;

  printf("\r\nSocket State  Loc_Port   Rem_IP    Rem_Port cTimer\r\n");
  printf("--------------------------------------------------------\r\n");
  for(i=0; i<TCP_MAX_SOCKETS; i++) {
    pSocket = &tcp_socket[i];
    switch(pSocket->state) {
      case 0: sprintf(state, "%s", "Free     "); break;
      case 1: sprintf(state, "%s", "Closed   "); break;
      case 2: sprintf(state, "%s", "Listen   "); break;
      case 3: sprintf(state, "%s", "Syn_Sent "); break;
      case 4: sprintf(state, "%s", "Syn_Recvd "); break;
      case 5: sprintf(state, "%s", "Establish."); break;
      case 6: sprintf(state, "%s", "Fin_Wait_1"); break;
      case 7: sprintf(state, "%s", "Fin_Wait_2"); break;
      case 8: sprintf(state, "%s", "Closing   "); break;
      case 9: sprintf(state, "%s", "Time_Wait "); break;
      case 10: sprintf(state, "%s", "Close_Wait"); break;
      case 11: sprintf(state, "%s", "Last_Ack "); break;
      default: sprint(state, "%s", "Unknown! "); break
  }
  if (pSocket->state < 2)
    printf(" %2d   %s\r\n", i+1, state);
  else if (pSocket->state == 2)
    printf(" %2d   %s  %4d\r\n", i+1, state, pSocket->local_port);
  else
    printf(" %2d   %s  %4d   %d.%d.%d.%d\t%4d  %d\r\n", i+1, state,
                                  pSocket->local_port,
                                  pSocket->remote_ip[0], pSocket->remote_ip[1],
                                  pSocket->remote_ip[2], pSocket->remote_ip[3],
                                  pSocket->remote_port, pSocket->cTimer);
}
  printf("--------------------------------------------------------\r\n");
}
```

This routine displays each entry of the socket's table. It displays different fields, according to the socket state. This routine is provided for debugging and educational purposes.

Lab 8: Working with TCP segments

Lab 8 introduction

In this Lab, we will use TCP-based connections to transfer data between the board and the PC.

Lab 8 target support

This Lab supports both types of boards. Select the appropriate target board from the 'Configuration drop-down menu' in the Workspace window.

Lab 8 options setting

This Lab requires the debug_tcp option to be set.

Lab 8 utilities used

In this Lab, we will use the TCP Console Panel to handle connections and transfer data. See the 'Getting Started' guide for help on this utility.

Lab 8 instructions

Complete the steps according to Chapter 12 (see section 12.6). Once the Lab is running, follow the Lab 8 exercises. If you use the LPC-P212X board, you must make the dial-up connection before sending or receiving any TCP segment. In Windows XP, check that the Windows Firewall is configured to allow outgoing destination unreachable ICMP packets, or deactivate the Firewall for this Lab.

Lab 8 exercises

- Start the TCP Console Panel utility using 192.168.0.30 as the remote IP address (or 192.168.0.51 for the LPC-P212X boards) and 1066 as the remote port. Initiate a TCP connection from the TCP Console Panel, and verify that the SYN message arrives at the board. However, the destination port 1066 is not bound to any socket. Check this, pressing the 'S' key to see that all sockets in the table are in the 'free' state. Verify the TCP Console Panel gets an error, indicating the connection could not be established. The board should respond with a Protocol Unreachable ICMP error. Note that in the Ethernet boards, this may not happen the first time, because the ICMP message may not be sent if the destination MAC address is not found in the ARP table. Instead, the 'ARP Entry not found!' message should appear.
- Analyse the received TCP messages. Compare their structure with the TCP message structure. Check that destination IP address and port value coincide with those specified in the TCP Console Panel. Capture the messages with Ethereal and analyse the messages.
- Press the 'h' key to see the available help. Press 'O' to open a TCP socket at port 1066. Now, initiate a connection from the TCP Console Panel. Check that a connection request message arrives at the board, and no ICMP message is sent to the TCP Console Panel. This is because a TCP socket is now open and listening at port 1066 (press the 'S' key to check this). Verify that connection request messages is accepted and the connection is established. Examine the handshaking with Ethereal.
- Press the 'J' key to reject all subsequent TCP connection requests. Initiate connection from the TCP Control Panel, and verify that all connection request messages are rejected (an RST segment is sent to the PC). Check this with Ethereal. Use the 'J' key to accept TCP connection requests again.

- Once you get a TCP connection established, send data from the TCP Console Panel. Analyse the data segment received in the board. Press 'D' to send data to the PC. Check if the 'Hello World!' data is received in the TCP Console Panel. Press the 'S' key to see if a new socket was created and it is handling this connection. Close the connection from the TCP Console Panel (using the Disconnect button), and verify the FIN message arrives at the board. Press 'S' to check the previously opened socket is now closed (in the 'free' state). Examine this using Ethereal.
- When a TCP connection has been established, press the 'S' key many times and check the connection timer (cTimer) is continuously decremented. Send data from the TCP Console Panel and verify the cTimer is re-started from 1200 (the TCP_DEF_cTOUT value). If no activity is detected, the cTimer will time out, and the connection will be ended. Press the 'S' key and verify the previously assigned socket is now free.
- While a TCP connection is established, press the 'R' key to enable the Retransmission Test mode. The code was slightly modified to not process the ACK messages from the PC (while the socket is in the TCP_SOCKET_ESTABLISHED state), so the socket retransmission timer (rTimer) will time out, and the data will be resent. Now, press the 'D' key and check the 'Hello World!' data is sent to the PC. Although the ACK received from the PC is displayed, it is not processed so, once the rTimer expires, the data is retransmitted. Verify each time the data is retransmitted that the PC acknowledges the data but it is not displayed in the TCP Console Panel, because the PC's stack recognizes this data as duplicated (with the same sequence number). Check that the time between each retransmission is duplicated following a back-off algorithm. Examine the segments with Ethereal. Once the data has been retransmitted several times, the socket is closed. Press 'S' to verify this. Press 'R' again to disable the Retransmission Test mode.
- Open several instances of the TCP Console Panel simultaneously. Try to connect each instance with the board. Try to transfer data from each instance to the board, and vice versa. Note that the 'D' option sends data to the last socket that establishes a connection or receives data from the PC. Press the 'S' key and verify that several sockets are opened at the same time. This exercise corroborates that the TCP implementation supports multiple connections simultaneously.

18

UDP-based and TCP-based embedded server applications

Now that our TCP/IP stack has implemented a Transport layer, we may start using it to remotely manage our embedded application. Even though most Internet applications use Application layer protocols such as SMTP, FTP or HTTP, sometimes it is convenient to use the Transport layer directly for our communications needs. In this chapter, we will see how this type of communication allows us to efficiently manage any embedded system application from the Internet.

18.1 Introduction

In Lab 1 (Chapter 13) we saw how the simulated application can be managed from the console, using the following commands:

- *Start cycle* (s): it starts the application process cycle.
- *Get parameters* (p): it gets the current parameters from the application process.
- *Cycle* (c): it sets/clears the cycle variable, so the application process runs continuously.
- *Board activity LED* (l): it enables/disables the board activity LED.

Now that the embedded system has an embedded TCP/IP stack, we could use the Transport layer to transmit the above commands from any device connected to the network/inter-network. In this way, the application could be remotely managed from any place in the world.

In order to implement the above, we need two components:

- A **client component** running in any device, which allows us to send the necessary commands to the embedded system using the TCP/IP Transport layer, in order to manage the embedded application.
- An **embedded server component** running at the embedded system, which responds to the commands sent from the client component.

As the Transport layer offers two protocols for data transfer, two versions of the above components can be implemented: the UDP-based and the TCP-based components.

18.1.1 The client component

The client component may be any software application that can transfer data using any of the TCP/IP Transport layer protocols. Even an embedded system with TCP/IP communications could accomplish this.

In our case, we will use a Windows (Microsoft Operating System) Desktop application, which is able to communicate with an embedded system using TCP or UDP. The application sends commands and gets responses from the embedded system in order to control and monitor the embedded application. The communication view shows the embedded system responses. A graphical view of the simulated application allows the user to see what is happening in the embedded application in a remote fashion.

The following screenshot shows a client component, called **Application Control Panel**, used in the present chapter's Labs.

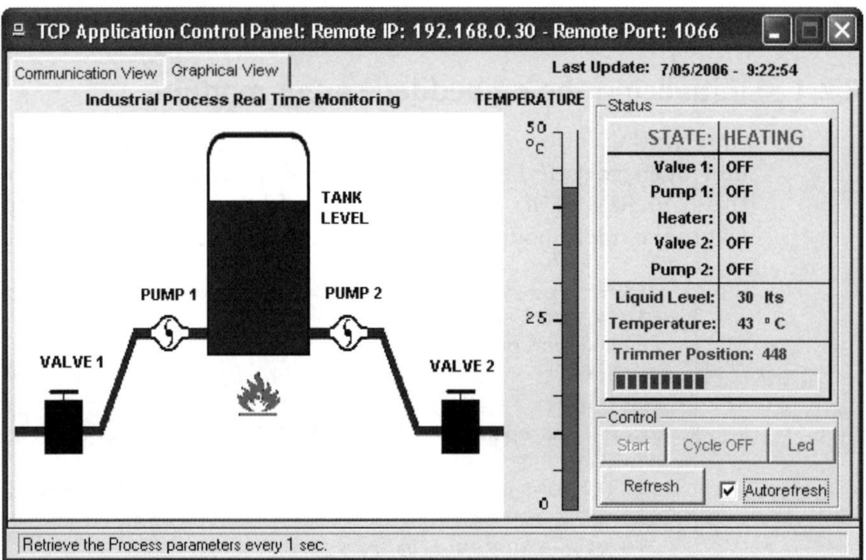

18.1.2 The embedded server component

In order for the client component to manage the embedded application, an embedded server must be running at the embedded system. This embedded server receives commands from the client component and responds to those commands, either performing some action or sending the requested information. Depending on the transport protocol the embedded server uses to communicate with the client component, a UDP-based or a TCP-based embedded server version will be required.

18.2 Implementing the UDP-based embedded server

Like any other server, the embedded server is an application waiting for a client's request, and responding accordingly. In this case, the embedded server is waiting for requests at port 1066. When a client request arrives at this port, the **udp_process( )** routine from the **udp.c** module uses the socket event handler to notify the application with the UDP_EVENT_DATA event, and passes the data to it. The embedded server parses the request and assembles the response. Then, the response is sent using the **udp_send( )** routine. However, before this can happen, the embedded server module must be properly initialized. The **udp_server.c** module implements this embedded server.

18.2.1 Initializing the embedded server module

The initialization routine opens a UDP socket at port 1066. The **udp_open_socket( )** function is called with the desired port value, the UDP_CHKSUM_SEND option, and the address of the **udp_control( )** routine, where the **udp.c** module will notify when data arrives at this port.

```
void udp_server_init(void) {
  unsigned short port;

  port = 1066;
  socket = udp_open_socket(port, UDP_CHKSUM_SEND, udp_control);
  if (socket > 0) {
    printf("UDP Socket %d created, port %d\n", socket, udp_get_port(socket));
  }else {
    if (socket == UDP_INVALID_SOCKET) {
      printf("Error opening a socket: increment UDP_MAX_SOCKETS=%d\n",
                                                        UDP_MAX_SOCKETS);
    }
    if (socket == UDP_PORT_ALREADY_USED) {
      printf("Error opening a socket: Port %d already used\n", port);
    }
  }
}
```

If the **udp_open_socket( )** function returns an invalid socket, the corresponding error is shown.

18.2.2 Handling the events

In order to receive the events from the **udp.c** module, a call-back function is declared when the socket is opened. The address of this function is saved in the socket's event handler, so when an event occurs, the **udp.c** module notifies the call-back function about this event. In our case, the call-back function is named **udp_control**.

The following code shows the **udp_control( )** call-back function implementation:

```
static void udp_control(int soc_handler, char event,
                        char *srcipaddr, unsigned short srcport,
                        unsigned short data_index, unsigned short data_len) {
  int i;

  event = event;                  //avoid compiler warning
  data_len = data_len;            //avoid compiler warning
  if (soc_handler != socket) {
    printf("The socket handler is erroneous! %d %d\n",soc_handler, socket);
    return;
  }
#if debug_udp_server
  printf("Socket: %d",socket);
  switch(event) {
    case UDP_EVENT_DATA:
      printf(" - Event: Data Available");
      break;
    default:
      printf(" - Unknown Event: %d",event);
      break;
  }
  printf(" from IP address: %d.%d.%d.%d Port: %d\n",
                *srcipaddr,*(srcipaddr+1),*(srcipaddr+2),*(srcipaddr+3),srcport);
  printf("Command: %c\r\n", rx_buf[data_index]);
#endif
...
```

When the **udp.c** module calls this call-back function, the event and its associated parameters are passed. The first two lines just avoid a compiler warning, as these parameters are not used in the routine (event is used only when the debug_udp_server option is set). After this, the socket passed is validated against the previously saved when the socket was opened at the initialization routine. If they differ, an error is shown.

If the debug_udp_server option is set in the **debug.h** file, the passed parameters are displayed for debugging purposes. The command received from the client is also shown. After this, the routine processes the request (data received), and assembles the response accordingly. That is, for the s, c, or l commands, the corresponding variable is set and the 'OK' response is assembled; for the p command, the application parameters are copied into the response; and for any other request, the 'ERROR' response is assembled, indicating the command is unrecognized. The last step is to send the data using the **udp_send( )** routine at the Transport layer. The next code fragment shows how the above is implemented:

```
...
switch(rx_buf[data_index]) {
  case 's':              // start
   if (state == STOP) {
     state = STARTED;
     i = sprintf(&tx_buf[data_index],"OK");
   } else
     i = sprint(&tx_buf[data_index],"ERROR");
     break;
  case 'c':              // cycle
    if (cycle)
      cycle = 0;
    else
      cycle = 1;
    i = sprintf(&tx_buf[data_index],"OK");
    break;
  case 'p':              // get parameters
    i = sprintf(&tx_buf[data_index],"S=%d A=%d H=%d B=%d L=%d
                                               T=%d R=%d C=%d",
            state,valve1,heater,valve2,liquid,temp,ADC_Read(),cycle);
    break;
  case 'l':              // Board Activity Led
    if (led_enable)
      led_enable = 0;
    else
      led_enable = 1;
    i = sprintf(&tx_buf[data_index],"OK");
    break;
  default:
    i = sprintf(&tx_buf[data_index],"ERROR");
    break;
}
udp_send(socket,srcipaddr,srcport,i);
}
```

Lab 9: UDP-based embedded server

Lab 9 introduction

In this Lab, we will monitor and control the embedded application through a network/Internet connection, using the UDP protocol.

Lab 9 target support

This Lab supports both types of boards. Select the appropriate target board from the 'Configuration drop-down menu' in the Workspace window.

Lab 9 options setting

This Lab requires the debug_udp_server option to be set.

Lab 9 utilities used

In this Lab, we will use the UDP-based Application Control Panel to remotely manage the embedded application. See the 'Getting Started' guide for help on this utility.

Lab 9 instructions

Complete the steps according to Chapter 12 (see section 12.6). Once the Lab is running, follow the Lab 9 exercises. If you use the LPC-P212X board, you must make the dial-up connection before executing the lab exercises.

Lab 9 exercises

- Start the UDP-based Application Control Panel using 192.168.0.30 as the remote IP address, (or 192.168.0.51 for the LPC-P212X boards), and 1066 as the remote port.
- From the Application Control Panel, select the Communication View tab and press the 'Start UDP' button. Then, send the 'l' command. Verify the data is received at the board, and the Board Activity LED is disabled. Use the same command again to enable the LED.
- Use the 's' command in the Application Control Panel to start the application process cycle. Check the yellow LED is blinking, indicating the process has started.
- Use the 'p' command to get the application process parameters. Send this command several times, and verify the parameters vary according to the process cycle state.
- Use the 'c' command to have the process running continuously.
- Set the Application Control Panel Auto-refresh option in order to get the application process parameters automatically every one second. Select the Graphical View tab and verify the figure reflects the application process cycle in a graphical fashion.

18.3 Implementing the TCP-based embedded server

The TCP-based version of the embedded server works in the same way as its counterpart (UDP-based), but it uses TCP as the transport protocol. The **tcp_server.c** module implements this. The first step in the implementation is to initialize the module.

18.3.1 Initializing the embedded server module

The initializing routine opens a TCP socket at port 1066, and if there are no errors, it puts the socket in the listen state in order to accept incoming requests.

The **tcp_socket_open( )** function opens a TCP socket at port 1066, and saves the address of the **tcp_control( )** routine (the call-back function) for future reference. If there are no errors, the **tcp_listen( )** routine puts the socket in the listen state.

```
void tcp_server_init(void) {
  int socket;
  unsigned short port;

  port = 1066;
  socket = tcp_socket_open(port, tcp_control);
  if (socket > 0) {
    printf("TCP Socket %d created, port %d\n", socket, tcp_get_port(socket));
  }else {
    if (socket == TCP_INVALID_SOCKET) {
      printf("Error opening a socket: increment TCP_MAX_SOCKETS=%d\n",
                                                       TCP_MAX_SOCKETS);
    }
    if (socket == TCP_PORT_ALREADY_USED) {
      printf("Error opening a socket: Port %d already used\n", port);
    }
    return;                    // Error
  }
  if (tcp_listen(socket) < 0) {
    printf("Error: socket %d can not put in LISTEN state\n", socket);
    return;                    // Error
  }else {
    printf("TCP Socket %d listening on Port %d\n", socket, tcp_get_port(socket));
  }
}
```

18.3.2 Handling the events

The **tcp_control( )** routine is used as a call-back function which the TCP module will notify for occurred events. Each time this routine is called, an action is performed according to the notified event. See this function implementation:

```
static void tcp_control(int soc_handler, char event,
                        char *srcipaddr, unsigned short srcport,
                        unsigned short data_index, unsigned short data_len) {
  int resp;

  data_len = data_len;                          //avoid compiler warning
  switch(event) {
   case TCP_EVENT_CONN_REQ:
     if (debug_tcp_server)
       printf("Connection Request from IP: %d.%d.%d.%d - Port: %d\n",
              *srcipaddr,*(srcipaddr+1),*(srcipaddr+2),*(srcipaddr+3),srcport)
     resp = tcp_conn_accept(soc_handler);
     if (resp == TCP_SOCKET_ERROR)
       printf("Accept Error: no free socket available\n");
     else {
       if (debug_tcp_server)
         printf("Socket %d created\n", resp);
     }
     break;
     ...
```

The code implements a switch( ) statement based on the notified event. If the event is a TCP_EVENT_CONN_REQ (Connection Request), the **tcp_conn_accept( )** function is called in order to accept the incoming request. The following code shows the process for the rest of the events:

```
  ...
  case TCP_EVENT_ESTABLISHED:
    if (debug_tcp_server)
      printf("Connection Established with IP: %d.%d.%d.%d - Port: %d\n",
                *srcipaddr,*(srcipaddr+1),*(srcipaddr+2),*(srcipaddr+3),srcport);
    break;
  case TCP_EVENT_DATA:
    if (debug_tcp_server)
      printf("Event: Data Available from IP: %d.%d.%d.%d - Port: %d\n",
                *srcipaddr,*(srcipaddr+1),*(srcipaddr+2),*(srcipaddr+3),srcport);
    command[soc_handler] = rx_buf[data_index];
    printf("Command: %c\r\n", command[soc_handler]);
    if (tcp_send_data(soc_handler, create_response) == TCP_SOCKET_ERROR)
      printf("Error sending data: TCP already have data to send!\r\n");
    break;
  case TCP_EVENT_SEND_COMPLETED:
    break;
  case TCP_EVENT_CONN_CLOSED:
    tcp_socket_close(soc_handler);
    if (debug_tcp_server)
      printf("Socket %d closed\n", soc_handler);
    break;
  case TCP_EVENT_RESET:
    printf("Error: Socket %d was Reset\r\n", soc_handler);
    break;
  case TCP_EVENT_rTOUT:
    printf("Error: Socket %d Timed Out\r\n", soc_handler);
    break;
  case TCP_EVENT_cTOUT:
    printf("Error: Connection in socket %d Timed Out\r\n", soc_handler);
    break;
  case TCP_EVENT_CLOSE_REQ:
    tcp_conn_close(soc_handler);
    break;
  default:
    printf("Unknown Event: %d\n",event);
    break;
 }
}
```

When the TCP_EVENT_DATA event is notified, the command is saved to process it later and the **tcp_send_data( )** routine is called to send the response. Remember that the data to send will be later filled in the transmit buffer by the **fill_buffer( )** routine (in this case, it is named as **create_response( )**).

If the TCP_EVENT_CLOSE_REQ event is notified, the **tcp_conn_close( )** routine is called to close the connection. When the TCP_EVENT_CONN_CLOSED event is informed, the socket is closed with the **tcp_socket_close( )** routine. For the rest of the events, a message is shown in the console.

18.3.3 Processing the commands

Each time a TCP_EVENT_DATA event is notified, the received data should have the requested command. As the TCP send data mechanism requires the application to inform it of the address of the routine which will fill the transmit buffer with the data to send, the command is saved to be later processed when the application fills the data to send. The routine that creates the response and fills the transmit buffer is the **create_response( )** routine. See its implementation in the following code:

```
int create_response(int soc_handler, unsigned short *position,
                                                        unsigned short *len) {
 int i;

 switch(command[soc_handler]) {
  case 's':                    // start
   if (state == STOP) }
     state = STARTED;
     i = sprintf(&tx_buf[TCP_DATA_START],"OK");
   }else
     i = sprintf(&tx_buf[TCP_DATA_START],"ERROR");
    break;
  case 'c':                    // cycle
   if (cycle)
     cycle = 0;
   else
     cycle = 1;
   i = sprintf(&tx_buf[TCP_DATA_START],"OK");
   break;
  case 'p':                    // get parameters
   i=sprintf(&tx_buf[TCP_DATA_START],"S=%d A=%d H=%d B=%d L=%d
                                                  T=%d R=%d C=%d",
               state,valve1,heater,valve2,liquid,temp,ADC_Read(),cycle);
   break;
  case 'l':
   if (led_enable)
     led_enable = 0;
   else
     led_enable = 1;
   i = sprintf(&tx_buf[TCP_DATA_START],"OK");
   break;
  default:
   i = sprintf(&tx_buf[TCP_DATA_START],"ERROR");
   break;
 }
 (*len) -= i;
 (*position) += i;
 return 0;
}
```

This routine processes the command accordingly, and fills the transmit buffer with the data to send (the response). After this, the passing parameters (len and position) are updated as required by the TCP send data mechanism.

Lab 10: TCP-based embedded server

Lab 10 introduction

In this Lab, we will monitor and control the embedded application through a network/Internet connection, using the TCP protocol.

Lab 10 target support

This Lab supports both types of boards. Select the appropriate target board from the 'Configuration drop-down menu' in the Workspace window.

Lab 10 options setting

This Lab requires the debug_tcp_server option to be set.

Lab 10 utilities used

In this Lab, we will use the TCP-based Application Control Panel to remotely manage the embedded application. See the 'Getting Started' guide for help on this utility.

Lab 10 instructions

Complete the steps according to Chapter 12 (see section 12.6). Once the Lab is running, follow the Lab 10 exercises. If you use the LPC-P212X board, you must make the dial-up connection before executing the lab exercises.

Lab 10 exercises

- Start the TCP-based Application Control Panel using 192.168.0.30 as the remote IP address, (or 192.168.0.51 for the LPC-P212X boards) and 1066 as the remote port.
- From the Application Control Panel, select the Communication View tab and press the 'Connect' button to be connected with the board. Send the 'l' command. Verify the data is received at the board, and the Board Activity LED is disabled. Use the same command again to enable the LED.
- Use the 's' command in the Application Control Panel to start the application process cycle. Check the yellow LED is blinking, indicating the process has started.
- Use the 'p' command to get the application process parameters. Send this command several times, and verify the parameters vary according to the process cycle state.
- Use the 'c' command to have the process running continuously.
- Set the Application Control Panel Auto-refresh option in order to get the application process parameters automatically every second. Select the Graphical View tab and verify the figure reflects the application process cycle in a graphical fashion.

▶

19

Sending e-mail messages: SMTP

This chapter introduces the SMTP protocol implementation, which will allow our embedded application to send e-mail messages around the world. The e-mail is a 'push technology' which allows the users to receive news and notifications without having to 'search' for them (unlike the 'pull technologies' where the user must search for them; for example, the WWW). This has an interesting application in embedded systems where the operator or supervisor can be warned about certain events, such as system reports, alarms, operator intervention requests, etc. In the present Lab we will have the opportunity to see how our embedded system 'talks' to the SMTP server, in order to accomplish its task.

19.1 Introduction

The **smtp.c** module implements the SMTP protocol used to send e-mail messages from the embedded system. This module provides the **smtp_sendmail( )** function, which requires the following parameters:

- **Recipient** (const char []): this parameter is used to provide the e-mail address of the destination user.
- **Subject** (const char []): this parameter is used to provide the text of the message's subject.
- **Body** (const char *): this parameter is used to provide the address of the message's body.
- **HTML_content** (char): this parameter is a flag which indicates if the message contains HTML (1) or plain text (0). This is necessary to include the appropriate 'Content-Type' header.
- **TagExpand_handler** (int *(TagExpand_handler( )): this parameter is used to pass the address of the function which implements the Tag Expand feature. This allows the messages to contain tags that can be dynamically 'expanded' or replaced with variable values. If this feature is not used, this parameter may be in zero.

It is worth noting that the **smtp.c** module is application independent, so it can be used in any embedded application without modifications. For this reason, the message itself and the Tag Expand implementation (which of course depend on the application) are implemented in separated modules.

The **console.c** module defines two body messages:

```
const char smtp_message0[] = "Hi:\r\nThis message is just to show you how emails are sent "
                        "from embedded systems\r\n\nBest Regards;\nSergio";

const char smtp_message1[] = "DATE: &20, &21,&22 &23\r\nTIME: &10:&11:&12 \r\n\n"
"This is a System Report from the Embedded Internet board:\r\n----------------------\r\n"
"STATE: &49 \r\nValve 1: &59 \r\nPump 1: &59 \r\nHeater:  &60 \r\nValve 2: &61 \r\n"
"Pump 2: &61 \r\n----------------------\r\nLiquid Level &62 ltrs \r\nTemperature: &63
                                                                              oC\r\n";
```

The **smtp_message0**[] consists of a simple text message, while the **smtp_message1**[] has a text message with tags. The tags consist of the '&' symbol followed by a 2-digit number. For example, the '&20' tag represents the day of the week, so it should be expanded to 'Saturday' (or any other day). In this way, our e-mail message may have inserted variable values, which are updated at the time the content is created. We need to provide a **TagExpand_handler( )** function which must expand these tags.

The following code shows how the **console.c** module uses the **smtp_sendmail( )** routine to send e-mail messages:

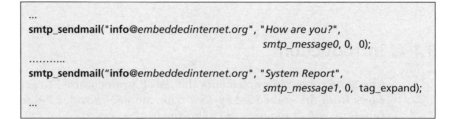

```
...
smtp_sendmail("info@embeddedinternet.org", "How are you?",
                                        smtp_message0, 0,  0);
...........
smtp_sendmail("info@embeddedinternet.org", "System Report",
                                        smtp_message1, 0,  tag_expand);
...
```

The first line calls the **smtp_sendmail( )** routine passing the destination e-mail address, the subject to include in the message, the address of the message's body, a zero value indicating the 'Content-Type' is text/plain, and finally a zero value indicating that no tags are included in the message. The second line calls the **smtp_sendmail( )** routine in a similar way, except for an address of the Tag Expand routine named **tag_expand( )**. This last is implemented in a separated module named **tagexpand.c**.

Once this routine has been called with the appropriate parameters, the **smtp.c** module makes everything that is necessary to send the message.

19.2 Implementing the SMTP module

In order for the SMTP module to send an e-mail, the following steps are required:

1 Establish a TCP connection with the SMTP server at Port 25.

2 When the '220' 'Ready' reply is received from the server, the 'HELO' command must be sent.
3 When the '250' 'Ok' reply is received from the server, the mail transaction begins:
   I The system sends the 'MAIL FROM:' command, specifying the sender e-mail address.
   II When a '250' 'Ok' reply is received, the system sends the 'RCPT TO:' command, specifying the recipient e-mail address.
   III When a '250' 'Ok' reply is received from the server, the system sends the 'DATA' command.
   IV When a '354' 'Start mail input' reply is received from the server, the system sends the e-mail header, the e-mail body and the End-Of-Message (EOM) indicator (<CRLF>.<CRLF>). This ends the mail transaction.
4 When the '250' 'Ok' reply has been received from the server, the 'QUIT' command is sent.
5 When the '221' 'Good bye' reply has been received from the server, the system closes the TCP connection.

The following sections show the code that implements the above steps.

19.2.1 The smtp_sendmail( ) routine implementation

This routine starts saving the address of the Tag Expand function into a pointer, and the e-mail recipient, subject and a body pointer into a structure named message.

```
void smtp_sendmail(const char recipient[], const char subject[],
                              const char *body, char html_content,
                              int (*TagExpand_handler) (char tagID,
                                     unsigned short pos, unsigned short len) ) {
  int socket = 0;
  TagExpand_SMTP =  TagExpand_handler;
  strcpy(message.recipient, recipient);
  strcpy(message.subject, subject);
  message.body = body;
  html = html_content;
  ...
```

The html variable saves the html_content value. All these parameters are saved into module's variables to be used later by other functions.

Next, a socket must be opened and a connection established with the SMTP server at port 25:

The **tcp_socket_open( )** is used to open a socket. As the port parameter is zero, the stack will assign a port value. The smtp_state_engine parameter specifies the address of the call-back function, which the stack will notify about all the events that have occurred.

```
  ...
  socket = tcp_socket_open(0, smtp_state_engine);
  if (socket > 0) {
    printf("TCP Socket %d created, port %d\n", socket, tcp_get_port(socket));
  }else {
    if (socket == TCP_INVALID_SOCKET) {
      printf("Error openning a socket: increment TCP_MAX_SOCKETS=%d\n",
                                                             TCP_MAX_SOCKETS);
    }
    return;                    // Error
  }
  SMTPstate = SMTP_initial;
  tcp_conn_open(socket, SMTPserver, 25);
}
```

Finally, the **tcp_conn_open( )** function is used to establish a connection with the SMTP server. The SMTPserver is a variable, which holds the SMTPServerIP value as it is assigned in the **stackcfg.h** file. This last also has the email address assigned to the embedded system:

```
...
// definitions for the SMTP.c Module
#define          SMTPServerIP    {192, 168, 0, 3}
#define          email           "Embedded Internet <test@embeddedinternet.org>"
...
```

In this case, the SMTP server is running in the PC with the IP address 192.168.0.3, but it could be in any other IP address as long as it is accessible from the embedded system.

19.2.2 SMTP state engine implementation

In order to accomplish the steps detailed above, a finite state machine is implemented. The SMTPstate variable will hold the current state of the FSM, initially set to the SMTP_initial value:

```
char SMTPstate = 0;
#define SMTP_initial          0
#define SMTP_ready            1
#define SMTP_from             2
#define SMTP_to               3
#define SMTP_data_header      4
#define SMTP_data_body        5
#define SMTP_data_EOM         6
#define SMTP_data_end         7
#define SMTP_quit             8
```

As stated above, the **smtp_state_engine( )** function will receive all the events regarding the connection. When the system establishes a TCP connection with the SMTP server, a TCP_EVENT_ESTABLISHED event is notified from the TCP module. If the debug_smtp option is set in the **debug.h** file, a message is shown in the console.

Immediately after the connection has been established, the SMTP server should send the '220' message. When this message arrives, the call-back function is notified with the TCP_EVENT_DATA event. Now, if the system corroborates that the '220' code was received, the 'HELO' command must be sent using the **tcp_send_data( )** function. Once the message is sent, the TCP_EVENT_SEND_COMPLETED event is notified. This last will make the FSM move to the next state, assigning the SMTP_ready value to the SMTPstate variable. In this way, the process follows until the FSM moves to the last state (SMTP_quit), according to the steps required to send the e-mail message.

This is the **smtp_state_engine( )** function implementation:

```
void smtp_state_engine(int soc_handler, char event, char *srcipaddr,
        unsigned short srcport, unsigned short data_index, unsigned short data_len) {

  int i;

  switch(event) {
    case TCP_EVENT_ESTABLISHED:
      if (debug_smtp)
        printf("Connection Established with IP: %d.%d.%d.%d - Port: %d\n",
                        *srcipaddr,*(srcipaddr+1),*(srcipaddr+2),*(srcipaddr+3),srcport);
      break;
    case TCP_EVENT_DATA:
      ...
      break;
    case TCP_EVENT_SEND_COMPLETED:
      ...
      break;
    case TCP_EVENT_CLOSE_REQ:
      tcp_conn_close(soc_handler);
      break;
    case TCP_EVENT_CONN_CLOSED:
      tcp_socket_close(soc_handler);
      if (debug_smtp)
        printf("Socket %d closed\n", soc_handler);
      break;
    case TCP_EVENT_RESET:
      printf("Error: Socket %d was Reset\r\n", soc_handler);
      break;
    case TCP_EVENT_rTOUT:
      printf("Error: Socket %d Timed Out\r\n", soc_handler);
      break;
    case TCP_EVENT_cTOUT:
      printf("Error: Connection in socket %d Timed Out\r\n", soc_handler);
      break;
    default:
      printf("Unknown Event: %d\n",event);
      break;
  }
}
```

The TCP_EVENT_DATA and TCP_EVENT_SEND_COMPLETED process will be seen later on. If the TCP_EVENT_CLOSE_REQ is notified, the **tcp_conn_close( )** function is called to close the connection. When the TCP_EVENT_CONN_CLOSED event is notified, the **tcp_socket_close( )** function is called to close the opened socket. For the rest of the events, a message is shown in the console.

The following code shows the process for the TCP_EVENT_DATA event:

```
...
case TCP_EVENT_DATA:
  if (debug_smtp) {
    printf("Event: Data Available from IP: %d.%d.%d.%d - Port: %d\n",
                *srcipaddr,*(srcipaddr+1),*(srcipaddr+2),*(srcipaddr+3),srcport);
    printf("Response: ");
    for(i=0;i<data_len;i++) {
      if (rx_buf[data_index+i] > 0x20)
        printf("%c", rx_buf[data_index+i]);
    }
    printf("\r\n");
  }
  switch(SMTPstate) {
    case SMTP_initial:
      if ( ! strncmp(&rx_buf[data_index], "220", 3)) {
        tcp_send_data(soc_handler, create_mail);
        return;
      }
      break;
    case SMTP_ready:
      if ( ! strncmp(&rx_buf[data_index], "250", 3)) {
        tcp_send_data(soc_handler, create_mail);
        return;
      }
      break;
    case SMTP_from:
      if ( ! strncmp(&rx_buf[data_index], "250", 3)) {
        tcp_send_data(soc_handler, create_mail);
        return;
      }
      break;
    case SMTP_to:
      if ( ! strncmp(&rx_buf[data_index], "250", 3)) {
        tcp_send_data(soc_handler, create_mail);
        return;
      }
      break;
    case SMTP_data_header:
      if ( ! strncmp(&rx_buf[data_index], "354", 3)) {
        tcp_send_data(soc_handler, create_mail);
        return;
      }
      break;
    case SMTP_data_end:
      if ( ! strncmp(&rx_buf[data_index], "250", 3)) {
        tcp_send_data(soc_handler, create_mail);
        return;
      }
      break;
      ...
```

```
  case SMTP_quit:
    if ( ! strncmp(&rx_buf[data_index], "221", 3)) {
      printf("Mail Send Completed!\r\n");
      return;
    }
    break;
  default:
    printf("SMTP State: Unknown\r\n");
    return;
}
printf("Unexpected Response from Server!\r\n");
break;
...
```

At the very beginning of the process, if the debug_smtp option is set, the response from the SMTP server is shown. After this, a switch( ) statement allows the system to send the appropriate command or data according to the SMTPstate variable value. However, before this, the expected response should be received from the SMTP server. Otherwise, the 'Unexpected Response from Server!' message is shown in the console.

Looking at the **tcp_send_data**( ) function, the **create_mail**( ) function is declared as the routine which will be called to fill the transmit buffer with the data to send. This routine will be seen shortly.

The following code shows the process for the TCP_EVENT_SEND_COMPLETED event:

```
...
case TCP_EVENT_SEND_COMPLETED:
  switch(SMTPstate) {
    case SMTP_initial:
      SMTPstate = SMTP_ready;
      break;
    case SMTP_ready:
      SMTPstate = SMTP_from;
      break;
    case SMTP_from:
      SMTPstate = SMTP_to;
      break;
    case SMTP_to:
      SMTPstate = SMTP_data_header;
        break;
    case SMTP_data_body:
      SMTPstate = SMTP_data_EOM;
      tcp_send_data(soc_handler, create_mail);
      break;
    case SMTP_data_EOM:
      SMTPstate = SMTP_data_end;
        break;
    case SMTP_data_end:
      SMTPstate = SMTP_quit;
      break;
    case SMTP_quit:
      SMTPstate = SMTP_initial;
      break;
  }
  break;
  ...
```

Each time the system sends data, the TCP_EVENT_SEND_COMPLETED event is notified when the data has been successfully transferred. The process for this event simply defines the next state of the SMTPstate variable, according to the current state. There is an exception for the SMTP_data_body state case, where additional data is sent when the previously sent data is complete. This is the case in which the message's body and the EOM are sent in separated segments. As the server will not respond until the EOM has been sent, we need to send the EOM as soon as we are notified that the message body was successfully transmitted. The separation of the message body from the EOM is not strictly necessary, but it is convenient for educational purposes.

19.2.3 Creating the e-mail content

Every time the **tcp_send_data( )** function is used, the TCP module calls the **fill_buffer** call-back function, in order for the application to fill the transmit buffer with the appropriate data. Remember that the call-back function is called with the data buffer's position to begin from, and the maximum length of data (len) to be filled in the transmit buffer, as parameters. Once the data has been filled, these parameters must be appropriately updated, and the function must return indicating if more data is left in the data buffer to be sent (in case the application data is larger than the maximum length allowable in each segment). In our case, the call-back function is implemented in the **create_mail( )** function, and it is implemented as follows:

```
int create_mail(int soc_handler, unsigned short *position, unsigned short *len) {
  char tagID;
  int tot, resp;
  static int pending;
  int j=TCP_DATA_START;
  static int length;

  soc_handler = soc_handler;     // avoid Compiler Warning
  switch(SMTPstate) {
    case SMTP_initial:
      tot=0;
      memcpy(&tx_buf[TCP_DATA_START+tot], "HELO SMTP_Embedded_Server\r\n", 27);
      tot+=27;
      (*position) += tot;
      (*len) -= tot;
      break;

    case SMTP_ready:
      tot=0;
      memcpy(&tx_buf[TCP_DATA_START+tot], "MAIL FROM: ", 11);
      tot += 11;
      length = strlen(sender);
      memcpy(&tx_buf[TCP_DATA_START + tot], sender, length);
      tot += length;
      memcpy(&tx_buf[TCP_DATA_START + tot], "\r\n", 2); tot += 2;
      (*position) += tot;
      (*len) -= tot;
      break;
      ...
```

As the data to send (commands or e-mail messages) depends on the FSM current state, a switch( ) statement will process the data according to the SMTPstate value. That is, in the SMTPinitial state the 'HELO ...' command is copied into the transmit buffer. After this, the position and len parameters are updated. When the SMTPstate is in the SMTP_ready state, the 'MAIL FROM: ...' command is loaded into the transmit buffer. See the rest of the code for other states:

```
...
case SMTP_from:
  tot=0;
  memcpy(&tx_buf[TCP_DATA_START+tot], "RCPT TO: ", 9);  tot+=9;
  length = strlen(message.recipient);
  memcpy(&tx_buf[TCP_DATA_START + tot], message.recipient, length);
  tot+=length;
  memcpy(&tx_buf[TCP_DATA_START + tot], "\r\n", 2); tot+=2;
  (*position) += tot;
  (*len) -= tot;
  break;

case SMTP_to:
  tot=0;
  memcpy(&tx_buf[TCP_DATA_START+tot], "DATA\r\n", 6); tot+=6;
  (*position) += tot;
  (*len) -= tot;
  break;

case SMTP_data_header:
  tot = 0;
  memcpy(&tx_buf[TCP_DATA_START+tot], "From: ", 6); tot += 6;
  length = strlen(sender);
  memcpy(&tx_buf[TCP_DATA_START+tot], sender, length); tot += length;
  memcpy(&tx_buf[TCP_DATA_START+tot], "\r\n", 2); tot += 2;
  memcpy(&tx_buf[TCP_DATA_START+tot], "To: ", 4); tot += 4;
  length = strlen(message.recipient);
  memcpy(&tx_buf[TCP_DATA_START+tot], message.recipient, length);
  tot += length;
  memcpy(&tx_buf[TCP_DATA_START+tot], "\r\n", 2); tot += 2;
  memcpy(&tx_buf[TCP_DATA_START+tot], "Subject: ", 9); tot += 9;
  length = strlen(message.subject);
  memcpy(&tx_buf[TCP_DATA_START+tot], message.subject, length);
  tot += length;
  if (html) {
    memcpy(&tx_buf[TCP_DATA_START+tot], "\r\nContent-Type: text/html\r\n", 27);
    tot += 27;
  }else {
    memcpy(&tx_buf[TCP_DATA_START+tot], "\r\nContent-Type: text/plain\r\n", 28);
    tot += 28;
  }
  memcpy(&tx_buf[TCP_DATA_START+tot], "\r\n\r\n", 4); tot += 4;
  (*len) -= tot;
  j += tot;
  SMTPstate = SMTP_data_body;
  length = strlen(message.body);
  // there is no break here intentionally!

case SMTP_data_body:
...
```

In the above code, the first two case statements copy the 'RCPT TO: …' and 'DATA' commands respectively. The next case statement, when the SMTPstate variable has the SMTP_data_header value, copies the e-mail message header into the transmit buffer. Here, the html variable is checked to include the appropriate 'Content-Type' header. After this, a blank line is inserted to delimiter the message header from the message body. Once the message header has been completed, the SMTPstate variable is moved to the SMTP_data_body state, and **no break** is used so the code will immediately continue with the SMTP_data_body case statement process. This is shown in the following code:

```
...
case SMTP_data_body:
  while (((*position) < length) && *len) {
    tx_buf[j] = *(message.body + (*position));
    if (tx_buf[j] == '&'  && TagExpand_SMTP) {

      tagID = ((*(message.body + (*position)+1)) - 0x30)*10 +
                  ((*(message.body + (*position)+2)) - 0x30);

      resp = TagExpand_SMTP(tagID, j, *len);
      if (resp == -2) {
        printf("Error: Tag &%02d not found\r\n", tagID);
      }else if (resp == -1) {
        return *len;              // the available space is not enough to expand the  tag...
      }else {
        j += resp;
        (*position) += 3;
        (*len) -= resp;
        continue;
      }
    }
    j++;
    (*position)++;
    (*len)--;
  }
  if ((*position) < length)
    return 1;
  else
    return 0;

case SMTP_data_EOM:
...
```

The while structure will loop as long as either the entire message body is copied into the transmit buffer or the maximum transmit buffer length is reached. In this loop, each message body character is copied into the buffer. If the character is a '&' (tag identifier) and the **smtp_sendmail( )** function was called declaring a TagExpand_handler, then the tagID is calculated (converted from its ASCII value into its numerical value), and the **TagExpand_SMTP** function is called (this is a pointer which points to the **tag_expand( )** function). If the **tag_expand( )** function returns –2, it means this tagID was not found. In this case, the '&' character remains unchanged. If the **tag_expand( )** function returns –1, it means that the buffer's available space was not enough to expand the tag, so the **create_mail( )** function returns, indicating that more data remains in the data buffer. Lastly, if the **tag_expand( )** function expands the tag successfully, the length of the expanded tag is returned. With this value, the position and len parameters are updated appropriately. Take into account that a tag such as '&20' may be expanded into 'Saturday', so the initial tag size (three characters) is now expanded to eight characters. This means that the actual message body length is different from that initially calculated. We will see more about this, in the next section where the **tag_expand( )** function implementation is shown.

If the character copied into the buffer is not a '&', it is left intact and the position and len parameters are updated accordingly.

Once the while( ) loop has ended, the position of the data buffer is compared to the body length, so if there is more data to be copied into the transmit buffer, a 1 is returned. Otherwise, a zero is returned indicating that there is no more data in the data buffer. Remember that we created data 'on the fly', so there is not actually a data buffer; this is just a way to indicate whether the application has more data to send. The rest of the code follows:

```
    ...
    case SMTP_data_EOM:
      tot=0;
      memcpy(&tx_buf[TCP_DATA_START+tot], "\r\n.\r\n", 5); tot += 5;
      (*position) += tot;
      (*len) -= tot;
      break;

    case SMTP_data_end:
      tot=0;
      memcpy(&tx_buf[TCP_DATA_START+tot], "QUIT\r\n", 6); tot+=6;
      (*position) += tot;
      (*len) -= tot;
      break;

    default:
      printf("SMTP State: Unknown\r\n");
      break;
  }
  return 0;            // It is supposed that the MAX Length is not exceeded
}
```

The last two case statements simply copy the EOM and the 'QUIT' command into the transmit buffer, respectively. It is worth noting that all case statements, except for the SMTP_data_header and SMTP_data_body, return 0 (last line of the above code), indicating there is no more data to send in the data buffer. This assumption may be taken only in those cases where the data length is so small that no more than one segment will ever be necessary to send the complete data.

19.2.4 Expanding tags

Tags are used as a way of creating dynamic data in an e-mail message or an HTML page. These tags are 'symbols' that will be replaced with the values they represent at the time the data is sent. Suppose we have the text 'Today is &20' where the '&20' is a tag that represents the day of the week. At the time this data is delivered, the tag would be expanded, creating the 'Today is Saturday' text. It seems very simple; however, there are some issues we need to consider. For example, note that the original text size was 12 characters, while the expanded text size is 17 characters. How can this affect it?

As we have already seen, when an application needs to send data using the TCP stream-oriented data send mechanism, it calls the **tcp_send_data( )** function, declaring a call-back function which will be called to fill the transmit buffer with the data to send. When this happens, the maximum length of data to fill the transmit buffer is passed, so if the available data to send is greater than this maximum value, once the data is copied, the call-back function returns, indicating there is more data to send. In this way, when the recently copied segment is sent and later acknowledged, the call-back function is called again to fill the buffer with the remaining data. This process continues until the application has sent all its data.

As we also saw, while the buffer is filled with the application data, if the '&' character is found, the **tag_expand( )** function is called in order to replace the tag with its corresponding value. Now, suppose the call-back function is filling the transmit buffer and a tag is found. Also suppose that the maximum transmit buffer length is 1460 bytes, and the application has already copied 1455 bytes, so only 5 bytes are available in order for the **tag_expand( )** function to expand the requested tag. What if this tag expands into more than 5 bytes? (as in the case with the 'Saturday' text). In these cases, the **tag_expand( )** function should return an error code (–1), indicating that the available transmit buffer space is not enough to expand the tag. Then, upon receipt of this error code, the fill buffer call-back function should return to allow the TCP module to send this segment, and complete with the Tag Expand in the next call-back function call.

Other issues may be presented when the tag is not found in the **tag_expand( )** function. In this case, there is no valid value with which to replace the tag, so an error code (–2) should be returned indicating this. Nevertheless, this situation may be an advantage in some cases. For example, let's consider the case in which the '&' character must appear in the message. In this case, this situation would represent an ambiguity. However, if the two following characters of the '&' define a tagID which is not found in the **tag_expand( )** function, an error is returned and the '&' is not replaced. In this way, we provide 'transparency' to the tag systems. The application rule would be: 'If an '&' must be in the text, just avoid defining this tagID in the **tag_expand( )** function.'

Finally, if the tagID is found, and there is enough space in the transmit buffer to expand the tag, the tag value is copied into the buffer and its length is returned. This length is used to update the **create_mail( )** function parameters. Let's see this code again:

```
...
case SMTP_data_body:
  while (((*position) < length) && *len) {
    tx_buf[j] = *(message.body + (*position));
    if (tx_buf[j] == '&' && TagExpand_SMTP) {

      tagID = ((*(message.body + (*position)+1)) - 0x30)*10 +
                        ((*(message.body + (*position)+2)) - 0x30);

      resp = TagExpand_SMTP(tagID, j, *len);
      if (resp == -2) {
        printf("Error: Tag &%02d not found\r\n", tagID);
      }else if (resp == -1) {
        return *len;                // the available space is not enough to expand the tag...
      }else {
        j += resp;
        (*position) += 3;
        (*len) -= resp;
        continue;
      }
    }
    ...
```

Notice that when the **tag_expand( )** function returns the length of the expanded tag, the *j* variable (which keeps the transmit buffer current position) and the len parameter are updated with this value. The position parameter is updated by 3 (the tag's length), because this parameter keeps the current position of the original message, which contains the tag.

The **tag_expand( )** implementation it is very simple, as the following code shows:

```
int tag_expand(char tagID, unsigned short pos, unsigned short len) {
  int i;

  switch(tagID) {
    case 10:
        ............
    case 11:
        ............
    case 20:
        ............
    default:
      return -2;
  }
}
```

This function is called with the tagID to expand the position of the transmit buffer (pos) indicating where to begin copying, and the length (len) of the available space in the transmit buffer, so the function does not override the buffer. A switch( ) structure allows the process of each tag individually. All existing tags must be declared in this structure. If the tagID is not found, the –2 code is returned.

Let's see the process for the '&20' tag as an example:

```
...
case 20:
  i = strlen(dow[DOW]);
  if (len<i)
     return -1;
  memcpy(&tx_buf[pos],dow[DOW],i);
  return i;
case 21:
...
```

The tag process consists of determining the length of the expanded tag. If len (the available space in the transmit buffer) is less than this value, a –1 is returned, indicating the available space is not enough to expand the tag. Otherwise, the tag is expanded into the transmit buffer, and the length of the expanded tag is returned.

As this process is similar for all tags, refer to the **tagexpand.c** module for the rest of the tags.

Lab 11: Sending e-mails

Lab 11 introduction

In this Lab, we will send e-mail messages from the embedded application using the SMTP protocol implementation.

Lab 11 target support

This Lab supports both types of boards. Select the appropriate target board from the 'Configuration drop-down menu' in the Workspace window.

Lab 11 options setting

This Lab requires the debug_smtp option to be set.

Lab 11 utilities used

In this Lab, we may use the free SMTP server program running in the PC. See the 'Getting Started' guide for help on this utility. If we wish to use any other SMTP server, we must set the SMTP server IP address and the sender e-mail address in the **stackcfg.h** file. This server should not require authentication for outgoing messages.

Lab 11 instructions

Complete the steps according to Chapter 12 (see section 12.6). Once the Lab is running, follow the Lab 11 exercises. If you use the LPC-P212X board, you must make the dial-up connection before executing the lab exercises.

Lab 11 exercises

- Change the e-mail destination address used in the **smtp_sendmail( )** function in the **console.c** module to the one you want. It is convenient to use your own e-mail address so you can check the results. If the Lab source code is changed, it must be rebuilt and downloaded to the embedded system in order for the changes to take effect.
- If the free SMTP server is to be used as the SMTP server, start this program. This program needs an Internet connection in order to send the e-mail messages.
- Press the 'h' key to see the available commands. Press the 'e' key to send an e-mail with a simple text message. See the responses from the SMTP server. Use Ethereal to analyse the 'conversation' between the SMTP server and the embedded system. Use your e-mail client program (such as Windows Outlook Express) to check if the message is received.
- Press the 'E' key to send an e-mail, which has tags in the text message. Once the e-mail arrives, check the embedded application variable values. Start the application process cycle and send e-mail messages every 10 seconds, until the process cycle ends. Compare the received e-mail messages and verify that the process's variables have the adequate values according to the process cycle state.

20

An embedded web server: HTTP

We have arrived at one of the most exciting and successful applications used in the Internet: the World Wide Web. In this chapter we will see how an embedded web server can be implemented that delivers HTML pages and images, allowing users to control and monitor the embedded application through a graphical and standard environment, using any desktop Internet browser. In the present Lab, we use the implemented embedded web server to monitor and control the application control process presented in the previous Labs. We will also see how to send e-mail messages from the embedded system through the web page. As a special bonus, we will send an e-mail from the system console, with a system report showing the application process in a graphical view.

20.1 Introduction

Typically, a web server delivers documents requested by browsers (web clients). When an HTTP Request arrives, the web server processes the command (GET, POST, etc.) and searches for the requested document, which is delivered to the browser. If the requested document is not found, a '404 Not Found' message must be sent. If the command requested is not recognized, a '501 Not Implemented' response must be sent.

If the command is a POST, the client is submitting data to the server for its processing. The web server should parse the submitted variables and process them accordingly. Once the HTTP Request has been processed, the HTTP Response must be assembled and sent to the client.

The above suggests that a file system must be implemented. This file system should have the entire web server documents loaded, before the web server is started.

20.2 Embedded web server implementation

20.2.1 Overview

Our embedded web server implementation is divided into two modules: the http.c module, which provides all the necessary web server routines that are application independent; and the web_server.c module, which provides the application-specific implementation. For this reason, the http.c module is included in the TCP/IP Stack files group, while the web_server.c module is in the application's source file group. In this way, the TCP/IP stack can be ported to any application without modifications.

When the web server is initialized, the http.c module opens a TCP socket at port 80 and puts it in the listen state, to accept incoming requests from the web clients. In addition, the http.c module declares the **tcp_control_process( )** routine to receive event notifications from the tcp.c module.

Figure 20.1 shows how an HTTP Request is processed by our web server implementation.

When the HTTP Request is received by the **tcp_process_segment( )** routine in the tcp.c module (1), the **http_control_process( )** is notified with the TCP_EVENT_DATA event (2). Then, the **HTTP_process( )** function is called in order to process the request (3).

If the HTTP Request command is a GET, the **getFileName( )** function is called to retrieve the file name from the Request-Line (4). If the command is a POST, the **process_POST( )** routine implemented in the **web_server.c** module is called in order to process the variables submitted by the browser (A). The **http.c** module provides the **parse_variable( )** function which helps this task (B). Once the POST data has been processed, the **getFileName( )** function is called to retrieve the requested file name. If the HTTP Request command was not recognized (other than a GET or POST), the –2 value is returned, indicating the requested command is not implemented (5).

When the **getFileName( )** gets the requested file name, the **HTTP_process( )** function must search this file in the file system. In case the requested file name was not found, the –1 value is returned indicating that the page was not found. Otherwise, the file system index is returned (5).

Once the **HTTP_process( )** returns a value, the requested document may be retrieved from the file system. If an error code was returned, an appropriate error page is addressed. With this, we are in a position to send the HTTP Response to the browser. **The tcp_send_data( )** routine is used for this purpose (6).

As we know, the **tcp_send_data( )** routine calls a call-back function to fill the transmit buffer (7). In this case, the **create_content( )** function creates the HTTP Response loading the status-line, the Content-Type header, the empty-line and the message-body (the requested page). Once the transmit buffer is filled, the **tcp_send( )** routine is called (8) in order to send out the HTTP Response (9).

20.2.2 Implementing the file system

The http.c module defines the following structure to support the file system:

```
struct {
  char              filename[13];
  const char        *contentpointer;
  unsigned short    contentsize;
  const char        *filepointer;
  unsigned short    filesize;
} filesystem[NUMBER_OF_FILES];
```

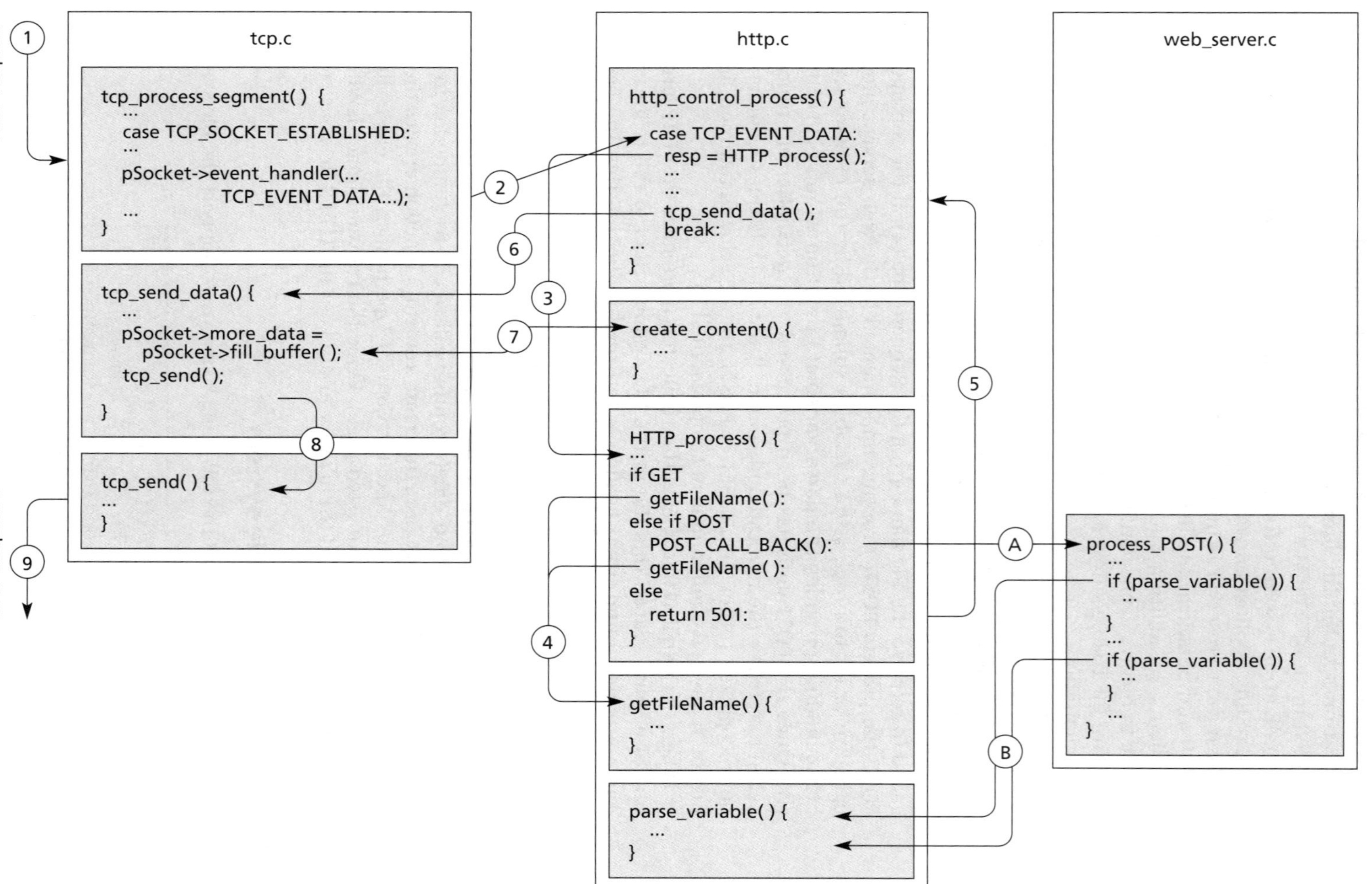

Figure 20.1 HTTP Request Processing.

The NUMBER_OF_FILES defines the maximum number of files supported, and it can be configured in the **http.h** header file. The structures on page 459 represents a table where each entry provides the file properties. The filename field holds the name of the file, as it will be requested by the browser in each request.

According to the type of file, the web server must include the appropriate 'Content-Type' header in the response. For this, the following file types are defined in the **http.c** module:

```
const char text[] = "Content-Type: text/plain\r\n";
const char html[] = "Content-Type: text/html\r\n";
const char gif[]  = "Content-Type: image/gif\r\nCache-Control: max-age 10000\r\n";
const char jpeg[] = "Content-Type: image/jpeg\r\nCache-Control: max-age 10000\r\n";
const char app[] =  "Content-Type: application/octet-stream\r\n";
```

The contentpointer field is a pointer that points to the corresponding 'Content-Type' string, while the contentsize field holds the 'Content-Type' string's size. The next field in the table is a pointer field named filepointer, which points to the start of the file's content. The last field, named filesize, holds the size of the file.

The **filesystem_add( )** routine inserts the file properties into the filesystem table:

```
void filesystem_add(int i, const char *filename, char type,
                                        const char *file, int filesize) {

  if (i >= NUMBER_OF_FILES) {
    printf("FileSystem Error: Increment the NUMBER_OF_FILES parameter\r\n");
    return;
  }
  memcpy(filesystem[i].filename,filename,13);
  switch (type) {
    case HTML:
      filesystem[i].contentpointer = html;
      filesystem[i].contentsize = sizeof(html)-1;
      break;
    case TEXT:
      filesystem[i].contentpointer = text;
      filesystem[i].contentsize = sizeof(text)-1;
      break;
    case GIF:
      filesystem[i].contentpointer = gif;
      filesystem[i].contentsize = sizeof(gif)-1;
      break;
    case JPEG:
      filesystem[i].contentpointer = jpeg;
      filesystem[i].contentsize = sizeof(jpeg)-1;
      break;
    default:
      filesystem[i].contentpointer = app;
      filesystem[i].contentsize = sizeof(app)-1;
  }
  filesystem[i].filepointer = file;
  filesystem[i].filesize = filesize;
}
```

First, the routine checks the table index against the size table. Then, the file name is copied into the **filename** field. The **switch( )** structure allows the appropriate file's '**Content-Type**' parameters to be saved in their respective fields. Finally, the address of the file and the file's size are copied into the **file** and **filesize** fields, respectively.

The **web_server.c** module initializes the file system through the **filesystem_init( )** routine:

```
void filesystem_init(void) {
  int i=0;

  filesystem_add(i++, "index.htm", HTML, index, sizeof(index)-1);
  filesystem_add(i++, "setup.htm", HTML, setup, sizeof(setup)-1);
  ...
  ...
  filesystem_add(i++, "valve.jpg", JPEG, valve, sizeof(valve));
  filesystem_add(i++, "pumpon.gif", GIF, pumpon, sizeof(pumpon));
  filesystem_add(i++, "pumpoff.gif", GIF, pumpoff, sizeof(pumpoff));
}
```

In this way, each file must be added to the file system table using the **file system_add( )** routine. The **html_pages.h** file contains the HTML documents, while the **graphics.h** file allocates the images. Once the file system is loaded, the web server can be started.

20.2.3 Starting the embedded web server

The **web_server.c** module provides the **web_server_init( )** routine, which is called from the **main.c** module at start-up. See this routine implementation:

```
void web_server_init(void) {

  filesystem_init();
  http_server_init(80, process_POST, tag_expand);
}
```

The first line initializes the file system as we have seen already, while the second line starts the embedded web server.

The **http_server_init( )** routine, allocated in the **http.c** module, opens a TCP socket at port 80, and puts it in the listen state. The **web_server_init( )** routine calls this function passing the port, the address of the **process_POST( )** function, which will process the data submitted by the browser, and the address of the **tag_expand( )** function, which will expand the tags used in the HTML pages. This last function is implemented in the **tagexpand.c** module, as we saw in the previous chapter. See the **http_server_init( )** implementation:

```
void http_server_init(unsigned short port,
        int (*POST_handler) (unsigned short data_index, unsigned short data_len),
        int (*TagExpand_handler) (char tagID, unsigned short pos, unsigned short len) ) {

  int socket;

  POST_CallBack = POST_handler;
  TagExpand_HTTP = TagExpand_handler;
  socket = tcp_socket_open(port, http_control_process);
  if (socket > 0) {
    printf("TCP Socket %d created, port %d\n", socket, tcp_get_port(socket));
  }else {
    if (socket == TCP_INVALID_SOCKET) {
      printf("Error opening a socket: increment TCP_MAX_SOCKETS=%d\n",
      TCP_MAX_SOCKETS);
    }
    if (socket == TCP_PORT_ALREADY_USED) {
      printf("Error opening a socket: Port %d already used\n", port);
    }
    return;               // Error
  }
  if (tcp_listen(socket) < 0) {
    printf("Error: socket %d can not put in LISTEN state\n", socket);
    return;               // Error
  }else {
    printf("TCP Socket %d listening on Port %d\n", socket, tcp_get_port(socket));
  }
}
```

The address of the **process_POST( )** and **tag_expand( )** functions are saved for later references, in the POST_CallBack and the TagExpand_HTTP variables, respectively. After this, a socket is opened, and, if there are no errors, it is put in the listen state. The socket is opened, declaring the **http_control_process( )** routine as a call-back function for event notifications. Now that the web server has been started, it is ready to accept incoming requests.

20.2.4 Handling the events

Each time an event occurs, the **http_control_process( )** routine is notified. The code overleaf shows the event processing.

In this routine, we see how each event is processed. The first five event processes TCP_EVENT_CONN_REQ, TCP_EVENT_ESTABLISHED, TCP_EVENT_DATA, TCP_EVENT_SEND_COMPLETED, TCP_EVENT_CONN_CLOSED will be described in the following sections. The rest of the event processes basically display the event.

```
static void http_control_process(int soc_handler, char event, char *srcipaddr,
        unsigned short srcport, unsigned short data_index, unsigned short data_len) {
  int resp;

  switch(event) {
   case TCP_EVENT_CONN_REQ:
     ...
     break;
   case TCP_EVENT_ESTABLISHED:
     ...
     break;
   case TCP_EVENT_DATA:
     ...
     break;
   case TCP_EVENT_SEND_COMPLETED:
     ...
     break;
   case TCP_EVENT_CONN_CLOSED:
     ...
     break;
   case TCP_EVENT_RESET:
     if (debug_http)
       printf("Error: Socket %d was Reset\r\n", soc_handler);
     break;
   case TCP_EVENT_rTOUT:
     printf("Error: Socket %d Timed Out\r\n", soc_handler);
     break;
   case TCP_EVENT_cTOUT:
     printf("Error: Connection in socket %d Timed Out\r\n", soc_handler);
     break;
   case TCP_EVENT_CLOSE_REQ:
     break;
   default:
     printf("Unknown Event: %d\n",event);
     break;
  }
}
```

20.2.4.1 Accepting connection requests

Before the browser sends an HTTP Request to the server, a TCP connection must be established.

When a TCP connection request arrives at port 80, the **http_control_process( )** routine is notified with the TCP_EVENT_CONN_REQ event. Then, the **tcp_conn_accept( )** function is called in order to accept the connection. When the TCP connection is established, the TCP_EVENT_ESTABLISHED event is notified. In both cases, when the debug_http option is set in the **debug.h** file, debug information is displayed in the console.

```
...
case TCP_EVENT_CONN_REQ:
  if (debug_http)
    printf("Connection Request from IP: %d.%d.%d.%d - Port: %d\n",
                    *srcipaddr,*(srcipaddr+1),*(srcipaddr+2),*(srcipaddr+3),srcport);
  resp = tcp_conn_accept(soc_handler);
  if (resp == TCP_SOCKET_ERROR)
    printf("Accept Error: no free socket available\n");
  else {
    if (debug_http)
      printf("Socket %d created\n", resp);
  }
  break;
case TCP_EVENT_ESTABLISHED:
  if (debug_http)
    printf("Connection Established with IP: %d.%d.%d.%d - Port: %d\n",
                    *srcipaddr,*(srcipaddr+1),*(srcipaddr+2),*(srcipaddr+3),srcport);
    break;
    ...
```

20.2.4.2 Receiving the HTTP Request

Once the TCP connection has been established, the browser sends the HTTP Request. When this is received at the server, the **http_control_process( )** routine is notified with the TCP_EVENT_DATA event:

```
...
case TCP_EVENT_DATA:
  if (debug_http)
    printf("Event: Data Available from IP: %d.%d.%d.%d - Port: %d\n",
                    *srcipaddr,*(srcipaddr+1),*(srcipaddr+2),*(srcipaddr+3),srcport);
  resp = HTTP_process(data_index, data_len);
  file_index[soc_handler-1] = resp;
  if (debug_http_file) {
    if (resp == -2)
      printf("Serving: 501 Command Not Implemented!\r\n");
    else if (resp == -1)
      printf("Serving: 404 Page Not Found!\r\n");
    else
      printf("Serving %s\r\n", filesystem[resp].filename);
  }
  if (tcp_send_data(soc_handler, create_content) == TCP_SOCKET_ERROR)
              printf("Error sending data: TCP already have data to send!\r\n");
  break;
...
```

If the debug_http option is set, a message is shown indicating that data has arrived. Then, the **HTTP_process( )** function is called. This function should return the file system index for the requested document, or an error code if an error was found. The function's response is saved in the file_index[] variable, to be processed later. An array is used in order to allow multiple simultaneous connections. In this way, the requested document index is saved independently for each socket.

If the debug_http_file option is set in the **debug.h** file, a message is shown displaying the **HTTP_process( )** response. After this, the **tcp_send_data( )** function is called to send the HTTP Response.

20.2.4.3 Closing the connection

Once the HTTP Response has been sent, the **http_control_process( )** routine is notified with the TCP_EVENT_SEND_COMPLETED event. As the TCP connection is no longer needed, the server will close the connection using the **tcp_conn_close( )** routine (in the HTTP Response, we use the HTTP/1.0 version to avoid HTTP/1.1 Persistent Connections feature, which leaves the connections opened, so consuming too many sockets).

```
..
case TCP_EVENT_SEND_COMPLETED:
  tcp_conn_close(soc_handler);
  break;
case TCP_EVENT_CONN_CLOSED:
  tcp_socket_close(soc_handler);
  if (debug_http)
     printf("Socket %d closed\n", soc_handler);
  break;
  ...
```

Once the connection is closed, the TCP_EVENT_CONN_CLOSED event is notified. Upon this, the **tcp_socket_close( )** routine is used to close the socket opened by the **tcp_conn_accept( )** function to handle this connection.

20.2.5 Processing the HTTP Requests

The **HTTP_process( )** function is in charge of searching the file system index of the document requested in the HTTP Request. If it is not found, the –1 error code must be returned, indicating that the '404' 'Page Not Found' message should be sent to the browser. In addition, if the command is a POST, the post call-back function must be called, in order for the **web_server.c** module to process the submitted variables. If the requested command is other than a GET or POST, the –2 error code must be returned, indicating that the '501' 'Command Not Implemented' message should be sent to the browser. See the code on page 467.

This function checks the first characters of the Request-Line in the HTTP Request, to see if the command is a GET or a POST. Otherwise, the –2 error code is returned.

```
int HTTP_process(unsigned short data_index, unsigned short data_len) {
  int i;
  char filename[13];

  if ( ! memcmp(&rx_buf[data_index],"GET",3)) {
    getFileName(filename, data_index+5);
    for(i=0; i<NUMBER_OF_FILES; i++) {
      if ( ! strcmp(filesystem[i].filename, filename))
        return i;
    }
    return -1;        // page Not Found (404)
  }else if ( ! memcmp(&rx_buf[data_index],"POST",4)) {
    if (POST_CallBack(data_index, data_len))
      getFileName(filename, data_index+6);
    else
      strcpy(filename, "index.htm");
    for(i=0; i<NUMBER_OF_FILES; i++) {
      if ( ! strcmp(filesystem[i].filename, filename))
        return i;
    }
    return -1;        // page Not Found (404)
  }else {
    return -2;        // command Not Implemented (501)
  }
}
```

If the command is a GET, the **getFileName( )** is used which copies the requested document's file name into the filename variable. Then, the filename content is searched in the file system. If it is found, the file system index is returned. Otherwise, the –1 error code is returned instead.

If the command is a POST, the **process_POST( )** call-back function is called (the POST_CallBack pointer was initialized with the address of this function in the **http_server_init( )**). After processing the posted variables, the **process_POST( )** function returns 1 if the 'Update' button was submitted, or 0 if the 'Cancel' button was pressed (if it is used in the HTML page form). In this last case, as the operation was cancelled, the **index.htm** page should be sent to the browser. Once the call-back function has been returned, the corresponding file is located in the file system, and the file system index is returned. Otherwise, the –1 error code is returned, indicating the requested page was not found.

The **getFileName( )** function is used to retrieve the name of the requested document from the HTTP Request. This function is called with the address of a variable into which the file name must be copied, and the receive buffer's start position at which to begin the search, as a parameter. See this function implementation overleaf.

The function starts looking for the space character (0x20), in which case it means that the file name was omitted (for example, 'GET / HTTP/1.1'). In this case, the **index.htm** file name must be copied and the routine returns.

```
void getFileName(char *p, unsigned short start) {
  int i;

  if (rx_buf[start] == 0x20) {              // if GET a space (GET / )
    strcpy(p, "index.htm");                 // return index.htm (default page)
    return;
  }
  for(i=0; i<13; i++) {
    if (rx_buf[start+i] == 0x20) {
      *p = '\0';
      break;
    } else {
      *p++ = tolower(rx_buf[start+i]);
    }
  }
}
```

If there is a file name in the Request-Line, the characters are copied from the receive buffer into the filename variable (passed as a parameter), until the maximum file name's length is reached (13 characters) or a space is found. In this last case, as the file name has less than 13 characters the string terminator '\0' is used. Please note that the **tolower( )** function is used to convert letters into their lower case equivalent; just in case the command has the file name in upper case.

20.2.6 Processing POST commands

The **web_server.c** module must provide a call-back function to process the POST commands. This function is called each time a POST command is found in the HTTP Request, in order for the application to process the submitted variables from the browser. Let's see what a POST HTTP Request looks like:

```
POST /setupok.htm HTTP/1.1
Accept: image/gif, image/jpeg, */*
Content-Type: application/x-www-form-urlencoded
Referer: http://192.168.0.30/setup.htm
Host: 192.168.0.30
Content-Length: 81
Connection: Keep-Alive
Cache-Control: no-cache

dow=Tuesday&month=March&dom=28&year=2006&hour=12&min=27
&sec=25&led=on&send=Update
```

This HTTP Request starts with the POST command, the **setupok.htm** file, and the HTTP/1.1 version in the Request-Line. After this, several headers appear. The empty-line separates the headers from the message body, where the POST request sends the submitted data to be processed.

In order to process the submitted data, we need to find the empty-line, which indicates the beginning of the message body (which contains the data). Then, we must 'parse' the data for the searched variables, which will appear in the 'variable=value' format. The '&' character is used as a separator between each data pair. The following code shows how the **process_POST( )** function is implemented:

```
int process_POST(unsigned short data_index, unsigned short data_len) {
  int i=0;
  int j;
  char value[200];
  char to[50], subject[50], message[200];

  #if debug_web_processpost
    printf("POST: DataIndex %d - Data Len %d\r\n", data_index, data_len);
  #endif

  while(i < data_len) {
    if (rx_buf[data_index+i]=='\r') {
      if (rx_buf[data_index+i+1]=='\n' &&
          rx_buf[data_index+i+2]=='\r' &&
          rx_buf[data_index+i+3]=='\n') {

        i += 4;
        break;
      }else {
        i += 4;
      }
    }else {
      i++;
    }
  }

  #if debug_web_processpost
    j = i;
    printf("POST data: ");
    while(j < data_len) {
      printf("%c", rx_buf[data_index+j]);
      j++;
    }
    printf("\r\n");
  #endif
  ...
```

This code starts displaying the POST data index (where the HTTP Request begins in the receiver buffer) and length, if the debug_web_processpost option is set in the **debug.h** file. After this, a while( ) structure loops until the empty-line (the '\r\n\r\n' sequence) is found. When this happens, the i variable contains the buffer's position where the POST data begins. Then, this data is displayed if the debug_web_processpost option is set.

Now that we have the data to process, we need to define the variables to search. That is, our web server application must process three different forms, as defined in the **mail.htm**, **applic.htm** and **setup.htm** pages. Those pages are included in the **html_pages.h** file.

The **mail.htm** page contains a form that allows the user to enter the destination e-mail address, the subject and the message. Then, the 'Send' button must be pressed to send the email message. This button is defined with the following tag:

```
<input type=submit name=mail value=Send>
```

where 'mail' is the name of the button tag, and its value is 'Send'. When the user presses the 'Send' button, the 'mail=Send' pair is submitted with the data. For this, we must search for the 'mail' string, and check if its value is 'Send'. If so, the rest of the variables are parsed, and the e-mail message is sent. See the following code:

```
...
if (parse_variable(&rx_buf[data_index+i], "mail", data_len-i, value)) {
   if (!memcmp(value, "Send",4)) {
      if (parse_variable(&rx_buf[data_index+i], "to", data_len-i, value)) {
         strcpy(to, value);
      }
      if (parse_variable(&rx_buf[data_index+i], "subject", data_len-i, value)) {
         strcpy(subject, value);
      }
      if (parse_variable(&rx_buf[data_index+i], "message", data_len-i, value)) {
         memcpy(message, value,200);
      }
      smtp_sendmail(to, subject, message,0,0);
      return 1;
   }
}
...
```

The **parse_variable( )** function is implemented in the http.c module, and it is used to parse the value of a variable. This function is called with the memory buffer address where the POST data begins, the string to search, the length of the data in the buffer, and a variable where the value of the searched string should be copied, if it is found.

For example, the **parse_variable**(&rx_buf[data_index + i], 'mail', data_len – i, value) returns 0 if the 'mail' string is not found in the receive buffer (rx_buf[]); or it returns 1 if it is found. In this last case, the string's value is copied into the passed parameter (value[]).

If the 'mail' string is found, its value is checked against the 'Send' string. If they match, the rest of the form variables are searched, and their values are copied into the respective variables. After this, the **smtp_sendmail( )** routine is used to send the e-mail message, and the process_POST( ) function returns 1, indicating the POST was successfully processed (not cancelled, in case there is a 'Cancel' button in the form).

The rest of the **process_POST( )** code processes the other two forms in a similar way, so will not be described here. Refer to the source code to follow their implementation.

The **parse_variable( )** function is found in the **http.c** module, and it is implemented as follows:

```
int parse_variable(char str[], char var[], unsigned short len, char value[]) {
  int i=0;
  int j=0;

  while(i < len) {
    if (var[j]=='\0')
      break;
    if (str[i] == '=') {
      while(str[i]!='&' && i<len) {
        i++;
      }
      j=0;
    }
    if (str[i] == var[j]) {
      j++;
    }else {
      j=0;
    }
    i++;
  }
  ...
```

The i variable is used as an index for the buffer data, while the j variable is used as an index for the string containing the name to be searched. Then, a while() structure loops to process the buffer data, so the i index is incremented to pass through the buffer. For each buffer character, the first character of the string is compared; if they match, the j index is incremented to compare the second character with the following buffer character. Otherwise, the j variable is reset to start again from the first character of the string. When an '=' character is encountered in the buffer, the i variable is incremented until it points to the '&' separator, and the j index is reset to start comparing the string from its first character. The loop ends when either the '\0' (string terminator) is found or the complete buffer is processed. In this case, if j=0 the string was not found. Otherwise, the string was found in the buffer, and the i value points to the '=' character, which separates the variable from the value.

In this code, if j is zero when the code exits from the previous while(), the string was not found, so the function returns with 0. Otherwise, i is incremented so it points to the buffer data where the 'value' is found. This last must be copied into the value[] variable, which was passed as a parameter. The j variable is reset and it will be reused to index the value[] variable. Then, each character of the 'value' is copied into the value[] variable, until either the '&' separator is found or the buffer data ends. After this, the '\0' string ter-

```
...
if (j==0) {
   return 0;
}else {
   i++;
   j=0;
   while(str[i] != '&' && i<len) {
      if (str[i] == '+')
         value[j] = ' ';
      else if (str[i]=='%') {
         value[j]  = str[i+1]<='9' ? (str[i+1]-'0')*16 : (tolower(str[i+1])-'a'+10)*16;
         value[j] += str[i+2]<='9' ? (str[i+2]-'0') : (tolower(str[i+2])-'a'+10);
         i +=2;
      }else
         value[j] = str[i];
      i++;
      j++;
   }
   value[j] = '\0';
   return 1;
}
}
```

minator is added to the value[] variable, and the function returns with 1 indicating the searched variable was found and its value was copied into the last parameter passed. If 'URL encoding' is used in the posted data, the characters are properly decoded (the '+' is converted into a space, and the '%' is replaced by the character whose hexadecimal value coincides with the 2-digit number that follows the '%' character).

20.2.7 Creating the HTTP Response

Once the HTTP Request has been processed by the web server, the response must be created and sent. The **tcp_send_data( )** function is used to send the HTTP Response to the browser.

When the **tcp_send_data( )** function has been used, the **create_content( )** call-back function is called to fill the transmit buffer with the data to send. In this way, the requested document must be sent in the body of the HTTP Response message, while the header must be created according to the response. As we already saw, the response header consists of the status-line and the message headers. The empty-line separates the HTTP header from the body of the message.

The constants set out at the top of page 473 are defined to create the responses.

The **page404**[] and **page501**[] strings are used when the '404' 'Page Not Found' or '501' 'Command Not Implemented' messages must be returned, respectively. Note that these strings already include the headers and the body of the messages.

The **status200**[] and the **empty-line**[] are used to create the header of the response when the requested document is delivered. In addition, the header uses the 'Content-Type' strings (**text**[], **html**[], **gif[]**, etc.) as defined in section 20.2.2.

```
const char page404[] =  "HTTP/1.0 404 Not Found\r\nContent-Type: text/html\r\n\r\n"
                        "<HTML><HEAD><TITLE>File Not Found</TITLE></HEAD>"
                        "<BODY><H4>The requested page was not found! </H4></BODY>";

const char page501[] =  "HTTP/1.0 501 Not Implemented\r\nContent-Type: text/html\r\n\r\n"
                      "<HTML><HEAD><TITLE>Method Not Implemented</TITLE></HEAD>"
                 "<BODY><H4>The requested method was not implemented!</H4></BODY>";

const char status200[] = "HTTP/1.0 200 OK\r\n";

const char empty_line[] = "\r\n";
```

Here is the **create_content( )** function implementation:

```
int create_content(int soc_handle, unsigned short *position, unsigned short *len) {
  char tagID;
  int resp;
  int j=TCP_DATA_START;
  unsigned short pos;

  pos = *position;
  if (file_index[soc_handle-1] == -2) {
    strcpy(&tx_buf[j], page501);
    (*position) += (sizeof(page501)-1);
    (*len) -= (sizeof(page501)-1);
    return 0;
  }
  if (file_index[soc_handle-1] == -1) {
    strcpy(&tx_buf[j], page404);
    (*position) += (sizeof(page404)-1);
    (*len) -= (sizeof(page404)-1);
    return 0;
  }
  ...
```

This function is called from the **tcp.c** module, with the following parameters: the socket handle, the position of the application data from where to begin loading the buffer, and the maximum allowable length of data to be filled into the transmit buffer. Although the position parameter keeps track of the absolute position within the application data, we need a variable that keeps track of the position relative to each message. For this, we define the pos variable, which is assigned the content of the position pointer each time this routine is started.

We must remember that the value returned by the **HTTP_process( )** function was saved using the file_index[] variable. Then, if this value is –2, the **page501**[] string must be copied into the transmit buffer, to be sent as the response. Then, the parameters are updated accordingly, and a 0 is returned indicating to the **tcp.c** module that no data remains in the application buffer. In a similar way, if the **HTTP_process( )** response was –1, the **page404**[] is copied into the buffer to be sent, the parameters updated, and a 0 returned. Note that we are supposing that the length of these messages is always smaller than the len parameter. Otherwise, we should check the len parameter to see if the buffer is full.

If the requested document was found in the file system, we need to create the HTTP Response including the document in the message body:

```
...
// fill the status line
while(pos < sizeof(status200)-1 && *len) {
  tx_buf[j++] = status200[pos];
  pos++;
  (*position)++;
  (*len)--;
}
if (*len==0)
  return 1;
pos -= (sizeof(status200)-1);
...
```

First, we need to copy the status-line into the transmit buffer. The while() structure copies each character from the status-line into the transmit buffer, and it updates the position and length passed as a parameters. The while() loops until either the complete status-line is copied or the buffer is full. In this last case (*len = = 0), the function must return with 1, indicating that more data remains in the application to be sent. However, if the buffer is not full, the pos variable is updated and the code continues.

```
...
// fill the Content-Type line
while(pos < filesystem[file_index[soc_handle-1]].contentsize && *len) {
  tx_buf[j++] = *(filesystem[file_index[soc_handle-1]].contentpointer + pos);
  pos++;
  (*position)++;
  (*len)--;
}
if (*len==0)
  return 1;
pos -= (filesystem[file_index[soc_handle-1]].contentsize);

// fill the empty-line
while(pos < sizeof(empty_line)-1 && *len) {
  tx_buf[j++] = empty_line[pos];
  pos++;
  (*position)++;
  (*len)--;
}
if (*len==0)
  return 1;
pos -= (sizeof(empty_line)-1);
...
```

In the above code, the 'Content-Type' header and the empty-line are copied into the buffer in the same way as we did with the status-line.

```
...
//fill the body of the requested page
while((pos < filesystem[file_index[soc_handle-1]].filesize) && *len) {
  tx_buf[j] = *(filesystem[file_index[soc_handle-1]].filepointer + pos);

  if (tx_buf[j] == '&' && (filesystem[file_index[soc_handle-1]].contentpointer == html ||
                    filesystem[file_index[soc_handle-1]].contentpointer == text)
                 && TagExpand_HTTP) {

    tagID = ((*(filesystem[file_index[soc_handle-1]].filepointer + pos+1)-0x30)*10) +
            (*(filesystem[file_index[soc_handle-1]].filepointer + pos+2)-0x30);

    resp = TagExpand_HTTP(tagID, j, *len);
    if (resp == -2) {
      printf("Error: Tag &%02d not found\r\n", tagID);
    }else if (resp == -1) {
      return *len;          // the available space is not enough to expand the tag...
    }else {
      j += resp;
      pos += 3;
      (*position) += 3;
      (*len) -= resp;
      continue;
    }
  }
  j++;
  pos++;
  (*position)++;
  (*len)--;
}
if (pos < filesystem[file_index[soc_handle-1]].filesize)
  return 1;
else
  return 0;
}
```

In the above code, the **while( )** structure copies the requested document into the transmit buffer, one byte at a time. This **while( )** structure will loop until either the complete document is copied into the buffer, or the buffer is full. For each copied character, the '&' character is checked in order to detect tags. Tag detection may occur only in HTML or TEXT files (to avoid those cases where a binary or image file contains the '&' character as normal data) and if a **TagExpand_handler( )** function was declared in the **http_server_init( )** initialization routine.

If a tag is encountered, the **tag_expand( )** function is called (the **TagExpand_HTTP** variable has the address of this function). If the function returns a –2, it means the tag was not found, so the code simply displays a message indicating this (remember that this may be intentional in order to use the '&' character in a document as normal data). If the function returns –1, it means that the buffer space was not enough to expand the tag. In this case, the **create_content( )** function must return with a value greater than 0, indicating that more data remains in the application to be sent. Once the **tcp.c** module has sent this segment, the **create_content( )** function will be called again to proceed filling the buffer with the rest of the data, from the position where it was left the last time.

Finally, if the **tag_expand( )** function returns any other positive number (the size of the expanded tag), the transmit buffer position must be updated by this quantity, but the application data position must be updated by 3 (the size of the original tag). The continue statement redirects the process to the top of the loop.

If the '&' character was not found in the tag, the parameters are updated normally and the routine follows with the next character to be copied.

Once the while( ) structure has ended, the pos variable is compared to the document's size. If the pos value is smaller than the document's size, it means that the document was not completely copied, so a 1 must be returned, indicating that more data remains in the application to be sent. Otherwise, the complete document was copied, and a 0 must be returned.

Lab 12: Serving the World Wide Web

Lab 12 introduction

In this Lab, we will access the board from the Internet browser using the embedded web server implementation. In addition, we will use the SMTP protocol implementation to send an HTML-based e-mail message reporting the application status.

Lab 12 target support

This Lab supports both types of boards. Select the appropriate target board from the 'Configuration drop-down' menu in the Workspace window.

Lab 12 options setting

This Lab may use the debug_http, the debug_http_file, and the debug_web_processpost options. Initially, these options are turned off.

Lab 12 utilities used

We use Internet Explorer (web browser) to access the embedded web server. We will need an SMTP server if we want to send e-mail messages from the embedded webserver. See Lab 11 for its configuration. In order to add your own graphics, a utility is provided in the accompanying CD, which converts the image file into the appropriate string definition, as shown in the graphics.h file. See the 'Getting Started' guide for help on this utility.

Lab 12 instructions

Complete the steps according to Chapter 12 (see section 12.6). Once the Lab is running, follow the Lab 12 Exercises. If you use the LPC-P212X board, you must make the dial-up connection before executing the lab exercises. **Important**: See the Lab 12 Notes in the 'Getting Started' guide.

Lab 12 exercises

- Open the Internet browser and enter the http://192.168.0.30 address (or http://192.168.0.51 for the LPC-P212X boards). The Web Control Panel main page should appear. Select the 'Setup' option to move on the 'Setup Page'. Adjust the Real Time Clock with the current Date and Time. Optionally, uncheck the LED Control option to see how the Board Activity LED may be disabled/enabled from the web page. Press the 'Update' button to submit the form. Verify if the Real Time Clock and the Board Activity LED have been set up accordingly.
- Select the 'Application' option. The Application Web Control Panel should appear. This web page presents a graphical representation of the Application Control Process, showing a tank, two valves and two pumps. In addition, a thermometer displays the tank liquid temperature. On the right of the web page the Control Panel from where the user can start the cycle and set some options appears. The panel shows the variables states and the liquid level and temperature. Press the 'Start' button in the panel to start the process cycle. Press the 'Refresh' button every 10 seconds to see how the control process variables are updated following the process cycle. Place the mouse over the valves or the pumps to display their state. Placing the mouse over the tank's liquid or the thermometer's mercury, the liquid level and temperature will be shown, respectively. Check the 'Cycle continuously' option and press the 'Refresh' button to have the control process running continuously. Check the 'Autorefresh' option and press the 'Refresh' button to have the web page refreshing automatically every 10 seconds. The refreshing period may also be changed if necessary.
- Select the 'Send email' option. The Send e-mail form should appear. Ensure that the correct SMTP server is configured in the **stackcfg.h** file (if the free SMTP server is being used, it should be running in the PC). Fill the 'To:' field with the destination e-mail address, the 'Subject:' field with the message subject, and the 'Message:' field with the message content. Then, press the 'Send' button to send the e-mail. After a few seconds, verify whether the e-mail has arrived at its destination.
- Select the 'About' option to see the '*Embedded Internet*' book index. This page shows how photos and logos can be delivered by the embedded web server.
- Use the debug_http_file option to see the file name the web server is serving. Use the debug_web_processpost option to see the data submitted by a form (with a POST command). Use the debug_http option to debug the operation of the embedded web server. The above options may be used simultaneously. Please take note that the debug options use the **printf( )** function which makes the system response very slow. For this reason, this Lab turns this option off initially. Use Ethereal to capture the HTTP messages and analyse these packets.
- Use your own HTML pages and images. Use the provided utility to convert from the binary format (JPG, GIF, PNG, etc.). Any file format supported by the browser can be used in your web pages.
- **Bonus:** Now, that we have dealt with HTML pages, press the 'E' key in the system console to send an HTML-based e-mail message. This command sends a system report e-mail message informing the Application Control Process state in a graphical way. In the message body, the **applic.htm** document is sent (as it is used in the embedded web server), but this page uses the <BASE href=www.embeddedinternet.org/book/SMTP/> label which makes the images being downloaded from the *Embedded Internet* web site. See the **smtp_message2[]** string definition in the **console.c** file.

PART III

Embedded Internet applications

'This is where the theory starts making sense...'

21

Remote monitoring, access and control

We have arrived at the applications. This is where the acquired knowledge and effort really make sense. After all, the applications are the 'justification' of the embedded systems' existence. In these chapters, we will describe only some of the possible applications. The list of applications mentioned here does not limit, in any way, the possibilities the embedded systems have when they are enabled with TCP/IP communications. Only our imagination limits this application field. It is worth noting that we will use the expressions 'Net-enabled' and 'Internet-enabled' interchangeably. Although the last expression would indicate that the Internet is accessible from the embedded system, both expressions indicate that a TCP/IP stack implementation enables the embedded system to have networking communications. The fact that a network is connected to the Internet will only affect the scope of the embedded system communications.

In this chapter we will see how embedded systems' applications can greatly benefit from remote monitoring, access and control when they are Net-enabled.

21.1 Introduction

Typically, an embedded system is an embedded processor with an application software designed for a specific task. By contrast, desktop PCs are based on hardware and an operating system oriented to a wide range of applications.

With the advent of networking technology, PCs started to connect between themselves, taking advantage of networking. These networks grew up to their maximum expression: the Internet. Similarly, embedded systems can take advantage of networking, interconnecting with each other; even with desktop PCs. In this way, the embedded application can be remotely accessed and controlled.

Although embedded systems present many ways in which they can communicate with other systems, there is one in particular that gives embedded systems the best benefits: TCP/IP. The following are some of the advantages of embedded systems using a TCP/IP stack:

- Use of the 'Internet backbone' infrastructure for communicating data over long distances (worldwide) and multiple locations, at the lowest cost.
- As TCP/IP is a widely adopted standard, the embedded systems will be able to communicate with other devices, such as PC, PDA, Web pad, phones, appliances and other embedded systems, in a straightforward manner.
- Taking advantage of the high availability of web browsers supported by many devices (PC, PDA, Web pad) to be used as a Web interface to remotely access the embedded system, providing a standardized user interface.
- Taking advantage of the Internet e-mail infrastructure in order to send messages to any user at any location in the world.
- Communicating with other Net-enabled embedded applications, exchanging information and data.
- Consuming services delivered from the Internet by various companies or other devices, e.g. weather information, to automatically take the appropriate action.

The next sections will show some of the many embedded Internet applications for Remote monitoring, access and control.

21.2 Universal GUI console

Embedded systems implementing a TCP/IP stack may provide a Web interface using a web browser running at any device. This way, embedded systems can be accessed without the need to provide a keyboard/LCD display.

Although a serial interface would also allow any PC's serial application (such as Hyperterminal) to access the embedded system, the graphical interface and a rich set of controls provided by the HTML pages make the browser the best choice as a system console. In addition, although communication over serial interfaces is limited to 15 metres (50 feet) (recommended), implementing a TCP/IP stack extends communication all over the world. Even though with a serial interface connected to a modem, we can extend communication over the world using conventional telephone lines, the costs are very high.

Figure 21.1 shows how embedded systems implementing a web server to handle a GUI console interface can be locally (through a LAN) or remotely (over the Internet) managed. It is interesting to add a Java Applet to the HTML pages, which implement the embedded system GUI interface. In this way, the applet may extend the ability to draw graphics in the browser, windows, messages, etc., so presenting better graphics and user interaction. It also allows programming to enable a socket to be connected directly to the embedded system, so the data shown in the browser can be updated continuously.

21.3 Home automation

Many systems installed at home could be Net-enabled to take advantages of the networking benefits:

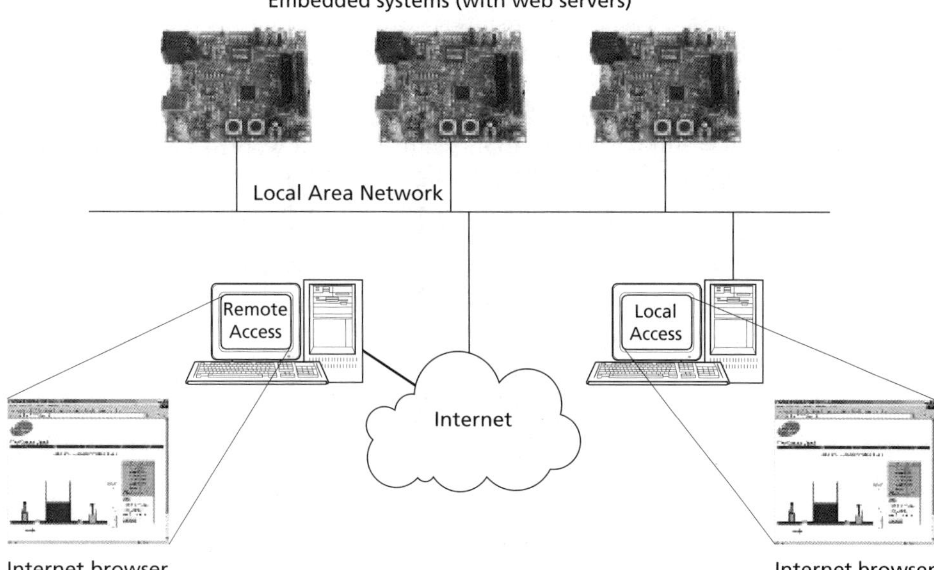

Figure 21.1 Embedded systems access through a GUI console.

- Security system
- Doors, windows, and garage locking systems
- Central air conditioning system
- Heating system
- Lighting system
- Irrigation system
- Entertainment systems (TV, DVD, home theatre)
- Computers

There are three ways in which these systems could benefit from a network connection:

1. They could be managed from a centralized point, using a browser running in a PC or perhaps in a wireless Web pad.
2. They could interact between each other, or with a master device, taking different actions according to a determined procedure.
3. They could be remotely monitored, controlled and operated from any remote point outside the home.

Figure 21.2 shows many home devices, which are normally controlled by embedded systems. If these devices were Net-enabling, they could offer additional benefits. If an internal Local Area Network were implemented, these devices could be managed from a centralized point. A wireless Web pad could be used to control all devices in a very comfortable way, from any point at home.

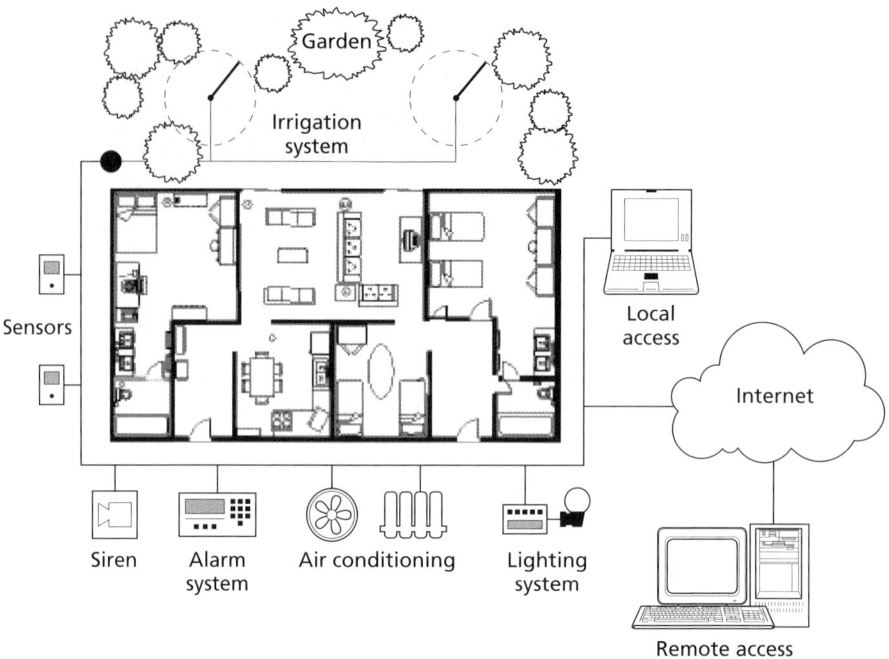

Figure 21.2 Home automation with NET-enabled embedded systems.

21.4 Industrial automation

In any industrial or factory plant, collecting and analysing information from plant floor machinery and processes is of great value to plant engineers and managers. Having this collected information in a centralized point allows supervisors to easily manage the plant without the need to move to each physical point where the process is developed. With embedded Internet, these centralized points may even be outside the plant, so supervisors may analyse the plant's performance at any time, from any place in the world.

Again, embedded systems controlling the processes could be connected between each other, allowing the synchronization of the processes, or the adoption of some common contingency strategy in case an alarm was detected at some point of the manufacturing line. Figure 21.3 shows a factory with industrial machinery connected to a local LAN and an Internet connection, which allows both local and remote access from the factory floor plant and from the central office located in the city.

Another important area where embedded Internet may contribute is in those manufacturing plants that work with their parts providers using a 'just-in-time' strategy. In these cases, as soon as the parts are consumed in the final product assembling, the suppliers must be notified in order to replace those parts. This whole process may be automated using embedded Internet, which allows the plant manufacturing process to be connected to the provider systems that ultimately process the part replacement orders automatically.

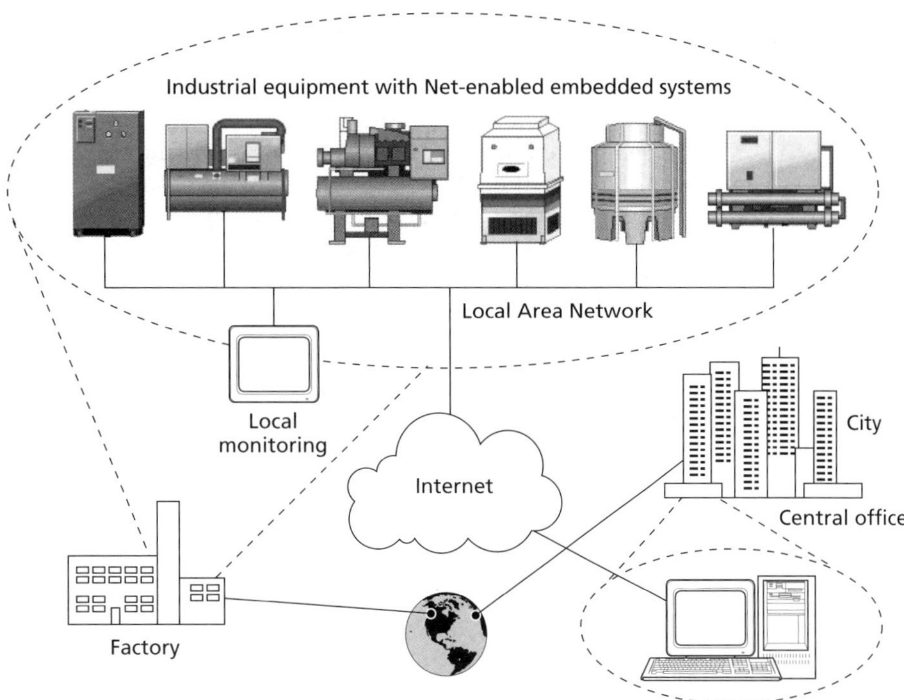

Figure 21.3 Remote management of an industrial plant.

21.5 Telemetry – virtual instruments

There is no doubt that in the telemetry field (taking measurements at a distance), the embedded Internet plays an important role. There is no better way to transmit measured data to any place than using the Internet infrastructure.

Imagine an embedded system registering the weather conditions in distant zones. This data may be sent to a server, which can process it and publish the results on a web page. This information can be accessed from a web browser anywhere. In order to transmit the data from the embedded system to the server, and assuming that no telephone lines or permanent Internet connections are available in such distant zones, a mobile (cellular) phone could be used which may access the Internet through a PPP connection, on a time basis. An alternative is to consider the use of RF transceiver modules, which transmit the data to the nearest point where a broadband Internet connection is available. These RF modules present an RS232 interface, which can be easily interfaced with the embedded systems.

The term 'virtual instruments' refers to a software component that displays the results of a measurement taken by a remote instrument installed somewhere other than where the software is running. That is, the 'real' instrument that takes the measurements is installed in one place while the software that shows the measurement results (the 'virtual' instruments) is running in a different (and perhaps very distant) place. In this way, the 'real' instrument takes the measurements, while the 'virtual' instrument displays the results to the user. From the user's point of view, the software that shows the results is the instrument; although it is considered 'virtual' as the 'real' measurements are taken by another system in a remote place.

Many software companies offer 'virtual' instruments, such as software components in a form of OCX, ActiveX, DLL, etc. These components can be easily integrated into any application. In this way, we may use the embedded system to collect the measured data, and to have it transmitted to the software, which ultimately displays it using the 'virtual' instruments.

Figure 21.4 shows 'virtual' instruments representing the 'real' measurements performed in an industrial plant located in a remote point.

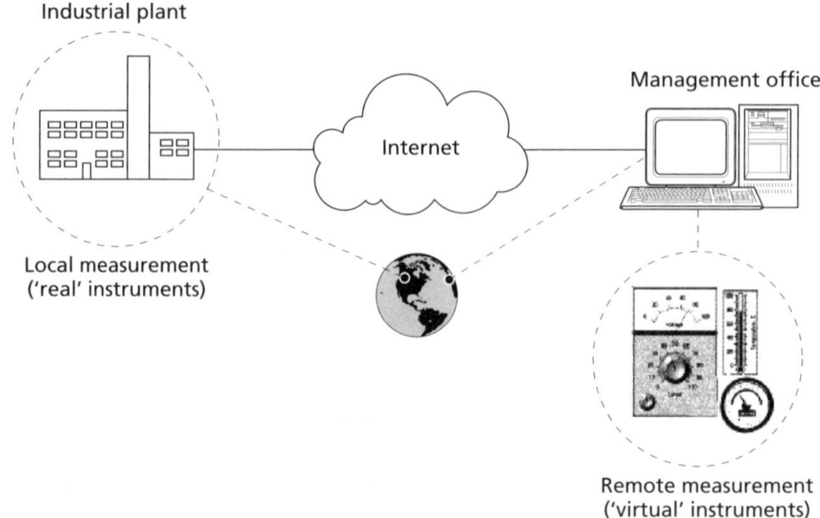

Figure 21.4 A 'virtual instrument' application.

21.6 Telemedicine applications

Telemedicine is the exchange of medical information via electronic communications to improve a patient's health status. Among the many services telemedicine provides is Remote Patient Monitoring (RPM), which heavily relies on embedded systems.

RPM consists of devices collecting data from the patient, and sending it to a monitoring station where a specialist may interpret it accordingly. Among the many devices that may be used in RPM, are the following:

- blood monitoring systems
- cardiac monitoring systems
- heart rate monitors
- respiratory monitoring systems
- vital sign monitoring devices

- electronic stethoscopes
- neurological monitoring systems
- urine monitoring systems
- home based cancer-screening tests.

Figure 21.5 shows how the patient's health status information can be monitored from the hospital, avoiding the physical presence of the examined person. In fact, embedded systems used for home care do not really need to be always connected. They can store the information and then connect at planned intervals, to send the data to a server for processing. The home telephone line may serve for this purpose, avoiding the need for a permanent Internet connection.

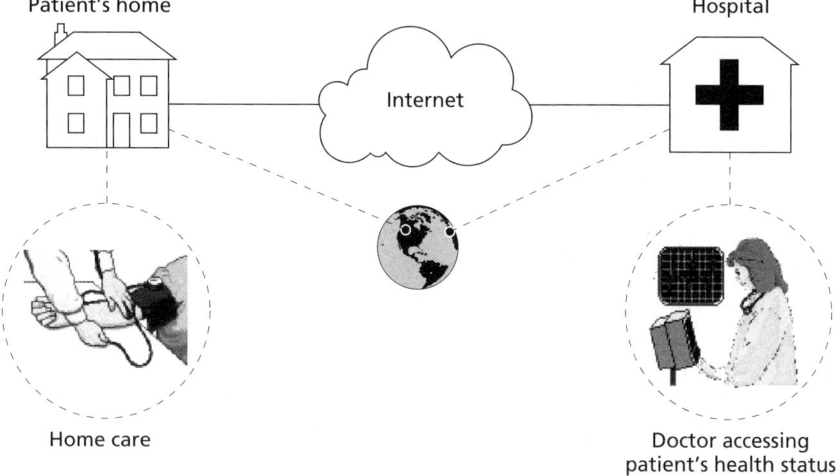

Figure 21.5 Telemedicine allows remote patient monitoring.

21.7 Commercial applications

The following are only some of the possible uses of Net-enabled embedded systems in commercial applications.

21.7.1 Price verifier

Typically, a price verifier is a TCP/IP network ready terminal for on-line price verification, used in supermarkets, retail stores, and outlets. As shown in Figure 21.6, an internal barcode scanner reads the product code when the product's barcode is presented under its beam (1). This code is sent to the host (2), where the product description, price and possibly other data are retrieved from the host database. This information is sent back to the device (3), in order to show it through its internal LCD display (4).

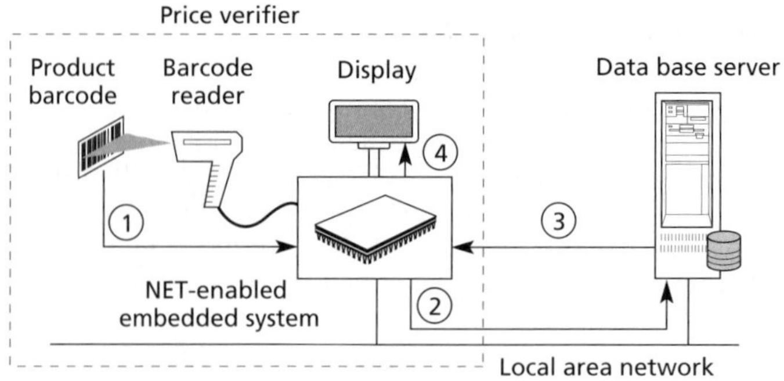

Figure 21.6 A price verifier embedded system.

In large installations, many of these devices are connected to the network, and distributed among the sales area. All these devices are connected to a host when a price verification operation is requested. This system allows the customer to verify the prices of the products on-line and perhaps get additional information about the product (like 'this offer is only for today…' or 'only 3 items left in stock…').

21.7.2 Vending machines

Even though vending machines have been around for a long time, Internet-enabling brings new possibilities, such as remote monitoring of the stock and the collected coins in order to know when products should be replenished or the money collected. This information could save time and money, avoiding either unnecessary trips to service the machine or a loss of sales from leaving the machine without stock.

Figure 21.7 shows a vending machine connected to the Internet, in order to report its status. Typically, this connection could be performed via a telephone line, or cellular equipment, depending on availability. The machine could be connected on a time basis, or to monitor certain events, in order to advise about any abnormality.

Additional benefits may be gained from the security perspective, if we take into account that any vandalism can be detected.

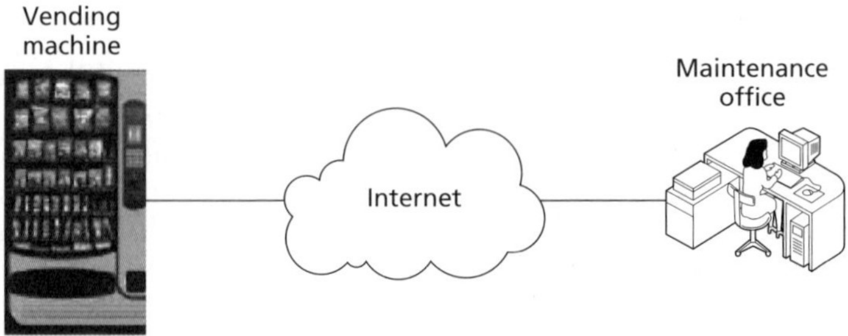

Figure 21.7 NET-enabled vending machines.

21.8 Street controllers

There are many kinds of controllers installed on the streets. Such controllers, like the street lighting and traffic lights controllers, are independent units covering defined areas. Although these controllers fulfil their function by themselves, they would greatly benefit from working in an interconnected way, in terms of synchronization. Additionally, as these controllers are distributed around the cities, it is expensive to move each controller every time parameters need changing or supervision is required. If they were Internet-enabled, they could be remotely accessed from any point.

21.8.1 Street lighting controllers

In many countries, street lighting controllers are used for energy-saving purposes. These controllers manage the electrical power supplied for illumination, obtaining up to 40% savings in their energy consumption. Additional savings come from maintenance and replenishment costs, since lamp life is increased when they are used under less 'stressed' conditions (lower voltages). In addition, the controller determines when the lamps must turn on and turn off, according to the time the sun sets and rises, which varies throughout the year.

These kinds of controller may be remotely managed when they are Internet-enabled. This allows supervisors to access and change, if necessary, any operation parameter at a distance. In addition, reports may be obtained remotely, from the electrical power meter included in the controller. Figure 21.8 shows how many lighting controllers may be monitored from a centralized point, even those located in different cities. Another important benefit from these controllers when they are Internet-enabled is that they can communicate with each other, meaning that synchronized operations are possible.

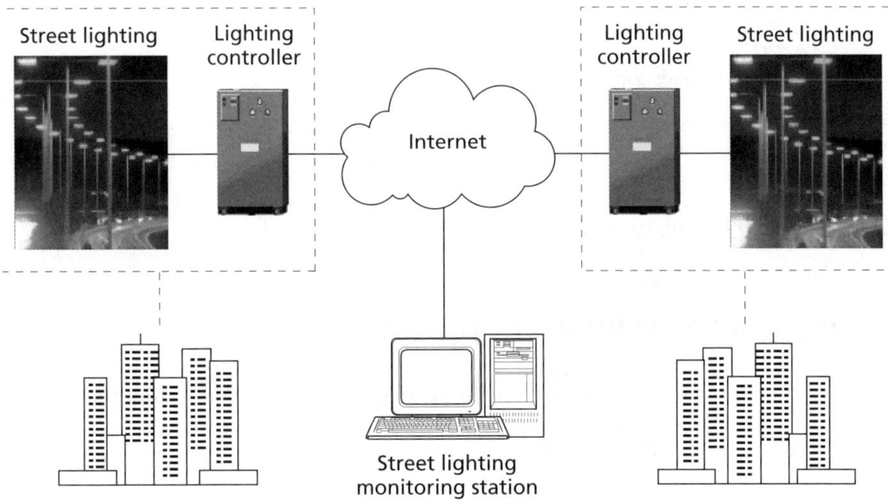

Figure 21.8 Street lighting controller remote monitoring.

21.8.2 Traffic Light controllers

Traffic light controllers are commonly used in street intersections, to order vehicular and pedestrian traffic. Although these controllers can work independently from each other, communication among them or with a central base allows them to work in a synchronized manner. Synchronization is very important as it reduces unnecessary vehicle stops and delays through more efficient traffic signal timing. In addition, special cases such as emergencies can be efficiently handled and accidents avoided, if they can be detected in some way.

Having these controllers Internet-enabled means they can be monitored and accessed by a central base, allowing a better coordination and a faster response to the changing traffic conditions. See Figure 21.9 for an implementation. Additionally, most of these modern controllers have special circuits for 'burned-out' light detection. Accessing this information remotely makes the maintenance of traffic lights more efficient.

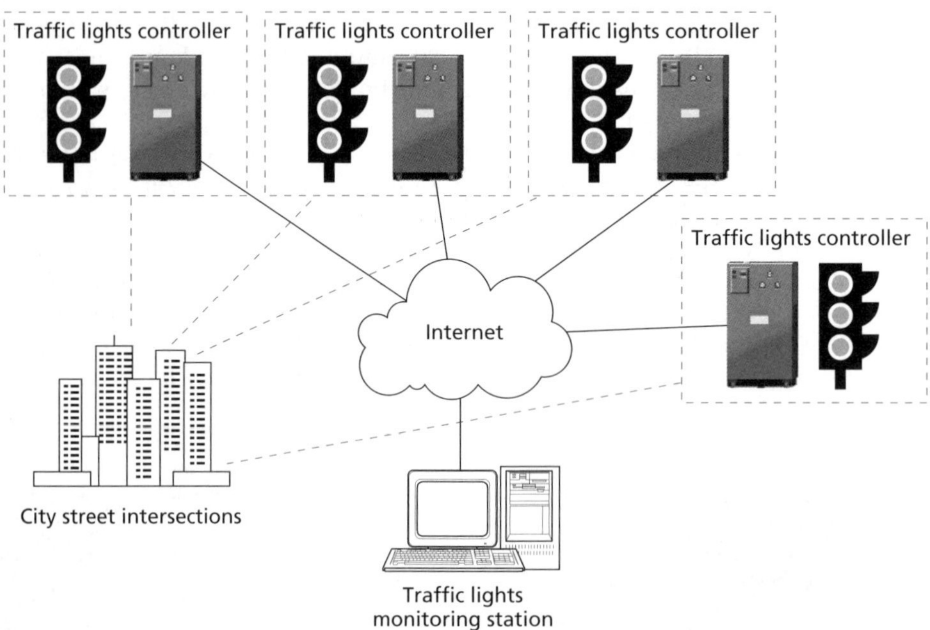

Figure 21.9 Traffic lights controller remote monitoring.

21.9 Data collection applications

There are many applications where data must be collected periodically. That is the case with the gas, water and electricity meters installed in residential and industrial addresses. The field workforce has to visit each end-point in order to read the consumption, to later input it to the billing system.

With automatic meter reading (AMR) technology combined with mobile collection systems, the field workforce's job is drastically simplified, saving time and cost. Such systems allow meter end-points to send the data to vehicles equipped with radio transceivers, collecting the data that later will be transferred to the billing system. These systems avoid the physical inspection of each meter end-point, saving a lot of time and money.

A further advance may be obtained by combining wireless and Internet technology. Net-enabling the meter end-points through the use of radio technology to connect these points to the nearest network-fixed point with internet access, remote metering and monitoring may be performed online, sending the data to centralized or distributed database servers, allowing access to this information from any web browser.

Figure 21.10 shows how information is collected from the meters, using a wireless link to the nearest point where the Internet is available. From this point, the information is sent to the main office, where it is processed, to be later entered into the billing system. This generates the appropriate reports necessary for an invoice to be distributed to each customer.

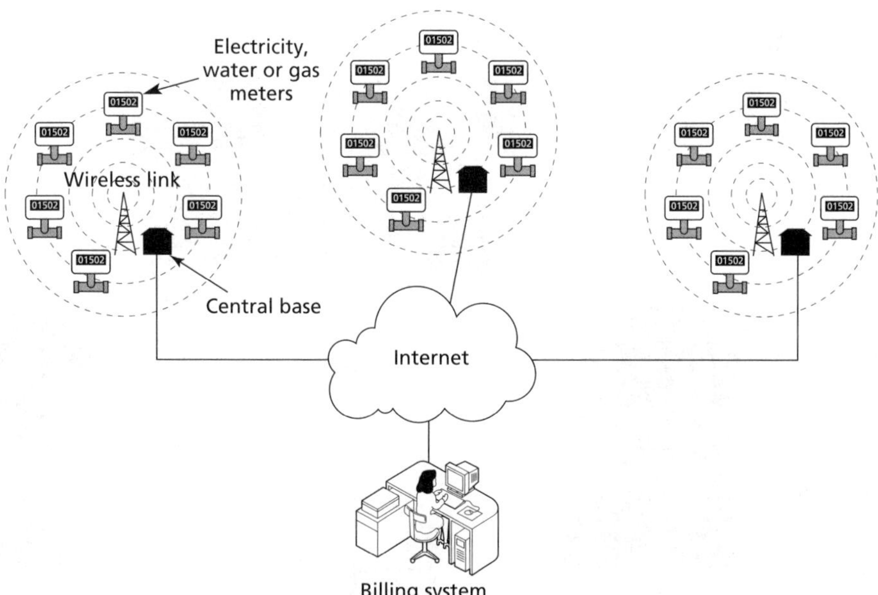

Figure 21.10 A data collection application system.

21.10 Information and advertising systems

There are many information systems installed in many places. Typically, these systems consist of large electronic LED displays providing moving messages with information such as news, weather forecasts, traffic conditions and perhaps advertisements which, ultimately, pay for the services in many cases.

Although these electronic displays are controlled with embedded systems, most of them need a user to load the message to be shown manually, or through the use of a computer, where the message is edited and later downloaded into the display controller using a serial interface. The idea of Internet-enabling these displays is to allow the information to be downloaded automatically from a central base, without the need to move to each location where the display is installed. The following sub-sections will describe different types of these information systems.

21.10.1 LED displays in public street

Many cities offer attractive points for installing these kinds of display. Typically, many people will see them, and they can provide news and other interesting information. If these display controllers are Internet-enabled, the information may be constantly updated from a central base, creating an 'online news channel' which may be effectively used as a vehicle to advertise.

Figure 21.11 shows displays installed in the street, which are remotely managed from a central station. The news and advertisements are downloaded into the displays using an Internet connection.

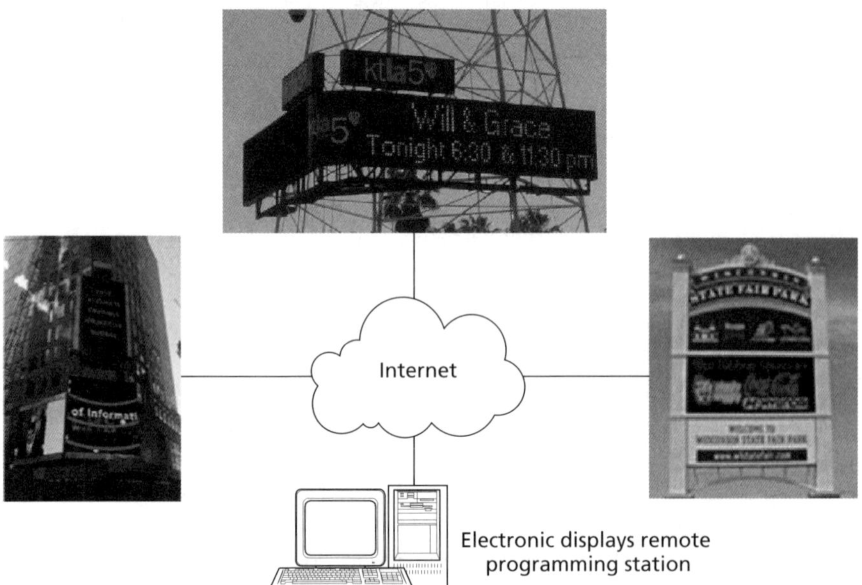

Figure 21.11 Electronic displays in the street.

21.10.2 LED displays in public transport

When people use public transport and they sit, they tend to stare at a fixed point in front of them. This provides a good opportunity to install a moving message display to communicate travel schedules, news and advertising.

Figure 21.12 shows a bus that has an LED display installed. The embedded controller may get an Internet connection using a mobile (cell) phone. Once it gets the connection, the information may be periodically updated from a server. In addition, a remote programming station may be used to modify certain parameters in the display controllers.

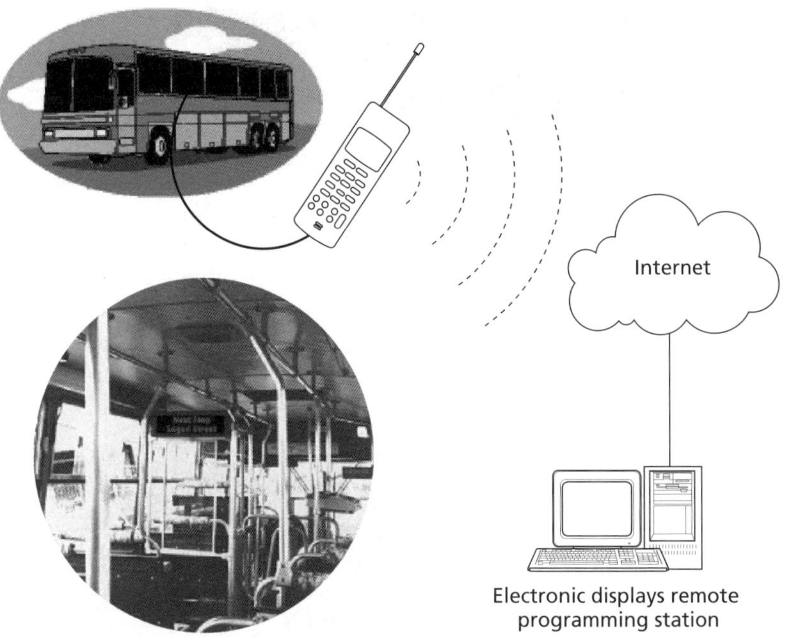

Figure 21.12 Electronic display in a bus.

21.10.3 LED displays in intelligent transportation systems

Vehicular traffic may greatly benefit from these displays installed in the road, highway or motorway. In fact, such equipment forms part of the 'Intelligent Transportation System' (ITS), which refers to transport systems applying information system technologies to avoid potential congestion problems. In addition, ITS goals include the improvement of transport safety and reduction of transportation times, fuel costs, air pollution and vehicle wear.

Figure 21.13 shows a motorway where an electronic LED displays important road conditions, to allow people to choose the best route. The fact that this information can be managed from a remote station allows operators to take important information from several points and devices (such as IP-cameras, position and speed detectors, and other sensors), and to communicate the advice in order to help drivers make the smartest choice.

Figure 21.13 Electronic displays on a motorway.

22 Security and surveillance applications

Security and surveillance systems were developed to protect our lives and goods. They are found in most commercial buildings, industrial installations and even in our own houses. Their uses are constantly increasing and their technology is improving. This chapter shows how such important systems may benefit from the embedded Internet technology.

22.1 Intruder alarms

Intruder (or burglar) alarms are used in stores, businesses and homes to detect intruder presence and avoid thefts. They can greatly benefit when they are connected to the Internet. We will start by reviewing conventional alarms, and then we will analyse the Internet-enabled case. Finally, we will see the benefits to network-enabled alarm elements (sensors, detectors, etc.) of distributing the 'intelligence' of the alarm among these elements, and monitoring them from a remote point.

22.1.1 Conventional alarms

Typically, most advanced alarms consist of an embedded system with some kind of detectors distributed through the building. For example, glass breakage detectors are used in windows, while magnetic sensors are attached to doors. Passive infrared motion sensors are used for detecting human movement, covering strategic zones in the building. Push buttons may be installed to manually activate the alarm, in an emergency. A control panel with a keypad and LED indicators (or an LCD display) are used to 'arm' and 'disarm' the alarm system, among other functions.

When an intruder presence is detected by a sensor, the embedded system receives this signal and sets off the alarm, alerting the building's neighbours. More sophisticated systems make a phone call, allowing a Monitoring Service Centre (MSC) to receive the alarm and act accordingly.

Figure 22.1 shows a typical alarm installation. The control panel has an embedded system, which provides 'centralized intelligence'. Each time a sensor detects activity (glass breaking, a door opening or movement), the embedded system is signalled in order for the embedded application to take

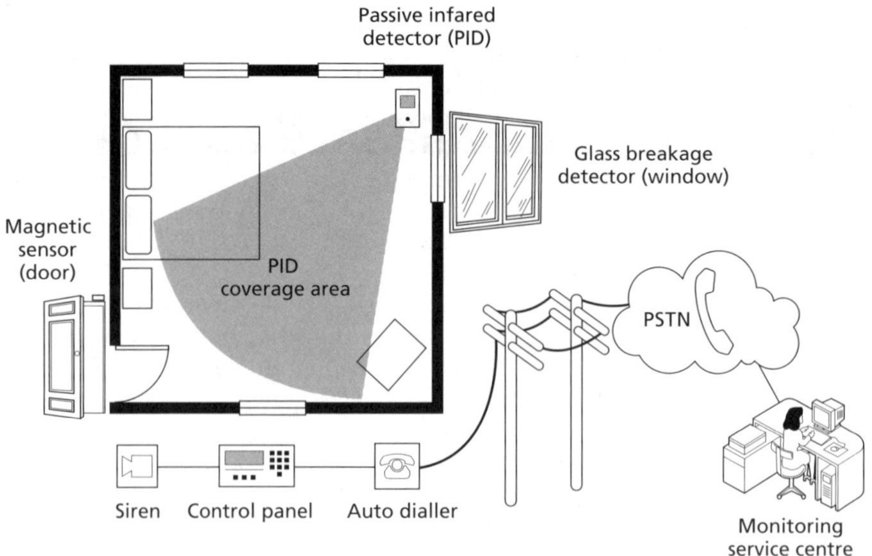

Figure 22.1 A typical intruder alarm system with monitoring service.

the appropriate action, such as to sound the siren, turn on some building lights or dial the MSC to inform them about the alarm activation.

Even when an alarm is connected to a monitoring service, when some events happen (alarm activation, alarm 'armed', alarm 'disarmed', etc.), they are not really monitored 'online'. They are only connected when such events happen. If we wish our alarm system to be monitored 'online', we need to install an exclusive phone line to the alarm system, while the MSC should have one line installed for every alarm system it supervises.

22.1.2 Internet-enabled alarms

If we provide an Internet broadband connection to the alarm system, we can have the MSC monitoring our installation 'online'. This means that it can not only receive news of events occurring, but it can also supervise the alarm state remotely. In this way, it can check if installed sensors and detectors are working properly, ensuring they will be ready when required.

This permanent link between the MSC and the supervised alarm system allows a better integration between them, and a higher performance in the supervision task. In this way, the MSC can be considered as a 'virtual extension' of the monitored alarm system.

22.1.3 Network-enabled alarm components

An advance on the previous systems would be distributing the 'centralized intelligence' of conventional systems among the alarm components, and Net-enabling them. In such case, each component (sensor, detector, PID) would behave as an independent unit with its own processing and networking capabilities.

A natural benefit of this arrangement is the remote management of each individual component from a distant place, like the MSC. Under this scheme, the MSC would act as the 'remote' control panel. That is, the MSC would receive the state of each sensor, and, if necessary, would take the appropriate action, such as activating the siren or calling the police to report the event.

Another benefit from this schema is redundancy, as the case when the 'central embedded system' hangs up, where any sensor detecting an event could signal the siren to trigger the alarm. On the other hand, even more, it could directly report the event to the MSC, if the local LAN is connected to this centre via the Internet.

Figure 22.2 shows how each alarm component may be connected to a local LAN and, through the Internet, to the MSC. In this configuration, each device has the capability to process and communicate detected events to an 'event processor' which may have defined the necessary action for procedure policies. The control panel would provide a keypad/LCD display for user intervention, and a 'minimal intelligence' to act in case communication with the MSC was not possible. Otherwise, the MSC would receive all reported events and would act accordingly. In this distributed alarm configuration, the alarm devices and the MSC are fully integrated through the inter-network.

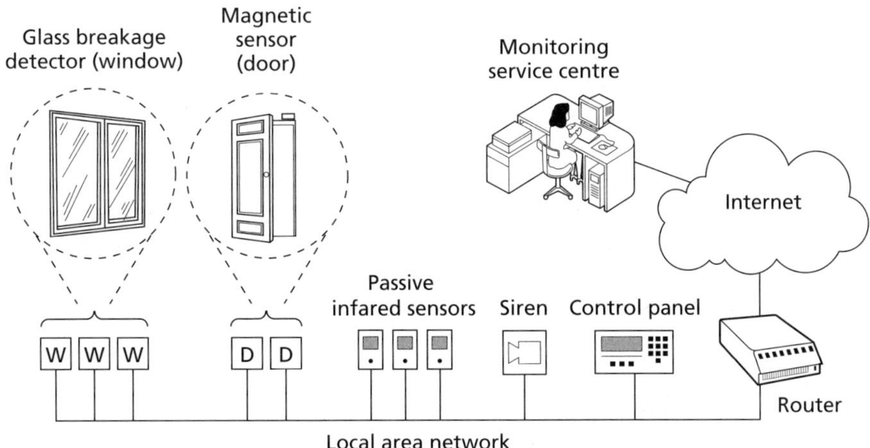

Figure 22.2 Net-enabling the alarm system components.

22.2 Video surveillance applications

Video surveillance systems are used in many places such as banks, offices, airports, stores and even in homes, to help security personnel in their activities. Video cameras are installed in strategic places, allowing operators to watch several areas of activity, from a centralized point.

Traditionally, analogue solutions called closed-circuit television (CCTV) were used for this purpose. Such equipment consists of analogue cameras linked to video monitors via cables or alternative direct means, forming a closed circuit over which the captured images are transmitted. Videotapes were used for the video recording.

Currently, analogue systems are being replaced by digital video surveillance systems (DVSS) that offer better video content processing and transmission. Advanced features such as motion detection and facial recognition are easily implemented by these digital systems. In addition, digital video allows systems to send a video stream to any server over TCP/IP networks. The server may display or record this information using appropriate software.

22.2.1 Digital video surveillance systems

Basically, digital video surveillance systems (DVSS) consist of three modules:

1 **Video capture module**: this module consists of a set of cameras and a video encoder. The video image is captured and compressed using a video-coding standard.
2 **Network interface module**: this module processes the video coded stream and delivers it to the network.
3 **Base station**: this module receives the video stream from the network, and it monitors every video channel. It also controls the camera's setting.

Figure 22.3 shows how the video images captured by the digital cameras are encoded and sent to a video server through the Internet. The video server uses special software, which allows many video channels to be displayed simultaneously. This software may also control some camera settings. As the figure shows, other servers might store the video stream for recording or back-up purposes.

The fact that these digital video surveillance systems use the TCP/IP networks or the Internet to transmit the captured images means the existing IT infrastructure can be used, making the integration with other systems easy and avoiding the installation costs for proprietary solutions such as CCTV systems.

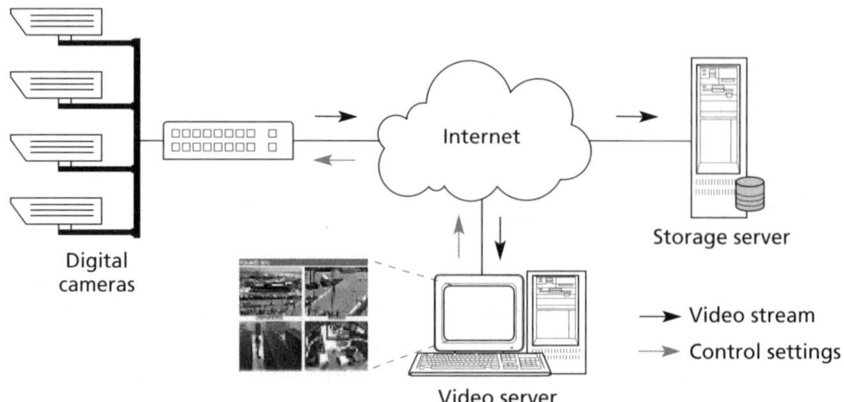

Figure 22.3 A digital video surveillance application.

22.2.2 IP camera

The concept of an IP camera (or network camera) relies on a stand-alone unit, which can be connected to the Internet, allowing users to access it from a standard Internet browser to view the live, full motion video captured, from any distant point. Basically, an IP camera consists of a digital camera connected to an embedded system with an embedded web server. This way, when a user connects to the IP camera using the web browser, the embedded web server delivers the live video captured by the camera.

Figure 22.4 shows how a user may address the remote IP camera using the web browser, and see the live video captured by the remote camera, through the Internet. Although this concept may be associated with the DVSS described in the previous section, the crucial difference is that while such systems transmit video stream continuously to servers, the IP camera only sends video images under request, when they are accessed by a user from a web browser. Another difference is that while DVSS are mostly used for private surveillance activities, most IP camera installations are open for public use, although, of course, they could implement a password protection in order to restrict their use.

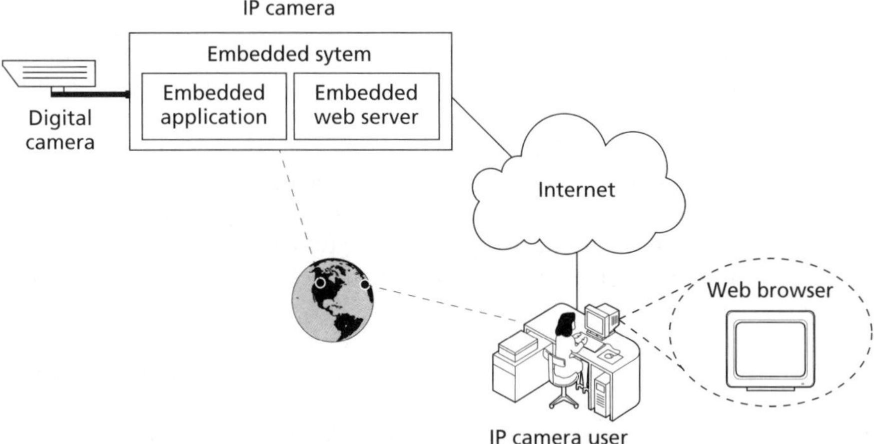

Figure 22.4 The IP camera (or network camera).

22.3 Integrated access control systems

Sometimes, there are specific areas where access must be restricted for some reason. In these cases, the access control systems fulfil this requirement, providing access for authorized personnel, but prohibiting entry for unauthorized persons. In other cases, it is necessary to keep track of an employee's work time, or provide a ticket to control the time a car is parked so the fee can be calculated. Several devices may contribute in these tasks. While most of the devices in Figure 22.5 may work as independent units, their storage

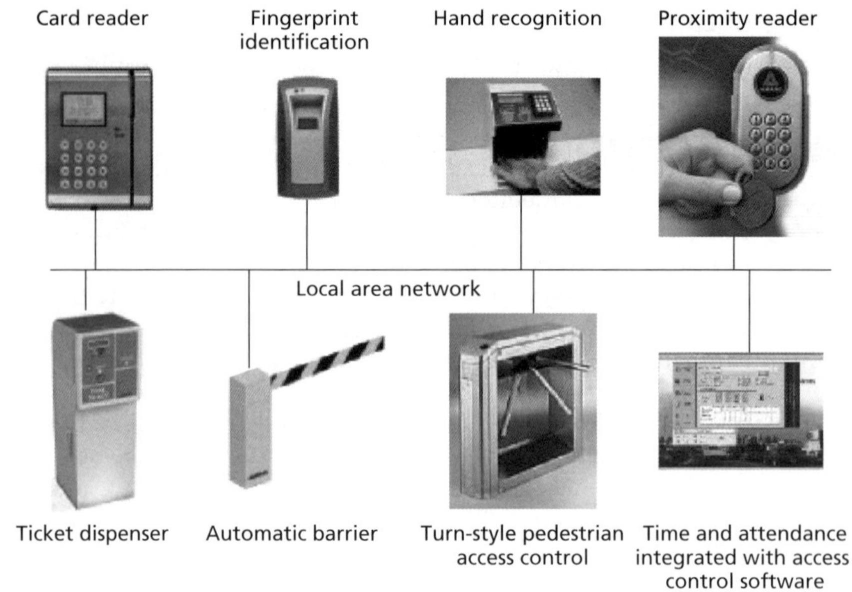

Figure 22.5 Network-enabled access control devices.

capacity is limited in some way. For example, fingerprint identification devices should store the biometric information of all authorized people. When the number of these authorized people is too high, the device's storage capacity may be insufficient.

Net-enabling the above devices gives the advantage that each device can communicate with a central desktop server, which extends the storage limit to 'virtually' any size. Another advantage is that devices may work 'online' with control software running at the server, so each device's activity may be monitored.

In addition, if a person's authorization access must be immediately revoked, it can be done directly from the server's control software, without the need to physically move to the device to update this information. Automatic barriers and door controllers may be directly controlled from the control software, to allow access to authorized individuals.

23

Tracking applications

Tracking applications provide real time information, which is used for security activities, efficiency operations and customer service improvements. Although some of the systems described here may still work without the use of the Internet, it will always provide a better way to integrate embedded systems with the available IT infrastructure.

23.1 GPS tracking systems

The Global Positioning System (GPS) is a satellite-based navigation system consisting of 24 satellites placed in orbit by the US Department of Defense. These satellites circle the earth twice a day and transmit information to Earth. GPS receivers take this information and use 'triangulation' to calculate the user's location. At least three satellites are needed to calculate a 2D position (latitude and longitude), while four are needed to calculate a 3D position (latitude, longitude and altitude). Once the user's location coordinates are known, the user's position can be shown on a digital map using a computer.

Installing a GPS system (and a communication channel) in a vehicle provides a way to send a vehicle's information to a central base. Many vehicle parameters such as position, speed, track, trip distance and distance to destination, among others, may be known from this point. Using the Internet as the communication channel between vehicles and the Monitoring Service Centre (MSC) may provide many additional benefits, such as tracking vehicles from any point in the world; downloading the route, weather, and much more information from a web server to the vehicle. Transit trip planning systems may provide 'online' information and assistance to those vehicles that require it.

Figure 23.1 shows a vehicle with a GPS receiver installed. The GPS information is submitted to the MSC where the vehicle's location is shown in a digital map using a computer. In this way, an operator may know the vehicle's exact position at any moment. A GSM/GPRS (global system for mobile communication/general packet radio service) system is used in the vehicle to provide an Internet connection. An optional information panel may be installed in order to display information downloaded from the MSC or any other web server.

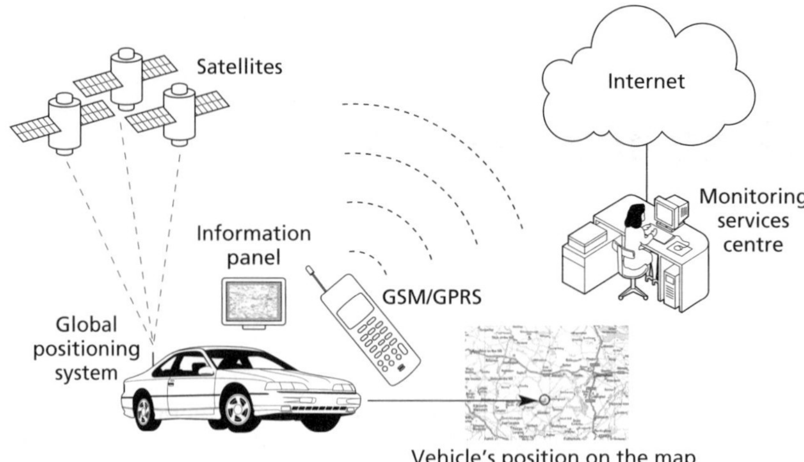

Figure 23.1 The GPS tracking system connected to the Internet.

Vehicle tracking systems provide a way to recover the vehicle when it is stolen. In addition, the vehicle may be remotely controlled by the Internet: to enable/disable the starter motor, to lock/unlock the doors, to honk the horn, etc. Although conventional systems may still work without an Internet connection, this contributes many services to the vehicle's user and makes possible tracking.

It is worth noting that this system is suitable for tracking not only cars, but also trucks, buses, police cars, emergency ambulances, motorcycles, and even people and pets. In some cases, such as tracking people and pets, a small radio frequency transmitter is used to send the data to a central base.

23.2 Automatic taxi dispatcher

Vehicle tracking systems may be integrated with an automatic job dispatcher system to provide a solution to a taxi fleet, increasing fleet efficiency, reducing operating costs and providing a better customer service while drivers work in a safe and equitable environment (and avoid 'favouritism').

Figure 23.2 shows how this system works. When the customer calls (1) the taxi dispatcher centre, the receptionist notes where the customer is (2), which is input into the automatic job dispatch system. This system keeps track of the taxi fleet, using GPS tracking, which transmits the taxi's whereabouts and state (free/busy). Having this information, the automatic job dispatch system sends a message to the customer's nearest free taxi, which receives the job and instructions with customer details through the in-vehicle data terminal (3). With this information, the Taxi moves to pick up the passenger (4).

This system eliminates the 'favouritism' perceived by some drivers, as the dispatch is fully automated and chooses the correct vehicle according to its

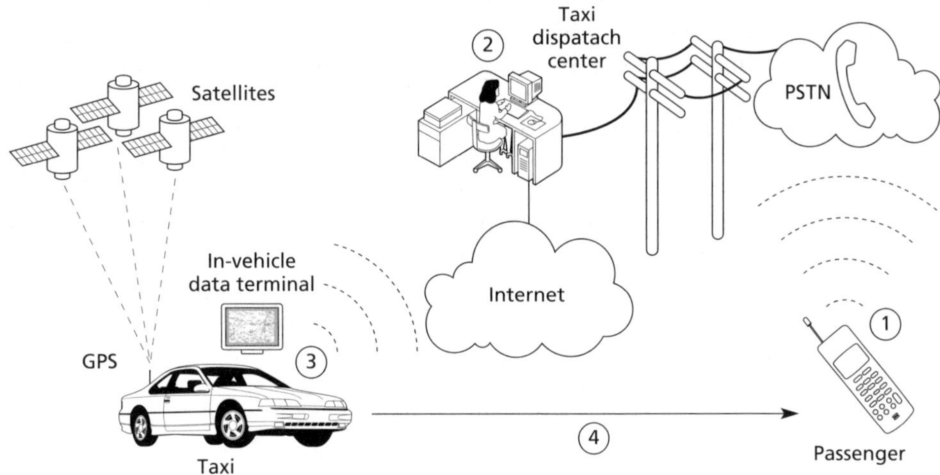

Figure 23.2 Automatic taxi despatcher system.

position, efficiently distributing the work. This also reduces the customer's waiting time, increasing customer satisfaction. The drivers work in a safer environment as anti-theft and panic alarm features are integrated into the system, protecting drivers' and passengers' lives.

23.3 Public transport tracking

Many factors such as traffic congestion and accidents make it very difficult for public transport operators to deliver a service according to schedules. This has a negative impact on the quality of service provided to the passenger.

A Real Time Passenger Information (RTPI) system provides bus riders with real-time information about the expected times of arrival at any given stop. In this way, the waiting time in the bus stands is minimized so users may use their time more efficiently. Users may access real time maps, which show vehicle locations, and they may receive alerts on their mobile phones or wireless devices which notify the time the next bus will be arriving at their stop. This alert's anticipation time may be selectable for each user.

In an RTPI system, every bus unit has a GPS receiver, which provides the bus's position at any time. This information is sent to a central base, which has an Internet connection. From this point, the data is sent to a central location, where it is processed and analysed. This process's 'predictions' are delivered to the bus's users via a variey of ways, such as the Internet, alert messages to mobile phones, information displays at the bus stops, etc. The resulting 'predictions' are adjusted as the bus travels along its route. Many factors such as traffic, time of the day, weather conditions, accidents, breakdowns, etc. are taken into account in this process.

Figure 23.3 shows how an RTPI system is implemented. Each bus unit has a GPS receiver, which provides the bus's position data at any time. This data is transmitted to a base station, which uses the Internet to send the data to a central location. From this point, and after the data is processed, information is delivered to information electronic displays installed in bus stops, and it is available to see 'online' via the Internet. Subscribing users receive alerts to their mobile phones and wireless PDAs. A Tracking Monitoring Centre's operator may supervise the complete operation from an Internet connection.

Security is a major concern, especially on school buses. In these cases, parents may monitor the bus location via the Internet, and they could estimate the time at which the bus would arrive at home. In addition, using a radio frequency identification (RFID) electronic chip embedded in the student's identification card, an RFID reader would identify each student as they boarded the bus. In this way, parents not only could find the bus on a map in real time, but they would also know if their child was travelling on this bus.

Some cities have implemented an Transit Trip Planning System, which uses Internet Geographical Information System (IGIS) that allows travellers to find the most efficient bus itinerary trip possible based on the start and end location, as well as the travel date and time. This service is provided through kiosks connected to the Internet, and installed in airport, train, and bus terminal stations. This system may be integrated with RTPI systems to provide information that is more 'accurate'.

For short-distance public transport services, the major concerns centre on fulfilment of the scheduled commitment, and the number of passengers transported over the authorized capacity. With these tracking systems, applicant authorities can easily control the service they provide.

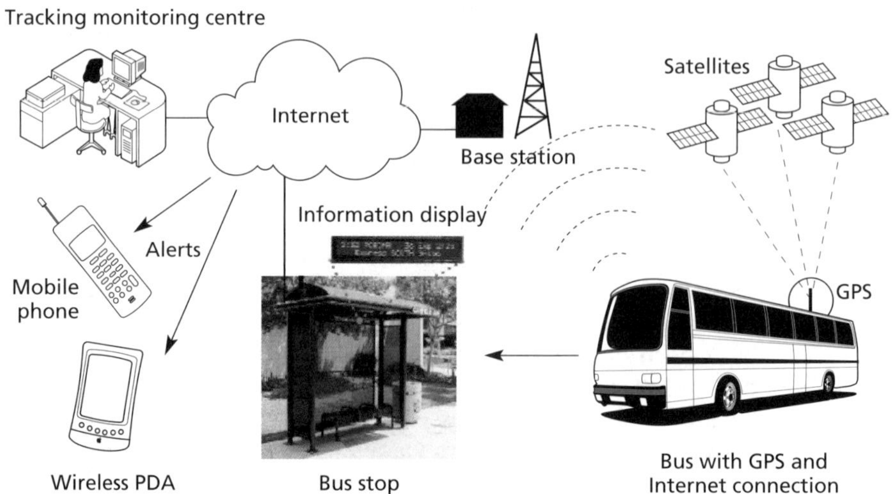

Figure 23.3 Bus tracking system.

23.4 Shipment tracking systems

Shipment tracking systems are used by many shipping companies to efficiently manage their tasks, while at the same time they improve the customer service, telling customers where their shipment is at any moment. Figure 22.4 shows a typical shipping route. It begins with a customer giving the shipment to the shipping company's receptionist. A barcode label (or perhaps an RFID label) is attached to the boxes as a shipment identification (1). This label allows a fast identification of the shipment, as it is moved along the warehouse.

While the box is transferred from this point to other warehouses (2), the truck uses a GPS system to provide the location data at any time. This information is submitted via an Internet connection, using GSM/GPRS. Once the user's box is in the destination warehouse (3), it is prepared for its final delivery.

In its final trip, the shipment may be located using GPS installed in a van (4). When the successful delivery occurs (5), the captured signature for proof of delivery is submitted to the system, using the Internet connection available in the van. In this way, the customer may know in real time when the shipping was delivered and who signed the reception sheet. Users may follow the complete process using a web browser through an Internet connection.

As this case shows, embedded systems can provide a complete solution by integrating seamlessly with the company's IT infrastructure.

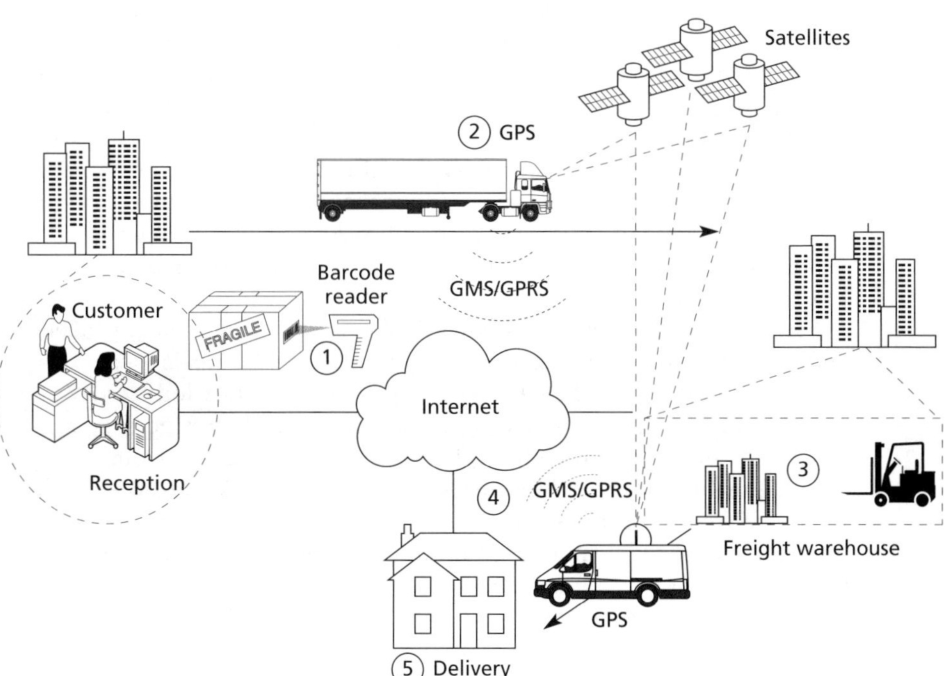

Figure 23.4 Shipment tracking from reception to delivery.

24

Outsourcing embedded code: using Web Services

Throughout the book, we have seen how embedded systems can be connected to the Internet and how to take advantage of the available resources. This chapter will show how embedded systems may outsource code using a concept that is becoming popular: Web Services. After introducing the concepts and protocols behind Web Services, we will see the necessary steps to implement this kind of solution for the embedded world, using a real application case. Finally, Lab 13 will be presented for those who want to learn more on this subject in a very 'hands-on' way.

24.1 Introduction

Embedded systems have limited resources compared with desktop computers. Large memory space and high processing power are necessary for some complex algorithms or CPU-intensive processes. In addition, embedded applications requiring the use of an embedded database make the situation worse.

Providing embedded systems have an Internet connectivity, they can use Internet resources, so these complex tasks can be resolved remotely in external servers. In this way, with few resources we can get great results using 'external intelligence' provided by desktop servers connected to the Internet.

Figure 24.1 shows an embedded application calling a local procedure (1) and a remote procedure (2) through the Internet. In this last case, the caller routine could pass the necessary parameters needed to resolve the requested functionality. Once processed, the called routine may return the results to the caller procedure. These results may come from a very complex algorithm, or a CPU-intensive calculation, or perhaps a set of records retrieved from a database. In this way, the embedded system may benefit from the use of the available 'external intelligence' without the need of additional resources.

The above concept could be implemented by developing proprietary solutions. For example, a TCP connection could be established between the embedded system and the remote server. Then, the embedded application sends a message with the name of the remote function requested and

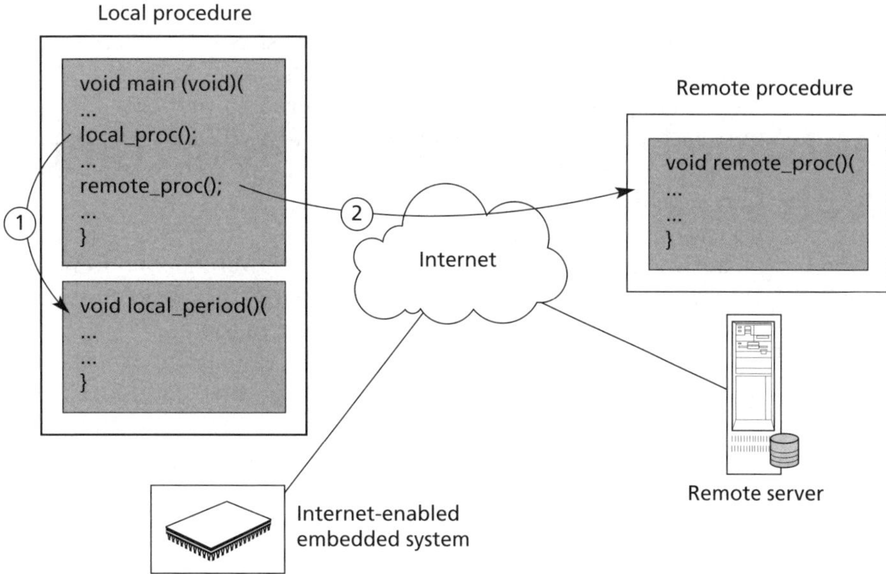

Figure 24.1 Calling a remote procedure through the Internet.

its parameters. The remote server may process this message; it calls the requested function, and sends back a message with the function results. Of course, these messages should be properly formatted according to a determined protocol. Once the response is sent, the server should close the TCP connection.

Although the above is possible, a better solution is reached using standard procedures, messages, and protocols. This is obtained using Web Services.

24.2 Web Services

24.2.1 Introduction

Web Services are a standardized way to call a remote procedure over the Internet. They allow a distributed computing schema to work independently from the technology, language and device. This means any device connected to any server anywhere on the Internet.

Web Services are offered by servers, which expose a piece of functionality through a web interface. A client may consume this functionality from its application, using standard Internet protocols such as HTTP (HyperText Transport Layer), SOAP (Simple Object Access Protocol) and XML (eXtended Markup Language). HTTP is used as the transport protocol, to move messages between clients and servers. For secure transmissions, HTTPS (Secure HTTP) can be used instead. These message formats are defined according to the SOAP protocol. The SOAP messages are encoded using XML. The advantage of using HTTP (or HTTPS) as a transport protocol is that most firewalls allow HTTP traffic in order for users to browse the Internet.

Figure 24.2 shows a typical scenario where some Web Services are consumed from an e-commerce company website page. When a user accesses the Shopping Cart web page (1), and after choosing the items he or she wants to buy, a shipping cost estimation is required so that this can be added to the purchase price. Rather than implementing this cost estimator locally, the shipping company's service is used by way of Web Service. So, the Shopping Cart page uses the Shipping Cost Calculation Web Service (2) and informs the user about the charge to apply in this case. In a similar way, when the user makes the payment, a Payment Processing Web Service from a payment processing company is consumed (3). When this Web Service returns, the transaction details are provided and shown to the user.

In this way, a diversity of functionalities may be exposed and consumed through the Internet, in a seamless manner. Instead of locally developing the required functionality, it is consumed from the functionality provider using the Web Services. Additional benefits are obtained from the maintenance point of view, because any change in the Web Service functionality is instantly reflected in the client when it is used, avoiding the need to reinstall or modify any code in the client.

The scenario is very similar for embedded systems consuming Web Services from the Internet, since they would also consume the services through a Web Service call over the Internet.

Although we have only considered embedded systems consuming Web Services, it could also be possible to have them exposing Web Services to any other devices. In this case, for example, a web page could consume an embedded Web Service to get environmental measurements, each time a user accesses the page.

Typical applications for exposing Web Services are currency conversion, specific format validations, spell checkers, language translators, credit card transactions and bank operations. However, this list by no means exhausts

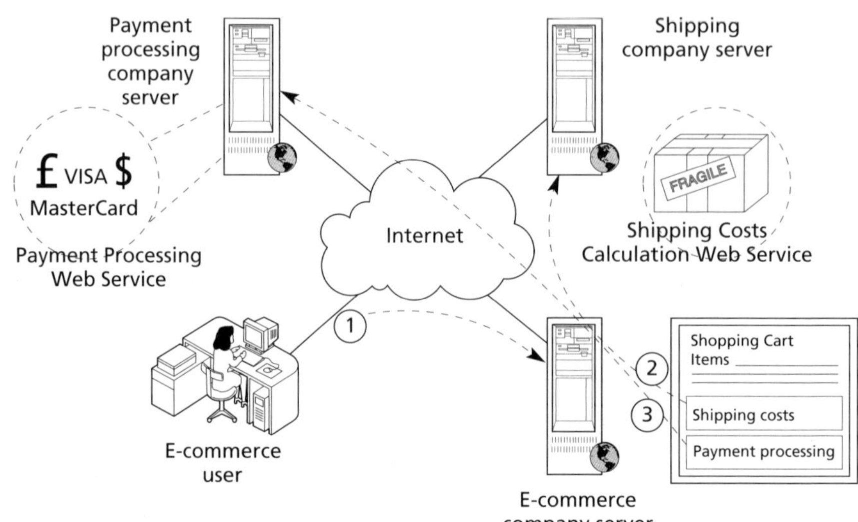

Figure 24.2 Exposing and consuming web services scenario.

the possibilities. If embedded systems require a specific functionality not found in the Internet, it may even be possible to develop our own Web Services to supply this functionality, and submit them to the Internet.

Additional advantages of using Web Services rather than proprietary protocols are the tools available for Web Service development. These include the use of the existing Web Service infrastructure, the possibility of installing our own developed Web Services in low-cost sharing hosting plans (they usually do not allow customer applications other than web pages running in these servers), and the ever-growing kind of Web Services available on the Internet.

24.2.2 Standards for Web Services

In order for a Web Service to be used, first it must be advertised, to have potential clients made aware of it. Then, the client must know the web service Interface specifications, in order to be able to correctly call it. A number of protocols have been developed to help in these tasks, as follows:

- **UDDI (Universal Description, Discovery and Integration)**: The UDDI database is a central repository of available Web Services. Developers can access the UDDI registry to search for a Web Service functionality.
- **DISCO (Discovery Protocol)**: It allows dynamic discovery of all Web Services located on a particular website.
- **WSDL (Web Service Description Language)**: It allows specifying in a WSDL document each method of a Web Service and the parameters it accepts and returns. That is, it specifies the interface of the Web Services. This document is considered like a contract that specifies the SOAP messages to send to the Web Service and the messages to expect in return.

Figure 24.3 shows the required steps in order for an application to use a Web Service. The first step is to search for a Web Service that provides the desired functionality (1). The UDDI Registry provides this information. Once it is found, we will be redirected to the Web Service vendor site. Using the DISCO

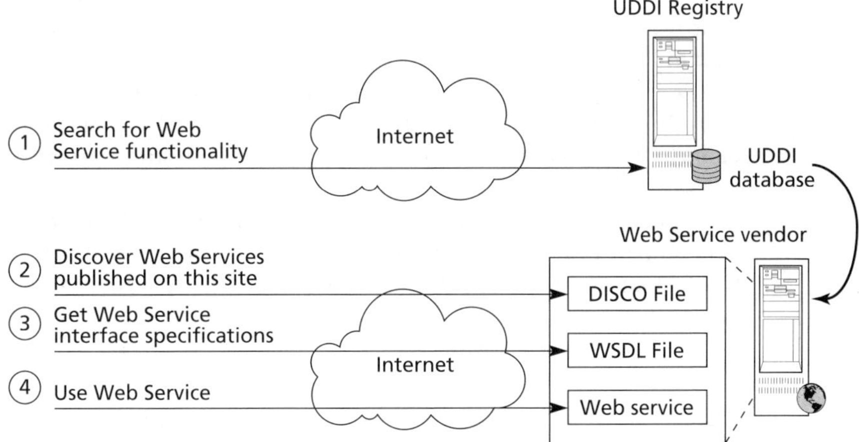

Figure 24.3 Web Service standards.

file, we will discover the Web Services available on this site (2). The next step is to get the Web Service Interface specifications using the WSDL file (3). From this point, we have all the information to correctly use the Web Service (4).

24.2.3 Web Services transport protocols and bindings

Currently, ASP.NET supports only HTTP as the transport protocol. However, three styles of binding to HTTP are supported: SOAP (versions 1.1 and 1.2), HTTP GET and HTTP POST. Although support for the HTTP GET/POST binding is more limited than for SOAP, in our embedded applications they may prove more convenient as they present simpler message structures, as we will see later.

In order to enable or disable one or more of the above bindings, the **<add .../>**, **<remove .../>** or **<clear />** elements may be used in the **web.config** file: The clear element clears all settings that are inherited from parent configura-

```
<configuration>
   ...
   <system.web>
      ...
      <webServices>
         <protocols>
            <clear />
            <add name="HttpSoap"/>
            <add name="HttpSoap12"/>
            <add name="HttpPost"/>
            <add name="HttpGet"/>
            <add name="Documentation"/>
         </protocols>
      </webServices>
   </system.web>
</configuration>
```

tion files. The add element enables the binding, while the remove element (not used above) disables it. The Documentation option provides documentation for the Web Service.

Let's see an example. Open the Internet Browser and enter the following link: **http://www.embeddedinternet.org/Book/WebServices/MathService.asmx** and the screen at the top of page 511 should appear in the Internet browser.

This screen shows the four implemented methods for that Web Service. Clicking on the 'Service Description' link, we will get a WSDL document with the formal description for each method and the parameters it accepts and it returns.

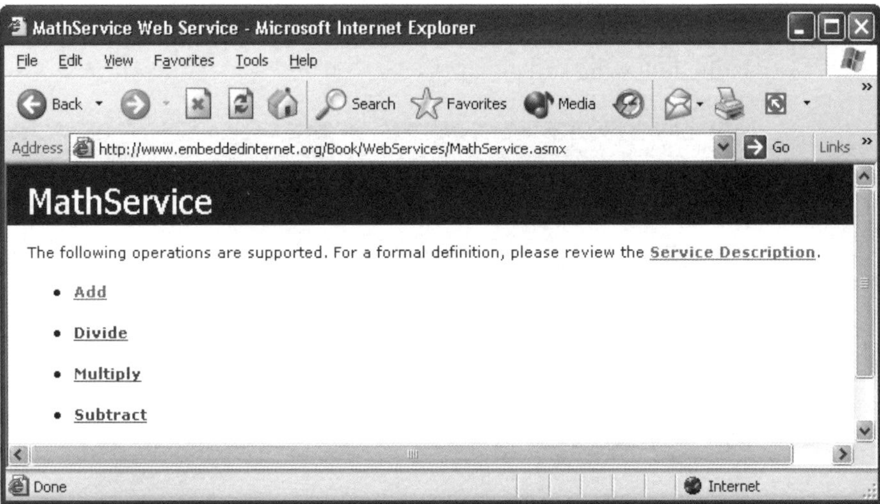

In order to test one of the above methods, make a click in the appropriate link. For example, making a click in the 'Add' method link, we get the following screen

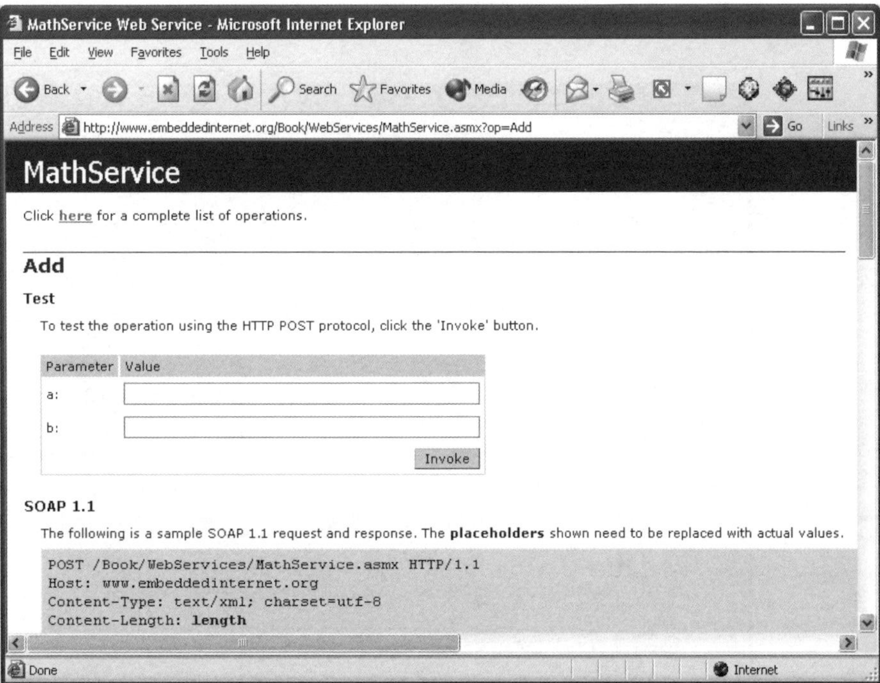

Then, entering numerical values for both parameters (a = 1 and B = 2), and pressing the 'Invoke' button, we will get the result that the method returns, as the following screen shows:

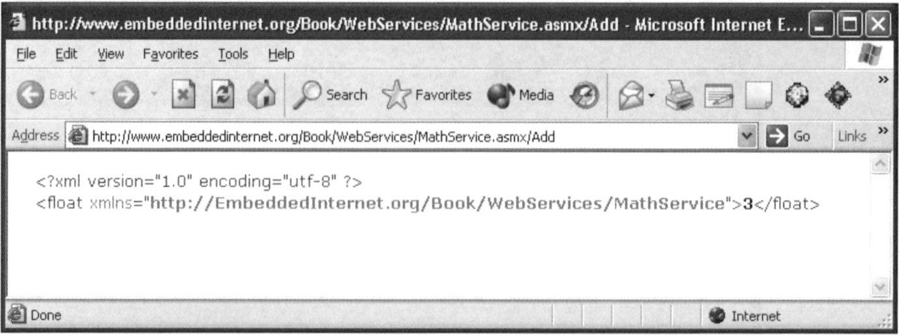

The invoked method returns a message encoded with XML including the Add operation's result (3).

In the previous screen, where the Test Invoke option appears, the Web Service Documentation presents the appropriate Request and Response messages format, for each of the enabled bindings. The following screenshots show the message format for the SOAP1.1, SOAP1.2, HTTP GET and HTTP POST bindings:

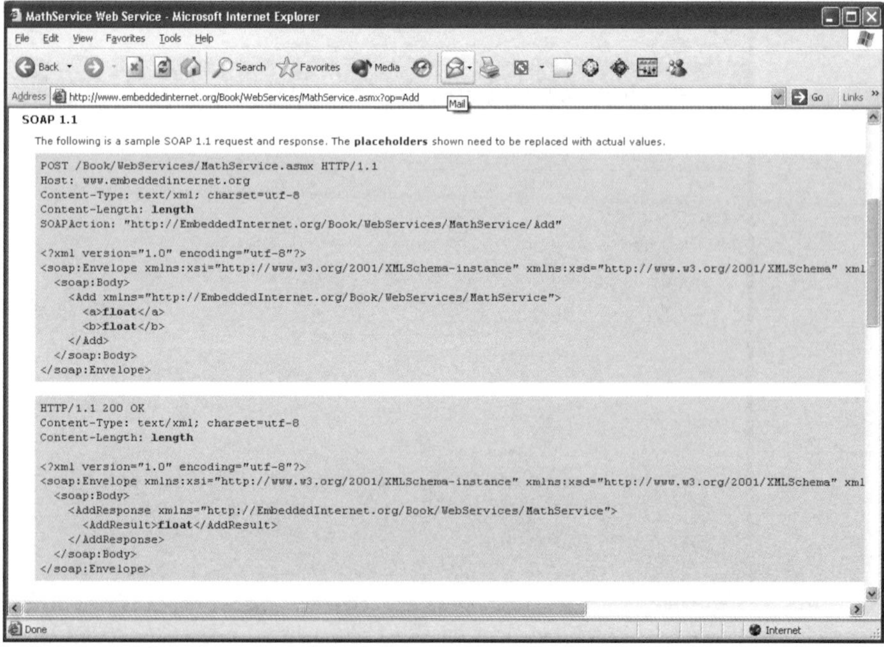

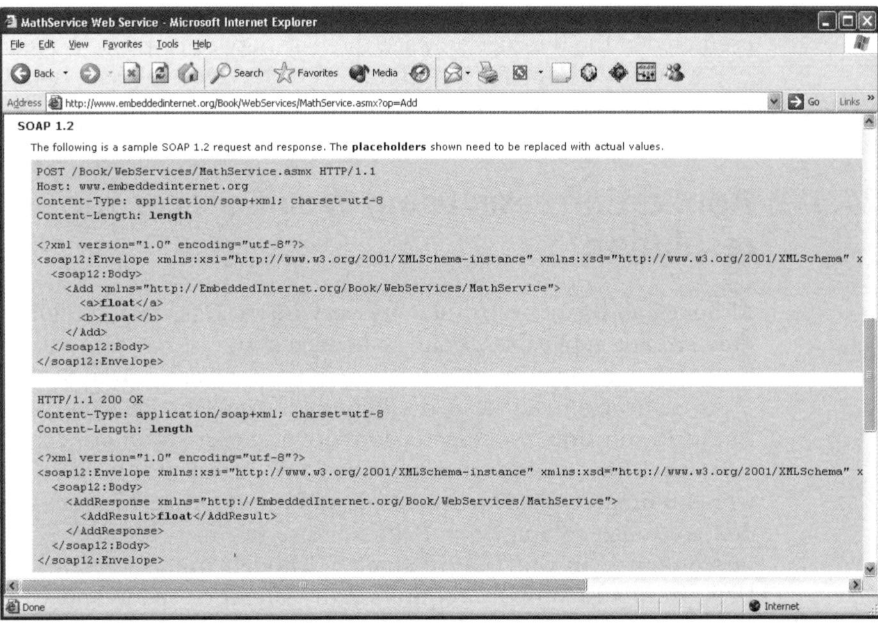

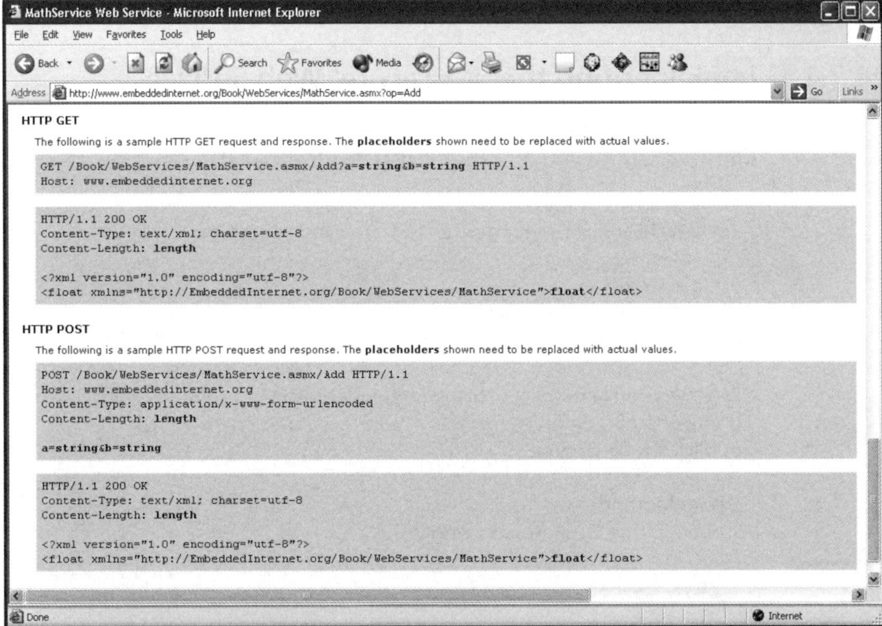

As the above screens show, the HTTP GET and HTTP POST message formats are the simplest and most convenient for their use in embedded applications. In addition, the HTTP GET binding allows the use of the Web Service to go through the HTTP URL syntax, as follows: **http://www.embeddedinternet.org/ Book/ WebServices/MathService.asmx/Add?a=1&b=2** where `Add` is the invoked method, and a and b are the required parameters. When the above URL address is entered in the Internet browser, the Web Service response is received.

For further information about Web Services, please visit **http://msdn.microsoft.com/webservices/webservices**.

24.3 Application case: using Web Services for DNS resolution

Although all the above results are very interesting, they do not mean much if they are not applicable to our embedded systems. For this reason, we will see how embedded applications may benefit from the use of Web Services.

As we have already seen in Chapter 11, the Domain Name System uses the Name Resolution process to convert a server's domain name into its IP address. This resolution process involves a set of queries to DNS servers, which ultimately provide the requested information. In order for our embedded systems to query a DNS server, it must have the DNS protocol implemented in the TCP/IP stack. Although this is certainly possible, the DNS protocol's support requires more memory space and CPU processing power for its execution. Instead of this, embedded systems may 'outsource' this service using a Web Service, which would provide the DNS resolution.

24.3.1 Implementing the 'DnsService' Web Service

The following code, written in C# (C-Sharp), implements the DnsResolve( ) method, which returns the first IP address of the requested domain name:

```
<%@ WebService Language="C#" Class="DnsService" %>

using System;
using System.Web.Services;
using System.Net;

[WebService(Namespace="http://EmbeddedInternet.org/Book/WebServices/DnsService")]
[WebServiceBinding(ConformsTo = WsiProfiles.BasicProfile1_1)]
public class DnsService {

  [WebMethod]
  public string DnsResolve(string dn)
  {
    try
    {
      IPHostEntry iphost = Dns.GetHostEntry(dn);
      return iphost.AddressList[0].ToString();
    }
    catch(Exception ex)
    {
      return ex.Message;
    }
  }
}
```

Here the [WebMethod] attribute indicates the method entry, and the dn string is the domain name that must be resolved. The **Dns.GetHostEntry( )** method resolves the domain name into an IP address list (it may have more than one IP address), and the first encountered IP address (**iphost.AddressList[0]**) is returned.

The above code is found in the **DnsService.asmx** file, which must be published in any hosting service with ASP.NET 2.0 support.

24.3.2 Testing the 'DnsService' Web Service

Once the above file has been published in a web server, the Web Service can be tested from an Internet Browser using the following URL syntax: **www.embeddedinternet.org/Book/WebServices/DnsService.asmx/DnsResolve?dn=www.intramarket.com.ar** and we should get the IP address or the 'No such host is known' message where the domain name could not be resolved.

24.3.3 Using the 'DnsService' Web Service from an embedded system

Once the Web Service has been implemented and tested, the next step is to implement the Web Service Consumer into the embedded application. The **webservice.c** module provides this implementation:

```
void webservice_call(char * dn) {
  int socket;
  unsigned short port;
  char wsIPaddress[4]  = wsIP;

   p_dn = dn;
   socket = tcp_socket_open(port, webservice_control);
   if (socket > 0) {
      if (debug_webservice)
         printf("\r\nTCP Socket %d created, port %d\n", socket, tcp_get_port(socket));
   }else {
      if (socket == TCP_INVALID_SOCKET) {
         printf("Error opening a socket: increment TCP_MAX_SOCKETS=%d\n",
                                                          TCP_MAX_SOCKETS);
      }
      if (socket == TCP_PORT_ALREADY_USED) {
         printf("Error opening a socket: Port %d already used\n", port);
      }
      return;                    // Error
   }
   tcp_conn_open(socket, wsIPaddress, 80);
}
```

The **webservice_call( )** routine is called from the **console.c** module in order to resolve the domain name passed as a parameter. The passed parameter is a pointer, which is saved into a **p_dn** variable (a *char pointer* variable declared at the beginning of the **webservice.c** module) for later use. Then, a socket is opened declaring the **webservice_control( )** routine to receive events from the

tcp.c module. If there are no errors, the **tcp_conn_open( )** routine is used to establish a connection with the Web Service server, whose address is configured in the stackcfg.h file.

Once the connection has been established with the server, the tcp.c module calls the **webservice_control( )** routine passing the TCP_EVENT_ESTABLISHED event. The following code shows the process for this event:

```
static void webservice_control(.......................) {
 ...
 switch(event) {
  case TCP_EVENT_CONN_REQ:
    ...
    break;
  case TCP_EVENT_ESTABLISHED:
    if (debug_webservice)
        printf("Connection Established with IP: %d.%d.%d.%d - Port: %d\n",
                   *srcipaddr,*(srcipaddr+1),*(srcipaddr+2),*(srcipaddr+3),srcport);

    if (tcp_send_data(soc_handler, create_query) == TCP_SOCKET_ERROR)
      printf("Error sending data: TCP already have data to send!\r\n");
    else
      if (debug_webservice)
        printf("The WebService Request was sent!\r\n");
    break;
  case TCP_EVENT_DATA:
    ...
```

Once the connection has been established, the embedded application uses the **tcp_send_data( )** function to send the Web Service Request to the server. The **create_query( )** function is declared to fill the transmit buffer when appropriate.

The Web Service Request fulfils the HTTP GET binding, and it uses the following constants:

```
const char wsreq1[] = "GET /Book/WebServices/DnsService.asmx/DnsResolve?dn=";
const char wsreq2[] = " HTTP/1.1\r\nHost: www.embeddedinternet.org\r\n\r\n";
```

Between the above strings, the queried domain name must be inserted. Then, when the **create_query( )** function is called to fill the buffer, the Request is composed.

```
int create_query(int soc_handler, unsigned short *position, unsigned short *len) {
 int i=0;

 i += sprintf(&tx_buf[TCP_DATA_START + i],wsreq1);
 i += sprintf(&tx_buf[TCP_DATA_START + i],p_dn);
 i += sprintf(&tx_buf[TCP_DATA_START + i],wsreq2);
```

```
  if (debug_webservice)
    printf("Web Service Request: \r\n%s", &tx_buf[TCP_DATA_START]);

  (*len) -= i;
  (*position) += i;
  return 0;
}
```

As the above code shows, the defined strings (wsreq1 and wsreq2) and the queried domain name (pointed by p_dn) are copied into the buffer, in the appropriate positions. If the debug_webservice option is set in the **debug.h** file, the Web Service Request is shown in the console.

Once the Web Service Request has been processed by the server, the Response is sent back to the embedded application. When this Response has been received by the **tcp.c** module, the **webservice_control( )** routine is called with the TCP_EVENT_DATA event. The following code shows the rest of the process for the Web Service Response:

```
...
case TCP_EVENT_DATA:
  if (debug_webservice) {
    printf("Event: Data Available from IP: %d.%d.%d.%d - Port: %d\n",
           *srcipaddr,*(srcipaddr+1),*(srcipaddr+2),*(srcipaddr+3),srcport);
    printf("\nWeb Service Response:\r\n");
    for(i=0;i<data_len;i++) {
      printf("%c", rx_buf[data_index + i]);
    }
    printf("\r\n\n");
  }
  start = search_string("http://EmbeddedInternet.org/Book/WebServices/DnsService",
                                        data_index, data_len);
  size  = search_string("</", data_index + start, data_len - start);
  printf("IP address: ");
  for(i=0;i<size-4;i++) {
    printf("%c", rx_buf[data_index + start + 2 + i]);
  }
  printf("\r\n");
  tcp_conn_close(soc_handler);
  break;
case TCP_EVENT_CONN_CLOSED:
  tcp_socket_close(soc_handler);
  if (debug_webservice)
    printf("Socket %d closed\n", soc_handler);
  break;
...
```

If the debug_webservice option is set, the Web Service Response is shown at the console. After this, the response is parsed in order to extract the result of the domain Name Resolution. For this, we use the **search_string( )** function which returns with the receive buffer position where the passed string was found. Once we have the start and size of the result in the Response, we can show it at the console. Then, as the Web Service Consume has finished, the connection is closed and the opened socket is closed.

24.3.4 Executing Lab 13: resolving DNS domain names

In order to test the complete solution, we can load the Lab 13 in the embedded system hardware, and run the embedded application. The following screenshot shows the embedded system console with the entered domain name (1) and the Web Service Request message (2) (the debug_webservice option was set in these examples).

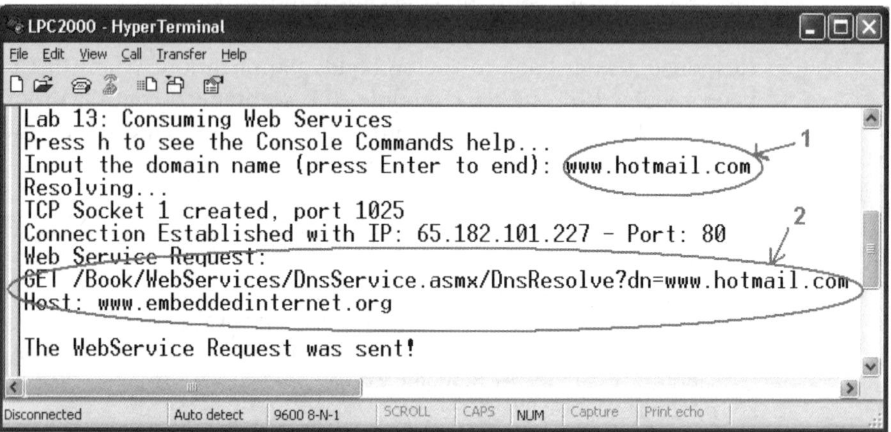

The following screenshot shows the Web Service Response received by the embedded application. This response consists of a header (1) and the body (2) that contains the query result. Finally, the IP address is extracted and shown (3).

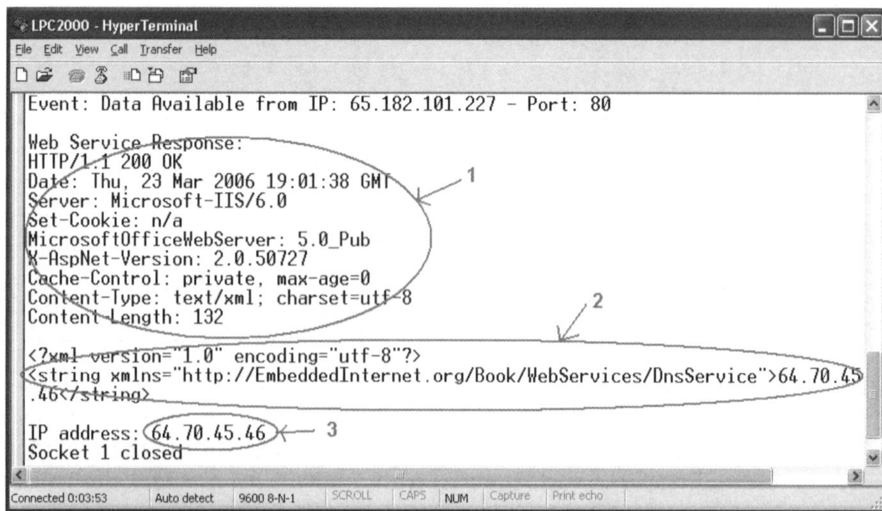

Lab 13: Consuming Web Services

Lab 13 introduction

In this Lab, we will consume a Web Service from our embedded application to resolve a domain name.

Lab 13 target support

This Lab supports both types of boards. Select the appropriate target build from the 'Configuration drop-down menu' in the Workspace window.

Lab 13 options setting

This Lab uses the debug_webservice option. Initially, this option is turned off.

Lab 13 resources used

We will use a Web Service published in the **www.embeddedinternet.org** web site. In order to use a Web Service published in another server, set its IP address in the **stackcfg.h** file. As the server's IP address may change from time to time, it is convenient to check this using the DnsService Web Service from a web browser, as explained in section 24.3.2.

Lab 13 instructions

Complete the steps according to Chapter 12 (see section 12.6). Once the Lab is running, follow the Lab 13 exercises. If you use the LPC-P212X board, you must make the dial-up connection before executing the lab exercises. If the Web Server is published on the Internet, the embedded system must have Internet access.

Lab 13 exercises

- Press the 'e' key to select the DNS resolution option. Enter the domain name, and press the Enter key to start the process. After some time, the console should display the resolved IP address. Try with different domain names. When a domain name is not found, the 'No such host is known' message is shown.
- Set the debug_webservice option in the **stackcfg.h** file. Build the Lab and download the code into the embedded system. Now, the Web Service Request and Response messages should be displayed each time a domain name is resolved. Verify the message formats with the HTTP GET binding message format.
- Use Ethereal to capture the packets in the network, and compare them with those shown on the console.

Appendix A

Bluetooth and IEEE 802.11 wireless LAN

In Chapter 3 we saw Ethernet as the most common LAN technology that enables devices to communicate with others at layer two, while in Chapter 4 the Serial protocols were examined, which provide a point-to-point solution in modern networks. With those technologies devices are able to have Internet access, and run any application protocol to start to benefit from the advantages that the Internet offers. However, in contrast with those 'wired' technologies, new wireless solutions were developed for such cases where a wire connection was not available or applications where the use of wires was somewhat cumbersome. In order to extend the Internet access with other solutions, this appendix provides an overview about two wireless technologies that are being rapidly adopted: Bluetooth and 802.11 Wireless LAN.

A.1 Bluetooth

A.1.1 Introduction

Many devices, such as personal digital assistants (PDAs), laptops and mobile (cellular) phones provide a way to interconnect, in order to gain Internet access, synchronize internal calendars, 'To-Do lists', telephone and e-mail directories, etc. For such purposes, they use cables for device interconnections.

However, there are compatibility problems with the way that different devices use proprietary connectors, special cables and different synchronization methods. Some of them provide an infrared port, which certainly resolves most of the incompatibility problems, although with some limitations, as we will see.

In order to overcome the above limitations, a special interest group (SIG), initially formed by communication companies such as Ericsson and Nokia and computing companies such as IBM, Toshiba and INTEL, started the design of a royalty-free, open specification technology for a universal short-range wireless communication method that allows all devices to connect to each other. The code name assigned to the project was Bluetooth, and the initial SIG was later joined by several companies from both the communication and computing worlds. In 1999, the first version of Bluetooth specification was published.

The main goal of the Bluetooth project was the development of a single chip, low-cost and low-power radio-based wireless network technology that supports both voice and data, allowing devices to implement an ad-hoc network (a network that does not require additional infrastructure, like *access point* devices and others). (See Fig. A.1.) In this way, two or more Bluetooth devices may implement a Wireless Personal Area Network (WPAN).

The potential use of Bluetooth is not limited to mobile phones, PDAs and computers, but it may be incorporated in any device and/or appliance that can present communication possibilities (e.g. camera, keyboard, mouse, headset, phones, speakers). Any kind of digital device requiring a communication method would greatly benefit from the use of this technology. As the cost of incorporating this technology is comparable to the cable and connectors cost, the Bluetooth market increases enormously.

A.1.2 Comparing Bluetooth and infrared (IR)

The IR technology has been used in many computer devices as a way to provide a point-to-point wireless communication at a very low price. However, its limitation comes from the fact that devices require a direct line of sight to effectively communicate, as in the case of the popular TV, VCR or audio equipment IR remote control.

Bluetooth, on the other hand, allows both point-to-point and multi-point communications, so many devices may be communicating among themselves at the same time. In addition, it does not require a direct line between devices, and it covers a larger transmission range.

A.1.3 Bluetooth technology overview

As Bluetooth was designed with the global community in mind, it operates in the 2.45 GHz unlicensed radio band, globally available. This band is reserved for industrial, scientific and medical (ISM) use for wireless communications

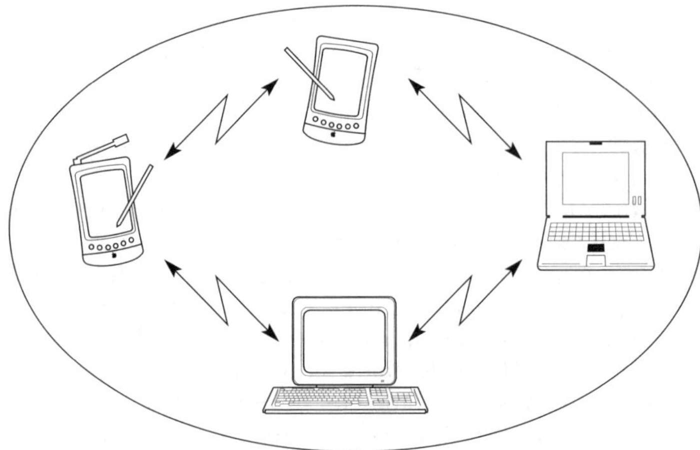

Figure A.1 An ad-hoc wireless LAN.

at short distances, on a global basis (some exceptions exist for France, Spain and Japan).

Bluetooth uses a frequency-hopping technique, where a carrier is shifted in discrete increments of frequency, based on a pattern generated by a pseudo-random code sequence. The transmission is spread over a wide frequency band. With this technique, the effect from signal interference and fading is reduced.

There are 79 RF channels spaced 1 MHz apart, in the range from 2402 to 2480 MHz. As the frequency hopping occurs at a rate of 1600 hops per second, each hop duration is 625 μs. During this time slot, the packet transmission occurs, although a packet can last up to five time slots in length. The carrier is modulated using the Gaussian-shaped frequency shift keying (FSK) technique, achieving a symbol rate up to 1 Mbit/s.

Bluetooth is based on a master–slave communication scheme. In order to support full-duplex communications, a time-division duplex (TDD) technique is used. All packet transmissions start at the beginning of the time slot, where the master devices use the even-numbered time slots and the slave devices use the odd-numbered time slots.

Bluetooth classifies devices in three power classes, according to the power requirement that determines the signal level and transmission range. While devices with Power Class 1 have a maximum output of 100 mW and a range of 100 m, devices with Power Class 3 have 1 mW as maximum output and 10 m as a transmission range. Devices with Power Class 2 are limited to 2.5 mW as the maximum output.

In addition to the power classes, the standard also defines three reduced power operating modes, intended for battery charge conservation. The three modes, in a decreased power requirement order are: **sniff mode**, where the operating rate is reduced; the **hold mode**, where the device does not participate in a Bluetooth network, although it retains its active member address; and the **park mode**, where the device does not retain its active member address.

A.1.4 Bluetooth interfaces

In order to provide flexibility, the Bluetooth specification defines four physical interfaces: Universal Serial Bus (USB), RS-232, Universal Asynchronous Receiver Transmitter (UART) and a PC card. In this way, the Bluetooth may be integrated with a PC's motherboard through the UART interface, or provided as a stand-alone module interfaced through USB or RS-232.

A.1.5 The PicoNet

A PicoNet is a collection of Bluetooth devices synchronized to the same hopping sequence. One device acts as a *Master* which determines the hoping pattern, while the rest act as *Slaves*, which must synchronize with the master's hopping. Each PicoNet has a unique hopping sequence.

A PicoNet may be composed of only one Master (M) and up to seven Slaves (S). Two additional types of devices may be found: Parked (P) devices, which are not actively participating in the PicoNet but they can be reactivated in just milliseconds, and Stand-By (SB) devices, which do not participate in the PicoNet. Up to seven Slaves may be actively participating in the PicoNet and more than 200 devices may be parked, where any of them may switch to a Slave mode to actively participate in the PicoNet. If the PicoNet already has seven Slaves, one of them must be parked to allow a Parked device to switch to the active mode.

A PicoNet may be started with two or more devices, where any device may act as a Master (the device that establishes the PicoNet automatically becomes the Master device). The synchronization process begins with the Master sending its clock and device ID. The hopping pattern is determined by the Master's device ID consisting of a 48-bit worldwide unique identifier. The Master's clock determines the phase in the hopping pattern. Every device, after adjusting its internal clock with the master's clock, may participate in the PicoNet. Active devices (Slaves) are assigned with a 3-bit **Active Member Address (AMA)**, while the Parked devices are assigned with an 8-bit **Parked Member Address (PMA)**.

All devices in a PicoNet have the same hopping sequence and share the available 1 MHz channel. Then, as more users are added, the throughput per user drops very quickly. In this way, the available 80 MHz bandwidth is not used efficiently. For this reason, devices are grouped, forming more than one PicoNet. These groups of PicoNets form a ScatterNet.

In a ScatterNet, as each PicoNet has its own hopping sequence, different channels are used by each PicoNet at any given time. Then, the 1 MHz channel is only shared by the PicoNet users and not by every user from the ScatterNet. A device may participate in different PicoNets synchronizing the hopping sequence from that PicoNet. Having devices going back and forth between different PicoNets, inter-PicoNet communication is possible.

Figure A.2 shows a ScatterNet formed by two PicoNets, and the different types of devices. Here, two PicoNets form a ScatterNet. Inside each PicoNet, there are many Slaves synchronized with one device which acts as a Master. Other devices marked as Parked are also synchronized with the Master, although they do not actively participate in the PicoNet (they are not 'connected'). Stand-By devices are not synchronized at all.

A.1.6 The protocol stack

The Bluetooth specification includes a protocol stack. However, Bluetooth does not strictly follow the 7-layer OSI reference model, because of its complexity due to the use of radio frequency communications, and its operation with telephones, modems and other devices. Instead, the protocol stack is divided into four layers:

- **Bluetooth Core Protocols:** Radio, Baseband, Link Manager Protocol (LMP), Logical Link Control and Adaptation Protocol (L2CAP), and Service Discovery Protocol (SDP). See the following section for more information.
- **Cable Replacement Protocol:** RFCOMM. It emulates a serial line interface (RS-232) allowing legacy applications to run over Bluetooth.

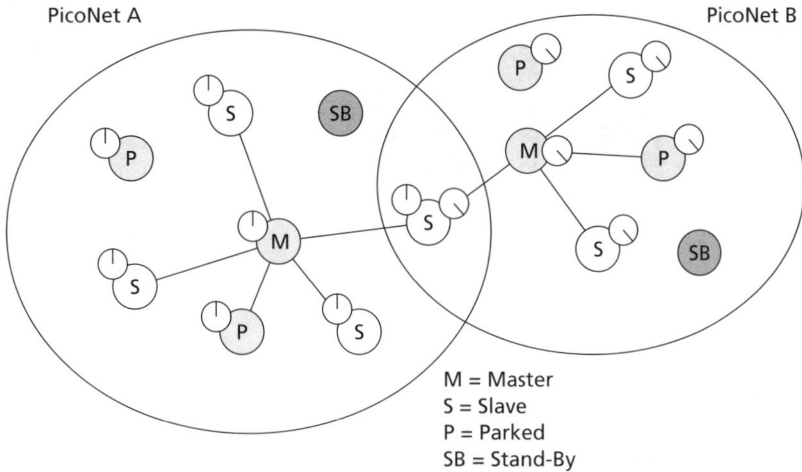

Figure A.2 Two PicoNets forming a ScatterNet.

- **Telephony Control Protocols:** TCS binary, AT modem commands. It describes a bit-oriented protocol for call control signalling allowing the establishment of voice and data calls between Bluetooth devices.
- **Adopted Protocols:** vCal, vCard, OBEX, WAE, WAP, TCP/UDP/IP, PPP. Those protocols were adopted to be used under Bluetooth. For example, the internet applications may use the TCP/IP stack through the use of PPP over Bluetooth.

Figure A.3 shows the Bluetooth protocol stack. Audio applications, after encoding, use the base band layer directly. In Bluetooth, the simple audio model enables any device to send and receive audio data between themselves, just by opening an audio link.

The Host Controller Interface provides a command interface for the base band and Link Manager, and access for the control/status hardware registers.

A.1.6.1 Bluetooth core protocols

A.1.6.1.1 *Radio layer*

The radio specification defines those aspects related to the carrier frequencies and output power. These specifications have been described in the section describing the Bluetooth technology.

A.1.6.1.2 *Base band layer*

This layer defines the frequency hopping and time division duplex (TDD) techniques used for interference mitigation and medium access, the physical links and many packet formats.

A.1.6.1.2.1 Frequency hopping / time division duplex (TDD) scheme

As the ISM band in which Bluetooth operates is open to anybody, many kinds of devices such as cordless phones, microwave ovens and baby monitors,

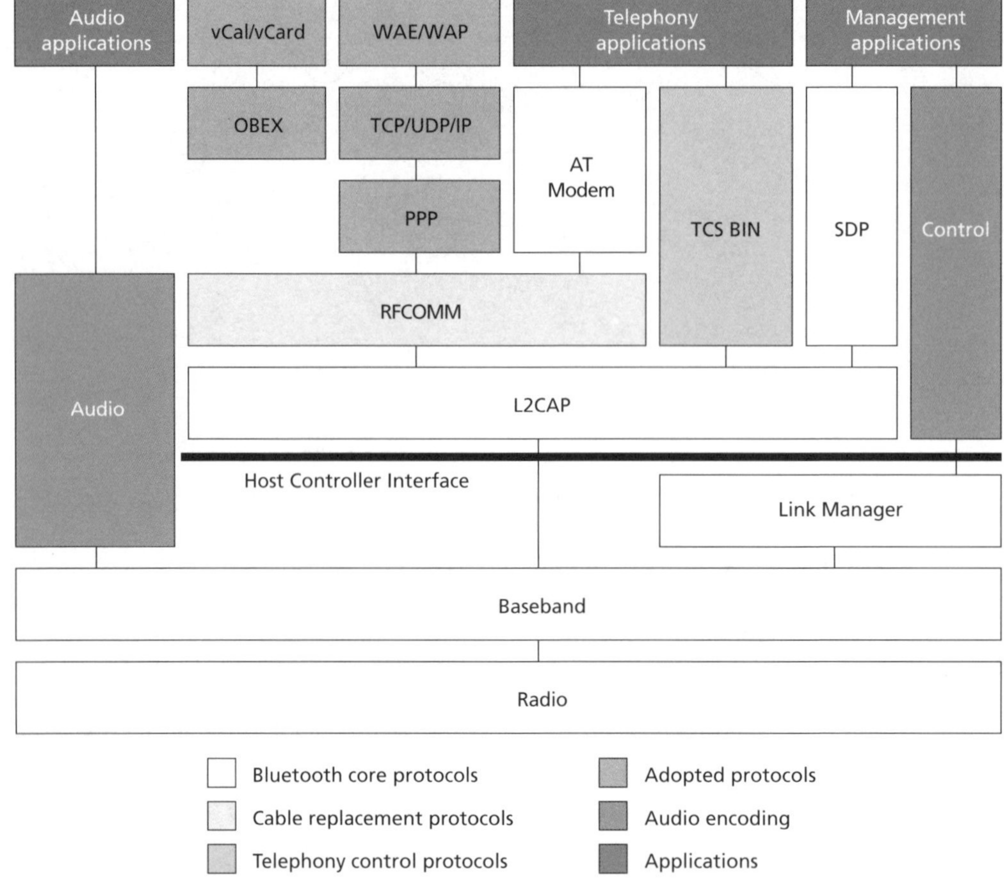

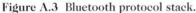

Figure A.3 Bluetooth protocol stack.

may be operating and interfering in this frequency range. In order to avoid this interference, a spectrum-spreading technique is used. In this way, the range from 2402 to 2480 MHz is divided into 79 channels spaced 1 MHz apart. Transmission occurs in any of these channels, following a sequence determined in a pseudo-random fashion. Slave devices must be synchronized with a Master, which dictates the sequence of channels to follow at any given time. In this way, as different frequencies are used during overall transmission, the possible interference is reduced.

Frequency-hopping occurs at 1600 hops per second, defining a time slot of 625 μs, over which packets are transmitted. In Figure A.4 we can see how the channel frequency changes ($f_k, f_{k+1}, f_{k+2}, \ldots$) for each time slot. A TDD scheme is used to alternate the Master and Slave devices transmission. While the Master transmits using the even slots, the Slaves use the odd slots. Normally, packet transmission occurs during a time slot, although some packets may use three or five time slots. In these cases, the frequency of the channel is maintained during the multi-slot packet transmission, and the normal sequence is restored after this.

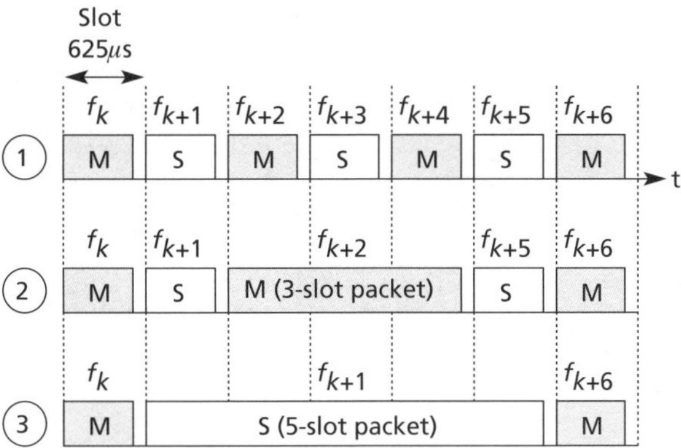

Figure A.4 Frequency-hopping / TDD techniques

A.1.6.1.2.2 Physical links

The Baseband layer enables the physical RF link between Bluetooth devices in a PicoNet. This layer specifies two types of physical link:

- **Synchronous connection-oriented link (SCO):** This type of link supports symmetrical, circuit-switched, point-to-point connections as typically used for voice. The Master reserves two consecutive slots (forward and return slots) at fixed intervals to define these links. The Master may support up to three SCO links with the same or different Slaves, while these last ones may support up to two SCO links with different Masters or up to three SCO links with the same Master. The SCO links are used for audio packets, or a combination of audio and data. Each SCO link carries voice at 64 kbit/s, and different schemes of forward error correction (FEC) can be applied. A continuous variable slope delta (CVSD) voice-encoding scheme is used to avoid voice retransmissions (which would not make much sense, as a voice needs transmission in real time).
- **Asynchronous connectionless link (ACL):** This type of link supports symmetrical or asymmetrical, packet-switched, point-to-multipoint connections as typically required data transmission. ACL connections are controlled by the Master using a Polling scheme. A Slave may answer only if it was addressed in the preceding slot. These types of links are only used for data packets. Packets may use one, three or five slots. The data may be protected using a 2/3 FEC (forward error correction) scheme and a CRC field. For reliable transmissions, a fast automatic repeat request (ARQ) scheme may be used.

In the same RF link, both types of packets may be transmitted in a multiplexed way. Figure A.5 shows an example transmission between a Master and two Slave devices. SCO and ACL links are mixed, where Slave #1 supports both an SCO link and an ACL link with the Master. Notice that the SCO link is at fixed slot intervals (six slots in this case). Slave #2 maintains an ACL link with the Master. As the ACL works under a Polling scheme, a Slave only transmits when the Master addresses it. When no data is available, the slot may be empty.

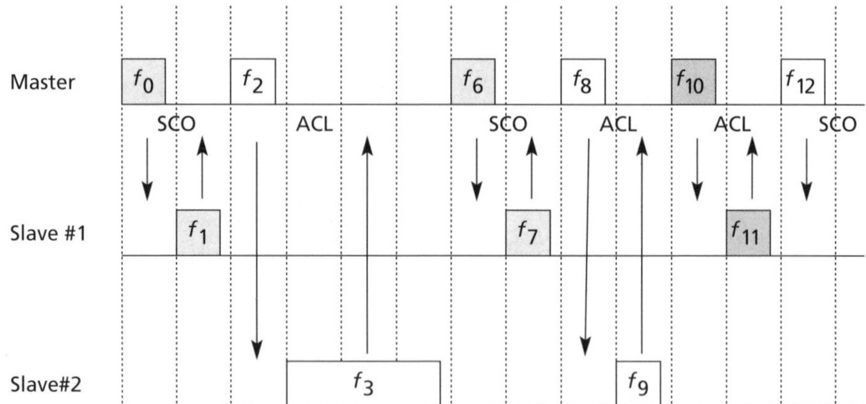

Figure A.5 Synchronous connection-oriented and asynchronous connectionless links.

A.1.6.1.2.3 Packet formats

Packets exchanged between a Master and Slave devices have the format shown in Figure A.6. The field description is as follows:

- **Access code:** it is used for timing synchronization and signalling purposes. It may represent a channel access code (CAC) which identifies each PicoNet during transmissions, a device access code (DAC) during paging, or an inquiry access code (IAC) during inquiry. It is composed of the following subfields:

  Preamble – 4 bits: it is used to indicate the arrival of packets to the receiver.
  Synchronization – 64 bits: it is used by the receiver for timing synchronization.
  Trailer – 4 bits: it is used only if the packet header follows the access code.

- Packet header: if it is used, it contains link control (LC) information using the following subfields:

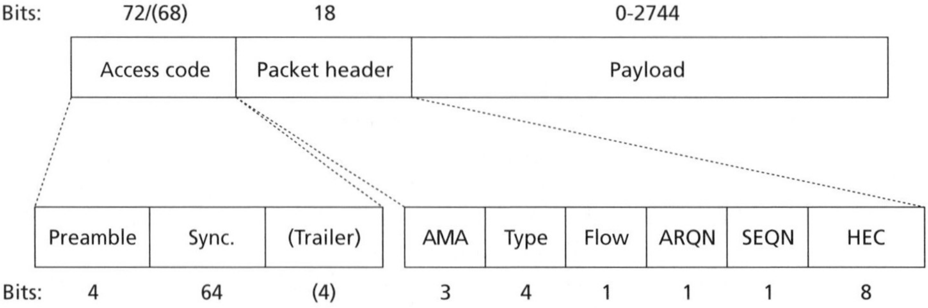

Figure A.6 Bluetooth packet format.

Active Member Address (AMA) – 3 bits: it is used to identify each Slave device in a PicoNet. As the '000' address is reserved for broadcast to all Slaves from the Master, only seven Slaves may be actively participating in the PicoNet.
Type – 4 bits: it is used to specify the type of packet. There are four different packet types for SCO links, and seven packet types for ACL links. It also indicates the number of slots the packet uses.
Flow – 1 bit: it is used for flow control of packet over ACL links. Flow=0 stop the data transmission, while Flow=1 resumes it.
Automatic Repeat Request (ARQN) – 1 bit and **Sequence Number (SEQN)** – 1 bit: they are used to implement a simple alternating bit acknowledgment system.
Header Error Check (HEC) – 8 bits: it is used to check the integrity of the header. If the HEC does not check, the whole packet is discarded.

- **Payload:** it is used to carry the voice or data depending on the packet type. For SCO packets, the HV1 and HV2 packet types include the audio information and FEC protection in the payload field. The HV3 packet type uses the payload only for audio information. The fourth type of SCO packet type, the DV, mixes voice and data for which the payload includes the audio information, a FEC sub-field, a payload header, the data and a CRC sub-field. The ACL packets may consist of DM1, DM3 or DM5 packets where the payload contains a header (8 bits for single slot, 16 bits for multiple slots), the data, an FEC sub-field and a CRC. Other three packet types, named DH1, DH3 and DH5, have a similar structure but without an FEC sub-field. Lastly, a seventh ACL packet type, the AUX1, consists of a header (8 bits) and the payload.

A.1.6.1.3 *Link Manager Protocol (LMP)*

The LMP is the module that sets up and controls the link between Bluetooth devices. A synchronization process is performed each time a packet is received. It also controls the device power modes, the transmission mode (Master/Slave), and the connection states of the unit in a PicoNet. As not all devices support all the available features, the LMP is in charge of the capability of negotiation. LMP also contributes to security in generating, exchanging, and checking link and encryption keys.

A.1.6.1.4 *Logical Link Control and Adaptation Protocol (L2CAP)*

The L2CAP is a data link control protocol that multiplexes higher-level protocols, and it offers logical channels between Bluetooth devices with quality of service support. It is only available for ACL links, providing three types of logical channels: connectionless, connection-oriented and signalling. Besides the multiplexing functions, L2CAP also provides segmentation and reassembly.

A.1.6.1.5 *Service Discovery Protocol (SDP)*

This protocol allows a device to query for the available services and their characteristics from other devices in radio proximity. A service record and service attributes are used to describe the discovered services. After a device knows about the available services, the device may select the desired one. After this, a connection between two or more Bluetooth devices can be established.

A.1.7 Usage models and profiles

Different usage models allows users to have different functionalities. In order for devices to select the appropriate components necessary for each usage model, a profile is defined. In this way, for example, a *fax profile* may need some components configured in order for devices to have the fax functionality, while the *dial-up networking profile* or the *basic printing profile* may need another configuration to enable functionality to devices with such usage models.

A.2 IEEE 802.11 wireless LAN

A.2.1 Introduction

The IEEE 802.11 standard specifies the wireless LANs implemented in many products available today. This standard belongs to the 802.X family (which includes the 802.3 Ethernet, 802.5 Token Ring, etc.), specifying particular physical and medium access layers for each technology, but presenting a common interface to higher layers maintaining interoperability. That is, if the underlying technology changes, only the lower layers must be changed, as the higher layers are technology-independent (see the IEEE 802 Model in Chapter 3).

The initial goal of the IEEE 802.11 standard was to specify a wireless LAN offering asynchronous and time-bounded services, supporting infrared and radio (using spread spectrum transmission techniques) as physical mediums, power management and operating in the 2.4 GHz ISM unlicensed radio band, which is available worldwide, with data rates of 1 Mbps as mandatory, and 2 Mbps as optional.

A.2.2 Network architecture

The IEEE 802.11 wireless LANs may present two different network architectures: an ad-hoc wireless LAN (forming a peer-to-peer network), or an infrastructure-based wireless LAN (using access point (AP) devices).

In Figure A.7, we see how many devices (named as stations) communicate, forming two independent Basic Service Sets (BSS). Each group constitutes an ad-hoc wireless network where each device may communicate to the others without the use of any additional infrastructure. However, stations from different BSS cannot communicate to each other. The separation of the two (or more) BSS may be produced by the distance between them (they must be out of the wireless coverage area), or by using different carrier frequencies. In this last case, the BSS may be physically overlapped without interference. This network architecture is also called peer-to-peer architecture.

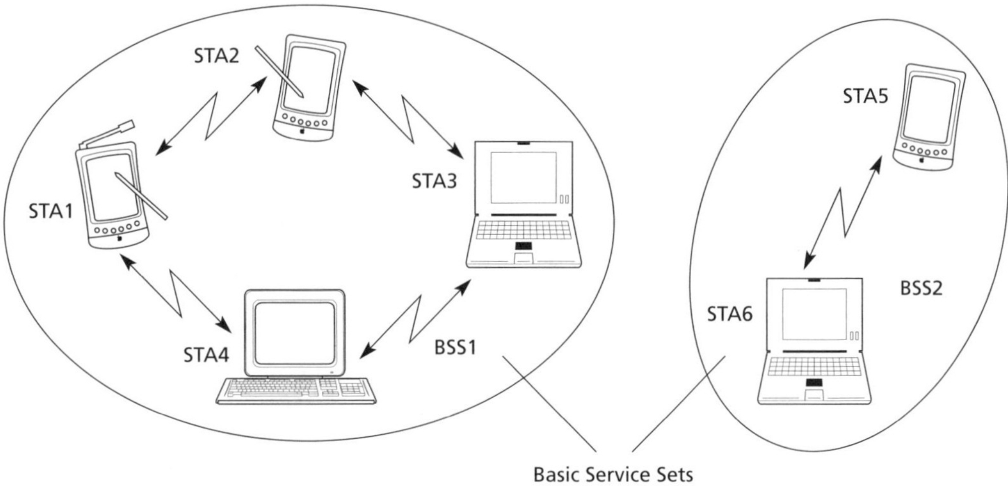

Figure A.7 IEEE 802.11 ad-hoc wireless LANs.

Figure A.8 shows an infrastructure-based wireless network. In this type of network architecture, all stations (or nodes) within a certain wireless coverage area are connected using an AP, forming a BSS. In this way, stations STA 1, STA 2 and STA 3 may all be interconnected through the AP.

A distribution system (DS) connects several APs and handles the data transfer between them. In this way, a single network is formed and the wireless coverage area is extended. The resulting new wireless network is called Extended Service Set (ESS). Now, all stations are connected, so for example, STA 1 can transmit to STA 4 (even when they are at different BSSs) using the provided infrastructure.

The DS also connects the ESS to a wired LAN (Ethernet, Token Ring, etc.) through the use of a portal device. Now, the whole network allows transmissions between any wired or wireless stations. Each ESS has its own identifier which the station needs to know in order to participate in the wireless LAN.

As stations can physically move, they may select the best AP (perhaps with the best signal level) and associate with it. This feature is called roaming and it is supported by the AP. Besides that, the AP provides synchronization, power management support and medium access control for the BSS that each AP controls.

A.2.3 IEEE 802.11 protocol architecture

As we saw in Chapter 3, the IEEE developed the IEEE 802 model in order to standardize LANs (including both wired and wireless versions). This model relates with the two lowest layers of the OSI Reference Model, that is, the Physical and Data Link layers.

The IEEE 802 model provides a different set of PHY and MAC layers for each network technology, and a single Logical Link Control (LLC) layer which allows a common entry point for upper layers, independently of the underlying network technology. In this way, different technologies such as Ethernet, Token Ring and Wireless may coexist in a single network, while the

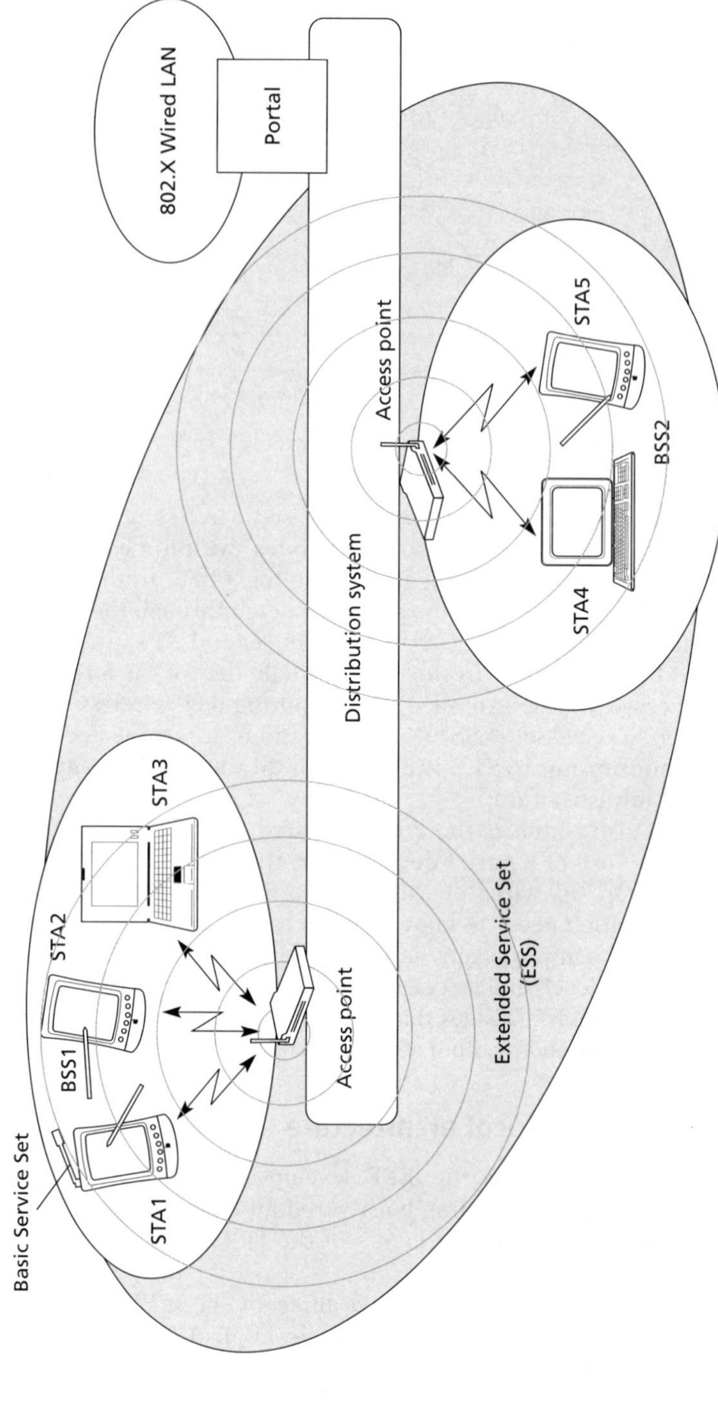

Figure A.8 IEEE 802.11 infrastructure-based wireless LAN.

upper layers of the protocol remains the same. Figure A.9 shows how this is possible in terms of protocol layers.

As occurs with the other standards describing different network technologies (as 802.3 for Ethernet, 802.5 for Token Ring, etc.), the IEEE 802.11 standard covers only the *physical* (PHY) and the *medium access* (MAC) layers. However, in this case, the PHY layer is further subdivided into the Physical Layer Convergence Protocol (PLCP) and the Physical Medium Dependent sublayer (PMD), as Figure A.10 shows.

The PLCP sublayer provides the clear channel assessment (CCA), which consists of a carrier sense signal, and a common PHY service access point (SAP) independent of the transmission technology. The PMD sublayer is in charge of modulation and encoding/decoding of signals. While the PMD sublayer depends on the particular wireless medium, the PLCP sublayer adapts the PMD capabilities to the PHY service offered to the MAC layer. The MAC layer, as we will later see, provides the medium access, as well as encryption and fragmentation.

Both PHY and MAC layers include management entities (PLME and MLME respectively), which provide the management service interfaces through which the layer management functions are invoked. While the PLME includes tasks such as channel tuning and PHY management information base (MIB) maintenance, the MLME is related to authentication mechanism, encryption, synchronization and association of stations with the AP, stations roaming between different APs, power management and the MAC

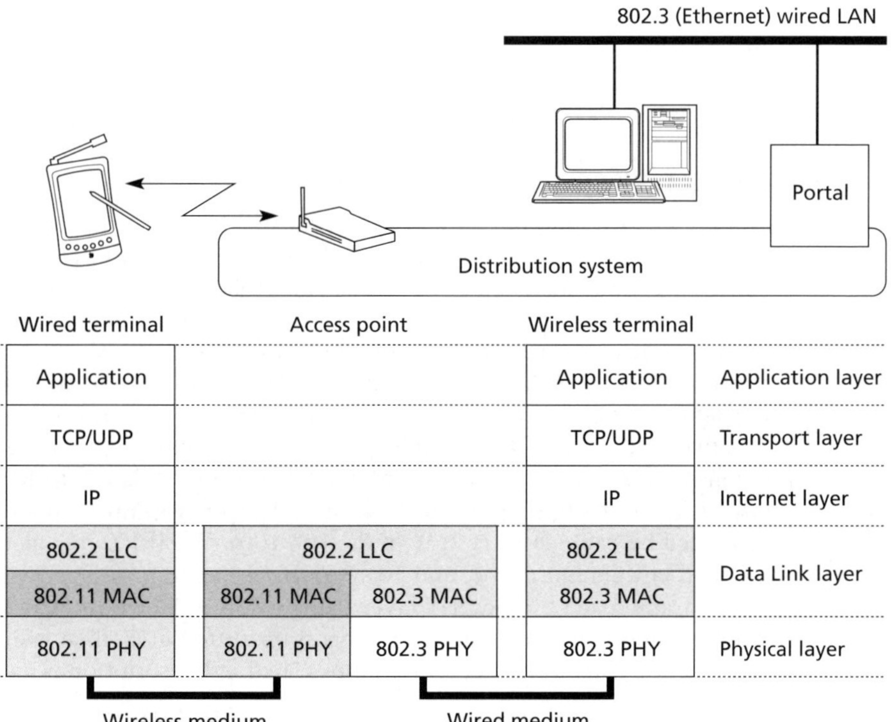

Figure A.9 Protocol architecture in an infrastructure wireless LAN.

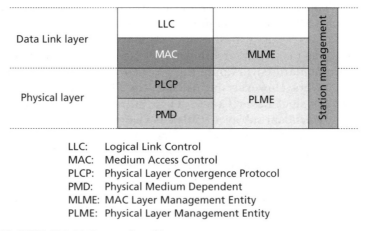

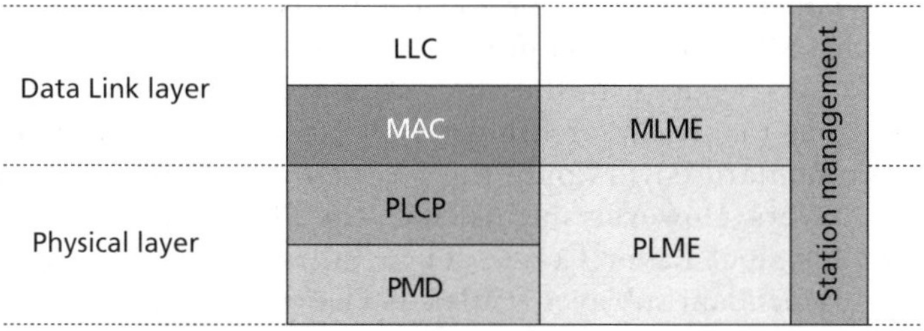

LLC: Logical Link Control
MAC: Medium Access Control
PLCP: Physical Layer Convergence Protocol
PMD: Physical Medium Dependent
MLME: MAC Layer Management Entity
PLME: Physical Layer Management Entity

Figure A.10 IEEE 802.11 Protocol architecture.

MIB maintenance. Besides this, an independent-layer Station Manager entity must be present in each station, for additional higher-layer functions. This Station Manager entity interacts with both PLME and MLME.

A.2.4 IEEE 802.11 Physical layer (PHY)

The IEEE 802.11 standard supports three different physical layers; two of them are based on radio transmission using the worldwide available ISM band (at 2.4 GHz), while the third layer is based on infrared. In order for the MAC layer to control the medium access, the PHY layer must provide a clear channel assessment (CCA). Also, the PHY layer offers a SAP to the MAC layer.

A.2.4.1 Frequency Hopping Spread Spectrum

The Frequency Hopping Spread Spectrum (FHSS) technique uses 79 hopping channels (23 channels in Japan) with 1 MHz of bandwidth in the 2.4 GHz ISM band. The transmitter uses different channels for transmission following a pseudo-random hopping pattern. The receivers must be synchronized with the transmitter in order to use the same pattern and receive the transmission appropriately. In this way, several networks may be operating in the same wireless coverage area without interference, using different hopping patterns.

A two-level Gaussian shaped FSK (frequency shift keying) is used as modulation to achieve the 1 Mbps mandatory data rate, while a four-level GFSK is used for the 2 Mbps optional data rate. The maximum transmit power is restricted by each country: 1 W in the US, 100 mW EIRP (equivalent isotropic radiated power) in Europe, and 10 mW/MHz in Japan.

The frame used by the PHY layer using FHSS is shown in Figure A.11. The PLCP preamble and header are always transmitted at 1 Mbps, while the payload may be transmitted at 1 or 2 Mbps. The field description is as follows:

- **Synchronization**: it consists of 80 bits with the '01010101….' pattern and it is used for synchronization of receivers. The CCA uses this field for signal detection.

PLCP preamble		PLCP header			
Sync	SFD	PLW	PSF	HEC	Payload
Bits: 80	16	12	4	16	variable

Figure A.11 The IEEE 802.11 PHY FHSS frame format.

- **Start Frame Delimiter (SFD)**: it consists of 16 bits with the '0000110010111101' pattern used to indicate the start of the frame.
- **PDU Length Word (PLW)**: it is used to indicate the length of the payload (in bytes). With 12 bits, it ranges between 0 and 4095.
- **PLCP signalling field (PSF)**: it is used to indicate the data rate of the payload. The '0000' indicates 1 Mbps, while '0010' indicates the 2 Mbps data rate.
- **Header Error Check (HEC)**: it consists of 16 bits checksum to protect the PLCP header using the $G(x) = x^{16} + x^{12} + x^5 + 1$ polynomial.
- **Payload**: it carries the MAC data which is scrambled using the polynomial $S(x) = x^7 + x^4 + 1$ for DC blocking and whitening of the spectrum.

A.2.4.2 Direct Sequence Spread Spectrum

The Direct Sequence Spread Spectrum (DSSS) technique is a spread spectrum method separated by code (and not by frequency as FHSS does). It consists of taking the user's bit stream and performing an Exclusive-OR (XOR) with a code pattern, called **chipping sequence**. The resulting operation appears as random noise, and the original user's information may be recovered only by using the same pseudo-random code sequence used by the transmitter.

The IEEE 802.11 implementing DSSS uses the sequence '10110111000' known as the **Barker code**, which presents robustness against interference and multi-path propagation effects. The 802.11 DSSS PHY uses the 2.4 GHz ISM band offering 1 Mbps and 2 Mbps data rates. The modulation scheme used is differential binary phase shift keying (DBPSK) for 1 Mbps data rates, and differential quadrature phase shift keying (DQFSK) for 2 Mbps transmissions. The maximum transmit power is 1 W in the US, 100 mW EIRP in Europe and 10 mW/MHz in Japan.

Figure A.12 shows the frame format used by 802.11 PHY layer using DSSS. The PLCP preamble and header are always transmitted at 1 Mbps, while the payload may be transmitted at 1 or 2 Mbps. The field description is as follows:

PLCP preamble		PLCP header				
Sync	SFD	Signal	Service	Length	HEC	Payload
Bits: 128	16	8	8	16	16	variable

Figure A.12 The IEEE 802.11 PHY DSSS frame format.

- **Synchronization**: it consists of 128 bits of scrambled ones. This field enables the receivers to perform the necessary operations for synchronizations.
- **Start Frame Delimiter (SFD)**: it identifies the beginning of the frame, and it consists of the '1111001110100000' 16-bit pattern.
- **Signal**: it specifies the modulation used; a value of 0x0A indicates 1 Mbps with DBPSK modulation, while 0x14 indicates 2 Mbps with DQPSK modulation.
- **Service**: this field is reserved for future use, but a value of 0x00 indicates that the frame is IEEE 802.11 compliant.
- **Length**: this 16 bits are used to indicate the time (in microseconds) required to transmit the payload.
- **Header Error Check (HEC)**: this field is a CRC-16 frame check sequence (FCS) over the Signal, Service and Length fields, using the $G(x) = x^{16} + x^{12} + x^{5} + 1$ polynomial.
- **Payload**: it carries the MAC data which is scrambled using the polynomial $S(x) = x^{-7} + x^{-4} + 1$ for DC blocking and whitening of the spectrum.

A.2.4.3 Infrared

The IEEE 802.11 PHY layer based in infrared uses near visible light in the 850–950 nm range. As the reception is based on diffuse IR transmission, a clear line-of-sight path between transmitter and receiver is not required, allowing point-to-multipoint communications. However, the wireless coverage area is limited to approximately 10 m, and their use is restricted to work inside buildings.

The standard defines a slot of 250 ns where the presence of a pulse in the slot represents a 1, and the absence of a pulse in the slot represents a zero. Some fields are transmitted using this scheme, while the rest of the fields use pulse position modulation (PPM). These last fields are transmitted at 1 Mbps using 16-PPM, or at 2 Mbps using 4-PPM. The 16-PPM maps four bits into a 16-position symbol (16 bits where only one bit is 1 and the rest are all zeroes), while the 4-PPM maps two bits into a 4-position symbol.

Figure A.13 shows the frame format used by the PHY layer based on infrared. The field description is as follows:

- **Synchronization**: this field consists of a sequence of alternated presence and absence of a pulse in consecutive slots. It has a minimum of 57 slots and a maximum of 73 slots, terminating in the absence of a pulse in the last slot. With this field, the receiver can perform synchronization and others tasks.

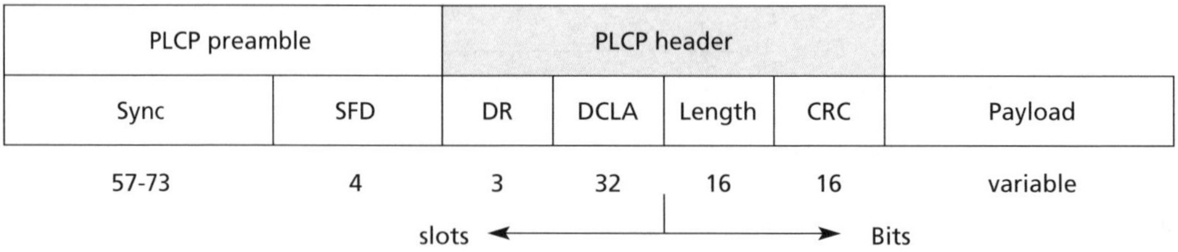

PLCP preamble		PLCP header				
Sync	SFD	DR	DCLA	Length	CRC	Payload
57-73	4	3	32	16	16	variable

slots ← → Bits

Figure A.13 The IEEE 802.11 PHY Infrared frame format.

- **Start Frame Delimiter (SFD)**: this field consists of a binary '1001' sent in four slots, and it indicates the start of the frame.
- **Data Rate (DR)**: it indicates the rate at which the Length, the CRC and the Payload fields will be sent. A binary value '000' indicates 1 Mbps, while '001' indicates 2 Mbs. This field is sent in three slots.
- **DC Level Adjustment (DCLA)**: this field is used by the receiver to stabilize the DC level after the Sync, SFD and DR fields. It consists of 32 slots where a different value is used according the DR field:

  DR = '000' (1 Mbps) DCLA = '00000000100000000000000010000000'
  DR = '001' (2 Mbps) DCLA = '00100010001000100010001000100010'

- **Length**: it is an unsigned 16-bit integer that indicates the length (in bytes) of the payload. It is sent using the PPM format.
- **CRC**: it is a 16-bit CRC calculated over the Length field. It is sent using the PPM format.
- **Payload**: it is a variable-length field (from 0 to 2500 bytes) which carries the MAC data. It is sent using the PPM format.

A.2.5 IEEE 802.11 Medium Access Control (MAC) layer

The MAC layer has the primary function of controlling access to the wireless medium. However, other tasks such as fragmentation, authentication, encryption, power management, synchronization and roaming are also assigned to this layer.

A.2.5.1 Access mechanisms

The IEEE 802.11 defines three access mechanisms: the mandatory CSMA/CA, an optional method using RTS/CTS extension and a polling method. The first two methods, providing **distributed coordination function (DCF)**, offer asynchronous service and they may be used in both ad-hoc and infrastructure-based wireless networks. The third method, providing **point coordination function (PCF)**, offers both asynchronous and time-bounded services, but it may be used only in wireless networks using an access point (infrastructure-based networks).

For these methods, a series of parameters are defined which provide the waiting time for medium access. They are based on the slot time, which is fixed according to the medium propagation delay, transmitter delay and other parameters that depend on the PHY. Table A.1 shows some typical values.

Table A.1

Parameters	Access priority	FHSS (μs)	DSSS (μs)
Slot time	–	50	20
Short Inter-Frame Spacing (SIFS)	Highest	28	10
PCF Inter-Frame Spacing (PIFS)	Medium	78	30
DCF Inter-Frame Spacing (DIFS)	Lowest	128	50

A.2.5.1.1 *Access mechanism using CSMA/CA*

In the carrier sense multiple access with collision avoidance (CSMA/CA) method, each node must 'listen' to the medium before transmitting. If the medium is idle for a DIFS duration (DCF inter-frame spacing), a node can access the medium at once. If the medium is busy, the nodes have to wait for a DIFS time plus an amount of time determined by a random back-off time chosen by each node. When this time interval ends, if the medium is idle, the node can access the medium. If the medium is still busy, the waiting cycle is restarted. However, the back-off timer is not reinitialized, so the node will have more probabilities to access the medium for each new cycle. (See Figure A.14 (a).) In this way, the DIFS time ensures a gap between contiguous frame sequences, while the random back-off time helps to avoid collisions as each node has different delays plus the DIFS time.

In the case of unicast messages, the receiver answers with an acknowledgement (ACK) frame to indicate to the sender the receipt of the message. In this case, the node sending the ACK only has to wait for a short inter-frame spacing (SIFS) which is shorter than the DIFS, ensuring the ACK is transmitted with a higher priority (and without collisions). (See Fig. A.14 (b).) If no ACK is received by the sender, a retransmission occurs for a limited number of times.

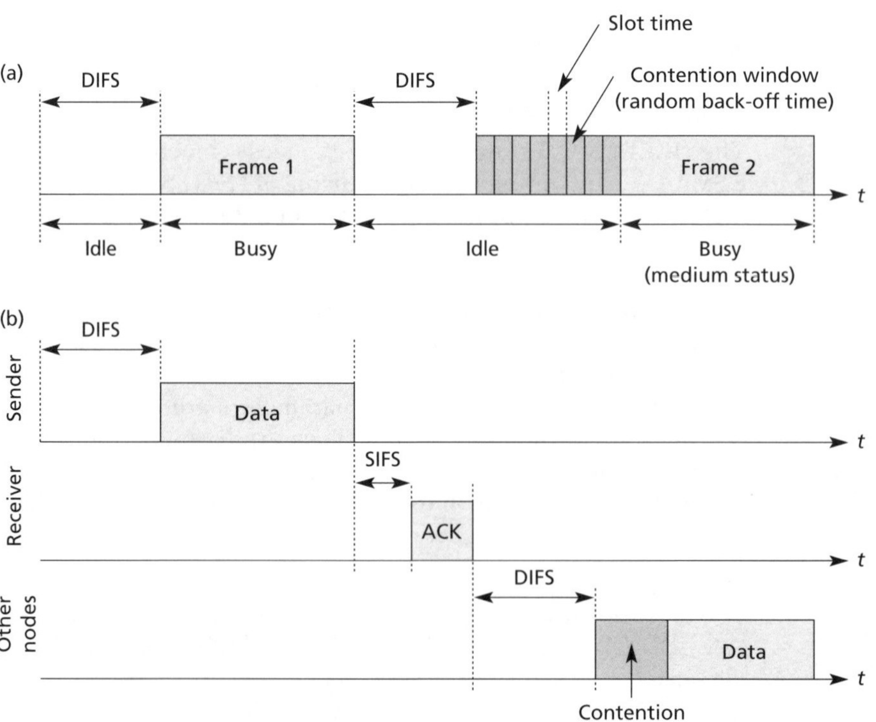

Figure A.14 Access mechanism using CSMA/CA.

A.2.5.1.2 *Access mechanism using RTS/CTS*

This additional (and optional) mechanism was developed to deal with the problem of hidden terminals. This is the case where a terminal (between two others) can receive from the other two, but those terminals cannot receive each other. Then, those stations may sense the medium as idle, and send a frame causing a collision at the receiver in the middle.

To avoid the above problem, two control packets are used: RTS (Request To Send) and CTS (Clear To Send). The whole transmission begins with the transmission of an RTS frame containing the address of the receiver and the duration of the whole transmission. In this way, each node receiving this information sets its **network allocation vector (NAV)** which specifies the time the node must wait to try to access the medium again. This mechanism (virtual reservation mechanism) reserves the medium for one sender and it provides contention for nodes trying to access the medium.

The receiver of the RTS must transmit a CTS frame, indicating the duration again. All the nodes receiving this frame, adjust its NAV accordingly. Owing to the problem of hidden terminal, the set of nodes receiving the RTS frame may be different from the set receiving the CTS frame. In this way, every node is informed about the duration of the transmission, and they will not attempt to access the medium, avoiding possible collisions.

After receiving the CTS, the DATA frame is sent, and the receiver sends the ACK frame. With this last one, the whole transmission ends, and the medium becomes idle.

The RTS frame is sent after waiting for a DIFS (plus a random backoff time if the medium was busy). But subsequent frames (CTS, DATA and ACK) are sent using the SIFS time, so these messages have the highest priority. Then, collisions can only occur at the beginning of the transmission, when the RTS is sent. (See Fig. A.15.)

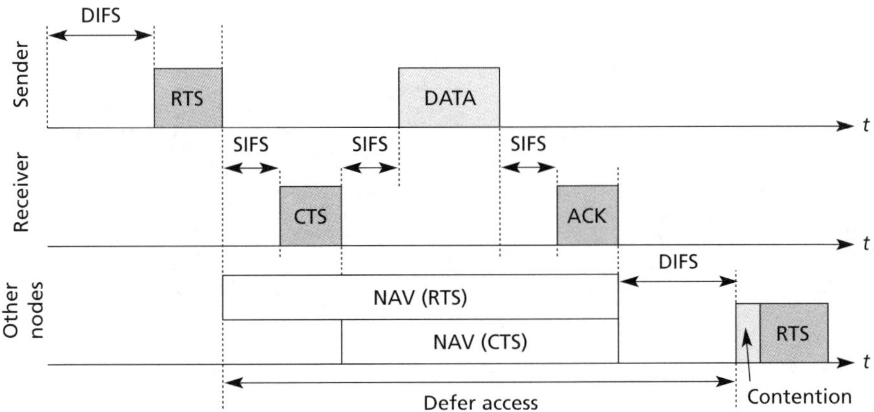

Figure A.15 Access mechanism using RTS/CTS.

A.2.5.1.3 *Access mechanism using polling*

The two above mechanisms cannot guarantee a maximum access delay (thus, a minimum transmission bandwidth). For this reason, the standard defines a **Point Coordination Function (PCF)** to provide a time-bounded service. The PCF is implemented using an access point AP which polls the nodes controlling the medium access. Thus, ad-hoc networks that are not based using an AP cannot use this function.

This PCF works on top of the DCF, so the whole transmission cycle is divided into two periods: the **contention-free period**, where the AP polls each station, and the **contention period**, where either of the two methods providing DCF can be used.

During the contention-free period, the PC (Point Coordinator or Access Point) waits for a PIFS period (medium priority access but greater than the contention period mechanism which uses DIFS) to access the medium. Once this happens, the PC sends data $\mathbf{D_1}$ downstream to the first node. After a SIFS period, this node can answer and upstream data $\mathbf{U_1}$. After a SIFS period, the PC can poll the second node $\mathbf{D_2}$, and this continues until the last node is polled. After this, an end marker ($\mathbf{CF_{end}}$) is sent indicating the end of the contention-free period.

In Figure A.16, we can see how the NAV indicates the duration of the contention-free period, so every node knows when this period may end. However, sometimes this NAV may need adjustments, as some nodes may not have anything to answer when they are polled. For example, the PC sends the $\mathbf{D_3}$ frame, but as the node has nothing to send, the PC waits for a PIFS period (greater than the SIFS period in which the node should answer) to send the next poll.

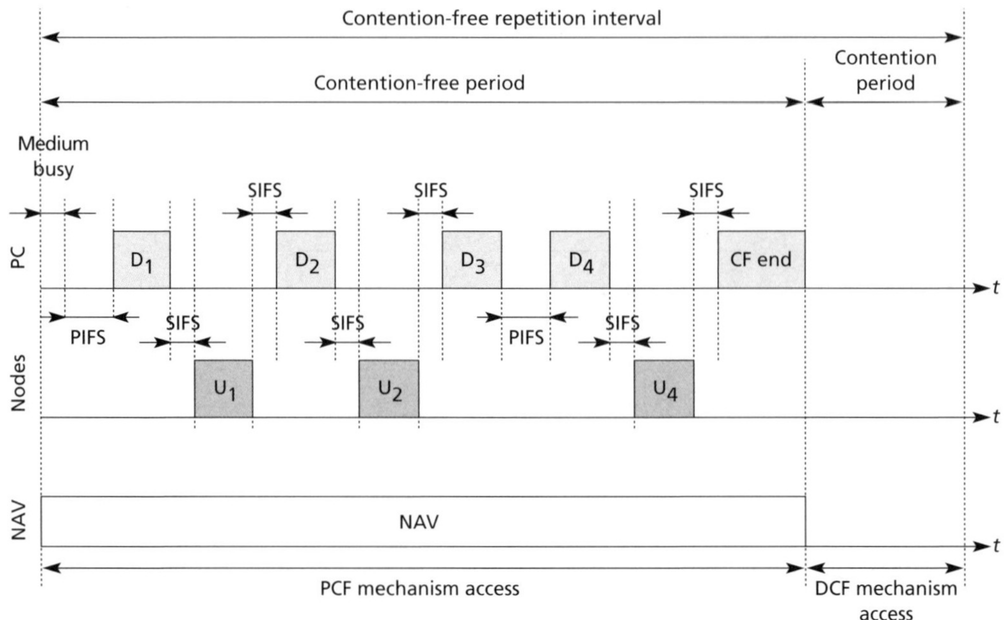

Figure A.16 PCF Polling mechanism.

Once the **CF_{end}** indicates the end of the polling cycle, the content period begins, where the nodes try to access the medium using one of the DCF methods. As these methods use a DIFS period to access the medium, the nodes have a lower priority than a PC that uses a PIFS period.

A.2.5.2 MAC frame formats

The MAC frames are carried by the Payload field of the PHY frame. Although there are many different types of MAC frames, they all share the first two bytes, called the Frame Control field. The rest of the MAC frame structure depends on the frame type. Figure A.17 shows the MAC frame formats.

The Data Frame is used to transmit information. The ACK Control Frame is used to acknowledge the received frame. The RTS/CTS Control Frames are used in the DCF to avoid the hidden terminal problem. The PS-Poll Frame is used in power management. The CF_{end} Frame is used by the PCF polling mechanism.

The Frame Control field description contains the following elements:

- **Protocol Version**: it is fixed at 0, and it represents the current version.
- **Type/subtype**: the type determines the function of the frame (00 = Management, 01 = Control, 10 = Data). The subtype determines if the frame is a data frame, an ACK, RTS, CTS, PS-Poll, etc. The complete information is given in the standard.
- **To DS / from DS**: To Distribution System/from Distribution System. See MAC Addresses Interpretation in the next section.
- **More Fragments**: it is set to 1 if another fragment follows.
- **Retry**: it is set to 1, if this frame is a retransmission.
- **Power Management**: if it set to 1, the station goes into a power-save mode after successful transmission.
- **More Data**: it is used to indicate to the receiver that the sender has more data to send, in addition to the current frame.
- **WEP**: the Wired Equivalent Privacy field indicates that the 802.11 security mechanism is applied.
- **Order**: if it set to 1, the received frames must be processed in strict order.

The Data Frame field description contains the following elements:

- **Frame Control**: see the Frame Control Field Description (above).
- **Duration/ID**: if the value of this field is less than 32.768, it indicates a Duration value to update the NAV in the access mechanisms. If the value is greater than 32.768, the field is used as an identifier.
- **Address (1 to 4)**: see MAC Addresses Interpretation in the next section.
- **Sequence Control**: it consists of a Fragment Number, which numbers each fragment; and a Sequence Number, which is used to filter duplicates.
- **Data**: it is the data transferred from the sender to the receiver.
- **FCS**: it is 32-bit checksum calculated over the whole frame.

Frame Control Field (bits)

Protocol Version	Type	Subtype	To DS	From DS	More Frag.	Retry	Power mgmt.	More Data	WEP	Order
2	2	4	1	1	1	1	1	1	1	1

Sequence Control (bits)

Fragmt Number	Sequence Number
4	12

Data Frame (bytes)

Frame Control	Duration /ID	Address 1	Address 2	Address 3	Sequence Control	Address 4	DATA	FCS
2	2	6	6	6	2	6	0-2312	4

ACK Frame (bytes)

Frame Control	Duration	RA	FCS
2	2	6	4

RTS/CTS Control Frame (bytes)

Frame Control	Duration	RA	TA	FCS
2	2	6	6	4

PS-Poll Frame (bytes)

Frame Control	AID	BSS ID	TA	FCS
2	2	6	6	4

CF_{end} Frame (bytes)

Frame Control	Duration	RA	BSS ID	FCS
2	2	6	6	4

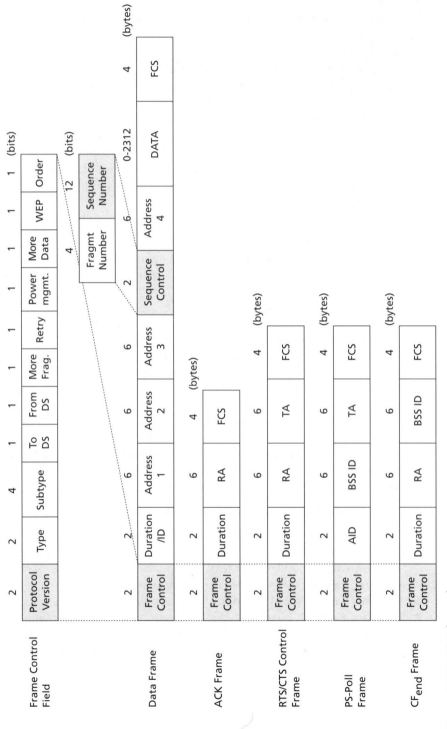

Figure A.17 MAC frame formats.

The ACK, RTS, CTS, PS-Poll and CF_{end} Frames Field contain the following elements:

- **Frame Control**: see the Frame Control Field Description (above).
- **Duration** (in all frames except PS-Poll): it is used to update the NAV in the access mechanism. For the CF_{end} frame, this value is set to 0.
- **AID** (only in PS-Poll Frame): it is the value assigned to the station transmitting the frame, by the AP in the current association.
- **RA, TA, BSS ID**: See MAC Addresses Interpretation in the next section.
- **FCS**: it is 32-bit checksum calculated over the whole frame.

A.2.5.2.1 *MAC addresses interpretation*

Table A.2 shows the interpretation of the fields that involve MAC addresses. Address 1 is always interpreted as the physical receiver of the frame, whereas Address 2 is the physical transmitter of the frame. Address 3 and 4 are used to identify the logical destination and source when the transmission occurs through intermediate devices (as access points). Row 1 represents an **ad-hoc network communications**, where transmission occurs between two stations without the use of the infrastructure. The BSS ID identifies the basic service set. Row 2 shows a case where a frame is *sent to a station from an AP* in an infrastructure-based network. In this case, while the transmitter is the AP (identified by BSS ID), Address 3 specifies the logical sender of the MAC frame (the originator of the message). In row 3, *a station transmits a frame to an AP* with another station as final destination, as indicated by Address 3. In row 4, a station transmits a frame to another station in a different BSS, using *two APs interconnected by the distribution system*. While Addresses 1 and 2 specify the physical addresses of the two access points within the distribution system, Addresses 3 and 4 indicate the original destination and source of the frame (the station's MAC addresses).

Table A.2

#	To DS	From DS	Address 1	Address 2	Address 3	Address 4
1	0	0	DA	SA	BSS ID	-
2	0	1	DA	BSS ID	SA	-
3	1	0	BSS ID	SA	DA	-
4	1	1	RA	TA	DA	SA

DS: Distribution System
DA: destination address
SA: source address
RA: receiver address
TA: transmitter address
BSS ID: BSS identifier

A.2.5.3 MAC management

As we saw in Figure A.10, the MAC Layer Management Entity (MLME) plays an important role in tasks such as synchronization, roaming, power management and others. We will examine some of them in the next paragraphs.

Synchronization is required in stations for many tasks, for example, to follow the hopping sequence in a FHSS system, in a PCF polling mechanism, for power management, etc. As all stations have their own internal clock, they must receive external information to adjust their clock with the rest. In an infrastructure-based network, the AP sends a beacon frame (Type = '00' Subtype = '1000') periodically, which contains a time stamp. If the medium is busy at the moment the beacon frame was to be transmitted, the transmission is deferred. However, the beacon interval is not shifted, and the time stamp carried reflects the real transmission time and not the scheduled time. In an ad-hoc network, without an AP, each station tries to send a beacon frame, but only one will make it for every beacon interval. In this case, since many stations are competing to send a beacon frame, a random back-off algorithm is applied. Every time the stations receive a beacon frame, their internal clocks are synchronized.

In order for an infrastructure-based wireless network to cover large areas or many rooms in a building, more than one AP may be needed. The **roaming** service allows devices to 'move' between AP, so the user can physically move into different areas, without the service being disrupted. For this process, a station starts scanning for another AP. This can be accomplished by sending a probe frame (active scanning) or by listening for a beacon (passive scanning). Once the station decides on a particular AP (if more than one is available), it sends an association frame to this AP. If this is successful, the station has roamed to this new AP.

As most wireless devices are battery powered, a power-saving mechanism is very important in these cases. For this reason, the MAC management is involved with **power management**. In order for a device to save power, the transceiver should be off (sleep mode) when no network activity is detected. This is not a problem in transmissions because the device knows when they will happen, so it can switch the transceiver on to transmit the message, and then it goes to the power-save state. But in reception, if the transceiver is idle (sleep), how will the device know if there is a frame for it? The solution is to have the stations awake at regular intervals, where the AP sends a **traffic indication map (TIM)**, which consists of a list of stations for which the AP has buffered frames to send to. Those stations will stay awake to receive the frame, while the rest can go to a sleep state to save power. For ad-hoc wireless networks, each station transmits an **ad-hoc traffic indication map (ATIM)** frame, so each station knows when to go to a sleep state, or stay awake to receive a frame. This mechanism clearly demonstrates that all stations must be synchronized for appropriate work.

A.2.6 IEEE 802.11 supplements

The main reason for the IEEE 802 standards is to provide standardization for local and metropolitan area networks, covering the Physical and Data Link layers according to the OSI Reference Model. While the process of the IEEE 802.11 standardization was developed only slowly, the Physical layers quickly evolved in their capabilities, and some enhanced proprietary solutions were offered in the market. Then, a series of supplements were published to cover that evolutions. The best known are the IEEE 802.11b, IEEE 802.11a and IEEE 802.11g supplement specifications.

A.2.6.1 IEEE 802.11b

The 802.11b standard specifies a new PHY layer called 'Higher-Speed Physical Layer Extension in the 2.4 GHz Band' offering up to 11 Mbps. The MAC layer specification remains the same as in the 802.11 standard.

The new PHY layer offers extensions to the DSSS system built on the data rate capabilities, providing 5.5 Mbps and 11 Mbps payload data rates in addition to the 1 Mbps and optional 2 Mbps of the 802.11 standard. These new higher data rates are achieved using 8-chip complementary code keying (CCK) as the modulation scheme. For the lower 1 Mbps and 2 Mbps data rates, the same 11-chip Barker sequence as in the 802.11 standard is used.

In addition, the standard defines two PHY frame formats. The mandatory, called **long PLCP PPDU** format, is similar and interoperates with the 802.11 PHY frame format shown in Figure A.12. In this case, while the preamble and header are transmitted at 1 Mbps using DBPSK, the payload may be transmitted at 1, 2, 5.5 or 11 Mbps. For this, the Signal field uses the 0x0A value indicating 1 Mbps, 0x14 for 2 Mbps, 0x37 for 5.5 Mbps and 0x6E for 11 Mbps data rates.

The second PHY frame format, called **short PLCP PPDU** format, uses a shorter synchronization field consisting of 56 bits of scrambled '0' bits, and the SFD field consists of the '0000010111001111' pattern which is a mirror of the pattern used in the long format SFD field. In this way, although receivers not configured to use this short header will not detect this SFD, they still sense the medium as busy. While only the preamble is transmitted at 1 Mbps using DBPSK, the header is transmitted at 2 Mbps using DQPSK. The payload is transmitted at 2, 5.5 or 11 Mbps (but not at 1 Mbps).

As the standard operates on certain frequencies in the 2.4 GHz band, where 14 central frequencies were defined, and the spacing between centre frequencies should be, at least, 25 MHz for minimal interference, three channels are used with the following specifications:

US	Europe
channel 1 (2412 MHz)	channel 1 (2412 MHz)
channel 6 (2437 MHz)	channel 7 (2442 MHz)
channel 11 (2462 MHz)	channel 13 (2472 MHz)

A.2.6.2 IEEE 802.11a

The IEEE 802.11a standard specifies a new PHY layer named 'High-speed Physical Layer in the 5 GHz Band', offering up to 54 Mbps using an orthogonal frequency division multiplexing (OFDM) system. The MAC layer specification remains the same as in the 802.11 standard.

The radio frequency LAN system is initially aimed at the 5.15–5.25, 5.25–5.35, and 5.725–5.825 GHz US unlicensed national information infrastructure bands. The OFDM system provides payload data rates of 6, 9, 12, 18, 24, 36, 48 and 54 Mbps, where 6, 12 and 24 Mbps are mandatory. The system uses 52 subcarriers that are modulating using binary or quadrature phase shift keying (BPSK/QPSK), 16-quadrature amplitude modulation (QAM), or 64-QAM. Forward error correction coding is used with a coding rate of 1/2, 2/3 or 3/4.

There are eight channels defined for the two lower bands (36, 40, 44, 48, 52, 56, 60 and 64), and four in the high band (149, 153, 157 and 161). The central frequency for each channel is given by 5000 + 5 * Channel Number (MHz). Each channel is 20 MHz spaced, and its bandwidth is 16.6 MHz.

The PHY frame format is quite different from the other versions, owing to the nature of the OFDM system. More information is found in the appropriate standard.

A.2.6.3 IEEE 802.11g

This standard supplement introduces new modulation schemes and an OFDM system, allowing data rates above 20 Mbps at the 2.4 GHz band. It should be backward compatible to 802.11b. This new scheme will benefit from the better propagation characteristics at 2.4 GHz compared with those at 5 GHz used in the 802.11a version. More information is found in the appropriate standard.

Appendix B

Internet Next Generation: IPv6

This appendix is intended to provide just an overview about one of the most important changes in the Internet in the last years: the new version of the Internet Protocol. Also called Internet Next Generation (IPng), this new version has been developed for many years and it still under discussion. Owing to the importance of this layer inside the overall TCP/IP work, the transition must be carefully planned. Some of the most important aspects of the new version of IP, as well as the modified ICMPv6 and the new IPv6 Neighbor Discovery protocol will be seen in the following sections.

B.1 Introduction

The present version of the Internet Protocol (IPv4) has been working for more than two decades. It has worked well as the Internet has grown from a small inter-network to the present giant where millions of devices are connected using it.

However, with the continuous growth of the Internet, sooner or later, the IPv4 had to be replaced. One of the main problems associated with it is the relatively small 32-bit IP address size, which means the available address space is almost exhausted. Although some improvements allowed the address space to resist the exaggerated growth of the Internet, the address space needed to be expanded. This is the main motivation for the next version of IP.

As IP is the foundation of TCP/IP, the replacement for the new version is not an easy task. For this reason, the designers took the challenge as an opportunity to redesign the protocol for the needs of the present Internet. A related protocol like ICMPv4 was upgraded to support the changes. Also, the new specifications impact on protocols such as ARP, RARP, DHCP and DNS, which had to be revised. Even more, a new protocol – called IPv6 Neighbor Discovery Protocol – was designed in order to take over some tasks previously performed by other protocols in IPv4, and to add new functions.

As a result, the designers not only had to deal with the protocol changes, but they also had to plan how the transition to the new Internet would be put into effect. IPng (IP Next Generation) or IPv6 has been developed for several years, and it has been tested in a real IPv6 network for many years. However, it will take some time and effort to have IPv6 fully working.

B.2 Internet Protocol version 6 (IPv6)

The new upcoming version of the present IP protocol (IPv4) is version 6 (version 5 of the IP was used for experimentation with Internet Stream Protocol, so the number 6 is assigned to the next version to avoid confusion). The specifications are described in a series of RFC documents published in December 1998, where RFC 2460 'Internet Protocol, Version 6 (IPv6) Specification', RFC 2461 'Neighbor Discovery for IP Version 6 (IPv6)', and RFC 2463 'Internet Control Message Protocol (ICMPv6) for the Internet Protocol Version 6 (IPv6) Specification' are the most important. Other documents such RFC 2464 and 2472 describe the transmission of IPv6 packets over Ethernet and PPP links respectively.

IP addressing in the new version of IP is also described in RFC 3513 'Internet Protocol Version 6 (IPv6) Addressing Architecture', and RFC 3587 'IPv6 Global Unicast Address Format'. Many other documents describe several protocol changes to support the IPv6.

B.2.1 IPv6 major changes and additions

The new version of the Internet Protocol (IPv6) was designed to correct some problems the current version (IPv4) presented. Perhaps the most important is the change in the IP address size to get a larger address space. However, other improvements were added. The following are the most important changes and additions in the new version of IP:

- *Larger IP address*: As the IP addresses are 128 bits long, the resulting available address space is really large.
- *Better use of the address space*: With such a large address space, it can be divided hierarchically, allowing better use.
- *Global unicast addressing*: This addressing allows multiple levels of network and sub-network hierarchies. A new way to generate IP addresses from the underlying hardware addresses allows an easy mapping between both addresses.
- *New type of addressing; Anycast*: This new type of addressing introduces new functionality, difficult to implement in the previous IP version.
- *Datagram format using extended headers*: The IP header has been redesigned with new features. The header may be easily extended, if more control information is required.
- *Support for security*: The authentication and encryption headers have been designed to support security.
- *Support for quality of service*: For those applications that require quality of service support, new features have been included.
- *Auto-configuration and renumbering*: A method has been defined for some devices to automatically configure their IP address (and other parameters), without using a server (such as in DHCP). The IP addresses may also be renumbered when necessary.
- *Improved fragmentation and reassembly*: These processes have been improved, giving more efficient routing.

The following sections describe only some of the changes of the new version of the IP protocol.

B.2.2 IPv6 addressing

The lack of available address space is one of the biggest problems of the present version of the Internet Protocol, and it was the main motivation for the upgrade to a new IP version. Although some aspects of the addressing characteristics changed in the new version, others remain as in the present version. The main change is the creation of a new address type.

B.2.2.1 IPv6 new address type: Anycast

The new version supports three address types:

- *Unicast addresses*: the same as that used in IPv4.
- *Multicast addresses*: used when a message must be sent to all devices in a group. Although IPv4 supports this address type, not all devices have it implemented. In IPv6, its support is a requirement.
- *Anycast addresses*: used when a message must be sent to *any* member of a group, but not to all of them. The selected member of the group to whom the message is sent is the easiest to reach. Anycast addresses mean that more than one device shares the 'same IP address' (the Anycast address), so this implies the removal of the uniqueness requirement for IP addresses.

The broadcast address defined in IPv4 is no longer supported in IPv6.

B.2.3 IPv6 address size and notation

In IPv6, the IP address size is 128 bits (16 bytes). It is really big compared with the 32 bits (4 bytes) of the IPv4. As a result, the address space is exceptionally large (2^{128} = 340 282 366 920 938 463 463 374 607 431 768 211 456 IP addresses).

In order to shorten the IPv6 address notation, the hexadecimal system is used grouped into eight 16-bit words, separated by colons. For example:

FF25:01C5:0000:0000:0000:48A3:7E41:036B

Using zero compression, where a sequence of zeroes may be replaced by a double-colon, the above address would be represented as:

FF25:01C5::48A3:7E41:036B

When an IPv6 address using zero compression is presented, in order to know how many 16-bit words with zeroes the double-colon represents, we need to insert as many of them as necessary to complete the full IPv6 address size (16 bytes).

If we have the following address:

FF25:01C5:0000:0000:0000:48A3:0000:036B

only one of the two strings with zeroes may be compressed. Obviously, with the compression of the first, we get fewer notations. In addition, the leading zeroes can be suppressed, so the above address may be reduced to

FF25:01C5::48A3:0:036B

Special addresses, like the IPv6 loopback address 0:0:0:0:0:0:0:1, may be reduced to ::1 .

There is a mixed notation used in IPv6 addresses that embed IPv4 addresses, where only the last four bytes of the address (the IPv4 portion) is shown in decimal notation. For example:

FF25:01C5::48A3:65.182.106.65

As the IPv6 addresses have the first *n* bits representing the Global Routing Prefix (like the Network ID in IPv4), the IPv6 address must use a slash and a prefix length (in decimal), indicating the number of bits of the prefix portion. For example:

FF25:01C5::48A3:0:036B/48

B.2.4 IPv6 address space allocation

Table B.1 shows how the RFC 3513 'Internet Protocol Version 6 (IPv6) Addressing Architecture' presents the initial assignment of IPv6 address space.

Table B.1

Allocation	Prefix (binary)	Fraction of IPv6 address space
Unassigned	0000 0000	1/256
Unassigned	0000 0001	1/256
Reserved for NSAP allocation	0000 001	1/128
Unassigned	0000 01	1/64
Unassigned	0000 1	1/32
Unassigned	0001	1/16
Global unicast	001	1/8
Unassigned	010	1/8
Unassigned	011	1/8
Unassigned	100	1/8
Unassigned	101	1/8
Unassigned	110	1/8
Unassigned	1110	1/16
Unassigned	1111 0	1/32
Unassigned	1111 10	1/64
Unassigned	1111 110	1/128
Unassigned	1111 1110 0	1/512
Link-local unicast addresses	1111 1110 10	1/1024
Site-local unicast addresses	1111 1110 11	1/1024
Multicast addresses	1111 1111	1/256
The 'unspecified address', the 'loopback address', and the 'IPv6 addresses with embedded IPv4 addresses' are assigned out of the 0000 0000 prefix space.		

B.2.5 IPv6 Global Unicast Address format

Since most part of the Internet traffic consists of unicast messages, a large block of assigned addresses is dedicated to unicast addressing. This block is easily identified by the '001' first three bits. The IPv6 Global Unicast Address format is shown in Figure B.1. The Global Routing Prefix is used for routing. The first three bits are '001' to indicate a unicast address. The rest of the bits (45) may be used, creating different levels to construct a hierarchical structure. Each level may have as many bits as we need in order to reflect the actual Internet structure. The Subnet ID identifies a subnet within the site. The Interface ID provides a unique identifier for each host interface.

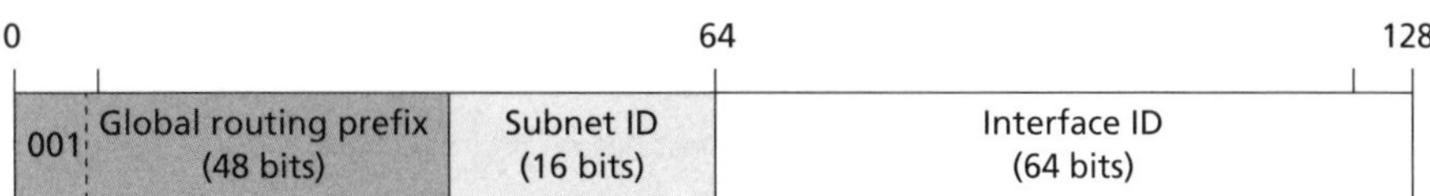

Figure B.1 IPv6 Global Unicast Address format.

As the Interface ID consists of 64 bits, instead of assigning an arbitrary number for each host, we could better map the underlying data link hardware address (MAC address) into this field. As a result, the mapping between the IPv6 address and the MAC address would be direct. In other words, the ARP protocol would not be needed using this technique. This last will work as long as the hardware addresses do not exceed the 64 bits in length.

In the case of Ethernet, with a 48-bit MAC address, the mapping used is very straightforward; the first 24 bits of the Interface ID (the left-most of the 64 bits) are taken from the first 24 bits from the 48 bits of the MAC address; the last 24 bits of the Interface ID (the right-most of the 64 bits) are taken from the last 24 bits from the 48 bits of the MAC address. The 'middle' 16 bits of the Interface ID are filled with FFFE; finally, we change the universal/local bit from a zero to a one. In this way, we map a 48-bit MAC address into a IPv6 Modified EUI-64 Identifier, as defined by the IEEE.

B.2.6 IPv6 datagram format

The IPv6 datagram was redesigned from the previous version. Although all datagrams have a fixed-length header as in IPv4, the most important change consists of the addition of extension headers, which provides flexibility in that some control information is carried only when needed. Options are also supported in IPv6, although implemented as an extension header. While some fields were just renamed to better reflect their use, others were eliminated. A new field allows Quality of Service support. Figure B.2 shows the IPv6 datagram format and the header fields. The IPv6 datagram consists of a header, zero or more optional extension headers and the data which encapsulates the upper layer protocol information.

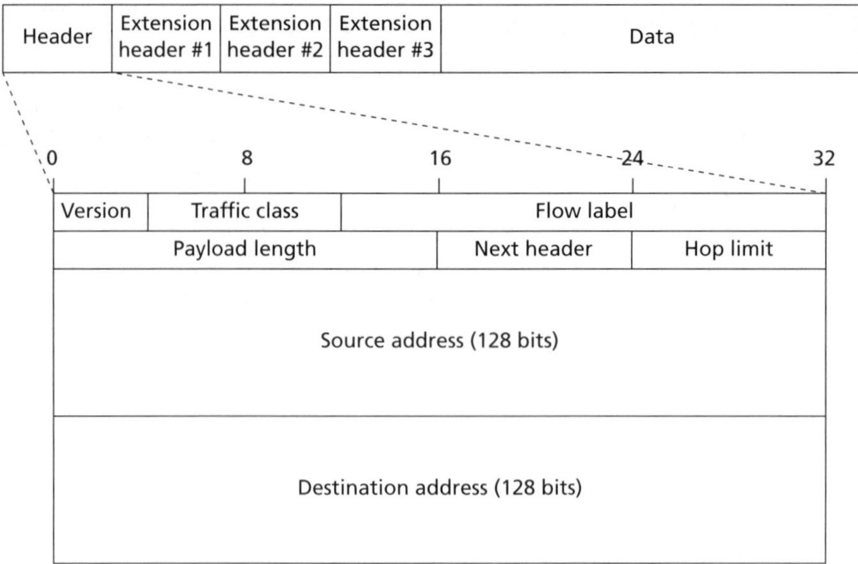

Figure B.2 IPv6 datagram format and header fields.

The header is a 40 bytes fixed-length structure with the following fields:

- **Version** (4 bits): it identifies the version of the IP which generates the datagram. For IPv6, this field contains 0110 (6) in binary.
- **Traffic Class** (1 byte): This field is used for Quality of Service support, and it uses the Differentiated Services (DS) method as defined in RFC 2474.
- **Flow Label** (20 bits): This field is used to provide a 'unique label' for a sequence of datagrams in a flow, so the routers handle those datagrams in the same way. This is very useful in real time datagram delivery, as it is used in a video stream sent over an IP inter-network. See RFC 2460 for more information.
- **Payload Length** (2 bytes): it specifies the number of bytes of the payload (Data), including the extension headers if they exist. As it does not include the header, this field indicates the total length of the IP datagram less than 40 (header size).
- **Next Header** (1 byte): this field specifies the value of the first extension header in the datagram. If the datagram does not have an extension header, this field simply indicates the 'Protocol' of the message encapsulated in the payload. See the next section for more information.
- **Hop Limit** (1 byte): it replaces the Time-To-Live (TTL) field in the IPv4 datagram. As this field value is decremented each time the datagram passes through a router (hop), this name better reflects how this field is used.
- **Source Address** (16 bytes): it specifies the 128-bit IP address of the originator of the datagram.
- **Destination Address** (16 bytes): it specifies the 128-bit IP address of the ultimate intended recipient of the datagram.

B.2.7 IPv6 datagram extension headers

Extension headers are used to include control information only when needed. An IPv6 datagram may have zero or more extension headers. They are included between the header and the data payload. Table B.2 gives the available extension headers.

Table B.2

Extension header	Length	Next header value (dec)	Description	RFC
Hop-By-Hop Options	variable	0	It is used to carry optional information that must be examined by every node in the packet's path.	2460
Routing	variable	43	It is used to specify the route (or multiple routes) for a datagram.	2460
Fragment	8	44	It contains fragment information, when the datagram contains a fragment of the original message.	2460
Encapsulating Security Payload (ESP)	variable	50	It is used to carry encrypted data to secure information.	2406
Authentication Header (AH)	variable	51	It is used to carry information to verify the authenticity of encrypted data.	2402
Destination Options	variable	60	It is used to carry optional information that needs to be examined only by a packet's destination node(s).	2460
The specific format for each extension header is given in its corresponding RFC document.				

If more than one extension header is included in a datagram, the following order is recommended:

IPv6 header (*always present*)
Hop-By-Hop Options extension header
Destination Options extension header (*if Routing extension header is used*)
Routing extension header
Fragment extension header
Authentication Header extension header
Encapsulating Security Payload extension header
Destination Options extension header (*with options for the final destination*)
Upper-layer header (*for example: a TCP segment*)

The Extension headers included in the IPv6 datagram are 'linked' among themselves forming a chain. For this purpose, the *Next Header* field is used. For example, suppose an *IPv6 datagram* carrying a *TCP segment*, and including *Routing* and *Fragment* extension headers. The *Next Header* field of the *IPv6 Header* will contain the value 43 indicating that the first extension header included is a *Routing* extension header (*Next Header* value of 43). The *Routing* extension header will also contain a *Next Header* field with the value 44, specifying that the next header in the sequence is a *Fragment* extension header. Finally, this last will have a *Next Header* value of 6, indicating that the next header is a *TCP Header*. In this way, the *Next Header* field of the last Extension header indicates the '*Protocol*' encapsulated in the payload. Figure B.3 shows this.

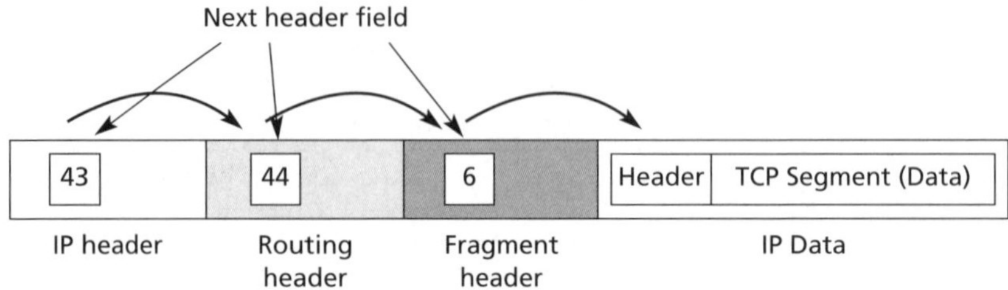

Figure B.3 IPv6 datagram headers chain.

As the IPv6 datagram consists of a sequence of many types of headers (IPv6 header, zero or more extension headers, and the header of the upper-layer protocol encapsulated by the datagram payload), the *Next Header* field indicates the type of the next header in the sequence. The last *Next Header* field indicates the 'Protocol' type of the encapsulated message (or the type of header of the last header in the sequence), as specified in the IPv4 header field (1 for ICMPv4; 6 for TCP; 17 for UDP; etc).

In the case where the datagram has no extension headers, the *Next Header* field of the IPv6 *header* will indicate the 'Protocol' encapsulated in the payload.

B.3 Internet Control Message Protocol version 6 (ICMPv6)

In order to support the changes the IPv6 presents in comparison to the previous version IPv4, a new ICMP was developed. This is known as ICMPv6, and it is described in RFC 463 'Internet Control Message Protocol (ICMPv6) for the Internet Protocol Version 6 (IPv6) Specification'. As in the original protocol, ICMPv6 was developed to communicate error messages when certain problems were encountered on an inter-network. The following error messages are defined:

- **ICMPv6 Destination Unreachable**: it should be generated by the router (or by the IPv6 layer in the originating node) in response to a packet that cannot be delivered to its destination, for reasons other than congestion.
- **ICMPv6 Packet Too Big**: it must be sent by a router in response to a packet that cannot be forwarded because the packet is larger than the

MTU of the outgoing link. (In IPv6, for efficiency reasons, the routers are not allowed to fragment a datagram to avoid them spending time doing this; instead, this responsibility falls on the hosts.)

- **ICMPv6 Time Exceeded**: it is used to notify that the sent datagram reached a zero value in its Hop Limit field.
- **ICMPv6 Parameter Problem**: it is used by a node to notify that it cannot complete processing a packet, because it found a problem with a field in the header or extension header.

Other types of messages, called informational messages, are used for diagnostic purposes, as well as to implement the IPv6 Neighbor Discovery (ND) protocol. The following are the informational messages:

- **ICMPv6 Echo Request and Echo Reply (RFC 2463)**: They are used for a basic connectivity test between nodes, and they implement the known 'ping' utility for the IPv6. Every node must support these messages.
- **ICMPv6 Router Advertisement and Router Solicitation (RFC 2461)**: Because a host needs a router in order to send datagrams to other hosts in a different network, every host must be able to localize a router to use it. Router discovery consists of Router Advertisement messages sent from the routers to the host, and Router Solicitation messages sent by the host to prompt for a router. These messages are based on a router–host communication.
- **ICMPv6 Neighbor Advertisement and Neighbor Solicitation (RFC 2461)**: They are used to determine the existence of neighboring hosts on the same network, including the exchange of information such as the link-layer address (used for address resolution). These messages are based on host–host communication.
- **ICMPv6 Redirect (RFC 2461)**: As a host may have more than one router by which it sends datagrams to other networks, it is possible that the host does not know the best route for each network destination. Then, if a router receives a datagram and it realizes that for that destination another router would be more efficient, the router sends a Redirect message to the originator of the datagram, informing this situation for future transmissions. In this way, hosts may learn which routers are more efficient for a given network destination.
- **ICMPv6 Router Renumbering (RFC 2894)**: It is used to allow routers to be renumbered, changing their prefixes (Network Identifiers). This is very useful in large networks migration processes.

The full description of the ICMPv6 messages and their formats may be found in their corresponding RFC documents.

B.4 IPv6 Neighbor Discovery (ND) protocol

As we have seen in Chapter 5, one of the most important aspects of an internetwork is that each device can communicate to others, as if they all were in the same local network. However, this is true only from the upper-layers point of view, because from the lower layers, each device must know if the destination device is in the same local network in order to make a direct delivery, or send the message to a router for indirect delivery. This decision is taken with the help of the IP addressing scheme (Subnet Mask).

If a direct delivery is required, then the device needs to know the hardware address of the destination device. For this task, the ARP protocol is used. For indirect delivery, the host must have a local router configured. ICMPv4 provides Router Advertisement and Router Solicitation messages for these purposes.

All the above indicate that a device must have some knowledge about the hosts and routers localized in the same local network. In other words, it should be related to its neighbours. Although in IPv4 all these tasks are performed, they are provided by diverse protocols and solutions. In IPv6, a new protocol called IPv6 Neighbour Discovery was developed to group all these functions in a single place. The concept of a neighbour is applied to devices that are local to each other. Then, the Neighbor Discovery protocol is all about communication between local devices, with the purpose of knowing the device's neighbours and certain information about them.

The RFC 2461 'Neighbor Discovery for IP Version 6 (IPv6)' is the defining standard for ND, although as most of its functions are implemented using ICMPv6 messages, the RFC 2463 'Internet Control Message Protocol for IPv6' also describes in part the ND operation. The functions of the ND protocol are described in Table B.3:

Table B.3

Group	Functions	Description
Host–Router	Router Discovery	How hosts locate routers on the same network.
	Prefix Discovery	How hosts know address prefixes that determine direct or indirect delivery.
	Parameter Discovery	How hosts learn link parameters (as MTU or Hop Limit) to use in datagrams.
	Address Auto configuration	How nodes automatically configure an address for an interface.
Host–Host	Address Resolution	How nodes determine the hardware address from the IP.
	Next-Hop Determination	The algorithm to know where to send the datagram, looking the IP destination address.
	Neighbor Unreachability Detection	How nodes determine that a neighbour is no longer reachable.
	Duplicate Address Detection	How a node determines if the address it wishes to use is not already in use by another node.
Redirect	Redirect	How a router informs a host a better route for a particular destination.

Appendix C

Dynamic Host Configuration Protocol

In modern networks, each host must be appropriately configured. The necessary parameters depend on each network, so automatic configuration provides each device a way to adapt itself to different networks. For this reason, a configuration tool is very important in these cases. Such a tool is provided through a specifically designed protocol called Dynamic Host Configuration Protocol (DHCP). This appendix provides an overview about its operation and application, as well as its relationship with its predecessor, the BOOTP protocol.

C. 1 Introduction

In order for a device to connect to an inter-network, an IP address must be configured. For this, a manual method may be used by the network's administrator, who would manually configure each device with its assigned IP address. While in small networks this task is somewhat cumbersome, in large networks (with thousand of devices) it is almost impossible.

For this reason, a boot protocol (BOOTP) was developed, which provided automatic IP address configuration for devices. In fact, the BOOTP was initially developed for diskless machines which cannot save a configured IP address. In this way, a diskless host would configure its IP address in order to download a boot file from a given server through a network. Later, BOOTP was extended to provide hosts with other information as well.

In BOOTP, a client sends a message to a server, which looks up in a table to determine the IP address for that client (this table maps an IP address for each device's hardware address), and it responds with the configuration information. In this way, every client has previously assigned an IP address in a server table, which remains the same over time. In these cases, it is said that the device has a 'static' IP address.

In a BOOTP implementation, the administrators have the network configuration centralized in just one file into a single place (the server). Every change is performed from this file. However, every device that wants to use the network should have an IP address previously assigned with an entry in this file. If a guest user needs to connect to the network temporarily, the administrator must beforehand assign an entry for it in the file.

Although this scheme worked well, the 'static' IP assignation is not well adapted for modern networks. In such networks, the use of devices such as notebooks and handheld devices, which are frequently moved into different networks, demand IP address changes (the network ID portion of the address changes from network to network). In such cases, the administrator would need to continuously change the assigned addresses for these mobile devices.

In addition, it is very common for guest users to only need to connect to the network for a limited time, and after that they do not need the assigned IP address any more. In these cases, with the lack of IPv4 addresses, a 'forever' IP address assigned without a real use is a luxury at a very high cost.

The solution for the above problems is the 'dynamic' IP assignation. That is, rather than a device '*own*' an IP address that has been 'statically' assigned, the device '*leases*' an IP address that is 'dynamically' assigned by a server from a pool of IP addresses. The 'leased' IP address has a certain duration, after which the device should renew the lease. If this does not happen, this IP address returns to the pool to be available for other devices.

The 'dynamic' IP allocation allows a limited pool of IP addresses to be shared by several devices. Then, we may handle more devices than the available IP addresses, if all devices are not connected to the network at the same time. In the 'static' allocation, we need one IP address for each device, even when the device is not connected to the network permanently. In the case of mobile devices, they lease an IP address from the network, as long as they need it. After that, as they move to other networks, they lease different IP addresses from those networks.

C. 2 DHCP overview

The idea behind DHCP is to provide a central configuration parameters repository, where the network administrator may define the network-specific parameters. This information would be provided to each host, using an exchange of messages.

Owing to a weakness of BOOTP, which was in the 'static' allocation scheme used, the DHCP designers changed this scheme by a 'dynamic' allocation, but they took the original BOOTP protocol as a base, giving the DHCP protocol many improvements. DHCP was converted into a complete tool not only to configure a host's IP addresses, but also to configure many other parameters required by modern networks.

C. 2.1 DHCP dynamic allocation

The RFC 2131 'Dynamic Host Configuration Protocol' is the current document describing the DHCP operation. The main change implemented by DHCP from its predecessor BOOTP, is in the IP address allocation scheme. Now, the devices 'lease' an IP address for a certain period, and they must renew the lease as long as they need it. In this way, a limited pool of IP addresses may be efficiently shared between lots of devices. At the same time, temporary users, such as guest or mobile devices, may use the network, and after that, the temporarily assigned IP addresses return to the pool for subsequent assignments.

In dynamic allocation, an important decision is about how long lease duration will be. In short lease duration, the devices must be constantly renewing their IP addresses, while in long lease duration, the efficiency may not be so good because an IP address may be still assigned to a device, when it no longer needs it (supposing the device did not release the IP address as it should have). Common lease durations range from hours to weeks, or even months, depending on the dynamic of the environment (devices connecting and disconnecting more or less frequently) and the number of available IP addresses and types of users (guest clients, mobile clients, servers, etc.). Even though DHCP was developed with 'dynamic' allocation in mind, DHCP server implementations also support 'static' allocation and manual configuration.

C. 2.2 DHCP IP addresses lease

In 'dynamic' allocation, the host uses a leased IP address. This IP address was assigned by a DHCP server in the **allocation** process. The host may use this IP address for a period of time (as expressed in the allocation process). When this period of time has expired, the leased IP address becomes invalid. Then, before this period expires, the host should **renew** the lease with the same server. If the renewal is not possible, the host should **rebind** the lease with any other server. If both processes, renewal and rebinding, were unsuccessful, the lease terminates. If at any time, the host decides not to use the leased IP address any more, it may **release** the IP address, terminating the lease.

A DHCP client must implement two timers in order to know when a renewal or rebinding process is necessary. The first timer (T1) is set by default to 50% of the lease period. When T1 expires, the client should start the renewal process. If this process is unsuccessful, the second timer (T2) will expire, by default, to 87.5% of the lease time. Then, the client should start the rebinding process. Once a lease has been extended (renewal or rebinding), both timers are reset and started again.

C. 3 DHCP client/server communication model

DHCP consists of a series of messages between client and server devices, using UDP as the Transport protocol. One of the reasons why UDP is used is its simplicity and its support for broadcasts. Let's see why this last is necessary.

A device must be configured (a valid IP address and other parameters) to be part of a network. In DHCP, the device (a client) must contact a DHCP server to get network parameters. However, two questions arise:

1 How does the device know the IP address of one or more DHCP servers if it is not yet configured?
2 How can the client (without a valid IP address and trying to get one) communicate with a DHCP server in an IP network?

The answer is **broadcasting**.

The device broadcasts a DHCP message to port 67 (the well-known UDP port for DHCP servers) into the local network. In some cases, where the device already has a valid IP address and it knows the server IP address (as in the case of IP lease renewal), the device uses unicast messages. Once the device broadcasts a message, this last is received by all active DHCP servers on the network. And every server that is able to offer a lease for the device will reply to the client. But how may a server reply to a device without a valid IP address? The server has two possibilities: (1) it may reply to the host sending a unicast message using the layer two address (the device's hardware address is in the CHAddr field of the client request received by the server), or (2) it may reply to the host using broadcasting at layer three. For this reason, the client devices also use a well-known UDP port 68 (instead of a temporary port as they usually do), so each DHCP client implementation knows that it may receive DHCP server's messages through this port.

The first method of server replies is preferred as it does not have the performance problems associated with broadcasting messages. However, the client implementation should accept and forward to the IP layer any IP packets delivered to the client's hardware address before the IP address has been configured. Those DHCP client implementations that are unable to do this must use the Broadcast (B) flag in the DHCP message to indicate the server's response should be a broadcast at layer three rather than a unicast at layer two.

A third type of device other than DHCP clients and server, called **relay agents**, are used as intermediaries facilitating cross-network communication between clients and servers. These devices allow the use of only one DHCP server in a network structured as many subnets, avoiding the use of one server for each subnet. With fewer DHCP servers, the work of network administrators is reduced. Of course, for redundant reasons, only one server is not a good idea.

Using UDP does not guarantee that messages arrive at destination. This would be reflected in the implementation, where each time a sent message is not replied, this may mean that: (1) there is not any server listening on the network, or (2) the sent message did not arrive at its destination. Each time a message is sent by the client, it should start a timer. If the timer expires before the message reply arrives, the message should be retransmitted. After retransmitting the message a certain number of times, if the client still has not received replies, it then may conclude that no active servers exist on the network, or some network problems exist.

C. 3.1 DHCP client/server messages

The following messages are exchanged between DHCP clients and servers:

- DHCPDISCOVER: it is used by the client, which broadcasts the message looking for a DHCP server.
- DHCPOFFER: it is used by the server, in reply to a DHCPDISCOVER.
- DHCPREQUEST: it is used by the client in the following cases:
  - to notify the servers about the option it chose.
  - to verify its lease (if it is still valid, after re-booting for example)

- to renew the lease with the server which gave it the lease
- to rebind the lease with any other server.

- DHCPRELEASE: it is used by the client to inform the server that it will no longer use the leased IP address, which returns to the IP addresses pool, for future assignments.
- DHCPINFORM: it is used by the client to request configuration parameters other than the IP address. For example, clients with 'static' IP address may still use DHCP to get other parameters.
- DHCPDECLINE: it is used by the client to notify that the leased IP address is already in use, for which the client declines to use it. The server should mark this IP address as unavailable.
- DHCPACK: it is used by the server to acknowledge a client's request.
- DHCPNAK: it is used by the server to deny a client's request.

Figure C.1 shows a state diagram with the DHCP client process for the 'dynamic' IP address allocation. The overall process begins with the client in the **INIT** state, without a leased IP address. As the client does not know about any DHCP server on the network, it broadcasts a **DHCPDISCOVER** message, filling its own hardware address and a random transaction identifier, to later match the replies. It may also request a specific IP address, a lease time and/or other specific configuration parameters. After that, the client goes to the **SELECTING** state.

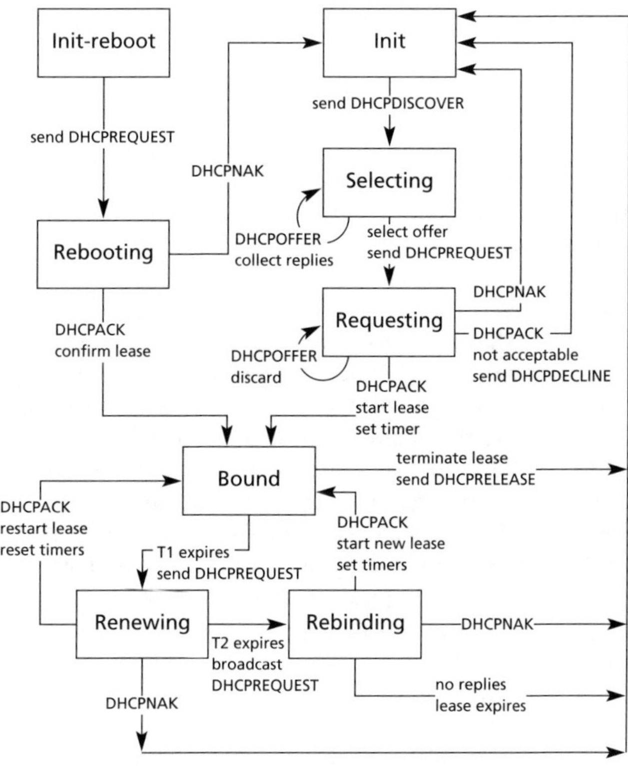

Figure C.1 DHCP client process for Dynamic IP address allocation.

Each server in the network receives the broadcasted message, and considers offering a lease for the client. If so, each server sends a DHCPOFFER message to the client, with the assigned IP address, the lease time and any other parameter requested by the client or programmed by the administrator to be included in the host's configuration. The servers are not required to satisfy the client's requirements used in the DHCPDISCOVER messages.

While the client is in the **SELECTING** state, it collects DHCPOFFER replies from the servers. If the client does not receive any DHCPOFFER, it should retransmit DHCPDISCOVER messages for some time. After a certain time and after having received some replies from the servers, the client must select one offer. A DHCPREQUEST message is then broadcast, to inform the servers which offer has been accepted. This message has a 'server identifier' option that allows each server to know which was selected. The client progresses to the **REQUESTING** state.

The client needs to wait for a reply from the selected server, which may confirm the lease with a DHCPACK message containing the configuration parameters; or it may reply with a DHCPNAK message, stating that 'the offered IP address is no longer available'. In this last case, the client must send another DHCPREQUEST choosing another offer (with a different server identifier), until a DHCPACK was received confirming the lease. If neither DHCPACK nor DHCPNAK is received, the client must retransmit DHCPREQUEST for a couple of times.

Once a DHCPACK is received, the client checks for IP duplication generating an ARP request for this IP address. If any device responds to the ARP request, than the allocated IP is already in use, so the client must send a DHCPDECLINE message to the server, informing that the IP address allocated is already in use by another device, and it must go to the **INIT** state. If the allocated IP address is not in use, finally the client accepts it and progresses to the **BOUND** state. The lease begins and the timers are started.

During the lease, the client may terminate it at any time sending a DHCPRELEASE message to the server which allocated the IP address. Then, the client goes to the **INIT** state.

Once in the **BOUND** state, the client uses the allocated IP address to operate in the network, during the lease time. But before this time expires, the client should renew the lease. When T1 expires, the client must send a DHCPREQUEST to the server that currently allocates the client's lease, in order to try to renew the lease. Then, the client progresses to the **RENEWING** state.

In the **RENEWING** state, the client is waiting for a renewal response from the server that has the current lease. If the server replies with a DHCPACK message, the lease is renewed, the timers are reset, and the client goes to the **BOUND** state. If the server refuses to renew the lease, a DHCPNAK is received by the client indicating that it must go to the **INIT** state and start the overall process again. Where no reply is received by the client, and the timer T2 expires, the client progresses to the **REBINDING** state.

In the **REBINDING** state, the client broadcasts a DHCPREQUEST message trying to find a server that will extend its current lease. Even when all servers receive this message, only those which have information about the client's lease will respond. The server that may extend the lease replies with a DHC-

PACK message, indicating the parameters that could be changed in this renewal. The client goes to the **BOUND** state, and the timers are reset. If the client receives a DHCPNAK, it must go to the **INIT** state to start a new lease process. If no replies at all are received by the client, eventually the lease expires, and the client will progress to the **INIT** state.

In case a client has a valid lease, and the device is re-booted, when it starts up, it should not start the overall process again. Instead, the client should confirm if the lease is still valid. For this, the client starts from a different state called **INIT-REBOOT**. The client sends a DHCPREQUEST to the server trying to confirm the lease it has. After this, the client goes to the **REBOOTING** state, waiting for the server's response. If the server replies with a DHCPACK, the lease is confirmed and the client goes to the **BOUND** state. If a DHCPNAK is received, the client must go to the **INIT** state and start over.

C. 4 DHCP message format

All the operation of DHCP is based on the exchange of messages between clients and servers. These messages have a specific format, which was based on the BOOTP message format for compatibility reasons (when DHCP was designed, BOOTP was already widely used). The fairly simple BOOTP message format was adapted for a more complex DHCP structure. For this, some existing fields in the BOOTP message are interpreted by DHCP in a different way, and some 'options' fields were used for 'mandatory' information. This approach allowed the BOOTP/DHCP interoperability. Figure C.2 shows the DHCP message format.

The field description is as follows:

- OP – Operation Code (1 byte): it specifies a Request from a client (value 1) or a Reply from the server (value 2).
- HTYPE – Hardware Type (1 byte): it specifies the type of hardware used in the local network. The values are the same from the Hardware Type field used in the ARP message format (see Chapter 5).
- HLEN – Hardware Address Length (1 byte): it specifies the length of the hardware address used in the local network, as used in the ARP message field. For Ethernet, this value is six.
- HOPS (1 byte): it is optionally used by relay agents to control forwarding of messages. The client sets this value to zero.
- XID – Transaction Identifier (4 bytes): a 32-bit random number used by the client to match the replies with the original requests. The server copies this value in its responses.
- SECS – Seconds (2 bytes): the client fills this field with the seconds elapsed since it began with the address acquisition or renewal process. The server may use this field as an indication to prioritize pending client's requests.
- FLAGS (2 bytes): only one bit is currently used, as a **Broadcast Flag** (B) which informs the servers and relay agents that the client's implementation is not able to forward IP packets to the IP layer without a valid IP address (before the stack is initialised), so the responses should be broadcast at layer three. The rest of the bits are reserved.

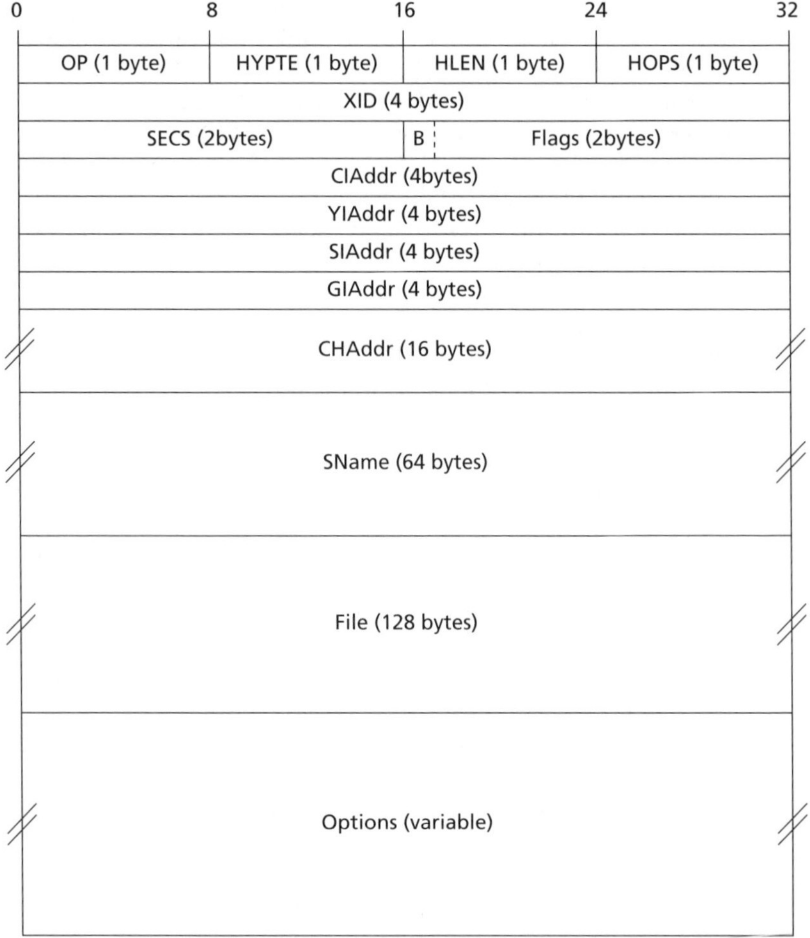

Figure C.2 DHCP message format.

- CIAddr – Client IP Address (4 bytes): this field is set to zero, except if the client already has a valid IP address (while it is in the **BOUND**, **RENEWAL**, or **REBINDING** states).
- YIAddr – Your IP Address (4 bytes): this field is used by the server to inform the client the assigned IP address.
- SIAddr – Server IP Address (4 bytes): this field is filled by the server with the IP address of the next server to use in bootstrap (it may be the same or a different server from the one sending the reply). The IP address of the server sending this reply is always included in the Server Identifier DHCP Option (Option Type 54. See section C.4.2).
- GIAddr – Gateway IP Address (4 bytes): it is used to inform the IP address of the relay agent whether clients and servers are in different sub-networks. This is not the default gateway IP address to configure in the client.
- CHAddr – Client Hardware Address (16 bytes): it is filled by the client with its layer-two address (hardware address).

- SName – Server Name (64 bytes): this field is used to send the name of the server sending a DHCPOFFER or DHCPACK message. The name is a null-terminated string, and it may refer to a fully qualified DNS name or a nickname. This field may also be used by the DHCP option overload feature.
- File – Boot Filename (128 bytes): this field may optionally be used by a client to request a particular type of boot file in a DHCPDISCOVER message, or it may be used by the server to fully specify the directory and filename of a boot file, in a DHCPOFFER message. This field may also be used by the DHCP option overload feature.
- Options (variable): this field is used to be filled with both 'optional' and 'mandatory' information to be exchanged between DHCP clients and servers. See the next section for more information.

C. 4.1 DHCP Options field

As we have already said before, for compatibility reasons, the DHCP message format is the same as that used by the BOOTP protocol, with a slight change in the last field. Originally, the BOOTP message format contained the Vend field (Vendor-Specific Area) as the last field. This consisted of a fixed-length 64 bytes of data that allowed vendors to customize BOOTP to the needs of different types of hardware. As this Vend field was defined as unstructured, each manufacturer could use it with a different format, so a 'magic cookie' was defined (the first four bytes of the field) in order for a device to identify the vendor and appropriately interpret this field.

With the development of modern networks, it was necessary to provide to each host other non-vendor-specific information in order for it to work properly. Certain parameters such as the subnet mask, default gateway (router) and local DNS, among others, needed to be configured in the host. However, the BOOTP did not have specific fields for these parameters. In order for BOOTP to support them, the RFC 1048 redefined the Vend field as the Vendor Information Extensions.

The Vendor Information extensions defined an internal structure for the Vend field. This field may contain many vendor information fields, where each of them consists of the following sub-fields: a Vendor Information Field Code (1 byte) defining the type, a Vendor Information Field Length (1 byte), and the Vendor Information Field Data (variable). In this way, both vendor-specific information and general parameters were carried in the Vend field. The special 'magic cookie' with value 99 130 83 99 was used to indicate that the Vend field is used with the Vendor Information extensions structure.

When DHCP was designed, based on the BOOTP message format, the Vend field name was renamed as Options, and the field now is variable in length, in contrast with the fixed-length 64 bytes of the BOOTP Vend field. The same 'magic cookie' is still used, and the options field maintains the same structure, although the sub-fields have changed their names:

Sub-field	Size (bytes)	Description
Option Code	1	It specifies the type of option.
Option Length	1	It specifies the length of the Option Data sub-field.
Option Data	variable	The data of the option.

There are two exceptions to the above structure; the Pad option type (value 0), used for padding if necessary, and the End option type (value 255), which is used to indicate the end of the option list within the Options field. Both options consist of only one byte (the Option Code), without the Length and Data sub-fields.

When the Options field has less than 64 bytes (the length of the Vend field in the BOOTP message), the field is padded with zeroes (Pad option) after the End option, to complete the 64 bytes in length.

The vendor-specific information, as defined for BOOTP, may still be used but as an option (Option Type 43). Figure C.3 shows the DHCP Options field format.

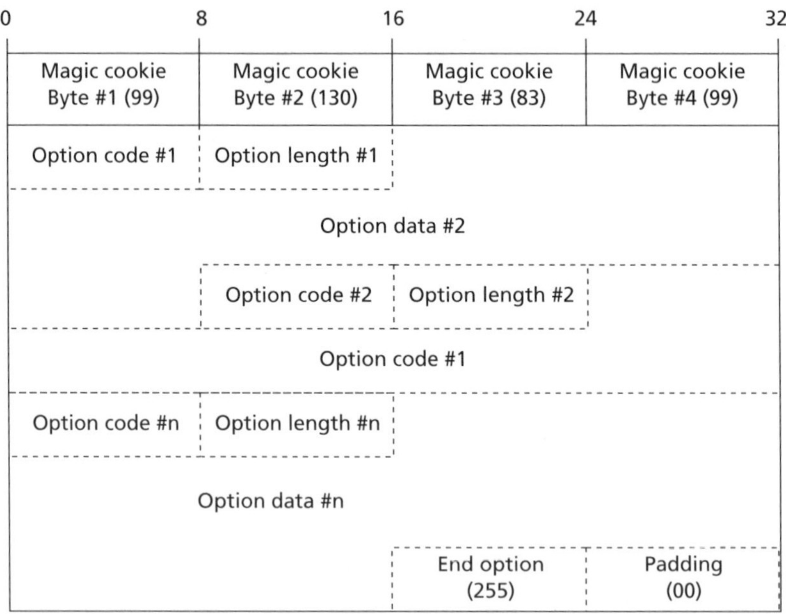

Figure C.3 DHCP Options field format.

C. 4.2 DHCP Option types

Table C.1 shows some of the DHCP Options that may be used in the Options field. The RFC 2132 'DHCP Options and BOOTP Vendor Extensions' provide a complete list of the options, which are categorized according to their purpose. The IANA website also provides current information for Options updates.

The complete set of available Options may be found in the appropriate RFC document, or in the IANA site (**www.iana.org/assignments/bootp-dhcp-parameters**)

Table C.1

Option category	Option Code	Data length (bytes)	Option name	Description
RFC 1497 vendor extensions	0	–	Pad	A 'filler' to align options.
	1	4	Subnet Mask	A 32-bit subnet mask for the client.
	3	Multiple of 4	Router	A list of 32-bit router addresses, in preference order.
	6	Multiple of 4	DNS Name Server	A list of 32-bit DNS name server addresses, in preference order.
	12	variable	Host Name	It specifies a host name for the client.
	15	variable	Domain Name	It specifies the DNS domain name for the client.
	18	variable	Extensions Path	It specifies the name of the file with vendor-specific fields. See option 43.
	255	–	End	A 'marker' indicating the end of the options.
IP layer parameters per host	22	2	Maximum Datagram Reassembly Size	It specifies the size of the largest datagram the client should be prepared to reassemble.
	23	1	Default IP Time-To-Live	It specifies the default value that the client should use for the TTL field for outgoing IP datagrams.
IP layer parameters per interface	26	2	Interface MTU	It specifies the MTU to use on this interface. The minimum value is 68.
	28	4	Broadcast Address	It specifies the address to be used for broadcasts on this interface.
Link Layer Parameters Per Interface	35	4	ARP Cache Timeout	It specifies the timeout, in seconds, for ARP cache entries.
	36	1	Ethernet Encapsulation	It indicates the type of encapsulation to use; Ethernet II (RFC 894) if value is 0, or IEEE 802.3 (RFC 1042) if value is 1.
TCP parameters	37	1	Default TTL	It specifies the default TTL value the client should use for outgoing TCP segments.
	38	4	TCP Keepalive Interval	It specifies the time (in seconds) the client should wait before sending a keep alive message on a TCP connection.

►

Table C.1 *Continued*

<table>
<tr><th>Option category</th><th>Option Code</th><th>Data length (bytes)</th><th>Option name</th><th>Description</th></tr>
<tr><td>DHCP extensions</td><td>50</td><td>4</td><td>Requested IP Address</td><td>It is used in DHCPDISCOVER to request a particular IP address.</td></tr>
<tr><td></td><td>51</td><td>4</td><td>IP Address Lease Time</td><td>It is used by the client to request a specific lease time, or by the server to specify the offered lease time. It is specified in seconds</td></tr>
<tr><td></td><td>52</td><td>1</td><td>Option Overload</td><td>It is used to carry options in the File and/or SName fields:<table><tr><th>Value</th><th>Meaning</th></tr><tr><td>1</td><td>The File field holds options.</td></tr><tr><td>2</td><td>The SName field holds options.</td></tr><tr><td>3</td><td>Both fields hold options.</td></tr></table></td></tr>
<tr><td></td><td>53</td><td>1</td><td>DHCP Message Type</td><td>Indicates the type of message:<table><tr><th>Value</th><th>DHCP message</th></tr><tr><td>1</td><td>DHCPDISCOVER</td></tr><tr><td>2</td><td>DHCPOFFER</td></tr><tr><td>3</td><td>DHCPREQUEST</td></tr><tr><td>4</td><td>DHCPDECLINE</td></tr><tr><td>5</td><td>DHCPACK</td></tr><tr><td>6</td><td>DHCPNAK</td></tr><tr><td>7</td><td>DHCPRELEASE</td></tr><tr><td>8</td><td>DHCPINFORM</td></tr></table></td></tr>
<tr><td></td><td>54</td><td>4</td><td>Server Identifier</td><td>It is used in replies to distinguish offers coming from different servers.</td></tr>
<tr><td></td><td>55</td><td>variable</td><td>Parameter Request List</td><td>It is used by the client to request a list of particular configuration parameter values.</td></tr>
<tr><td></td><td>56</td><td>variable</td><td>Message</td><td>It is used to indicate error messages and others.</td></tr>
<tr><td></td><td>57</td><td>2</td><td>Maximum DHCP Message Size</td><td>It is used to specify the maximum size of DHCP message allowed.</td></tr>
<tr><td></td><td>58</td><td>4</td><td>Renewal (T1) Timer Value</td><td>It indicates the client the value to use for this timer.</td></tr>
</table>

Table C.1 *Continued*

Option category	Option Code	Data length (bytes)	Option name	Description
	59	4	Rebinding (T2) Timer Value	It indicates the client the value to use for this timer.
	66	variable	TFTP Server Name	It replaces the SName field, when using the option overload feature.
	67	variable	Bootfile Name	It replaces the File field, when using the option overload feature.
Application and service parameters	43	variable	Vendor Specific Information	It is used to exchange vendor-specific information between clients and servers.
	68	Multiple of 4	Mobile IP Home Agent	A list of IP addresses of home agents the client may use in Mobile IP, in preference order.
	69	Multiple of 4	SMTP Servers	A list of IP addresses of SMTP servers the client may use, in preference order.
	70	Multiple of 4	POP3 Servers	A list of IP addresses of POP3 servers the client may use, in preference order.

C. 4.3 DHCP Option overloading

As DHCP uses the Options field to exchange lots of information, the size of the DHCP message might exceed the maximum datagram allowed by the UDP transport protocol. In this case, in order to downsize the message, we could still make use of the available space provided by other fields in the DHCP message which were not really specifically designed for the DHCP protocol. Specifically, we could make use of the SName (64 bytes) and File (128 bytes) which were used by BOOTP to provide information about the boot file to download, but are not required by DHCP.

DHCP allows the use of these fields as an 'extra' room for DHCP options. This feature is called **Option Overloading**, and it is indicated by Option Type 52 with one byte of data indicating if the SName, the File, or both fields are used to carry options. Inside each field, the options structure follows the same as for the Options field. In addition, if both fields were needed in the message, they may still send specific options within the Options field (Option Type 66 and 67).

Appendix D

Simple Network Management Protocol

The protocol overview (seen in the first part of the book) would not be complete without a look at the Simple Network Management Protocol (SNMP), which is a hot topic these days, especially in the embedded systems environment.

D.1 Introduction

As modern networks become larger and more complex, they become more difficult to manage. In small networks, the administrator may easily move around each network device to test and configure it. In larger networks, such as the Internet, this is almost impossible. For this reason, a 'network tool' had to be developed.

As all devices connected to a TCP/IP network share this protocol implementation, it makes sense to use the network itself as a way to communicate network management information between the network administration and the network devices. In this way, the network administrator could manage the network devices remotely.

The SNMP was developed for this purpose. Under this scheme, network administrators make use of special network devices, called **Network Management Stations** (NMS), to interact with other network devices, called **Managed Nodes**, to get information from them, as well as to modify some parameters.

Any network device connected to a TCP/IP network, such as routers, switches, printers and even embedded systems, can be a Managed Node, as long as it has the proper SNMP software implemented. This software consists of an **SNMP Agent**, which implements the SNMP protocol to allow devices to interact with the NMS; and an **SNMP Management Information Base** (MIB), which defines the type of information stored in the managed device. This information may be collected from the NMS and it can be used to control the managed device.

The NMS is a computer running an **SNMP Manager** software, which implements the SNMP protocol to communicate with the SNMP Agents; and one or more **SNMP Applications**, which allow a network administrator to use SNMP to manage the network.

Both the NMS and Managed Nodes are called SNMP entities. Figure D.1 shows a typical SNMP scenario. While the **SNMP protocol** specifies how information is exchanged between SNMP entities, the MIB defines the type of this exchanged information. A third component, the **Structure of Management Information** (SMI) specifies how MIB information is defined. These three components constitute the **SNMP Internet Standard Management Framework** defined for TCP/IP networks management.

D.2 The Management Information Base (MIB)

In order for a network administrator to manage a device, it may need to collect information from the device, as well as modify some information stored in this device. Then, we could create a set of commands for these purposes. However, as many different kinds of devices may be managed, the type of information each device may present can be very different, so it would be almost impossible to create a set of commands for each kind of device to be managed. For this reason, the device information should be stored as variables, and the commands could be 'generic' in the sense that they could work for any kind of device, independently of the characteristics each device could present.

When an NMS collects the device information, these variables and their values are sent from the device. When some device information has to be modified, the variable and its new value are sent to the device. In this way, no matter the kind of device, the manageable characteristics are represented by these information variables, called objects. Each device characteristic is described using an object. While some objects may be common to every device (such as the object describing the IP address of a device), other objects may describe unique characteristics presented in each device.

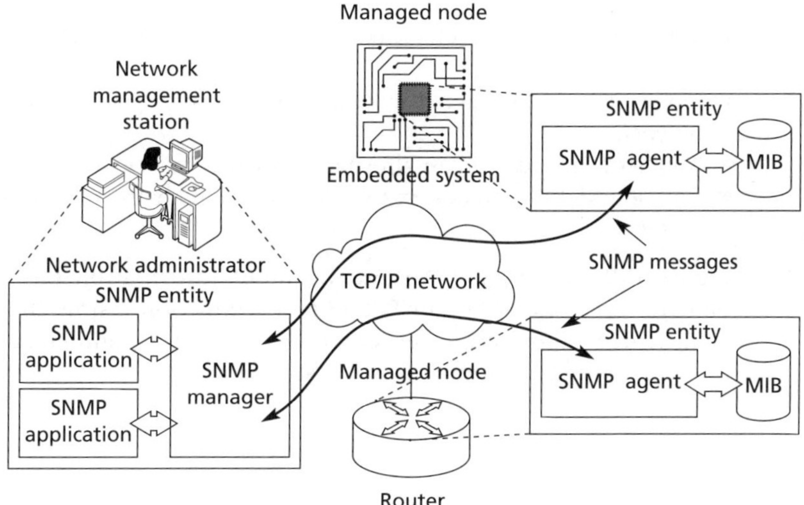

Figure D.1 The Simple Network Management Protocol model.

D.3 Structure of Management Information (SMI)

MIB objects allow SNMP to work with a wide variety of devices connected to a network. But, how are MIB objects defined? The Structure of Management Information standard specifies the rules to define MIB objects.

SMI establishes five mandatory characteristics and a variable number of optional ones, as rules to define an MIB object:

- Object Name: each object must be uniquely identified. An **Object Identifier** (OID) is used for this purpose. At the same time, an **Object Descriptor** provides the object with a textual name. See section D.3.1.
- Syntax: it defines the type of information that the object contains. Two categories are allowed:
  - *Base data types*: integer, string, unsigned, IpAddress, TimeTicks, etc.
  - *Multiple data elements*: a list or table of base types may be constructed to represent a set of values. They are also called columnar objects.
- Maximum Access: it defines the level-access for the object:
  - read-create: the object can be created, read, and written.
  - read-write: the object can be read and written.
  - read-only: the object can only be read.
  - accessible-for-notify: the object is accessible only via notification.
  - not-accessible: indicates an auxiliary object.
- Status: indicates the status of the object:
  - current: definition is current and valid.
  - obsolete: definition is obsolete and should not be implemented.
  - deprecated: definition obsolete, but maintained for compatibility.
- Description: provides a textual definition of the object.

The following optional characteristics may appear in the definition of an object:

- Units: a textual definition of the units associated with the object.
- Reference: a textual reference to another document, which provides additional information.
- Index: it is used when the object is a 'row' of other objects (columnar object).
- Augments: it presents an alternative for the Index clause.
- DefVal: it defines an acceptable default value for the object, when an object instance is created.

Figure D.2 shows an SNMP Management Information Base containing *n* objects, and the ipDefaultTTL object definition using the Structure of Management Information rules and the data description language called ISO Abstract Syntax Notation 1 (ANS.1) standard.

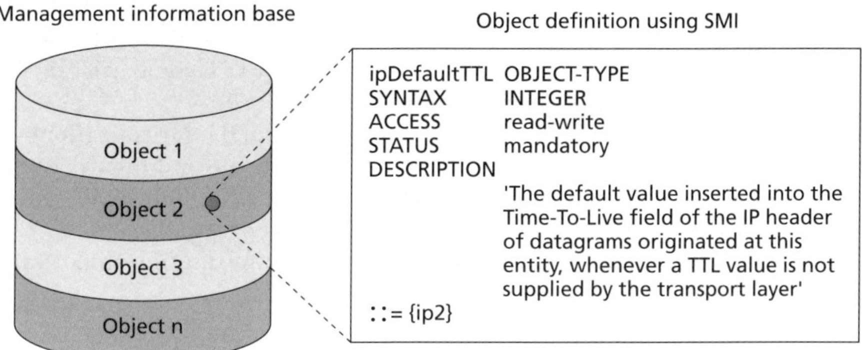

Figure D.2 SNMP Management Information Base (MIB).

D.3.1 The MIB Object Name Hierarchy

As we saw, each object name must be unique. As the number of possible object names could be immense, a plain naming system would be impractical. For this reason, a structured Object Name Hierarchy was proposed, like the one operating in the Domain Name System. In this way, each object characteristic would have a position in this hierarchy tree. As an attempt to standardize the object names in a global fashion, a single universal hierarchy was proposed, which would contain all the possible objects used in the world. Only a branch of this hierarchy would be dedicated for the MIB objects.

Each node of the tree is identified with both a label and an integer. In this way, each MIB object has two names; an **Object Descriptor**, which provides an easy reference for human interpretation, and the **Object Identifier (OID)**, consisting of a sequence of integers that specify the location of the object in the global hierarchy tree.

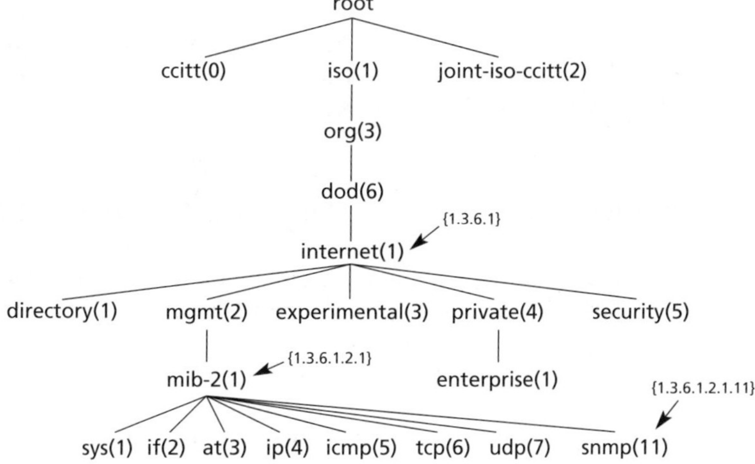

Figure D.3 Object Name Hierarchy.

Figure D.3 shows the Object Tree Hierarchy. The root of the global object tree has no label, and it has three children; ccitt(0), iso(1) and joint-iso-ccitt(2). The purpose of these nodes is for ITU/CCITT standards, ISO standards and joint standards, respectively.

Under the iso(1) node, we may find org(3) – Organizations – under which we find dod(6) – US Department of Defense – and finally we find internet(1). In this way, the Internet node may be specified using the text labels as 'iso.org.dod.internet', as well as {1.3.6.1} using its OID.

Every SNMP object is located under the Internet node. Under this node, we find the following nodes (among others);

- mgmt(2): it is used for MIB-II (version 2) objects.
- experimental(3): it is used for development.
- private(4): it has an enterprise(1) node under which private companies register their objects.

Under the mgmt(2) node, we find the mib-2(1) node with the following subnodes; system(1), interfaces(2), at(3), ip(4), icmp(5), tcp(6), udp(7), and snmp(11), among others.

For a complete reference, visit **http://www.iana.org/assignments/smi-numbers**.

D.3.2 MIB Object Groups and Modules

Each of the above listed nodes constitutes an MIB Object Group. That is, a collection of related objects is arranged forming an Object Group. For example, the ip(4) group contains objects related to the IP layer of the device. Each object name in this group is prefixed with the group code; in this case ip, as in the ipDefaultTTL object which defines the default Time-To-Live value for IP packets.

While for some groups implementation is mandatory, others are implemented as required. In this way, if the device has particular features, then the group providing these characteristics is implemented.

As new technologies appear, these groups needed to be constantly updated as with the standards describing them. As this approach was impractical, an MIB Module concept was defined, which comprises the groups of objects that specifically describe the new technology. For example, for Mobile IP objects, the mipMIB module was defined.

D.4 Simple Network Management Protocol (SNMP)

The SNMP is responsible for exchanging management information between Network Management Stations and Managed Nodes. Although the original SNMP specification was modified to allow its transport using many different protocol suites, we will refer exclusively to the TCP/IP suite.

In order for NMS (SNMP Manager) to manage Managed Nodes (SNMP Agents), a series of messages are exchanged. These messages are called Protocol Data Units (PDUs). The following PDUs are defined:

- GetRequest-PDU: the SNMP Manager uses this message when it needs to collect MIB information from an SNMP Agent. The message includes the MIB Objects whose values are required.
- GetNextRequest-PDU: the SNMP Manager uses it when it needs to collect managed information, which is presented as columnar data (tables) rather than single values.
- GetBulkRequest-PDU: it is used for columnar data, as the previous case, but to get all the data at once in the response.
- SetRequest-PDU: the SNMP Manager uses it when it needs to modify some object value at the SNMP Agent.
- Response-PDU: the SNMP Agent uses it in order to respond to an SNMP Manager's request. When the request is a GetRequest-PDU type, the Response-PDU message contains the solicited objects, or an error code, if an error occurs. When the request is a SetRequest-PDU, the Response-PDU message includes a successful message or an error indication.
- SNMPv2-Trap-PDU: it is used by the SNMP Agents when they need to inform the SNMP Manager about some event that has occurred. In this way, the SNMP Agents do not have to wait for an SNMP Manager to poll them, to inform of such events.
- InformRequest-PDU: these messages are used by SNMP Managers to exchange information between themselves.

An SNMP Manager implementation must be able to generate and send the GetRequest-PDU, GetNextRequest-PDU, GetBulkRequest-PDU, SetRequest-PDU, InformRequest-PDU and Response-PDU types; while it must be able to receive and process the Response-PDU, SNMPv2-Trap-PDU and InformRequest-PDU types, as well.

A SNMP Agent implementation must be able to generate and send the Response-PDU and SNMPv2-Trap-PDU types; while it must be able to receive and process the GetRequest-PDU, GetNextRequest-PDU, GetBulkRequest-PDU and SetRequest-PDU types as well.

Figure D.4 shows the SNMP Communication Model. Different cases are presented, where each case uses a different set of messages, according to the operation. The SNMP messages are sent using UDP as the transport protocol. The well-known port 161 is reserved for this purpose. That is, all SNMP entities should listen for messages in this port. A second well-known port 162 is reserved for SNMP Traps, so only SNMP Managers have to listen in this port too. In this way, SNMP Traps are kept separately from the other messages.

The maximum SNMP PDU size is limited by the maximum size of messages that UDP may transmit. For networks where the MTU is 1500 bytes, the maximum SNMP PDU size would be 1472 bytes.

Since UDP is an unreliable transport protocol, some messages could not arrive at destination. This means that SNMP applications should consider this possibility. However, most PDU types are confirmed; that is, for each GetRequest-PDU, SetRequest-PDU or even InformRequest-PDU type, a Response-PDU type is sent back to the requester, so this acts as a receive confirmation. An exception occurs with the SNMPv2-Trap-PDU types, which are unconfirmed.

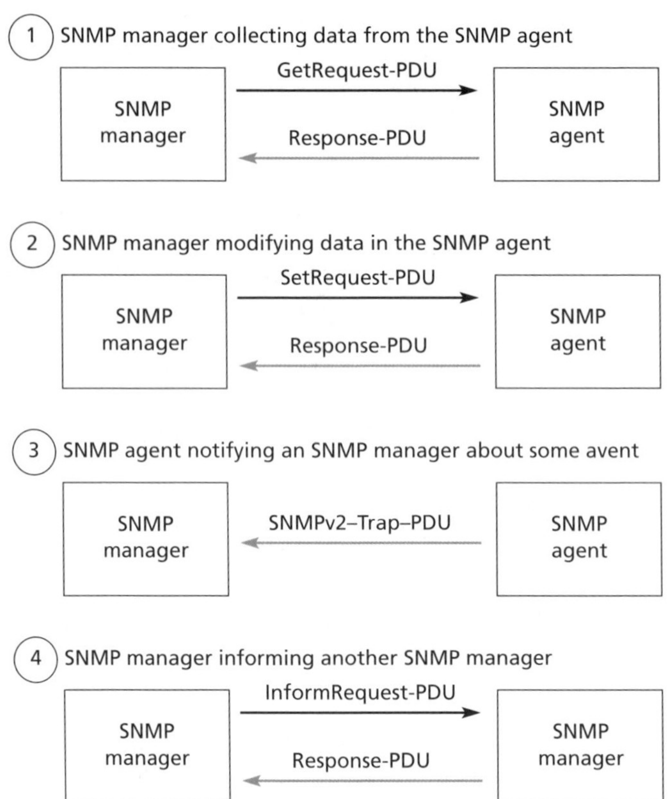

Figure D.4 SNMP communication model.

Security is provided through the following models:

- **User-based Security Model (USM)**: it is based on the user's access rights rather than on a machine-related security scheme.
- **View-based Access Control Model (VACM)**: defining views, the administrator can manage the kind of information accessed and who accesses it.

D.4.1 SNMP General Message format

Although the standards describe the SNMP message formats using ANS.1, we will use the same format we used for other protocols. The following are the SNMP message fields:

- msgVersion (integer – 4 bytes): it is set to 3, to identify the SNMP version number of this message.
- msgID (integer – 4 bytes): it is used as a way to match response messages to request messages.
- msgMaxSize (integer – 4 bytes): it informs the maximum message size supported by the sender of the message.
- msgFlags (octet String – 1 byte): it consists of a set of flags which control the processing of the message:

  - authFlag (1 bit): when set to 1, it indicates authentication is used.
  - privFlag (1 bit): when set to 1, it indicates encryption is used to protect the privacy of the message.
  - reportableFlag (1 bit): when set to 1, the receiver must send back a Report-PDU message, under those conditions that can cause the generation of the Report-PDU.
- msgSecurityModel (integer – 4 bytes): it indicates the security model used for this message. The default is 3 (USM).
- msgSecurityParameters (variable size): it contains the necessary parameters required to implement the security model used in the message.
- scopedPduData (variable size): it contains the scopedPDU where the transmitted PDU is included. The 'scoped' word refers to the SNMP context associated with the transmitted PDU. The field may be encrypted or in plain text, depending on the privFlag value. The scopedPDU is made up of the following sub-fields:
  - contextEngineID (octet String, variable size): it identifies which application the scopedPDU will be sent to for processing.
  - contextName (octet String, variable size): it names the particular context associated with the managed information contained in the PDU. The application that originates the message provides this value.
  - PDU (variable size): it contains the transmitted PDU. See next section for its description.

D.4.2 Protocol Data Unit (PDU) format

The last field of the above message description is the Protocol Data Unit, which consists of the PDU Control Fields and the PDU Variable Bindings. The PDU format is common for all PDU types, except for the GetBulkRequest-PDU (which will not be shown), and it contains the following fields:

- PDU Type (integer – 4 bytes): it indicates the PDU type:

0 GetRequest-PDU	5 GetBulkRequest-PDU
1 GetNextRequest-PDU	6 InformRequest-PDU
2 Response-PDU	7 SNMPv2-Trap-PDU
3 SetRequest-PDU	8 Report-PDU
4 Obsolete	

- Request-ID (integer – 4 bytes): it is used to match the request with the responses.
- Error-Status (integer – 4 bytes): it is used in a Response-PDU to indicate the result of the operation:

0 noError	7 wrongType
1 tooBig	8 wrongLength
2 noSuchName	9 wrongEncoding
3 badValue	10 wrongValue
4 readOnly	11 noCreation
5 genErr	12 inconsistentValue
6 noAccess	13 resourceUnavailable

14 commitFailed
15 undoFailed
16 authorizationError
17 notWritable
18 inconsistentName

- Error-Index (integer – 4 bytes): it contains a pointer that specifies which object generated the error (when Error-Status is non-zero).
- Variable-Bindings (variable): it provides a list of MIB objects identified by a name/value pair;
  - Object Name (Sequence of Integers): the object identifier. Example: 1.3.6.1.2.1.4.2
  - Object Value (variable): this field contains the value of the object, in SetRequest-PDU or Response-PDU messages.

Figure D.5 shows the SNMP message and its relationship with the Scoped PDU and the PDU (some of the above fields are not shown in this figure).

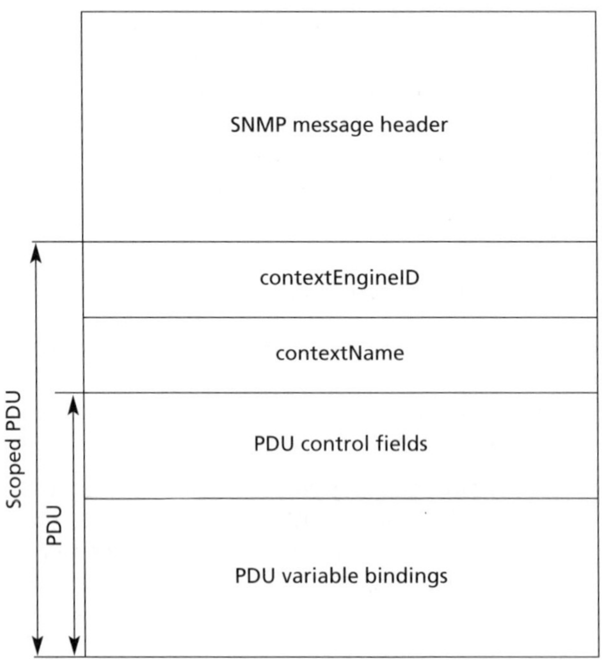

Figure D.5 An SNMP message format.

D.5 SNMP version considerations

The present documentation was based on the SMIv2 (RFC 2578), MIB-II and SNMPv3 (RFC 3416). However, for compatibility reasons it would be convenient to consider older versions for some implementations since SNMPv1 is still widely accepted and currently in use.

Appendix E

Administrator utilities

In this Appendix, readers may learn about utilities that will help them to put into practice some of the concepts given in the theory part of the book. As these utilities are found in any operating system TCP/IP implementation, no additional hardware or software than a PC is required, so they provide interesting exercises, or could even be used in a real case where a configuration or troubleshooting were needed. Although the described utilities are based on the Windows Operating System, they mostly exist in other systems such as Unix or Linux. Consult the Operating System documentation for details about its use.

E.1 Introduction

The TCP/IP application protocols were designed for end-users. As such, they are specifically designed to cover the user's needs. However, the TCP/IP network administrators have a different need when they configure or troubleshoot an IP network. For these cases, a set of utilities are provided to help administrators in their configuration, maintenance and troubleshooting daily tasks.

E.2 Host name

The host name utility allows the administrator to know the host name assigned to a host upon which the utility is run. This name may be a 'flat' name or a DNS name. This utility is very simple to use as it does not accept any argument, although other implementations may accept a –s (for short) parameter, indicating that only the short name must be displayed, rather than the fully qualified domain name (in case, it uses a DNS name).

In the example overleaf, the utility returns 'server' as the assigned host name. In order to change this host name, the Windows Control Panel must be used.

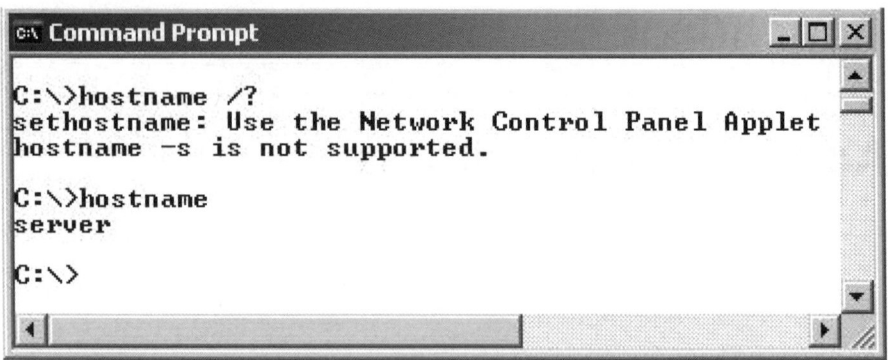

E.3 IPConfig

The ipconfig utility allows the administrator to inspect some TCP/IP configuration parameters. Table E.1 shows the optional arguments the utility supports.

Table E.1

Argument	Description
(none)	It displays the DNS suffix, IP address, subnet mask and default gateway for each interface on the host.
/?	It displays the utility's help.
/all	It displays more detailed information, including the interface MAC address, DNS and DHCP servers IP address, among others.
/release ["adapter"]	It releases the DHCP lease for the specified adaptor (or for all, if none is specified).
/renew ["adapter"]	It forces the renew of the DHCP lease for the specified adaptor (or for all, if none is specified).
/flushdns	It clears the host's DNS resolver cache.
/registerdns	Renews all DHCP leases and re-registers the DNS names.
/displaydns	It shows the contents of the host's DNS resolver cache.
/showclassid "adapter"	It displays the DHCP Class IDs associated with the specified adaptor.
/setclassid "adapter" [classid]	It modifies the DHCP Class ID for the specified adaptor.

The following screenshot shows the ipconfig with the /all parameter, returning the TCP/IP configuration information.

```
C:\>ipconfig /all

Windows IP Configuration

    Host Name . . . . . . . . . . . . : server
    Primary Dns Suffix  . . . . . . . :
    Node Type . . . . . . . . . . . . : Unknown
    IP Routing Enabled. . . . . . . . : No
    WINS Proxy Enabled. . . . . . . . : No

Ethernet adapter Local Area Connection:

    Connection-specific DNS Suffix  . :
    Description . . . . . . . . . . . : Realtek RTL8139 Family PCI Fast Ethernet
NIC
    Physical Address. . . . . . . . . : 00-08-54-18-5D-87
    DHCP Enabled. . . . . . . . . . . : Yes
    Autoconfiguration Enabled . . . . : Yes
    IP Address. . . . . . . . . . . . : 192.168.100.50
    Subnet Mask . . . . . . . . . . . : 255.255.255.0
    Default Gateway . . . . . . . . . : 192.168.100.1
    DHCP Server . . . . . . . . . . . : 192.168.100.1
    Lease Obtained. . . . . . . . . . : Tuesday, April 19, 2005 8:02:52 PM
    Lease Expires . . . . . . . . . . : Tuesday, April 19, 2005 8:03:02 PM

C:\>
```

In the Win95/98/ME versions, there is a graphics utility called winipcfg, which provides almost the same functions as ipconfig, but in a graphical environment.

E.4 ARP

The arp utility allows the administrator to inspect or modify the host's ARP cache table. The utility is called in three ways:

1 arp –a — displays the contents of the ARP cache table.
2 arp –s ip_addr mac_addr — allows a manual entry in the ARP table.
3 arp –d ip_addr — allows a manual deletion of the entry in the ARP cache table.

where ip_addr is the IP address, and mac_addr is the physical interface address.

Other parameters may be used to indicate a specific interface. The following is a screenshot of the arp utility.

```
C:\>arp -a

Interface: 200.112.136.74 --- 0x2
  Internet Address      Physical Address      Type
  200.112.136.1         00-06-2a-cf-84-54     dynamic
  200.112.136.2         00-e0-6f-2f-0b-91     dynamic
  200.112.136.35        00-e0-7d-fd-fb-3a     dynamic
  200.112.136.37        00-e0-6f-2e-9c-4d     dynamic
  200.112.136.60        00-10-dc-fd-4b-e7     dynamic
  200.112.136.66        00-a0-73-b2-04-22     dynamic
  200.112.136.80        00-0f-3d-16-cd-d8     dynamic
  200.112.150.10        00-aa-bb-01-02-03     static

C:\>_
```

E.5 Ping

The ping utility is one of the most well known and used, because of its usefulness. It allows the communication between two devices to be tested, where the user's device sends an ICMP message (Echo Request) to the other device, which must reply the message (Echo Reply) in order for the administrator to verify that both devices are correctly communicating through the IP layer. Because all TCP/IP stack implementations must support this, this utility has been widely adopted as a basic communication tool for diagnostic purposes.

Beyond this simple communication test, many other functions may be checked, like the number of packets sent, received and lost (if any), and the round trip-time (the time a packet takes from the moment it is sent and then received). The following screenshot shows the ping options, as are shown when ping is invoked without arguments.

```
C:\>ping

Usage: ping [-t] [-a] [-n count] [-l size] [-f] [-i TTL] [-v TOS]
            [-r count] [-s count] [[-j host-list] | [-k host-list]]
            [-w timeout] [-R] [-S srcaddr] [-4] [-6] target_name

Options:
    -t             Ping the specified host until stopped.
                   To see statistics and continue - type Control-Break;
                   To stop - type Control-C.
    -a             Resolve addresses to hostnames.
    -n count       Number of echo requests to send.
    -l size        Send buffer size.
    -f             Set Don't Fragment flag in packet (IPv4-only).
    -i TTL         Time To Live.
    -v TOS         Type Of Service (IPv4-only).
    -r count       Record route for count hops (IPv4-only).
    -s count       Timestamp for count hops (IPv4-only).
    -j host-list   Loose source route along host-list (IPv4-only).
    -k host-list   Strict source route along host-list (IPv4-only).
    -w timeout     Timeout in milliseconds to wait for each reply.
    -R             Trace round-trip path (IPv6-only).
    -S srcaddr     Source address to use (IPv6-only).
    -4             Force using IPv4.
    -6             Force using IPv6.
```

The following screenshot shows the ping utility 'in action'. See how the ping may also be used using DNS names, in order for the utility to resolve the name into its IP address.

```
C:\>ping www.yahoo.com

Pinging www.yahoo.akadns.net [68.142.226.32] with 32 bytes of data:

Reply from 68.142.226.32: bytes=32 time=276ms TTL=45
Reply from 68.142.226.32: bytes=32 time=282ms TTL=45
Reply from 68.142.226.32: bytes=32 time=242ms TTL=46
Reply from 68.142.226.32: bytes=32 time=239ms TTL=46

Ping statistics for 68.142.226.32:
    Packets: Sent = 4, Received = 4, Lost = 0 (0% loss),
Approximate round trip times in milli-seconds:
    Minimum = 239ms, Maximum = 282ms, Average = 259ms
```

E.6 Tracert

The tracert utility (Traceroute) is used to know the route a datagram takes, between two devices. The Windows traceroute utility implementation uses a ping message (ICMP Echo Request) to the destination device, starting with a Time-To-Live (TTL) that equals 1, and increments this value in the following messages. Actually, it sends three messages for each TTL value, and takes the round trip-time value for each response. Each time the message is forwarded, the TTL field is decremented; and when it gets a zero value, an ICMP (TTL Exceeded) error message is generated and sent back to the sender. In this way, the program may know the path the ping message takes (the IP source address of the ICMP error message) and the corresponding RTT value. The TTL value is still incremented, until a successful ping reply (ICMP Echo Reply) is received, indicating that the ping arrived at the intended destination, so the complete trace was obtained.

For each hop the ping message reaches, the RTT values are shown, as well as the IP address that the message gets. A reverse DNS query is also used to try to get the host DNS domain name of the corresponding IP address. By default, the maximum hops are 30, but this value may be modified using a -h parameter.

The following screenshot shows a traceroute example:

```
Command Prompt

C:\>tracert www.yahoo.com

Tracing route to www.yahoo.akadns.net [68.142.226.34]
over a maximum of 30 hops:

  1    24 ms    33 ms    64 ms  10.2.0.1
  2    28 ms    14 ms    42 ms  host005-pop12.bbt.net.ar [200.81.94.101]
  3   129 ms    58 ms     *     host130.200.80.32.ifxnw.com.ar [200.80.32.130]
  4    95 ms    50 ms   258 ms  r3noc-int-bsas-arg.bbt.net.ar [200.81.94.34]
  5    80 ms    84 ms    72 ms  host139.200.80.32.ifxnw.com.ar [200.80.32.139]
  6   196 ms   218 ms   299 ms  host193.200.62.0.ifxcorp.com [200.62.1.193]
  7   233 ms   232 ms   197 ms  border6.ge3-2.ifx-10.mia003.pnap.net [69.25.48.25]
  8   174 ms   264 ms   222 ms  core2.pc1.bbnet1.mia003.pnap.net [69.25.0.2]
  9   196 ms   191 ms   243 ms  sl-st20-mia-12-1.sprintlink.net [144.223.245.145]
 10   192 ms   197 ms   411 ms  sl-bb22-orl-10-0.sprintlink.net [144.232.20.78]
 11   206 ms   204 ms   208 ms  sl-bb24-fw-13-0.sprintlink.net [144.232.9.37]
 12   231 ms   210 ms   239 ms  sl-bb27-fw-14-0.sprintlink.net [144.232.11.74]
 13   262 ms   253 ms   268 ms  sl-st20-dal-1-0.sprintlink.net [144.232.9.136]
 14   222 ms   226 ms   216 ms  interconnect-eng.Dallas1.Level3.net [64.158.168.73]
 15   221 ms   204 ms   225 ms  so-1-2-0.bbr2.Dallas1.Level3.net [209.244.15.165]
 16   213 ms   237 ms   231 ms  as-4-0.bbr1.Washington1.Level3.net [64.159.0.138]
 17   274 ms   230 ms   284 ms  ge-3-0-0-53.gar1.Washington1.Level3.net [4.68.121.66]
 18   246 ms   272 ms   266 ms  63.210.29.230
 19   263 ms   285 ms   244 ms  UNKNOWN-206-190-33-73.yahoo.com [206.190.33.73]
 20   223 ms   281 ms   236 ms  p3.www.re2.yahoo.com [68.142.226.34]

Trace complete.
```

As we see, each line shows the round trip-time for each of the three ping messages sent with the same TTL value, the host name (if available) and the IP address of the hop where the sent messages passed.

The following parameters may be used in the tracert utility:

```
Command Prompt

C:\>tracert

Usage: tracert [-d] [-h maximum_hops] [-j host-list] [-w timeout]
               [-R] [-S srcaddr] [-4] [-6] target_name

Options:
    -d                 Do not resolve addresses to hostnames.
    -h maximum_hops    Maximum number of hops to search for target.
    -j host-list       Loose source route along host-list (IPv4-only).
    -w timeout         Wait timeout milliseconds for each reply.
    -R                 Trace round-trip path (IPv6-only).
    -S srcaddr         Source address to use (IPv6-only).
    -4                 Force using IPv4.
    -6                 Force using IPv6.
```

E.7 Netstat

The netstat (network status) utility provides information about the TCP/IP stack operation. Mainly, it provides the active TCP/IP connections, the route table contents, and the protocol statistics. The /? parameter invokes the netstat help, which shows the available options.

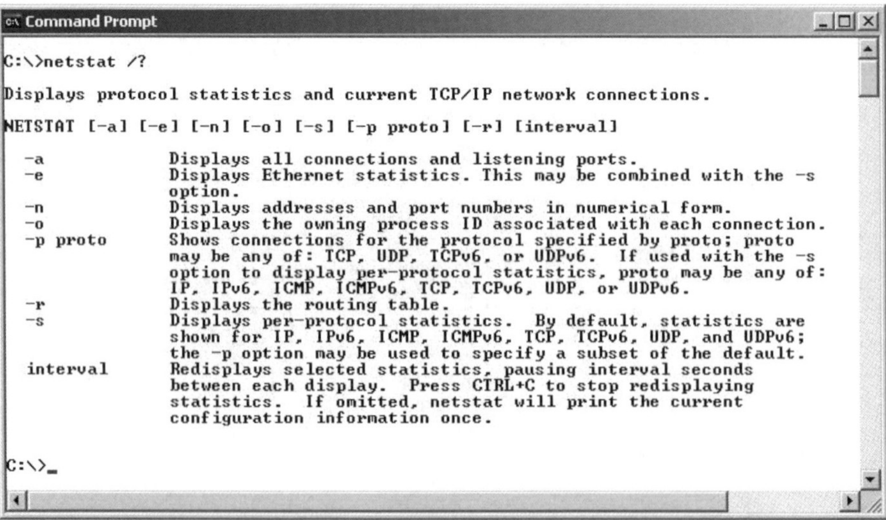

```
Command Prompt

C:\>netstat /?

Displays protocol statistics and current TCP/IP network connections.

NETSTAT [-a] [-e] [-n] [-o] [-s] [-p proto] [-r] [interval]

  -a            Displays all connections and listening ports.
  -e            Displays Ethernet statistics. This may be combined with the -s
                option.
  -n            Displays addresses and port numbers in numerical form.
  -o            Displays the owning process ID associated with each connection.
  -p proto      Shows connections for the protocol specified by proto; proto
                may be any of: TCP, UDP, TCPv6, or UDPv6.  If used with the -s
                option to display per-protocol statistics, proto may be any of:
                IP, IPv6, ICMP, ICMPv6, TCP, TCPv6, UDP, or UDPv6.
  -r            Displays the routing table.
  -s            Displays per-protocol statistics.  By default, statistics are
                shown for IP, IPv6, ICMP, ICMPv6, TCP, TCPv6, UDP, and UDPv6;
                the -p option may be used to specify a subset of the default.
  interval      Redisplays selected statistics, pausing interval seconds
                between each display.  Press CTRL+C to stop redisplaying
                statistics.  If omitted, netstat will print the current
                configuration information once.

C:\>_
```

The following screenshot shows the netstat utility providing statistics for the ICMP protocol:

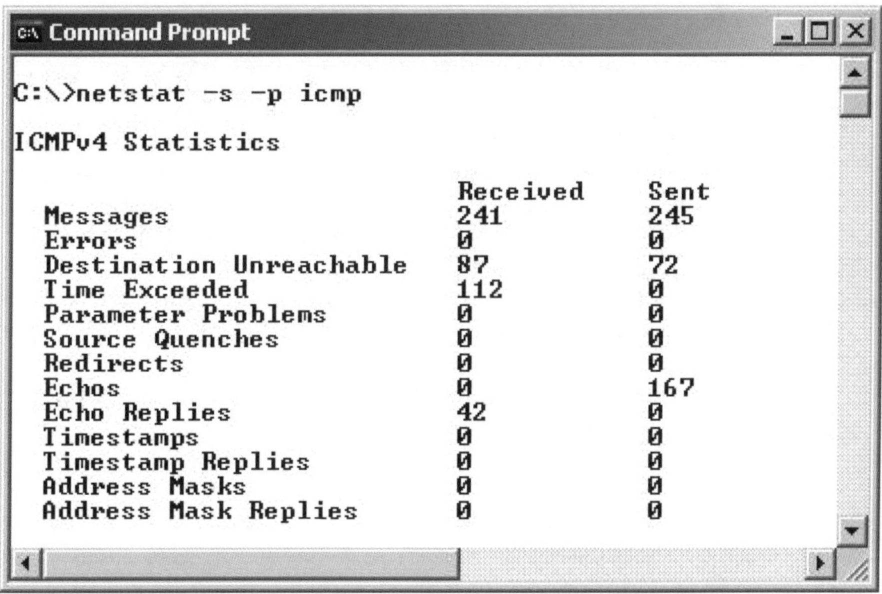

```
C:\>netstat -s -p icmp

ICMPv4 Statistics

                            Received    Sent
  Messages                  241         245
  Errors                    0           0
  Destination Unreachable   87          72
  Time Exceeded             112         0
  Parameter Problems        0           0
  Source Quenches           0           0
  Redirects                 0           0
  Echos                     0           167
  Echo Replies              42          0
  Timestamps                0           0
  Timestamp Replies         0           0
  Address Masks             0           0
  Address Mask Replies      0           0
```

The –r parameter may be used to show the route table contents, as the following example shows:

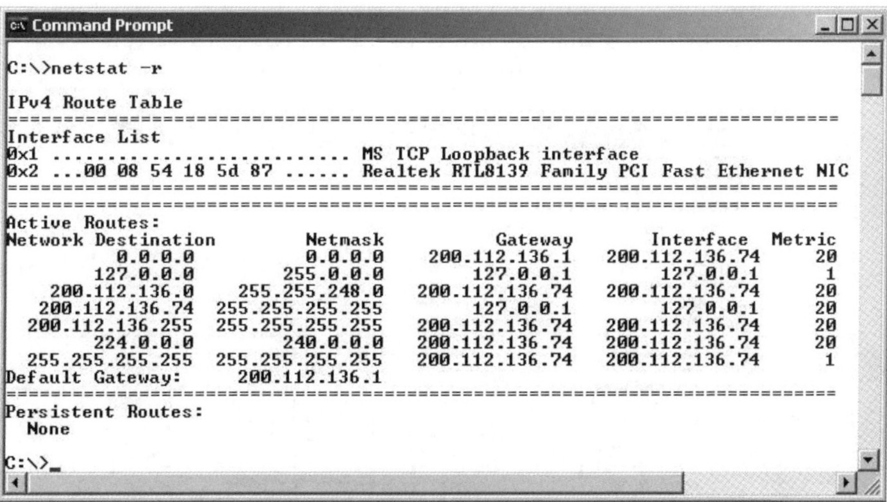

```
C:\>netstat -r

IPv4 Route Table
===========================================================================
Interface List
0x1 ........................... MS TCP Loopback interface
0x2 ...00 08 54 18 5d 87 ...... Realtek RTL8139 Family PCI Fast Ethernet NIC
===========================================================================
===========================================================================
Active Routes:
Network Destination        Netmask          Gateway       Interface  Metric
          0.0.0.0          0.0.0.0    200.112.136.1  200.112.136.74     20
        127.0.0.0        255.0.0.0        127.0.0.1       127.0.0.1      1
    200.112.136.0    255.255.248.0   200.112.136.74  200.112.136.74     20
   200.112.136.74  255.255.255.255        127.0.0.1       127.0.0.1     20
  200.112.136.255  255.255.255.255   200.112.136.74  200.112.136.74     20
        224.0.0.0        240.0.0.0   200.112.136.74  200.112.136.74     20
  255.255.255.255  255.255.255.255   200.112.136.74  200.112.136.74      1
Default Gateway:     200.112.136.1
===========================================================================
Persistent Routes:
  None

C:\>_
```

E.8 Nslookup

The nslookup (name server lookup) utility allows users to manually resolve DNS domain names into their corresponding IP addresses. It also allows the reverse resolution returning the domain name associated with a specified IP address. This utility operates under two modalities: non-interactive and interactive.

The non-interactive version of the nslookup utility uses the following syntax:

nslookup <host> [<nameserver>]

where **<host>** may be a domain name for which we wish to know its associated IP address, or it may be an IP address, in which case the reverse resolution will be performed, returning the associated domain name for this IP address. The optional **<nameserver>** parameter may be used in order for a different name server to be used to resolve the DNS query. If omitted, the host's default DNS server is used.

The following screenshot shows the non-interactive version of the nslookup utility, with both a normal and a reverse name resolution.

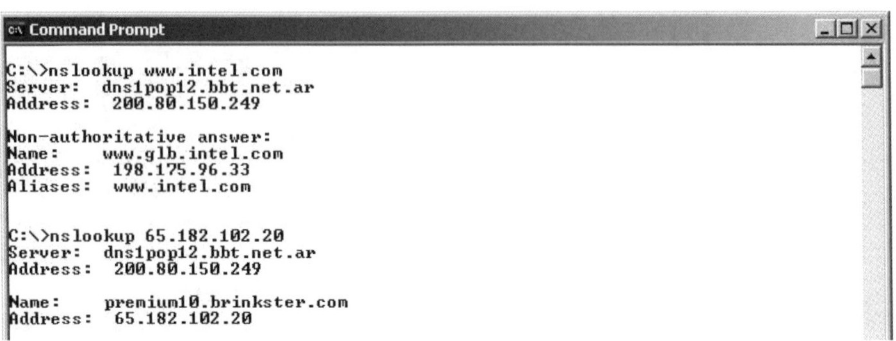
Command Prompt
C:\>nslookup www.intel.com
Server: dns1pop12.bbt.net.ar
Address: 200.80.150.249
Non-authoritative answer:
Name: www.glb.intel.com
Address: 198.175.96.33
Aliases: www.intel.com
C:\>nslookup 65.182.102.20
Server: dns1pop12.bbt.net.ar
Address: 200.80.150.249
Name: premium10.brinkster.com
Address: 65.182.102.20

The interactive version of the nslookup utility is invoked without additional parameters. When the utility prompt appears, the ? command will show the available options, as the following illustrates:

```
Command Prompt - nslookup

C:\>nslookup
Default Server:  dns1pop12.bbt.net.ar
Address:  200.80.150.249

> ?
Commands:   (identifiers are shown in uppercase, [] means optional)
NAME            - print info about the host/domain NAME using default server
NAME1 NAME2     - as above, but use NAME2 as server
help or ?       - print info on common commands
set OPTION      - set an option
    all                 - print options, current server and host
    [no]debug           - print debugging information
    [no]d2              - print exhaustive debugging information
    [no]defname         - append domain name to each query
    [no]recurse         - ask for recursive answer to query
    [no]search          - use domain search list
    [no]vc              - always use a virtual circuit
    domain=NAME         - set default domain name to NAME
    srchlist=N1[/N2/.../N6] - set domain to N1 and search list to N1,N2, etc.
    root=NAME           - set root server to NAME
    retry=X             - set number of retries to X
    timeout=X           - set initial time-out interval to X seconds
    type=X              - set query type (ex. A,ANY,CNAME,MX,NS,PTR,SOA,SRV)
    querytype=X         - same as type
    class=X             - set query class (ex. IN (Internet), ANY)
    [no]msxfr           - use MS fast zone transfer
    ixfrver=X           - current version to use in IXFR transfer request
server NAME     - set default server to NAME, using current default server
lserver NAME    - set default server to NAME, using initial server
finger [USER]   - finger the optional NAME at the current default host
root            - set current default server to the root
ls [opt] DOMAIN [> FILE] - list addresses in DOMAIN (optional: output to FILE)
    -a          -  list canonical names and aliases
    -d          -  list all records
    -t TYPE     -  list records of the given type (e.g. A,CNAME,MX,NS,PTR etc.)
view FILE           - sort an 'ls' output file and view it with pg
exit            - exit the program

> _
```

E.9 On-line tools

There are many web sites providing on-line tools, which may help the administrator in its tasks. One interesting site is **www.samspade.org**, which provides on-line utilities such as whois, IP whois, Traceroute, DNS and reverse DNS. It is also possible to download a great program called Sam Spade for Windows that provides many tools in a graphical environment. The next section gives a brief description of it.

E.10 Sam Spade (for Windows)

This program is a freeware, which provides many utilities such as ping, nslookup, whois, IP block whois, dig, traceroute, finger, SMTP VRFY, web browser, heep-alive, DNS Zone Transfer, SMTP relay check, e-mail header analysis, e-mail blacklist query and abuse address query. All these are presented in a graphical interface.

The following is a screenshot of the Sam Spade for Windows freeware program.

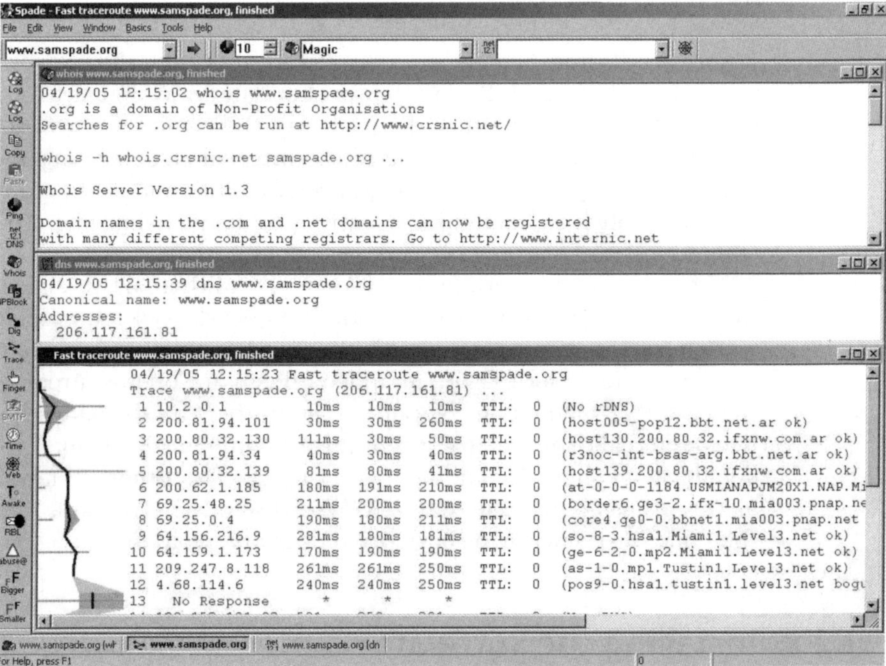

Appendix F

Network Protocol Analyser: Ethereal

In this last appendix, we will briefly look at an excellent tool which will allow us to first capture and later analyse network packets, in order to view what is going on in a real network, and better understand the protocols we learned in Part I of this book. This software will also help us in the protocol software development in Part II of this book, as we may inspect the packets we are receiving and sending, in order to debug the application.

F.1 INTRODUCTION

A Network Protocol Analyser is a software tool that allows users to capture network packets, and display that packet data in as detailed a way as possible. It also tries to recognize the packet (if the packet protocol is supported), in order to present it according to the internal structure depending on the packet protocol. Some of the best uses for this tool are in troubleshooting network problems, examining security problems, debugging protocol implementations, and learning network protocol internals.

The proposed Network Protocol Analyser is **Ethereal**, which is the software that analyses and displays the captured network packets. Actually, this software works in conjunction with the **WinPcap** software which allows the packet capture. Both Ethereal and WinPcap are open source software, and their latest available versions may be freely downloaded from **www.ethereal.com**. Refer to their corresponding user manuals to get further details about their use and operation. (*Note*: The Ethereal network protocol analyser has changed its name to Wireshark. Nevertheless, the software is the same. Visit **www.wireshark.org** to learn more about this.)

F.2 Installing the software

Execute the Ethereal software installer (.exe file) and follow the installer instructions. This program will install both the WinPcap capture software and the Ethereal protocol analyser software into the destination computer. After this, the Network Protocol Analyser will be ready to work.

F.3 Using Ethereal

F.3.1 Ethereal's user interface

After invoking the Ethereal software, the main window appears. Once we capture network packets, the following window will be shown:

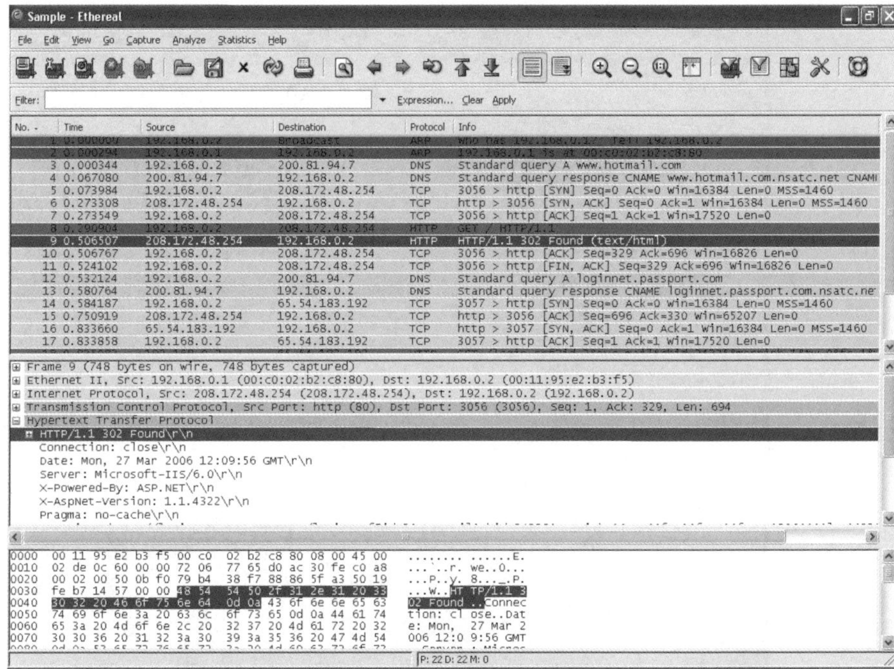

The following parts are shown in the main windows:

- The *menu* which is used to start actions.
- The *main toolbar* used as a quick access for some items from the menu.
- The *filter toolbar*, allowing display of only certain types of packets.
- The *packet list pane* which displays a summary of each packet displayed.
- The *packet details pane* which displays the packet selected in the packet list pane in more detail.
- The *packet bytes pane* which displays the data from the packet selected in the packet list pane, and highlights the field selected in the packet details pane.
- The *status bar* giving details about the current program state and the captured data.

F.3.2 Capturing packets

In order to start capturing network packets, choose *Options*... from the *Capture* menu. Then, the following window will appear (once an interface has been selected from this window, capturing can be started selecting the *Start* option from the *Capture* menu):

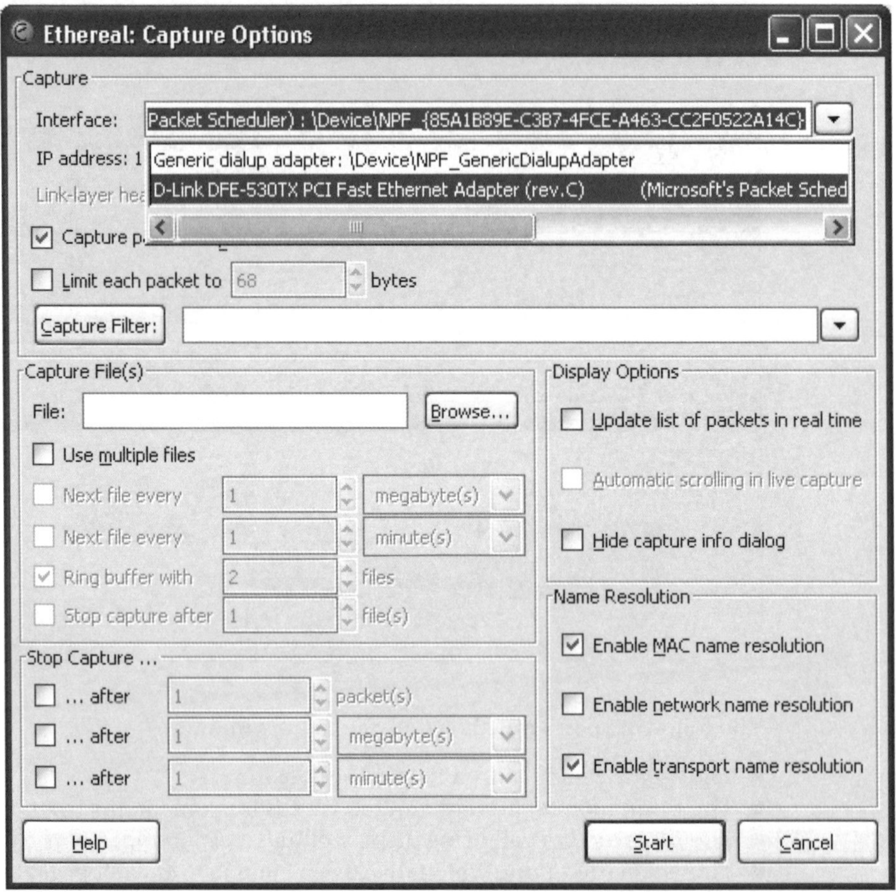

Despite its name, Ethereal may capture network packets from different interfaces, such as Ethernet and serial connections (PPP). So, the appropriate interface must be selected from where to capture the packets. As we will later see, a Capture Filter may also be used in order to capture only the desired packet types. The Start button must be pressed to start capturing the network packets.

While the network packets are being captured, the following window shows the capture statistics:

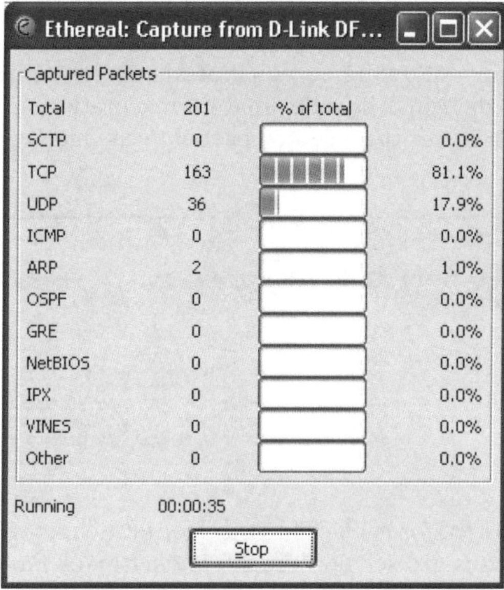

Pressing the Stop button, the capture process will end and the captured packets will be loaded into the *main window*, as shown in the above *main window* screenshot.

F.3.3 Analysing packets

Once in the *main window*, with the captured packets loaded, the process of analysing the packets may be started. For each packet we select in the *packet list pane*, the *packet details pane* will show the specific packet structure according to the packet protocol type.

```
Frame 12 (436 bytes on wire, 436 bytes captured)
Ethernet II, Src: 00:08:54:18:5d:87, Dst: 00:06:2a:cf:84:54
Internet Protocol, Src Addr: 200.112.136.74 (200.112.136.74), Dst Addr: 65.182.102.20 (65.182.102.20)
Transmission Control Protocol, Src Port: 4483 (4483), Dst Port: http (80), Seq: 3938177480, Ack: 6110136
Hypertext Transfer Protocol
  GET / HTTP/1.1\r\n
    Request Method: GET
    Request URI: /
    Request Version: HTTP/1.1
  Accept: image/gif, image/x-xbitmap, image/jpeg, image/pjpeg, application/x-shockwave-flash, applicatic
  Accept-Language: es\r\n
  Accept-Encoding: gzip, deflate\r\n
  User-Agent: Mozilla/4.0 (compatible; MSIE 6.0; Windows NT 5.0; .NET CLR 1.1.4322)\r\n
  Host: www.intramarket.com.ar\r\n
  Connection: Keep-Alive\r\n
  \r\n
```

This pane shows the protocols and protocol fields of the selected packet, using a 'tree' structure which may be expanded or collapsed as needed. The Frame line contains information generated by Ethereal, such as the time the packet arrived, its length and the protocols it contains. The rest of the lines indicate the fields for each protocol header used to encapsulate an upper layer protocol. In the above figure, we can see how an HTTP message is described, which is encapsulated by a TCP message, which is carried by an IP datagram, and finally encapsulated by an Ethernet frame.

As the following screenshot shows, the *packet bytes pane* shows the packet data in a hexadecimal representation and their corresponding ASCII characters, for the selected packet in the *packet list pane*:

```
0000  00 06 2a cf 84 54 00 08  54 18 5d 87 08 00 45 00   ..*..T.. T.]...E.
0010  01 a6 c2 42 40 00 80 06  3e 8a c8 70 88 4a 41 b6   ...B@... >..p.JA.
0020  66 14 11 83 00 50 ea bb  d1 c8 03 a4 55 37 50 18   f....P.. ....U7P.
0030  fa f0 63 0a 00 00 47 45  54 20 2f 20 48 54 54 50   ..c...GE T / HTTP
0040  2f 31 2e 31 0d 0a 41 63  63 65 70 74 3a 20 69 6d   /1.1..Ac cept: im
0050  61 67 65 2f 67 69 66 2c  20 69 6d 61 67 65 2f 78   age/gif,  image/x
0060  2d 78 62 69 74 6d 61 70  2c 20 69 6d 61 67 65 2f   -xbitmap , image/
0070  6a 70 65 67 2c 20 69 6d  61 67 65 2f 70 6a 70 65   jpeg, im age/pjpe
0080  67 2c 20 61 70 70 6c 69  63 61 74 69 6f 6e 2f 78   g, appli cation/x
0090  2d 73 68 6f 63 6b 77 61  76 65 2d 66 6c 61 73 68   -shockwa ve-flash
00a0  2c 20 61 70 70 6c 69 63  61 74 69 6f 6e 2f 76 6e   , applic ation/vn
00b0  64 2e 6d 73 2d 70 6f 77  65 72 70 6f 69 6e 74 2c   d.ms-pow erpoint,
00c0  20 61 70 70 6c 69 63 61  74 69 6f 6e 2f 76 6e 64    applica tion/vnd
```

In addition, for each field we select in the *packet details pane* the corresponding bytes are selected in the *packet bytes pane*. (Note that even when the PPP packets from the serial interface were captured, they are shown as frames under the Ethernet name in the packet details pane; and the Flag, Address, Control and FCS fields are not shown; only the Protocol and Information fields are shown.)

F.3.4 Saving packets into a file

We can save the packets into a file using the *Save As* option from the *File* menu. Several options allow us to choose the range of packets to save, such as the *captured* or *displayed* packets, *selected* or *marked* packets, and even specifying a *packet range*. Once the packets are saved into a file, they can be opened using the *Open* option from the *File* menu.

F.3.5 Marking packets

The packets listed in the packet list pane can be marked/unmarked using the *Mark Packet*, *Mark All Packets* or *Unmark All Packets* options from the *Edit* menu. In this way, we can save only marked packets to a specific file.

F.3.6 Colouring packets

In order for packets in the *list pane* to be easily differentiated, we may assign different colours for each packet's protocol type. If we select *Coloring Rules* from the *View* menu, we will get the window shown on page 593.

In this window, we can see how different colours are assigned to each protocol type. The protocols names must be entered in lower case. Other expressions may be composed, like 'ip.addr = = 65.182.156.25', using the *Expression* button.

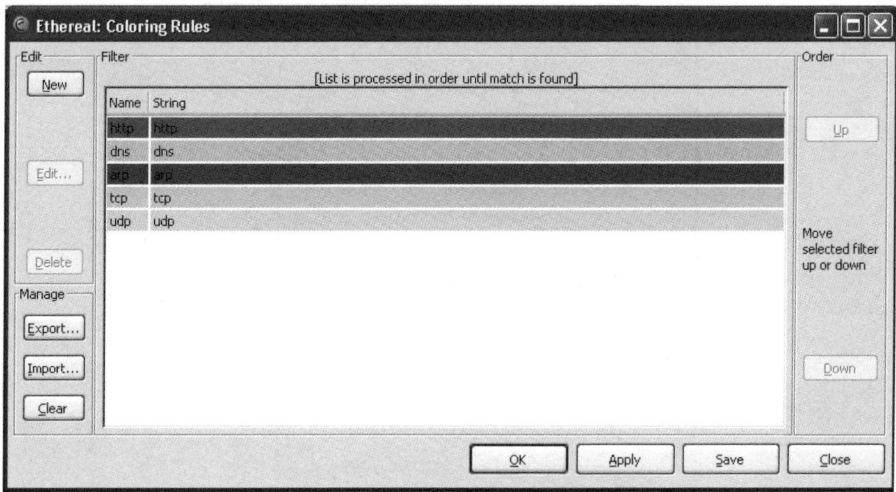

F.3.7 Filtering packets while viewing

Display filters allow us to concentrate on the packets we are interested in. They provide a way to select packets by protocol, or establishing conditions that specific protocol fields should meet, and only displaying those selected packets. The logical operators 'and', 'or', and 'not' may be used to combine conditional expressions. The selection criterion is specified in the *filter toolbar*.

Filter: tcp.port == 4483 ▾ Expression... Clear Apply

The following are examples of valid display filter expressions:

```
ip.addr = = 10.0.0.2
frame.pkt_len < 128
eth.addr != ff:ff:ff:ff:ff:ff
ip.addr = = 10.0.0.5 and tcp.flags.fin
eth.src[0:3] = = 00:00:83 or eth.src[0:3] = = 00:00:f3
```

The *Filter* button allows saving and later opening existent display filters, while the *Expression* button allows defining the filter expressions using the *Filter Expression* dialogue box, as shown overleaf.

F.3.8 Filtering packets while capturing

A filter language may be used to only capture those packets we are interested in. Some examples with valid syntax are:

```
host 200.136.152.20
tcp port 80
udp port 53
tcp src port 23 and not host 10.0.0.2
```

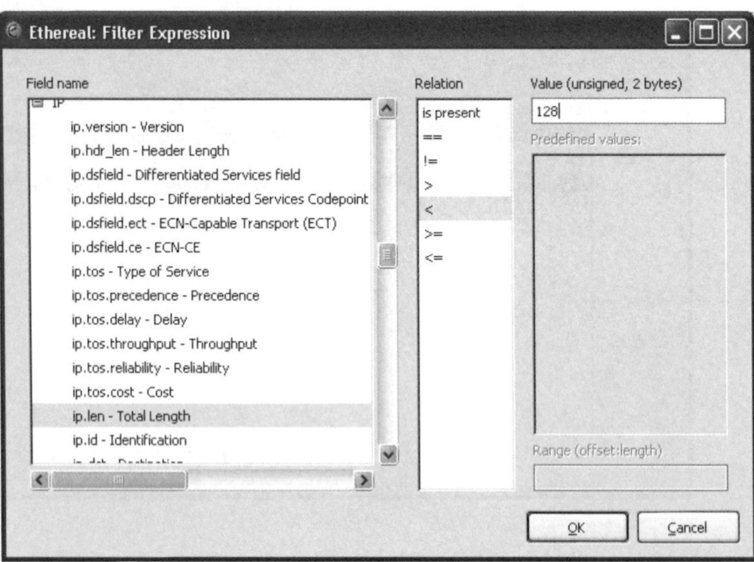

The *Capture Filter* window allows *Capture Filter expressions*, to be defined and saved. These may be used in the *Capture Options* window to specify the packets which must meet the filter expression to be captured.

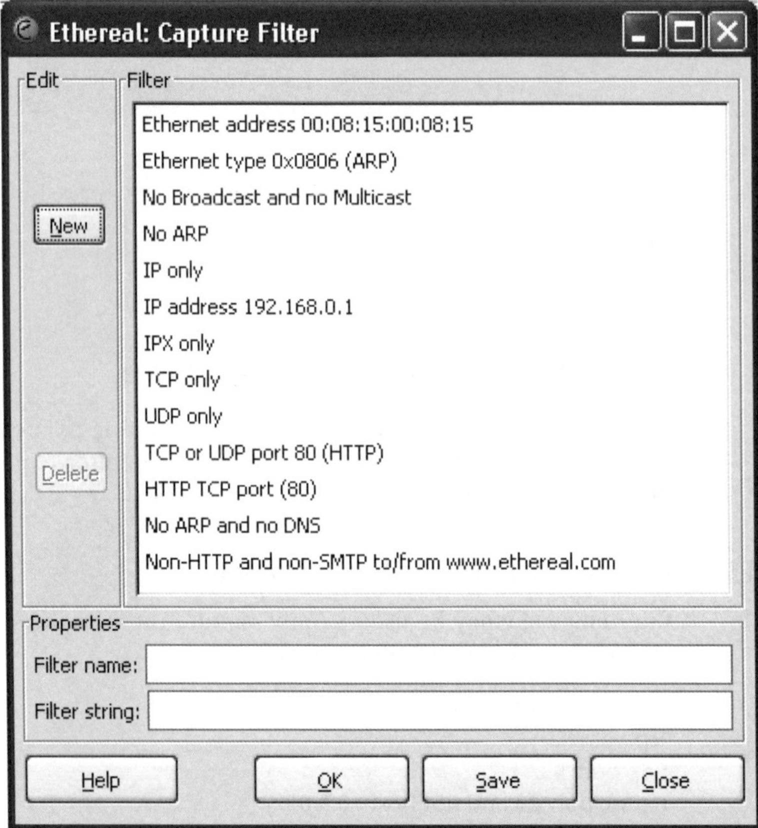

F.4 Where to go from here...

F.4.1 Ethereal capture samples

We provide sample capture files for the reader to use as a starting point for this tutorial. Additional samples are found in the software website. Using those samples, and trying to capture your own, will be a good way to learn how to use this tool.

F.4.2 Further information

The Ethereal features shown in this appendix are only the basic ones needed to start using this Network Protocol Analyser. Refer to the Ethereal User Guide that accompanies the software, to gain a complete overview of their possibilities and operation.

Index

LICENSING AGREEMENT

This book comes with a CD. By opening this package, you are agreeing to be bound by the following:

The files contained on this CD are copyrighted. THIS CD IS PROVIDED FREE OF CHARGE, AS IS, AND WITHOUT WARRANTY OF ANY KIND, EITHER EXPRESSED OR IMPLIED, INCLUDING, BUT NOT LIMITED TO, THE IMPLIED WARRANTIES OF MERCHANTABILITY AND FITNESS FOR A PARTICULAR PURPOSE. Neither the book publisher nor its dealers and its distributors assumes any liability for any alleged or actual damages arising from the use of this CD.